Trekking in Pakistan and India

THE SIERRA CLUB
ADVENTURE TRAVEL GUIDES

Adventuring Along the Gulf of Mexico, The Sierra Club Travel Guide to the Gulf Coast of the United States and Mexico from the Florida Keys to Yucatán, by Donald G. Schueler

Adventuring in Alaska, The Ultimate Travel Guide to the Great Land, Completely revised and updated, by Peggy Wayburn

Adventuring in the Alps, The Sierra Club Travel Guide to the Alpine Regions of France, Switzerland, Germany, Austria, Liechtenstein, Italy, and Yugoslavia, by William E. Reifsnyder and Marylou Reifsnyder

Adventuring in the Andes, The Sierra Club Travel Guide to Ecuador, Peru, Bolivia, the Amazon Basin, and the Galapagos Islands, by Charles Frazier with Donald Secreast

Adventuring in the California Desert, The Sierra Club Travel Guide to the Great Basin, Mojave, and Colorado Desert Regions of California, by Lynne Foster

Adventuring in the Pacific, The Sierra Club Travel Guide to the Islands of Polynesia, Melanesia, and Micronesia, by Susanna Margolis

Adventuring in the Rockies, The Sierra Club Travel Guide to the Rocky Mountain Regions of the United States and Canada, by Jeremy Schmidt

Adventuring in the San Francisco Bay Area, The Sierra Club Travel Guide to San Francisco, Marin, Sonoma, Napa, Solano, Contra Costa, Alameda, Santa Clara, San Mateo Counties and the Bay Islands, by Peggy Wayburn

Trekking in Nepal, West Tibet, and Bhutan, by Hugh Swift

Trekking in Pakistan and India, by Hugh Swift

Walking Europe from Top to Bottom, The Sierra Club Travel Guide to the Grande Randonnée Cinq (GR-5) through Holland, Belgium, Luxembourg, Switzerland, and France, by Susanna Margolis and Ginger Harmon

Trekking in Pakistan and India

by Hugh Swift

*with additional material by
Peter H. Hackett, M.D., Rodney Jackson,
John Mock, Haqiqat Ali, Helena Norberg-Hodge,
and Stephen Shucart*

Sierra Club Books   San Francisco

The Sierra Club, founded in 1892 by John Muir, has devoted itself to the study and protection of the earth's scenic and ecological resources—mountains, wetlands, woodlands, wild shores and rivers, deserts and plains. The publishing program of the Sierra Club offers books to the public as a nonprofit educational service in the hope that they may enlarge the public's understanding of the Club's basic concerns. The point of view expressed in each book, however, does not necessarily represent that of the Club. The Sierra Club has some sixty chapters coast to coast, in Canada, Hawaii, and Alaska. For information about how you may participate in its programs to preserve wilderness and the quality of life, please address inquiries to Sierra Club, 730 Polk Street, San Francisco, CA 94109.

Copyright © 1990 by Hugh Swift

Library of Congress Cataloging-in-Publication Data

Swift, Hugh.
    Trekking in Pakistan and India / Hugh Swift.
        p.   cm.

    Bibliography: p.
    Includes index.
    ISBN 0-87156-662-1
    1. Hiking—Pakistan—Guide-books.   2. Hiking—India—Guide-books.
3. Hiking—Himalaya Mountains—Guide-books.   4. Pakistan—Description and travel—Guide-books.   5. India—Description and travel—1981—Guide-books.
6. Himalaya Mountains—Description and travel—Guide-books.   I. Title.
GV199.44.P18S95   1990
915.491—dc20   89-10167
                                                                        CIP

Photographs are by the author unless otherwise credited.

Production by Felicity Gorden

Cover design by Bonnie Smetts

Book design by Robyn Brode

Maps by Tom Dolan

Composition by The Compleat Works, Berkeley, CA

Printed in the United States of America
10 9 8 7 6 5 4 3 2 1

Table of Contents

             An Infinite Variety of Green 374
             Trekking in Sikkim 374
                 Travel from and to Nepal 376

Chapter 13   Himalayan Natural History,
             by Rodney Jackson 377
             Introduction 378
             Life Zones 379
                 Aeolian Zone 383
                 Alpine Zone 383
                 Subalpine Zone 384
                 Temperate Zone 385
                 Subtropical and Tropical Zones 386
             Himalayan Fauna 387
                 Mammals 387
                 Birds 393
                 Reptiles and Amphibians 397
             A World in Transition: The Future
             of Himalayan Wildlife 398

Chapter 14   A Himalayan Medical Primer,
             by Peter H. Hackett, M.D. 401
             Preparation 402
                 Immunizations 404
                 Prevention of Malaria 406
             On Trek 406
                 Diarrhea 406
                 Respiratory Infections 412
                 Snow Blindness 413
                 Women's Health Concerns 413
                 Trauma 414
                 The Nitty Gritty: Lice, Fleas,
                   Bedbugs, and Scabies 415
                 Altitude Problems 416
                 Rescue 421
                 The Trekker's Medical Kit 422

Appendices   Appendix A: Maps 425

             Appendix B: Trekking Outfitters
             in Pakistan and India 430

             Appendix C: Afghanistan! 433

Acknowledgments

Many people have contributed important chapters or sections to this book, and without their kind assistance, the book would not be nearly as complete as it is. I would like to acknowledge the following people who have been particularly helpful with writing separate chapters: Peter H. Hackett, M.D., one of the world's foremost authorities on altitude sickness, an expert on wilderness medicine, and veteran of a solo ascent of Mt. Everest, wrote the authoritative chapter "A Himalayan Medical Primer." Rodney Jackson, the person who knows more about and has studied most extensively the elusive and symbolic snow leopard, contributed the excellent chapter "Himalayan Natural History." John Mock, an expert linguist and a wonderful trekking companion, has not only written the new "Introduction to Hindustani (Hindi-Urdu)," but has also updated the glossaries on Burushaski and Balti.

Further, I am extremely appreciative to these collaborators, each of whom is identified in the text, for writing the following sections or glossaries: Haqiqat Ali, for the "Wakhi Glossary"; Debra Denker, for "Making the Most of Being a Woman Trekker"; Tashi D. Lek, for "Kinnaur"; Helena Norberg-Hodge, for the "Ladakhi Glossary"; Tom Pritzker, for "The Temples of Spiti"; Pam Ross, for "Trekking with Children"; Stephen Shucart, a real Asia hand, for the "Introduction to Afghan Dari"; Gerry Spence, for his most eloquent essay on "Trekking as Metaphor"; Susan Thiele, for "The Trail to the North Side of K2"; Cameron Wake for "The Biafo-Hispar Glacier Traverse"; Ray Wallace, for "The Kaghan Valley"; Carmi Weingrod, for much of the chapter on Sikkim; Betsy White, for "Family Trekking in the Hispar Region"; and Jan Eric Zabinski, for "The Baltoro Glacier and the Trek to Concordia." Each of these sections or glossaries adds to this volume and has helped make it a better book. I am especially grateful for each person's contribution.

Some of the same people and others have assisted with providing information directly, through their writings, or by reading portions of the manuscript, and to them I wish to express my deep appreciation: William M. Aitken, Edwin Bernbaum, H. Adams Carter, Debra Denker, Diana L. Eck, K. Garnay, Ron V. Giddy, Richard Irvin, Scot MacBeth, John Mock, Christina Noble, Helena Norberg-Hodge, Rebecca Paxton, Tom Pritzker, Galen Rowell, Rahul Sharma, Rekha Sharma, Elizabeth Thukral, Gurmeet Thukral, and especially Ray Wallace.

Others threw up their hands when presented with such a maze of information, place names, and foreign language, but my intrepid copy-editor, Mary Anne Stewart, dedicatedly and good humoredly wrestled with the lengthy manuscript, and the book is far better as a result. *Shabash!* At Sierra Club Books, I am most appreciative to my editor, David Spinner, for bringing together into book form the myriad details of a difficult project, and to Felicity Gorden for overseeing its production. My thanks also go to Robyn Brode, the book's designer and compositor, who has done an exacting job beyond the call of duty.

Mushkeel Baba played hermit monk and typed the manuscript. And the Global Emperor provided inspiration, with his salute to "All and All of Globe" and his beaming shy, sly smile.

Thanks to Tom Dolan for his lettering on both old and new maps. And thanks also go to Benjamin Ailes for working especially hard to make excellent conversions of transparencies from color to black and white.

When I have visited their homelands, certain people have been especially helpful with answering my many questions, giving warm hospitality, and assisting me in many ways. I would particularly like to thank Mohammed Akram, Sayeed Anwar, Izzatullah Beg, Salahud Din, Ghulam Rasul Drasi, Anul Hayat Hunzai, Ghulam Mohammed Beg Hunzai, Ibadat Shah Hunzai, Saifullah Jan of Balenguru, Tawakhel Mohammed, Dad Ali Shah, Haider Ali Shah, Padam Singh, Mohammed Sirat, and Mohinder P. Soni.

Others have also answered unending questions, provided hospitality, and assisted by doing so much, but they have also trekked with me, and to them I am particularly grateful. The times we have shared have meant a great deal to me, and I will long remember them. I wish to thank Guda Ali of Pasu, Amanullah of Shimshal, Dambar Bahadur, Ghulam Nabi Balti, N. K. L. Chhultim, Abdul Ghani, Prem Singh Gurung, Ghulam Hussain of Balegaon, Mohammed Jan of Karma Ding, Dil Bahadur Rai, Ramazan, Danu Sherpa, Ajai Taj Singh, Ram Bahadur Tamang, and Zerbali of Yasin.

Acknowledgment is made for permission to reprint material from the following sources:

Mountain Monarchs, by George B. Schaller. Chicago: University of Chicago Press. Copyright © 1977 by George B. Schaller.

"Mr. Tambourine Man," by Bob Dylan. Los Angeles: Warner Bros. Music. Copyright © 1964 by Warner Bros., Inc. Used by permission; all rights reserved.

The Scottish Himalayan Expedition, by W. II. Murray. London: J. M. Dent and Sons Ltd. Copyright © 1951 by W. H. Murray.

That Untravelled World, by Eric Shipton. Kent: Hodder and Stoughton Ltd. Copyright © 1969 by Eric Shipton.

Throne of the Gods, by Arnold Heim and August Gansser, translated by Eden and Cedar Paul. New York: MacMillan, Inc. Copyright © 1938 by Arnold Heim and August Gansser.

A Walk in the Sky, by Nicholas Clinch. Copyright © 1982 by The Mountaineers, Seattle.

Vagabonding in America, by Ed Buryn. New York: Random House, Inc. Copyright © 1975 by Ed Buryn.

Preface

*I failed entirely to realize that the one book was as full of
grotesque blunders and inaccuracies as the other.*
Aleister Crowley, 1929
(on guidebooks available at the time)

The Himalaya invites superlatives. But superlatives become meaningless with repetition. Try this: talk with people who have been to the
Himalaya. Watch their eyes light up, note the animated voice and faraway
stare as they recall their trip. But neither their words nor mine can convey
the majesty or uniqueness of the Himalaya; only the direct experience of
smelling, hearing, and seeing will suffice.

This book is written to inform both those who have never visited the
Himalaya and to suggest further routes for those who have already gone
and want to peel another layer closer, walk another league farther toward
the evanescent soul forever hidden among these many ranges. This volume
is likewise for the armchair explorer who is content to learn about the
Himalaya from the steadfast confines of home turf, because essentially I
think of this book as an overview of the people and places of the Himalayan
regions of Pakistan and India.

The trails and passes of the Himalaya and Karakoram ranges in Pakistan and India are no longer unknown places. Remote and difficult of access,
yes, but the maps are there. One need only set forth. Pakistanis and Indians
as well as foreigners are discovering the delights of hiking among these
endless hills. No book or books could ever describe all the paths in the
mountains of these two countries, but this volume depicts the most popular
trekking routes and mentions most major valleys or regions.

Pakistan's government has not given much emphasis over the years to
tourism development. We in the West see few if any lush ads in the press,
and if we go to Pakistan, we may receive offhand advice upon arrival.
Pakistan as a whole has suffered from an equivocal image abroad. Head-
lines datelined Pakistan have often described civil unrest or another un-
seemly election postponement. But thousands of trekkers and climbers
have discovered the unadvertised secret that Pakistan's mountain regions
are an exciting world unto themselves, containing awesomely stunning
scenery and hill people who are gracious and hospitable.

India generally has a more benign image abroad: throngs of pilgrims
bathing in the Ganges, camel fairs in Rajasthan, limpid lakes in Kashmir.
India works hard abroad to promote tourism. But aside from a few short
trekking routes in Kashmir and in the vicinity of Leh in Ladakh, outsiders
are often at a loss to know where to trek in India's extensive hill regions.
Not Indians, however. They have begun to discover the joys of hiking, and

many now set off for the mountains in large groups. From the dry, remote canyons of Zanskar to the pine-forested valleys of Himachal Pradesh to the lush pilgrimage routes of Garhwal, India offers an exquisite feast of opportunities for the hiker.

This book gives you scores of suggestions for where to head in both countries. The Himalaya of Pakistan and India is far more than the Baltoro Glacier and Kashmir, as you'll see by a quick glance at the table of contents. Dare to follow that beckoning trail leading over the hill. It has been there for hundreds of years, just waiting for you to discover its mysteries.

Herein you will find an extensive revision of the portions of *The Trekker's Guide to the Himalaya and Karakoram* that describe Pakistan and India. When my plans for updating that book threatened to produce a hunk of wood pulp resembling an unwieldy doorstop, this book and its companion volume, *Trekking in Nepal, West Tibet, and Bhutan,* were born. If you have both books, you can see that the initial three chapters in each bear a strong resemblance to each other. It is beyond my powers of creativity to introduce the subject of Himalayan trekking and advise on preparation twice over. These beginning chapters are written to be complete in each book and to be entirely accurate for the regions they introduce. Every word of the introductory material herein is relevant to trekking in Pakistan and India.

But my heart truly lies in the hills: with the people to be met and the places to be visited. When it comes to writing the area descriptions that comprise the majority of this book, out come the well-thumbed journals, the maps floppy with use, the carefully protected slides, and the best books, whether brand new or written by Gypsy Davy and Lady Ba three generations ago. And up comes the phone: "Hey Wal, when you and Patti went up the Barpu Glacier . . ."

The nine descriptive chapters are arranged from west to east by region. Within each chapter, the valleys or regions discussed proceed either from west to east or outward in a natural progression from the principal town or towns. It's not always possible to say something smashingly unique about each valley or route described in this book. You may have to say, "Well, here's a valley we don't know much about, let's just walk up it and see what we find." Serendipity and chance plus determination often lead to memorable experiences.

It is my fervent hope that as you dip in and out of these pages, you will realize that a detailed step-by-step guide noting every trail junction is not only impossible to create, but beside the point. If this book can success-fully give you an easygoing approach to trekking, it will have achieved a lot. A helpful principle to keep in mind is to know where you are going and what will be required of you to get there.

The approximate number of days you will need to trek into and back from a destination or to go from one place to another is important. I have always given guidelines on approximately how many days or weeks you will require for a particular route. But hours? In Nancy Hatch Dupree's informative and delightful guide to Afghanistan (cited in Appendix C), she tells a story of Mullah Nasruddin, the fabled fictional character from Sufi folklore:

> Mullah Nasruddin was once asked how long it would take to walk to the next village. "Walk," he said. Half an hour later he came running up to say, "It will take you an hour and a half." Astonished, the traveller asked bewilderedly, "Why didn't you say so in the first place?" "I did not know how you walk," said Mullah Nasruddin.

Trekking with a local can not only ease your load and eliminate questions about routefinding, but introduce you to much that you might otherwise miss along the way. Good maps can also be an invaluable aid, and the U502 Map Series is often referred to (see Appendix A). The "Introduction to Hindustani (Hindi-Urdu)," the lingua franca of the hills, by John Mock, can go a long way toward helping you communicate directly with the locals, and the other six language sections can give you an additional entrée to talking with people. The more words you know in any understandable language, the more you will stand out from other foreigners who may have passed through. The locals always appreciate your speaking with them, and the rewards to you are equal to the efforts you make.

You will enjoy your trip to the Himalaya far more if you visit fewer locales in depth than if you try to visit too many places. The vagaries of getting confirmed tickets on local or international regional flights, the hard seats and jolting rides you may have to endure on buses, vans, or jeeps all render long-distance travel trying. Be careful not to use up too much energy moving from one region or country to another.

What is so compelling about trekking? On the trail, life is instantaneous; it's right before your eyes. The days expand, and life is fully lived. Reality isn't diffused through Channel 4 or the daily *Times*. You can't hide in your car or inside your home. There's no filter. Every day is new and different while hiking. Turning a corner on a path can take you into heaven or hell, or face to face with a villain or a saint. How angry can you get? How ecstatic? How weak? How strong? How much can you hate your damn porter? How grateful can you be to that saintly man? Why are you undergoing this insane torture? Why didn't you dare to try this exalted experience before? You are truly biting into life. While trekking, the immediacy of being, of existing, is tantalizing, frightening, intoxicating.

It has been rewarding but difficult to write this book. For as the journey across northern Pakistan and India has proceeded, I have recalled or imagined each remarkable area and each unique valley in turn. And I know how inadequately I have evoked these places and their strong, genuine peoples. If you go to even a single region depicted herein, you can learn far more about it than I am able to intimate here.

Have you had a great trek you would like to suggest for others? Or have you done one you'd like to tell me about, but not see in print? (I thoroughly respect confidences. I certainly haven't written about my own favorite secret places.) Did I tell about someplace that is too special to be mentioned? Or, as Crowley declaims above, did I write something misleading, incomplete, or inaccurate and get you into a fix? Additions, deletions, and changes are the stuff of trail descriptions. Comments, corrections, harangues? When not "over there" for months at a time, I am "over here" and would be glad to hear from you. Jot a note to me c/o Sierra Club Books, 730 Polk Street, San Francisco, CA 94109, U.S.A.

Hugh Swift
Berkeley, California

The Mir of Hunza's former palace rests above the poplars and fruit trees of Baltit and beneath the gorge leading to Ultar meadows.

1
Himalayan Trekking

There are many ways to enjoy mountains: some persons engage their passion by cutting steps into impossible ice walls, others entrust their lives to one fragile piton in a rocky crevice, and still others, I among them, prefer simply to roam the high country.

George B. Schaller, 1979

The Himalayan germ, once caught, works inside one like a relapsing fever; it is ever biding its time before breaking out again with renewed virulence.

Marco Pallis, 1939

Northern Pakistan and northern India

Travelers in the Past

The Himalaya is our highest mountain system, and it very effectively separates the South Asian subcontinent from the rest of Asia. Yet until the mid-eighteenth century, the Himalaya's countless isolated valleys within scores of autonomous princely states were virtually unknown to the outside world. Still, long before Europeans ever set foot there, in fact back into prehistory, the Himalaya had provided homes and trade routes for many people. The inhabitants, some of whom live at loftier elevations year round than any other mountain people, have for centuries maintained circuitous paths through terrain people could not otherwise traverse.

The Himalayan trails are an extraordinary mountain network. These tracks vary greatly, from wide, professionally made, stone-paved routes to treacherous talus paths and narrow, exposed ledges. Many extremely remote areas of the Himalaya are visited by shepherds, hunters, or wood gatherers who have no reason to document their excursions. Winter migrations continue: entire villages move south, threading the paths to escape the grip of snow, visiting traditional camps, and taking in the sights of such towns as Chitral, Gilgit, or Srinagar. Aside from these migrants and local householders who use the routes for access to field, pasture, and market, until quite recently only three types of traveler have used Himalayan trails.

Merchants and traders, the first group, have been important voyagers along the major trans-Himalayan trade routes for hundreds of years. Along the branches of the Silk Route in Chitral and Ladakh and the scores of winding paths leading north to Sinkiang and Tibet, people traveled carrying on the trade in *pashmina* (shawl wool), salt, tea, textiles, grains, spices, and more. During the heyday of trade on the Silk Route, crossing from the northern to the southern slopes of the great mountains was an immense undertaking. Tattered, indomitable caravans of Bactrian camels no longer enter the bazaars of Chitral, Gilgit, and Leh, but hundreds of traders still carry goods through the mountains by various methods. Cow-yak crossbreeds in Baltistan and mule, sheep, and goat caravans in the Indian Himalaya continue carrying goods in homespun woolen bundles. And people have always been beasts of burden in these ranges; once, four of us (two Westerners and two Tibetan porters) accompanied a merchant and village chief from Torpa village in Humla, Nepal, as he and his three hired porters carried his merchandise on their backs from Jumla to his store in far northwestern Nepal.

Since the days of small local kingdoms, emissaries of the prevailing rulers have visited remote areas. Government employees still travel the Himalayan trails in the line of duty, though civil servants often wear no uniform, hat, or identifying badge of their profession. Until recently, anyone carrying a portable radio and wearing stylish sunglasses might have been an official. Once, Chris Wriggins, my trekking companion, and I were descending from Jang Pass in central Nepal when we met a man with modish, wraparound dark glasses and a cloth-covered radio who asked several questions about our route. Later we were told that he was walking to his new position as police chief of Dolpo District.

The third traditional Himalayan traveler has been the pilgrim. From Baba Ghundi Ziarat in upper Hunza to Tashigang Monastery in eastern Bhutan, pilgrimage sites and the routes to them trace the mythological past of the Himalaya. The pilgrimages by foot that attract the greatest numbers of people take place in India: the Amarnath Yatra and gatherings of Tibetan refugees for an appearance by the Dalai Lama attract thousands, but religious-cum-trade festivals occur in many hill areas, particularly in Garhwal, with its many sacred shrines.

The 3,500-year-old Vedas, Hinduism's oldest spiritual teachings, recommend that the last third of a person's life be devoted to seeking the Ultimate in a state of voluntary poverty. The varieties of "renouncing individuals" (*sannyasi*) are many, but most ascetics are called *sadhu*s. A sadhu, whether he is independent or belongs to an order, will travel from shrine to shrine most of the year, rarely staying in one place longer than three days. Many older sadhus are well educated and have left their former professions. More than once I have had pleasant conversations in English with trident-carrying, ochre-daubed sadhus on the trail. During the summer months, those walking into the Indian Himalaya are joined for the Amarnath and Kedarnath *yatra*s (pilgrimages) and for the yatras to the sources of the Ganges by thousands of householders eager to assure themselves religious merit and a better place on the karmic wheel in the next incarnation. Muslims who live in the Himalaya believe the greatest pilgrimage to be the *haj* to Mecca. At home, Muslims traditionally consider travelers (called *muzzafer*) to be guests and offer them warm hospitality.

Mapping and Exploring the Himalaya

For a while, Alexander the Great's empire extended east to Chitral and the Indus Valley. The Kalash in southern Chitral and some families in the Hunza Valley still claim to be descendants of dissatisfied soldiers who did not follow "Sikander" home to Greece. After Alexander's forces departed south down the Indus River, nearly a thousand years passed before Chinese pilgrim-scholars began to filter across snowy Karakoram passes seeking the seminal texts of their Buddhist teachings. The best known of these Chinese was the indefatigable seventh-century pilgrim Hsuan Tsang. He arrived in the region called Gandhara, centered in the Peshawar Valley, and traveled for fourteen years in what is now Afghanistan, Pakistan, and northern India before returning to China by the Pamir caravan route.

At the beginning of the fourteenth century, Marco Polo made his voyage of discovery from Italy to China and back. He spread the message to both Orient and Occident of the riches each held for the other, nearly single-handedly opening the era of the great Silk Route. The trans-Himalayan branches of this trail stretched from Chitral to the Leh-Rudok route east from Ladakh. For many years the finest silk, tea, textiles, jewels, and other valuables were carried along several tracks through the Oxus,

Chitral, Hunza, and Indus valleys en route between Europe and China. With trade came cultural diffusion. Catholic missionaries began to move eastward. The first Christians into the mountains were two Portuguese Jesuits who established a church in the seventeenth century at the west Tibetan city of Tsaparang. The Society of Jesus also set up a missionary outpost in Lhasa, which passed to the Capuchins and operated until that order was expelled by the Chinese emperor in 1740.

Aside from these few incursions, trails within the Himalaya remained the exclusive domain of Asian traders, civil servants, and pilgrims until the mid-nineteenth century. The xenophobia of every Himalayan potentate successfully kept most Angrezi (foreigners, or, strictly, the English) away from the formidable ranges. Those who entered the foothills were immediately suspected of trying to learn a region's geography, of arranging lucrative trade contacts, or of endeavoring to influence local political sentiment. The grapevine among people on the trail passed along word of any approaching Angrezi, for such information traveled as rapidly as the swiftest person could walk. It was the rare Westerner who could disguise himself so skillfully or move so covertly as to avoid detection, although a few were successful.

Eventually, however, the expanding British presence in the Ganges and Punjab plains to the south brought pressures too great to be contained. By 1800 the British imperatively needed to know more about the Abode of Snow (*Hima-alaya* in Sanskrit) than the meager accounts previous travelers had brought back.

In 1803 Nepal's first British resident, the chief British official in Nepal, had a preliminary survey done, for up to then, the height of the Himalaya Range had not been understood. Even then, European scientists refused to believe the British survey work, maintaining that the Andes were the world's highest mountains. The unassailable trigonometric survey, begun in south India, was supervised by George Everest as it moved northward and undertook the Herculean effort to map the Himalaya and Karakoram. Not until 1845 was Dhaulagiri (26,810 feet) officially recognized as taller than the Andes' Chimborazo (20,703 feet), and only in 1852 did Mt. Everest (29,028 feet, named for Sir George) gain its rightful place in the record books.

In 1812 the British explorer and trader William Moorcroft and a friend named Hearsey disguised themselves as sadhus, crossing the Niti Pass in Garhwal en route to Lake Manasarowar and Mt. Kailas, the holy of holies for Hindus and Tibetan Buddhists. They went to find the goats that produce shawl wool, called pashmina, and when they returned they brought a herd of the long-haired goats to spur interest in the lucrative pashmina trade. During this trip, Moorcroft made the first accurate sketches of the sources and drainages of the Indus, Sutlej, and Ganges rivers. Eight years after that clandestine journey, Moorcroft journeyed northwest from the Sutlej River, then the limits of British control, with three hundred men and sixteen pack animals carrying textiles for barter. He did not return for three long years. Herbert Tichy noted in the 1950s that Moorcroft's name could

Five Balti shepherds await the first rays of the morning sun at their pasture above the Sherpikang Glacier.

still be seen scratched on the cave wall of the great Buddha at Bamian in central Afghanistan.

The Gurkha War of 1814–16 resulted in Nepal's western boundary shifting east, from the Sutlej River to the Mahakali, by order of the British-dictated treaty terms. This opened the Ganges River headwaters to outside scrutiny for the first time. In the 1830s G. T. Vigne, another independent British explorer, was the first Westerner to explore the Karakoram kingdom of Baltistan, conducting four journeys to that vertical, glaciated world. Most of its high peaks and major watersheds were known by the mid-1800s, but the arduous, valley-by-valley work of surveyors with plane-tables still remained to be done.

Despite these discoveries, large areas of the subcontinent's map were still marked UNEXPLORED in enticingly bold print: Nepal, Tibet, Sikkim, and Bhutan. To chart those sovereign, forbidden lands, in 1865 the Indian Survey began training carefully selected people from the hills, who traveled disguised as merchants, monks, pilgrims, or *fakirs* (Muslim aescetics). These men came to be known as the pundits, and their stories remain some of the most remarkable in the annals of Himalayan exploration. Each person's mission was to map a specific region within those forbidden kingdoms. They were able to fulfill their duty by allaying suspicion in a variety of imaginative ways: a Muslim mullah carried a special compass, said to point to Mecca; a Buddhist monk carried a *mala* (prayer beads) with one hundred beads for counting paces instead of the one hundred and eight beads traditional in Buddhism; a merchant liked to camp alone at the base of prominent hills that he would ascend; and one pundit hid his mercury for measuring altitude in a coconut. They used code numbers and names, and some of the men became famous: the Mullah, A-K, the Pundit, and Hari Ram, who first fixed the latitude and longitude of Lhasa. Later, in 1873, Hari Ram also visited Mustang, the last outsider on record to have done so until H. W. Tilman passed through the southern part of the region in 1950. Two of the pundits were away without contact for four years in the uncharted vastness of Tibet, Mongolia, and western China. The accuracy of the work they brought back astounded their university-trained British colleagues and the explorers of later years.

The Survey of India Quarter Inch Series sheets from the period 1914–24 that cover India, Nepal, Tibet, Sikkim, and Bhutan are drawn from information supplied by the pundits. Interestingly enough, the maps for these areas in the AMS U502 Series (see Appendix A) are taken in part from that early Survey of India Series. So presently we not only follow routes that were explored by the pundits, but some of us use maps derived from their drawings and measurements.

The explorer George Hayward, an Englishman who favored traveling alone in Afghan dress, explored the upper Yarkand River drainage in 1868–69. Then he visited the previously unknown cities of Kashgar and Yarkand before succumbing violently, "in the wilds of Central Asia," as he had predicted. It fell to the renowned explorer Francis Younghusband to cross the Mustagh Pass of the northern Karakoram in 1886, still probably the only traverse from Turkestan south into Baltistan. The height and extent of the entire Himalayan mountain system was essentially known by 1900, but as recently as 1937 Eric Shipton (known along with H. W. Tilman for the lightweight equipage of his mountaineering explorations) could exult while in the Karakoram:

> To the east and west stretched an unexplored section, eighty miles long, of the greatest range in the world. We had food enough for three and a half months, and a party equipped and fully competent to meet the opportunity. . . . Carrying three weeks' food which, with our equipment, was as much as we could manage without relaying, we set off up the Shaksgam. . . . We started by climbing a 20,000-foot peak to discover the lie of the land. . . . The next ten days were spent exploring the glaciers flowing north and west from K2, the second highest peak in the world.

The exploration by land of the Himalaya still has not been exhaustively completed, although some sites only recently reached by Westerners are now much frequented. The Khumbu Glacier, for instance, destination of hundreds of today's trekkers yearly, had never been seen by outsiders until Dr. Charles Houston and H. W. Tilman reached the southern base of Everest in 1950.

A Short History of Himalayan Trekking

No, not shooting; not rocks-collecting, not flowers keeping; not heads measuring, not mountains measuring; not pictures taking. This my Sahib and my Mem-Sahib traveling where their felt are liked, camping always high place to look the country.
Rasul Galwan, 1923

Until quite recently, high mountains put fear into the hearts of European and Easterner alike. The inhabitants of the Alps believed that dragons lived by glaciers (which is not surprising, for glaciers can emit frightening noises) and also assumed that survival overnight on a glacier was totally impossible. Only toward the end of the eighteenth century did mountain peaks, high-country lakes, and meadows begin to appear aesthetically pleasing to Westerners. On the full moon of August in 1786, the Frenchmen Gabriel Paccard and Jacques Balmat became the first of thousands to climb 15,782-foot Mont Blanc, the highest peak in the Alps.

Carrying only iron poles as aids, they went up and back 8,200 feet each way in one day, for they still believed it impossible to sleep on the mountain. The second ascent of Mont Blanc involved eighteen porters carrying assorted wines, brandies, and scientific instruments, proving, as we see in the Himalaya today, that there are different styles by which people can go into the mountains.

Beginning in the early nineteenth century, the British established summer "hill stations" on ridgetops at Murree, Simla, Mussoorie, Darjeeling, and other locations in British India well situated for viewing the eternal snows. Trekking and hunting enthusiasts on holiday set out from those well-furbished bases, and of course they began writing home about the glories of the Himalaya. In 1883 an Englishman named W. W. Graham was the first person known to have traveled to the Himalaya from England "more for sport and adventure than for the advancement of scientific knowledge." In those days, when travel was far more difficult than it is now, Graham certainly would have read the popular *Art of Travel* by Francis Galton, the period's required reading prior to an Asian trip. It was subtitled *Shifts and Contrivances Available in Wild Countries* and featured instructions on rope descents, making black powder, and defending a camp against marauders.

From the outset of travel into the Himalaya, a trek or a climb could be in either of two styles. Some people preferred to walk with a small group that ate the local diet and replenished food supplies along the way, eschewing large numbers of porters. Others traveled as befitted a proper *sahib* (then meaning any Westerner), with porters, servants, cooks, guides, and, if not all the comforts of home, enough to take the edge off. Each method of travel has had its enthusiastic participants, and trekking styles today have evolved from the parties that went into the Himalaya a hundred years ago.

A perfect example of the grand, well-provisioned approach to Himalayan trekking was carried off first class by Robert and Katherine Barrett in 1923–24. Well read in both Tibetan lore and *The Art of Travel*, this unique American couple left Kashmir and trekked for a year in Ladakh and Baltistan, calling themselves Gypsy Davy and Lady Ba. En route, they reached the Baltoro Glacier, made a winter camp above Leh, and stayed by Tibet's Pangong Lake before returning to British India. Their book, *The Himalayan Letters of Gypsy Davy and Lady Ba*, is a little-known classic, with an unexcelled map showing every night's camp and depicting the glaciers as firewater-breathing dragons.

Toward the beginning, Lady Ba wrote to a friend, "It is our pilgrimage to Mecca, this Himalayan journey. We go about in a sort of rapture. It may be years before we get back." Davy, in his fifties, went about in "neatly patched Shetlands" and liked to meditate on high viewpoints. The Barretts lived Tibetan style in handsome embroidered tents. They hired Rasul Galwan from Leh, the best *sirdar* (caravan foreman) of the day, and allowed him to outfit the caravan to his liking. Davy and Rasul had traveled together twenty years earlier, and it was Rasul's knowledge that bestowed their pilgrimage with an extra dimension. "Up to now," Lady Ba wrote, "the mountains have been earth to us, beautiful, austere, impersonal. To Rasul they are places, backgrounds for stories of people."

The opulent style of Gypsy Davy and Lady Ba's journey "to the high quiet places" cannot be duplicated today, but it is quite possible to go with a sizable crew, eat Western food, and maintain many amenities. However, many Himalayan travelers today, given limited bank accounts and recent innovations in lightweight gear, are taking an unencumbered approach to trekking. This style also had its enthusiasts in the days when few valleys had been breached by outsiders.

The first mountain explorer to advocate traveling lightly was Dr. Tom Longstaff, a British explorer and climber who made discoveries and ascents in the Gilgit valleys, Baltistan, Garhwal, and the Everest area at the beginning of this century. Another exponent of the unencumbered approach was the legendary British mountaineer Eric Shipton, who in 1934 amazed even Longstaff by telling him that he and Bill (H. W.) Tilman planned to travel to India by cargo ship, hire two Sherpas, and travel in the Himalaya five months for a total of £300. Not only were Shipton and Tilman £14 under budget for that trip, but they became the first Westerners to reach the meadows of the Nanda Devi Sanctuary and explore the three major sources of the sacred Ganges River. Shipton later wrote in his autobiography, "Bill and I used to boast that we could organise a Himalayan expedition in half an hour on the back of an envelope."

In 1949, several years before Nepal opened its doors to tourism, Bill Tilman, Maj. James O. M. Roberts, and two scientists were permitted to trek into the upper Marsyangdi and Kali Gandaki valleys to look about and climb a few peaks. Like Tilman, Roberts knew the mountains, but the major lived higher off the land on his trip than had Tilman and Shipton with their wheat flour, *tsampa* (roasted barley flour), butter, and tea. (Even the hardy Sherpas, while emphasizing that Shipton and Tilman were always fair, complained of the spartan diet they shared with these two Angrezi.) Major Roberts was fluent in Nepali, having commanded a Gurkha Rifles regiment, and had gone into the hills many times on recruiting missions. From time to time he did some climbing, once as leader of the only expedition ever sanctioned to attempt sacred Machhapuchhare ("The Fishtail"), but the climbers were stopped by sheer ice walls a respectful distance below the summit of the sacred peak.

When Jimmy Roberts retired, by then a colonel, he opened the first trekking agency, in 1965, called Mountain Travel. Roberts's idea was that, in order to trek comfortably in the exquisite and remote hills of Nepal, people would be willing to pay for porters, supplies, and Sherpas with know-how. It was a prescient decision, as events have proven, an idea that expanded in scope far beyond anything Roberts imagined at the time.

Today's Styles of Trekking

A hundred years ago, you would have been foolish to travel in some parts of the Himalaya without being capable of repelling a raid by the locals. As time has passed, however, the people who live in and govern the Himalaya have changed their minds a great deal about foreigners. Economics have been a factor in many areas. With population pressures and deforestation, hill people need income to purchase foods they can't grow, as well as other necessities they cannot produce, like clothing, kerosene, and cooking oil. Outsiders are now seen to be a source of revenue, not spies or representatives of a distant government.

Today's trekker has a number of options as to style. You can walk completely alone (recommended for very few except on the major routes) or with one or more friends; with just a porter; with or without friends (my own preferred style); with a sirdar and crew; or with a group arranged by a local outfitter or tour operator. The descriptions below can help you decide which style is closest to your inclination and means.

Note that while the manner in which you trek may differ in terms of convenience and the load you carry, the one doing the walking is always you. The first few days of a Himalayan trek can be daunting even though rationally you know that thousands of people (some of them quite out of shape) have preceded you, and that for countless thousands of mountain dwellers in the Himalaya, walking mountain trails is an everyday fact of life. A good way to break in is to hike in hills or mountains near your home before setting off halfway around the world to trek. Be sure you like hiking before buying your ticket to South Asia, if you're going there solely to walk.

If you are already in Asia and are considering a long hike, then you might try a short walk into the country to get a feel for the land and see whether you like trekking. There are easily accessible one-day walks you can take out of places like Chitral, Rawalpindi, Baltit in Hunza, Srinagar, or any of India's hill stations. You can practice your trekking act and shove aside mountains of inhibitions by carrying a small pack to or beyond the day-hike viewpoint, then setting up camp and staying for the night. Two quick considerations if you do this: do not sleep in a religious temple or shrine and be certain that you are well above town and away from a road. As at home, the laws and denizens of the city can be very different from country ways and people.

Another way to warm up for a longer trek, or to help decide which style of trekking fits you, is to walk solo or with a porter for a couple of days or more to get the feel of things. The danger is that in a day or two you will indeed have a feel for the trail, yet lack the gear or permission to continue. Returning to "Go" and reequipping can be most frustrating.

Here are the four basic styles of trekking.

Walking Alone or with Friends

Yes, to dance beneath the diamond sky with one hand waving free . . .

Bob Dylan, 1965

When we hike in the Sierra, Rockies, Appalachians, or the Alps, we plan for our food needs, take shelter, and head for the trail. This kind of trekking can be done in the Himalaya too, but several ifs and warnings are attached to going completely alone. The first-time trekker who will set off entirely alone is rare, although some have. My decision to go trekking for the first time was arrived at one day in 1971 during a delightful walk west of Pokhara. In the course of that hike I easily came to the realization that, yes, the trail just kept going along and all I had to do was follow it. Luckily, however, I met some Peace Corps volunteers who were about to leave also, and we agreed to trek together. By preference I like to explore new places alone, but I know that for the first two to three days of that trek, like any beginner, I was very glad to be with the PCVs, learning the ropes and more vocabulary.

Solo trekking is often easier for the young and intrepid. Walking alone is easiest if you are hiking on a well-trekked route in Nepal where there are plenty of inns. In Pakistan and India it can be more difficult to trek alone if you don't speak any Hindi/Urdu (or Hindustani as the language is often called collectively). Trekking alone can also be done by the strong Himalayan veteran who knows the ways of the land. Trekking solo, however, is not appropriate for women (see "Making the Most of Being a Woman Trekker"); remember that nowhere do local women walk alone beyond their village locale.

Trekking by yourself can be wonderful, but to do it you must be prepared to put more than walking along the trail into your day. If you plan to camp out and cook your own food, then you must have the stamina to do it. In many areas you may stay in homes or possibly rudimentary inns. In either a house or an inn away from the road, you will need to know some basic vocabulary in the local lingua franca (see the appropriate glossary at the end of this book), because locals in Pakistan and India do not know "trekking English" like innkeepers in Nepal. Also, you must be prepared for the funky environment of most homes. This includes smoke from the family fire, the inevitable squalling child, the distinct possibility of fleas or lice (see "Trail Sense" in Chapter 3), and the probability that family members will stay up much later than you and talk into the night.

Walking alone or with one or more friends over Himalayan periods of time (typically five days out or more) takes a knack that comes as you proceed. If you are intrepid enough to trek alone off the main routes, you probably have good trail sense, and should have a good map. A hundred-word vocabulary and a friendly disposition are two of the best assets for any foreign walker, but they are particularly helpful to the solo trekker. Just as families have often given the occasional local traveler shelter and a meal, the local traveler has traditionally reciprocated with news and gossip, the word-of-mouth newspaper. Since you are not fluent in the language and don't know the issues and personalities of the valley, you can talk with people about other subjects, such as their livestock, the children, or a neighboring valley, or you can ask and comment about the trail in the vicinity. Practicing your food words with the cook may lead to eating a better meal. You will be surprised how many subjects can be handled with a few words and how quickly you will learn new words if you jot them down and actively use the language.

You need to be alive to what is going on about you. Recently I met an individual trekker in Nepal who asked querulously, *"Mastey,* what means this *mastey?"* The fellow was four days up the trail and still didn't understand word number one: *"namaste,"* the Nepali word of greeting. He thought the children saying the word to him were asking for something. Individual trekkers can walk along, self-righteously burdened by their packs, and be quite out of touch with what is going on about them. This book aims to assist you in communicating with the locals you meet and being in touch with the land you are passing through.

A solo trek can be the most rewarding walk possible. It can bring you almost mystically close to both the people and land in a way impossible when traveling with a group. Carrying all your gear is the most tiring way to walk in the mountains, but you may be compensated by a very real freedom to come and go, getting in and out of trouble, or ecstasy, depending upon who you are.

Trekking with a Porter

There came a time when I realized that he was teaching me more than I was teaching him.

Edward W. Cronin, Jr., 1979

For a great many people, trekking with a porter who carries gear and (if there are no inns on your route) cooks, or trekking with friends and several porters, is the best way to walk in the Himalaya. This is particularly true for hiking in Pakistan and India, where trekkers and trekking are less well understood than in Nepal. Your companion can introduce you to his hill neighbors you will meet along the way, providing you with an entrée into local society. He can also explain to people why you are walking through their bailiwick. Going with a local person opens you up to much that might otherwise pass by unnoticed and spares you the labor of lugging all your belongings and food. If you show an interest in crops, forest plants, or people along the trail, your porter will be able to pass on much lore, because he knows the country. You will often be reminded that you may be the sahib, but he is the teacher.

Soon after you begin walking with a porter, a private vocabulary will develop, probably a pidgin version of English combined with Hindi/Urdu. Speaking even minimal Hindustani will set you apart from most all other trekkers. Using a modest amount of the local language or Hindi/Urdu, the lingua franca, is extremely important in establishing good relations with your porter. If your porter-guide-companion spoke English well, he would probably be working elsewhere. But if your porter wants to work for trekkers in the future, he will try to learn as much English while walking with you as he can.

Longstaff, Shipton, Tilman, and Murray walked the mountain trails with a similarly minimal approach to trekking. Because they trekked for months at a time and departed from trailheads that were farther from the ranges than the trailheads used today, they needed more than one porter to a Westerner. But everyone carried a load. If you are willing to carry at least a small load yourself, you and a friend can have a rewarding trek far into the Himalaya with one or at most two porters each. If you start getting too many people, you'll be hiring porters to carry the food for other porters. When I reached my mid-forties, I found that I couldn't carry the loads I could in my twenties and still have any energy by the end of the day. But that is only part of the reason why I have learned to prefer walking with a porter. Going with a local frees me to enjoy the walk, not just carry a load all day, and gives me the pleasure of walking with a good companion as well. And I can learn much more about local ways and have access to people that I never had when walking alone.

Do not assume that you can get a first-class porter on snap notice. If you must count every day of your time in the Himalaya, you should weigh the merits of trekking with a sirdar and crew, or with a group arranged by a local outfitter or tour operator at home. The important subject of whom to hire as porter and how to go about the process of hiring him is discussed in detail in the section "Trekking with a Porter" in Chapter 3.

Going with a Guide and Crew

It was clear that we must field a light party and live on the country, after the manner set by the pioneer of Himalayan climbing, Dr. Longstaff—a manner that subsequently lapsed but which had again been demonstrated by Shipton and Tilman in the nineteen-thirties.

W. H. Murray, 1951

If you want to walk a chosen route through the mountains for a limited time with several friends, and if expense is not a prime concern, then hiring a guide (the person called a sirdar in Nepal), cook, and porters is a good way for you to go trekking. By making arrangements with a tour operator at home or a trekking outfitter in Pakistan or India, or possibly by hiring a guide after you arrive (this can be tricky), you can go on a private trek with all of the comforts enjoyed by those who trek with a group organized by a tour operator. A trekking outfitter can do anything from merely arranging for a porter to completely outfitting a crew for you or your own group of friends.

If you have never been to Pakistan or India before, and want to have everything arranged for you when you arrive, you can write or call one or more of the established tour operators at home *at least* six months before you plan to leave. In the travel business this is called arranging an "FIT," meaning foreign independent travel. Tell the tour operator you choose where and for how long you or your group would like to walk, discuss terms, and you can have the company's local trekking outfitter completely outfit your trek before you arrive in Asia. Then you will not waste time in-country, and although working with a tour operator is more expensive, you can be reasonably sure that your group will have an experienced guide, adequate supplies, and a dependable crew. It is not easy to make these arrangements on your own in either Pakistan or India. The company you contact will make the arrangements for your trek through a trekking outfitter it works with in Islamabad or New Delhi. The tour operator at home and the trekking outfitter in Pakistan or India have already established working relationships (and probably the two companies have telex facilities as well), which greatly facilitate matters.

Alternatively you can write directly to a trekking outfitter in Pakistan or India and ask it to plan things for you. (See Appendix B, "Trekking Outfitters in Pakistan and India.") It can be somewhat difficult to make arrangements directly with a company halfway around the world in India or Pakistan. But on the other hand, the outfitters in these two countries have far less business than most companies in Nepal, and your file is less likely to get lost in the shuffle than it could in Nepal. Still, outfitters that you have contacted directly may possibly do little until you actually show up. Making arrangements directly with a company will definitely not be as expensive as going through a tour operator at home, but negotiating through international mail will take longer than asking a tour operator at home to handle your plans.

If you wait to organize a crew until you arrive, you will probably need at least a week to make plans. Again, once you are in-country, you can go to an outfitter and ask it to assist you to put together a guide and staff. It is not easy at all to put together a crew by yourself. You can go to a local shopkeeper who deals with tourists and ask him to assist you. In the chapters that describe the various areas, I will mention people that I know, but, as always: caveat emptor. These people aren't always going to be able to come up with an excellent choice on short notice. If G.M. or Dad Ali in Gilgit, for example, make a bad choice (based on who's in town at the moment), you'll just have to shrug it off and hope that any contacts you have made will serve you better the next time. You might try telling your hotel manager that you are looking for a trekking crew, but the hotel manager will merely put you in contact with a friend or family member who may not be well qualified. The outfitter may not be the best, it will just be his friend, or someone he owes a favor to. The busiest time of year for trekking in Pakistan and India is during the summer and early autumn before the snow falls. You will be unlikely to find experienced guides available then, but you might get lucky if a guide is free due to a cancellation.

If you sign with a trekking agency in Islamabad or New Delhi, you will pay a fixed price for everything and that will be it. But if you deal directly with a guide, you will make a verbal arrangement and then you must agree on everything. Any points left vague or open to interpretation may get hauled out later for renegotiation. If you go with an established outfitter, it will provide equipment, but if you hire a guide yourself, you may find yourself in the bazaar following him around as he purchases everything from pots to spices. Many people like to call themselves guides nowadays. You must always ask for a person's chits, his letters of reference from former employers. Read the letters carefully and form an intuitive sense of the man. Note particularly whether he has been along the specific route you want, and whether he is recommended by someone you know or know of. Be certain, too, that the chits are his and not on loan from a friend.

Trekking with a Group Arranged by a Tour Operator

So-called "adventure travel" is going mainstream. Many people now have the money for these foot-propelled vacations but would like everything arranged for them when they arrive. For these folks, there are numerous tour operators that offer treks in the Himalaya. The oldest of these companies have been sending people on walking excursions for over twenty years, and the best tour operators do an excellent job. Mountain Travel was the first tour operator to send people from the United States to Nepal and elsewhere, but it has been joined by a host of competitors, each with its own flashy catalog. Organized trekking groups from Japan, England, Germany, France, Italy, Australia, and the United States fan out in many seasons, sometimes with itineraries leading to obscure places or with sophisticated specialities. Before long, some enterprising company will offer a tour to observe the making of hand-rubbed *charas* (hashish) as the participants wend their way over hill and dale.

If you go with an organized group, you can have confidence to trek that you might not have otherwise. But you need to be realistic about your abilities before deciding to go. Groups may have a physician along, and the leader can be helpful in calming beginners and advising on pace, but you must be physically fit and prepared to leave behind many comforts of home.

The first thing many people ask when they inquire about going with an arranged group is, "Who will I be going with? Who is already signed up?" I've found that people who join trekking groups (particularly the longer, more vigorous walks) tend to be self-selecting. Indeed, on a group trek you will be walking with people who are initially strangers, but people usually get along just fine with each other and you will always find some congenial souls with whom to become friends. One of the unfortunate characteristics of group travel is that people are generally inclined to relate exclusively to others in the group and often miss opportunities to meet locals or other trekkers along the way.

Recently a man on a group I was escorting became ill and could not continue. He and his wife stayed behind with a Sherpa, and when he was ready to walk again, the three of them retraced their steps back the way we had come. When we met again in Kathmandu, they told me that the return by themselves had been the most rewarding part of the trek. They had been able to walk utterly at their own pace and get to meet the locals much more easily than had been possible with the group. They didn't hesitate to seek out their own encounters and paint their own canvas. Yet many people prefer the companionship and sociability engendered in group trekking.

One question you should ask before deciding which group to sign up with is, Who is the group leader and what are his or her qualifications? How many times has the escort been over the route before? Does that person speak any of the local dialect or Hindi/Urdu? Your escort can assist you to learn much, much more about where you are going if he or she is familiar with the region and its inhabitants. Group members trekking with a savvy leader can become more knowledgeable about an area than individual trekkers who just put their heads down and start walking. In order to stand out from the crowd, tour operators need to have both good leaders and good outfitters (agents) in the country where the trip takes place.

An important feature to keep in mind about group treks is that the participants agree to a set schedule. They all know, before leaving, where they will be on any day of the trek, and no one can follow an individual impulse to set off on an overnight side trip, to rest for a day, stay in an interesting village, or climb a tempting minor peak. Group trekking is active, but by no means adventurous. The group must always camp together, although they certainly don't need to walk in a cluster. For many, the security and comradeship offered by groups is the ideal way to go. Group trekking has opened windows to remarkable areas and foreign cultures that participants might otherwise not be able to experience.

Making the Most of Being a Woman Trekker *by Debra Denker*

[Debra Denker has traveled in Tibet and trekked in India, Pakistan, and Nepal, sometimes with her mother, Maria Denker. She has kindly contributed the following thoughts for women who go trekking.]

Being a woman gives you wonderful, sometimes unique, opportunities to get to know local people while trekking. You will probably have very different experiences, depending on whether you are trekking with a porter-guide, with a group, with another woman, or with a male companion. The composition of your group will affect how local people relate to you, but ultimately it's your own attitude that will make or break your relationships with people along the trail.

In some cultures where men and women live separately, being a woman gives you a special chance to relate to the female half of society. Even in Buddhist and Hindu cultures where men and women live and work closely together, women respond to other women with spontaneous sisterhood, and children respond to women as mother or aunt figures. You can enrich your trip immensely by learning about a hundred simple words and phrases of the local language. Learn to ask questions like, "How many children do you have?" and to answer other people's questions about you and your family. Bring pictures of your own family if they're not with you. Local people are just as curious about you as you are about them. It always helps to have a respectable profession, such as teaching, writing, or photography, that you can tell people about in the local language. When all else fails, use sign language. Be spontaneous! One of my fondest memories is of my mother, Maria Denker, and a lama (a Tibetan Buddhist priest) from Mustang making hand shadows of animals by firelight on the wall of a lodge near Muktinath in Nepal.

Whether you are with a friend or with a group, pictures and small instruments, such as wooden flutes or harmonicas, make great conversation starters. Children also like to sing into tape recorders, and are thrilled to hear the playback. In a home or inn you can often enter the kitchen and watch women cook, make *chang* (beer), or churn butter tea. They'll be flattered by your interest, and you may be able to lend a hand in cleaning grain or even making bread. An exception, of course, is in Hindu households: non-Hindus are outside the caste system, and thus we would be viewed as ritually polluting their food and kitchen.

Trekking completely by yourself isn't advisable; in fact, it's just plain foolhardy. Remember that local women don't walk alone beyond their village. If you are not traveling with anyone, it is safest to hire a porter-guide from a reputable outfitter.

One of the difficulties of being female is that local men will sometimes be overly interested. The best way to handle this is to make clear at the beginning your lack of reciprocation. Generally, a sweetly uttered "But I think of you as my brother" is enough to make any male back off and, in fact, treat you with great respect. [Unfortunately, the introduction of video-cassette recorders and the X-rated films that may accompany them have sometimes given a wildly inaccurate impression of Western women to the locals.] Remember that you are far safer trekking escorted in the hills, as compared to traveling in Latin America or at night through any city in the United States.

Dress is very important, perhaps more so for a woman than for a man. If you want to be culturally sensitive and avoid misunderstandings, shorts and halter tops are definitely not recommended. Aside from being reveal-ing, they are impractical, and you will end up scratched, bitten, and sun-burned. Some women like to wear the *chuba*, the wraparound Tibetan robe, but usually Tibetan and Sherpa women walk better in them than we do over long distances. They are nice for lounging around a lodge, however, and people always appreciate foreigners who dress as they do. Learn from the local women and make sure your local dress actually goes together and is not a hodgepodge of styles or cultures that locals will look at oddly.

I have personally found *shalwar kameez*, the baggy trousers and long loose shirt worn in Pakistan and northern India, to be comfortable, practi-cal, and acceptable for trekking nearly anywhere. Loose cotton trousers for summer, loose wool trousers for winter, and especially long skirts, if you can walk in them, are also recommended. Remember that in remote areas a woman in pants may not be recognized as a woman. Nude bathing (unless you are with village women in a private place) or even wearing a bathing suit under an enticing waterfall is not recommended. If it's hot, it's nicer to bathe in your clothes and let them dry on you anyway.

If you have long hair, wear it in braids to keep it untangled and out of the way. Even better, let a village woman or girl braid it for you in the local fashion. I find a scarf or other head covering helps keep the dust out of my hair and the direct sun off my head.

A mundane but important consideration is what to do when you have your period. Bring plenty of tampons or sanitary napkins from home, because you won't necessarily find them in the bazaar, or they won't be the right brand, or they will be very expensive. Disposal is another problem. One could burn the stuff, but lots of brands don't burn easily. Never burn sanitary or toilet materials, including facial tissues, in a kitchen fire or stove (considered sacred in Hindu or Buddhist locales), only in a private campfire out of sight of locals. Inns will have marked toilets, and one can deposit used sanitary materials in these, unless you think the night soil will be used as fertilizer. The most ecologically conscious thing to do is to wrap tampons or sanitary napkins up in layers of plastic and take them back to a city for disposal. If you're absolutely sure they are biodegradable, it's okay to bury them, but like toilet paper they should be buried deep enough. (Note that many women temporarily lose their period when they travel overseas and sometimes for a month or two after they return. This is nothing to be concerned about.)

Personal cleanliness is sometimes hard to maintain, especially if you are trekking in a cold season and tend to wear your clothes for days at a time because it's too cold to undress. Panty liners are useful, and a babywipe at the end of the day does wonders for one's mood and feeling of cleanliness.

Many women have problems with cold hands and feet. I recommend a hot-water bottle, to be filled last thing at night from the kettle. This can also provide lukewarm washing water in the morning. Be sure, too, that you take a warm-enough sleeping bag and perhaps down booties.

Whoever you are, however you trek, you can make the most of your experiences by being open to people around you and by going out of your way to be friendly, whether you've learned a little language, or play the flute, or simply smile and use sign language.

Trekking with Children   *by Pam Ross*

I don't dare shout, but my heart is beating very fast.

Robert Rushing, age thirteen,
about to depart for Asia, 1971

[Pam Ross has lived in Nepal and assisted her husband Charles Gay as escort on several group family treks. They have walked with their grade-school-age son Forrest on these and other hikes in various regions of Nepal. Pam has many words to the wise about hiking with children.]

Do you really want to take your kids with you to the Himalaya? For many first-time trekkers, the prospect of staying happy and healthy while walking in the mountains of Asia is daunting enough without the added responsibility of making sure that their offspring have a good time as well. Certainly you should already know that you enjoy traveling, camping, and hiking with your child before you contemplate a family trek in the Himalaya. In fact, having a child along can enrich the experience of trekking and encountering a new culture, and it definitely opens doors into that culture. Aside from parental anxiety, there is absolutely no reason why children can't trek successfully.

How will taking your offspring along change the trek? As every parent knows, lack of energy is never the problem. Boredom or lack of perseverance is what causes a child to say, "I'm tired, I need to rest," and then to spend the entire rest time climbing the nearest steep rock and jumping off the top. Having other kids along makes both walking and playing more enjoyable for most children. Go with friends or join a group of other families; some tour operators offer family treks.

Plan on relatively short days: four or five hours of walking, with lots of fifteen-to-twenty-minute stops to throw rocks in rivers, climb things, watch insects, etc. Plan on a two-hour stop in the middle of the day (most group treks do this anyway, so the staff can prepare a hot meal for everyone). While walking, be ready sometimes to tell stories or play word games with your child instead of drinking in the spectacular scenery in meditative silence.

Hire an extra person to carry each child under eight. The wives of Sherpas often do this job in Nepal, and a wife or other female relative of your staff member may be able to do this in Pakistan or India, so long as there are no young children at home. Even if your children end up walking most of the time, it's great for them (and you) to know that they can be carried if they need it, if they get sick, or if you have to get over a pass to reach a good campsite. Himalayan terrain is steep and often difficult, and even if your children's porters never carry them, it's reassuring to have someone who holds their hand in dicey places, carries their raingear and sun hat and rock collection, and picks up their gloves when they leave them behind. There are two options for child-carrying packs: your own child carrier, which can be simple or high-tech, and has the advantage of being the one your child is accustomed to, or the local type of woven basket, which can be cut down to make room for the legs and easily padded with a sleeping bag. These baskets work beautifully, especially for older kids, and have the advantage of being good load carriers when the child is walking.

Can you keep your children healthy on a trek? This is the big question, the one that makes people think you're crazy for even considering taking a child trekking, but there's no reason, given adequate precautions and the cooperation of the child, why your kid shouldn't stay just as healthy as you. Read Chapter 14, "A Himalayan Medical Primer" and follow Peter Hackett's advice. The only extra risk with children is that they do tend to put their dirty hands (and other even less savory objects) in their mouths. I dealt with this problem quite successfully when my son Forrest was three years old by starting a big campaign of "no hands in mouths" as soon as we left the United States. To reinforce this idea, we *both* painted on bad-tasting stuff designed to stop nail biting. He loved reminding me not to bite my nails, and soon got into the habit of washing his hands before eating anything. A thumb-sucker would be more of a challenge—perhaps regular cleaning with alcohol pads would do it.

Pediatric solutions of some common medicines are available over the counter in the large cities of Pakistan and India. Carry child dosages of whatever you take in your medical kit. (Cough syrup is especially important for those night coughs that keep everyone awake.) *Travel note:* For long plane flights I highly recommend a kiddie sleeping medicine. The one my pediatrician prescribed was aptly called Noctec, but anything that induces sleep will do.

Altitude sickness in children (who are beyond the infant stage) has not yet been documented as any more likely to occur than it is with adults. Obviously it is important to acquaint yourself with the early symptoms of the disease and to make sure your child drinks plenty of fluids and reports any headaches or nausea. The key is awareness to both your own and your child's physical state, and willingness to rest for a day or descend if it seems warranted.

Should special food or equipment be carried? Most children like the rice-and-lentil diet, and many enjoy the sweet, milky tea served in most parts of the Himalaya. Some suggestions for extras to bring from home: soy sauce to flavor rice; powdered drink mixes to mask the taste of iodine in water and to promote fluid consumption; and granola bars, dried fruit, or nuts for quick treats on the trail. These items are generally not available in India and Pakistan (with the exception of dried fruits and nuts).

Your child's clothing and sleeping bag should be just as good as yours, with the additional reminder that a child who is being carried is not generating heat of his own and should be warmly dressed. A warm hat is particularly important.

A few small, familiar toys are definitely worth taking: tiny stuffed animals, pens and notebooks, a small tape player with earphones and kids' music and stories. Keeping a daily journal (for younger children, drawing pictures plus a narrative dictated to you) is a wonderful occupation and the best possible souvenir. Having a teacher assign the task may make this more palatable for some kids.

A tent provides welcome privacy for a child who may be overloaded with attention from the local villagers. For all but the most gregarious child, the constant attention of strangers gets to be too much from time to time. This is when a child needs to be able to retire to a tent for some quiet with familiar playthings.

Diapers and toileting are a problem in the mountains. Disposable diapers are not all that disposable where there is no garbage pickup. Probably the best solution is to bury used diapers *deeply* once a day. On organized treks the staff digs a latrine, and a separate hole for diapers could be dug nearby. Check to make sure the hole is covered properly before you leave any campsite, otherwise dogs will dig things up. Do not attempt to burn diapers: they don't burn easily, and such fires are offensive to the locals. Older kids may object to the lack of proper facilities. Have your child practice ahead of time, outdoors if possible, and, if in doubt, buy a small plastic potty or cut the seat out of one of the folding stools commonly carried on organized treks.

How can you foster interaction with local kids? For Himalayan villagers, the arrival of trekkers is a lot like having the circus pull into town. You are definitely a show, and even on the few better-traveled routes, foreign kids are still a rarity. The traditional cultures along the trail are very family-oriented and are usually thrilled to see that trekkers do indeed reproduce and travel as families, but to turn the existing fascination and goodwill into meaningful interchange requires some effort. Despite what we'd all like to believe, kids do not instantly overcome language and cultural differences and play together, especially if it's with a new set of kids each day.

An English-speaking local staff person can help to get games started. In many villages, children play a version of duck-duck-goose that any kid can learn to play in two minutes. Tug-of-war is known everywhere, as are different forms of tag. Take a ball and a frisbee. But please do *not* take small gifts to hand out to kids: this practice just starts them begging.

If your child is of school age, try to visit a school. English is taught from the early grades, and participation in an English class would be enlightening for your child as well as the students. And the game of naming things in English and the local language can be fun any time there is an opportunity for one-on-one play.

A valuable relationship to foster is that between your child and an English-speaking local staff person who can expand your child's observation into learning. How the locals go about their daily lives (the details of food production, animal husbandry, and housekeeping) are always more fascinating to kids than the names of towns, the elevations of peaks, or the names of deities. Mountain people are of necessity excellent naturalists, with a vast knowledge of the plants and animals around them. And children specialize in minute observations of the natural world. Identification of animal droppings found along the trail is fun and so is birdwatching, especially with a good picture guidebook.

Like many activities that people don't often do with kids, trekking in the Himalaya requires some extra effort and advance planning, but the rewards of sharing one of the great adventures of your life with your children are great indeed. Even if your children don't remember the specifics of the trek in a few years, the experience of visiting a culture where people live in harmony with their mountain environment without roads, machinery, or modern entertainment is bound to make a lasting impression.

Musical accompaniment at the Hemis Festival in Ladakh.

2
Before You Leave

There is no happiness for him who does not travel, Rohita!
Thus we have heard. Living in the society of men, the best
man becomes a sinner. . . . Therefore, wander! . . . The
fortune of him who is sitting, sits; it rises when he rises; it
sleeps when he sleeps; it moves when he moves. Therefore,
wander!
Aitareya Brahmanan in the Rigveda, 800–600 B.C.

As often as possible, do what the others are not doing: go
off-season instead of on, go in bad weather instead of good,
walk when others ride, laugh when others cry. . . .
Ed Buryn, 1971

To Begin . . .

Many of us tempt ourselves for years with the possibility of going to the Himalaya. Scenes from books or films come to mind, and we imagine ourselves being in those faraway places. We fantasize about trekking north of the world's highest massifs into land indistinguishable from Tibet, or of walking up a glaciated pass between two medieval valley kingdoms. When the decision is finally made, it is as if you had been walking up a rolling hill and imperceptibly crossed its ridgeline, finding yourself going down the far side. You *are* going. Many people follow the crowds and go trekking first in Nepal where trekking is big business. But more and more often, people are beginning to discover the people and trails of Pakistan and India—cultures and paths that have seen fewer foreigners, but which are equally challenging and fascinating. This book covers some remarkable regions, those areas "less traveled by."

Eric Shipton could organize his excursions to the Himalaya "in half an hour on the back of an envelope," but you will require considerably more time and at least two full-size sheets of paper for making lists of immunizations to get, visas to obtain, and more. My second overland trip to Asia was completely organized on less than three weeks' notice, from inspiration to departure. This can be done and we proved it, but if you take such a hasty approach, you will be ill prepared and may be exhausted by the time you reach Asia. Three months is a much better minimum time to consider planning such a sojourn. A Himalayan trek requires planning, and you can begin several aspects of preparation at once.

Physical Conditioning

If you plan to trek in addition to sightseeing, you should initiate or continue a good conditioning program. Vigorous exercise that strengthens the cardiovascular system, lungs, and legs is the best way to prepare yourself for Himalayan walking. Running, swimming, bicycling, and cross-country skiing will help toughen you for walking in country so vertical that you may trek steadily uphill for days at a time. The best exercise, of course, is to hike uphill and down, carrying a day pack if you are going with a group, or more if you will be carrying any weight in the Himalaya. Exercise continuously for sixty to ninety minutes every couple of days, or even more often if you have the time, and certainly work up to that much exercise before leaving. Even this amount of training will not fully condition you for a full day of walking day in and day out, but it will help strengthen your system to the point that your body can accept the rigors of trekking. Backpacking in your favorite hilly location is the best approximation of what you will do in the Himalaya and will help remind you of your physical capabilities. One of the many joys of a Himalayan trek is that you get far beyond the achy-muscles-and-groggy-evenings stage of hiking by the end of the first week. If you have done no physical preparation at all, however, it will take far longer than a week on the trail. Many people who either don't get in condition or set off on a whim don't get far without wishing fervently that they were in shape. Spur-of-the-moment trekkers are sometimes forced to turn back by ailments that might not have occurred had they been physically prepared.

Background Reading

This book describes many trekking possibilities in Pakistan and India, but you will enjoy your trip more if you do some background reading. After perusing the trail descriptions herein, you may have a greater interest in two or three areas and might want to seek out additional reading about them. The annotated bibliography at the back of the book will lead you a long way toward gathering all the information you will need or can absorb.

My own favorite book on the regions of Chitral and Hunza is John Staley's *Words for My Brother*. The book is a relatively recent one but can be difficult to locate, like some of the regions it describes. The persistent person who is able to find a copy will be well rewarded. Books like *Into India*, by John Keay, or *Portrait of India*, by Ved Mehta, make excellent introductions to India. Eric Newby's *A Short Walk in the Hindu Kush* remains one of the classic books on this part of the world. Newby, his friend Hugh, and their crew of three Afghans trekked in Nuristan, Afghanistan, in 1956. With minimal paraphernalia, they walked in the Panjshir Valley, then tried to reach the top of 19,880-foot Mir Samir, reading how-to-climb books on the ascent. After failing in three attempts, they had an eventful look at their real objective, the rarely seen Ramgul Valley in the region of Nuristan. Newby experienced and hilariously detailed many predicaments and pitfalls facing the neophyte trekker.

Aside from your other reading, try to absorb some vocabulary and sentence structure from John Mock's "Introduction to Hindustani" and, if possible, look over the more localized glossaries corresponding to the regions you plan to visit. These glossaries may ultimately be the most helpful part of the book once you arrive in South Asia. Every word learned is another opportunity to talk with the locals when you are walking through their homelands.

Maps

As you narrow down the areas you are interested in and begin planning your trek, you need to consider purchasing maps. When you are trekking, a map can be one of your most instructive sources of information. The U502 Series map sheets for Pakistan and India remain by and large the most accurate maps available for the regions covered in this book. For specific information about these maps and others, be sure to consult Appendix A, "Map Information." The maps in this book, while drawn to scale, are meant only to give you an overview of the regions covered. Do read the appendix to learn the range of maps available, and consider purchasing more thorough maps before you leave.

If maps are difficult for you to comprehend, you can familiarize yourself with them in several ways. When you fly in a plane and look down, what you see is very similar to a map. You can become accustomed to route finding as you read by following the paths described on a map. Once in the Himalaya, you can read towns off the map and talk with locals about them even if you haven't figured out the exact relationship of one place to another. If at first a map appears to be a jumble of lines, you can become more at ease with the whole process of map reading by constantly comparing your map with the lay of the land as you walk through the countryside. Use a map to figure out alternate routes. Ask the locals about those paths and try them if you want to see some different trails from the ones other trekkers are taking, or from the ones described herein.

Some people like to mark their maps with colored felt-tip pens, using one shade for the main rivers and another for the ridgelines. Such lines following valley bottoms and ridges can particularly help you visualize the country shown on photocopied or one-color maps. Don't hesitate to make notes right on a map or its border if your reading of the land disagrees with what the map shows.

Passport and Visas

All citizens of the United States need a current passport for travel abroad. If your passport has expired (or is within six months of expiration, in the case of travel to India), you will need a new one. Most post offices in the United States can give you passport application forms or you can apply at one of the passport agencies operated by the State Department in major cities. For a first application, you will need a certified copy of your birth certificate, a driver's license, and two identical recent photographs one to one and a half inches high. For a renewal you will need your old passport and new photographs. You should also get at least a dozen smaller photos for visa applications.

All United States passport holders need a visa for Pakistan. Visas are granted for up to three months, and the first entry must be within three months of date of issue of the visa. A small fee is usually charged. Multiple-entry visas may also be given if requested. With a double-entry visa, for instance, you can travel north from Hunza out of Pakistan into Sinkiang in China, visit Kashgar and vicinity, then return with no difficulty. Extensions of stay up to six months total in one year can be granted. Extensions are granted at district police stations but are rarely given for long periods of time. It is better to request a three-month visa when you initially apply at home. Even then, Pakistani bureaucrats can be capricious in the amount of time they allot, or will be instructed to give a visa stamped something like "Authorized Duration of Each Stay: To Be Determined at the Port of Arrival in Pakistan." But when you apply, you can always try for as long a period of time as you may need.

The various areas where you can trek in northern Pakistan are considered to be in either "open," "restricted," or "closed" zones. The status of any particular region is apt to change somewhat from year to year, but in Chapters 4, 5, and 7, I try to give you as clear an idea as possible of the official status of every area discussed. Open zones can be visited without permits of any kind; closed zones are closed, period. To confuse the issue, some areas are not mentioned in the list of treks published annually by the Pakistani government. Officially, restricted zones can only be visited after an application process, which needs to be initiated *several months* before your projected arrival in Pakistan. For full particulars of this process and the necessary forms to initiate it, you should write to: Deputy Chief, Tourism Division, College Road, Sector F-7/2, Islamabad, Pakistan. Ask for the current edition of "Trekking Rules and Regulations." If you wish to climb a peak in Pakistan that is higher than 19,680 ft., you should ask for the current edition of "Mountaineering Rules and Regulations." Trekking in restricted areas requires hiring and outfitting a licensed guide and complying with various other regulations. It is easier to undertake the application process if you arrange with an outfitter in Pakistan ahead of time to submit the application on your behalf. A list of outfitters is found in Appendix B. Further information about trekking regulations is found in Chapter 3 under "Pakistan's Trekking Policies."

Citizens of most countries, including Commonwealth countries, need visas to enter or transit India. Please note this if you plan to stop overnight in India or even change planes there in transit. The Indian visa can be validated for single, double, or multiple entries. It can be issued for up to a three-month stay, and the first entry must be within six months of the date of issue. A fee will be charged, probably depending on the number of entries requested. The visa is extendable for three more months once you are in-country. Extensions are granted at district police stations. Please check current regulations carefully when you apply for an Indian visa, for these regulations can change. Whatever stipulations are in force at the moment are applied to the letter. For example, a friend was flying en route to Bhutan when transit visas became required for India. When he landed at Calcutta just to change planes, he had a great deal of difficulty. Be sure to have a valid visa before you reach India.

To travel in Sinkiang you will need a Chinese visa. The procedure involved in obtaining visas for individual travel to China was once quite involved, but this lengthy process has been eased. Check with the Chinese embassy or nearest consulate for the present formalities. Visas for China can be obtained overnight (during working days) by applying at the Chinese consulate or approved travel agencies in Hong Kong. If you are traveling to Sinkiang with a group, your travel agent or tour operator will assist you in getting your visa. There is a Chinese embassy in Islamabad, Pakistan, but it would be better to have a visa for China before you reach Pakistan.

One important note on filling out visa application forms: if you plan to go trekking in a hill area, don't let your enthusiasm spill across the visa application. You may well be better informed on hill geography and restricted regions than the person who issues your visa. If you put words like Chitral, Baltistan, Ladakh, Zanskar, or Kashgar on the line that says "Places to Be Visited," you may invite unneeded complications. Visa applications have been turned down by ill-informed bureaucrats who have read these exotic names on visa applications and assumed the regions to be restricted. Play it safe and just put "Rawalpindi, Swat, and Gilgit" or

"Delhi, Agra, and Srinagar" on your application. Once issued, your Pakistani, Indian, or Chinese visa will be good for any unrestricted region in the designated country.

To get a visa for Pakistan, India, or China, you must first request an application from the particular country's embassy or consulate. After filling out the visa application, mail it back with any necessary payment and photos, a self-addressed stamped envelope (SASE), and your passport. To be absolutely safe when mailing your passport, send the letter by express or registered mail and include postage on the SASE sufficient for your stamped passport to be returned likewise by registered mail. Allow as much as three weeks for each visa to be processed. In many cities there are visa services that, for a fee, can obtain visas for you far faster and more easily than you can get one on your own.

In the United States, you can obtain visas for Pakistan, India, or China at the following addresses:

Embassy of Pakistan, 2315 Massachusetts Avenue NW, Washington, DC 20008

Consulate General of Pakistan, 12 East 65th Street, New York, NY 10021

Embassy of India, 2107 Massachusetts Avenue NW, Washington, DC 20008

Embassy of the People's Republic of China, 2300 Connecticut Avenue NW, Washington, DC 20008.

India also has consulates that can issue visas in New York, Chicago, and San Francisco. China also has consulates that can issue visas in New York, Chicago, Houston, and San Francisco.

Immunizations

Although immunizations are rarely required for entry into Pakistan, India, or China, you would be very wise to get several shots prior to leaving home (and quite foolish not to get them). For information on immunizations, please see Chapter 14, "A Himalayan Medical Primer," by Peter H. Hackett, M.D.

Saman: The More-Than-Enough List

In Hindi and Urdu, the word for "belongings" or "gear" is *saman*. You must be the final judge of what saman to take when you go trekking. To have a good idea of what you'll need, keep in mind your requirements when you go hiking at home. Remember that if you are going walking in summer, the weather in the mountains of Pakistan and India can be quite hot as well as cool. Be prepared with light clothes as well as clothing for cool weather. And remember that you can always buy lightweight duds or have them made before you leave the last good-size bazaar town.

To assist you with what you may need in Asia, I have compiled the following rather exhaustive list. It is divided into six categories so that you can visualize what you will be adding to your pack or duffle if you wish to trek on your own carrying camping and cooking gear, or if you go into the high snows off the trail. Not everything is applicable to everyone's use; the equipment in category 5, for instance, is only for those intending to walk up snow peaks or along glaciers. Far more important to your enjoyment while walking than the latest synthetic piles, miracle fabrics, and fancy gear are prudence (in high places or changeable weather) and enthusiasm for the trekking experience.

Here are the six categories, then the More-Than-Enough List, item by item:

1. Clothing and Personal Gear
2. Camping Equipment
3. Cooking Equipment
4. Miscellaneous
5. Gear for the Snows and Glacier Walking
6. Optional Accessories

Clothing and Personal Gear

If you are going to be walking in the Himalaya for any length of time, the chances are good that you will need most of the clothing listed here. If you are going to be walking in snow or on a glacier, you may have to help equip a porter with clothing essentials acquired locally. As you choose what to pack, keep in mind that you will be hand-washing the most used items in cold stream water.

Underwear. Three pairs are enough. Wash and rewear.

Bras. For women, a couple. Bras are recommended for modesty in traditional societies.

Tampons or sanitary napkins. These will be difficult or impossible to locate in the local bazaar. (See "Making the Most of Being a Woman Trekker" in Chapter 1.)

Socks. Take three pairs of both thin liner socks and heavier outer socks. Liner socks of nylon or cotton are good. Wool or a blend with mostly wool (not synthetics) should be your choice for outers. You must have, at minimum, two complete changes of socks plus an extra pair in case you need another layer. Keep washing your socks, and your feet will thank you by not blistering (given well-broken-in hiking boots or shoes).

Tights. For women, at least one pair for warmth.

T-shirts. Take several. T-shirts with snazzy designs on the front make great gifts for your porter or anyone you would like to give a present to.

Lightweight shirts. You should have one or two loose-fitting wash-and-wear shirts.

Medium-weight to heavyweight shirt. Two button-down pockets on your upper-altitude shirt will come in handy. Wool's still best.

Long, loose-fitting walking skirts. Long skirts are recommended for women. I am also advised that they can be very practical when you must dodge off the trail. The baggy, locally made pants described below are also appropriate for women and offer wonderful freedom of movement.

Loose-fitting trekking pants. For men or women, a pair of pants in addition to those you wear on the plane. Loose pants are a must if you want freedom of movement on the trail. Baggy pants are always worn in Pakistan and usually in India's hilly areas (except by those sophisticates who wear running suits). In the West, the nearest we have to Himalayan-style pants are knickers. These give room for the knee to bend unconstricted, but many are much too tight in the crotch and pelvis unless you make or buy yours large on purpose. Jeans are much too tight for trekking, and if they get wet, they take forever to dry.

Far better than knickers is the Muslim *shalwar*, those wonderfully comfortable pajama-style pants with a drawstring at the waist. As soon as you arrive in Pakistan or India, consider having a local tailor measure you for a pair to take on your trek. After measuring you, the tailor will know how much cloth is necessary. You can then purchase the material (dark colors hide stains), and the pants can be sewn within hours. I always ask the tailor to make the ankle openings just wide enough to fit around my trekking boots. For me, walking in shalwar is the only way to go except on tricky, exposed places off the trail, where the voluminous material can snag. These pants breathe when the temperature is hot yet seem to retain heat during cold weather. Their primary asset is that they permit unrestricted leg movement in any direction without rubbing. And the locals always appreciate it when you wear clothes like theirs.

Thermal underwear. (The shirt is optional.) Polypropylene is the favorite material nowadays. In winter, raw weather, and in high camps, if you wear long johns under your pants or shalwar and the rest of your body is kept warm, the wind will have to become quite intense before you become uncomfortable. For most treks, even with several high camps, these two garments will be enough cover on your legs. (If you carry rain chaps or rain pants, you will have a third layer.)

Rain pants or chaps. Coated nylon or Gore-Tex rain pants are great for rain and wind, but I've always done fine with just rain chaps. If they are tied at one end, you can carry *atta* (wheat flour) in them.

Down, pile, or fiberfill jacket or parka. You will want to have a good down or pile jacket or a down or fiberfill parka on most treks to ensure comfort. Don't take an expedition parka, however, unless you are going up a high peak or have extremely slow metabolism. Remember that you can always add layers. If you trek with a porter, he can use your down jacket to sleep under, with his own blanket beneath him. A synthetic-fill jacket will be better if you trek in the monsoon, but remember that fiberfill jackets take up more room. You may want to add a woolen sweater if you are trekking in the fall or winter.

Trekking boots. Medium- to lightweight trekking boots of your preference are best to walk in. For the rugged terrain of the Karakoram and western Himalaya, you need the ankle and overall foot support of good-

Glaciers can be very dangerous. If this crevasse was hidden by snow and you fell in, you could be a goner if you weren't roped-up (photograph by John Mock).

quality hiking boots. Your new boots *must be broken in*. Never take boots to the Himalaya without being certain that the boots and your feet are well acquainted. Some people like to wear running shoes while trekking, but if you sprain your ankle, you'll feel mighty silly hobbling out to a roadhead or airfield on the other side of the world for lack of a pair of shoes that would adequately protect you. Many people are quite satisfied to trek in running shoes, but please be sure to walk carefully if you choose to wear them. If you plan to do any glacier walking, it would be foolhardy not to wear good boots, given the slippery surface of glaciers. Do be extremely careful where you put your boots when you are not wearing them: trekking boots (and sleeping bags) can disappear faster than any other items in the mountains.

Some boot manufacturers now make hiking boots that cannot be resoled. When their soles wear out, you must toss away the boots. Consider this when you purchase your next pair. When you go to get your boots resoled, be sure the repairman knows his business. Before you head overseas, you might take along some Barge cement or Shoe Goo II if you have any qualms about how your soles will last. Remember: "Comfort of foot is pleasure of mind."

Running shoes or tennis shoes. Running shoes are useful as backup footgear, around camp, when you are not carrying much, must ford a fast-moving stream, or have blisters. If you will be walking on a little-traveled route in Zanskar or Baltistan, you should definitely have lightweight shoes for fording the inevitable streams. Light shoes are great for switching off with your regular footgear, but beware of taking them as your only shoes (see the previous discussion of trekking boots). When you wear them on the trail, walk carefully until you get the feel of them. Some kinds of treads are tricky; they tend to grab and can throw you off balance. If you hire a porter for a trek with a snow pass or glacier walking, he can wear your running shoes for those sections, unless, like one man I hired, he already has mountaineering boots with full-length steel shanks!

Insoles. Your feet may become more fatigued than you expect, and a soft cushion beneath them can give some relief. Insoles can also help keep a foot from rubbing when a boot stretches from extensive use. In a pinch, you can cut your own innersoles from the end of your foam pad.

Moleskin. This padding is used to cushion broken skin. Some people prefer Elastoplast or Second Skin to moleskin. Any kind of tape can partially protect rubbed skin (if it's clean) from further harm. Be sure to take some sort of preventive measure if you even begin to feel a hot spot.

Gloves or mittens. For chilly mornings and high passes, you'll be glad to have hand protection. Wool, polypro, or pile is best.

Umbrella. That's right, a bumbershoot. Many cognoscenti of the Himalaya would never be without one. It is your best protection against the tropical or alpine sun: with an umbrella, you always have shade. Also, in the rain, an umbrella is superior to a poncho (which tends to soak you in perspiration), and it provides a quick line of defense against charging Tibetan mastiffs. When you take backlit photos, an umbrella is excellent for shading the camera lens. If you're in Hunza or Kashmir and see a ripe mulberry, apricot, or cherry tree, flip the umbrella upside down, whack the branch above you, and you've got the world's most refreshing snack. In Pakistan and India, an umbrella is called a *chatta*. Chattas are used by sadhu, funky trekker, and Sir Edmund Hillary alike. I always recommend umbrellas to people I trek with and they bring them along, sometimes unwillingly. But the believers multiply after a couple of hours in direct sunlight.

Hat. A warm wool stocking cap, pile cap, or down hood is the best instant regulator of body temperature. Because more than 40 percent of the body's heat exits from the head, a thick cap will go a long way toward keeping heat in. If you don't plan to use an umbrella in the sun, take a lightweight wide-brimmed hat. Remember that a brimmed hat will keep the sun off, but you will sweat like Victoria Falls in one when it's hot. You *must* have something with you to keep the sun off your head.

Money belt or pouch. A thin, sweat-proof money belt that holds trekking permit, passport, immunization booklet, traveler's checks, and currency is most convenient for such valuables. It is the trekker's equivalent of the amulets that Buddhists, Hindus, and Muslims often wear around their necks. Before you begin trekking, your money belt should be fastened around you, but on the trail it can be buried in your pack. Your passport may be needed along the way for identification, so don't become separated from it. At night you can slip your money belt into your sleeping bag.

Handkerchiefs. Handkerchiefs or bandanas are great; take one or two large ones for swabbing sweat, carrying walnuts, and playing peek-a-boo with kids.

Poncho and groundcloth. Sometimes extra baggage, sometimes necessary protection, a poncho may serve as your groundcloth, raingear, or extra padding. Be sure that yours has a hood, grommets in the corners, and snaps along the sides.

Sleeping bag. What makes for a proper sleeping bag is up to you. Don't be awed by Himalayan heights and overequip yourself for trekking. A three-season bag will be fine for most treks. I have used a bag containing 26 ounces of goose down and one that had 42 ounces of goose down. The latter was always too warm below 6,000 feet but fine in colder weather, particularly those winter nights at 16,000-foot elevations. Carry your sleeping bag inside your duffle or pack, if possible: "Not good to tempt rain, damage, or theft, sahib."

Foam pad. A ½-inch-thick or, preferably, ⅝-inch-thick closed-cell foam pad under the proper sleeping bag will keep you cozy on a Karakoram glacier. Therm-a-Rest pads are becoming very popular, but if you have one, take a repair kit also. Use a pad everywhere you sleep to keep out the chill and damp.

Sleeping sack. Last in this category, I list a personal favorite. Fold an old sheet lengthwise and sew it closed across the bottom and along the open side to about 10 inches of the top. You can also get one of these made up for you from a thin length of cloth in the subcontinent, anywhere there's a tailor. The sleeping sack that results goes into your bag at night to protect it from dirt and nighttime sweat. Washing a sleeping sack several times is a lot easier than washing a sleeping bag once.

Camping Equipment

The clothing and gear on the previous list are needed by most trekkers in the Himalaya. You will not need to carry your own shelter if you trek with a group, plan to sleep only in houses or inns, or decide to chance the rain. Most trekkers, though, need at least a tent in order to camp.

Tent. A sturdy, rainproof tent can make all the difference. Having a tent means you can camp anywhere with a flat spot and reachable water. Your poncho tied to a tree or pole may suffice if need be.

Cooking Equipment

In order to trek fully self-contained, a few cooking implements (in addition to food, which is discussed in the next chapter) are necessary. These items can be bought locally, but local versions will be heavier than the lightweight models you can bring with you.

Stove. A reliable kerosene stove that you can clean anywhere is preferable to cooking over a wood fire (unless you are in a heavily forested area of Kashmir, Himachal Pradesh, or Garhwal). Kerosene is available in Himalayan bazaars; it burns with a hotter flame than gasoline (petrol) and, unlike gas, will not explode. Like many people, I have found the MSR X-GK model to be the lightest and best kerosene-burning stove. Keep it well wrapped in plastic or in an outside pocket; it can dribble smelly fuel when it is broken down. MSR now also makes another kerosene-burning stove called the Internationale, and Coleman also makes one. As the wood-fuel crisis spreads and standards of living rise in the mountains, kerosene-burning stoves are slowly coming into greater general use. This helps to assure that you can buy fuel in the darnedest places; ask for it at stores and large homes that may double as stores. Local makes of stove are heavier and bulkier than Western models. Also, Asian stoves are less fuel efficient and less well built. Note that white gas, used in many popular models of American camp stoves, is not available in Asia. Carry a filter for the local kerosene, which can be filthy.

Fuel container. Your fuel must not leak away, so think again before waiting until you reach the trailhead bazaar to buy your fuel container. Carry enough fuel, and use a sturdy container or containers.

Nesting cookpots. A minimum of two cookpots, or billies, is needed. Bring some, or purchase a pair in the local bazaar. The Asian variety is heavier but can be given as part of a tip to your porter when the hike is over.

Stuffbags. To carry bulk rice, flour, sugar, and other foods, you need nylon or cotton cloth bags with drawstrings at the top. In the United States they are called stuffbags; in Asia they have other names, and tailors can make them quickly.

Freeze-dried food. If your style of trekking includes freeze-dried food, bring packets from home. Remember that freeze-dried foods may not have enough calories or bulk, ingredients you need a lot of when trekking.

Miscellaneous

This is a long list, but look it over carefully. Many articles are light-weight and might be needed on the trail; others can be omitted. Large and important items are listed toward the beginning. Many of the following (such as a backpack) are unnecessary if you go on a group trek.

Backpack. As with a tent and a sleeping bag, you will have to choose for yourself what you want in a pack. A single-compartment, top-loading pack is the best for me. A broken zipper on an "easy access" pack is quite a nuisance, and that situation can be averted by using a zipperless, top-loading model. Try to avoid using a pack that has no sweat-evaporating back panel or webbing, or you will find that both back and pack become drenched with sweat during summer or lower-elevation trekking. If you plan to go by yourself or go long distances with a porter, take a large-volume pack. Mine holds more than 5,800 cubic inches, and it has been quite full several times. Your porter may use a tumpline when he carries your pack. If you go with an organized group, you will need only a dufflebag.

Stuffbags. You will need various sizes and colors to put things in.

Iodine crystals, solution, or tablets. See Chapter 14, "A Himalayan Medical Primer." Some form of water purification utilizing iodine is abso-lutely essential. Don't leave without it. If you drink an iodine solution soon after the 10 to 20 minutes needed for the iodine to decontaminate the water, the taste of the water is remarkably unaffected. Treated water that has been standing overnight will have a much stronger taste.

Medical kit. A small but complete medical kit should accompany you. See Chapter 14.

Maps. Take the best maps you can. The old Army Map Service U502 Series maps are quite helpful for Pakistan and India. Be sure to read Appendix A, "Map Information."

Notebook and informative materials. Carrying a notebook is almost a necessity for the traveler. Before leaving home you can make notes in it, including addresses and other information you think you'll need, and tape photocopied glossary pages or other information to it. After arrival in Asia, you owe to your future memories a record of events and places, even if what you've noted is cursory. Use your notebook, or you will forget the color and small touches of a special experience, despite its vividness at the time. Don't forget to take photocopied information about the regions you will be visiting. If there are photographs of locals, these pages can be helpful in making friends.

Day pack or shoulder bag. A day pack or locally made shoulder bag (called a *jhola*) is good for day hikes as well as for trekking. On a day walk above a town or high camp, the day pack or jhola contains food and water.

Toilet kit. The toilet kit may include toothbrush and toothpaste, mirror, comb, soap (one bar for washing yourself, plus a laundry bar, available locally, for clothes), washcloth, and dental floss. The floss is important to have, for it is unavailable in South Asia, and a sliver of meat or husk in your teeth can be painful.

Toilet paper. Take it, buy it in the bazaar, or use *Time* magazine's international edition for a wild juxtaposition of timeless mountains and ephemeral news stories. Burn the used paper. Or you might do it the way the locals do: with a pebble or the left hand and water poured from a bottle.

Watch. A reliable watch will help you know when to rise for an early start or how much light is left on cloudy days. Some people keep a few extra inexpensive watches in their packs. They barter their "only" watches and later replace them with others to be used again as trading material. Locals can be quite sophisticated in their knowledge of watches, so don't take the cheapest ones available. A small alarm clock or watch with an alarm is helpful if you need to catch local transport (which sometimes leaves very early in the morning).

Enamel cup. Purchase a large enamel cup in a hardware store or in any well-stocked bazaar. If you try to use it at a teahouse, the *chai-wala* (tea-seller) will still pour the tea into his own (perhaps unsanitary) cup first to measure the amount. A cup that holds at least 20 ounces is preferable; some entire meals of soup or tsampa will be eaten from it.

Spoon. A large soup spoon will enable you to mix food and eat nearly anything.

Can opener. Weighing about 2 grams, the G.I. or P-38 can opener is the best for the trail.

Pocket knife. A good knife is always necessary; try to get one with a small pair of scissors attached.

Flashlight. An absolute must: for those obligatory nocturnal trips, for the time you find yourself benighted on the precipice trail, and for every other imaginable and unimaginable occurrence in the dark in village or wilderness. Take extra batteries and bulb. Some people prefer a headlamp with a longlasting lithium battery.

Water bottle. Another absolute necessity. Your water container should hold 1 to 2 quarts or liters. Don't compromise on quality.

Sewing kit. Needles, strong light and dark thread, numerous safety pins, and a few feet of 2-inch-wide ripstop repair tape compose a good, minimal sewing kit. You may wish to carry extra clevis pins or eyebolts (for repairing your pack) in the sewing kit. *Note:* Safety pins make excellent, lightweight gifts: take plenty.

Thick garbage bags. A plastic garbage bag placed inside your pack, around your sleeping bag, or lining your duffle will provide excellent protection from rain or sweat. Garbage bags (with rubber bands or cord) can always be used as gaiters in a pinch.

Boot protector. Take Sno Seal, mink oil, or your favorite boot grease, if you have leather boots. You will be surprised how much punishment your boots will suffer on a long trek, compared with a shorter outing at home.

Lip balm. Your lips will quickly chap when trekking. Without question, take some form of lip grease with a high sun protection factor (SPF) on any trek.

Suntan lotion. Many people need suntan lotion, although others do fine using only an umbrella or hat. If you burn easily, take lotion with a high SPF (15 or above).

Cord. Twenty to forty feet or more of nylon cord has a multitude of uses. And few gifts please a person from the hills more than a nice length of nylon cord.

Photographs. Photographs are great icebreakers. Everyone likes to see "fotos" of your family, your home, and such places as stores or roads with cars. Pictures of single objects are better understood than, say, a shot of Manhattan's skyline. In the roadless hills, pictures of automobiles can set off wonderful discussions. The photograph I take that causes the most comment shows my sister milking a goat, a very large-uddered goat, the sight of which provokes exclamations of envy and awe.

Sunglasses. These are useful for low and medium elevations; for walking on snow you need glacier goggles.

Spare glasses. If you use prescription glasses, take a spare set in a hard case.

Insect repellent. Insect bites are usually a minor problem unless you trek in the middle of the monsoon. Take strong insect repellent if you are especially sensitive to bites.

Bug powder. Even if you don't cross the threshold of a single dwelling in the Himalaya, you may still acquire those tiny things that itch and bite in the night, merely by walking down a path in town or camping somewhere that has recently been frequented by livestock. I have found that if bed bugs or fleas have materialized, lethal powder (available in Asia) is helpful for dusting clothes and sleeping bag (see "The Nitty-Gritty" in "Trail Sense" in Chapter 3).

Odds and ends. You should always have a candle, large and small rubber bands, plastic bags (available in most bazaars), tape, and extra pens.

Gear for the High Snows and Glacier Walking

With a little more saman you can head for the high snows and try for the summits, or walk along a glacier in the Karakoram.

Mountaineering or glacier goggles. With nothing about but sun and snow at the tens of thousands of feet on the upper part of a glacier, your eyes will fail painfully unless protected from the immense amount of direct and reflected light. Be sure to use goggles with high-altitude lenses. Carry good dark glasses or goggles for your porter if you are going with one, for he, like you, can get snow blind without eye protection.

Glacier cream. Get high-altitude glacier cream or lotion with a high SPF (15 or higher) to protect your face from strong radiation and reflection. Be sure to put it under your nostrils and on your ears.

Extra mittens. Protect your fingers from the possibility of freezing in the heights with at least two pairs of good hand protection made of wool, pile, or polypro.

Cold weather headgear. Carry a thick wool, pile, or polypro balaclava or down hood that will keep your head warm in penetrating winds.

Gaiters. Walking through deep snow will be a very unpleasant experience unless you can cover the opening between your pants and boots; gaiters accomplish this best. A good stopgap to keep the snow out is plastic or garbage bags held on with rubber bands or cord above and below your cuffs.

Crampons. Take crampons only if you are quite certain you will be going well above the highest trails onto steep icy or snowy slopes. Many people, including me, have naively carried crampons about for weeks, only to return with them unused. High passes on almost any intervalley route will not require crampons, because other people will have blazed the way (although you may possibly need gaiters in such a place).

Ice ax. An ice ax provides a bit of panache, but it weighs a pound or more and is not needed for trekking unless you plan to walk high along a glacier or onto a steep snow-covered peak.

Climbing equipment. If you are a technical climber, take your gear, for the sky's the limit. You may be able to find used climbing gear for rent or purchase in Skardu, Gilgit, or private homes up-valley from those towns (ask around, but don't count on finding exactly what you need).

Rope. You should carry rope if you plan to walk into the back country of Baltistan or Zanskar, because of the unbridged streams you are likely to encounter. Rope is also essential if you are walking on the upper part of a glacier where the moraine gives way to snow. Glaciers are often covered with snow that can hide crevasses. To walk high on a glacier, all members of your party must be roped together and have equipment for crevasse rescue.

Optional Accessories

You may want to take along some of the following to record or illumine the world you will be visiting.

A good book. Most people have time for a good novel when trekking. A paperback with trading potential is best, in case you finish it and want to swap with someone en route. Some people prefer guides to the flora or fauna (see the bibliography). Remember H. W. Tilman, on the traditional mountaineer: "His occupational disease is bedsores, and a box of books his most cherished load."

Camera and film. For a few tips about camera equipment and use, see the "Tips on Photography" that follow. Some people going to the Himalaya say, "I'm not going to take a camera, because with one, I wouldn't really *see* things there." This notion loses out in the long run, however, as memories fade and nothing is left to remind you of the place you went, except perhaps a friend's photographs.

Cassette recorder. Using a cassette recorder, you can make friends with people by playing music: yours or theirs. When you return home, tapes from your trip will lend impact to a slide show.

Binoculars. Some people prefer a lightweight monocular. Either way, field glasses are required if you want to observe animals or birds.

Compass. Many people find a compass useful, particularly high up in foggy weather or when trekking across a place like the Deosai Plains. As to using a compass for naming those white peaks on the horizon, I defer again to H. W. Tilman, who wrote, "The identification of very distant peaks is a harmless and fascinating amusement so long as the results are not taken seriously."

Altimeter. Handy for getting approximate elevations when you are wandering the high country or traversing out-of-the-way routes.

Frisbee. Not appropriate for impressing stuffy village elders with your seriousness of purpose, a frisbee can nevertheless be a good icebreaker.

Postscript to the More-Than-Enough List

From trekking boots to monoculars, this is a fairly exhaustive list, and you couldn't carry everything on it plus food and walk very far. No matter how you trek, whether funky or fancy, pare this list down to what is appropriate for you. Again, if you are not going with a group, I recommend hiring a porter to haul some of your gear and cook your food. Trekking with a lighter pack will enable you to enjoy, not merely endure, the entire trek and allow you to better assimilate and record the experience. Comparing the many items on this list to the small jhola of gear that many locals carry for days of walking makes us realize how far we Westerners have drifted from needs to wants.

Tips on Photography

In the Himalaya, the distance from home and extremes of temperature make special preparation necessary for the photographer, whether beginner or professional. Some of the following hints should be helpful. The nearest qualified camera repair shop will be far away when you are trekking, so take a well-built camera. For most people, a 35 mm single-lens reflex camera is the best for Asia. Zoom lenses are handy but heavy. You might want to use a wide-angle lens, say 24 mm or 28 mm, and a telephoto of 100 mm or more. Beyond these lenses, the sky's the limit, but you will have to carry what you take. Think twice before relying on a camera that utilizes an electronic mechanism unless the camera can also be operated manually. What would you do if the electrical system failed? To preserve your equipment, minimize sudden temperature changes. For example, don't move a camera directly from your sleeping bag into subfreezing outside air. Avoid extremes in temperature or dampness if at all possible. Change film in the shade and be very careful that dust and grit do not enter the camera when you replace film or lenses.

To protect your lens, use an ultraviolet filter. Use a polarizing filter to reduce haze, increase contrast and color saturation, and dramatize clouds and sky, but remember to take the polarizer off when not shooting in direct sunlight. If you take only one filter, a polarizer is the best; it will bring out a richness in sky and land colors like no other filter. If you want to compensate for the great difference in light between the ground and sky, you can use a split-neutral-density filter. Carry a camel's-hair brush with blower and lens cleaner to clean your lenses. If your camera requires batteries, carry plenty of extras, especially if you will be trekking in late fall or winter. The cold can deplete your batteries' power very quickly. Some people use ski poles, a lightweight monopod, or an aluminum camera clamp as a tripod, as a larger tripod can be heavy and clumsy to carry. A motordrive is excellent, for portraits in particular. Your subject may very likely assume a frozen, serious pose, then break out into an appealing smile as soon as you've taken the picture. With a motordrive, you've got both shots: the serious mien your subject desires and the relaxed image you want.

When taking pictures of people, put them at ease with a smile and perhaps some soft words. In Muslim regions you should be sure that you have a woman's assent before you take her photograph (unless you have a long-enough lens that you will not be intrusive). Some locals do not want to have their pictures taken; please respect this. Other people may ask for payment. This is not at all advisable. If a foreigner took your photograph, would you ask for money? Fill-in flash is good for taking pictures of people in daylight because dark complexions are very difficult to photograph in the light. Aim your light meter toward your subject's face to get a good exposure when taking pictures of people. When taking scenics, aim the light meter at the ground, never at the sky, to get your reading. It can be difficult to get accurately metered photographs on a sunlit glacier or a snow-covered landscape because light meters do not read the light correctly in such bright situations. Take off the polarizer (which only confuses the metering further) entirely for the shot and underexpose slightly to get a well-exposed photograph. Likewise, it is difficult to get good photographs in the middle of the day because the light is too harsh. Remember that the camera doesn't see things the way we do. The most vivid photographs are almost always taken before midmorning or after midafternoon.

If you want to photograph frescoes in monasteries, you will probably end up with reflected glare if you use a flash that is attached to your camera; more elaborate equipment with strobes aimed at 45-degree angles to the wall will be necessary. Finally, state-of-the-art camera gear is definitely less important to the results of your photography than your rapport with the person you are photographing, care in composition, and the indefinable matter of your "eye."

Be certain to carry enough fresh film to last the entire trip. It may be difficult to get fresh film most places in Pakistan or India. You can get Kodak print film and Fuji and Agfa slide film in Rawalpindi and Lahore in Pakistan. Some Kodak films are available in New Delhi and Srinagar in India, but prices for film in any of these places will be on the expensive side. Kodachrome 25 and 64 slide film can be carried and used for at least a year with no falloff in image quality, providing that you take reasonable care to keep it away from high temperatures. The chemicals in these films are made to last, whereas the chemicals in professional films are meant to be used at the time of purchase. Films utilizing E-6 processing (such as Ektachrome and Fujichrome) can be developed immediately if you find a processing lab that has the appropriate imported equipment. If you will be traveling for a long time, expose a roll of E-6 film in Asia and have it developed to make sure your camera is still functioning. Some people like to use Fujichrome 50 (or 100) slide film, particularly because of the way it renders greens, while others say the green effect is too garish. Kodachrome 25 still has the finest grain of any film and renders skies beautifully, but is difficult to use in low-light situations.

Don't let your film or loaded camera pass through the metal-scanning machines at airports, despite what any signs may say about no damage to film. Scanning machines *can* harm your film. Exposed film is at the most risk. If your film is in one of those lead-lined pouches and the inspector behind a scanning machine is curious, all he or she has to do is crank up the dial and *really* fry your film. You should hand-carry all film on flights. Checked baggage is not only subject to possible loss, but it is very often passed through X rays out of your sight at airports: an unadvertised added feature of modern life. Never mail home exposed film from anywhere in South Asia. Hand-carry it only or mail it from Japan. Film that is mailed from South Asia may be exposed by inspectors looking for contraband, stolen by someone who will sell the film as unused, or lifted by someone who wants the uncanceled stamps on the package.

Reaching South Asia

In 1973 I flew from New York City to London and traveled overland as far as Kathmandu for a total of $260 in transportation expenses. But of course a price like that is now history, as is the overland route itself presently for Americans. Europeans can still travel overland from Europe to South Asia by taking the southern route through Iran (which prohibits passport holders from the United States, England, and Canada) and crossing into Pakistan. But relatively few people make that still-adventurous trip these days.

As of 1989 you may fly round trip from either coast of the United States to Rawalpindi or New Delhi for about $1,200 and up, depending on the airline. Flights from Europe and Australia to South Asia are significantly cheaper. The APEX fare (Advance Purchase Excursion fare) is probably your least expensive choice. Tickets bought at APEX rates can't be changed without substantial penalties, so don't change your plans once such a ticket is bought. You can find out about the various types of flights by calling a travel agent experienced with international travel. Shop around for travel agents by checking the Sunday travel section of your local paper, or the classified telephone directory. Keep in mind that the cheapest flights can have various riders attached to those low fares. Or you may find that if you book what appears to be an inexpensive flight, you'll have to overnight between connecting flights for a day or two someplace where the hotel expense will drive up the total cost of the voyage.

Remember that you should check in two and a half hours prior to departure on international flights, because some airlines overbook notoriously. And check your baggage from home to your point of departure for the international flight. Then recheck your baggage for the international flight. Luggage very often goes astray at the point between the internal and international carrier.

Confirm, confirm, and reconfirm air tickets for both in-country and international travel anywhere in South Asia. Before you leave to go trekking, reconfirm your seat home if you are traveling on your own. If you are with a group, the tour operator's local agent should do this for you. Check to be sure reconfirmation will be done. If you don't absolutely ensure that you have a seat, your name may be mysteriously dropped from the manifest.

If you are without reservations for a hotel at your point of arrival, do not be concerned. Rawalpindi and New Delhi have plenty of hotel space, from $3-a-day specials to five-star accommodations. Preconfirmed, computer-made reservations are not absolutely necessary. Unfortunately, many international flights arrive at Rawalpindi-Islamabad or New Delhi in the middle of the night, when it can be very hard to get into any hotel. Note what time you will be arriving and factor that into your plans. The arrival areas in the airports at both Islamabad International and Indira Gandhi International Airport (in New Delhi) have booths operated by the respective tourism development corporations personnel, whose job is to assist you with arranging lodging. And your friendly, scheming taxi driver will always be glad to take you to a hotel. No matter where you are and what you may be told at first, remember that in Asia the outcome of a situation is never known until that situation is completely resolved. Information as first stated can always be amended, and *there is* a vacant hotel room.

Estimating expenses for your trip to South Asia is difficult to do, for you can spend vastly different amounts of money in Pakistan or India depending on your standards of lodging and cuisine. An approximate rule of thumb is that your costs will be slightly less than your normal monthly living expenses at home. Trekking costs are higher in Pakistan and India than they are in Nepal, and in the various chapters on the different regions I attempt to give you a rough idea of what rates are for porters circa 1989. If you are trekking with a prearranged, organized group, most of your in-country expenses will be taken care of, and the only extra money you will need is for a few meals, tips, and any souvenirs that you buy.

Take sufficient funds with you. Having money sent is difficult, subject to delay, and will probably produce only local currency, not dollars. If money must be sent, your best bet is through American Express in Rawalpindi or New Delhi (see "Sending and Receiving Mail").

Sending and Receiving Mail

Mail may take up to three weeks to travel between North America or Europe and South Asia, no matter which direction it is going. The best kind of mail to send or receive is always an aerogramme. It is safer from theft than ordinary envelopes because it cannot contain any enclosures and does not have any uncanceled stamps that could be detached and sold for reuse.

Advise your correspondents to underline or capitalize your family name when they address your mail, to ensure that the letters held for you are filed correctly. If you are going trekking with an outfitter, you can have your mail sent in care of their address. Should you be trekking with an arranged group, your tour operator at home will direct you where to send your mail. Otherwise, you can have mail sent to you in care of your embassy.

The poste restante (general delivery) system is not overused in Pakistan, so you should have no trouble getting your mail through it in any city or large town. Have mail sent to Your Name, Poste Restante, City, State, Pakistan. If you use American Express (AMEXCO) traveler's checks, you can collect your mail in care of (c/o) American Express, Rahim Plaza, Murree Road, P.O. Box 96, Rawalpindi, Pakistan. Mail sent there will be held for thirty days (no packages). Mail can also be sent c/o your embassy in Islamabad or c/o the American consulate in Peshawar if your passport is from the United States.

A useful address in north India is c/o American Express, Wenger House, Connaught Place, New Delhi, India. There you can expect a colorful, international queue and efficient, professional handling of your mail. Note that in New Delhi, AMEXCO is open for clients' mail only part of the day. If you are not a client of AMEXCO traveler's checks, mail can be sent to you in New Delhi c/o your embassy, but the diplomatic enclave is some distance from the center of the city, whereas AMEXCO is in the midst of New Delhi. You can also receive mail c/o Poste Restante in New Delhi. Your mail will be delivered to the post office on Bhagat Singh Marg due west of Connaught Place in New Delhi. If you will be in Ladakh, Kulu, or elsewhere in the mountains, your mail will be held in large towns when it is addressed to you there c/o Poste Restante. Be sure to have the sender indicate which state the town is located within.

Mail service to and from China is quite good. Letters to Kashgar can be sent in care of the General Post Office, Kashgar, Sinkiang, People's Republic of China.

Seasons for Trekking

Most people trek in Pakistan and India during the spring, summer, and early fall. In the spring, you can trek beginning in March at the earliest, but you will find snowy conditions then at any place above 8,000 feet in elevation. The snows melt as spring advances, but it is still apt to be snowy above 10,000 feet until May or later. Conditions vary from place to place, depending on whether you are on a north- or south-facing slope and depending on whether there is forest cover. Snow conditions will also vary from one year to another, depending on how much snow has fallen over the winter. In April and May, the sun-scorched premonsoon weather across the plains (in places like Peshawar, Rawalpindi, and New Delhi) can be blistering, so try to get into the hills then as fast as possible.

The subcontinent's life-giving monsoon comes from the southeast: it normally arrives in Sikkim about June 5 and reaches Garhwal ten days later. The monsoon causes muddy trails, obscures the view, and brings out leeches in Himachal Pradesh and Garhwal, but in those places, as well as in Kashmir, it also gives rise to a profusion of greenery. Monsoon rain is not continual, but in Himachal Pradesh and Garhwal it should be expected for a few hours daily at least through September and sometimes into October. Often the rain falls at night. By the time the monsoon reaches Kashmir, particularly in Ladakh and northern Pakistan, the rains have broken up and often fall as occasional storms, rather than daily showers.

Autumn can be magnificent in the mountains once the monsoon relents, but by October any place in northern Pakistan or Ladakh can be quite chilly at night. If you are not traveling too high, however, autumn can be the best season, as anyone knows who has experienced the fall colors in Hunza or Kashmir. Autumn is a great season to visit the Central Himalaya in Himachal Pradesh or Garhwal. The air is bracing, the crops are in, and the peaks glisten like diamonds.

No matter what the region or season, vicious localized storms can occur anywhere in the mountains, particularly in mid- to late afternoon or at night. So be prepared. Remember that Himalayan climate is primarily dependent on two factors: elevation and time of year. Because of the vertical distances involved in many treks, you may encounter widely varying temperatures (a drop of 3.5 degrees Fahrenheit for every 1,000 feet gained in elevation). Be prepared for cold weather after the sun goes down whenever you are above 10,000 feet, except for clear days in midsummer.

3
Arriving in Pakistan and India

India is a carnival and Pakistan is a tent revival.
Bruce Valde, 1980

Introducing Pakistan and India

Unlike the view from Kathmandu, Nepal, where the high, white himals can be seen gleaming to the north on a clear day, the the landscape surrounding Pakistan's Islamabad International Airport and India's Indira Gandhi International Airport in New Delhi can be quite a letdown to the arriving trekker. The Margala Hills above Islamabad are not particularly lofty, and New Delhi in the level plains is often enveloped in haze. Neither city has a "scene" like Kathmandu's Thamel area, crammed with used trekking goods shops and inexpensive restaurants serving Western food. Rawalpindi, Islamabad's larger neighboring city, and New Delhi are urban areas with populations in excess of a million, and the newcomer can be swallowed up in their wide boulevards and teeming alleys. Each of these two metropolises has its fascinating old parts of town and interesting traditions, but unless you are willing to stay around and learn about them, these cities may be only jumping-off places for heading north to the Himalaya. You'll get closer to the mountains only when you head up-country to towns like Chitral, Gilgit, Skardu, Srinagar, Leh, Manali, or Joshimath, which you will read about in the chapters that describe the different hill regions.

The present chapter first discusses Rawalpindi-Islamabad and New Delhi, but only cursorily, for this is not a book about cities of the plains. Next, the trekking regulations for Pakistan and India are summarized. Lastly are sections on equipping yourself locally, food, trekking with a porter, acculturation, trail sense, and trekking as metaphor.

Rawalpindi and Islamabad

Van not going. My bus going.

Bus conductor in Rawalpindi, 1980

Most people reach Rawalpindi and the nearby capital city of Islamabad via Islamabad International Airport, located east of Rawalpindi. Visitors tend to stay in 'Pindi, as it is usually called, for it is larger and has many more hotels than Islamabad. Rawalpindi (1,700 feet) is divided into an old city and a new city or cantonment (called cantt) that are separated by the railroad tracks. The new city was developed when the British began to settle in 'Pindi during the last century and built a completely new town with colonial buildings and wider streets next to the existing city with its bazaars and *galis*, the winding lanes mostly too narrow to admit vehicles. Originally Rawalpindi was a village of Rawals, a tribe of yogis. Today the two cities have a combined population of about one million.

In Rawalpindi cantt (also called *saddar*), several inexpensive hotels are situated near the hospital just northeast of the Mall, a main street in the midst of town. Other, plush hotels are nearby on the Mall. The Rawalpindi Tourist Information Office of Pakistan Tourism Development Corporation (PTDC) is also on the Mall at Flashman's Hotel. After establishing your quarters, head for the PTDC Tourist Information Office and ask for the separate trekking section (which is actually part of Pakistan Tours Ltd.) to get the latest information on any newly opened trekking areas up-country.

'Pindi's old city has many cheap hotels in the crowded, bustling Raja Bazaar area, but these places are mainly for the young and devil-may-care. Don't fail to try the delicious, rich yoghurt, called *dahi*, in milk shops scattered about the old city. If a shop is out of yoghurt, then you have probably found one of the better places; be sure to return later. Wherever you are, you'll see crowds of men wearing shalwar kameez, the national dress of pastel-colored, pajama-like floppy pants (shalwar) and shirt (kameez) with long tails that hang down. Two blocks north of Flashman's Hotel are several stores that sell ready-made shalwar-kameez, if you want to purchase these airy clothes for trekking (highly recommended).

In contrast to less restrictive customs in most mountain villages, you'll see few women on the streets of 'Pindi, reminding you that Pakistan remains a rather conservative Muslim society. Pakistan has an often-undeserved reputation as a country where foreign women are apt to have difficulties. Actually, Pakistani men have a real respect for women, but Western women are considered not worthy of respect if they transgress the traditional rules of decorum and modesty. Women should cover their arms and legs (even in very light clothing) in public, and in these down-country cities, they should walk with another person, either male or female.

Islamabad, which means "The Place of Islam," is Pakistan's new, carefully planned capital city. It is located 8 miles north of Rawalpindi's city center, but the two cities are growing together so that they are nearly contiguous. Many trekkers miss Islamabad entirely unless they are going to restricted areas and need trekking permits (see "Pakistan's Trekking Policies," following). Lok Vrisa, the National Cultural Center and Museum off Link Road, has exhibits, handicrafts, and examples of dress from different regions in Pakistan. A supervised International Camp Ground lies near Zero Point on the southern edge of the city. To reach most embassies in Islamabad (including the Indian embassy) from Rawalpindi, take a cab or the Route 2 minibus from Rawalpindi cantt. The Indian embassy is open from 9:00 A.M. to 12:00 noon Sunday through Thursday at 482 F Sector G64, Islamabad.

If you have a half day or more at your disposal, a pleasant walking excursion would be to the cave tomb of the area's most important saint, Bari Imam. You may rent a taxi, but most people take a shared van that leaves from Rawalpindi. At the departure point in saddar, ask the van drivers which vehicle goes to Nirpur Shahan, or just say "Bari Imam." Your van will go north of Islamabad to Nirpur Shahan near the base of the Margala Hills. Ecstatic singing with musical accompaniment called *qwawali* is performed at the roadhead shrine area, particularly during the yearly Urs (death anniversary) of Bari Imam, celebrated about the beginning of May. From there, walk past the shrines of other saints, fakirs, and *malangs* (religious mendicants) along a path that leads in 3 miles to the whitewashed cave shrine visible on the rock face.

It is possible to leave Rawalpindi in different ways for other major destinations along the venerable Grand Trunk Road that connects the northern plains cities, or for Gilgit and Skardu to the north. You can take one of the daily flights from 'Pindi to Gilgit if you want to visit Hunza, or to Skardu if you plan to trek in Baltistan. Information on these flights and other transport north is found at the beginning of Chapters 5 and 7 respectively, which discuss these regions. If you want to travel southeast from 'Pindi to Lahore near the border with India, or northwest to Peshawar, you can take an air-conditioned coach operated by PTDC that leaves from Flashman's Hotel. PTDC also operates a van service to Gilgit departing from Flashman's. Check at the Tourist Information Office for fares and schedules. Several companies offer a rapid transport service, called flying coaches, that plies between 'Pindi and Peshawar or Lahore. These companies are located not far north of the railroad underpass on Murree Road across from Liaquat Bagh, "Liaquat Gardens." If you want slower, more inexpensive transportation and a real cultural immersion, take a small van west from Raja Bazaar in the old city to the Pir Wadhai Bus Station. Eleven-passenger vans and garish, chrome-ornamented buses that look as if they have been designed by Jules Verne on psychedelics leave from this pulsating terminal. Hawkers extoll the merits of their vans or buses with lungs that would do any evangelist proud. Pir Wadhai is only for those with real mettle.

A note on crossing from Lahore to India: The easiest way to cross from Pakistan to India or vice versa is by taking a flight between Lahore and New Delhi. Flying may be the only way to cross directly between the two countries, for two reasons: India's volatile Punjab State, east of the only permitted border crossing between the two countries, is sometimes entirely closed to foreigners. Or the border checkpoints themselves may be closed to all travelers because of the strained relations between the two nations. A plane flies between the two cities at least five times a week. Some days the flight is operated by Pakistan International Airlines (PIA), other days by Indian Airlines (IA), India's major domestic carrier. If you are in Pakistan it will be easier to get a confirmed booking at short notice on the IA flight, but you may be able to book your seat only at the IA office next to Faletti's Hotel in Lahore.

If the land border is open for international travel and the Punjab in India is not restricted, you can either take the train or go by road. Check to be sure that the border is open on the day you want, for sometimes the frontier is only open certain days of the month. A daily train leaves the Mughal-style Lahore Railroad Station about midday for the border and continues to Amritsar in India. At Amritsar you can book a seat on one of two evening trains for New Delhi or take a train to Pathankot or Jammu if you want to go directly to Himachal Pradesh (see Chapter 10) or Kashmir (see Chapter 8). In addition to the train, it may be possible to take the road between Lahore and Amritsar. The border post on the Pakistan side is called Wagah; in India the checkpoint is named Attari Road. Buses from Lahore to the border can be found at the depot across from the Lahore Railroad Station, or you can rent a taxi to reach the frontier much more quickly, for Wagah is only about 9 miles due east. If you go by road and are carrying much luggage, note that you must walk 200 yards or more between the Pakistani and Indian checkposts. When you are carrying a lot of gear, the train is far easier, even if it takes more time. Regulations often change at this land border; be sure to check carefully before leaving for it. You may need to be on a through bus between Lahore and New Delhi.

New Delhi

In India one never gets to the bottom of things.

John Keay, 1973

Indira Gandhi International Airport at New Delhi is often the Western traveler's muggy introduction to India. If you are arriving on a long-haul flight, you will very likely reach New Delhi between 1:00 and 3:00 A.M., thanks to the vagaries of international scheduling. At that time of night you are probably best advised to take a taxi the 10 miles to the center of New Delhi at Connaught Place. Alternatively, you can take a three-wheel scooter, which is less expensive but slower. A passenger bus called E.A.T.S. (Ex-servicemen's Airlink Transport Services) operates between the airport and Connaught Place, except in the middle of the night, when you are likely to arrive. As you are conveyed toward town, India begins to caress you with image and fragrance: your driver lazily swings around two cows bedded on the pavement and lights a small conical *beedie,* the workingman's pungent miniature cheroot. An oxcart carrying sugarcane creaks and rolls through thick jasmine-ladened air as you swish past a succession of buildings unchanged since they were constructed during the British Raj (the British rule). A few years ago I was one of the only passengers on the E.A.T.S. bus, and the driver asked where I wanted to go. I hesitated, then said I'd get off at the Imperial Hotel. But the driver could easily tell that I wasn't material for the multistar Imperial. So I asked him if he crossed on Tolstoy Marg (street) near the Imperial. He laughed and correctly surmised, "Oh, you are wanting Mr. Soni's Guesthouse."

Near Connaught Place you will find hotels of every type. I favor Mr. Soni's Guesthouse, located, like several others nearby, in a home, just west of Jan Path near the Indian Oil Building. These modest homes feature tiny private rooms and shared baths. The acting manager, who may be any member of the family, is always ready to give tips, answer questions, or maybe discuss politics, as Delhi *wala*s like to do (in Hindi or Urdu, wala describes a maker or doer of anything). If you prefer to stay in an inexpensive place in old Delhi, then the Pahar Ganj area, within easy walking distance of Connaught Place, is the place to find a hotel. Be forewarned, though, that the street scene in Pahar Ganj jammed with peddlers, rickshaws, taxis, and ambling cows can be too frenetic for some. And there are some bad actors in Pahar Ganj. Don't for a moment believe that you can't find a hotel room, despite what the calculating taxi drivers at the airport (here or in 'Pindi) may say. If the first place is full, you can be sure to find accommodation with a bit of perseverance.

The Mughal-built Red Fort and nearby Chandi Chowk Bazaar are two of the old city's attractions. Chandi Chowk teems with people: turbaned Rajasthanis, bearded Sikhs, lean Biharis, shalwar-clad Muslims, country folk clustered for safety, uniformed schoolchildren, hawkers, beggars, foodsellers. If you're in Chandi Chowk, ask for Paratha Wala Gali, the alley of paratha-makers, a place that has existed since Mughal times. There are still a couple of small, smoky eateries selling delicious, greasy *parathas*, wheatcakes cooked in oil, just what you need to get your digestive system ready for hill food. Nearby is Jelabie Wala Gali, where you can fatten up with *jelabies*, sticky sweets, before or after you return from the hills. Particularly in the narrow lanes of old Delhi, foreign women can be subjected to occasional grabs at their anatomy. This is called "Eve teasing." If you see the culprit, point him out and insult him; bystanders will roar with delight, and he probably won't do it another time.

New Delhi is dotted with numerous landscaped tombs and gardens. For example, Jantar Mantar, a group of pink-painted observatory structures just off Parliment Street south of Connaught Place, is a relaxing place to cool off beneath the trees. If you find yourself withering in Delhi's summer heat, visit the nearby air-conditioned U.S. Information Agency Library on Kasturba Gandhi Marg. Several miles to the southeast of Connaught are the quiet, pleasant gardens surrounding Humayun's Tomb, a fine place to visit.

To help you find your way around town, ask for a city map at the main Tourist Information Office, 88 Jan Path, not far from Connaught Place. New Delhi is a city of seven to eight million people, so a map can be one of your best guides to town. If you are flying anywhere, particularly to Kathmandu in the fall, be certain to confirm, confirm, and reconfirm your reservations. You may hear that no seats remain for a flight; in that case, you might be happily surprised if you nevertheless show up at the airport ninety minutes before flight time with cash or an open-dated ticket in hand and clearly establish with the people behind the counter your interest in a seat. The "duty officer" is the person who can really help: he is in charge.

New Delhi has good bus connections with many hill towns from the Inter State Bus Terminus (ISBT) on Qudsia Marg just north of Kashmiri Gate in the old city. From the ISBT you can get direct buses to Shimla, Dehra Dun, and Hardwar, with connections for Dharmsala, the Kulu Valley, and the yatra roadhead towns in the upper Ganges watershed. Further information on traveling from New Delhi to the hills up-country will be found in the chapters that concern each area.

India's extensive railway system is readily available to foreigners, who may request seating and sleeping reservations from the quota set aside for tourists. Try to get a posher first-class ticket or a two-tiered sleeper in second class, which is softer than a three-tiered bunk in second class. To obtain a reservation, go to New Delhi Station, located on Chelmsford Road near Pahar Ganj north of Connaught Place. To have sleeping space in second class on an overnight train, you will have to book a sleeper reservation in addition to your seat. Overnight sleeper trains run to Amritsar for Lahore, Jammu, to connect with buses for Srinagar (but only if the Punjab is open to foreigners), and east to Varanasi (Benares) or Patna, where you can connect with flights to Nepal. You can take a morning train to the incomparable Taj Mahal in Agra (and even stay overnight to see it in all its moods), then still have a confirmed reservation from the nearby rail junction of Tundla. This reservation system is quite effective. When you approach the railway coach hand-numbered on the back of your ticket through the throng on the platform, it is always comforting to find the mimeographed reservation list and see your misspelled name with your assigned berth number alongside.

As you settle into your seat on the Indian train, just as when you take a seat on a bus in Pakistan, you will be mingling with Asia. Those you meet may nod kindly (perhaps in the rotating side-to-side fashion that is so difficult for Westerners to comprehend) and say *ahcha*—meaning, roughly, "good"—act reserved, or engage you, the Angrezi, in conversation. Often people will mirror your demeanor, as people are wont to do anywhere. Whether meeting Asia for the first time or returning for the fifth, remember what Arthur, a British traveler, said in 1967: "Everyone finds his own India."

Trekking Regulations in Pakistan and India

The two primary considerations about walking in the subcontinent's mountains are historic and political. Traditionally, the many Himalayan kingdoms from Chitral to Bhutan were reluctant to admit any outsiders, unless a person was a government official, trader, or pilgrim. For centuries, Western foreigners were definitely unwelcome. Today's policies in Pakistan and India have slowly evolved from these historical attitudes, as well as from the knowledge of China's extreme sensitivity to having foreigners approach the frontier. Trekkers, in the best sense, are the Western world's contemporary equivalent of the Hindu yatri, the pilgrim who walks long distances on yatra, "pilgrimage."

Pakistan's Trekking Policies

In the 1970s when I visited the Tourism Division in Islamabad to apply for permits to trek, I was greeted with disbelief and skepticism. That was the end of the era when a Westerner who merely wanted to walk in remote regions was suspected of wanting to ferret out information or to have some other ulterior motive for going hiking. Why, it was believed, would people from such an advanced country want to endure the difficulties of tramping through rugged terrain unless they were financed by a private or government agency and bent on some sort of mischief?

The modern era in Pakistan's official attitude toward trekking began in the spring of 1982, when the Tourism Division announced many areas to be "open zones" where "foreigners are allowed to trek without permit and guide, etc." From the Kalash valleys in Chitral to the Hushe Valley in eastern Baltistan, numerous trekking routes were recognized, and trekking without a permit was permitted in many of them. The Tourism Division has divided some of Pakistan's mountainous regions into three categories—open, restricted, and closed. Other areas good for trekking have not been listed. If an area you are interested in is not near a border (see the last paragraph in this section), or in a Pathan tribal area in the North-West Frontier Province, or in Kohistan in the Indus Valley, where you would not be welcome, then you may generally assume that it is all right to trek there. The rules and regulations at the time of this writing stipulate, however, that unspecified treks in restricted zones need a permit.

In the open zones (or areas) you are free to trek without a permit up to an elevation of 6,000 meters (19,685 feet). Going above 6,000 meters has been defined as mountaineering, which technically requires a permit, guide, and a fair amount of red tape. For restricted zones, a permit is required, and you are further required to trek with an approved guide. If you want to trek in a restricted area, you will either have to contact an outfitter (see Appendix B, "Trekking Outfitters in Pakistan and India") or apply on your own several months in advance. Entry is not permitted to closed zones. The status of an area can change from one year to the next, so be sure to check before you go. You can find out what category a particular region is in by writing for the current edition of the booklet titled *Trekking Rules and Regulations*, available from: Deputy Chief, Tourism Division, College Road, Sector F-7/2, Islamabad, Pakistan.

For information about arranging mountaineering expeditions, write to the same address and request the booklet titled *Mountaineering Rules and Regulations*. Mr. Sayeed Anwar, who works for PTDC out of the trekking office at Flashman's Hotel on the Mall in Rawalpindi, is Pakistan's foremost trekking expert. Sayeed has been everywhere and can be of great assistance.

Note that Pakistan has a 10-mile closed zone along its northern borders with Afghanistan, China (with the exception of the route along the Karakoram Highway), and India.

Regulations in India

Of all the countries on the South Asian subcontinent, India has the most straightforward policy regarding trekking. No permits are required for trekkers in its mountainous areas. As long as your visa is valid, you may walk as long as you like, with the following important proviso: no foreigners may cross north of what is called the Inner Line. The exact location of this line varies in distance from place to place along the northern border. The Inner Line runs directly along the road west of Kargil in Ladakh. There, the road is only 1 mile south of the disputed cease-fire line (officially called the Line of Control) that forms the border with Pakistan. Near the western border of Nepal, the Inner Line is some 50 miles south of the Tibetan border. In the Indus Valley of Ladakh, the Inner Line is more than 50 miles from the frontier. In northeastern India, the Inner Line follows the border of India's state of Assam, which precludes foreigners from even reaching Arunachal Pradesh ("Arunachal State"), which lies beyond Assam. For this reason, the Himalayan regions in Arunachal are not covered in this book. The location of the Inner Line across northern India will be noted in Chapters 8 through 11.

The exception to the above guidelines is Sikkim, where permits are required for anyone who wishes to enter. Permits for going into Sikkim are issued by the Ministry of Home Affairs in New Delhi and may require at least three months to process. See Chapter 12, "Sikkim," for more details.

Using Local Gear

In contrast to Nepal, where virtually any item of trekking equipment is available for purchase or hire, specialized hiking gear can be very difficult to locate in Pakistan or India. You might be extremely lucky and find a Western-made lightweight stove or tent in Gilgit, Skardu, Srinagar, or someone's home near the roadhead, but you'd be naive to go expecting that you'll find such items. And if you do unearth something, you will pay handsomely for the use of it. Part of the joy of trekking in these two countries is that you won't be tripping over other hikers along most routes. Since trekkers are few, however, virtually no used equipment is available. If you arrive without a needed item of equipment, you will have to be inventive in searching out your needs and be prepared to get by on less than, or something different than, what you might wish to have.

Many items locally made and available in hill bazaars are appropriate for trekking. The following list covers gear that you can expect to find in the major bazaar towns you will pass through before you hike away from the roads.

Kerosene. Kerosene, called *myTTi-ka Tel*, is the only fuel you can expect to buy in the hills. So take a stove that uses kerosene, for wood is rarely available in Pakistan or Ladakh.

Cigarettes, loose tea, and matches. These lightweight items are always appreciated as gifts. If you have qualms about giving cigarettes, take tea, matches, or sewing needles.

Small-denomination currency. Stock up on small notes; with them, you can bargain to the rupee and never need change. You can obtain bills from a bank.

Pack for your porter. You may not be able to find a locally made woven basket like the *doko* of Nepal. Still, there are several choices of a container for your porter's load. You can buy a burlap sack from a merchant or bring a sturdy duffle bag from home. Your porter could also use your pack to carry gear. If you are in the hills of India, he may want to use a tumpline from his home to help carry the load.

Rope. Rope, called *rassi*, will hold together the porter's load. Purchase enough to give to your porter as a tip and for possible use during stream crossings.

Fuel and water containers. Sometimes excellent watertight plastic containers for fuel are available in the larger bazaars.

The articles below have already been described in "*Saman:* The More-Than-Enough List" in Chapter 2. These items are noted here as well because they may also be purchased locally, but only in large bazaars.

Stove. Kerosene stoves can be found, but they are less sturdy and much heavier than Western-built models.

Enamel cup. A 20-ounce or larger size gives you an all-purpose cup and bowl.

Nesting pots. Cooking pots are sold by weight; you should get at least two. You may also want to buy a teapot.

Umbrella. Umbrellas are available in the bigger towns. If you haven't brought one from home, be sure to purchase a model that is good for rain as well as sun.

Pants. You can have loose-fitting pants made at a tailor shop. You will have to make it a two-step process by having the tailor measure you to determine how much material you need. Then purchase the cloth and take it to the tailor. If you have him make the cuffs small, dust will be kept out.

Food in the Hills

Our own experience coincides with that of Shipton and Tilman, who proved how economically one can live in the Himalayas. . . . Our diet consisted mainly of rice, barley, wheat, and millet . . . we enjoyed the most excellent health throughout, on an almost strictly vegetarian diet. . . .

Arnold Heim and August Gansser, 1938

The Local Diet

A good, balanced diet with adequate calories is essential for enjoyable trekking. Depending on your weight, activity level, and individual metabolism, you are likely to need between 3,000 and 4,500 calories to sustain you during each day of vigorous trekking, and these calories should come from a mixture of proteins, carbohydrates, and fats. Approximately 1 pound of pure protein or carbohydrates will provide 1,800 calories, and 1 pound of fat (only for Eskimos!) will give 4,500 calories. Carbohydrates (such as wheat, rice, and sugar) provide energy quickly; the energy from proteins and fats becomes available later but lasts over a longer period of time.

A local person eats about 2 pounds of grains each day, which provides approximately 3,200 calories that are primarily from carbohydrates. The grains are supplemented with *dal* (lentils), milk (if available), and salt. Vegetables, dairy products, legumes, eggs, and sugar are also consumed if they are obtainable. On this repetitive diet, porters can carry enormous loads through difficult terrain day after day, and many trekkers have enjoyed good health and fitness following the local example. If you rely primarily on local grains, your total dry weight of food per person-day will be about 2½ pounds. The key to a grain-based diet, however, is to eat enough of it. You really have to stuff the food in, and that takes practice and determination. Eat those *chapatis* (wheatcakes)!

You may want more variety than the local diet provides, however. From local markets you can add fresh and dried vegetables, occasional canned goods, dried fruits, nuts, spices, and even sometimes chicken or other meat. From home, bring packaged sauces and such luxuries as chocolate bars, cocoa powder, drink mixes, or other high-calorie, low-weight favorites. But keep in mind that with such additions you may easily end up carrying 3 pounds of food per person-day. If what you bring from home is freeze-dried foods, your total food weight can be lower than 2 pounds per person-day. Bringing freeze-dried rations probably won't be worthwhile, however, unless so much of your trekking route will be through uninhabited country that supplies aren't otherwise available. If you do bring freeze-dried foods, be sure to read the labels to determine whether the food you plan to bring contains enough of those all-important calories.

These supplements are not essential, however. The local diet can be perfectly adequate for nourishment. Indeed, this diet is in line with the theory of protein complementarity popularized by Frances Moore Lappé, who explained in *Diet for a Small Planet* how to get your complete protein requirements without the need for meat protein by using four basic food groups in three basic combinations. Wrote Lappé:

> The combination of grains plus beans, peas, or lentils evolved spontaneously, becoming the center of the diet in many different parts of the world—rice and beans in the Caribean, corn and beans in Mexico, lentils and rice in India, and rice and soy in China. . . . Only recently has modern science truly understood what must have been known intuitively by the human race for thousands of years.

The four basic food groups are:

1. Grains: rice, wheat, barley, corn, millet
2. Legumes: lentils, beans, peas, peanuts
3. Milk products: cheese, yoghurt, butter, *lassi* (similar to buttermilk), milk
4. Seeds: sesame, sunflower

The three basic combinations are:

1. Grains and legumes
2. Grains and milk products
3. Seeds and legumes

We Westerners are often surprised that we can trek for weeks eating only the locally available foods and emerge fit and amply nourished. My friend Chris Wriggins and I lived and trekked for nine weeks in western Nepal eating foods entirely from the first three groups (with the addition of eggs when possible) and finished lean but strong. A high-bulk diet like the locals' in ample quantities is very sustaining, but, again, you must eat enough of it, as locals do (and it can be difficult).

Available Foods

The items on the following lists are not the only foods you will find or can expect to eat while trekking; remember also that not all items will

A shepherd's or trekker's lunch of tea, yoghurt, and wheatbread.

be found everywhere. Some localities are food deficient and far from roads where supplies can be jeeped or trucked in. In those places you will have to offer a good price to make the sale of rations to you worthwhile. This is the case in regions like northern Chitral and Zanskar. In places like these, keep in mind the value of traveling with as few people as possible and purchase small amounts of food from several families. When buying food in the hills, check the appropriate glossary for the proper local words. And remember that your porter-companion can be your best asset when it comes to purchasing food.

If you are going into a very remote area or along a Karakoram valley glacier, be certain to carry enough food; the extent of your foot travel will often depend on the amount of food you can carry and obtain in the hills, and people have had to turn around for lack of it.

The most difficult time of year to get food in the hills is early spring before the harvest. Fall is the easiest time. Remember to ask about fruits in season, such as mulberries (the earliest-ripening hill fruits, available in early summer), grapes, apples, and luscious apricots, the tastiest found anywhere on earth. You'll be better off getting these delicious products directly from the tree of the person who raises them, rather than from a bazaar, for fruit in town can often be washed in unsavory places before it reaches the market.

Food Available at Large Bazaars

Whole milk powder. Next to grains, I take more milk powder than anything else into the mountains. Milk is excellent food, whether taken in tea, or mixed with properly treated water. The best way to hydrate the powder (which tends to cake) is to mix it with a few ounces of cool water in a cup. Amul, a large Indian milk-producer's cooperative, makes high-quality milk powder that is available in India. Excellent tinned milk powder from Europe can be purchased in Pakistan.

Peanut butter. Only available in India. Peanut butter makes a good topping for chapatis and is an excellent source of protein.

Jam. Most local jams are excellent. Take plastic containers to repackage jam and any other food that comes in jars.

Butter. You can find canned butter in both countries, usually imported in Pakistan and locally made in India. Or buy it fresh if you are in the high pastures during the summer. Butter or *ghee* (clarified butter) can be an important source of calories in the trekking diet.

Dry soup mixes. Brought from home or purchased locally, dry soup packets come in handy; they add flavor to soups made on the trail and are a quick topping for grain dishes.

Dried fruit. This is excellent food and can be found in markets across northern Pakistan and in Kashmir. Dried fruit can also be found in the hills. One spring in Chitral I survived on dried fruit and local wheatcakes.

Noodles. Instant noodles have reached the subcontinent. In a pinch, two to four packets make a meal. The cost and bulk of instant noodles can add up, but the weight will not. Long, dry noodles, usually called chow mein, are often available in large bazaars; if so, you can carry along several meals of them also. Remember to take enough; everyone's appetites will be gargantuan on the trail.

Salt. Moderate use of salt is a necessity when trekking because of the large amount used up in extensive exercise and the limited amount of sodium occurring naturally in the local diet. Try to purchase granulated salt. Sometimes in remote areas only rock salt may be available. If so, ask the shopkeeper to grind it for you, because pulverizing salt can be very difficult to do yourself.

Sugar. Sugar is absorbed rapidly into the blood, providing quick energy when needed; it is usually taken with tea, and it helps make some foods, such as tsampa, more palatable.

Spices. There are two types of spices, hot (like chilies) and sweet. Get some powdered hot spices to flavor the basic dal, vegetables, and chapatis or rice. You can find cumin, cayenne, turmeric, and other components of curry powder. Sweet spices, such as cardamom, ginger, cinnamon, and cloves, can be used in tea or curries. Also, check whether your porter wants the explosively hot peppers that some locals favor. If so, for a few rupees he can season his food to his own liking.

Coffee. You can purchase instant coffee in India in the larger bazaars, but coffee may be harder to find in Pakistan.

Tea. Get plenty of high-quality tea; don't buy lesser-grade "dust tea." A gift of tea is always appreciated by people in the hills.

Biscuits. "Biskoot" is an Anglo-Hindustani word for what we in North America call crackers and cookies. Biscuits are fine for snacks and in quantity can sustain you if necessary when you miss a meal, but they are uniformly disappointing when damp. Squeeze the package; if the biscuits don't snap when they break, they are wet. Both countries have manufacturers that make fine foods, but stay away from off-brands or you may end up with poor-quality biscuits or as much paper as product.

Candy. A good picker-upper for those day-long uphill tramps. Individually wrapped sweets are safest.

Canned foods. Who knows what you may find here or there in a store. Sometimes quality isn't up to Western standards, sometimes it is. When buying canned food, examine the tin for signs of expansion, which indicates spoiled food.

Food Usually Available in the Hills

Grains. Grains in one form or another will form the bulk of your diet on the trail. Wheat flour and rice are the most popular grains by far, but others are to be had, and some grains may be found in different forms. In Ladakh, Zanskar, and the upper villages in Baltistan you'll find roasted barley (most often ground into flour called *sattu, nasphe,* or *tsampa*). Plan on ½ pound of grain (1 cup) per hiker per meal. Your porter will probably eat half again that much grain. To determine the total amount of grain needed, multiply 1 pound by the number of person-days (1½ pounds per person-day for each porter). The accompanying table shows at a glance how the different grains can be prepared and served.

Common Ways to Prepare and Serve Grain

	Whole grain, to boil	*Flour for fried graincakes*	*Roasted flour for tsampa*	*Other form*
Rice	X			pounded
Wheat		X		
Barley		X	X	roasted, whole grain
Millet	X	X		
Corn		X	X	roasted, whole grain
Buckwheat		X		
Oats (in tins)	X			
How to serve	rice and millet with butter, dal, vegetables or yogurt	with butter, yogurt, peanut butter, fruit, or jam	eaten in tea or milk with sugar, butter, cheese, yogurt, or jam	from your hand

Dal. Lentils are called *dal*. With rice or chapatis they form an important part of the diet, so be sure to carry some. Well-stocked bazaars sell many kinds of dal, and you can also buy it in lower elevations where it's grown. If you will constantly be at high elevations, get a quick-cooking type of dal (orange-colored *masur dal* cooks quickest) or plan to use only flour.

Peanuts. A legume like dal, peanuts (also called groundnuts) combine with grains to form a complete protein, and they are a great snack. Ask for peanuts, and if you can find them, they may be raw or roasted.

Milk products. These include milk, buttermilk, lassi, yoghurt, cheese, butter, and ghee. Fresh milk products can be purchased seasonally in hill markets, but you can also ask along the trail, and people will tell you if you can buy dairy foods. Remember that they produce the full protein complement, if eaten with grain. If you reach the upland summer pastures, you can trade for, or more likely buy, delicious, just-produced milk foods. Buttermilk is generally given away, but the other products are usually sold.

Himalayan butter is nearly always of excellent quality and often comes protected in skins. Travelers of yore who complained of being served rancid butter in salt tea probably were not used to the rich taste of upland butter, particularly if it came from yak or yak-hybrid milk. Butter comes fresh from the summer pastures and has always been a cash crop, so you will have to pay well for it. Ghee, often misunderstood by Westerners to be inferior to butter, is actually a refined, pure product made by clarifying butter. Ghee is food from the gods.

Caution: Raw milk may contain harmful bacteria. Before drinking milk, be sure it has been boiled.

Eggs. Virtually the most complete protein you can eat comes from eggs. Those you can buy along the trail are from chickens that run around, scratch in the earth, and eat all manner of food. Consequently these eggs, although small, have a deep-orange yolk and a rich, full flavor that is rare in the West. For their weight, eggs are some of the most nutritious food you can carry. In Gilgit, Srinagar, or Leh, you may get down-country egg-farm eggs with pale yellow yolks. These still have good protein but are not as rich in nutrients as the local product.

Cooking oil. Edible oil (often called *vanaspati*) from one of many sources will be needed if you are not able to find butter for cooking. Most meals require vanaspati. Beware of mustard oil, *toori til*, which tastes distinctly fishy.

Vegetables. Most vegetables are available only in season, and few are grown extensively. Potatoes, called *alu*, are the principal exception: they are being introduced in numerous areas. Squash, pumpkins, and root vegetables will keep into the winter and can be purchased by request, when you are able to locate them. As time goes on and as people begin to realize their nutritional benefits, more and more vegetables will be introduced into hill communities.

Honey. Sometimes you can buy delicious honey, particularly in Himachal Pradesh and Garhwal. Finding honey unexpectedly can lift your spirits, like seeing a rainbow or coming across a big shade tree in the middle of the day.

Meals While Trekking

If you have only some of the foods listed above, you can eat well while trekking. You may carry additional food from home, but if you or your cook is capable, you will learn that a grain-based diet can be quite adequate. Trail food, though not in endless variety, is usually fresh and can be cooked temptingly with butter and spices. When your palate becomes accustomed to the locally grown food, prepared foods like glucose biscuits (with preservatives) begin to taste suspiciously artificial. Once, while hiking in Baltistan, we had been using *atta* (wheat flour) from the Punjab plains that was purchased in Skardu. Then we resupplied with delicious locally grown and milled flour, and the bag of Punjabi atta promptly disappeared into the bottom of our Balti companion's sack until all the local grain was finished.

During most trekking days you will have two large meals and an additional pause for tea. The concept of two main meals a day is very deep-seated in South Asia. Don't try to tamper with this custom if you are trekking with a porter or staff. Trekking groups adhere to this schedule: what is lunch for the trekking group is actually morning *khaanaa* (food) for the local staff.

A typical day's meals when you are trekking with a porter will begin with a simple breakfast. After arising, you'll probably have tea (or possibly coffee) while striking the tent and preparing to leave. You might supplement this with biscuits, porridge, chapatis, or any other food left over from dinner. After walking a good portion of the distance you will cover that day, everyone stops for up to a couple of hours while khaanaa is cooked. This break for the morning meal usually occurs during the heat of the day before the afternoon breezes begin. The time for khaanaa will vary with the terrain, personnel, and when you began the day's walk. You can wash, explore, snooze, or catch up on your journal while food is cooking. In the afternoon, tea is usually made first, while camp is set up, and dinner comes later. The evening meal may well be chapatis fried in butter or oil and washed down with dal, or whatever vegetables you may have found recently.

Trekking at high elevations (above 10,000 feet) requires a few meal changes, for higher up dal never completely cooks and even rice is difficult to soften. In the uplands, most meals are of soups, chapatis, potatoes, or tsampa.

Porters: Windows to Their World

The person you hire to carry your gear may be called a porter, but he will be far more than that. He will be your entrée into the homes of a local society that may not be familiar with outsiders, let alone outsiders from a foreign country. He will also be your guide to the proper trail, your translator, your cook, and, yes, he will carry your saman. The subject of trekking with a porter was introduced in Chapter 1 in the context of choosing your preferred trekking option. This section provides specifics on the who, where, and how of porter hiring and gives you an idea of what it is like to trek with a porter.

Who Will Porter for You?

A man who may occasionally porter for foreign trekkers is usually taking time off from work at home to earn some needed cash. The principal exception to this is the Braldu Valley in Baltistan, where portering for mountaineering expeditions and group treks walking up the Baltoro Glacier has become an important and expected addition to the local economy. Most likely your porter will be a local farmer, but more specifically, you're likely to find several different types of people who might be available.

The first person you meet may speak some English if he has worked for trekkers or mountaineering expeditions before, but he may be expensive because of his language ability and experience with Angrezi. He may be willing to carry for a paid trip into the hills, however, even at less-than-expedition salary. Otherwise, he may be a person who can help locate the right porter for you.

A younger person who needs income can be a good porter, but try to find out that you are hiring someone who knows the countryside. Avoid the pidgin-English-speaker who has little experience in the hills and who may quickly falter, like a lad I once started walking with on the high, rugged path into the Nanda Devi Sanctuary.

An older man can be an excellent porter if you can find him and he wants to go. Often older porters are the hardest-working, most reliable companions: wise to the old ways, knowledgeable about the land, and delighted to point out trail lore. Often older men will have chits, letters of recommendation from former employers, like venerable Haji Hussein in the Hushe Valley's Machilu village in Baltistan. He quickly produced several glowing, but worn chits that were over thirty years old.

If someone has good, individually written chits (not counting a form letter from an expedition), you have probably found an excellent person to trek with you. Some travelers find their porter can interpret all of nature's wordless hints, signs, and scents. These people have hired the right person. Others feel differently: "Porters are mostly local men of uncertain occupation and unsteadfast habit, notorious for giving trouble." The author of that statement trekked with a companion so "desperate to get under way" that virtually the first people who agreed to carry were hired.

Often the people who happen to be at the roadhead or in the bazaar when you first arrive are not the ablest or sturdiest. The best strategy may be to wait overnight for word to get around and for people to come in from the fields before hiring anyone. This can save more time in the long run than does barely slowing down to consider whom you are hiring in your haste to leave. You or your group can move faster and more comfortably with a good, motivated porter. A few hours' delay or an overnight halt at the beginning can often save a lot of time and difficulty later.

If you want to hire a guide, who will in turn hire his own crew of porters, you must ask to see any letters or chits held by someone claiming this status, as noted in "Going with a Guide and Crew" in Chapter 1. Many people hire a guide through previous contacts or through an outfitter in Gilgit, Skardu, New Delhi, or a major hill town. You may also make advance arrangements for a guide and staff by mail. The guide you hire as leader will then enlist his own crew of porters and be responsible for them.

Where and Whom to Hire

If there are only one or two of you, then wait until you reach the trailhead bazaar before engaging a porter. If you are several people and you need a crew, then you are probably better off hiring a competent guide. If you are going to cross several passes in Chitral or are on a long trek in Himachal Pradesh, you may only be able to hire people who will go partway with you, and you'll have to change porters. In Pakistan, many porters will be reluctant to go too far away from their homes, particularly if it means leaving the valley in which they live. That means you may have to change porters en route.

When you reach the place where you will first be hiring someone, you can expect one of two or three situations. First, there may be no one immediately about who is interested in working. Don't be in the least concerned. This is Asia, and the telephone works by word of mouth. Tell whomever you think can help that you need a porter: the jeep or bus driver on the way, a hotel manager or cook, or a few nearby shopkeepers. Spread the word as soon as possible. Think about this process as you would about finding a hotel room: like the inevitable room, a good porter will certainly appear.

In a second likely scenario you may find an accomplished guide with a good command of English. If you need him and a crew, you're set. Otherwise, you can ask for his assistance. Drink tea with him and ask him to help you find a person to porter. Given a day, he should be able to refer a friend or two to you.

Remember that in Asia, word passes around in mysterious ways; serendipity is a very real phenomenon. In Gilgit once, two members of a group trek were strolling along an irrigation canal above town. They met a man and began chatting in pidgin English, telling him that the forthcoming trek needed an assistant cook. One thing led to the next, the man was hired because he had good experience, and he proved to be a better cook than the head cook.

Reaching Agreement

When you are discussing portering with someone, you need to decide more than just how many rupees per day he will be paid. You might work up to the subject of wages by discussing and agreeing on other points first, as noted in this section. State your position or offer, then say, *"Thik hay?"* ("Okay?"). If he agrees, he'll answer, *"Thik"* ("Okay!"), and that will be settled. Keep in mind that wages differ from person to person, as at home. One man will go for 60 rupees per day when another won't budge for less than 80. Salaries will depend on the amount of work to be done, the person's need for money, and many other factors aside from experience and ability, for every porter prospect can carry and cook local foods. The following list covers the principal terms upon which you will need to agree:

Time. Some people are able to go with you for weeks, while others will walk only a few days or over one pass. Some men want only a couple of days' work (in which case you would have to change porters again soon), while others don't want to be bothered unless they are going to earn a substantial pile of money. To avoid misunderstandings later on, you should agree on roughly how many days the person will work for you or how far you will go.

Stages. You will need to recognize that, particularly in Pakistan, "stages," also known as "haltages"—the acceptable distance for a porter to walk in one day—are becoming increasingly "etched in stone." I have had trouble accepting these sometimes, for they can be rather short: *"This is a stage?* We've only walked a half hour since lunch!" One thing you can do is pay your porter a day's wages per stage, no matter how far you go in a day. This often works just fine. Or you can discuss the stages ahead of time and adjust your expectations to the conventional distances. Often the preset stages make sense, for there may not be other possible camping spots or places with water in the vicinity. On routes like the walk up the Baltoro Glacier, the stages are so fixed by tradition that they are unchangeable, but usually people walk double stages on the way back. Traditional stages are also an issue when determining days off and the number of days to be paid for the return journey.

Cooking. In a small group, it is much easier when everyone eats the same rations. Your porter is thoroughly familiar with cooking the food you'll be eating: let him do it. (If he is Hindu, make certain that he has no caste restrictions against taking his food from the same pot as you.) On the first evening of a trek in Baltistan, John Mock and I stopped with our porter to make camp. As I was putting the stove together, it became apparent that our porter was not inclined to make the chapatis. So John rolled up his sleeves and said in Urdu, "Well, I haven't made chapatis in five years, but I'm sure I can remember how. . . . " With that, our reluctant friend began to look most concerned; he washed his hands in the irrigation channel, and proceeded to make the evening meal.

Wages (including food). Try to learn the local wage scale; then be willing to add or subtract from it depending on the circumstances. In Hunza and Baltistan in Pakistan, wages for porters are higher than anywhere else in the Himalaya and are somewhat fixed by region. The person you want to hire is not a top-wage, high-altitude porter, but neither is he an ordinary load hauler, whose work is over the moment you reach camp. If you are going with only one person, he will be cooking for you, and that adds to his responsibilities. In 1977 we paid as little as 35 rupees per day in Baltistan to hire Mohammed Jaan for going up the Kondus Glacier and back, but by 1982 it was necessary to pay 65 (somewhat devalued) rupees in the same region. Now you'll have to pay up to or over 100 rupees a day thereabouts. If the person you are hiring has worked for expeditions and wants a high rate, explain with a twinkle in your eye that your bank is not as big as an expedition's. Offer a higher rate if you'll be walking on a glacier.

Don't give your porter a large advance before you leave for any reason or you may well never see him again. Likewise, don't pay him daily as you go, for the money may disappear. Just cover any immediate expenses as you proceed. Saving money for the morrow isn't thought of the same way in Asia as it is in the West. Nowadays people usually pay for their porter's food as part of the wages. It is proper for you to pay a half day's wages for every day the hiree must walk back to reach the point where you began (unless the return involves going by road, in which case you pay his fare).

Clothing. Remember that if you expect to trek high in elevation, you are responsible for your porter. Be sure that he has warm clothes, a coat, and blankets. Ask to see them, for he may not be thinking about the cold when you begin. You must look ahead and anticipate what the weather and elevation may bring. Be ready to camp near shelter at night or bring additional shelter for your porter. It is up to you to be responsible for your porter's well-being. Purchase a wide sheet of plastic for rain protection. Particularly if you are to be on snow or a glacier, you must provide for your porter-companion's warmth at all times: shoes, socks, coat, goggles, gloves, and a hat are the minimum requirements. If he does not have these six items, see that he borrows them or uses your spares. This should be arranged before leaving for the high country.

Bakshish. The universal Asian term for a gratuity means, in this case, a bonus. If your prospect is going to be working more than just a few days with you, then hint that some of your clothing or the locally purchased equipment will go his way when you are done with the trek. If by the end of the trek you have gone for some time together and gotten along well, there will be no question about giving him gear, extra food, or maybe even your Swiss Army knife (now that's talking, sahib!), along with an appropriate cash bonus.

Your relationship with your porter can hopefully become one of good companions on the trail. Using what David Snellgrove has called "a combination of quiet resolution and ingenuous friendliness," you can keep a warm spark within your group and foster good relations with those you meet. Be sure to walk with your porter in order to get to know him, particularly during the important first few days of a trek.

Your porter is the best lens to help you focus on and begin to understand this world you are entering. Remember that although you are his employer, he knows the country: it's his bailiwick. Leave route-finding decisions to him, particularly if you are within a couple of day's walk from his home. When I have shown interest, porters have pointed out all manner of flora, fauna, mineral deposits, tracks, and trails, and have told me stories about themselves, their families, and the country we were traversing. These insights can be among the most rewarding aspects of a trek. The porter we trek with is usually recalled more readily by us than we are by him, but some sahibs nonetheless enter the local lore and are remembered for years. And you will always be welcomed back to your porter-companion's home and village should you ever return.

Cross-Cultural Clues

The following observations about the culture you will be entering are offered in the hope of helping you get off to a good start and smoothing your way. From the moment you meet the immigration inspector at the airport who eyes your passport and looks for your visa, you will be forming impressions of whom and what you see. Whether observing or taking part in a situation, try to reserve some judgment and set aside preconceptions as much as you can. Your interpretation of what you see may or may not be correct. Try not to fume or be frustrated by inexplicable behavior or situations that cause delay. You are part of the dance and can't always change its tempo. You didn't go to Asia's hills to have the same kind of experience you would have at home or at a well-oiled resort where people are paid to be ingratiating.

Language. As stressed earlier, it is all to your advantage to learn as much Hindi-Urdu (colloquially called Hindustani) as you can, particularly if you are trekking on your own. Your time in Pakistan or India, as in any foreign country, will be completely different if you learn as many words as possible. Be sure to consult John Mock's fine "Introduction to Hindustani" in the back of the book. It is more than a glossary; you can begin speaking simple sentences after absorbing the section. On arrival in country you'll be able to begin trying words with the customs wala as he eyes your chattels. Don't be concerned with mispronunciation; you'll still be appreciated, and in the process, the invisible barrier separating you from him will be lowered.

Greet people in Pakistan or Kashmir with the Muslim world's universal *"Salaam alekwm,"* "Peace be with you." In most parts of India you'll say *"Namaste"* or the more formal *"Namaskar,"* which translates loosely as "Hello," or more correctly as "I honor the godhead within you." Then, in either country, you can proceed to *"Kyaa haal chaal hay?"* "How are you?" You can easily find English-speaking students, merchants, hotel employees, and others who will be most willing to help you with needed words or pronunciation. Trade words with the other person: what you need to know for what he wants to learn. Misunderstandings can be ironed out surprisingly often with the right word or phrase. Often travelers and locals misunderstand each other not through nonagreement but literally from noncommunication. Just a few words can help to establish a connection with shopkeepers, innkeepers, porters, and others who want to make themselves understood but can't, lacking the English.

The word *sahib*, pronounced "sahb," basically has come to mean "sir." It is not reserved for you as foreigner, and it can connote varying degrees of respect in various situations. *Barasahib* is used sparingly and may mean anything from "boss" to "governor." Some Westerners fall under the spell of the word sahib, as if by having it used on them, it confers a certain status. Don't be fooled.

Chai. Tea, or *chai*, the beneficent, deserves a brief paean here. All across South Asia most people drink, or wish they could drink, tea daily. To the world's billions of tea drinkers, the sipping of a cup is a refreshing break from the business at hand. Chai calms but revivifies; it cools a person in summer and warms the body in winter, an always-reliable balm. Important for the traveler, tea is quite safe to drink, whereas the fresh water it is brewed from may not be potable. Wherever you become involved, you may be asked to "take tea." Asking you to drink tea is a merchant's way of saying, "I'd like to get to know you better," or perhaps, "You look exhausted and this should help." Always pause to drink tea with officials if it is offered. To decline would be rude. In the middle of a long afternoon's hike, you might call a halt to the walking for a half hour by some inviting stream and brew tea. With every sip, you will appreciate the soothing, restorative value of chai, the traveler's magic beverage.

Bargaining. Like tea drinking, bargaining is a venerated Asian custom, but one that many foreigners need some time to feel at ease with. Bargaining is agreeing on a price or rate of exchange, and this process is usually played out with different mental attitudes on the part of local and visitor. The Westerner often considers bargaining akin to a duel between adversaries, whereas the shopkeeper or porter thinks of bargaining as a social exercise, not unfriendly at all, and at its conclusion, over and done. There is a matching of wits but never a winner or loser, and when the price or rate is decided, that is it: no paperwork, no bad feelings. You may prefer to begin practicing the bargaining process with small things; however, most ordinary items are fixed-price merchandise. For larger purchases, learn the ballpark price first. Think of bargaining as a good way to practice language; you can toss out words and see if they are understood. If your words are polite and firm, offered with a smile, and given with good humor, your bargaining stance should be a good one.

Asking questions. When you ask anyone for information, never imply the answer in the question. This is very important. To suggest in the question the answer you expect is human nature. But it is also human nature that people everywhere wish to please, so they are very likely to agree with you, even if the answer is not in the least bit correct ("Yes, it's only a half hour to Amarnath"). In urban or rural settings alike, anyone is likely to go along with you if you answer your question as you pose it. Don't say:

Are there two buses today to Manali?

Is the next bus at eight o'clock?

Does this path reach Krakal?

The questions would be better phrased:

When are the buses to Manali? (or, How do I get to Manali?)

When is the next bus?

Where does this trail go?

If the person understands your question and doesn't know your preference, you may hear, "Patta nahi" ("I don't know," literally "I've no information"), or you will get a more informative answer.

Public display of affection. In both Pakistan and India (as in all of traditional Asia), public display of affection (PDA) between the sexes is not understood. This is a difficult concept for many Westerners to comprehend, much less emulate in an attempt to be culturally sensitive. Men walking together or women walking together may hold hands as a sign of friendship, but men and women will never so much as hold each other's hand in public. Remember that in Indian cinema, with lascivious dancing sequences in every film, the scene is always cut just as the lovers are about to kiss each other. Strange (from our perspective), but true. PDA just embarrasses people in these countries.

Taboos. One's head is considered to be the most sacred part of the body, while feet are impure. Thus, patting children on the head should be avoided. Likewise, if you are sitting down with your legs extended, pull them in if someone needs to walk by. It is not polite to walk over any part of a person's body. These taboos apply to both Muslim and Hindu regions. Note also that the cooking fire is considered sacred in Hindu regions, so it is not appropriate to toss burnables of any kind in the hearth. Remember to take things from people with your right hand, and *always* eat using your right hand. The left hand is considered unclean because it is used for less sanitary activities.

Beginnings. Some of us fantasize about trekking and prepare for it so long that by the time we actually begin we are set askew for a couple of days, perhaps experiencing mild fatigue from the outset of walking, minor aches, or a haziness, a feeling of unreality. This is a dose of culture shock akin to the way people can feel when they alight from a plane in a new country, almost expecting the clouds to be altered, the very ground they tread to be different. Probably the few trekkers who do have these temporary symptoms undergo them not so much because they feel a letdown, a leaving go of expectations, but because they are either overloaded with beauty or repelled by the lower standard of living. Take things slowly for the first few days and let yourself become accustomed to your new surroundings. Asia is without a doubt different from home; let it come to you slowly.

Returning home. Many people (including myself) find that returning home from such an absorbing experience as trekking involves far more disorientation, more culture shock, than going to Asia in the first place. This disorientation may occur partly because trekking obliges you to become somewhat involved in a very different culture, not just be an observer of it. Often we find when we return to our own country that it appears foreign to us, not exactly the way we remembered it. Affluence, trendiness, self-centeredness, and other aspects of Western life can stand out in boldface after we have been immersed in a traditional culture. The return home can also be wrenching because of the issues that still await us. Often people go trekking when they are in one of life's passages: following graduation, between jobs, after the breakup of a marriage. Sometimes people go trekking to find out something for themselves about their physical abilities or about an abstract dilemma. More often the former type of question is answered than the latter.

The best thing you can do when you return home is to keep busy: plunge back into activity (after up to a week of letting jet lag run its course). By all means, tell your friends about your trip, show them slides, but remember that they are not seeing or hearing things exactly as you experienced them. And that's quite all right. Your own response to the trip will change over time as well. Our reasons for going trekking, or the answers we sought by going, do not crystallize until "reflection in tranquility," as the poet William Wordsworth said. But we can hope to return to our native land with a greater understanding of our own country and an enhanced ability to deal with our complex society at home.

With respect to returning home and dealing with the experience of extensive travels fully lived, consider the following words by John Staley from his fine book *Words for My Brother:* "What Kohistan gave Elizabeth and me was the different viewpoint: the viewpoint one has while 'living second lives' in a different environment, society and culture. But any insights we may have gained have to be integrated into our own lives, and not attributed to the lives of others."

Trail Sense

This book does not attempt to mention every trail junction and village along the trekking routes described: that would be impossible. Nor does this book tell you hour-by-hour distances. One person's hour is another person's hour and a half, as pointed out by Mullah Nasruddin in the preface. The person who takes longer to reach a place has probably gained more from the experience by stopping to look, talking with people along the way, and smelling the flowers, as it were. I will attempt, however, to give you a close approximation in days or weeks of how long it would take the "average" person to cover each hiking route that is described. My hope (as I mentioned in the preface) is that this book gives an approach to trekking that does away with the desire some people have for an exhaustively detailed guidebook. Consider the thought that it's what you *experience along the way* that is important, not just arriving at the place you will stay for the night.

Many variables are involved in walking, say, from one valley to another 12 miles away over a 16,000-foot pass. Heavily laden porters or neophyte trekkers might take three days, while those in a hurry might require a single day to traverse the same distance. Rather than setting day-to-day itineraries, I have limited myself to suggesting that a route may take four to six days, for example, or two to three weeks. If you want to plan a trek down to the day, either go with a trekking group or read a tour operator's catalog and note the number of trekking days allowed for a walk that appeals to you. If the route is easily passable, expect that you will take about as long as the organized group does to cover the same distance. But going this way won't be leaving you any time to follow that interesting side valley or rest somewhere that catches your fancy.

Treks follow different kinds of courses, and often you will have a choice of possible routes in a given area. You may walk up one valley, climb over a pass, and return down another valley. You might come back to your starting point by the trail you took, get there by a different path, or end up at another roadhead entirely. If you get off-route during your trek, it's not the end of the world. Taking the wrong trail may even turn into one of the highlights of the trek or lead you to an interesting encounter you would never have had otherwise.

Never forget that the routes described in this book are only a few of the multitude of possible trails you can follow. I've discussed many major routes and some others as well, but the possibilities are absolutely endless. People who strike off into the hills on local trails off the main trekking routes have completely different experiences than those who stick to well-worn paths. For a little over three months in the spring of 1982, two of us Westerners and our Nepali porter-companions walked every step of the way through India's hills on interconnecting paths from the Mahakali River on the Nepal border to Lamayuru Monastery in Ladakh. The vast majority of the time we saw no other foreigners, yet we passed through scores of villages and had refreshing and memorable interactions with the people we met along the way. This continued for three weeks as three of us walked across Baltistan in Pakistan. Many of the trails hiked during that long trek have not found their way into this book. It doesn't mean the paths we covered aren't interesting, it's just that there are far too many trails to mention them all. And that is just one of many wonders of the Himalaya: the possibilities for discovery are endless.

All the routes covered in this book (with the exception of glaciated areas) are along established paths, although as you walk, you may become misled by divergent tracks that lead to villages or grazing pastures other than the ones you are attempting to reach. The key is to keep your eyes open to where you are and where you're heading. Don't be shy about asking people the way, for locals who are unfamiliar with an area also ask directions. Most trails will be in good repair, but there can always be surprises, especially during or after the monsoon. The degree of difficulty from one trail to another will be related to the path's condition and the elevation you gain or lose as you proceed. I have tried to indicate the elevations at valley bottoms and passes or the approximate total elevation gains to reach most passes. If you are walking through particularly high elevations or hilly terrain, your pace will, of necessity, be slower than otherwise.

Trails themselves may be used differently from season to season: in the winter during low water, valley routes are often used, whereas higher paths have to be taken during times of the year when the snows melt and/or the monsoon brings precipitation. The walk to Shimshal in the Hunza Valley is a perfect example. In winter the Shimshal River can be jumped on stepping stones, and locals walk along the valley floor. But during the summer (when we trekkers are likely to be about) the river is a raging torrent that must be avoided by long detours on a sometimes-tricky path. Again, ask directions if you have any doubt at all about the way. Locals are always asking each other directions when unfamiliar with a trail.

The horizontal distance traveled each day on a trek may not be great unless you are in a relatively flat river valley. The day's distance will not reflect the day's labor if you have just spent many long hours descending 6,000 feet into a gorge and partially climbing up the other side. To take an extreme example, I have hiked less than a single horizontal mile in a hard day on a faint trail walking into the Nanda Devi Sanctuary in India. On the other hand, in the Yarkhun Valley of Chitral, Pakistan, I walked 29 map miles in one day even with a leisurely start and a lunch break. Your distance covered on any given day can therefore vary greatly. If you eat well, your average will increase after the first few days, as your body adjusts physically. Maybe by then you will have slowed down anyway, to take in interactions with locals along the way and to enjoy the scenery.

Particularly in the first week of a trek, don't set overly ambitious distance goals. Have an easy attitude toward trekking, and don't make it into an endurance contest. Experienced long-distance runners and hikers know that those who go the farthest and remain the strongest pace themselves at the outset. Later on, when your muscles and lungs are stronger, you can push yourself for a day or more. Then, when you ask yourself,

"Shall I try for that next ridge?" you can push on for it and know that your aches, parched throat, and empty stomach will not rest as markedly in your memory as the far view you saw by gaining the ridgetop.

In popular trekking areas, particularly in Pakistan, how far you walk in one day may be determined by traditional stages (see "Stages"). In more remote regions, where traditional stages have not become established, an average day's length can vary from group to group and person to person. If you are cooking your own food, you can call the halts as the conditions permit, but the two-meal schedule (as noted in "Meals While Trekking") will always apply. Rarely in the Himalaya do two days ever unfold exactly alike, but in general the day's journey is geared to the sun: because the cooler hours in the morning are preferred for walking, you will often rise with the sun's earliest light and cover much of the day's distance before the morning meal is cooked. By the time the first meal is over, afternoon breezes or clouds may have arisen to cool the air. After camp is made in mid- to late afternoon and you have had a chance to rest, the evening meal is eaten. Time of year is important to both the length of trail that can be covered in a day and the meal routine. In midsummer, prepare to go to bed before dark so you can walk in the dawn hours before the day's heat builds.

The physical act of walking through the Himalaya (whether or not you carry a pack) may require adaptation because of the scale of things, the order of magnitude involved. In these, the world's highest ranges, river-to-ridge elevation differences can be 2 or more vertical miles and encompass different climatic zones, not to mention numerous levels of settlements and fields. You will find yourself walking uphill for days at times, and when you have descended halfway down the other side of the ridge, you will find that going down is as hard on the legs as climbing is on the lungs. Pace yourself when walking, take rests, carry drinking water, and don't forget what you have learned from backpacking at home.

A trick to going downhill is to use the bent-knee style of walking. It takes a bit of doing until your upper-leg muscles strengthen, but when you can walk down trails in a bent-leg posture you will cushion your upper body, keep your weight directly over your feet, and save your stamina. Keep your weight over the balls of your feet when you descend. If your weight is over your heels, you may well fall backward. Watch how the locals walk downhill and learn from them. Westerners who rush heavily down a canyon and later complain of aching knees or, worse, who must remain immobile with swollen knee joints suffer from the malady known as sahib's knee. Only the foreign sahibs are foolish enough to put so much pounding pressure on their legs and knees.

One question people often have is what to do when nature calls. You will probably never see a local defecating. When you need to relieve yourself, go well off the trail and when you are done, bury or burn your toilet paper. You can always carry matches or a lighter for this purpose. Locals everywhere always use their left hand for cleaning themselves. In arid regions without forest cover, going out of sight can sometimes be tricky, but note the lay of the land and you should be able to sashay around a ridgeline or behind a rock.

Theft used to be unknown in the hills and is still extremely rare in untrekked areas. But thievery has started to become a concern in some regions, particularly in the Warwan Valley, just to the east of Kashmir. Trekking groups in this area have to be guarded by their staff, who rotate watches during the night. You need to be especially careful of all belongings whenever you are in the vicinity of a road. Many of the old ways vanish as soon as a road is built into a valley. Just like home, if you leave something behind when you leave a place, it probably won't be there when you come running back to find it. If the sahib doesn't care enough about his possessions to hang on to them, then someone else who appreciates their value will be glad to assume possession of them. The equipment we blithely carry with us would take most locals years to purchase.

Be as alert as possible to your surroundings, especially if no one in your group has been on the trail before. Fill water bottles before you leave the vicinity of a stream (especially in arid regions and upper altitudes) and before climbing passes. And avoid becoming benighted on a narrow trail far from the nearest-conceivable camping spot. In any case, do not head for a pass late in the day. When you are walking in high elevations, always carry water and fuel, and be sure you are ready to make a high camp. If you are trekking with a porter, give him some voice in any decision to stop or go. In the Himalaya, you always have much to learn; be open to your status as student.

As you walk into villages, remember that you are the best act in town. Imagine for a moment that in the town where you live or in a nearby national forest a Ladakhi were to amble along carrying a load of willow branches. If you lived in Srinagar, you would expect to see lots of tourists in certain parts of town, just as you would if you lived in London or Manhattan. In the countryside, however, unless you are trekking a frequented route, a foreigner is most definitely an oddity. You can almost gauge the degree to which foreigners are seen in a village by the response to you, especially by the initial reactions of the children. In any remote area, young children who are playing outside will run in fear at the sight of a strange foreigner approaching. Their older brothers and sisters will walk away, to reappear in a window or on the roof. On a well-trekked trail, however, kids' reactions will vary right on up to nonchalance. Often children will ask for candy or a pen, just to divert themselves. (Can you imagine children in the United States *asking* for candy from strangers?!) I have learned that if I camp near a village or stay in someone's home, inquisitive people may congregate at the campsite (until dinnertime, when the crowd disappears), or young, crying babies may keep the household awake. No matter what your mood when you reach a village, try not to let yourself forget that you are there entirely of your own accord.

Assume goodwill on the part of others. Travelers are often on their guard in new situations, but never do the Golden Rule and its corollaries apply better: expect the kind of treatment from villagers that you would

Juno from Baltit was Hunza's former court historian. He wears an old chogha and my glasses and playfully hints at how much they help his eyesight.

accord a foreign visitor at home (albeit a well-to-do visitor). Better yet, try to imagine how the locals might see you. In cities most people are honest, but in the provinces even fewer people are used to shucking outsiders. Agreed: there will be a fast talker about from time to time. But you will almost always be correct if you do assume that people's intentions are honorable. In Hindu India, you can be ready to explain that you are a *yatri*, a pilgrim, on pilgrimage, and your foot journey will be better understood. In Muslim societies, the *muzzafer*, or traveler, is recognized as a person away from home and hearth and therefore to be assisted. This can definitely be to your advantage in any region where traditions of assistance to travelers are maintained.

When you walk in the hills of Pakistan or India, you will be in country that has a human history going back thousands of years. In places like Hunza and Garhwal you'll be in cultures that trace their history to events so ancient they disappear into the mists of time and have been mythologized. Traditional cultures have elaborate social and, in some areas, caste systems, all of which will be totally invisible to you. As a visitor you are seeing only a slice of time, and much that will meet your eyes your mind cannot interpret. If you should meet the rare anthropologist, or any local who is competent in English, ask him or her just who is who in town, and you may be surprised: "Oh, he's the headman and the richest man in town" (an older man in well-used work clothes). "This chap just came back from school and has nothing to do" (a well-dressed man who speaks a little English). "She moved here from down-valley to marry" (a woman with a light complexion). To figure out the local cast of characters, you'll probably have to be told or must be an acute observer with language ability. Keep your eyes open to the interactions about you as you walk. As you become aware of the local customs, respect them, and note the courtesies that you see practiced by people about you.

Trekking rarely offers opportunities to acquire souvenirs in the hills, although you may be able to find handwoven textiles or needlework in some homes. Take photographs and keep a journal going (perhaps the most valuable objects you can take from your experience, and *you* have created them), or press flowers and tape music and conversations. But satisfy your acquisitiveness by purchasing mementos in places like Peshawar, Saidu Sharif and Madyan in the Swat Valley, Srinagar, or New Delhi. In these larger towns the souvenir industry is alive and well, but few genuine old relics are left in the mountains anymore. In Gilgit, Kareemabad (in Hunza), and Leh in the hills you can find some nice handicrafts.

Trekking as Metaphor

In the end, our endeavours were themselves our reward.
Sheppard Craige, 1978

Sometimes, however, it seems that journeys are undertaken for their own sake, with the intention of turning anything encountered on the road into a means of spiritual profit. This is best expressed in the [Tibetan] phrase gang shar lam khyer, *"to bring to the path (to enlightenment) whatever may happen." The journey is itself therefore regarded as being of equal importance to its goal.*
Michael Aris, 1975

The trail as metaphor is a broad and wonderful concept, for each person walks his or her own path through life, and each individual can be largely responsible for the direction that path may take. For many people, walking trails in the Himalaya is an experience all the more powerful because its metaphorical teachings are couched neither in words nor within a system of organized thought. The rhythms of the day and the days taken together acquire a connectedness, unity, and dimension that is missing in urban Western society.

This palpable realness about life on the trail is called "direct perception" in the Tibetan tradition. Pilgrimage has long been recommended as a means of salvation in both Tibetan and Hindu societies, not only for the merit that accrues in reaching a holy shrine or sacred phenomenon, but because of the character and inner strength induced by such travel.

After some days of adjusting to the walking routine, you will begin to pay little or no attention to your hesitant thoughts and will become better acquainted with the nuances of the endlessly changing land that you pass through. You may feel that each day is more intensely etched during these periods of time when your life is altered from its ordinary course. Your initiation may occur when you cross your first high pass: the tough, sweaty, lung-pounding climb with its uncertainties and teasing false passes is offset by the growing panorama below, the giddiness of the height, and your exultation at reaching the top. As you stand there between the past and the future, the present can be luminous.

High above the passes are rarely touched mountains where nature seems at its most monumental and visual metaphors abound. But we don't need to be a mountain climber to walk among breathtaking settings in such places as Hunza, Ladakh, and the high glaciers of Pakistan's Karakoram. In these exalted milieus we seem to be in the midst of amphitheaters where the multiple flows into the one, where some inexpressible explanation of reality presents itself. While trekking, we all read meanings into nearby landforms and the human interactions that occur within their aura. Many places have visibly metaphoric qualities. Glaciers appear dragonlike or riverlike, depending on perspective, and individual glacial features translate immediately into mushrooms, incisors, eyes, and vast galleries. Evocative also are individual peaks summed up in sacred, symmetrical Mt. Kailas in west Tibet, with its snow-filled couloir, the Stairway to Heaven, etched vertically toward the summit.

Few can fail to be touched by becoming, for a time, part of the Himalayan tapestry.

Recently I was fortunate to walk with a group in Nepal that included a most sensitive and compassionate man named Gerry Spence. The three-and-a-half week hike circling north of the Annapurna himal included a 17,770-foot pass, and the trek was physically challenging for him as it is for everyone, but never was a person more determined to make the most of a trek. Several times during the course of the walk we talked about trekking as metaphor. Afterward, I asked Gerry if he would be willing to write down some of his thoughts on this theme. He very kindly wrote the following provocative and eloquent words that complete this chapter:

Life, of course, is a matter of ups and downs like any trail in Nepal. When one is going up, and the way is steep and tiring and hot, the idea that there will ever be an easier time of it is only a vague belief. It is not real. The trail up and hard is real. The aching bones are real. But not the promised top. That will never come.

Yet when one reaches the top and takes a short breather, one is impressed with how soon the misery of the climb has been left behind. Already I have forgotten the pain of it. The sweat has dried. I see only the way ahead. Where I have been seems immaterial. Where I am going is what engages me.

We learn something, I suppose. We learn that the pain and the sweat are what life is about. It is sweet. It confirms life. It is the heart pounding and the lungs working. The pain confirms existence. The steps are like days. The top is like goals that when achieved seem unimportant, often silly. It is the process, the steps, the getting there, the human effort that is important.

But what are goals about? Well, what is mountain climbing about? One does not climb a mountain and stay there. One climbs a mountain and comes down in order to climb another. One could get on top of the mountain by merely flying up there in a helicopter. But for what reason? One can easily see that attaining the top is not the issue. The goal itself is not what life is about; rather it is the process of getting there. Yet the process and the goal cannot live one without the other. If only the process were important, we could just as well never leave the bedroom. We could walk as senselessly and as far on a treadmill.

It seems to me that goals give direction and purpose to life. They give texture and afford closure. They provide satisfaction that one can do what one has set out to do. They reaffirm our worth if the goal is worthy. They prepare us for even-greater challenges. In the end it is both the trip and our arrival at the destination that count. One needs the other.

To me trekking provides a goal that is slightly beyond me. It is important not to pick easy goals. Trekking as metaphor teaches that goals must be realistic, that they should be set just beyond our expected reach, that they should be carefully planned and thoughtfully executed and that we should utilize the best advice and engage the finest guide available. Otherwise a trek through either the Himalaya or life can be disastrous.

This business of choosing a guide: what guides are available to us for our trip through life? Our parents have never been where we are actually going. They took their trip, not ours. Our neighbors or friends are not equipped for this trip. They have their own equipment, their own talents that make them ready for an excursion through life quite different from ours. Where do we get a guide? Therein the metaphor breaks down as all eventually do.

There are no guides in life. One must find one's way through this trip alone. Although you may have companions, such as a spouse or children or friends, in the end you take the trip alone and find your way alone. Since no one has been on your trip before, no one can show you the way. They are too busy finding their own way.

The danger in trekking is our expectation that it will provide something for us. Like life, *we* must *take from it*. The problem is that in the end we take only ourselves into the trek. We cannot leave ourselves at home. If we are blind or uncreative, or dead inside or insensitive—if we demand to be thrilled and entertained—then the experience will be only a reflection of who we are.

We will pass many places and see many people who are strangers to us and who, when the trek is over, we will leave behind forever. How we treat them is not as important for them as for us. Our giving is like receiving. We can give little and receive little. Only the poor who have kept it all for themselves will remain poor on the trek. I say it is important to give a great deal or we risk receiving nothing. If we are truly caring about ourselves, we will see to it that we are richly rewarded by giving freely of ourselves.

A Chitrali hunter in an upper-valley hut. The skylight, framed by poplar poles, is called a kufal.

4

Chitral: Land of the Kho

Away from the rockfall . . . under the avalanche.
Old Chitrali Saying

[The Hindu Kush is] a wild, desolate, little-known country, a country of great peaks and deep valleys, of precipitous gorges and rushing grey-green rivers; a barren beautiful country of intense sunlight, clear sparkling air and wonderful colouring as the shadows lengthen and the peaks and rocks above turn gold and pink and mauve in the light of the setting sun.
W. K. Fraser-Tytler, 1950

Chitral and Swat

Peshawar: Gateway to the North-West Frontier

In order to reach Chitral, virtually everyone first passes through Peshawar, the colorful, enigmatic capital of Pakistan's Wild West: the North-West Frontier Province (NWFP). So, before we travel north to Chitral (which is the name of both a town and a district), here is a quick excursion through this fascinating city. Remember that if you visit Peshawar anytime between the months of April and September, the summer heat can be ovenlike, particularly in May and June prior to the monsoon.

Peshawar means "Frontier Town," a name given by the sixteenth century emperor Akbar the Great. The Peshawar we glimpse today is an amalgam of Buddhist, Mughal, Sikh, British, Pathan, Afghan, and present-day influences. Like Rawalpindi, the city is composed of an old town chockablock next to a British-built cantonment. The war in Afghanistan brought Peshawar once again back into the news as we heard tales of bombings, arms smuggling, and intrigue among different factions of the *mujahedeen,* the "holy warriors" who brought down the Russian-imposed government in neighboring Afghanistan. But for those familiar with the era of the British Raj in the North-West Frontier, tales of plots, anarchy, and conflict are nothing new, but only a continuation of Peshawar's long, tumultuous history. As with any town in Asia, we can enter Peshawar's world, yet are still apart from it; Peshawar is there to see, but never to know.

In 1977 when the mountain snows were deep across the Himalaya, I wintered for five weeks at the fifty-cents-a-night National Hotel in Peshawar's Qissa Khawani Bazaar around the corner from the old Street of the Storytellers and Cinema Road. During that time, I never failed to be absorbed by the bustling copper, jewelry, cloth, and money bazaars, and the crowded restaurants serving *keema* (chopped meat with barbecue sauce), *karai* (eggs fried with tomatoes and onions), chicken tandoori, and other specialties. Peshawar's gregarious people, Pathan, Punjabi, and Chitrali, assured me that the personality of the city's storied past is not in the least dimmed. That year an ancient tradition ended when, due to a fractious election campaign, the open carrying of rifles, pistols, and ammunition belts in public was disallowed. The practice has not been permitted since in Peshawar itself, but many men have bulges beneath their kameez from packing guns in shoulder holsters. A few miles west, in the Tribal Areas, only Pathan tribal law is obeyed, and most men openly carry rifles or pistols.

Several good, old-style hotels stand at the junction called Shuba, located at the edge of the old city near the railroad tracks. Most of Peshawar's better hotels are located in the cantonment within several long blocks of each other, west of the venerable Dean's and Jan's hotels and the Tourist Information Center (located at Dean's Hotel). The fame of Peshawari food, including spicy meat dishes, light *roti* (flat wheatcakes), and rich milk products, is justly renowned. Ask your hotel manager to recommend a restaurant, and he will gladly suggest several nearby establishments.

The bazaars of Peshawar's old city and the tranquil parks in the cantonment are its prime attractions. The Peshawar Museum contains some excellent pieces of Bactrian art, as well as wooden funeral figures from the Kalash valleys in Chitral that are finer than those now left in the valleys themselves. Just west of Chowk Yadgar's money market in the old city is a courtyard off the jewelry bazaar called the Shinwari Market. The important merchants from Chicken Sale Street in Kabul, Afghanistan, have migrated here and now peddle their rugs, jewelry, and other wares. For as long as Afghan refugees remain in and about Peshawar, go to the Afghan-inhabited village of Fakirabad north of town on Friday. There you will be able to see *buzkashi,* "goat grabbing," the Afghan national sport, in which two teams on horseback vie for possession of a headless goat or calf. Peshawar is truly a city of many cultures. While walking through a single park in the cantonment, John Mock, language expert extraordinary, observed a volleyball game in which Pashtu (the language of the Pathans) was spoken, a football game in which the players were using Afghan Dari, and a cricket match played in whites, in which Urdu was interspersed with English.

If you have the better part of a day to spare and restrictions against visiting the Tribal Areas have been lifted when you visit Peshawar, you might take a taxi or local bus to Landi Kotal Bazaar in the Khyber Agency (one of the seven agencies that comprise the federally administered Tribal Areas located along the Pakistan-Afghanistan border). Landi Kotal is located at 3,400 feet in elevation, 31 miles west of Peshawar and just beyond the Khyber Pass, only 5 road miles from the Afghan border. Landi Kotal is probably the only place on earth where people will come up to you and proudly volunteer, "This free country, Mistaar. No police here. What you want, I can get." If what you want is *charas* (hashish), opium, heroin, or locally made guns, copies of Uzis, AK-47s, Mausers, Berettas, Kalashnikovs, or merely an eyeful of such contraband with a later peek into Afghanistan from the upper story of a teahouse, then you have found it. Landi Kotal is truly the land of guns and drugs and the bane of responsible Pakistanis, and that is part of the reason it has often been closed to foreigners. Look, but don't buy, for you shouldn't fail to note that a customs inspection occurs on Peshawar's outskirts as you leave the Tribal Areas and return to Peshawar.

An hour's drive south of Peshawar is Darra Adam Khel, home to the Adam Khel Afridis and notorious as the manufacturing and sales center for locally manufactured guns. If Darra is off-limits to Westerners, you will be rapidly sent back to Peshawar, but if not, you will see enough gritty gun-making warrens and gun salesrooms to last you a long time. South of Darra over a low pass and out of the Tribal Areas is Kohat, a bustling, untouristed Pathan bazaar town.

When the border with Afghanistan reopens, daily buses will once again leave Peshawar for Kabul, passing through Landi Kotal and the Khyber Pass. Buses and planes (in good weather) leave daily for Chitral and Swat; see "The Road to Chitral" that follows for details. Vans and "flying coaches" leave Peshawar regularly for Rawalpindi.

On the Edge of the Subcontinent

The region of Chitral (now formally a district of the North-West Frontier Province) forms the northwestern roof of the South Asian subcontinent. The rugged Hindu Kush Range comprises Chitral's northern and westerly borders, while the imposing Hindu Raj Mountains isolate it from the south. Within Chitral, the Adamzada, the former ruling clan, proudly traces its lineage to the fourteenth-century Tartar emperor Tamerlane; Adamzada governors called *Mehtars* dominated the state for 350 years until about 1950, when Chitral's statehood ended. Surrounded by warlike tribesmen in Afghanistan and the unruly Pathan state of Dir to the south, Chitral's three and a half centuries of autonomy represent a hard-won freedom. Through Chitral's central valley, an arm of the great Silk Route led to the Boroghil Pass in the Hindu Kush. This path provided a low-elevation passage to the ancient Turkestani bazaars of Kashgar and Yarkand, but marauding bandits forced most caravans to abandon this route for the punishing five-pass eastern trail through the Karakoram Range in Ladakh. As the years pass, a few travelers and trekkers have begun to trickle into and start to discover Chitral, this intriguing, mountain-encircled land beneath the highest and easternmost ramparts of the Hindu Kush. But, of the three principal regions in northern Pakistan (Chitral, Hunza, and Baltistan), Chitral still remains the least visited, partly because it can be slightly more difficult to reach and also because it is less well known.

Late nineteenth-century photographs show that members of the mehtar's court wore the long, bulky Afghan turban and pointed sandals. Today the *pakol,* a handsome woolen, Tudor-style hat, is worn throughout Chitral, and its popularity has spread into Afghanistan as well. The occupation of the often hawk-nosed, blue-eyed, and sandy-haired Chitralis has evolved from warrior to farmer. Chitralis are not Pathans, like their neighbors in Dir District to the south, but the Pathan code of *melmastia,* hospitality, is nonetheless practiced in Chitral, particularly in the lesser-visited northern valleys.

This Muslim tradition of offering hospitality to the muzzafer, the traveler, is observed throughout Pakistan's northern areas, but in few places is it offered so genuinely as in Chitral. If someone should invite you to stay in his house, it will be an unforgettable experience. Most village homes in Chitral have a large family room called a *baipash.* In the middle of the baipash is a fireplace with homespun rugs arranged near it, upon which the family and neighbors sit. The mother ladles wheat flour from sturdy wooden chests along the rear wall and cooks tasty round wheatcakes over the fire. At the sides of the room are raised sleeping areas covered with straw and blankets. Some well-to-do people have a separate room especially for visitors called an *angotee* in which you would be lodged.

The warm hospitality Chitralis accord foreign visitors is the kind of experience only found in regions that rarely see foreigners. Before the spring wheat harvest some years ago, I was fed and sheltered in four upper valleys for three weeks. Such estimable offerings to the traveler are neither to be expected nor abused, however. It is best to carry food when you trek in Chitral, and you would be wise to hire someone to go with you who can act as intermediary and help smooth the way for you. For the individual trekker or couple, their local escort, and their Chitrali hosts, this reception in the home is mutually rewarding. You can carry safety pins or extra tea or salt from Chitral Bazaar to give any benefactor in appreciation, and a gift of currency as you leave would also be considerate.

The sport of falconry, once widespread, is now rarely encountered in Chitral (although some people raise falcons to sell to oil- rich Arabs), but the largest towns still field polo teams and rivalries are strong. Polo grounds in Chitral are situated on mountain passes (the Shandur and Shah Jinali) and in such other improbable locations as the 10,000-foot summer village of Lasht Khot, high above the floor of the Turikho Valley. In an old notebook, I find the following line: "Gole is played with a ball and stick 4 or 5 miles up- and down-valley *in the snow.*"

Chitral also has a strong musical tradition. The Chitrali sitar, a graceful string instrument, is heard daily at small workingmen's teahouses in Chitral Bazaar. The *chenai* and *dol* (oboe and drums) frenetically accompany all polo matches. Taped film music from India and Pakistan in Hindi and Urdu, the down-country national language, is played in most Pakistani towns, but often the music heard on cassette recorders in Chitral District is recorded by local musicians from small villages in the Turikho and Yarkhun valleys.

Chitral became a district of Pakistan's North-West Frontier Province in 1969, and only since then have its people been directly affected by the regulations that accompany central government. The district was formerly insulated from the national government because of its relative inaccessibility north of the Lowari Pass. Now new federal buildings have been constructed, and a larger bureaucracy has arrived. Near one government building, by the corner of a new stone wall, a Muslim religious mendicant, called a *malang,* has lived for years in a small mud-and-canvas home covered with morning glory vines. His entreaties caused the stone wall to be diverted around his humble abode, and he continues to live in his traditional dwelling. The malang has successfully resisted a corner of the future. Yet, like the crockery mender and the camel caravans from Turkestan, he too will someday vanish.

The U502 Series maps covering western Chitral are restricted and not available. The *Mastuj* sheet (NJ 43-13) provides an extremely accurate rendition of Chitral north of the town of Maroi along the main valley. The small southeastern portion of Chitral along the Golen Gol and upper Shishi Valley is found on the *Churrai* sheet (NI 43-1), which also portrays the northern Swat Valley. The lower regions of the Kaghan Valley are on the *Mardan* sheet (NI 43-5), most of the valley's forested areas are on the *Srinagar* sheet (NI 43-6), while the uppermost stretches can be found on the *Gilgit* sheet (NI 43-2).

The Road to Chitral

A quick glance at a map would lead the casual observer to think that the town of Chitral is easier to reach than either Gilgit or Skardu, which lie farther to the north, because Chitral lies closer to the level plains. But appearances are deceiving for two reasons: Chitral's airport cannot accommodate the Boeing 737 jets that the lengthened runways to the north are now capable of handling, and the road north from Peshawar over the steep, rain- and snow-prone Lowari Pass remains subject to landslides and is difficult for vehicles larger than jeeps to negotiate. As a result of the crowded and often sporadic air service to Chitral, many people have to travel by road, a ride that usually takes the better part of two days from Peshawar.

Chitral Bazaar can be reached by two road routes and the connection by air. First, the option of flying. PIA schedules a daily plane from Peshawar to Chitral, but bad weather can force cancellation of these flights, particularly the second flight that is often added on in summer. In the spring of 1987, the plane did not fly for thirty-two days, causing vociferous demonstrations in Chitral. The fifty-minute flight is made aboard a venerable forty-seat Fokker Friendship plane that must be booked from several days to more than a week in advance (although there are plans to lengthen the airstrip and fly in larger planes). The PIA office in Peshawar is located on Shahrah-e-Pahlavi Street in the cantonment. However, you may have more luck in getting a confirmed seat if you ask a local travel agency to book the flight for you, because a travel agency may be more likely to get you on one of the few seats reserved for tourists. If you get on the flight, try to sit on the left side in order to see the virtually roadless, self-governed Pathan tribal areas of Mohmand and Bajaur and, beyond to the west, the knifelike upper ridges of the Hindu Kush in Afghanistan. In recent years this flight has often been diverted to the east over the Swat Valley because of occasional harassing ground fire from Afghanistan. If the plane takes its normal course, it will cross over the town of Dir, then not far above the road on the Lowari Pass, and begin to descend into Chitral, flying east of the dry lower gorges of the Kalash valleys. Due north lies Tirich Mir, at 25,264 feet the highest mountain in Chitral and the entire Hindu Kush Range.

The less-used land route to Chitral proceeds west from the town of Gilgit, in the part of Pakistan called the Northern Areas, along a jeep road that is being widened but which is far longer than the road from Peshawar. The route taken by this road toward Chitral District is mentioned in the context of describing the valleys upriver from Gilgit in Chapter 5, "Gilgit and the Hunza Valley," so only the busier, direct road north of Peshawar will be discussed here.

The best place to find out about land transportation to Chitral is at the

PTDC Tourist Information Center at Dean's Hotel on the corner of Shahrah-e-Pahlavi Street and Islamia Road. PTDC may run their own vehicle to the town of Dir at the southern base of the Lowari Pass, or possibly all the way to Chitral. If they don't have their own vehicle, they will be able to tell you of the best transport service currently in operation. This may be a private company that leaves from the bus station 2 miles east of town on the Grand Trunk Road, or the Government Transport Service (GTS) from its terminal on the Grand Trunk Road near Hashtnagri Gate. In 1974, before the road to Dir was widened and paved, my sisters Betsy and Pat and I groggily took the rattley, pink Dir Bus Service vehicle that left at 2:00 A.M. from Namak Mandi, Peshawar's old salt market. We learned that most of the passengers had arrived the previous evening, sleeping until departure on beds inside the bus station and on its mud roof. That day the bus had three flat tires on the rough road, and the trip to Dir took fifteen hours.

The road northward leaves the hot Peshawar Plain and snakes up the steep, dry ridge topped by the Malakand Pass. This hill is the first geomorphic hint of the great tangle of ranges to the north: the Hindu Kush, Hindu Raj, and Karakoram. On the pass, a large British-built fortress is manned by Pathans in khaki, their shiny uniform insignia reading MALAKAND. Northward from this low pass, the foreboding mountain vastness was once well guarded by the three princely states of Swat, Dir, and Chitral. They remained semiautonomous until the early 1960s, when direct federal authority was imposed state by state.

The teeming Malakand Bazaar north of the pass is the last large village until your bus crosses the Swat River and begins to leave the Swat Valley for the hill district of Dir. On a ridge just beyond the river crossing is a small fortress where Winston Churchill served his military apprenticeship and wrote some lurid newspaper dispatches about British encounters with bloodthirsty, sword-toting Pathan tribesmen. At an alfresco checkpost near Chakdarra Bazaar, you may be asked to register and present your passport, a custom that remains from the time when Dir State had a degree of autonomy. Across the road from the checkpost is a metal tablet identifying the nearby fort as one formerly garrisoned by Scottish Highlanders.

Once in Dir District, you may be able to join others on the roof of the bus for the ride to Dir Bazaar. The absorbing scenery as viewed from the roof is unobstructed, and other passengers who choose the roof often like to converse. Once I talked for several hours with a policeman returning to duty in Dir after he had taken a prisoner to jail in Peshawar. Leaning on our baggage, we discussed Islam, the local penal code, and the hard-headed intransigence of Dir-walas, as all the while the tree-covered foothills of the Hindu Raj Range rose about us.

Beyond the Chakdarra checkpost the road bears to the west, crossing a ridge and entering the lower Panjkora Valley. When the British were finally able to negotiate with the fusty nawab of Dir to build the road in the 1930s, gunfire from across a tributary in the nearby Mohmand Tribal Area necessitated constructing the road on this ridge route out of rifle range. As you ride along the wide Panjkora Valley with its "river from five districts," you can see into the federally administered Tribal Area of Bajaur. As recently as 1960, Arnold Toynbee wrote that neither Briton nor Pakistani had ever entered Bajaur, and even now, few roads penetrate this "free country," as it has been considered by its self-governed inhabitants. A Swiss acquaintance who learned the Pushtu language and dressed wholly in local style lived for some time in Bajaur during the late 1970s. He said that the walled family compounds in Bajaur all had watchtowers that were manned throughout the night by men who would call out, "Be awake. Be watchful." The symbol of the Bajaur Scouts, the local constabulary, is a tall watchtower. As you approach Dir Bazaar, the Panjkora Valley narrows, becoming more heavily wooded. Such rich timber is seen elsewhere in Pakistan only within the Swat and Hazara districts. Vast improvements on the road to Dir were rapidly completed in 1977 after a shoot-out between government troops and Pathan irregulars from Dir over the sensitive matter of timber rights. More recently the same issue caused the air force to fly strafing runs with jets over some areas of Dir to get the government's point across.

By now, you've got the idea. Dir's dusty bazaar may be the least hospitable town you will ever encounter. Be on your best behavior here: look people square in the eyes as you greet them with *"Salaam alekwm"* and think hard before you wander off the main street. You don't have to go far to take a walk on the wild side here: I have had stones thrown at me for walking away from the bazaar. Women should be well clothed (arms and legs covered) and stay with their male escort. Who knows? You may have a fine time here, but a word to the wise is always advisable in Dir. Formerly Dir was an obligatory overnight stop where travelers between Peshawar and Chitral were required to change vehicles. Jeeps used to be necessary for crossing the Lowari Pass, but in mid- to late summer when the road over the pass is clear of snow, you may be able to continue across the pass in a larger vehicle. A GTS booking office is situated in the main bazaar. At the north end of town are several small shops that make a Dir specialty: high-quality pocket knives. The single-blade knives are so well known and the originals produced in such small quantity that imitations are sold in Peshawar.

If you take a jeep over the Lowari Pass as most people do, get ready for a rocking, rolling, reeling ride and batten down the hatches by wearing sturdy clothes and a hat for the dusty (or perhaps muddy) ride. After you cross the bridge north of Dir's bazaar, the narrow road begins to climb toward the pass as one tight curve follows another. Just to the west below the road, you can see the south end of an unfinished tunnel meant to provide year-round access to Chitral beneath the Lowari Pass. Work on this immense project has been alternately slowed and stopped by difficulties with politics, funding, and water seepage, much to the anger of Chitralis, some of whom die yearly each winter from avalanches while crossing the Lowari Pass on foot (for the road can be closed by snow from late November until late May, depending on how much snow has fallen in any given year). Pines and deodar (East Indian cedar) dot the rocky *nala* (nala is a common

Hindustani word meaning "stream" or "side valley") en route to the pass.

In 1959, it took six days for the Italian Mt. Saraghrar expedition to traverse this route from Peshawar to Chitral (versus one and a half to two days now), since the road did not then include such amenities as bridges. Fosco Maraini's well-written account of that expedition and the religious and cultural history of Chitral in *Where Four Worlds Meet* remains an excellent introduction to the region. If you travel far enough in Chitral, you may agree with Maraini that the whole region is virtually unexplored. The road over the 10,200-foot Lowari Pass was completed in 1950, and as you cross the top, you enter Chitral District. The route leading down from the north side of the pass descends in an unending series of switchbacks. When my sisters and I returned south from Chitral, we rode in a jeep through pouring rain. I sat to the left, on the outside of the sociable, unperturbed driver, and while we hung on for our lives, the jeep skidded and sloshed around these muddy hairpin turns and the driver practiced his English with us, gleefully spelling out, "r, a, i, n, c, o, a, t: raincoat!"

Chitral Bazaar

As soon as you arrive in the town of Chitral, 52 miles north of the Lowari Pass, you will need to register at the Foreigner's Registration Office east of the main street in Shahi Bazaar. Once, when I was doing so, the civilian-clad policeman assigned to tourists and visiting VIPs looked up as he was noting my particulars in his ledger and waxed philosophical: "Where do we come from, where are we now, and where will we go? That is the question."

The town of Chitral (4,840 feet) is located on the west bank of the Chitral or Kunar River, a watercourse that is called the Yarkhun near its headwaters, then the Mastuj, the Chitral, and finally the Kunar to the south as it drains into Afghanistan. Steep, dry ridges rise from either side of the north-to-south-trending valley, and the bazaar of small shops follows the same orientation. East of the main Shahi Bazaar is Shahi Mosque with its round, graceful domes. Just above the river and next to the mosque is the fortress palace formerly occupied by the mehtar, where British, Sikh, and Chitrali soldiers fought off a local rebel force for six and a half weeks in 1895 until a relief column arrived from Gilgit (another relief force crossed the Lowari Pass and arrived several days later). Chitral's gently rolling polo field lies at the southern edge of town. Keep asking when the next match will be held or wander by in the late afternoon, for small pickup games often occur in summer. A polo tournament is held every June, and an annual festival with polo matches occurs in midsummer. Lodgings in town range from the modestly up-scale Chitral Mountain Inn to my former favorite, the dirt-floored Shabnam ("Dew") Hotel, which serves meals to a varied, colorful clientele ranging from traveling salesmen to local wags. The Shabnam and Chitral Mountain Inn are situated in the southern part of town called Ataliq Bazaar, named for the *ataliq,* the man who once acted as tutor to the mehtar. Tasty meals may be ordered at the Mountain

Inn in advance by those not in residence. Many visitors to Chitral stay at other, moderately priced hotels in Shahi Bazaar, like the Tirich Mir View.

The town's slow-paced way of life has been rocked in recent years by the arrival of refugees and mujahedeen from Afghanistan, just over the range of mountains to the west. Tented refugee camps have grown near town, and the outsiders have constituted an often-unnerving presence, muscling in on the local transport business and setting up their own shops and restaurants in town to compete with the locals. This is not to mention the occasional bombing raids, originating from Afghanistan, that once jolted this southern part of Chitral District. As the refugees return home, these aggravations will dwindle, but Chitral, like most of the NWFP, may never be the same.

Mohammed Akram, Chitral's experienced tourist officer, can be of assistance with the logistics and planning of your trek. The PTDC Hotel, where he works, is on the north end of Shahi Bazaar, the northern part of town. Don't overlook the manager or an assistant at your hotel, who is a mine of information about prices and shops. He will also gladly act as your tutor in Urdu or Khowar, expanding your vocabulary from this book's Khowar glossary and correcting your pronunciation. In the bazaar, you can be certain to find most of the basic foodstuffs for trekking: rice, atta (wheat flour), pulses, cooking oil, some vegetables in the summer, tea, sugar, and locally dried mulberries and apricots. In case of temporary shortages, you should bring canned food and powdered milk with you from Peshawar.

Short Walks from Town

Two steep, scenic walks begin directly from Chitral Bazaar. A fine but unshaded day hike follows the dry, rocky trail leading from the residential area called Haryankot, just west of the main Shahi Bazaar. This path, which is used mostly by shepherds, takes you some 3,000 feet up to the place called Birmogh Lasht ("Plain of Walnut Trees"), where there is an abandoned, mud-walled building that was formerly a summer residence of the mehtars. It has sweeping views of the valley and magnificent Tirich Mir, the broad snowy summit dominating the northern aspect. If you don't want to climb all the way, just walk up for twenty minutes or so for a bird's-eye view of town. As you climb, you'll see that there are higher hills rising above those you can see from the bazaar.

An overnight walk leads to the old royal compound of Biron Shal at 10,000 feet. The Biron Shal trail begins behind the deputy commissioner's office, soon entering a scattered deodar forest that becomes thickly wooded with pine as you gain altitude. This narrow valley is a game sanctuary, and owing to its proximity to the civil authorities who enforce its regulations, wildlife can be viewed there if you are a patient, lucky observer. Snow leopards have been seen above Biron Shal. This is the valley where wildlife biologist George Schaller took the first photographs of a living snow leopard in the wild. Good luck in sighting one.

An easier walk would be to cross the bridge across the main river just north of town and stroll up the gently sloping alluvial fan through the town of

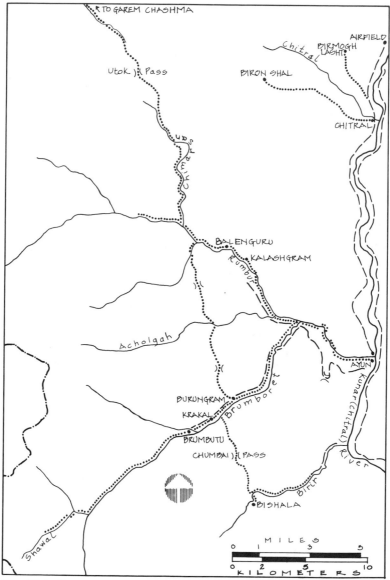

The Kalash valleys

Danin. Here you'll pass homes, fields, a wooden mosque or two, and see rural life away from the busy bazaar. If you wish, you can walk beyond town up into Danin Gol (*gol* means "stream" or "valley" in Khowar).

The Kalash Valleys

When the Afghan king Abdur Rahman Khan converted the non-Muslim Kalash people (who lived northeast of Kabul) by the sword in 1895, the name of their locality, Kafiristan, "Land of the Infidels," became Nuristan, "Land of Light" or "Land of the Enlightened." Since then, segments of three narrow, well-forested valleys in Pakistan that adjoin Afghanistan upriver from Ayun village in Chitral District have become the only region populated by non-Muslims in a 100-mile radius. *Please note* that in order to visit the Kalash valleys, foreign visitors need to get a permit from Chitral's deputy commisioner, whose office is located west of Ataliq Bazaar and uphill from the Chitral Mountain Inn.

The three thousand Kalash who live in these valleys, called Birir, Brumboret, and Rumbur, have been encroached upon by their Islamic neighbors. They seem to have maintained their joie de vivre and unique way of life, but their time as a culturally distinct people is fast ticking away, particularly since tourist-bearing roads have been built into all three valleys and since staunchly Islamic Afghan refugees have flooded into the upper regions of the valleys. Kalash women still wear five large braids and the *cheo*, a black woolen homespun dress, red-beaded necklaces by the dozen, and an exceptional headpiece (shaped differently in each valley) covered in cowric shells, beads, and trinkets that flow down their back. The Kalash women are often very attractive and have an outgoing manner that is disarming, delightful, and unexpected in a region where purdah is generally practiced. Young women have approached me to examine an article of my clothing or equipment and then expressed considerable amusement at my inability to understand their spirited comments. But they have now learned to be quite vociferous in demanding rupees if you pick up a camera. Bring photographs of your own family and the women will be very interested. After looking at your family photos, they may possibly pose willingly for you so that your family can see them (after you explain this in sign language).

You greet a Kalash person with *"Esphad,"* the local salutation, comment by saying *"Prusht"* ("Good," "Okay") to just about anything, and explain where you are going by using your destination and *"parai"*; for example, *"Brumbutu parai"* means "I'm going to Brumbutu." Though they have their own language, most Kalash (particularly the men) know more Urdu or Khowar than you, so you can use words from either of those glossaries. An article in the October 1981 *National Geographic* magazine by Debra Denker (who wrote "Making the Most of Being a Woman Trekker" in Chapter 1) will tell you more about the Kalash and their winter festival of Chaomos.

To reach the valleys, take a jeep from the jeep compound in Chitral's Ataliq Bazaar either the 10 miles south to Ayun (where you can begin walking into the valleys) or all the way in to one of the valleys. If you elect to walk from Ayun, follow the south bank of the sparkling river west up its narrow valley. At the end of a two-hour walk, after you cross many log bridges, the river divides. The southern stream fork leads to the Brumboret Valley; the northern fork of the river is the mouth of the Rumbur Valley. From Brumboret you can walk south over a pass to the Birir Valley or north over two steep ridges to Rumbur (more on these routes follows).

The Brumboret and Birir Valleys

Several hours' walk from the river junction along the south fork will bring you to Burungram, the first sizable village in Brumboret Valley. Some small stores are open here and a rudimentary inn or two snoozes beneath the walnut trees. Note that some inns in the Brumboret and Rumbur valleys are operated by Kalash, while others are run by outsiders. If you are aware of this, you can decide whom you would rather stay with, given the choice. Another mile up-valley from Burungram, note the exceptionally large stone houses at Krakal. Kalash homes are solidly built of logs and stone, but these houses at Krakal are particularly sizable. The last and largest town in Brumboret is Brumbutu, at the end of the jeep track. By making advance reservations through the office of the steno (the district commissioner's secretary in Chitral Bazaar), you can reserve a room in the pleasant government rest house at Brumbutu for up to three nights. The manager will provide meals on request and guide you through the small nearby fish hatchery. Small private lodges are also located there.

In one very long day you can walk from Brumbutu to the pastures of Shawal and back, but you may want to carry food and stay at Shawal's meadows for the night. To reach them, walk up the main valley from Brumbutu and continue about 4 miles, until you reach the last small grove of pines (if it is still there). Here the path to Shawal begins to ascend above the valley floor, and you pass a last lone pine tree and begin climbing talus slopes. The narrow gorge you have entered divides, with the right-hand path leading to another pasture. For Shawal, stay left; a stiff further climb will bring you to a meandering stream in lush pastureland. This large rocky cirque is called Shawal. When I arrived, hot and tired, some herdsmen were playing a game remarkably similar to quoits that involved the pitching of flat, heavy rocks toward a distant stake. With much good-natured banter, the teammates urged on their own side and disparaged the efforts of the opposing players. Shawal is only one of the summer pasture areas reachable from all three of these valleys. If you are walking with a Kalash escort, let him know you are interested in visiting some pastures and he can show you the way to those used by people from his own village.

From Krakal, partway up the Brumboret Valley, the most southerly Kalash valley of Birir may be reached via a trail that crosses the main stream on a small bridge. Once on the south bank, follow the narrow

A Kalash woman from the Rumbur Valley in Chitral weaves a strap for her new shoulder bag.

tributary valley ahead of you to the south and climb steeply upward 3,500 feet, over the Chumbai Pass. The town of Bishala in Birir sits on the valley floor below. This narrow valley was the first Kalash valley entered by a jeep road. The jeep track lies down-valley from Bishala and leads out to the main road along the Chitral River south of Ayun.

The Rumbur Valley

The easiest way to walk into the Rumbur Valley is to take the north fork of the river up-valley from Ayun. A harder walk into Rumbur that may require the better part of two days leads north from Batrik village just up a side valley from Burungram in the Brumboret Valley. This hilly route is beautiful but strenuous: well wooded and uninhabited, it offers you the opportunity to see the remaining valley of the Kalash. The trail can be confusing at times, however; side paths (used by livestock) can take you off course, and an intervening valley must be followed before you reach Rumbur. Hiring a local person to guide you would be best. The first ridge you reach has an enormous oak tree at the top and an excellent view of Tirich Mir. The intermediate valley is called the Acholgah Gol; from it you climb another steep ridge, descend to a small stream, and follow it through a narrow rock defile. There you are a mile upstream from the hamlet of Balenguru. This small village is shaded by tall walnut trees and is the uppermost Kalash town in Rumbur. In the 1970s a British anthropologist from Oxford lived in Balenguru for fourteen months conducting an in-depth study of these special people and their language. Only 4 miles of the Rumbur Valley are still populated by the Kalash; Muslim villages are located both above and below the towns inhabited by Kalash.

An ambitious trek north from upper Rumbur takes you over the 15,270-foot Utak An (*an* means "pass" in Khowar) to the popular hot springs at Garem Chashma in the Lutkho Valley. For this walk you should definitely take a guide from Rumbur and enough food to last three days. Your route follows the Chimarsan Gol, an hour's walk upstream from Balenguru. The going is tree shaded at first as you follow the right bank of the Chimarsan along a typically narrow valley. Several hours up, the trail crosses the stream and begins to rise toward the pass, 4,000 feet above. This pass should not be attempted before June, owing to its elevation, and after a winter of heavy snow it may not be open until July. The first village north of the pass is Putrik, halfway from the Utak An to Garem Chashma.

The Lutkho Valley

The Lutkho Valley is not inhabited by Kalash. It lies equally as far north of Chitral town as the Kalash valleys are south, and it is the western-most region of Chitral. Note that in order to visit Garem Chashma or any place in the Lutkho Valley, *you must get a permit* from the district commissioner's office in Chitral. The permit will probably be good for both the Kalash valleys and Lutkho. Lutkho's most popular spot with tourists is the town of Garem Chashma ("Hot Springs" in Urdu) and its enervating hot waters. A hotel here has a pool of naturally warm water so deep that you can dive in. Garem Chashma is not far down-valley from the Dorah Pass, a major artery into Afghanistan. During the recent Afghan war, this small town was an important resupply point for mujahedeen, and a great deal of lapis lazuli (mined not far away in Afghanistan) has been carried through here on its way to Peshawar, where it is bought by international gem dealers. Steve Shucart, an experienced Asia hand who buys, cuts, and polishes lapis lazuli and other gems (and is the author of this book's informative "Introduction to Afghan Dari") tells great tales of going to Garem Chashma and wading through rooms ankle deep in rough lapis-bearing stones, then paying for his purchases in $100 bills. The Afghan mujahedeen who sold him the lapis immediately bought ammunition with the money and prepared to return to help free their homeland.

The local language here in the Lutkho Valley is called Yidgah. Lutkho is known for the fine quality of its cloth, called *puttee,* handwoven from the wool of sheep, goats, and yaks. The best puttee is named *mogh,* after the town of the same name, and is woven solely from lamb's wool. Puttee is woven into foot-wide strips, then sewn into the characteristic *pakol* or *chogha,* the Chitrali hat and cloak.

When the hostilities in Afghanistan cease, experienced trekkers can consider walking north of the main Lutkho Valley into the Owir Valley west of Tirich Mir. This valley runs right up to the Afghan border. Perusal of a good map will present other interesting possibilities for hikers in the Lutkho Valley. Jeeps travel frequently from Chitral Bazaar to the towns of Garem Chashma and Shogore in Lutkho. Shogore has a large government compound; its long front veranda is lined with stained glass panels and ibex horns set in the woodwork. Inside, embroidery hangs on the walls, and faded Turkoman carpets recall the past, when caravans traveling between Afghanistan and Chitral carried less lethal cargo than they have recently.

Into the Southern Hindu Raj

Interesting treks can be undertaken into the narrow valleys of the infrequently visited Hindu Raj Range in southern Chitral. This range, a branch of the Hindu Kush, marks Chitral's entire eastern boundary, but this section looks only at the southern part of these mountains, where they divide Chitral District from northern Dir and upper Swat districts. These walks have not been classified by Pakistan's Tourism Division. A good way to get into these mountains is to drive into the upper part of the Shishi Valley and walk on a rarely traveled path into the midst of the Hindu Raj Range.

To reach the Shishi Valley, you must take a jeep from the jeep compound in Chitral's Ataliq Bazaar to the large town of Drosh, 26 miles south of Chitral on the road to the Lowari Pass. Drosh is the headquarters of the Chitral Scouts, an elite unit of Chitralis, four thousand strong, whose symbol is a pair of Markhor horns and whose principal job is to keep watch over the scores of passes between Chitral and Afghanistan. At Drosh you will have to change jeeps (unless you have been extremely fortunate and found a vehicle going directly to the Shishi Valley) and retrace your way 3 miles north into the Shishi Valley. Somewhere along the line you should find a porter-escort and with him ride (or walk partway) to Madaglasht, 25 miles up the Shishi Valley. Continue up the valley on foot from Madaglasht, a village originally settled by Farsi-speaking Persians from Afghanistan who made breech-loading muskets for the mehtars. The valley's walls to either side are very steep, with few trees, as in most of Chitral District except the Kalash valleys and the southernmost Kunar Valley.

Beyond the highest village, Dhaulatabad, the 13,700-foot Dok An at the head of the valley is ascended by a small path. Keep to the southern side of the gorge and follow the steep upper trail onto the northern ridge. From the pass, the village of Ustur is 8 miles down to the north in the Golen Gol. At Ustur, three routes are possible.

The first and shortest route follows the trail 9 miles down-valley through a gorge with precipitous walls to the main valley, where you meet the jeep road. Walking 2 miles down the road by the thundering torrent (here known as the Mastuj River) will bring you to Koghozi, a large town 15 miles north of Chitral Bazaar. Wait in Koghozi at the large teahouse for a jeep going south.

Secondly, from Ustur, you can walk 9 miles up the Golen Gol to the summer settlement of Dukadaki. Climbing 4,000 feet up the steep ridge north of Dukadaki will take you to a 15,000-foot pass. After you leave Dukadaki, there will be no water until you are well over the pass and into the Reshun Gol. A day's walk down the Reshun Gol on the far side of the pass will bring you to the large village of Reshun, 35 miles by jeep north of Chitral Bazaar. In the vicinity of Reshun, the deep red and violet coloring of the hills is most extraordinary.

The most ambitious trek from Ustur leads farther up the Golen Gol to the northeast and the difficult, snow-covered Phargam An (16,590 feet). Note that you can reach this pass by walking directly up the Golen Gol or by coming over the Dok An into the Golen Gol from the Shishi Valley. For this walk you must hire a local guide, and you may need to pay him well, because he knows the Phargam is not easy to cross. The Phargam An lies between an unnamed 20,000-foot peak to the south and 21,500-foot Buni Zom, the highest point of the entire Hindu Raj. From either Madaglasht or the mouth of the Golen Gol you will probably need six days to reach the town of Rahman at the road in the Laspur Valley northeast of the pass. Be ready to ford some large streams as you descend to Rahman. Eleven miles north of Rahman is the large town of Mastuj, and there, at the junction of the Laspur and Yarkhun valleys, you can get a jeep to Chitral Bazaar. The road from Rahman up the Laspur Valley to the south leads in an equal distance to the Shandur Pass and, beyond, to the Ghizar Valley and eventually to Gilgit (see "The Passes East from Chitral").

Chitral's Upper Valleys

Upper Chitral is a beautiful area of dry but colorful rounded ridges and sharp, snow-capped mountains. Summer pastures are found in small tributary valleys and along the higher ridges where snowmelt permits wild grasses to grow. Along the base of the main valleys are villages surrounded by lush fields wherever the combination of flat land and adequate irrigation is found. Like everywhere in northern Pakistan and Ladakh, these green oases complement and render even more beautiful the pastel colors of the stark mountains that dominate the landscape.

The two principal valleys in northern Chitral are the Turikho and the Yarkhun; they run parallel to one another in a southwest-to-northeast direction and are connected by several passes. Northwest of the westerly Turikho Valley is the smaller Tirich Valley. Most places in these valleys are not classified by the Tourism Division, except the Shah Jinali Pass, which is considered to be a closed area (this will hopefully change after the situation stabilizes in nearby Afghanistan). Every place in Chitral discussed from here on until the end of the chapter (including the Phargam An, upper Golen Gol, and the trail from the Golen Gol to Reshun, all mentioned in "Into the Southern Hindu Raj") is depicted in excellent detail on the highly accurate *Mastuj* sheet (NJ 43-13) of the U502 map series noted in Appendix A, "Map Information."

Wherever you go in upper Chitral, you will have to take a jeep from the town of Chitral to get there. The jeep compound for all rides north (including Garem Chashma in the Lutkho Valley) has been located off the west side of Shahi Bazaar, 50 yards north of the Chitral Gol, but the compound may move elsewhere because it is outgrowing its present location. A jeep's average speed up-valley or down-valley may only be 10 miles per hour, owing to the wriggling, narrow roads. The driver may stop 20 to 30 miles up-valley for a meal, and you should be certain to eat first before wandering about, or you risk finding the victuals already finished when you return. More than once I have gone hungry after strolling about to see the village, much to the innkeeper's consternation and my own.

Jeep rides anywhere in northern Pakistan are dusty, cramped experiences, but the country they lead to and through makes them worthwhile. You'll know this from experience if you have already crossed the Lowari Pass by jeep. There are two ways to ride long distances in a jeep. The first and most comfortable, but by far the priciest way to go, is to "book" a jeep only for yourself and anyone with you. To do this, you must negotiate a price with the driver or shopkeeper you are dealing with. You would do well to take competing bids from different drivers as well as the local tourist office, which is also in the jeep transport business. If there is room left and you want to, you can always sell the remaining space to any comers. Keep in mind that every driver has an assistant. Before you leave town, the driver may put a couple of heavy sacks of rice or atta in the back of the jeep. He may make an extra profit for delivering these, but carrying them could also be to your benefit, for they provide extra traction, which is often needed on icy or muddy stretches. Yes, this is all part of the fun of jeep rides.

The other, more common, way to ride a jeep is to buy room on one carrying cargo and passengers. Usually there is a set charge for the distance you'll go, although since you're a foreigner, the price may get jacked up a bit. When going up-valley, your pack and any other luggage will be weighed, and you will pay additionally for it based on weight. You will be wedged among your many fellow passengers, sitting on several hundred pounds of goods the driver is transporting. I have counted sixteen riders plus cargo on a single jeep. Jeeps going back down-valley (to Chitral, Gilgit, or Skardu) usually carry only passengers, and transportation costs are generally less then, for the driver makes his money primarily on the cargo he carrys north. Some words to the wise: arrange your gear very carefully before a jeep trip, because your luggage will definitely be sat upon, probably by several people at a time. Keep your camera with you in a shoulder bag, cushion all fragile objects, and hope for the best. The front seat in a jeep is a desirable location but difficult to obtain for anyone except a local woman or official. Wear a hat and keep your composure; the torture won't last forever. After the ride's over, you can brush the dust off and begin walking.

The first valley in northern Chitral covered here is the Turikho Valley, sometimes called Rich Gol.

Turikho: Home of the Kho

The towns and their surrounding oases in the Turikho Valley often lie high above the river and seem especially well manicured. Here you will often see rosebushes and flower gardens, and, except for the high relief of the land, you might be walking through English countryside of an earlier age. The poplar trees grow tall in irrigated areas of Turikho, yet the dry wastes between villages are as unsupportive of life as anywhere in northern Pakistan.

To reach Turikho, take a jeep 60 miles from the town of Chitral to Warkup (about 7,500 feet in elevation), the uppermost village you are likely to get a ride to hereabouts. You could also jeep to the large town of Drasan, about a day's walk down-valley from Warkup. At the mouth of the Turikho Valley, right above the point where the Rich Gol flows into the main Mastuj (Chitral) River, is the Kuragh defile, a narrow ravine where the jeep track is chiseled out of the valley walls. At the end of the nineteenth century, a British-led force of Sikhs was wiped out here by locals. As you pass through the Kuragh, with gray waters thrashing a few feet away, it is not hard to imagine how a relatively few marksmen could decimate a large force in this claustrophobic defile.

The path through Turikho lies on the east side of the valley most of the way north of Warkup. About 4 miles along the trail north of Warkup you cross a dark, evil-looking slurry called the Melph Gol. *Melph* means "black" in Khowar, and this stream is well named, for it must be the thickest, most sediment-choked watercourse to slough downward anywhere in the Himalaya. Cup your hands and let the murky water drain out. In seconds a layer of dark particles will have come to rest in your palms. Rain is the next village, with its poplar-encircled polo field. Right by the polo field is a small shop selling prepared food, the last eatery you're likely to encounter in the valley. A granite rock on the northern outskirts of Rain has a large petroglyph of a Buddhist *stupa* (a tall reliquary shrine) clearly outlined on it, recalling the era over seven hundred years ago when this valley was Buddhist. The rock lies directly on the trail and across the valley from a wide tributary lazily swinging into the main river from the west. This is the mouth of the Tirich Valley, discussed in the next section.

The Turikho Valley south of Shagram village (about 4 miles up-valley from Rain) is correctly called Mulikho, meaning "Lower Land of the Kho," while above Shagram is Turikho proper, the "Upper Kho Country." The Kho are the Chitrali people, who originated in Turikho, according to legend. Shagram still houses part of Chitral's royal family. I was given kind hospitality by a red-haired polo-playing prince in Shagram the first time I passed through in 1977. Seven years later I was fortunate to meet him at home again, for by this time he had become a lawyer with an office in Chitral town. We discussed what had happened in our lives since our last visit and the freak rainstorm three weeks previous that had wreaked havoc from Peshawar to uppermost Chitral, killing eight people in Turikho alone and blocking roads throughout Chitral.

Not far north of Shagram is the large Khot ("Cloud") Gol, which enters the main river from the east. An interesting high walk out of the Turikho Valley would be to ascend this valley and cross the 14,000-foot Knot An at its head to reach the central Yarkhun Valley. The best path up the Khot Gol is the one on the northern side, which climbs above the valley floor and in about 4 miles passes the town of Lasht Khot ("Cloud Plain") with its polo ground. In the vicinity of Lasht Khot you should hire a local to guide you to the pass, for the trail is little used and misleading stock trails are numerous. As you climb the Khot Valley, you begin to see west to the Hindu Kush peaks behind the nearby ridges. Walking up this long hill is tiring yet invigorating, and as with every high climb, you are rewarded by nature's unfolding panorama. At the Khot Pass, spires of the Hindu Raj ahead appear extremely rugged. The steep, unmaintained trail from the pass down to the Yarkhun Valley crosses from the left to the right bank of the Khutan Gol some 1,500 feet below the pass and descends along a ridge. At the Yarkhun Valley floor, walk north to reach the small village of Dizg, by a long green meadow, or trek south 2 miles and cross the river to the large town of Brep, situated on a wide alluvial fan.

Back in the main Turikho Valley, a two-day walk from Shagram will bring you to Rua, the northernmost permanent settlement in Turikho, at an elevation of 9,400 feet. Along the way the trail passes many villages and the large Ziwar and Uzhnu side valleys to the west. Both of these major tributaries lead to upper-valley glaciers, support no permanent villages, and are known to host scattered herds of ibex in their upper reaches. Fosco Maraini's 1959 Saraghrar expedition followed the Ziwar Gol on its approach march, and it was this area that he called virtually unexplored.

A grandly scenic, nearly level 5-mile walk beyond Rua village will bring you to Moghlang, where three large glacial streams converge to form the main valley. On inspection, Moghlang itself turns out to be a lone, solidly constructed hut used intermittently by herdsmen and hunters. It rests on a low rise above a large spring and commands an excellent view both down-valley and up the glaciated tributary gorge to the west. Several hundred yards west of Moghlang, the large Rahozan Gol emerges from the north. That valley leads to Bala Bughdu (another shepherds' quarters) and a profusion of glaciers from the Hindu Kush peaks that border the Wakhan Corridor of Afghanistan. East of Moghlang, the large Shah Jinali Gol comes into view between magnificient high buttresses.

You can follow the Shah Jinali Gol some 10 miles east to the wide, rolling meadows of the 13,300-foot Shah Jinali Pass, the "Black Polo Field." The route to the pass is little used but not difficult, with the exception of one obstacle. At some point between 5 and 8 miles up the valley you must cross the main stream from the north to the south bank. You may be able to make the crossing early in the morning by wading the river when the waters are low at a place where the stream is braided. If fording is too daunting, continue up-valley and keep your eyes peeled for a place where the river flows several hundred feet below the surrounding meadows in a narrow canyon. There, on August 24, the people I was traveling with were able to scamper across a snow bridge at the base of these two dicey, precipitous slopes of crumbly rock.

At the Shah Jinali Pass you are 5 air miles from the Wakhan Corridor of Afghanistan, and hereabouts grow rhubarb, anise, and mint. Several miles northeast of the pass is a 19,050-foot mountain that doesn't look particularly special in the morning light. But if you see this peak toward the end of the afternoon on a clear day, you'll know why the locals call it Ishperu Zom, "White Mountain." At this time the peak's nearly perpendicular, jagged pincushion slopes glow with an awesome white brilliance. An hour's walk below the pass is Ishperu Dok, a summer settlement inhabited by villagers from Yoshkist, located down-valley a few hundred feet above the Yarkhun River. From Yoshkist you can return southward down the Yarkhun Valley to Mastuj. The Turikho-to-Yarkhun route (or vice versa) makes an excellent trek. If you give yourself at least ten days' walking time from Warkup to Mastuj, you will be able to explore and enjoy some places along these scenic valleys and meet a few of their hospitable inhabitants.

To the Base of Tirich Mir and Over Zani An

Just north of Rain village, the Tirich Valley branches west from the main Turikho Valley. There is now a small jeep track partway up the valley, but so few vehicles ply the road that you can walk along it and may not encounter any motors at all. This narrow watershed curves back to the southwest and slowly rises toward the various glaciers that descend from the northern slopes of Tirich Mir. The compact villages in the Tirich Valley have grass-floored groves of apricot trees and mosques with straw-covered entrance porches. People from these villages have worked for various expeditions climbing Tirich Mir (25,264 feet), Noshaq (24,580 feet), Istor-O-Nal (24,269 feet), and Saraghrar (24,111 feet). Consequently, here in the Tirich Valley, unlike the other valleys in Chitral, you are apt to see a person wearing mountaineering boots or leading an animal by a length of climbing rope. A two-day walk up the valley from its mouth brings you to Shagram, a different village than that of the same name in Turikho. Beyond Shagram, another day's walk takes you to the last summer settlement just below the Lower Tirich Glacier, north of Tirich Mir.

Tirich Mir, like Rakaposhi and Nanga Parbat to the east, is known for being the home of *peris*, a word usually translated as "fairies" in English. But fairies who live in these areas refer to anthropomorphic supernatural beings that are by no means effete, although they are usually female. Peris appear (albeit rarely now) to people who transgress onto their snowy domain, but stories of their doings are legend in Chitral, the Gilgit River valleys, including Hunza, and around Nanga Parbat.

The Tirich Valley parallels the Turikho Valley and is separated from it by a 15-mile-long flat-topped ridge that averages 12,500 feet in elevation. The ideal way to reach this ridge, for its unsurpassed views of the high peaks in both the Hindu Kush and Hindu Raj, is to climb Zani An (12,500 feet). Zani An is situated between Shagram in the Tirich Valley and Drasan, the largest town in Mulikho, 58 miles from Chitral Bazaar. The pass is 3,000 feet above Shagram and a mile higher than Drasan, thus it is most easily approached from the Tirich Valley, because the climb is 2,000 feet less from this side. The ridgetop in both directions from the pass is quite level, inviting you to stroll along it and view the spectacular Hindu Kush peaks from Tirich Mir to Saraghrar and north. To the east, the Hindu Raj, including Buni Zom, and a copper-hued area near Mastuj are also visible. The play of light on the Hindu Raj and Hindu Kush is a breathtaking sight as the day progresses, and passing a night on the ridge would be an ethereal experience. A permanent lake on the ridge 2 miles southwest of the pass makes toting all the water you might need unnecessary (my fingers are crossed as I write this, for I've not seen the lake except on the exceedingly accurate *Mastuj* sheet). I climbed Zani An in late April with villagers who were going from Shagram to get supplies. We left at 3:00 A.M. so they could reach Drasan on the other side and return home the same night. They walked a total of 8,000 feet up and an equal distance down that day, carrying loads 5,000 feet up on the return! As we approached the snow-covered ridge at sunrise, an unforgettable display of rose, gold, then yellow light played on the towering snow peaks: a celestial view. If you want to climb the pass from the south, begin walking up the steep slope at the Zani Gol, a mile down-valley from Drasan.

Yarkhun: The Painted Valley

East of Turikho is the upper part of Chitral's main valley, a region called Yarkhun. The Yarkhun Valley is wider and grander than Turikho and far longer than its neighbor to the west, extending to the Chiantar Glacier at the easternmost tip of Chitral District. At the southern extremity of Yarkhun, next to the mouth of the Laspur Valley, is the important town of Mastuj. This fair-size town is reached from Chitral Bazaar (72 miles south) by jeep and lies along the road connecting Chitral and Gilgit. Mastuj (about 8,000 feet) perches several hundred feet above the junction of the Laspur and Yarkhun rivers. Here you'll see a Chitral Scouts garrison in the old British fortress and a couple of small inns. In summer and fall, jeeps from

Chitral can usually drive directly up to Mastuj and a ways up-valley as well, but other times the bridge across the swollen Laspur River just downriver from town may be impassable for vehicles.

The trail along the wide, 38-mile-long corridor of the lower Yarkhun Valley from Mastuj north to the Gazin Gol sweeps past low alluvial fans, many of them cultivated, and also crosses long stony wastes. The route is generally quite level, and long, map-devouring distances can be traversed in a day. For much of this distance you can follow a path on either side of the river. The Yarkhun Valley cuts a wide swath between a succession of precipitous spurs vividly colored in ochre, gold, gray, and rust: a majestic setting whose colors change during the day with the play of light. Yarkhun has more arable land than Turikho, as seen by the large towns of Chapali, Brep, Bang, and Miragram.

At Brep, several hours' walk north of Mastuj, you can be quite certain of finding an inn, but north of here, you will probably have to stay in your tent or a home's guest room, if invited. The rock outcropping in the center of Brep on which a school now stands formerly supported a Chinese fortress. Yarkhun was once famous far and wide for the quantity and quality of its hashish, but since the 1970s, when concerted efforts to stamp out production were made by the central government, both availability and potency have diminished. Most residents of Yarkhun are Ismaili Muslims, locally called Maulavi (see "The Ishkuman Valley" in Chapter 5). This valley was once a lawless and therefore little-used branch of the famed Silk Route; the Chitrali two-string bow (which shoots rocks, not arrows) and the occasional horseman with breechloader recall that era. People in upper Chitral love to put a stone in the pocket of their two-string bow and offer the bow to the occasional Angrezi. Then they lean back and wait for the fun. There is a trick to using these bows, and unless you know how to release them, you are almost certain to whap yourself with the rock.

At the Gazin Gol, a path leads east into the midst of the Hindu Raj and over a moraine-covered glacier for part of the way to the scenic Thui Pass, noted in the next section. North of Gazin, the valley narrows and bends directly north until it reaches Yoshkist at the base of the trail to the Shah Jinali Pass. Then the Yarkhun turns east and widens again as you pass some of the last large villages, inhabited by Wakhi people, the same ethnic group found in the Gujal region of upper Hunza. Hereabouts you are north of the Hindu Raj, the valley floor is higher than 10,000 feet in elevation, and the glaciers descending from the Hindu Raj nearly reach the river. Ahead lies the 12,400-foot Boroghil Pass, a wide, grassy, but politically closed door to the Pamir Range in Afghanistan's Wakhan Corridor.

The highest reaches of Yarkhun are a windswept land of grasses, streams, and glaciers, home to yak, wolf, and the rare Marco Polo sheep. Because of its proximity to Afghanistan's Wakhan region, this area is considered sensitive, and it is difficult to get official permission to come here. Silently congratulating ourselves on having gotten as far as Lasht village (because we were escorting a group and traveling with a government-approved guide), John Mock and I began a short late-afternoon stroll upriver. We met the local schoolmaster, who promptly burst our bubble by nodding up-valley and asking, "Are you going to upper Chitral?"

The Passes East from Chitral

Instead of walking west from Yarkhun into Turikho via the Khot and Shah Jinali passes described in the section on Turikho, you could take a path from Yarkhun leading east to the Gilgit River watershed. These routes are described here from north to south. Of these passes, the Thui An may be considered closed, but if so, hopefully it will become open in time. The first three routes lead to the upper reaches of the Gilgit River watershed; the fourth pass leads southeast into the Swat Valley.

The most tantalizing pass eastward is the 14,400-foot Thui An, offering sheer views of 20,300-foot Thui peak to the south. Thui Pass connects the Gazin Gol in the upper Yarkhun Valley with the Thui Gol of the Yasin Valley in the Gilgit watershed. Thui An is used by locals and has been crossed by trekkers. It is a great walk, but if alone, you are advised to go with a local, for to reach the pass you have to walk on easily negotiable but unmarked routes that traverse glaciers along both valleys below the pass. The western approach up the Gazin Gol is fairly straightforward if you go with a local; the walk up the eastern side will be described in "The Yasin Valley" in Chapter 5. (The glaciated 15,000-foot Darkot Pass, farther east up the Yarkhun Valley and also situated between Yarkhun and the upper Yasin Valley, is too crevassed to be suitable for hikers. This pass is even closer than the Thui An to the Afghan border, so it is unlikely to be derestricted in the future.)

The Chumarkhan Pass (14,200 feet) is the shortest route to follow between Yarkhun and the Gilgit River watershed. From the Chitral side, the pass is approached through the Zagaro Gol, a tributary leading east from Chapali village, 7 miles north of Mastuj. The main trail up the east side of the Yarkhun Valley passes through Chapali and joins with the wide path leading east to the Zagaro Gol. Follow this canyon for 5 miles until you reach the first large tributary from the southern (left) bank. There you cross the main stream on a bridge and begin a stiff 3,500-foot climb to the Chumarkhan Pass. All trees are left behind soon after you leave the valley floor, and in the lower reaches of the ascent, you'll pass several herdsmen's huts. If the hour you reach the stream junction is past early afternoon, consider camping either there or within 1,000 feet above, because water is usually scarce near the pass. When you descend from the pass, you will be at Barset village in the scenic upper Ghizar Valley.

The Chumarkhan Pass itself is a wide and rolling plain. If you are approaching it from the Barset side, you may have some difficulty differentiating the pass trail from the various side routes taken by stock in the summer months. Stay toward the center of the wide, rocky plain, angling back toward the middle of it if the route you have taken diverges toward the hills. You can purchase (or may be given) delicious milk products in the pass area during the summer months.

The 12,250-foot Shandur Pass is the traditional route between Chitral and the Gilgit River watershed, but the distance between Mastuj and Barset via the Shandur is 10 miles longer than the path across the Chumarkhan Pass. A jeep road now crosses the Shandur Pass, and this is the route you will take if you ride between Gilgit and Chitral. Like the Shah Jinali and Chumarkhan passes, the Shandur is quite wide and level. On the eastern side of the pass is a lake, next to which is a locally famous polo ground. Most summers, usually in August, polo matches are played here between teams from Chitral and Gilgit, and the event is definitely worth attending if you are in the area.

Accessible by midsummer from the Laspur Valley is the 15,630-foot Kachhikhani Pass, leading south into the Swat Valley (described in the next section). From the village of Sor Laspur, a town at the western base of the route to the Shandur Pass, the trail to the Kachhikhani continues up-valley for 9 miles to the Kachhikhani Gol, the first sizable tributary on the east bank of the Laspur River. The little-used route up this tributary continues an additional 10 miles to the top of the pass. When you first encounter the icy moraine of the upper-valley glacier, begin to look for a side glacier to the east that joins the glacier you are following. This is the narrow opening that you take to the pass itself from the Kachhikhani Gol. The route leads through the Hindu Raj Range into the Swat Valley's Ushu Gol and south to the trailhead near Matiltan village, where a road goes to the large town of Kalam. Hiring a porter-guide is the best strategy for finding your way across this pass, as neither the northern nor the southern approach to the pass is straightforward. And getting lost is not the only potential hazard to the crossing of the Kachhikhani. South of the pass you are in country inhabited by Pathans who tote rifles and who may be distinctly unfriendly to Westerners. You would be foolhardy to walk in this area unescorted. Note carefully the caution at the end of the next section.

The Swat Valley

Bordering Chitral on the southeast is the Panjkora Valley, most of which lies within the region called Dir (not an area to trek in, as indicated in the preceding section, "The Road to Chitral"). The valley east of Dir is Swat, which, like Dir and Chitral, was once an autonomous princely state. Swat is not a large valley, but it is lovely and fertile, and along with the Kaghan Valley (see below), it is the hill region that is most accessible to the large cities of Lahore and Rawalpindi. From the second century B.C. until the ninth century A.D., Buddhism flourished in Swat, and the vale was the birthplace of Vajrayana (Tibetan) Buddhism. In the eighth century, the historical figure who has come to be known as Guru Rimpoche or Padmasambhava left Swat, or Uddiyana as it was called then, and embarked on his long journey of conversion through Ladakh and Tibet. The Nyingma sect of Buddhism that he taught is still followed in many regions within

Ladakh, Tibet, and Nepal. Scores of archeological sites in Swat recall its Buddhist era, a period that lasted in a small way until the sixteenth century.

The upper valleys of Swat Kohistan, "Swat's Land of Mountains," rise up to steep, pine-covered ridges that lead toward scores of snow-clad 18,000-foot peaks. Unlike Chitral and the Gilgit River valleys to the north and east, Swat receives monsoon rain and has an alpine flavor reminiscent of the Rockies or Alps. Many of Swat's peaks were first climbed by the British in the days of empire. The Vale of Swat is well touristed by Pakistanis during the summer as far up the valley as the town of Kalam, but the most scenic northern areas are less often visited, and with good reason, as you will see.

The Swat Valley is accessible from Islamabad by plane to Saidu Sharif, or from Peshawar or Rawalpindi in half a day by van. The van will probably take you as far as Mingora, where you must change to another van or the slower bus for the remaining ride up-valley. Note that in Saidu Sharif, 5 miles southeast of Mingora and off the main valley road, the venerable Swat Hotel houses a government Tourist Information Center (TIC). Also in Saidu Sharif, Swat's capital when it was an autonomous state, you can book rest house rooms for the upper valley. Particularly in Saidu Sharif, but also in Madyan and elsewhere in Swat, you can find some of the most interesting souvenirs anywhere in northern Pakistan, including wooden chairs, embroidery, shawls, semi-precious and precious stones (emeralds from Swat are world famous), and silver jewelry. Forged antiques, from coins to stone carvings, are a flourishing business in Swat. Let the buyer beware. At the town of Khwazakhela north of Mingora, a road heads east for Besham Qila in the Indus Valley (see "The Karakoram Highway up the Indus Valley to Gilgit" in Chapter 5). This is a lovely drive of at least three hours over the Shangla Pass to Besham Qila, and is said to have been a section of the Silk Route between Peshawar and Gilgit.

Thirty miles north of Mingora is the pleasant town of Madyan in the last open stretch before a pine-clad gorge leads to Swat Kohistan and, in another 30 miles, Kalam. Numerous day hikes out of Madyan suggest themselves if you wish to stop here. Kalam's bazaar, which can also be reached by the Kachhikhani Pass (described in the last section) is the farthest point up-valley where basic food commodities are available.

The Ushu and Gabrial valleys, north and west of Kalam respectively, are the best trekking areas in Swat, but note the next paragraph. Each of these valleys has a rest house, reservable from the TIC in Saidu Sharif. In upper Swat, look for the unique mosques constructed entirely of wood that are found in most villages. These mosques have a quiet beauty despite their modest size. Three miles south of Kalam is a small village hidden above a bluff with a wooden mosque in its center. A day's walk to the ridgeline east of that village will take you to grand, Swiss-like vistas.

Upper Swat's many stockades are reminders that the valley and its neighboring districts are Pathan. If you trek anywhere off the roads outside

Kalam or in the Ushu and Gabrial valleys, you must be absolutely certain to go with a reliable local guide. Robberies and worse have occurred in upper Swat. Guns have been turned on foreigners in these northern valleys. It is best not to trek at all in Swat's uppermost regions unless you have solid assurance from the local tourism official or a reliable outfitter that the people going with you are trustworthy. At least one of your companions will have to be armed. Swat is a beautiful and accessible region, but you must be very careful before you consider doing anything more than a day hike along the roads.

Murree and the Galis

If you are in Rawalpindi or Islamabad awaiting a permit or flight and have a day or more to spare, then you can quickly get up from the warm lowlands to Murree (circa 7,000 feet), the nearby hill station originally built by the English. North of Murree are the Galis, a series of small resort towns along the same steep, lilac-forested ridge running south to north between the Jhelum River to the east and the large town of Abbottabad in the flatlands to the west. During the busy summer season, all of these towns, especially Murree, will be filled with vacationers from the big cities, but you'll always be able to find a room somewhere. Check with the Tourist Information Center at Flashman's Hotel in 'Pindi; they may be able to help you with suggestions, if not reservations.

The easiest way to reach Murree is by taking a flying coach from one of the companies on Murree Road in Rawalpindi, or a van from Bank Road in 'Pindi. The ride will take about two hours. Murree's jumbled mass of weathered wooden and newer stone buildings explodes with people on holiday between May and September. The largest crowds are found strolling along the Mall and nearby lanes. But you can find quieter forest paths, especially down the west side of the main ridge. If you want a longer walk, fill your water bottle and try following the ridgeline north out of town. Murree is the place where the British explorer (and, later in life, mystic) Francis Younghusband was born in 1863.

If you want to go beyond Murree, you can go north to the Galis, which are far more compact and less bustling. You can reach the Galis by going to Murree and changing to a bus going north, but you might be able to get to them just as quickly by taking a flying coach or van from Rawalpindi to Abbottabad and changing to another vehicle there. Gali means "lane" or "alley" in Hindi or Urdu, but here the Galis are a group of settlements, each with its own hotels, located on a road with steep drop-offs that winds along north of Murree. Some of these towns are Barian, Sawar Gali, Khaira Gali, Changla Gali, Dunga Gali, and Nathia Gali, the northernmost and perhaps most pleasant of all. Nathia Gali is a small English island, and leading away from town in several directions are pleasant trails. On a clear day you can see massive Nanga Parbat far in the distance. Take lunch and follow the track north to Miranjuni, at 9,470 feet, the highest point from Murree north along the entire ridge.

The Kaghan Valley   *by Ray Wallace*

[Ray Wallace has twice studied Urdu in Lahore and has visited the Kaghan Valley four times. "Wali," as he is known to his many Pakistani friends, is an inveterate fisherman and with his wife Patti Cleary has visited many areas in northern Pakistan.]

The Kaghan Valley lies north of the Galis and southeast of the Indus River. Trekking in the Kaghan Valley area offers the opportunity to see yet another side of the mountains and peoples of Pakistan. In addition, the Kaghan Valley provides an alternate route to or from Gilgit and the Northern Areas that avoids much of the long, rough ride up the Karakoram Highway (KKH) or the uncertainty of the flight. Travelers with enough time and a desire to see more of Pakistan than the mighty mountains and glaciers of the north may want to consider a trip to the Kaghan Valley, where one can fish, take day or multiday hikes into the forested side valleys, or perhaps walk over the Babusar Pass into the Kohistan region of the Indus Valley.

The Kaghan Valley, named for the town of Kaghan rather than for the Kunhar River, which flows the length of the valley, is located in the Hazara region of Pakistan. The valley extends for some 100 miles from the town of Balakot to the 13,600-foot Babusar Pass. The local population is friendly and easygoing and speaks Hindko (a language spoken by the hill people in Hazara), Pushto, and/or Urdu. The region is alpine in geography and climate, with forests and meadows dominating the landscape below peaks that reach over 17,000 feet. On my first visit I was reminded of the mountains surrounding Sun Valley, Idaho.

The area is reached by road via the towns of Abbottabad, Manshera, and Balakot. A direct flying coach from Murree Road in 'Pindi to Manshera offers comfortable, air-conditioned service. Seats should be booked in advance, as they are often full. In addition many vans (known locally as "wagons") run from 'Pindi to Abbottabad, where you can change vehicles and usually find quick transportation to Manshera or Balakot. In Balakot, morning and afternoon buses leave for the towns of Kaghan or Naran as well as private vehicles that depart as soon as they are full. In the spring the road between Kaghan and Naran may be closed by snow to all vehicles or passable only with four-wheel drive. Thus, if you are determined to proceed to Naran before about mid-June, you may find yourself having to walk up-valley from Kaghan or Naran (which is fine—just don't let the snow put you off).

Balakot, Kaghan, and Naran offer a broad range of hotel accommodations, but since this valley is a popular vacation spot, rooms may be booked full during the busy season from June through August. If you travel earlier or later in summer, you will have a better chance of avoiding the crowds. The journey from 'Pindi to Naran can be completed in one day by vehicle, but like all travel in Pakistan, it may take a little longer than expected.

The road from Balakot (the scene of a famous battle in 1831 in which

Ahmed Shah Brelwi was defeated by the Sikhs) ascends along the Kunhar River through lovely forests and the villages of Paras, Shinu, Jared, and Mahandri. In this last village is a handsome rest house next to the river. While I was staying there in 1986 during Ramadan (the month of fasting), the considerate *chokidar* (watchman and caretaker) awoke me before dawn so I could breakfast with those who would fast until sunset! The valley is somewhat narrow along this stretch and the views are limited, but as you ascend, the surrounding peaks come into view. It is possible to leave the main road on this stretch and explore the side valleys. One spot that is popular with the locals and renowned for its beauty is Shogran. This village, surrounded by peaks and forests, is east of the main Kunhar River in a side valley located just 2 miles below Jared in the main valley. The mountains in this area are by no means the giants of the Karakoram, but they do exceed 17,000 feet and are quite impressive.

Just before Naran the valley widens, and the flow of the river slows, making Naran one of the prime trout fishing areas in Pakistan and giving the valley a wide-open feel with many lovely vistas. In Naran you will find all types of hotel accommodations, from the lovely PTDC hotel at the north end of town to the small hotels that hug the roadside. My own favorite is a small unnamed place on the east side of the road just south of the junction with the side road to Saiful Maluk Lake. The staff members are friendly and are experts at preparing the trout you bring back from a day along the river.

Depending on the season, the fishing can be very good indeed. If you want to try your luck, you'll need to purchase a license from the Fisheries Office, located off the main road on the way to Saiful Maluk Lake. You can rent fishing equipment in Naran, and it is a good idea to hire a guide for the day. Every season certain parts of the river are closed to all fishing, so it is important to know which areas are open during your visit. If you're serious about fishing, you may want to pick up some "spinners" at a reasonable price in 'Pindi.

Most visitors to Naran pay a visit to Saiful Maluk Lake (10,500 feet) 6 miles east of town. If the road is open, you can arrange transportation by jeep. If the road is closed, it is an easy, gradual three-hour walk, and the lake is a lovely spot for a picnic. The rest house on the lakeshore affords impressive views of the surrounding mountains, particularly 17,356-foot Malika Parbat. If you do plan to trek over the Babusar Pass at the head of the valley, you could make the lake the first stop on your journey, followed by a walk to the village of Lalazar 6 miles north of the lake and continuing on to rejoin the main valley at the village of Battakundi.

One of the most interesting features of the Kahgan area is the Gujar (herder) families you'll see along the way bringing their animals up to the summer pastures. The Kahgan Valley is one of their most popular destinations in Pakistan, and you'll find them camped along the road in their tents or moving up the valley with their goats, sheep, and pack animals. The Gujars are generally quite friendly and usually have a cup of tea ready for the visitor. But be advised that they keep some large, loud dogs around their camps for security!

Even though the trail over the Babusar Pass is an easy one to follow, I suggest you have a local man along for the trip. Not only can he carry a good part of your load and help with the camp chores, but he also knows the best places to camp and is expert at fording streams, something you may have to do between Lulusar Lake and the pass. In addition, he can help you with your Urdu at no extra charge. The porter my wife Patti and I hired in 1986, Mr. Muhammed Bashir from Naran, was such a joy that we insisted he travel to Gilgit with us and trek with us in the Northern Areas.

If you are walking directly up-valley from Naran to Babusar "Top," you should allow at least four to six days to cover the 50 miles. Since this is a seasonal jeep road, the going is generally very easy, but the road is only open a few months of the year, and since the opening of the KKH this road is not heavily traveled. Consequently, you may find slide areas and spots where the track is rough going. There are many fine campsites along the way, but the population is sparse and the best you can hope for in the few villages above Naran is a simple teashop. Thus you should plan to have all the food and fuel you will need for the journey, as there is no guarantee that supplies will be available along the route. The gentle slopes are treeless after the village of Battakundi, and there is no firewood. If you travel before July, you can count on walking on snow part of the time and will find that the planks from the bridges across the river have been removed for the winter. Those planks are stored close by, however, and you can place them across the bridge to speed your journey. The road hereabouts opens in July.

Perhaps one of the loveliest spots to camp on this trail is at Lulusar Lake. Located just before the final grade to Babusar Top and surrounded by tall peaks, Lulusar is just one of the many high-elevation lakes that sit along the crest of the ridge. From Lulusar you are just a half day's walk from Babusar Pass. At the pass itself a magnificent view extends north to the Karakoram Range, but you must hike east about a mile above the pass to get a good view of Nanga Parbat. The view is a fine one indeed, and it would be possible to camp on this ridge to enjoy the sunrise. However, the only water you'll find at the pass comes in the form of snow, so carry some water from the river if you're unsure about snow at the pass and want to spend the night.

It is a steep two-hour walk down from the pass to Babusar village, the first town on the Kohistan side of the pass. Early in the season this descent can begin with an exhilarating glissade from the top of the pass. You'll find a rest house in town that may or may not be open. It might be possible to find transportation from the village to Chilas, but the road is sometimes closed by slides. Thus you may find yourself walking to Chilas at the KKH in the bottom of the Indus Valley (see "The Karakoram Highway up the Indus Valley to Gilgit" in Chapter 5). You are strongly advised not to camp out alone on the Kohistan side of the pass. So, either stay at the guesthouse in Babusar village for the night or walk all the way down to Chilas. But remember, it is a full day's walk to Chilas, and during the summer the temperature rises dramatically as you descend down towad the Indus. Plus, the residents of Kohistan often approach foreigners with an aggressive curiosity that can be quite disconcerting, especially if women are in your group. No matter how you arrive in Chilas, you'll be required to register at the police station when you get there.

The Kahgan Valley is a low-elevation area of Pakistan that most trekkers don't see. With its forests, lakes, and high meadows it is an especially lovely part of the country. Trekking in this area is particularly nice when the road over the Babusar Pass is closed or when you leave the main valley road to wander in the mountains. With the assistance of a local person who knows the territory, the possiblities for day hikes and side walks are unlimited. A trek through this valley provides an opportunity to make your own way into the Northern Areas and offers glimpses of the people and geography of both Hazara and Kohistan. For those with the time and interest, this peaceful, lovely valley offers an interesting and enjoyable destination.

5

Gilgit and the Hunza Valley

Even paradise loses its luster when you can't leave.
Dad Ali Shah, 1987
(When Gilgit and Hunza were temporarily stranded by air
and land from down-country because of cloudy weather and
landslides that blocked the Karakoram Highway.)

*To travel hopefully is a better thing than to arrive, and the
true success is to labor.*
Robert Louis Stevenson, 1881

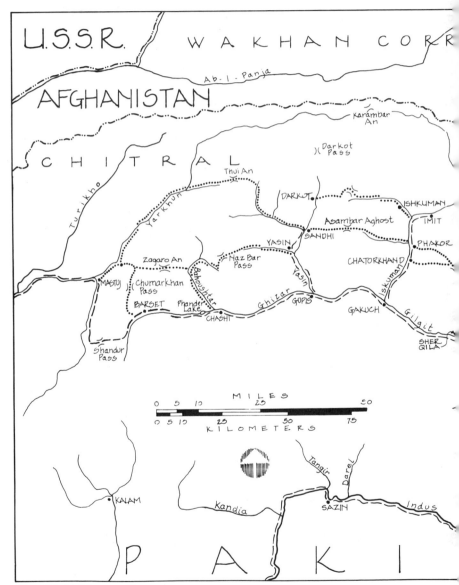

The Gilgit River valleys

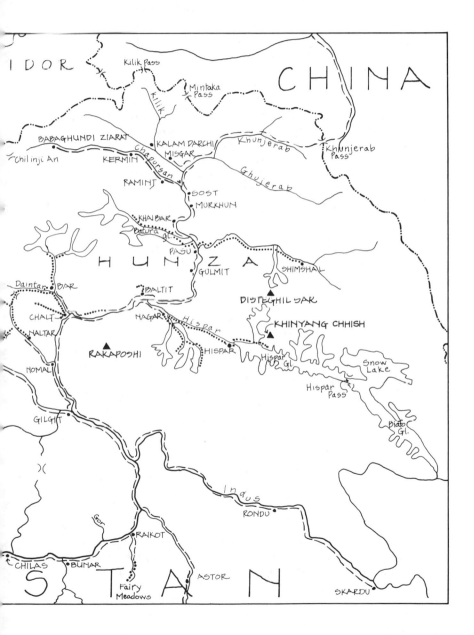

The Gilgit River Valleys

The four principal tributary valleys of the Gilgit River—Ghizar, Yasin, Ishkuman, and Hunza—reach into glacier-clad gorges and toward remote, knife-edged peaks. There are few places in the world where you can step off a major road as you can in the Hunza Valley and rapidly reach glaciated valleys so dicey that even the local inhabitants now rarely venture into their forbidding jaws. Stretching west to east from the Hindu Raj Range to the Karakoram and from the semilawless reaches of Indus Kohistan south of Gilgit to the Pamir Range on the northern border, these valleys and the passes that connect them have remained largely places of mystery to the outside world. Within the last hundred years, until the British assumed tentative control of these lands, the area comprised over a half dozen independent states, each with its own ruler whose decisions were law. But with the opening of the Karakoram Highway (KKH) along the Indus River to Gilgit and north to Sinkiang in westernmost China, as well as a lengthened runway at Gilgit that can handle Boeing 737 jets, Gilgit and the Hunza Valley in particular are rapidly being discovered by the outside world.

Tourism and commerce, once extremely limited in this area, are increasing rapidly. And the ancient traditions and customs of these valleys are disappearing as jeeps, trucks, and buses bring contemporary gadgets and modern ideas to people whose lives less than a generation before were virtually identical to their ancestors one and two hundred years ago. This chapter first follows the KKH up the parched Indus River gorge to Gilgit, the administrative and commercial center of the region, then looks at Gilgit itself. Then, from west to east, it looks at each of the four valleys in turn. The west-draining Ghizar Valley and the Yasin and Ishkuman valleys are moderately large, but the Hunza Valley is different. This remarkable valley has many tributaries with feasible hiking routes, and thus Hunza is described at much greater length than the other tributaries of the Gilgit River.

Several U502 Series maps depict the regions described in this chapter. Most of the lower Indus River gorge is shown on the *Churrai* sheet (NI 43-1) and the *Gilgit* sheet (NI 43-2). The Ghizar and Yasin valleys are seen on the reliable *Mastuj* sheet (NJ 43-13). The Ishkuman and Hunza valleys are found on the less reliable *Baltit* sheet (NJ 43-14), while the Hispar region, the Shimshal Valley, and the upper areas near the Khunjerab Pass are on the *Shimshal* sheet (NJ 43-15).

The Karakoram Highway Up the Indus Valley to Gilgit

The land route most of the way from Rawalpindi to Gilgit follows the Karakoram Highway up the deep Indus River gorge. If flights are booked or you want to see an imposing, desolate gorge cutting into the Himalayan Range, take the land route to Gilgit and you definitely won't be disappointed. The best way to go by road to Gilgit (if you don't book your own vehicle, which is rather expensive) is to take a fifteen-passenger van, often locally called a minibus or a wagon. You can reserve a seat on a van at the Pakistan Tours Ltd office (PTL is a division of Pakistan Tourism Development Corporation or PTDC) in Flashman's Hotel on the Mall, Rawalpindi, or you can ask the information officer there where to get the best van if theirs is booked. Vans also leave from the Modern and Park hotels in 'Pindi's Raja Bazaar. Try to get a front seat (difficult to finesse) or at least a seat by the window and avoid taking a bus, which travels a good deal more slowly than a van. Expect the trip to take an absolute minimum of twelve to fourteen hours, *inshallah* ("if God wills"). The maximum time for the trip? Well, be sure to pack a meal or two and also water, for you could possibly get stranded near a landslide (or, less likely, between two of them) somewhere along the way in the depths of the Indus gorge. Now for the marathon, nerve-rattling, neck-swerving, mind-boggling ride to Gilgit.

You'll probably begin the trip by following the Grand Trunk Road west over the insignificant ridge called the Margalla Pass, a place that the noted British historian Sir Olaf Caroe considered to be the boundary between the South Asian subcontinent and Central Asia. Then you pass the turnoff to Taxila, an extensive series of archaeological sites from successive civilizations dating from 600 B.C. to 600 A.D. that stood at the cultural crossroads of China, India, Central Asia, and the West. Next you swing south of Wah, a town favored by the Moghuls, who built elegant gardens and pavilions here in the sixteenth century. The route turns off the Grand Trunk Road at Hassan Abdal, a place that to the passerby appears to be merely a cluttered intersection. But this site was once sacred to Buddhists and is still important to Muslims (a shrine to the saint Baba Wali lies above on a hill) and also to Sikhs, a group of whom are permitted to travel from India each spring to visit the Panja Sahib Gurdwara. This temple was built in honor of Guru Nanak, the founder of the Sikh religion, who is said to have left the imprint of his hand here on a rock.

Three miles north of Hassan Abdal you enter the Hazara region of the North-West Frontier Province and continue past the bustling town of Haripur to Havelian, the railhead and official beginning of the Karakoram Highway. Next is the large town of Abbottabad, where a road branches east to the hill town of Murree and its neighbors, the Galis (see "Murree and the Galis" in Chapter 4). North of Abbottabad the road meanders through gentle hills in Hazara, a tranquil but very conservative area where women are rarely seen without the veil, unless they are members of the nomadic Gujar clan. Hereabouts you'll pass through country with emerald green rice paddies, fields of corn, fruit trees, and pines. But after Batagram, the land begins to change: now the road twists downward in a drier canyon en route to its rendezvous with the mighty Indus River.

At Thakot (2,515 feet in elevation and 123 miles from 'Pindi), the KKH leaves Hazara and enters Swat District, crossing to the right bank of the Indus over the first of the more than ninety graceful suspension bridges built by Chinese engineers that lie between here and the northern border. Not far from Thakot is the bustling town of Besham Qila (also called just Besham). At Besham, a good road from the Swat Valley joins the KKH;

this was the way I first approached the route up the Indus Valley in 1974 when the unpaved road was still called the Indus River Road. Here at Besham, Ray Wallace (he was introduced in the last chapter as author of a section) who has lived and studied in Pakistan, met a Pakistani geologist who related how he was tirelessly accompanied by locals during his mapping excursions in the countryside. When he asked why they were so interested in his rock sampling, they replied, "We know why you've come. You're here to find the gold."

As you proceed north on the KKH, you enter the region called Kohistan, "Land of Mountains." This area was formerly known as Yagistan, "Land of the Ungovernable," or "The Rebellious Country." As you continue for the next few hours and see the grim, bearded visages of the Kohistanis, you can imagine how intractable their forebears must have been. As recently as 1977, thousands of these tribesmen surrounded camps housing Pakistani and Chinese engineers and road workers, because the Kohistanis felt they had not been adequately compensated for their land given up for construction of the KKH and because, in any case, they just didn't like the intrusion of the road. It took thousands of soldiers backed by artillery and jets to get the government's point across and allow road work to recommence. Again, in 1988, shoot-ups between Sunnis and Shiites resulted in burned villages and scores of deaths. So much for jumping off your vehicle and trekking up an intriguing side valley in Kohistan. Attitudes change very slowly all along this valley as far north as Gilgit, and the reasons why a foreigner would want to wander afield are not understood hereabouts.

The town of Pattan is Kohistan's administrative center and was the hardest-hit village when an earthquake struck Kohistan in 1974, killing thousands of people. Here the Indus flows through a V-shaped gorge with scattered trees and small homes that cling to the steep, brown slopes as if camouflaged. The rocky hills are particularly steep in this part of the gorge, and in the 1960s road workers had to lower themselves down on ropes to drill and set the first charges of dynamite. Between four hundred and five hundred Pakistanis and Chinese lost their lives building the KKH, and more were killed in this stretch than anywhere else. All told, over fifteen thousand Pakistanis and ten thousand Chinese worked on the KKH, and they used 8,000 tons of dynamite, removing 30 million cubic yards of earth and rocks to complete the road. The KKH was officially dedicated in 1978, but the last Chinese engineers stayed until late 1979, and up to 1981 foreigners needed permits to travel on the road. It will still be many years until the mountains stop moving onto the KKH, and you may conceivably find yourself temporarily marooned between two landslides. Don't worry: you will get where you're going. *Muzzafer khana*s (travelers' inns) are scattered along the way, and you can eat dal and roti and sleep on a *charpoy* (rope bed) for the night while listening to someone tell you about another time when landslides were worse. If the blockage is particularly severe, you may possibly have to leave your vehicle and walk across the landslide, then climb aboard another conveyance to continue your journey.

In winter and spring, the Indus glides by a lovely deep blue, but during the summer and early fall, when most outsiders see the river, its waters roil southward the color of milk coffee and the clear streams from numerous nalas instantly disappear in the brown mainstream. Temperatures can be blazing during midday in summer all the way to Gilgit, so travel with a full water bottle. Above Pattan the road crosses to the left bank of the river, and a little farther on, just before the river trends easterly, the Kandia Valley joins the Indus. For experienced trekkers with an armed local escort, a week's walk up and back down the Kandia Valley could be an exception to the rule of "no trekking in Kohistan." Kandia is actually part of Swat District, and like upper Swat, it has some lovely wooden mosques. In addition, sturdy hikers with a local guide might be interested to know that there are about three passes between 15,000 and 17,000 feet in elevation that lead from Kandia into the upper Swat Valley.

Near the town of Sazin the blind turns and stomach-turning precipices below the road diminish as the valley widens, and scattered sandy beaches appear below on the riverbank. Almost directly across the river to the north of Sazin is the mouth of the Tangir Valley. Tangir and the neighboring valley of Darel, which debouches into the Indus 6 miles to the east, are known for their lush terrain high above and out of sight from the main valley, and also for their intractable inhabitants, many of whom live in homes that have square towers with gun slits. Tangir and Darel remained totally independent during the British colonial era, but in 1952 both valleys voluntarily joined Pakistan. Blood feuds going back many generations exist in valleys like these throughout Kohistan and the North-West Frontier Province, and the only place a person involved in such a feud is truly safe is in the sanctuary of his home or the local mosque. When you meet Kohistanis, never doff your hat to them, for this would be taken as an insult. A police officer once stationed in Kohistan said, "There was only one problem: murder. Murder, murder, murder."

East of Sazin the KKH leaves the North-West Frontier Province and enters the administrative region called the Northern Areas. You will be traveling in the Northern Areas for the rest of this chapter and all of the time you are in Baltistan, discussed in Chapter 7. The principal town in this west-to-east part of the Indus Valley is Chilas, an inhospitable and sun-bleached place. Here at Chilas (about 3,900 feet in elevation and 280 miles from Rawalpindi) the road descending from the Babusar Pass and the Kaghan Valley joins the KKH (see "The Kaghan Valley" in Chapter 4). At Chilas is an up-scale hotel, called the Midway Hotel, where anyone may stay, but particularly people who are en route to the Shangri La Hotel in Baltistan.

The most interesting sites in the Chilas vicinity are various rocks where ancient petroglyphs can be seen. Over the past four millennia, Kushan, Buddhist, and Hindu conquerers, merchants, missionaries, and pilgrims carved symbols and inscriptions onto various large boulders glazed dark brown by oxidation of their iron content. At the different sites you can see the likenesses of horses, serpents, ibex, stupas, and figures of Buddha. These petroglyphs were made by some in triumph and by others in gratitude for safe passage. One site is located near the bridge leading across the Indus to Tangir and Darel, and two sites are found near Chilas. Complete information on all the petroglyphs in the Northern Areas can be found in *Rock Carvings and Inscriptions in the Northern Areas of Pakistan,* by Karl Jettmar, noted in the bibliography. At Chilas a footbridge crosses the Indus north to the Kiner Gah (*gah* means "stream"), where rock carvings are found near the bridge and more can be reached after a short climb. These carvings were probably made by Buddhist pilgrims of a bygone era as they traversed these high mountains from south to north and back again. A path (also noted in the latter part of the next section) can be followed up the Kiner Gah to Gilgit, a walk that will take roughly five days. But this route should only be taken by experienced hikers with an armed local escort who knows the way.

East of Chilas this dry gorge becomes even deeper, because high above and out of sight to the south rises Nanga Parbat (26,650 feet), the westernmost peak in the Great Himalaya Range, a mountain so gargantuan it is more a range than a single massif. At the hamlet of Bunar, the Bunar Gah debouches into the Indus River from the south. Following this valley up for 6 miles, then the easterly Diamir Gah for an equal distance, takes you to the Airl Gah. Up the Airl Gah to the south is the way to the 17,000-foot Mazeno Pass, a difficult route over the western ridges of Nanga Parbat. The technical part of this path is the uppermost few hundred feet of the northern side of the pass. The south side of the pass leads you down to the Rupal Glacier and toward the towering south face of Nanga Parbat (this area and the pass are also noted in "Astor and the South Face of Nanga Parbat" in Chapter 7). Along the KKH east of Buner, the small Gor Valley drains into the far side of the Indus from the north. Near this place a landslide in 1840 blocked the Indus River for six months, forming a lake that reached as far up-valley as Gilgit. When the dam broke, a wall of water flooded down the Indus Valley for hundreds of miles and inundated the plains south of the mountains, wiping out an army of Sikhs camped on the bank of the river near Attock.

In this area you are north of Nanga Parbat in the second-deepest gorge on earth, as measured from the peak to the base of the valley. (The Arun Valley, in eastern Nepal, from the summit of Makalu to the Arun River, is the greatest vertical drop.) It is utterly incongruous to drive up this ovenlike gorge in summer, knowing that nearly 4 miles above are shimmering snowfields. At Raikot village, the Raikot Valley joins the Indus. From the village a road angles up a steep ridge and leads up the valley as far as a hotel, the Shangri La (in the same chain as the Midway and Shangri La in Baltistan). A long day's walk above the roadhead takes you to the pastures called Fairy Meadows, below the Raikot Glacier. If you give yourself four days, you can have a fine, leisurely paced round trip from the roadhead to beyond Fairy Meadows and back. As always, it is advisable to hire someone to walk with you. You can walk up the west side of the glacier to the point marked 14,954 on the *Gilgit* sheet (NI 43-2) of the U502 Map Series.

Just upriver from Raikot, the KKH crosses to the north (right) bank of the Indus. Now the Indus Valley bends to the north, and as you move away from Nanga Parbat you can begin to see its snows miles above the valley floor. The large Astor River empties into the east side of the Indus in the lower portion of this northerly trending area. This valley to the east of Nanga Parbat is discussed in Chapter 7 on Baltistan, since it is adjacent to the Deosai Plains of Baltistan and is not a part of the Gilgit River system, even though it is administered and usually approached from Gilgit. North of the Astor River and also on the east bank of the Indus is the sun-bleached town of Bunji, headquarters of the Northern Light Infantry. The KKH crosses a clear tributary stream on a suspension bridge, then passes through the town of Jaglot, where the road from Bunji and the Astor Valley crosses the Indus to join the main KKH.

Not far north of Jaglot the Gilgit River joins the Indus from the west. Here in a parched wasteland is a brief stretch of road where you can look right at the junction of these two mighty rivers. In summer the waters from the Gilgit River are a grayish black, while the Indus is light brown in hue. From here on, the KKH follows first the Gilgit River, then the Hunza Valley to the road's terminus on the border with Sinkiang, China, at the Khunjerab Pass. A mile up the Gilgit Valley, the road to Baltistan diverges northeast from the KKH, crossing the Gilgit River on its way up the Indus. It is uncanny to think that just 10 miles away up the Indus gorge the river bends to the southeast and continues from there in the same direction for some 500 miles to its source north of sacred Mt. Kailas in western Tibet.

The KKH continues almost due west along the Gilgit River valley, crossing dry alluvial fans, and in a dozen miles passes south of the Bagrot Valley, a tributary nala with a road that leads directly north to the southern base of Rakaposhi, the 25,550-foot peak overlooking the main oases of Hunza. Soon you see a long suspension bridge over the Gilgit River that leads to the town of Dainyor with its many green fields, located at the mouth of the Hunza Valley. The KKH crosses that bridge, carrying on into the gorge of the Hunza River. Further description of the KKH will be in the section that follows on Hunza, for the remainder of the road follows the Hunza Valley. Five miles beyond the bridge up the Gilgit Valley lies the large, prosperous town of Gilgit.

Gilgit

The town of Gilgit (4,900 feet in elevation and 365 miles from Rawalpindi) is a large entrepôt, said by official publications to have a population of twenty-five thousand, an estimate that likely also includes some surrounding towns. It is a place travelers must pass through and pause at on the way to or from their excursions in Hunza, or between Chitral and Baltistan, but it is not a destination in itself, particularly in the hot midsummer months. In the past, the town was alternately fought over, plundered, and ignored. Today Gilgit is growing rapidly, and you'll see many diverse people here: taciturn local Shina-speaking farmers and shopkeepers, outgoing Hunzakuts (as people from Hunza are called), rugged Kohistanis visiting the bazaar, and steely-eyed Pathan truck drivers or businessmen. Although two-humped Bactrian camels led by Turkomen from Kashgar no longer plod into the main bazaar, Gilgit is becoming a key transit point for trekkers because of its location between Chitral and Baltistan and just south of Hunza.

Planes from Islamabad-Rawalpindi arrive daily in Gilgit now that the airstrip on the eastern edge of town is being lengthened to accommodate jets. The former small, stone-walled passenger terminal used to have four waiting rooms, and the signs to them provided insight into down-country Pakistan: Men's Lounge, Women's Lounge, VIP Lounge, and VVIP Lounge. If you arrive by air, the main bazaar in Gilgit is a short mile away, and to get there you can grab a small van or whatever vehicle seems to be taking passengers. Gilgit's main street runs generally east-west, paralleling the river. We will look quickly at Gilgit from east to west, beginning at the airport, but first two places to keep in mind that are not on the main street.

East of the airport and away from town is the area called Jutial, where there are numerous military compounds and one or two small lodges (the Tourist Cottage here is popular with budget travelers). Farther east in Jutial and back from the main road leading to the KKH is the Serena Inn, the poshest place in town and the only one with a view of Rakaposhi, the tip of which is just visible from the hotel. Behind the Serena at the base of the rocky slopes are some rock carvings.

Back at the airport is a road (diverging north from the main Airport Road) that leads near the river to the Chinar Inn, the PTDC-operated hotel in town. The official Tourist Information Center and local office of Pakistan Tours are at the Chinar Inn, and the tourist officer there is a good person to speak with if you want to book a jeep or discuss the better-known trekking locations. Near this hotel are a couple of other hostelries, the best of which is the Hunza Inn, and Chinar Bagh (*bagh* means "garden"), a cool, shady grove of chinar or plane trees next to the river where locals have picnics. Here you may hear a military band practicing in the mornings, its piping almost drowned out by the roar of the river. At Chinar Bagh is the larger of the two bridges in town that cross the Gilgit River to its north bank.

Now to swing westerly through Gilgit, beginning at the airfield. Note that for a rupee or two you can squeeze into a small Suzuki van and ride from one point to another along the length of Gilgit's long bazaar. Near the airport is the local office of Waljis Travel, where you can inquire for booking jeep transport or hiring a guide or porter. At the end of the runway, Airport Road meets the main road coming from the KKH, and this artery, generally known as Airport Road also, continues west into town. Along this stretch are some hotels, Masherbrum Tours (a bus company) with daily departures for Skardu in Baltistan, an office for vans (mini-bus or wagon, they are much the same) to 'Pindi, and the government-operated Northern Area Transport Company (NATCO) office. NATCO has jeeps for hire and runs a scheduled bus service to Rawalpindi and several destinations in Hunza. It also has a monopoly on passenger transport from the upper

Hunza Valley over the Khunjerab Pass into China. Just west of the cinema and south of the main street is the PIA office. Be sure that your PIA ticket to Rawalpindi is reconfirmed at least once prior to the day before you leave, or your name will disappear from the manifest. Near here is also a store specializing in goods from China brought down the KKH. At some of the many shops along Airport Road you can find trekking supplies and foodstuffs.

The main street now divides. Angling south is Jamaat Khana Bazaar, named for the Jamaat Khana, the Ismaili "House of Assembly," found on the corner. In Jamaat Khana Bazaar are several souvenir and general merchandise stores owned by Hunzakuts and an inn or two. A street running west of and parallel to Jamaat Khana Bazaar has shops run by people from Nagar, and there you can inquire about jeeps leaving from this vicinity and going straight to Nagar in the Hunza Valley (see "Nagar" that follows). The fishery office for the Gilgit River valleys is also located on this street. If you want to get a temporary fishing license, the fishery office is the place to do it, and Samiullah Khan is the person to speak with, if he is available (note the different rates for day, week, month, or season). Samiullah has written an informative brochure entitled "Trout in Northern Areas," and he can be very helpful. Either he or one of his staff can explain the limits on how many fish can be caught and make suggestions on good locations for fishing. The NAWO office (the Northern Areas Works Organization repairs roads and undertakes other public works projects in the Northern Areas) on this street is the place to make reservations for the various rest houses scattered about the Gilgit River valleys. NAWO rest houses can be found (from west to east) at Teru, Phander, Gupis, Yasin, Gakuch, Imit, Naltar, Nomal, Chalt, and Nagar. If you have a proper chit and aren't expecting snappy service, you may enjoy staying at one or two of these rustic rest houses. Food can usually be prepared at these places by an appointed cook who lives near each rest house and who can be found sooner or later. If you bring some eatables, that will make it easier for the cook (or more likely his wife, who will do the actual cooking) to get started. South of and approximately midway between the street where the NAWO and fishery offices are located and Jamaat Khana Bazaar is the district commissioner's office and nearby is the hospital.

At the east end of Jamaat Khana Bazaar the main street turns north, then west again at Saddar Bazaar, where more shops offer general merchandise and food; you'll also find the police station and post office. To the north is a narrow street of shops and greasy spoons that leads to a bridge across the Gilgit River. Just west of the bridge is the large fenced-in polo field surrounded by stands for spectators. With luck you can see a polo match; ask the host at your hotel or other local acquaintances when the next match will be played. Gilgitis say polo was first played here, while the same claim is made in Chitral and Baltistan.

West of the polo field is Punial Bazaar, where you are most likely to find cargo jeeps that will accept passengers going to the Ghizar, Yasin, or Ishkuman valleys (note the two paragraphs on long-distance jeep rides in

"Chitral's Upper Valleys" in Chapter 4). The farther away from Gilgit you want to go, the harder it may be to find a ride. You'll have to ask all your contacts in town and just keep trying if you want to go west of Phandar in the Ghizar Valley. During the summer, however, there may be occasional scheduled passenger service as far as Mastuj in Chitral. The roads west up the various valleys upriver are slowly being widened and paved. As improvements to these roads are made over the years, it will become easier and easier to find better and faster transport up these valleys (with a consequent increase in tourism and a lessening of the hospitality traditionally offered to travelers).

It would be impossible to leave Gilgit without mentioning two Hunzakuts who have had shops and been fixtures in town for many years. Dad Ali Shah's shop, which sells handicrafts from Hunza, trekking gear, and other items, is located at the Park Hotel on the main street in the eastern end of town. Easygoing Dad Ali is a born storyteller. Ghulam Mohammed (G. M.) Baig Hunzai has his Mohammed Book Stall in Jamaat Khana Bazaar. G. M. is involved in social work, and he regularly searches out interesting books in English and Urdu and is known far and wide as a bookseller. Both men are mines of information about the area; they each have contacts throughout the regions covered in this chapter and can be helpful in recommending lodgings and porter or guide contacts. G. M. and Dad Ali can make suggestions for transportation if you are going somewhere out of the ordinary and their shops are likely to be your best bets to find any used trekking gear. But used equipment can be hard to come by in Gilgit, and what there is will, without doubt, be priced at what the market will bear.

Near Gilgit is a Buddha carved into a stone face, a remnant of the era over seven hundred years ago when Buddhism held sway across much of what is now the North-West Frontier Province, the Northern Areas, and Afghanistan. To see this rock carving, take a local van west from Punial Bazaar or walk along the irrigation canal west of town continuing past numerous walled compounds, green fields, and the suburb of Napur to the Kargah Nala. South of the main road and up this nala, a large rectangular niche well above the trail frames a ten-foot-high standing Buddha. The Kargah Nala is now a game sanctuary. You could take a day hike up this nala, for it has many trees and makes a pleasant walk if the weather is not too warm.

More ambitious trekkers could consider a trek south that begins in this nala and eventually crosses the 14,000-foot Shinghai Gali en route through high pasture lands to the Indus Valley at Chilas. This trek is unclassified by the Tourism Division and would take about six days. You should absolutely go with a local to show you the way, for the route is not clear, especially in the high country, and as you proceed farther south you will be in a region inhabited by Kohistanis. If you can't find a local who feels comfortable accompanying you, don't attempt this walk.

Next, the Ghizar, Yasin, Ishkuman, and Hunza valleys are discussed, traveling generally from west to east and proceeding up-valley as we visit each valley in turn. The Ghizar, Yasin, and Ishkuman valleys are all reached by traveling west up the Gilgit Valley from Gilgit, either by cargo jeep or a small passenger van. When the road up-valley from Gilgit is widened, scheduled transport will undoubtedly service each valley.

The Ghizar Valley

This valley is the westernmost extension of the Gilgit River and provides the road link between Gilgit and Chitral. Ghizar was ruled alternately by the Khushwaqt clan of Mastuj and its own raja (local potentate) in the town of Gupis near the mouth of the valley, 68 miles west of Gilgit. If you want to walk in the Ghizar Valley and are coming from Gilgit, you should get a jeep that will take you at least as far as the pleasant rest house at Phander overlooking the lake of the same name. I once got stuck in Gupis without a ride and, having no patience, decided to hoof it up the lower Ghizar Valley. This decision was soon regretted, for the long two-day walk between Gupis and Phander is along a hot, dry, narrow gorge with nothing to recommend it. Near the turquoise blue Phander Lake, however, the valley widens considerably, becoming more striking and colorful.

From the village of Shamran just east of Chashi in the Ghizar Valley (down the hill and east of Phander), a pleasant walking route leads north up the large tributary valley called the Bahoushtar Gol, a game reserve. From the road here at Shamran you could walk north, then west up a side valley and over the steep 16,500-foot Zagaro An into the Zagaro Gol, which flows down to Chapali north of Mastuj in Chitral's Yarkhun Valley. Or you could walk east out of the Bahoushtar Valley up the Ano Gol over the 16,300-foot Nazbar Pass to the Nazbar Nala, which flows east into Yasin. An hour's walk north of the Ghizar River up the Bahoushtar, you begin traveling through country that is inhabited only by occasional shepherds. Because both the route over the Zagaro An and the path over the Nazbar Pass are little traveled, you should take a local person to indicate the way, help carry supplies, and cook (either of these treks could be done in four to six days). The path up the stream valley called the Bahoushtar Gol is plain enough, but when the tributary Zagar or Ano gols are reached some 11 and 15 miles upstream, respectively, the tracks become difficult to follow. The upper approaches to either pass are unmarked and rarely used by locals. My notes on the route up the Nazbar Pass (the one I've crossed) go on for two pages, reminding me that the way is not at all straightforward. Views from the Nazbar Pass stretch along the Hindu Raj northeast to the Darkot Pass area and southwest to Buni Zom in Chitral.

Trekking from the town of Yasin (see the next section) over the Nazbar and Zagaro passes to Chapali in the Yarkhun Valley, or from Yasin across the Nazbar Pass and down the Bahoushtar Gol to Phander, then along the Ghizar Valley and over the Chumarkhan Pass to Chapali, would make for a very nice traverse of the Hindu Raj. The former route would be shorter and more difficult (because of the steep Zagaro An), and the latter would be longer and not so tough. Allow about a week for the former route and

*Amanullah, a schoolmaster in Shimshal, proudly wears the white woolen chogha
made by his wife.*

eight to ten days for the latter; these trails are all in an open zone. These routes and all the paths in the Ghizar and Yasin valleys (except the easterly trails out of the Yasin Valley) are well depicted on the *Mastuj* sheet (NJ 43-13) of the U502 Map Series.

The little-used jeep road up the main Ghizar Valley continues west from Phander through Teru and a few other villages to Barset, the valley's last town, situated on a barren, windswept plain. Poplar and fruit trees are grown on the village oases (except Barset, where it is too cold), and the nalas emptying into the Ghizar River are usually sparkling clear. North of Barset is the 14,200-foot Chumarkhan Pass, the ideal trekking route into Chitral's Yarkhun Valley (see "The Passes East from Chitral" in Chapter 4). Beyond Barset, the main valley turns south, and in 6 miles the road turns west and climbs up a side valley to the 12,250-foot Shandur Pass (140 miles from Gilgit), which demarcates the boundary between the Ghizar Valley and Chitral. On the Ghizar Valley side of the wide pass area is a polo ground where an annual match is played between teams from Gilgit and Chitral. For about a week in August (the date is not fixed), this *maidan* (flat meadow) in the midst of nowhere comes to life, sprouting rows of tents. The prime minister often shows up, jeeps galore run back and forth from Gilgit and Chitral, and songfests fill the air of the warm summer night.

The Yasin Valley

Like the Ghizar Valley, the Yasin has ties to Chitral that are at least a century old. Running north to south, parallel to and east of Chitral's Yarkhun Valley, the wide Yasin Valley enters the Gilgit River near the town of Gupis. Warshikgam is the valley's name in Khowar, the Chitrali dialect that is understood by some locals. The primary language in Yasin, though, is Burushaski, as spoken in Hunza many miles distant. This valley has many ties with Hunza, and marriages are still arranged between prominent families in both places. The town of Yasin (8,000 feet elevation and 84 miles from Gilgit) has a pleasant rest house at the southern end of town with an apricot-tree-shaded garden; reservations for the rest house must be made at the NAWO office in Gilgit. From the town of Yasin you can walk directly west to the Nazbar Pass, as mentioned in the preceding section. The upper Nazbar Nala is a game reserve, adjoining the game reserve along the Bahoushtar Valley. It will take two short days from Yasin to reach the base of the pass, but the way to the last rocky stretch of scree leading to the pass is not straightforward, so take a local with you if you walk this way.

North of Yasin, you could head for the Thui Pass, the western approach to which is briefly noted in "The Passes East from Chitral" in Chapter 4. With any luck this pass will be unrestricted by the time you read this (in any case, it is not near a sensitive border area as is the Darkot Pass to the north). To reach this pass, walk north from Yasin along the jeep road for an hour to the Thui Gol, the first major tributary entering the main valley from the west. Like all valleys large and small hereabouts, the Yasin is at its loveliest at either end of the day when the golden light slants down upon the irrigated green fields and sere magenta hillsides, emphasizing the rich colors that wash out in the bright light of midday. Follow the small road west up the Thui Gol, and before too long, if you have sharp eyes, in a wheat field near the village of Ishkaibar you may see a boulder with petroglyphs of stupas and tridents. As our group ascended this valley, our accompanying friends from Hunza remarked, "Here they speak *pure* Burushaski!" (the tongue spoken in the mid Hunza Valley). After a half day's walk up the valley, the road becomes a path as it crosses back and forth from the north to the south bank of the river. One village blends into another, and every settlement is shaded by poplar and fruit trees. To the west beyond Das village, the steep peak-encircled side valleys hide their secrets, chiding you that you can't explore every hidden redoubt.

Gradually the Thui Nala turns to the north, narrowing as you pass the last permanent homes. Up to this point you can find your way with no difficulty, but before you head onto the Aghost Bar Glacier (*bar* means "stream"), which leads toward (but does not extend to) the pass, you should hire a shepherd to show you the way along the glacier at least as far as the upper valley. Locally infamous is the martial ex-havildar (a low-ranking noncommissioned officer) Yakin Shah, whose many chits include one that reads, "He can teach close order British military drill at 13,000 feet if the situation calls for it." If you go with Yakin, whose summer quarters are at Sholtali, near the base of the glacier, you *will* toe the line. Like many glaciers, the crevassed Aghost Bar is trickiest near its mouth, where the ice underlying the rocky surface is melting, making for slippery going. Sometimes the route here changes from week to week. A mile up the glacier to the north is the Kalandar Gum Glacier, the "Lost Wanderer" Glacier. The locals, with some hilarity, say that two people once went up that nala and "they never came back."

After several hours' walk, you get off the glacier and proceed uphill north of and parallel to it, soon reaching a flat valley. Unless practices have changed, you will see a rare sight hereabouts, for these meadows are so difficult to reach that the herdsmen do not bring their sheep and goats up the glacier to graze. Grass and flowers are uncropped, munched on only by the occasional ibex. High above to the south, the northern slopes of Thui I (20,310 feet) are so steep that one wonders why the mountain's hanging glaciers don't avalanche at once in an explosion of stinging ice particles. These peaks of the Hindu Raj Range, like those farther south in Chitral, are not particularly high for this part of the world, but they make up for it in precipitousness. The last climb to the Thui Pass (14,400 feet) angles easily up a gray scree slope. When Tom Dolan, who made the fine maps for this book, got 50 yards from the top, he began running euphorically. At the top of the pass, the eleven-year-old son of our wily Chitrali porter distinguished himself by singing several songs, accompanied by a flute and a chorus of Hunzakuts. The beat was pounded out on an upturned red plastic bucket. Then the porters from Yasin led a series of cheers: *"Amreekah zindabad"* (*zindabad* means "long live"), *"Pakistan zindabad,"*

"Leeder zindabad," ending with *"Jaan sahib Zindabad"* (this for John Mock). After everyone had disappeared down the western side of the pass into Chitral, John and I remained, savoring the view and the quiet. John noticed a piece of paper beneath a flat rock and extracted an inscrutable chit written to me by a Nepali with another group that had preceded us over the pass.

There are two ways to walk east from the Yasin Valley to the neighboring Ishkuman Valley. The southern route follows the Asam Bar Valley, located on the east side of the Yasin Valley a mile south of and across the main river from the Thui Gol. You will probably have to cross a bridge due east of Yasin village to reach the east side of the main valley. Then walk north to Sandhi and trek east up the Asam Bar Valley to 14,500-foot Asambar Aghost (*aghost* means "pass"), which is at the valley's head and south of 19,020-foot Asambar Peak. Continue east from the pass down the Asambar Gol to the Ishkuman River. A short hour's walk south of this confluence is a bridge to Chatorkhand, the largest town in the Ishkuman Valley. Allow about three days to trek from Sandhi in the Yasin Valley to the Ishkuman Valley. The second way to walk from the Yasin Valley to the Ishkuman is to walk north up-valley from the town of Yasin as far as Darkot village (which is south of the restricted and glaciated Darkot Pass, which leads to Chitral's upper Yarkhun Valley). At Darkot (or before), hire a local to take you east to the Anesar Bar and the 16,000-foot Ishkuman Aghost. It should take about three days from Darkot to reach the Ishkuman Valley; you will pass through Ishkuman village not long before reaching the valley floor.

The Ishkuman Valley

East of and parallel to the Yasin Valley is the Ishkuman, which has the distinction of dividing the most easterly slopes of the Hindu Kush and Hindu Raj ranges from the most westerly peaks of the Karakoram Range. From the midvalley town of Imit you can see Koz Sar (21,907 feet) south of the 17,000-foot Chillinji Pass, which connects Ishkuman with the Chapursan Valley, a tributary of the Hunza River. Like most peaks in the Karakoram, Koz Sar has steep, gray, sharp-angled slopes above serrated ridges, between which flow torrents spawned by milky snowmelt. West of the Ishkuman Valley from Koz Sar are the sienna-colored ridges of the easternmost Hindu Raj. Up-valley from Imit, both the river and the upper valley are called the Karambar.

Chatorkhand, with its small bazaar and teahouses, is halfway to Imit from the valley's southern terminus at Gakuch on the Gilgit River (all three of these towns are reachable by jeep from Gilgit within a day). Chatorkhand (7,000 feet elevation and 57 miles from Gilgit) is the residence of an Ismaili religious leader called a *pir*. The pir in Chatorkhand, whose title is ancestral, is one of the most venerated religious leaders living in this region. Pir Sayyed Karim Ali Shah, the incumbent, has done extensive work on the grounds of his residence. He is an avid gardener and if at home would surely provide hospitality for any who carry vegetable or flower seed samples.

In the valleys of Turikho, Yarkhun, Ghizar, Yasin, Ishkuman, and Hunza, the reform Ismaili branch of the Shia sect is a significant, often predominant, part of the population. The Ismaili sect developed during the ninth century in Iraq. Locally called Maulavi, Ismailis follow Prince Kareem Aga Khan, said to be a direct descendant of Mohammed through Mohammed's daughter Fatima (who married the Prophet's cousin, Ali). When the Aga Khan (the traditional title given the leader of the Ismaili sect) visited the Northern Areas in 1983 on the occasion of the twenty-fifth year of his reign, many villages whitewashed stones on hillsides spelling out "Welcome Our Hazar ('present') Imam" in both English and Urdu. You may still see these greetings when you visit the Gilgit River valleys. Since Prince Kareem Aga Khan is a living Imam (a divinely appointed, infallible successor of Mohammed), the forty-ninth in succession, he can initiate change and modernization, which is accepted by Ismailis. As the Aga Khan speaks English, it is considered an important language, and educated Ismailis often know some English, a great help to foreign visitors. Ismaili women generally do not wear veils, and education of women is given great emphasis. Education and social action are very important in Ismaili communities. The Aga Khan Rural Support Program (a branch of the Aga Khan Foundation) has a large office in Gilgit and many projects in the valleys of the Gilgit River watershed that benefit the community at large. In Karachi, Ismailis operate a 720-bed hospital in conjunction with Harvard University.

The walks west from Ishkuman to the Yasin Valley were noted in the previous section. You can also hike east to Naltar, a tributary of the lower Hunza Valley: from Chatorkhand, hike east up the Hayul Gol to the 16,000-foot pass below Khaltar Peak (19,310 feet). An alternate route from the village of Phakor, a few miles north of Chatorkhand, goes up the Phakor Gol to the same pass. Beyond the pass lie a clear lake and the green meadowlands of the upper Naltar Valley. Figure a four- to five-day walk between Chatorkhand, or Phakor, and Naltar. The trail up from Naltar to this pass is discussed in "Naltar," following.

The Incomparable Hunza Valley

Eric Shipton, a person well experienced with the world's highest mountains and not one given to exaggeration, called the Hunza Valley "the ultimate manifestation of mountain grandeur." Lord Curzon, once viceroy of India, said, "The little state of Hunza contains more summits of over 20,000 feet than there are of over 10,000 feet in the entire Alps." A topographic map of the region (about half the size of the state of Connecticut) has so many 500-foot contour lines that in places they form near-solid masses. Glaciers abound in this valley, including the 30-mile-long Batura and the immense Virjerab and Hispar glaciers. The Nubra, Braldu, Hushe, and Saltoro rivers are born in the glacier-laced Karakoram; the Shyok River encircles the eastern flanks of the range; but only the Hunza River actually cuts from north to south completely through the Karakoram Range. The Hunza River has its origin in name at the juncture of the Kilik and Khunjerab nalas, some 100 miles from the river's mouth near Gilgit. Carving a gorge between 25,000-foot peaks and receiving the waters of scores of glaciers, this is by far the largest and grandest tributary of the Gilgit River watershed. From the hot lower gorge of the valley to the uppermost reaches of the KKH as it snakes toward the windswept border, mudslides and avalanches bedevil both the road and Hunza's settlements. Road and villages alike are granted a precarious existence wedged into the narrow, low recesses of this fragile land.

Most of the Hunza River watershed was once Hunza State, which was semiautonomous until 1974. The Hunza Valley is composed of "Hunza proper" (as Hunzakuts call it) in the midvalley, while the larger upper-valley region is called Gujal and is populated by the Wakhi-speaking ethnic Wakhi. Nagar, another former state, is located in two areas, and you will visit its narrow glaciated canyons as you proceed up the valley. Nagarwals speak Burushaski with their own accent, and as strict Shiites they differ from their neighbors, the reform-minded Ismailis of Hunza who live across the valley. Once these differences involved pitched battles and kidnappings, but modern times have mellowed the valley's inhabitants. Still . . . one warm summer day I asked a man in Baltit, Hunza's former capital, where the haze came from that was obscuring the valley. "Oh, that haze," he replied. "It comes from Nagar."

The Hunza Valley was difficult for foreigners to enter earlier this century, when permission from the Mir (the ruler of Hunza State) was required for entry. If permission was granted, the visitor faced a track with an unending series of precipices overhanging the raging, mocha-colored river. But as of May 1986, when the Khunjerab Pass was opened for travel to Sinkiang, China, the main valley from end to end can once again be seen by outsiders. We can only imagine the difficulties faced four generations ago by those traveling the former Kashgar-to-Gilgit branch of the Silk Route, which once traversed the length of the valley. Some of Hunza's populace, then known as Kanjutis, were feared brigands who plundered caravans, both those plying up or down the valley and other caravans farther afield in western Turkestan. Until Hunza was merged with Pakistan in September 1974, no police force had ever existed in the valley. In times past, the large caravans provided sufficient funds, willingly or by force, and individual Hunzakuts never paid taxes to any authority outside the region. Until 1975, the only form of taxation was payment in goods to the Mir. Today's Hunzakuts are likely to earn money as drivers, by working for the government, doing part-time work in Gilgit, or as trekking or expedition porters, cooks, or guides. Now, with severe overpopulation of Hunza's few arable alluvial fans, thousands of locals must work at down-country businesses or the civil service, and sizable populations of Hunzakuts have migrated to Islamabad and Karachi.

The isolation once imposed by Hunza's magnificent gorges led to the wholly indigenous "pure" diet of the locals before they were exposed to British influence at the end of the last century. Hunzakuts say that when the British came, they brought five food-adulterants with them: sugar, spices, tobacco, tea, and *dalda* (vegetable oil). Hunzakuts often still bemoan the passing of pure food in the local diet. With the end of their pure diet and other changes brought to the valley by outside influences, the longevity formerly ascribed to the populace is now a historical footnote. One of Hunza's renowned old men was henna-haired, wrinkly-faced Wazir Ali Murad, belovedly called Juno, "Little One." I first met Juno when he was the oral historian on the Mir's council of ministers. When the Mir's court, the state's supreme authority, was still in session, Juno would discuss the precedents to any case, based completely on memory. With twinkling eyes, Juno loved to say, "People tell me I'm 105 years old." Everyone agreed that Juno had lived so long because he was without cares, a person truly happy with life.

The famous "Hunza water" is locally called *mel*; it is a grape wine that can be very tasty when well made. *Arak,* from the tall mulberry trees, is crystal clear, potent firewater, but it can be difficult for outsiders to acquire either of these liquids.

Four clans live in Hunza, and each is said to have originally come from a different region: Dramatin from Tartary, Barataling from Russia, Kurukutz from Persia, and Broung from Kashmir. Hunzakuts are proud of their heritage, friendly in a taciturn way, and quite individualistic: reminiscent of down-east New Englanders. Until grains and other foods could be brought in by road, Hunza was a food-poor valley, for it lacks enough flat, irrigable surfaces for cropland. Before the spring wheat or barley harvest, it was not unusual for even the last of the previous year's apricots to give out. The strength, individuality, and warmth attributed to the Hunzakuts has by no means disappeared, but as the rate of tourism continues its rapid upturn, the spontaneous hospitality accorded visitors has become diluted. Profit-making inns have been built along the main valley to cater to visitors, and you are far less likely to be offered hospitality in someone's home. If you speak a smattering of Urdu, Burushaski, or Wakhi from one of the glossaries, you will surprise people and may open yourself to experiences denied the casual tourist.

This section on the Hunza Valley will proceed up-valley from Gilgit through Nagar, Hunza, and Gujal, describing sites of interest and trekking possibilities en route. Every area in the Hunza Valley up to, but not including, Chapursan is officially considered an open zone, even the dicey Hispar Glacier. Most treks in this valley aren't particularly long ones, since access from one side valley to another is often impossible and it is usually necessary to return down a tributary nala the way you came. But the ways back offer different views, and the scenery in Hunza is never dull. There are exceptions to the matter of short treks, of course: the Hispar-Biafo walk and the hike to Shimshal and beyond are two examples. Walks in the upper nalas are easier to connect, but many of these routes are restricted (although the intrepid can figure things out for themselves with a good map). The *Baltit* sheet (NJ 43-14) of the U502 Map Series covers the regions described in the Ishkuman section, and from here on to the end of the chapter, with varying degrees of reliability (exceptions to this coverage are the Hispar

Glacier and Shimshal walks, for which you will need the *Shimshal* sheet [NJ 43-15]). Porter fees in Hunza and Baltistan are the highest in Pakistan. Unfortunately for trekkers, mountaineers, who often have large sums of money at their disposal, have come to this area and inflated porterage rates. You may well have to pay over 110 rupees a day (about $7) for a porter, and more if you want someone who calls himself a guide (and who won't carry anything, but will hire others to carry the saman).

You must be very careful on any of these walks that involve glaciers. In fact, a flashing red light should go off in your brain if you plan any glacier walking. Read the section called "Glaciers and Dragons" in Chapter 7 to familiarize yourself with the dangers of glacial terrain. The KKH now makes it possible for people to step from a comfortable vehicle practically directly onto a glacier, and in so doing the unwary can walk into a heap of trouble. I once talked with a traveler who had walked on glaciers before but had just increased his already-healthy respect for them. He had set out alone from Pasu one sunny morning intent on doing an easy day hike. In order to continue where he wanted to go, he found it was necessary to walk onto the Pasu Glacier. Soon after he did so, he slipped on a few pebbles. Without warning he slid utterly out of control into a fiendishly slippery, funnellike trap. In an instant he was neck deep in a bottomless pool of ice-cold water, gasping for breath and grabbing for a nonexistent handhold. Desperately he braced himself on the lip of the pool with one waterlogged shoe and his hands, arching himself out of the water onto the shiny ice. He had almost drowned, less than a mile from the KKH. If you, good reader, ever venture onto a glacier, never go alone and always travel with a local.

Now to explore Hunza. Every place or trailhead described in the remainder of this chapter is reached via the KKH from Gilgit, with the exception of Naltar (discussed next). The locations up to and including Baltit and Kareemabad can be reached directly any day of the week in two to three hours by taking a jeep or van, or, in the morning or early afternoon, a slower, brightly decorated bus from Gilgit. Vehicles also go daily to Pasu or Sost, but try to leave in the morning if you want to arrive before too late in the day. If you won't be hiking in the high country, keep in mind that Hunza can be beautiful in the spring and autumn: the apricots bloom in April, and the poplar and fruit trees shine like gold in October.

Naltar

The Naltar Valley, a game sanctuary, is due north of Gilgit and about two hours' drive away. The settlement of Naltar (8,300 feet) offers many pleasant day-hiking possibilities, and you can also take walks of four days or longer west to the Ishkuman Valley or north to Daintar (see the next section). The best way to reach Naltar is by jeep from Gilgit. Jeeps leave often in summer and early fall, and you can find out about getting one by making a few inquiries in Gilgit. The direct route to Naltar crosses the Gilgit River right at Gilgit and follows the west bank of the Hunza River within sight of the KKH on the opposite bank. En route you will pass the

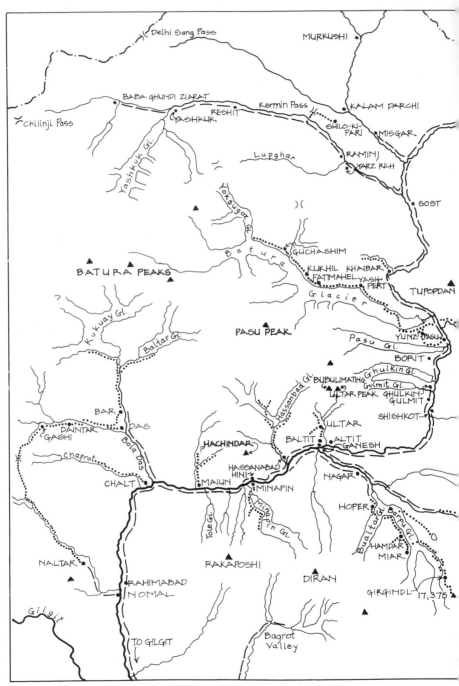

The Hunza Valley (The reliability of this map varies.)

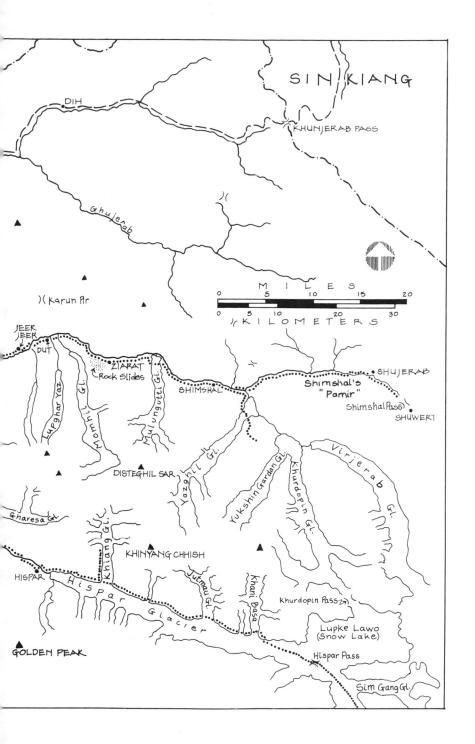

small village of Nomal at the mouth of the Naltar Nala. You can also reach Nomal via a footbridge from the KKH directly across the Hunza River, but if you come this way, it may be difficult to find a vehicle with room going up to Naltar. Better to get a jeep in Gilgit. At Nomal the jeep track begins its twisting journey up to Naltar.

Naltar town has a few shops and inns (which are expensive for value because the proprietors know there is little competition) and a NAWO rest house you can book in Gilgit. Nearby is is a climbing school that also teaches mountain and winter survival. The wide valley is grandly scenic, thickly forested with pines and larch in places, and 19,000-foot peaks rise above the valley. The path up-valley from Naltar begins on the north bank of the stream, then crosses back to the south side after a few miles, climbing through forests and passing shepherds' huts. Eight miles beyond the village is an exquisite clear lake, with plenty of lovely camping places and good vistas along the wide meadows. The way up-valley is easy as far as the mouth of the upper valley's glacier. If you want to walk from here to Daintar or to Chatorkhand (or Phakor) in the Ishkuman Valley, hire one of the local Gujar shepherds to show you the way. The path north to the Daintar Valley climbs 1,500 feet above the glacier to the last huts on a grassy shelf. Then you must follow a faint path to the northeast up a grass- and talus-covered ridge to the pass, which is about 15,550 feet high. The route to Chatorkhand or Phakor follows the tricky main valley glacier to a pass that is slightly higher than the one to Daintar. From this pass the valley to the north takes you to Phakor, while a westerly canyon leads to Chatorkhand.

Chalt, Chaprot, and the Bar Valley

North of the Naltar Valley are the Chaprot and Bar valleys. These valleys are reached from the KKH, so we'll follow the KKH up from Gilgit to reach them. Leaving Gilgit, your vehicle skirts the airport run-way on the east end of town, then passes the suburb called Jutial and crosses a few dry alluvial fans. Joining the KKH, the road turns north, crossing the Gilgit River on a large suspension bridge and passing through the large oasis of Dainyor, a town where many Hunzakuts live. Beyond Dainyor the road curls in and out of several nalas, entering the lowest reaches of the Hunza Valley, here a dry, rocky, and uninspiring V-shaped gorge. If it has rained heavily recently, you may be slowed or stopped at a place where avalanches of loose, gray conglomerate periodically inundate the road. But most days you will whiz right along to Rahimabad (or Matum Das), a small hamlet watered by a large spring where your driver may stop for tea or to pick up a fresh joint of meat to take to a relative's hotel up-valley. North of Rahimabad your vehicle barrels along at the base of the rock ridges that are the westernmost outliers of Rakaposhi. Across the river lies Nomal at the base of the Naltar Valley, and north of Nomal on the west side of the gorge you can still see some fragments of the original road clinging to a series of impossibly steep precipices and cliffs.

A forty-five-minute drive from Gilgit, the valley opens up and the Hunza River bends to the east, now north of the Rakaposhi massif. To the north across the valley you can see the irrigated fields of Chalt (6,560 feet, pronounced "Cha-lit" by the locals), a town that was formerly part of the state of Nagar. If you have not taken a jeep or van that is going directly to Chalt, the driver will let you off at the link road connecting Chalt with the KKH, and you can walk across the narrow bridge to town. The British flew the flag in this far corner of their colonial empire from a small fortress in Chalt, and in 1891 a force of Nepali Gurkhas, Kashmiri Dogras, and British from the Chalt fort engaged and defeated the Hunza-Nagar army at Nilt, several miles up the Hunza River.

For those who want to explore these rarely visited and readily accessible tributary valleys, the NAWO rest house at Chalt is an excellent takeoff point (remember to get a chit to stay at the rest house before leaving Gilgit). Providing the water for the orchards and fields of Chalt is the Chaprot Nala. In the 1930s the British explorer R. C. F. Schomberg wrote, "The Chaprot Valley is lovely, more beautiful than any other valley in the Gilgit Agency [as the area was then called], and it is far more accessible than many better known." Chaprot is a small side valley located between the Naltar Valley to the south and the Daintar Valley to the north, and you could wander up into it for a couple of leisurely days. Once you got a little way up the Chaprot Valley, you would have a fine view of Rakaposhi. Somewhere up the north side of this valley is a route into the adjacent Daintar Valley to the north.

Just east of Chalt, the large Bar (or Bola Das) Valley running north into the northwestern massifs of the Karakoram emerges into the Hunza Valley. A narrow jeep road runs for some miles up the east side of the valley's dry lower stretches, but few vehicles traverse it. You can book a vehicle in Chalt to take you up this road, or just walk up the Bar Valley. As you proceed along this valley, the first large tributary you reach some 6 miles up is the Daintar Nala, flowing from Daintar, a summer grazing settlement to the west.

The trail to the Daintar Nala crosses a bridge to the west side of the main valley, then winds up on steep cliffs south of the Daintar Nala and across the mouth of the valley from Das, a small village on a bluff between the two streams. As you climb, you'll begin to have a view of Rakaposhi, but the gleaming peak disappears as you enter the narrow valley. The path eventually reaches an irrigation ditch and follows it into the narrow, dry canyon, then crosses to the north side of the stream (near here is a side trail that angles up northeasterly to cross the 10,550-foot Talmutz Pass to join the Bar Valley below Bar village). The way leads back to the south bank and arrives at Daintar, a permanent village surrounded by fields and pastures with forested slopes above. Across the valley is the river's major water source, a glaciated stream flowing in from the north. Several hours up is Gashi, the village's summer settlement. Nearby a path leads up, often steeply, to the pass that takes you to the Naltar Valley (see the preceding "Naltar"). You'll need a local to show you the way, at least from Gashi to the pass. This circle route from Chalt to Naltar, or vice versa, takes about five to six days, or more if you linger to explore byways in the Daintar Valley.

Continuing up the main Bar Valley north of the Daintar Nala, you reach Bar village, where you can hire a local to show you up the valley to the summer pastures. Not too far from Bar the valley divides into two branches, each glaciated. Along the easterly side is the Baltar Glacier, in the smaller of the two valleys, but one with good pastureland. Up this nala, you will see a two-pinnacled peak called Beka Brakai Chok and many feeder glaciers; at the head of the valley is an immense perpendicular massif over 22,500 feet high. The larger, main-valley trail angles to the northwest and follows the Kukuay Glacier; if you go far enough up this glacier, you will see that it has two main arms, the easterly of which, like the Baltar Glacier, has its sources in the peaks that rise above the head of the Batura Glacier (approached from Pasu up-valley). Figure at least five days to a week above Chalt if you want to explore the settlements of this upper valley. The existing maps of the Daintar and Kukuay areas are not accurate or detailed. A crossing was made earlier this century from the Daintar Nala to the Ishkuman Valley by the British explorers Sir George Cockerill and Sir Francis Younghusband. This route and any others from the Bar Valley to the Ishkuman Valley undoubtedly require technical aids.

Of Maiun, Apricots, and the Hassanabad Nala

As the KKH continues up-valley beyond Chalt, it remains in Nagar as long as the road lies on the south bank of the Hunza River. Not far beyond Chalt on the northern side of the Hunza River is the former boundary of Hunza State. The jeep bridge at Sikandarabad ("Alexander's Town") gives access to the northern side of the river at the Bar Valley, and soon another bridge leads off the KKH to the village of Maiun. You could walk over to Maiun carrying five to seven days' worth of supplies and trek into the nala north of town with a local, for this valley extends into the massif for a good distance. The stream divides after a long day's walk, and the glaciated valleys up either tributary can be followed for several days with the aid of a villager who knows the way. Check out one or both of these valleys (and let me know what you found and how you liked the walk); very few foreigners have been up this way.

The KKH crosses several streams that tumble down the flanks of Rakaposhi, just minutes below the mouths of the glaciers that spawned these tributaries and seconds before they disappear into the Hunza River. One such glacier, the Tole, is known for supplying ice to cool the soft drinks sold in Gilgit (that's why your cola had pebbles in it). The road enters Hunza proper as it crosses to the north side of the river and passes through the village of Hini. Here you have a classic, postcard-perfect view, albeit somewhat foreshortened, of 25,550-foot Rakaposhi, the "Crown Jewel of Hunza," towering over the Pisan Glacier. This is as close to the peak as the vehicle-bound viewer will ever get. Rakaposhi, like Tirich Mir and Nanga Parbat, is believed to be the home of fairies who may play tricks on humans when people get too close to their snowbound homes. The peak is also called Dumani, a Shina name meaning "Two Princesses."

The narrow gorge opens out as the road continues easterly, soon revealing Hunza's green breadbasket, an interconnecting series of villages, irrigated fields, and poplar and fruit trees that begins at Hassanabad and nearby Aliabad, just beyond the large Hassanabad Nala. Before the KKH was built, Hunza's Mir kept a rest house in Aliabad, where incoming visitors were greeted and fed. Arriving by foot in 1974, when Hunza State still existed, my brother Ken and I were taken to this rest house by a young lad and offered delicious apricots. The golden fruit was lying ungathered on the ground and as we ate, we were told that good luck will befall anyone hit by a falling apricot, according to Hunza lore. Apricots are called *ju* in Burushaski, but the correct pronunciation is elusive. Once in Gilgit, while repeatedly trying to master the word under the tutelage of the Hunza Inn's manager, I paused, and he said, "You see. It is very difficult to say." Of the more than twenty-five cultivated types of apricots, only two kinds do not have delicious, almondlike seeds. One variety, called Shikandar, is considered to have aphrodisiac qualities: "Shikandar is dangerous," I was told by Ayub from Pasu with a wide grin. Dried apricots are called *battering* in Burushaski. Apricot season begins in early July and extends for months as the fruits ripen farther up-valley. During this time, from Chitral to Baltistan, piles of broken apricot shells lie next to flat rocks, on which the shells are cracked.

Hunzakuts believe that for apricots to be digested properly, the seeds, called *hanee*, must be eaten after the fruit. Indeed, I have found that fresh apricots, unlike many fresh fruits, can be eaten in quantity without tempting gastrointestinal fate, but I've always been sure to eat the seeds afterward. Some people take strong exception to this, however. I quote from a letter written by R. V. Giddy, an experienced British climber and trekker: "I would take issue with you about eating large quantities of apricots. Indeed, in South Africa where I was brought up, there was something known as 'Apricot Sickness.' This was a generic term for diarrhea. Eric Newby in his *Short Walk in the Hindu Kush* mentions the dire effects of gorging on apricots and I seem to remember that in the American classic on privy building, *The Specialist,* the narrator calculated that a Sears Roebuck catalog would last so many months 'TAKING INTO ACCOUNT APRICOT TIME!' "

At Aliabad are several small hotels, a bank, and an office of the government gemstone corporation. Here, or better yet, at Hassanabad, you can engage a local to accompany you up the Hassanabad Nala, which begins gently but quickly turns gritty. This is a walk for hikers who like narrow paths and steep climbs. The locals have found the going so rough that few of them still take their flocks up to the old traditional pastures. The path leads up the nala, passing a tributary to the west, then splits as the valley divides into two glaciated upper valleys, the Shisper and the Mutsutsil. The glacier here is one of the most active in the area, retreating and advancing over the years. Several generations ago, it advanced over 5 miles down the main valley within 6 months. By 1954 the glacier had retreated into the two upper valleys, but by 1980 the two upper-valley glaciers had rejoined in the main Hassanabad Nala. In 1986, when Ray Wallace and his wife Patti Cleary walked up here with Suleman, their porter friend from Hassanabad, the glacier still extended into the main nala and in moving down the valley had ripped out the access trails built by locals. People in Hunza and Nagar say that glaciers have sexes and try to descend to join with each other. A lot of sexual imagery gets involved in glacier discussions, and one story even recounts the union of two glaciers producing the first Hunzakut.

The Shisper Glacier occupies the nala to the right (the east), and if you go this way, stay on the true left side of the glacier. The path is steep and heavily eroded higher up, but very spectacular as you gain elevation. Only goats go up this way because of the tricky trail; you can follow this side for about two days.

The western side valley leads to the Mutsutsil Glacier. Just as you reach this glacier, a tributary to the north leads to a 25,000-foot peak called Sangri-marmar ("Marble Rock"), which climbers often attempt. Below Sangri-marmar are some abandoned stone summer huts. Higher up is a pond, but between the huts and the pond, water can be difficult to find. At the Mutsutsil Glacier you can walk alongside and on the glacier itself for three to four days, and you will find a small lake partway along.

Kareemabad and Baltit

The 6-mile-long fertile oasis beginning at Hassanabad contains small villages among terraced fields and is the center of the former state. Not far beyond Aliabad a link road branches uphill to the north of the KKH and is the direct way to Kareemabad and Baltit (65 miles from Gilgit and ranging 500 feet up and down the hill at roughly 7,800 feet in elevation), two adjoining towns that once together served as Hunza's capital. Now, because of their inns and their spectacular location overlooking Rakaposhi and the green fields of Hunza and Nagar, these two towns, Kareemabad in particular, function as the focus of Hunza for most visitors. Some tourists in groups drive up to Kareemabad from Gilgit, arriving in the heat of day, then return to Gilgit first thing the next morning, having "seen" Hunza. If you are riding in a vehicle that does not go direct to Kareemabad, you will be taken as far as the town of Ganesh on the KKH and should disembark there. At Ganesh you are some 800 feet below Kareemabad. You can grab a vehicle going up the steep connecting road (or wait for one to materialize) or stroll up to town at your own pace. If you are in Kareemabad and want to go up-valley, walk down to the KKH and you can expect to get a bus at Ganesh around 10:00 to 11:00 A.M.

At Kareemabad are inns, shops, the Mir's home, and the large Samar-

kand Canal, also called the Barbar or Dulla,* accompanied by a long row
of large poplars. Pleasant footpaths shaded by poplars usually accompany
canals, and these walkways make excellent routes for day hikes to towns
as far away as Aliabad. From these paths you have dramatic views south
to Rakaposhi, seen here in all its glory, and directly across the valley to
rounded 23,700-foot Diran. From along the upper canals west of town you
can look up the Hispar Nala, which leads past the village of Nagar, and
beyond you can see the top of yellow Golden Peak above the unseen Barpu
Glacier. While walking about, you may hear a person hollering loudly to
someone else far away, the local version of lung distance. When Ray and
Patti were in Hassanabad talking with the village headman about hiring a
companion for walking up the nala, the man simply raised his head, cupped
his hands, and bellowed, "SULEMAAAAAAAN."

Practice your Burushaski with those you meet; people will enjoy it, and
you may be asked in for tea. Burushaski is a complex language with four
genders, and it is a "language isolate," unrelated to any other tongue. Hunza
was an autonomous, self-governed state for six hundred years, and the
people's beliefs regarding clan, social interaction, birth, marriage, death,
and a myriad of other cultural customs remind us that this is a very intricate
but nonmaterial society. With the building of the road and the resulting
inevitable dissolution of many ancient tenets, times are rapidly changing
in Hunza. Fortunately scholars, both local and foreign, are studying and
writing about Hunza's unique culture so that it will not be lost to posterity.

As you walk up the jeep road above Kareemabad, the town blends
into Baltit, with its polo ground and school beyond, and the nearby Jamaat
Khana A little farther up you reach a low stone wall beneath poplar trees
where the town's elders like to sit and greet their friends. Across the way
is an ancient low building housing a throbbing century-old grain mill. If
you walk up from this intersection, then turn right, you will reach Baltit's
five-hundred-year-old castle (pictured on the cover of this book), perched
on crumbling, perpendicular conglomerate above the maw of the Ultar Nala
and dominating the town. The castle, which formerly housed the Mir
(known to Hunzakuts as the Thum) and his ancestors before him, is definitely worth a visit, so try to locate the chokidar, who will unlock it and
show you around for a small fee. Inside, you first climb a wooden ladder,
and in an upper room you may still be able to see a small collection of
fading photographs featuring potentates of yore, both Asian and European.
The rooftop views are unparalleled, and here on the roof the Mirs once
held their daily court. An early Mir chose the castle site well; even today
only a small, square memorial to Queen Victoria a steep scramble up the
cliff high above Baltit has a more spectacular position. Until the early

---

* Is this correct? Are Barbar, Dulla, and Samarkand all names for the same canal?
As I wonder about this, I can imagine sometime in the future a friend from Hunza
saying, with reference to this or any other mistake, "What you have written about
Hunza is good. *But there is one thing I must tell you* . . ."

1980s this memorial was faithfully whitewashed, an appropriate gesture from the denizens of the last princely state on the subcontinent.

Across the Ultar Nala east of Baltit and Kareemabad is the town of Altit, reached from Kareemabad by a road that passes beneath an arch (which supports a canal). The road to Altit rapidly switchbacks down to the Ultar Nala, then climbs to Altit's polo ground. Not far ahead is a castle, built centuries ago by craftsmen from Skardu, that, like Baltit's castle, stands in a highly precarious setting. The castle with its delicate tower teeters directly over the angry, roiling Hunza River, 1000 feet beneath. Below the castle, a rope bridge used to cross the river, but this ancient bridge has been replaced by a newer, Chinese-built model carrying the KKH and capable of supporting vastly heavier loads. At Altit's castle, the Mir would live for several days each spring during Bo Pho, the seed-sowing festival. Gheenani, Hunza's spring harvest festival, is still celebrated, but in far fewer locales than formerly. The Mir's "Sunday bungalow" is near the Altit castle amidst an orchard garden with some of the world's sweetest apricot trees. In ancient times, the northern boundary of Hunza did not extend beyond Altit, but that was before Hunza gained power and Gujal, as the upper valley has always been called, came to be part of Hunza.

Water Flowers and the Path to Ultar

The crops in this vicinity, as in all areas of the Hindu Kush and Karakoram, grow only because of irrigation, and in this small section of the valley in particular, the amount of irrigated land is very extensive. The canal (here called a "channel" in English, or a *gotsil* in Burushaski) that provides water for most villages from Baltit to Aliabad emanates from the Ultar Nala above Baltit. This canal—the Samarkand, Barbar, or Dulla (see earlier footnote)—was once known as far away as Kashgar. The massive amount of labor involved in keeping this and other canals in repair is shared by the villagers, and fines are levied on those who do not work and cannot find a replacement. Tempers flare over water allocation in the spring, when water needed for the growing crops is low, and inevitably, litigation in the government court system over water rights has begun to appear. When the Ultar Nala is in spate during the summer, men stay day and night at the head of the canal to guard against too much water entering the Dulla. Another man camps at the point a mile west of Kareemabad where the water is divided into smaller channels.

The glacial water from Ultar carries brightly reflecting mica and other minerals, locally called "water flowers," which give the liquid a glittering life of its own even as it quietly slips by in an irrigation canal miles away from the steep Ultar Nala. This same water often gives foreigners' stomachs undesired lives of their own, but Hunzakuts extoll the healthful, nutritive qualities of the water they drink from the channel. However, if asked, they will also admit that most of the drinking water they take from the nala has been collected in the early morning when the mineral content of the water is lowest, or that they let the water settle for hours before drinking. Many households in Baltit and Kareemabad get their drinking water from a tap near the Jamaat Khana, which has clear water carried by pipe from a spring not far up the Ultar gorge.

The Ultar Nala is a fine example of the type of ravine often found in the Karakoram, where a stream issuing from a few mammoth ax slices cut from sheer walls hides far more than meets the eye. Near Kareemabad and Baltit you can see Bubelimating ("Bubela's Peak"), a granite pinnacle that up to the time of writing has frustrated all climbers; next to this needle is the round 24,700-foot Ultar Peak, also unclimbed. But Ultar's narrow gorge conceals pastures and a glacier that cannot be seen from the valley floor.

The walk up Ultar's steep nala can be an unforgettable experience, and depending on who you are, how fast you walk, and how far you go, you could make this a day hike or stay for several nights. Some visitors return from this nala thankful to be alive, and others barely mention the tricky route but praise the scenery. Some walk up in the heat of morning and don't get far; others leave early and reach the shepherds' hut several thousand feet up, ecstatic with exhilaration. Some people walking back have missed a turnoff, gotten off-route, and become benighted on the precipice where the high, recently built Karimyari Channel pours its water down a steep rock face near Queen Victoria's memorial. Others descend happily with the shepherds they've made friends with. Ultar seems to be a peculiar crucible for the foreigners who approach it.

Before you leave for Ultar, check with the manager of your inn to be sure the path is safe. For a few weeks in midsummer when the weather is clear and temperatures warm, the stream can be so high it inundates the width of the narrow gorge not far up the nala. You might also ask the manager to have his wife make you a loaf or two of *phiti,* the round, local-style bread that is great to take for food anywhere in the valley. Carry tea, sugar, and anything else (in addition to your own wheat flour and other rations) that you might want to trade with the shepherds for their milk products. The last tips apply to any treks in Hunza and elsewhere in the Northern Areas: carry protection for your head (if not an umbrella, then a wide-brimmed hat, for both sun and sudden rainstorms can be vicious) and get started early in the cool of morning.

The trail to Ultar begins in Baltit at the path leading up beside the mill, 100 yards west of the old castle. When you reach the ridge, you descend a few feet and follow the canal to enter the narrow gorge. The way leads up, sometimes quite steeply, on the west side of the cold stream that thrashes downward, freshly released from its glacial source. You pass a tiny fenced orchard, a small meadow perfect for resting, then a tricky, loose, rocky slope and, above, the Karimyari Canal. The views are sweeping across the valley to Diran, and above, the swooping Ultar Glacier, resembling a giant's roller coaster, comes more clearly into sight.

A couple of hours' walk above town are the meadows, holding pens, and stone huts where five months a year men from Kareemabad and Baltit take turns herding the village sheep, goats, and a few cattle. The rich dairy foods that come from those pastures include milk, *(mamu)*, buttermilk *(diltar)*, butter *(maltash,)* and a delicious white cheese called *burus*. If you are interested in how the milk products are made, you can learn a great deal about age-old customs by observing the men as they go about their daily chores. Butter, for instance, is made by sloshing milk back and forth in a goatskin called a *tharing,* which rests on a person's lap. The men make butter together and swap stories, like their wives and daughters below at the water spigot near the Jamaat Khana.

Other pastures extend high above the shelters. To reach the ridgeline called Hon, walk straight up the hill directly above the huts. The going gets steeper as you go, and wildflowers with vivid colors grow in the higher areas. Across the wide bowl, Ultar's noisy icefall drops steeply, but part of it now lies below you, and you can begin to see its white upper catchment basin. With some backing and forthing, and by using your hands for support, you will come out on the ridgeline thousands of feet directly above Baltit. Here at Hon you can see the entire crescent of green within Hunza and Nagar, four of Rakaposhi's glaciers, and vistas beyond of Nagar's long valley glaciers and distant Karakoram peaks. If you carefully work your way just a little distance down the other side, you can pass the night at a rounded, grassy knoll, as I once did, drinking in this intoxicating view far above the valley and watching the sun set on the high peaks.

Other walks from the shepherds' huts up to Ultar's high pastures suggest themselves, but be careful that you don't get up into a place where you can't get down, like a kitten in a tree (for a few anxious moments I thought this had happened to me when I was descending from Hon). The men at the pastures would just as soon not have any more stories to tell each other about rescuing frightened foreigners.

Nagar: Roses and Glaciers

Of the former autonomous states within Pakistan, Chitral, Swat, and Hunza are the most often referred to, but Nagar, once a state in its own right, is equally magnificent. Nagar includes the Chaprot and Bar valleys and the entire south bank of the Hunza River from those valleys to the fertile Hispar Nala (across the valley from Baltit). Rakaposhi, Diran, and the 38-mile-long Hispar Glacier (the world's third-longest glacier outside the polar caps) are all within the confines of Nagar. The region has more fields and trees than central Hunza, and its people are usually lean and dark haired, unlike Hunzakuts, who may have brown or sandy hair. Nagarwals are Shiite and speak Burushaski with a different accent than their neighbors across the Hunza River. Nagar is a more conservative region, not as attuned to tourism as Hunza; you will rarely find an inn in Nagar, but for trekkers going away from the towns, this needn't matter.

To reach villages like Minapin in the main part of Nagar, get off a vehicle at the south side of the KKH bridge leading to Hini and walk up-valley along the jeep road. You can also cross the Hunza River on a bridge just below the KKH downriver from Hassanabad and then walk or possibly take a jeep up to the main oases in Nagar. To reach the Hispar Nala, you can cross the large KKH bridge at Ganesh and walk or jeep directly up the parched right bank of the lower Hispar Nala to a bridge connecting with Nagar's main jeep road (the one coming from the bridge at Hini). Now to look at some of the hiking possibilities in Nagar proceeding up-valley from Minapin.

Walking up to the pastures behind Minapin makes for a pleasant hike of two to three days. When I decided to go up this way and was asking directions in the village, a discussion ensued among the villagers. Whether they were questioning my safety in walking alone, or whether they were discussing my right to go at all, I couldn't be sure, but I was able to put whatever concerns they had to rest and set out up the main trail. That was some years ago, however, and by now enough outsiders will have gone so that your reasons for going should not be misunderstood. The path rises behind town, with a fine view of Hini across the valley, then you dip down to cross the stream. From the bridge the way ascends for some distance up a dry hill to a gentle slope forested with juniper and rosebushes. If you continue following the path, you will reach the pastures used by shepherds from Minapin. My intention was to climb the steep ridge to the west, and after resting during the heat of the day, I scrambled to the top. Perched on the narrow, wooded ridge, I could look to one side at Diran and the Minapin Glacier and turn my head to view the steep, narrow Pisan Glacier. As the light dimmed, an avalanche exploded several hundred yards away on the slopes of Rakaposhi, and I could imagine the fairies playing tenpins for their amusement.

Another route up from Minapin follows the ridge to the east of the Minapin Glacier. A small path along this ridge leads to the base of Diran, but only try this route with a local who knows the way. The Minapin Glacier has been quite active, advancing and retreating noticeably over the years, because its upper basin is very large compared with the steep, narrow slot down which the lower end flows. You can see the snout of this glacier if you walk off the main path toward the glacier as you are walking up to or down from the pastures.

Nagar's wide, fertile oasis, mirroring Hunza's across the river, holds no particular side treks of interest, but the steep narrow nala directly across from Baltit near Sayyar village can be ascended by hikers who like a rugged walk. This is another approach to Diran (in addition to the route along the Minapin Glacier noted in the last paragraph), a mountain that can be climbed with only a few technical aids. By now you have reached the Hispar Nala, a watershed so large it deserves its own sections.

To the Barpu Glacier Meadows

The jeep road along the west side of the Hispar Nala at first contours along a dry hillside, then reaches irrigated fields and the town of Nagar with its unused polo field lined with tall poplars. Nagar was the capital of

Nagar State, and the Mir's family lives here. Just beyond Nagar village the raging waters of the Hispar River branch off to the east and the river's headwaters at the long Hispar Glacier, a two-day walk away (see the next two sections). A bridge across the river here near the town of Nagar leads to the jeep road that goes along the east (right) bank of the river to the KKH near Ganesh in Hunza. The narrow road continues along up from Nagar town among well-irrigated meadows and two more villages that lie between a steep ridge and a dry lateral moraine that extends for miles. Finally the road peters out near a small rest house at Hoper (locally called Holshal), 3 miles from the village of Nagar. If you wish, you can book a jeep to bring you this far. You can pitch your tent at the rest house, although its caretaker will probably ask for a small fee should you do so. If you plan to continue much farther, it would be best to hire a porter from one of the villages along the way. As you have been progressing up this valley, behind you rise the high peaks above Baltit, including Bubelimating and Ultar Peak, looking impenetrably steep.

For the past several miles the lateral moraine you have been paralleling has been hiding a glacier, which lies not just behind, but hidden well below, the old, crumbling moraine. About 200 yards before reaching the Hoper rest house, follow an obvious path to the crest of this moraine and take a steep switchback trail down to the Bualtar Glacier. The Bualtar flows directly away from the high peaks you see a few miles to the southwest. It is obvious that the glacier is melting rapidly, for it now lies over 200 feet below its former lateral moraine. You cross the glacier on a route taken by locals that is marked by sporadic cairns. On the far side, leave the glacier and ascend a path to the north (left) that leads to the left side of the larger Barpu Glacier, which joins the Bualtar just below where you have crossed. The path now passes clusters of rosebushes and rises up, paralleling the left side of the Barpu Glacier en route to the summer settlements of Hapa Kund, Hamdar, and Miar. You can reach Miar, the last pasture up the western upper branch of the glacier, in an easy two-day walk from the village of Nagar. The Barpu Glacier is one of the few in the Hunza Valley that is pure white, almost completely free of the rocky morainal covering that most valley glaciers accumulate. The towering peak with the sheer north face that you see at the end of the valley is 23,000-foot Golden Peak.

From this trail on the west side of the Barpu, you can go to two places, but in order to reach either of them, you must cross the glacier to its right (east) side. If you are crossing the Barpu, be sure to go with a local who knows the best path. The first route is to climb the high ridge east of the glacier to the pastures at Gutens and a small lake at the 15,000-foot level. Sayeed Anwar, Pakistan's most accomplished trekker, who hails from Chalt down-valley, went here with some friends and reports that the view is superb.

The second route from the east side of the glacier leads to Girgindil, the last summer pasture area up the eastern upper branch of the glacier, a trek that takes about five days round trip from Nagar (or up to a week if you do any looking around). To reach Girgindil, you have to walk onto the glacier twice, but a few cairns will help you find the way. If you go early enough in the summer, you'll see lots of wildflowers and a nice stand of junipers on the way. When Ray "Wali" Wallace and Patti Cleary walked to Girgindil, they went with a guide from Nagar. Before they left Nagar, they were approached by a man who told them please not to disturb the Mir of Nagar's goats, and they assured him they wouldn't. So if you go this way, be sure not to make off with any of the Mir's goats. From Girgindil, you can take a beautiful day hike up to the point marked 17,375 on the *Baltit* sheet (NJ 43-14) of the U502 Map Series, where you will be within hollering distance of Golden Peak's perpendicular north face. One nice aspect of the walks along the Barpu Glacier (in addition to the great scenery) is that although you do cross a glacier in one or more places, the going is not particularly steep, nor is the way difficult as it is up the Hassanabad Nala and on some of the routes in Gujal.

Hispar and Biafo Glaciers

In recent years, some intrepid souls have been making the rugged trek east from Hispar village onto the Hispar Glacier, over the 16,900-foot Hispar Pass, and down the Biafo Glacier into Baltistan's Braldu Valley, a couple of hours' walk upstream from the village of Askole. This walk follows next to or on some 65 miles of glacier, takes about two weeks (definite stages are becoming accepted for this walk), and needless to say, is only for the sturdy. Most people who do this traverse go from Hispar to the Braldu, taking porters from Hispar village who have been before and who charge stiff rates. One of the main reasons for going this way is that trekkers have not encountered difficulty with permissions on the Hispar side. Officials expecting payoffs can set up obstructions in Askole, although this route has been classified as being in an open zone, where permits are not needed. A good outfitter in Gilgit (or their main office in 'Pindi or Islamabad) will be willing to help you find the right porters, given adequate notice. You will have to pay handsomely to make arrangements through an outfitter, but chances for safely completing the trip are certainly greater if you make arrangements this way. Word has it that the walk is best done in spring or early summer before the winter snow has melted (revealing underlying crevasses). Galen Rowell, the well-known climber, writer, and photographer, did this route in the latter half of April with two friends. He said that the Biafo contained more wildlife than he had seen anywhere in the Karakoram and "the greatest display of granite spires in the entire Karakoram, marching up the glacier like organ pipes in an ordered procession."

If you don't want to do the entire Hispar-Biafo traverse, you could walk along the lower parts of either glacier for several days. Betsy White and her family did just that, and she tells of their experiences in the next section. For information about the Biafo Glacier, look at "Along the Biafo Glacier" in Chapter 7. Also see "The Biafo-Hispar Glacier Traverse" in the same chapter.

Family Trekking in the Hispar Region   *by Betsy White*

[Betsy White and her husband, Gene, lived in Pakistan for six years and have each returned there six times. Betsy wrote her dissertation on women and Islamic society and works with the Asia Foundation, while Gene is a water resources engineer who has consulted on many projects in Pakistan and elsewhere. They both speak Urdu and Pashtu.]

On June 28, 1987, our party assembled at the airport in Islamabad: the Davis family, consisting of Del and Andrea and sons Guy, eighteen, and Wade, sixteen; and Gene and Betsy White and daughter Laura, sixteen. We set off by minivan to drive up the Karakoram Highway, since the forty-seat Fokker plane was completely booked in advance by outfitters and locals. Food and water, good books for the adults, and a Walkman for each teenager were essential for survival of this long drive. After sixteen hours of careening around curves on the alternately paved and gravel highway perched hundreds of feet above the river, we reached Gilgit at 10:00 P.M. In the morning we set out to buy supplies and found some good boots and an ice ax for one of the boys. Expedition gear provided to porters is sold in Gilgit and Skardu, just as in Kathmandu, but in much smaller quantities.

Our two jeeps left Gilgit for Nagar at 11:00 A.M., loaded with baggage and our small party. The teenagers rode in the open jeep, while the parents, more sensitive to the effects of the sun, rode in the closed vehicle. We had hoped that the jeeps would take us to the end of the road in the Hispar Valley, but instead they left us at the town of Nagar to bargain for porters and transport farther up the valley. In Nagar, the boys napped and photographed while Gene and Del (who had previously gone with Gene up the Batura Glacier) began lengthy negotiations with the potential porters. Andrea, Laura, and I hiked up a hill for the view and were invited into the garden of an attractive bungalow, where we had tea with the wife and daughter of a local government official.

Later, the entire male population of Nagar came out to watch us cook and eat. The fascination was increased by the presence of an attractive young girl. Even in the mountains, where the *burka* (veil) is seldom worn, women are rarely seen in public and hide from the sight of persons who live outside the immediate family or neighborhood. Most girls do not attend school and are married before they reach Laura's age. Each driver and several porters inquired whether she was married, and some tentative marriage proposals were made, very properly, to her father. The Davis boys distracted what would have been uncomfortable amounts of attention directed at Laura by photographing, throwing things with, and generally interacting with the throngs of young boys in the villages. In 1977, I led a Mountain Travel trip in Pakistan that included a seventeen-year-old girl and her mother. The guide fell in love with the girl, and while no unpleasant events occurred as a result, it was awkward for her. Having several young people, rather than just one, on a trip makes it more fun for everyone.

The men of Nagar were hard bargainers, insisting upon very short stages for each day, to be paid at the then-standard daily rate of 110 rupees a day. Adding rest days and return days brought the total portering cost far over our estimates, and we found we had not brought enough rupees to engage the porters for the whole two weeks. We would have to set up a base camp somewhere and disengage the porters in order to afford the high expense of carrying to and from the mountains.

We left in the morning, the porters in a wagon behind a tractor and ourselves in a single overloaded jeep. After 14 miles the rugged road finally ended in the Hispar Valley near an unfinished bridge. We crossed the river in a *garroti* (a wooden box) on a cable and continued on a trail that hugged the cliffs, sometimes far above the raging Hispar River, sometimes so close to the river that we were sprayed by the torrent. In the late afternoon we again crossed the river, this time on a suspension bridge with many planks missing, and hiked up a high shoulder to the large village of Hispar with its many irrigated fields and orchards. Camping on the porch of the village guesthouse, we were again surrounded by a curious crowd of men and children, some seeking medical treatment.

The foot of the giant Hispar Glacier is 3 miles up-valley from the village, and the next day we again crossed the river on another garotti below the glacier. The trail follows moraines on the north bank of the Hispar and passes through several pastures where animals graze. In the late afternoon we found a campsite on a moraine leading up a side valley toward the peak called Kinyang Chich (or Khinyang Chhish, 25,762 feet). The only good water was runoff from a huge icicle descending from a cliff above the camp. The next day we walked further along this side valley, descending huge scree slopes down to the glacier and climbing back up to a series of meadows and boulder fields on the moraines. We settled on a campsite in a meadow traversed by a small stream where three scruffy horses were grazing. The porters departed after being paid, although their leader said he would stay in the area to hunt.

We set up three North Face tents, one for each couple and one for the teenagers, found a good spot for cooking, and designated a latrine area. Then we could all pursue individual interests: photography, reading, rockclimbing, listening to music, and painting. The following day it snowed and rained a little, but the boys and men all did a rockclimb anyway. On July 4, Laura's birthday, Gene, myself, and the three kids hiked up the glacier to its next side-valley junction, discovering granite walls larger than El Capitan in Yosemite Valley. Seeing all those potential rock routes was frustrating for Guy, who is an excellent 5.11 rockclimber. On July 5, Gene and I did a snow climb to a point on a ridge about 17,000 feet high. The following day Del and his sons did the same climb, while Andrea, Laura, and I hiked up a 15,000-foot point and Gene did a solo climb. July 7 saw us again scrambling on rock towers around camp while some took baths in the icy stream.

We departed for Hispar village the next day, and after one night hiked on to the end of the road, where a truck met us for the drive to Kareemabad in Hunza. Here the kids walked around the village, buying handicrafts, and up the canyons, taking photographs. Kareemabad is very different in 1987 from the first time I visited in 1974, but the apricots are still delicious. While we had not climbed anything spectacular, the trip was a success. Both families had enjoyed it, and we were all better friends than ever. We even began discussing our next expedition as we rode down the Karakoram Highway. Although we hadn't gotten as far up the Hispar Glacier as we had planned, we did reach some fascinating vertical country and were able to climb and scramble well up into it.

Into Gujal

Just beyond Ganesh village below Kareemabad, the KKH crosses the Hunza River on a large, graceful bridge. Within walking distance from the bridge right on the roadside is Haldikish ("Place of the Rams"), also known as the Sacred Rock of Hunza. This large rock has many carvings from different eras and in varying scripts. From here up-valley for some distance the Hunza River flows in an arid, V-shaped gorge that is sparsely populated. In a few miles the riverbed curves to the north, and as you proceed along this deep gutter, the main peaks of the Karakoram tower above out of sight, for here the river is cutting between the highest summits of the range. Now you are entering the region called Gujal, the largest area within the Hunza Valley.

As you continue northward through Gujal, you will meet the friendly Wakhi, a people of ancient Persian stock from Turkestan who more recently have come from the Wakhan region of Afghanistan. Wakhis speak Wakhi, an old Indo-Iranian dialect, and are Ismaili like the Hunzakuts. In Wakhi, bread and tea are called *putok* and *choi,* and you may eat and drink lots of both when you go trekking in Gujal. If you talk with a Wahki as if you are in Hunza, he may correct you by gesturing down-valley and saying, "Hunza proper is down there. This is Gujal."

Several times in the past century, mud and rock slides thundering out of the nala near Shishkot village have blocked the main Hunza Valley. In 1974, a large mudslide sent down from this glacier destroyed some homes in Shishkot, buried a new bridge under 60 feet of silt, and created a 7-mile-long lake that didn't drain for three years. Most years, when the glacier isn't so frisky, it is possible to walk up the nala, even making a circle trek and returning down a neighboring canyon, a walk of up to a week in duration. For the specifics of this route, you'll have to speak with a local and hire him to show you the way.

At Shishkot the KKH crosses to the west side of the river and soon reaches Gulmit (about 8,000 feet). Gulmit, within a lushly irrigated acreage of orchards and fields, was once the summer residence of the Mir. Now Gulmit has a couple of lodges, and the town is a very attractive one to visit for a couple of days. Just above the lodges is the Hunza Cultural Museum. Here is a depiction of a typical home, as well as other displays, including a snow leopard pelt. If you follow the stock trail leading beyond the town's cultivated fields and walk over the moraine, you soon reach the Gulmit Glacier. This noisy, active glacier descends from an ice-covered

A woman tends the boiling pot of kurut at a hut used in the summer along the Batura Glacier in the Gujal region of the Hunza Valley (photograph by John Mock).

24,000-foot peak, as does its larger sibling, the Ghulkin Glacier, situated beyond a serrated ridge to the north.

Another walk from Gulmit goes to Ghulkin village, reached by a link road that goes west from the KKH not far north of town. At Ghulkin you are between the Gulmit and Ghulkin glaciers and somewhat away from the road. Longer, multiday walks are possible alongside and on both glaciers, which have a common upper cirque, and you can walk up one and down the other with a local who knows the way. The Ghulkin Glacier comes very close to the road, and travelers on the KKH are often struck with a rush of frigid air while passing by the glacier. The Ghulkin is one of those capricious glaciers that likes to toy with man's improvements in the area, and sometimes in summertime it sends down torrents of water or morainal rock that submerge the KKH and halt traffic. With the help of your inn's manager, you can engage an escort from Gulmit or Ghulkin if you want to explore either or both of these tricky, unstable glaciers.

Pasu and Its Summer Pastures Along the Batura Glacier

Near Gulmit the valley widens dramatically. The KKH crosses the raucous streams of the Gulmit and Ghulkin glaciers, then passes the town of Sesoni. In this stretch of valley you begin to see Tupopdan, a multi-pinnacled ridge culminating in a 20,000-foot peak. Tupopdan is a giant pincushion of sheer, knifelike spires, a sui generis mountain rising straight up from the plain and dominating this section of the valley. The Wakhi village of Pasu (8,500 feet elevation, 102 miles from Gilgit, and the home of Haqiqat Ali, author of the Wakhi glossary) lies on a low alluvial fan just north of the stream bounding down from the large Pasu Glacier. In 1962 a wall of water roared out of the Shimshal River gorge, just upriver from Pasu, washing more than half of Pasu's homes down the Hunza River, but Pasu now has at least sixty houses. You have several inns to choose from here, so you won't have any difficulty finding a place to stay. North of town a flat, stony plain stretches for 2 miles. When I first came here, this desert was the site of the Chinese headquarters for construction of the KKH. After the road was finished, the camp was torn down and the plain reverted to being an arid waste. But with the help of the Aga Khan's Rural Support Program, locally headquartered in Gilgit, work is proceeding on building a large canal from the Batura River to the north, and soon this large plain will be fertile. Pasu is the place to begin walks along the Batura Glacier or up the Shimshal Valley, but you can also take some shorter hikes, so I'll mention a few of them first.

A nice outing is the circular walk along the north edge of the Pasu Glacier, up to the small shepherds' huts at Yunz, then back to Pasu from the north. This is the hike taken by the person who almost made a fatal slip when he found he had to walk onto the Pasu Glacier for a short distance before climbing the steep, rocky hill to Yunz. If you go to Yunz, you would be well advised to take someone from Pasu with you, even a boy who could show you the way. At the ridge between the two glaciers, you have views of both the Pasu and the much larger Batura Glacier. It is also possible to walk west along this ridge to some other summer camps, but if you do so, be sure to engage someone from Pasu to accompany you.

An easier walk is the one to clear but salty Borit Lake. To reach the small community of Borit and its lake, walk south from town on the KKH until you cross the Pasu Glacier, then angle up the south side of the next hill. If you don't feel sure of the route, keep walking on the KKH and you'll soon reach a small link road that you can follow to Borit, which is very pleasantly located among sizable moraines.

Routes lead along both sides of the Pasu Glacier, but in recent years, trekkers have begun walking to Pasu's summer pastures along the north side of the 30-mile-long Batura Glacier, which flows west to east at a ninety-degree angle to the main valley (and thus the route in and back is the same). The mighty Batura's snout lies about 3 miles north of Pasu. Usually the glacier rests demurely up its side valley, but in 1971 the Batura became rambunctious and slid to the end of its nala, pushing the KKH most ignominiously into the Hunza River. Two temporary bridges, one on each side of the glacier, had to be constructed to divert the road. Villagers from Pasu graze their sheep, goats, cattle, and yaks in various pastures, and should you want to visit the meadows, plan to be gone from about four days to a week, depending on how long you want to look around and how far you want to go. In Pasu, it is the women and children who take the animals to pasture, leaving in the first half of May and returning about the third week in September.

If you want to visit the pastures, it is best to go with someone from town, for he can introduce you to people who would otherwise be hard to speak with and guide you across the tricky sections of the Batura and for some distance along its north side. You could try to communicate with the women using Wakhi words from Haqiqat Ali's glossary, but it is still much more proper in this traditional society to go with an escort. You can learn far more about the Wakhi way of life if you walk with a local, and best of all, instead of being a stranger, you will be treated like a guest.

The way from Pasu to the Batura Glacier leads north toward Tupopdan along the road to the Batura's low moraines, then angles through them until you begin to approach, then parallel, the south side of the glacier. At some point as you are walking along, your escort will turn right and begin crossing the rocks on top of the glacier. When I came here with Guda Ali (known in Pasu as the village's strongest man), on the ground a large arrow made from rocks marked the route onto the glacier, but that marker was, of course, only temporary. Now you wind across the glacier for an hour or so, wending your way up and down the rubble-covered hills of ice. Toward the north side but still on the glacier is a stony resting place called Zakzak, where clear water can be found. From here the going is sometimes rough as you continue up on the glacial stone pile beneath a vertical rock wall. Finally the way leads off the glacier, and you walk along gentle ground to Yashpert, the first large grazing area, which can be reached in a full day from Pasu. Yashpert lies at the base of a white scree slope dotted with scattered juniper trees; a good spring is nearby, and log huts abound, some used by people, others by animals. At Yashpert you can see Disteghil Sar ("Sheepfold in the Hills," 25,868 feet), the highest peak in Hunza, rising to the east, south of the Shimshal Valley. From here, where you are slightly above the glacier, the Batura looks like a river with frozen, rolling waves that are best seen in the morning or late afternoon light.

Beyond Yashpert the different pastures follow one after another for an easy day's walk: Shindiat, Fatimahel, Kukhel, and Guchashim. The path from one small settlement to the next is gentle for the most part and does not go onto the glacier again, passing willow and juniper trees in the lower stretches and following meadows, moraines, and streamlets. At Fatimahel, "Fatima's Meadow" (Fatima was Mohammed's daughter), you are directly north of Pasu Peak, at about 25,540 feet almost as high as Rakaposhi. An icefall cascades down nearly from the top directly onto the glacier, making this perhaps the longest icefall in the world. Just before you reach the last settlement of Guchashim, a two-pronged side valley leads to the north. The eastern branch, the steeper of the two, is called Sherrin Maidan, "The Sweet Pasture," and up it is a route to Khaibar village (in the main valley north of Pasu). The northern and larger branch is called Waltum Nala, and a high pass at its head leads to the Lupghar Valley, a tributary of Chapursan, a large valley to the north that you'll soon learn about.

Arriving at Guchashim, Guda Ali and I met Guda's wife and his younger son; soon we were gorging on fresh bread, yoghurt, and tea made from an herb that grows in the nearby meadows. Beyond Guchashim you can walk for an hour or more along sloping pastureland strewn with pink flowers, past a small lake, and to the junction of the Yoksugoz Glacier, which enters the Batura from the north. This junction makes a good stopping point for most trekkers. Some people from Pasu push their yaks across the Yoksugoz to another pasture, called Poopshikargah, where the yaks graze undisturbed for the summer. From this pasture above the Batura and Yoksugoz, you can see Batura I, II, and III, whose steep northern slopes fall into the upper reaches of the main glacier. And the Batura Glacier itself? It disappears out of view around a bend, where its uppermost basin lies encircled by some of the westernmost peaks in the Karakoram Range.

Each year fewer and fewer of the families from Pasu go up to their traditional pastures alongside the Batura. The money economy that is entering the valley makes less inviting the hard work of herding and milking the animals and making the butter and *kurut* (a popular food flavoring made from the dried residue of boiled buttermilk and wheat flour and used in soups and other foods throughout the Northern Areas and west across Afghanistan). Still, some families continue to go to their upland pastures, and as you and your friend from Pasu approach his family's hut, or that of a friend, a woman will emerge and wave by twirling her upraised right hand in small circles. Then the two may kiss each other's hand, in time-honored fashion reminiscent of Central Asian custom north of the border. As you are invited into the small building where the kurut is boiling away on a yak dung fire, you will be glad you came (even if your eyes smart until you sit down beneath the smoke) and you'll know that you've truly found Gujal.

The Tricky Path to Shimshal

Ghulam Mohammed Baig Hunzai in Gilgit told me the old saying: "If Karun doesn't get you, then Shams will," regarding the difficult hike up the Shimshal Valley to the village of Shimshal. Karun is Karun Pir, the now-unused high pass that people used to take into the gorge, and Shams refers to the tricky scree slopes (where rocks often fall from above) that still must be traversed. And this is not to mention the dry, rocky path the traveler follows most of the way in, or the slippery Mulungutti Glacier that must be crossed. No, the route to Shimshal is not for most people, but it is now open, and some trekkers have been walking there. So here goes. The map to use (although it has few place names on it) is the *Shimshal* sheet (NJ 43-15) of the U502 Map Series, the only sheet in the series from Chitral to Bhutan that has a 1,000-foot contour interval. Take a guide and porter from Pasu or go with a Shimshali returning home, if you should meet or be introduced to one in Gilgit or Pasu. Locals may tell you it is a five-day walk from Pasu to Shimshal, but three days is enough (and the Shimshalis do it in less than two days at a pace that would leave most of us Angrezi dragging). So figure a minimum of eight days to Shimshal and back and possibly many more if you want to go slowly or take any of the many possible side treks. If the sky is clear and you are walking in summer, you would be wise to leave Pasu soon after dawn (Guda Ali and I left at 5:00 A.M.) or late in the afternoon, for the midday heat can be intense. Be sure to carry a full water bottle.

At the base of spiky-peaked Tupopdan and directly across the main Hunza Valley from the Batura Glacier, the Shimshal River snakes out of its narrow gorge. The mouth of the valley is so narrow that unless the light is just right, you can't even see where the river emerges. The path to Shimshal begins by crossing the metal erector set-like Bailey bridge that was constructed over the Hunza River to divert the KKH when the Batura Glacier swept the road away in 1971. Then you angle up a talus slope at the base of Tupopdan, cross a low notch, and enter the narrow lower gorge. At the notch you have a fine view from Pasu north along the flat valley floor to the rock-covered Batura Glacier. As you walk along the base of Tupopdan, the first part of the route into the canyon is barely a path, since the talus slides down to obliterate the footprints of those who have preceded you. Where the path follows close to the thundering torrent, a cool breeze from the water can raise gooseflesh. When the river smashes against a wall or over a submerged rock, the mica-bright froth resembles ocean waves on a stylized Japanese painting.

The first place where people sometimes halt for the night (if they are going slowly or have left in the late afternoon) is a large cleft called Jeer Jeer, where the sandy beach extends beneath an overhanging rock. A tiny spring of water trickles out just to the left of the shelter's entrance. The next possible resting spot is a tiny, inhospitable place with one stone shelter, called Shugardan. If it is not too late in the day, if your porter is agreeable, and if you have energy, cross the river ford (only knee deep when we crossed in midafternoon in late July, usually a time of high water), then take the bridge to the south bank of the river and keep going to the camping ground called Dut (meaning "Rope Bridge," in reference to a former bridge to the river's north bank). To the north across the Shimshal River are the black, 7,000-foot-high slopes leading to the now-unused Karun Pir Pass. Dut is located on the bank of the Lupgar Nala where there are a few willows and a spring near the high-water mark. The two shelters at Dut, one on either side of the nala, are traditionally used by travelers, but beware of tiny critters if you sleep inside. The narrow Lupgar Glacier lies to the south, invisible from the trail, but you might want to walk the relatively short distance up this side valley to Kuk near the mouth of the glacier. It is possible to walk two short days up the Lupgar Glacier with a local who knows the way.

Beyond Dut you round a low ridge and cross the noisy Momhil Nala, a stream the color of liquid graphite in its narrow slot, bashing downward from the unseen Momhil Glacier above. Again, a side trail leads to the Momhil Glacier, and with a guide you could walk two to three days up the glacier, which reaches to the western base of Disteghil Sar. The main trail upriver, often blasted out of the solid rock, climbs the hillside, and shortly the valley opens out from the narrow gorge you have been following since you entered the canyon. For claustrophobes it is nice to have a view, but

The track to Shimshal is best traversed by intrepid hikers. Here, Guda Ali waits for an avalanche to subside before proceeding.

what you are looking at is fearsome because now you can see some of the 3,000-foot-high scree slopes you must cross: the most dangerous part of the walk. Thousands of feet above the trail, large rocks are imbedded in compacted powder. When a breeze wafts across this conglomerate, rocks dislodge and tumble down the unstable talus, setting off avalanches of dust, pebbles, and rocks. Speed (difficult in the slippery footing) and adrenalin are your best assets for crossing the several talus bowling alleys. Follow your escort, who will show you where to walk, then take you to pure springs beyond at the edge of the river.

Langar, a second rest house (which needs fumigation), lies beyond and within sight of the easternmost scree. This place was named in honor of Shah Shams (or Shams-i-Tabriz), a saint said to have once visited the valley. Sacred though it may be, Langar's water source is a ways upriver, so consider walking a little farther to Shikarzuoi, a large grove of willows and wild roses irrigated by a clear stream of water.

The valley widens as you proceed along sandy bottomland, then you'll pad up a dusty narrow slit onto a high alluvial fan with thornbushes and a few small fields of spindly wheat. The wide Mulungutti Glacier descends from the massive, sheer north face of Disteghil Sar, now standing in clear view to the south. It is possible to walk up both sides of this glacier to the base of Disteghil Sar. The Mulungutti, like the Barpu and Pasu glaciers, is known as a white glacier, with virtually no rubble to reduce the glare. Your friend will find a route across the glacier, which has no cairns because the glacier's flow is constantly changing the configuration of its surface. Your escort may use a long wooden staff with a short metal pick at the end that many locals carry to steady themselves and chop footholds in ice.

After you climb the high moraine on the far side of the Mulungutti, you will be rewarded with the sight of Shimshal's green fields spread out foreshortened in the distance. The town may look close, but it takes two hours to reach, and you must cross two streams en route. The old part of the main village is a cluster of mud-walled homes, while newer houses are scattered about. The largest building in town is its green-roofed Jamaat Khana. Shimshal boasts schools for both boys and girls, and after arriving I soon met Amanullah, the headmaster of the girls' school (funded by the Aga Khan). The population is well over a thousand, but in the summer most villagers are in the pastures to the northeast, an area Shimshalis belovedly call their *pamir*. Some of these meadows lie beyond the Shimshal Pass, and they are some of the few pastures in the South Asian subcontinent that extend north of the main Himalayan-Karakoram watershed. These remote meadows are a reminder of the larger region in this vicinity called Raskam—an area once claimed by the Mir of Hunza. You may need special permission to walk into the Shimshali's pamir, which is guarded by local "border levies."

In 1889 the British explorer Francis Younghusband came into these pastures from Turkestan to the north and successfully negotiated with the notorious Kanjuti (Hunza) raiders, based in Shimshal, to stop plundering Silk Route caravans, explaining to them "that the Queen of England was naturally very angry at her subjects being raided." His mission accomplished, Younghusband returned north and never attempted to pass through the dreaded lower Shimshal gorge. That remained for Eric Shipton and Michael Spender to do in 1937. These two Englishmen were mapping the region, traveling with five Nepali Sherpas. When Roland and Sabrina Michaud arrived in Shimshal with their son Romain in 1974 (Guda Ali was one of their porters), they were the first Westerners in twenty-seven years to walk up the gorge. Along with the British explorer Schomberg, they are even today clearly remembered in Shimshal. Mohammed Nayab, a well-respected village elder, still remembers Shipton's visit.

Guda Ali, Amanullah, and I walked to the meadows at Yazghil, an easy walk from town that involves crossing the lower flow of the 15-mile-long Yazghil Glacier. When we arrived at the lone herders' shelter, we were greeted in traditional fashion by two men who walked toward us with their arms extended and carried our packs the remaining few yards to the hut. Later I learned that both men had traveled with Schomberg forty-nine years before. We sat conversing on a flat stone platform covered with blankets, and soon a large bowl was brought out of the stone hut by a young boy. It contained *dekun-malda,* a mixture of crumbled wheat bread, cheese, and yoghurt molded into an island surrounded by liquid butter.

From the ridge above the shelter you can see the lower portion of the Virjerab Glacier and the tip of the Khurdopin Glacier, the longest glaciers in the valley, both over 20 miles in length. The Yazghil and these latter two glaciers can be ascended (as well as the Yukshin Gardan, which emerges near the mouth of the Khurdopin) if you go roped with someone who knows the way. A route to the Hispar Glacier lies over a difficult, technical pass at the head of the Yazghil Glacier. This remarkable valley offers many possibilities for glacier walking and climbing, but remember: know where you are going and what it will require of you if you strike out into these uninhabited areas. And provide well for the safety of everyone who travels with you. Your return to the main valley will be back down the main gorge.

Unknown Chapursan

North of Gujal's Batura Glacier, the KKH and the Hunza River enter a narrow gorge and squeeze by the western flanks of Tupopdan. High on an isolated fan near the western tip of Tupopdan lies the village of Khaibar, a town with both Burushaski- and Wakhi-speaking residents. Unlike the villages in most of Pakistan's far northern areas, Hunza's villages are often situated on fans that rise hundreds of feet up from the turbid Hunza River, and Khaibar follows the pattern. If you were to climb 4,500 feet up the nala behind Khaibar, you would find that it levels off for several miles at around 13,500 feet. Here you'll have excellent perspectives on Tupopdan, and near the head of the valley is the tricky route over to Sherrin Maidan north of the Batura Glacier. The Khaibar Nala pasturing area is used by some villagers, although many local people take their stock to the vast, rolling pastures in the Khunjerab and Ghujerab nalas to the north.

The road continues through the narrow gorge, crosses the river to the east bank village of Gallapan, and reaches Murkhun. The high, now-unused trail up to Karun Pir Pass and the Shimshal gorge climbs up the north side of the Karun Pir ridge from the wide nala behind Murkhun. Up-valley 3 miles from Murkhun is the village of Gircha with a large spring of pure water. From Murkhun to Sost the valley widens dramatically, and you have an increasingly grand view of the precipitous northern slopes of the main Karakoram Range.

Across the valley from Sost lies the wide, 45-mile-long Chapursan Valley, trending west to its head at the glaciated 17,000-foot Chillinji Pass, which leads to the Karambar River in the upper Ishkuman Valley. Chapursan has been restricted over the years, but its status may well change after the war in Afghanistan ends if Russian troops withdraw from Afghanistan's Wakhan Corridor, just a few miles from the upper reaches of the valley. Chapursan is traversed by a little-used jeep road made under the supervision of Imam Yar Beg Sani, Hunza's master road-builder and raconteur who built the trail into Shimshal and rebuilt the road to Astor, among other achievements. But the road needn't deter trekkers interested in meeting Chapursan's hospitable Wakhi (who include the accomplished mountaineer Nazir Sabir) or taking an interesting side trek. Expect to take up to ten days if you want to walk into upper Chapursan and back, and plan to carry your rations with you. Be sure the valley is open to travel by foreigners, or that you have permission to travel there, for you will be asked for your papers. Unless you cross a high pass south from Chapursan's Lupghar

Valley tributary, your return will be back down the valley the way you came.

In 1986 Jean-Michel Strobino and Hélène Laffargue, two inveterate Himalayan trekkers from France, were fortunate to become some of the first Westerners to visit Chapursan since Schomberg went in 1932 (and they were most probably the first foreigners in this generation to visit both Shimshal and Chapursan). Along with two friends and Iman Ali, their excellent Wakhi guide, they reached Baba Ghundi Ziarat, the sacred pilgrimage shrine toward the western end of the valley. As they walked, people called them *Schomberg do,* "the second Schomberg." It seems the locals did not remember the gritty Britishers Wilfred Thesiger or W. H. Tilman, both well known by their writings, who each traversed Chapursan at different times, leaving via the Chillinji Pass. Jean-Michel and Hélène were told, "Here is the place where Schomberg took tea; you must take tea here. This is where Schomberg camped; you must camp here."

The bridge across the Hunza River to Chapursan lies just up-valley from Sost, and the road into the valley briefly follows the north bank, then crosses to the south bank, where it remains. The hills above the valley floor are almost uniformly dry, for Chapursan gets little rain and most vegetation results from irrigation. Here in the lower valley the scree-covered hills are pale yellow, but as in Nepal's Mustang region, much of Chapursan's splendor, particularly in its upper reaches, is derived from the many subtle shades of color in the surrounding landscape. The homes are low with flat roofs, and some houses have poplar trees to provide shade. Beyond Yarzrich village the large Lupghar Valley branches to the south. Lupghar does not have any permanent settlements, but several summer pastures are scattered along the nala, and high passes lead to the Waltum Nala and the Yoksugoz Glacier, a tributary of the Batura Glacier. Just west of the Lupghar tributary is Raminj, the only Burushaski-speaking village in the valley.

Farther along the main valley is the village of Kermin, and north across the river is the path up to Shilo-ki-Pari, the town's summer pastures, which lie along a ridge. At these pastures you can see Disteghil Sar to the southeast and well up the Kilik Nala toward the northernmost point in Pakistan. The Kermin Pass on this ridge leads to the border post of Kalam Darchi north of Misgar, a village also reached by a side road from the KKH (see the next section). West of Kermin in the main valley the track follows the wide, level Chapursan River due west, and the hillsides become tinged with pink, ochre, and maroon. Zudkhun is the last permanent village in the valley, and not far beyond it to the south is the mouth of the Yashkuk Glacier, the largest glacier in the valley, which has several summer settlements along its west side. Up-valley from the Yashkuk Glacier is Chapursan's most sacred location.

At the far edge of a flat meadow lies Baba Ghundi Ziarat, the "Shrine of the Baba from Ghund," a small, white, pyramid-roofed shrine surrounded by a low stone wall and a second outer wall. Colored flags tied to poles in the small compound have been left by pilgrims to flutter in the wind. The legend of Baba Ghundi has different versions, but this is the story Jean-Michel and Hélène were told: When the valley was inhabited by unbelievers, a respected religious leader from Ghund (in Wakhan) came to preach the true religion. The people said they would become and remain believers, but when Baba Ghundi returned, only an old widow named Kampire Dior had remained pious. The baba told her to climb a high rock near her home the next day and wait for him there. Then the baba sent down an avalanche of large rocks that killed everyone except her. Even now the large rocks from this cataclysm are still visible along the valley for many miles, and one giant boulder is larger than all the rest. Baba Ghundi is buried at the ziarat, and the old woman rests beneath the large boulder. She is further remembered by tall, black Kampire Dior, the mountain that bears her name. To this day no one is allowed to sleep in the cleft below the boulder, and a flame is kept burning there at night. Each year two people from Chapursan and two from Shimshal are in charge of watching over the rock and Baba Ghundi's ziarat. Jean-Michel and Hélène, being pilgrims (and as tradition dictates), paid to have a goat sacrificed in Baba Ghundi's memory and shared its sustenance with their traveling companions and the shrine's guardians.

From Sost to the Khunjerab Pass

The village of Sost (9,100 feet elevation and 125 miles from Gilgit) used to be a tranquil Wakhi village but has now become Gujal's unlikely boomtown. The Khunjerab Pass (or Khunjerab "Top" as it is usually referred to locally), on the border between Pakistan and China, has been crossed on the road by construction workers, officials, and goods trucks since 1973. But on May 1, 1986, the Khunjerab was opened to foreigners and Pakistanis for travel between Hunza and Kashgar in Sinkiang Province. Since then, Sost has been the customs, health, and immigration checkpoint on the Pakistan side and the place where people depart for or arrive from China, even though it is 54 miles from the pass. If you intend to cross into China, you will either have to stay in Gulmit or Pasu and leave *early* in the morning for Sost, or stay in one of the new hotels in Sost (a better idea). Leaving Pakistan, you will have to finish immigration formalities by mid- to late morning, depending on when the vehicle you take is leaving for the pass. On the Pakistan side, all travelers ride in vehicles operated either by NATCO or PTDC. Buy your ticket as soon as you can after you arrive in Sost. If a vehicle is available, you can book it for the 54-mile trip from Sost to the pass and return to Hunza or Gilgit if you do not intend to enter China. You should, however, check in Gilgit with the tourist officer at the Chinar Inn to be certain that a permit is not required.

The Khunjerab Pass is open for travel from May 1 until mid- to late November, depending on snow and road conditions in the pass area. Note that the first two years the pass was open for travel, the road was closed because of snow by November 15. To enter China, you must have a valid Chinese visa, and if you intend to enter (or reenter) Pakistan, you will likewise require a visa. The pass area will be a lot colder than Sost, so be sure you have warm clothes in your hand baggage; once your luggage is stored on or in the vehicle, it will remain unavailable for the day. A full water bottle is a must, and several meals are strongly advised, for when meals are available in Sinkiang north of the pass, they may not consist of more than a bowl of noodle soup. Breakdowns and road blockages between Sost and Kashgar are not unknown. After all, this is a truly remote area, not like traveling from Boston to New York, or Manchester to London. If all goes well, you will travel from Sost to the Chinese immigration point at Pirali in Sinkiang, 31 miles from the border. At Pirali, after customs and immigration formalities are finished, you transfer into a Chinese vehicle for the remaining 53-mile ride to Tashkurgan. Going from Sost to Tashkurgan takes one to one and a half days. From Tashkurgan you travel to Kashgar (travel on the Chinese side of the pass is covered in "From Khunjerab Pass to Kashgar" in Chapter 6). Enough for rules and regulations, the fine points of which are bound to change.

What will you see and where will you be near as you drive north from Sost? A few miles north of Sost, the brown Kilik (or Misgar) Nala and the gray Khunjerab Nala join to form the Hunza River, each stream vying with the other to donate a more brackish contribution in summer when the glaciers up their respective valleys are melting. You will most likely be taking the KKH up the Khunjerab Valley, but first, here is a quick look up the Kilik Nala. A narrow jeep road zigzags up the dry slope less than 200 yards beyond the confluence of the Kilik and Khunjerab streams. This road leads to the town of Misgar, a green oasis on a plain high above the valley floor. It is a grand, heroic setting, across the open valley from a similar but arid shelf. During British rule, Misgar was the last outpost of civilization in the valley; at that time a telegraph wire stretched back to Gilgit. North of Misgar, mail runners carried messages on to the British consulate in Kashgar for a half century. Prior to the British Raj, this strategic and well-irrigated town had been fought over several times by the Kanjuti men from Hunza and the Kirghiz from Turkestan. It is from this valley north of Misgar that caravans of two-humped Bactrian camels from Kashgar carried pottery, spices, and silk south as recently as 1962. Four miles beyond Misgar along the Kilik Nala is Kalam Darchi, the border fortress and customs post, astride a stream junction. The western tributary here leads to the Kermin Pass trail and, farther along, the high Delhi Sang Pass. The Delhi Sang was crossed by Americans Jean and Franc Shor in 1950, when they were forced to divert into Hunza from the Wakhan Corridor of Afghanistan as they were retracing Marco Polo's route across Asia.

Up the main Kilik Nala from Kalam Darchi is a game reserve, and farther along lie the few summer shelters called Murkushi (a Wakhi word meaning "Much Rain"), at the junction of the Kilik and Mintaka nalas. Each of these nalas leads to a pass of the same name, and each pass has a long, flat top, like the Khunjerab Pass. The Kilik Pass is some 150 feet higher than the 15,450-foot Mintaka (which means "A Thousand Ibex"). In former times, the easier-to-ascend Kilik was used by the caravans from Turkestan more often than the Mintaka. But the Mintaka is said to be the pass crossed by Marco Polo en route to Kashgar in the thirteenth century. The Silk Route over the Kilik or the Mintaka Pass provided a single high point separating Kashgar (and China) from Gilgit, unlike the series of five severe passes north of Leh in Ladakh that had to be crossed if one took the caravan route through Kashmir and Ladakh. The route through Hunza was little used, however, because of the Kanjuti brigands likely to be encountered. The Kilik Pass is virtually astride the most northerly point in Pakistan and the South Asian subcontinent, and it lies less than 3 miles from the meeting point of Afghanistan, Pakistan, and China.

The second of the nalas forming the Hunza River is the larger Khunjerab, a Wakhi word meaning "the Red (or Bloody) Valley." Here the KKH follows the river along the bottom of a narrow, utterly inhospitable canyon of slate and shale. Soon the road turns north into the smaller of two narrow gorges. This is still the Khunjerab Nala, and the valley to the east is the Ghujerab. At the junction of the two valleys you enter Khunjerab National Park, a preserve of over 800 square miles that was first proposed by the eminent wildlife biologist George B. Schaller in 1973 and established in 1975. At the bleak outpost called Dih (or Dhi), your documents may be checked by a member of the Khunjerab Security Force, a unit composed of men from different parts of the Northern Areas. It was here that an army officer almost ejected my brother Ken and me from the jeep in which we were riding in 1974. But Ken managed to use his kind Urdu, and we were permitted to visit the last post higher up, where a Wakhi shepherd from Khaibar village treated us to a delicious meal of hot bread and soup.

At Kara Jilga ("Black Stream") the road again turns north into the smaller of two streams and begins a series of switchbacks. Now you are truly among the rolling Khunjerab and Ghujerab uplands used by the Wakhi to graze vast numbers of sheep, goats, cattle, and yaks that they drive up-valley each year. Formerly the Mir reserved vast tracts in these upper meadows for his own animals. These 13,000- to 16,000-foot grasslands pocked with marmot burrows resemble the Pamirs over the pass to the north far more than they do the Karakoram. At the level 15,400-foot Khunjerab Pass, the road is bisected by a white, bilingual memorial marker. To the side, a businesslike sign saying China—Drive Right reminds you that this is a crucial watershed. And you leave the immensely varied and fascinating Hunza Valley for Sinkiang and Chinese Central Asia.

6
Kashgar and the Roads to Pakistan and Tibet

Maachine yok? ("Don't you have a vehicle?")
Uighur shepherd riding a donkey, to author,
hitchhiking in the desert south of Kargalik, 1986

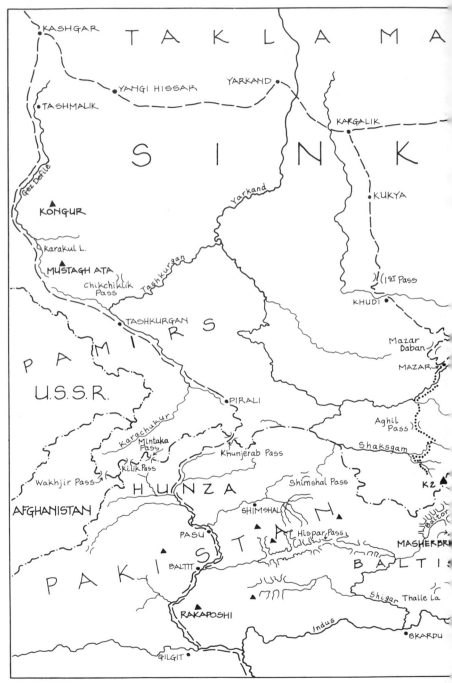

Southwestern Sinkiang

K A N

PISHAN

I A N G

KHOTAN

K U N L U N RANGE

HONG LIU TAN

Sanju
Pass

Chitai Daban

Very Dry

Wild
Ducks

SHAHIDULLA

Keycha
Daban

Suget Pass

NOT FAR
TO
TIBET

Yarkand

M I L E S

0   25   50   75

0   25   50   75   100

K I L O M E T E R S

Karakoram
Pass

A K S A I

C H I N

Siachen Gl.

SASSER
KANGRI

Nubra

HUSHE

T A N

DAHSAM

Shyok

KHAPALU

CONTROL

LINE OF

I N D I A

Pangong

LEH

L A D A K H

Indus

The Desert Route from Pakistan to Tibet

This book is about trekking in Pakistan and India, but two additional regions are briefly touched on as well: Afghanistan (see Appendix C), because of its potential for hikers, and southwestern Sinkiang (pronounced "Shinjang" and formerly known as Turkestan) in China, explored in this chapter. Here, the intention is not to include all of southwestern Sinkiang, but to describe the route through Sinkiang that traverses north of the Karakoram and the western Himalaya.

When the Khunjerab Pass opened to travel in 1986, it became possible for the first time to make an overland circuit north of the Himalaya. This chapter depicts the western part of that route from the Khunjerab Pass at the border of Pakistan through southwestern Sinkiang to the boundary of northwestern Tibet, with a quick stop-off in fabled Kashgar en route. Kashgar, the area's largest city, lies at the junction of two important roads: the road south to the border of Pakistan at the Khunjerab Pass and the far-longer route leading around the perimeter of the Takla Makan Desert. At the town of Kargalik, this latter road meets with a route going south across the western extremity of the Kun Lun Range and the high Aksai Chin Plateau to the border of western Tibet. The remaining part of this route through western Tibet north of the Great Himalaya Range is discussed in *Trekking in Nepal, West Tibet, and Bhutan,* the companion volume to this book.

Areas outside of Kashgar (and the other permitted cities in southwestern Sinkiang) and to either side of the roads covered in this chapter are rarely reached by trekkers because the authorities prefer that visitors come in easy-to-control groups and if not, that they stay in Kashgar and on the main road to the border of Pakistan at the Khunjerab Pass. Nevertheless, a few determined individuals have been able to reach these arid hinterlands and walk in them, and others will undoubtedly follow as long as Kashgar and the road to the border of Pakistan at the Khunjerab Pass remain open to foreigners.

This chapter, in keeping with the book's direction (moving from west to east) begins at the Khunjerab Pass, where the last chapter ended, and proceeds to Kashgar. After a brief discussion of this still-authentic Central Asian city, I describe the long, rarely traversed road from Kashgar to western Tibet. The Bartholomew map of the Indian subcontinent shows all of the area covered in this chapter, as does the Operational Navigational Chart ONC G-7 (see Appendix A, "Map Information," for more specific information about these maps).

From Khunjerab Pass to Kashgar

Descending from the Khunjerab Pass, you enter Sinkiang Uighur Autonomous Region of the People's Republic of China. If you are traveling with an organized group, you will be in your own separate vehicle, but if you are an individual traveler taking public transport from Hunza to Kashgar, your fellow passengers will be mostly Pakistani men and possibly a few Uighurs from Sinkiang returning from the haj (pilgrimage) to Mecca. The men from Pakistan huddle in the bus and wrap their shawls tighter in the chill air. In Kashgar they plan to buy consumer goods for resale back home and many will taste alcohol, forbidden in "Islamized" Pakistan. As one man said, "50 percent business, 50 percent *sherab* ('wine')." The road winds down to the east from the pass for 1,500 feet, then enters a wider valley and heads north, the direction it follows most of the way to Kashgar. The high, snowy peaks to either side of you are not as steep as the Karakoram, and those ahead are part of the lofty Pamirs, a knot of ranges that lie mostly in Russia.

Thirty miles from the border is Pirali, with its hotel and Chinese customs and immigration checkpoint. Here, all passengers switch to a Chinese vehicle after the entrance formalities are completed (the well-decorated Pakistani bus returns empty unless passengers are waiting to travel to Pakistan). A scramble ensues at Pirali as everyone tries to get his saman into the tiny square building for customs inspection, fill out the required forms, and finish the procedure in order to get a good seat on the next bus. Be sure to get a ticket for this bus, for you will probably be on it all the way to Kashgar (although you might try to buy a ticket only as far as Tashkurghan and stay there a day or two).

When you are done with the cursory customs inspection and involved stamping of passports, step outside into the fresh air. Just to the north of you, a side road ascends the U-shaped valley branching west. This valley, called the Karachukur, extends to the headwaters of the Tashkurghan River, the valley you are descending, but the Karachukur is much more than the source of a river. The valley's north rim rises up to the Taghdumbash Pamir and the Russian border, while to the south lie the Mintaka and Kilik passes leading into Pakistan's Hunza Valley at the northernmost point of the South Asian subcontinent. In the days when these passes were crossed regularly, the Kilik was said to be the easier route, but it did not become free of snow until later in the summer. In the seventh century, Hsuan Tsang, the Chinese pilgrim traveler, crossed one of these two passes en route to Buddhist pilgrimage sites in India. Marco Polo is said to have crossed the Mintaka Pass in the thirteenth century. Theodore and Kermit Roosevelt (the former having just been defeated for governor of New York State) and their friend Suydam Cutting, the naturalist and explorer, crossed the Kilik Pass in 1925 on their return from a Central Asian expedition during which they bagged specimens of Marco Polo sheep, pandas, and other animals for the Field Museum of Natural History in Chicago. British writer Peter Fleming and his Swiss traveling partner Kini Maillart rode up the Karachukur Valley in 1935, crossing the Mintaka into British India on their epic journey from Peiping. Five years later, Eric Shipton crossed the Mintaka on his way to a posting in Kashgar as British consul-general of the government of India. In 1947, his mountaineering companion Bill Tilman followed the same trail to join Shipton.

The short arc of mountains at the valley's head connects the Russian border to the north with Pakistan and comprises China's diminutive frontier with Afghanistan. The 16,145-foot Wakhjir Pass on the southern reach of this crescent forms the watershed between Chinese Sinkiang and the Wakhan Corridor in northeast Afghanistan. In the era of the Silk Road, the accessible Wakhjir was used by many traders. In 1891, during the "Great Game" between England and Russia for control of these farthest frontiers of their empires, the British lieutenant Francis Younghusband crossed the Wakhjir Pass. A few days later, after drinking and dining with the Russian colonel Yanoff, Younghusband was obliged by Yanoff to recross the pass under protest. In 1906, Aurel Stein went over the Wakhjir into Turkestan on the second of his archaeological expeditions. Like all the others mentioned who crossed from either Hunza or Afghanistan, he traveled along the same Tashkurghan Valley you are now following.

Although the seats may be hard on your bus, this tantalizing reminder of former travelers who took the same route on horseback should ease your ride as you drive north. Herds of sheep and goats graze the wide meadows, yaks forage on the heights, and occasionally Bactrian camels gaze abstractedly at your vehicle. No, the two-humped camels are not a mirage; you are now most definitely in Central Asia. The road follows the slowly descending Tashkurghan River, and the mountains lining the valley to the west are the Taghdumbash Pamir. The Soviet Republic of Tajikstan lies just across this range, so the area you are traversing is naturally considered sensitive. Finally, some 53 miles from Pirali, you reach Tashkurghan (11,800 feet), a town that second-century astronomer Ptolemy once called the extreme western emporium of China. If you have been coming from Sost, the immigration point in Hunza, it has been a long day.

Tashkurghan, which means "Stone Tower," is a market town of several thousand inhabitants with a bazaar, medical unit, and post office. Beyond the renovated Pamir Guesthouse is a low hill topped by the mud-walled ramparts of the old fortress, the Stone Tower of yore, a great place from which to view your surroundings. Consider dodging off your bus and roaming the sweeping countryside to the east for a day or two (don't head west, for the Russian border is less than 10 miles away in that direction). Tashkurghan sits at an important Silk Route junction. Down the Tashkurghan River to the east lies the ancient track to Yarkand and the high summer route to Kashgar. The truly intrepid might be interested in retracing this route, the former stages of which are noted in Peter Fleming's excellent *News from Tartary.* If you ever make this walk, my hat is off to you and I'd surely like to hear how it went. The route to the north, the old winter track to Kashgar, is followed by the present-day road. The population at Tashkurghan is largely Tajik, the eastern nub of millions who live in both the Soviet Union and Afghanistan. Tajiks are Muslim, of course, and they are tall, imposing people, as likely to be herdsmen as merchants.

If you are traveling from Tashkurghan to Kashgar, 175 miles away, you will probably reach your destination in a day, given good road conditions, but if you are coming from the other direction, the uphill ride may take two days. Leaving Tashkurghan, you head toward the massive 24,750-foot

Mustagh Ata, the "Father of Ice Mountains," which dominates the horizon 20 miles north of town. The unbroken snow ramp on the near, western, side of the peak probably serves to make Mustagh Ata the world's highest walk-up climb. But this is only theoretical. Soft snow conditions, exposure, and altitude on the mountain have stopped the likes of Swedish explorer Sven Hedin, Aurel Stein, and Shipton and Tilman. It was not until 1956 that Mustagh Ata was finally climbed by a Sino-Soviet expedition. At the base of the mountain across boggy meadows lie the mud brick homes of Subashi, a small Kirghiz village.

The Kirghiz who inhabit this region usually live during the summer in yurts, which they call *aq oey*, ("white dwelling") and which are moved from pasture to pasture as the season progresses. The Kirghiz can be extremely hospitable, if they have not been inundated with foreigners, as my traveling friend Betty Vermey and I rapidly discovered. We had arrived at nearby Karakul Lake in tow with a CITS (China International Travel Service) driver and factotum, who fortunately lacked keys for the isolated, ersatz CITS yurt we were supposed to stay in. He went to look for keys, and we immediately began walking back to the Kirghiz encampment we had just seen when we were driven by, imprisoned in the jeep. Most of the men were off with their herds, but the women, dressed in brightly colored scarves, sweaters, dresses, and pants, were most welcoming with no trace of self-consciousness. We watched as they made fresh round *nan* (wheat bread) in a small tandoori oven. Then we were invited to a nearby yurt, where we delightedly sat cross-legged on woven mats and had tea, warm nan, delicious fresh yoghurt, and *ayran*, a yoghurt drink. The circular yurts, although portable when dismantled, are very sturdily made of an inner wooden frame covered with canvas walls and felt roofs held on by handwoven ropes. The perimeter of the roofs is embroidered with maroon designs and tufts of yak wool. Inside, quilts are piled neatly to the ceiling, a reed screen partitions the kitchen area, and babies swing side to side in suspended cradles. If you are invited to visit a yurt, you needn't remove your shoes, but sit with legs crossed, and if you are offered nan, break it into small pieces before eating.

This Kirghiz summer camp we visited near the northern shoreline of Karakul Lake is overlooked by Mustagh Ata reflecting in the lake's clear waters. But to the north an equal distance away rises another solitary mountain, larger and higher than Mustagh Ata. Mt. Kongur (24,910 feet) is a giant massif ringed alternately by icy spurs and tumbling glaciers. Unlike its smaller sibling, Kongur reveals no obvious route to its summit, and the mountain was not climbed until 1981, when British climbers Peter Boardman, Al Rouse, Joe Tasker, and Chris Bonnington reached the summit.

Other Kirghiz summer settlements lie to the east, hidden from the road in the rolling hills between these two peaks. It may take a little doing to extricate yourself from a vehicle on the main road, but if you can get free and if you have some rations and feel explorative, strike out for a few days and see what you can find. The Marco Polo sheep that used to roam the high country beneath the melting snows have mostly been killed, but you may sight an occasional wolf and you'll surely meet some Kirghiz herders and their flocks.

The road to Kashgar heads down-valley, leaving the meadows of the Kirghiz and following the western, then northern base of Kongur. West of Kongur is Bulun Kul, the remains of a small stone fort. Here the land opens out into a wide, shallow lake, and beyond are high white sand dunes in the direction of the frontier with Soviet Tajikistan. Now the road enters the rapidly narrowing gorge of the Gez River as it descends between the flanks of Kongur and a peak to the north. The grasslands of the high country quickly become a pleasant memory as you spiral down into the arid Gez defile, the portion of the route that formerly made this track impassible during the high water of summer. At one narrow passage in the Gez defile that cannot be bypassed is a checkpost where passports may be scrutinized.

The air thickens and warms, the eroded copper, pink, ochre, and gray hills retreat, the river braids in its stony bed, then disappears from sight. Now the driver puts the gas pedal to the floorboard and you are skimming across wasteland, past the oasis of Tashmalik east of the road and toward fabled Kashgar.

Kashgar: Still an Authentic Central Asian Oasis

The names of some cities play in our minds like ancient rhythms: Kathmandu, Lhasa, Kashgar. Yet the vision dims when we arrive. Kathmandu's squares may be crammed with chartered tourists, Lhasa may have transmogrified into a Han city. But Kashgar? Kashgar is still Kashgar. Most of the town seems caught in a time warp. Hurry, though, if you want to see Kashgar (pronounced "Ka Shih" in Chinese) as it was. The city is slowly being rebuilt with the architecturally sterile buildings found elsewhere in China. Sinkiang (which means "New Dominion"), with a current population of some sixteen million people, the majority of whom are Uighurs, Kazakhs, Kirghiz, and other indigenous peoples, is expected to mushroom to over a hundred million, most of whom will be Han migrating from eastern provinces. Khotan, a large city east of Kashgar, already has a far larger percentage of Han than Kashgar, and plans are underway to similarly transform Kashgar.

If you are not arriving from Pakistan, the easiest way to reach Kashgar is by plane from Urumchi, Sinkiang's largest city, 925 air miles away. Flights are scheduled most days of the week, or you may take a bus to Kashgar from Urumchi (or the closer railhead at Korla) via Aksu. The hot, crowded three- to four-day bus ride across monotonous desert is, from all accounts, an experience to be missed if at all possible. Urumchi is connected to Peking by a daily flight, and to the heartland of China by daily rail service from Korla via Lanchow. To enter China you will need a visa, obtainable at any Chinese embassy or consulate (see "Passport and Visas" in Chapter 2).

Kashgar (4,230 feet) lies along the southwestern edge of the Tarim basin, just beyond the rolling sand dunes of the Takla Makan Desert. The city is a large oasis surrounded by sere wasteland and permeated with an aura of the sands. Homes and the walls that surround them are the bone-and-buff color of the desert. In the early morning, sweepers with long-handled brooms clean the streets. Dusty donkey carts creak and roll, carrying melons, alfalfa, or passengers into town between long rows of Lombardy poplars. Uighur men wearing embroidered pillbox hats and long cloaks stroke their beards and ceremoniously greet each other: *"Yok shu maaz?"* *"Yok shu maazaz."* ("How are you?" "I'm well.") Women with scarves over their caps and dresses, long or short, buzz with news as they shop for food. Melon, kabob, and knickknack meisters clamor for attention. Shops selling *'ash* (noodle soup) and street vendors of nan are ubiquitous. Sellers of hats, knives, and cloth and iron mongers each flog their wares in separate sections of town chockablock with rival merchants, as in most Asian markets.

Id Gah (or Id Kah) Square is the center of town, with the mosque of the same name facing its western side. Inside the walls of the mosque is a pleasant open-air, poplar-lined courtyard. Id Gah means "The Place of Id," or "The Place Where Id Prayers Are Spoken," and this explains the large courtyard, for ten times the usual number of people will come to the mosque to say prayers at the holy festival of Id. Later in the afternoon, the venerable building's front steps are draped with men young and old watching the passing show. Energetic storytellers and men who recite the holy *Koran* often attract a ring of listeners in the open square in front of the mosque. Nearby are alfresco restaurants serving greasy hunks of mutton and loaves of bread to rough-hewn customers. A tobacco vendor plays the local version of a guitar while waiting for his next sale. Cigarettes are hand-rolled conically in newspaper, and sometimes hashish (*mee sha* in Uighur) is surreptitiously added, for thousands of years ago Turkestan (as the region is still called by many residents) was the first place this substance was ever known to be used. The egg man's hard-boiled variety is dyed dark red, and his prospective buyers appear to be listening as they shake the white eggs to determine whether they are fresh. Across the square from the mosque is the crowded old market with its black-market money changers who write rates on their palms with ballpoint pens.

The street to the left of the mosque leads to an intersection called Ustung Bui. Here is a two-story teahouse-cum-restaurant where you can rest out of the sun and watch the world pass. In the mornings, local women sell delicious yoghurt *(kai-tik)* at Ustung Bui, stuffing all earnings inside their knee-high stockings. Other yoghurt sellers may come to your hotel. Yoghurt eaten with fresh, warm bread can make a delicious breakfast. Handy words to know in Uighur, in addition to using sign language, are *atha* (tomorrow), *rakh-med* (thank you), and *yak sher* (very good). Kashgar is quite warm in summer, but by no means insufferably hot, so don't let the threat of heat keep you from coming.

Four hotels (all government operated) cater to Westerners, but more will appear when the demand increases. The Kashgar Bingguan ("Kashgar Guesthouse") is the city's up-scale hotel, largely reserved for Western tour groups and visiting dignitaries. It is a couple of miles east of Id Gah Square, too far from town to be of interest to many people. Three-quarters of a mile west of the square is the Seman Hotel, the former Russian consulate; meals are served here, and it has rooms in widely varying price brackets. It used to have a sign in front that read Joint-Building Hotil with Civilization. Just inside the entrance gate is a white plaster statue of a camel arching its neck, ridden by a man shading his eyes with an upraised palm who peers at a distant horizon. The large dormitory at the Seman is, in all likelihood, the former banquet hall. Peter Fleming and Kini Maillart were invited there the last night they were in Kashgar, and about this soiree, Fleming wrote: "Turki and Chinese soldiers lounged everywhere; automatic rifles and executioner's swords were much in evidence, and the Mauser pistols of the waiters knocked ominously against the back of your chair as they leant over you with the dishes. . . . Nobody was assassinated." Directly across the street from the Seman is the Youyi Bingguan, the "Friendship Guesthouse" (although by now it may have another name), established to handle the overflow from the Seman. Small restaurants in the area come and go; the general practice seems to be to raise rates after a foreign customer becomes a regular.

Closer to Id Gah Square (take the street to the right of the mosque) is the Chini Bagh Hotel, none other than the old British consulate. You can almost see Eric and Diana Shipton in the enormous library reading Shakespeare or an autographed volume on Central Asian travel. Or see Fleming and Maillart coming up the drive, five and a half months on the road, hungering for a bath and a beer. Or see Tilman arriving for a bit of mountain bashing with Shipton. Or see the Hunzakut guards playing volleyball in the courtyard. In the rear of the consulate (whoops, hotel) is the circular porch where in 1934 Mrs. Thompson-Glover, the consul-general's indomitable wife, was struck in the shoulder by a bullet during one of the sporadic local rebellions. Chini Bagh means "Chinese Garden" in Hindustani, and appropriately, a well-watered garden of hollyhocks and marigolds lines the entranceway. This hotel is the home of a Chinese work brigade and has become the favorite residence of the many Pakistani businessmen-tourists who visit Kashgar each year. Other foreigners may stay here as well, but few now choose to. Do make a nostalgic visit to Chini Bagh.

Without a doubt Kashgar's big day is Sunday, the day of the weekly bazaar (*bazha* in Uighur). Monday through Friday the bazaar grounds and pavilions east of town (en route to the Kashgar Guesthouse) are deserted, but Saturday finds farmers and merchants arriving with their wares. On Sunday morning the dusty roads leading to the bazha are crammed with trucks, horse and donkey carts, and people on foot. The cast is of thousands. City people and country folk: Uighur, Han, Kirghiz, Tajik, and uniformed Chinese tax collectors trying, trying to collect a percentage from each seller. What's available? Everything under the Kashgar sun: dresses, blouses, shirts, trousers, knitwear, tie-dyed silk, cloth in many types and

Mutton patties and rice are served at Kashgar's weekly bazaar, to the accompaniment of a sing-song chant. The meal was delicious.

colors, women's shoes, shiny black shoes, tall leather boots, men's wooly pillbox hats, women's embroidered caps, jewelry, raw cotton, cotton quilts, woven rugs, reed room dividers, 15-foot-long poplar poles, window and door frames, wooden doors, wooden beds, locks, hinges and other hardware, medicinal herbs, spices hot and sweet, green and yellow melons, watermelons, slices of melon, apricots, peaches, apples, pears, heaps of peppers, potatoes, tomatoes, beans, radishes, carrots, joints of beef and mutton, freshly churned ice cream, noodle soup, mutton soup, mutton dumplings smothered with rice pilau (delicious), sheesh kebab, halyards, bridles and other tackle of all kinds, chickens, calves, cows, sheep, donkeys quiet and braying, horses (and a narrow runway to try them out), camels buff, beige, and brown, large and small, and bells for them to wear. Not to be missed.

Kashgar's long-distance bus station is located east of Id Gah Square on the first side street to the south of the boulevard running between the park and the giant statue of Mao with upraised arm (will this monument to a bygone era last?). This is probably the place where you will leave town for Korla, Urumchi, Yarkand, Kargalik, Khotan, or Pakistan, if you are not flying to Urumchi.

First, some hints on travel to Pakistan. You will need a valid visa for Pakistan, and presently Kashgar does not have a Pakistani consulate, so get your visa before you arrive. Be aware that the border doesn't open before May and that in 1986 and 1987, the first two years the border was open to travel, the Khunjerab Pass was closed by mid-November because of snow. People have told many tales of buses canceled without warning, buses breaking down on the way, and drivers who do not go the entire distance, leaving people off by the side of the road. So approach the whole endeavor with an easygoing attitude, or you may be in for frustration. There are, however, alternatives to going by public bus. You might be able to arrange a ride with a returning Pakistani who is hiring a truck or bus if you make it worth his while (but this could still entail delays). Check with the Pakistani contingent at Chini Bagh. The other alternative is to book a vehicle yourself in conjunction with other travelers. You may be able to hire a vehicle through the local branch of the Chinese Mountaineering Association (CMA), CITS, the local Kashgar Travel Service, or possibly the taxi company. It will take some time to find the various offices and negotiate a price (possibly playing one office off against another). If you plan to do this, get current reports from other travelers and learn from their experiences. However you go, carry some drinking water and enough food for at least a couple of days. Expect the trip to take at least three days to Sost in Hunza. After you arrive in Hunza, don't be in a rush to leave (see Chapter 5 for ideas on what to do in Hunza).

By the time you read this, the road will probably be open as far east as Khotan (Ho Tien in Chinese). If so, you can buy a ticket at Kashgar's long-distance bus station the day before you want to leave and head for any of the major towns along the way: Yangi Hissar (Ying Chi Sha), Yarkand (So Che), and Kargalik (Ye Cheng). This account will focus on the route from Kargalik onward to west Tibet, a trip that may well be restricted unless you are traveling with an officially sanctioned group. One suggestion if you want to travel by this route to Tibet would be to form your own small group in Kashgar with determined, like-minded individuals and hire a vehicle for the trip from CITS, the CMA, or the Kashgar Travel Service. Money talks in China, and regional tourist offices are often willing to arrange transportation. If you are willing to pay the expensive cost of a jeep, landcruiser, or bus to travel to western Tibet, the office where you are renting the vehicle may be able to give you some assistance in acquiring an "Alien Travel Permit" from the local police station, known as the Public Security Bureau (called Gong An Ju in Chinese). Note that in Kashgar, as in Lhasa, there are two Gong An Ju, the regular one and a separate one for foreigners. One may give a permit that the other doesn't. Keep trying. If you can get a vehicle, just go. Determination and patience are important in such endeavors.

From Kashgar to Kargalik and on to Western Tibet

A relatively well traveled road skirts the southern fringe of the Takla Makan Desert between Kashgar and Kargalik. As you leave Kashgar, the road passes fields of corn, cotton, sunflowers, and melons hedged with poplars, willows, and occasional tall stalks of cannabis. You meet trucks, tractors, and some buses, but very few cars, and traffic thins beyond Yangi Hissar, an hour beyond Kashgar. Yangi Hissar is known as the town where the bright daggers sold in Kashgar's old market are made. The mud-walled domestic compounds thin, and and the poplars surrounding them become even more dust covered. Now the arid wastes dominate the landscape until, for a short distance, the road actually passes through the shifting dunes of the Takla Makan Desert, a blank on the map, an empty quarter that sweeps for hundreds of square miles in a vast oval area through the midst of Sinkiang. Takla Makan is said to mean "after you go in, you don't come out," and whether this definition is true or not, the dunes certainly give that impression. Just passing through this penumbra of sand drifting across the pavement gives you an immense respect for the power of the desert to engulf man's humble constructions, like the road you are riding on.

Soon after you enter the sand's fringes, you are out again, however, and beyond lies the large oasis of Yarkand. Yarkand, like Kashgar, used to be surrounded by a 40-foot-high wall with gates that could be shut against invading raiders. The wall was encircled by a moat and was large enough to have a road on its top. The city has spread well beyond its former confines with the help of vast irrigation projects that utilize waters from the Yarkand River. Assuming that Yarkand is open when you read this, the city has not been open to tourism for as long as Kashgar, so you may attract something of a crowd if you wander around the large bazaar. The route through Yarkand is north of the main part of the city, and once beyond town the road crosses the main branch of the silt-laden Yarkand River on a low bridge. Now the pavement turns almost due south, a direction you will travel (if you are going to western Tibet) until you reach the same river much farther up its course. More flat fields surrounded by endless rows of poplars and willows disappear in the sleepy summer haze. You pass several towns, but after about an hour's drive you will reach Kargalik, approximately five hours' driving time from Kashgar.

Just at the place on the north edge of Kargalik where the road turns to the east in a sweeping, banked turn is a large truck compound to the west of the road. This compound and another next to it on the north are where trucks leave for the large town of Ali, located five days' drive south (five days by truck, less by landcruiser) on the bank of the upper Indus River in western Tibet. If you have a ride south to Tibet, all will be well and this compound may be just a brief blur as you go by. But if you are not in a vehicle that is going through to Ali, this compound may be the place to find a ride. However, it is probably still illegal for drivers to take foreigners south, so you may have difficulties in getting a lift here. If it is still not permitted for truck drivers to take you, they can be fined, so they may not want to be seen taking you with them (a difficulty I encountered). At the truck compound are rooms for rent and a small restaurant where you can take meals. If you are on the lam, you may have to attempt a 3:00 A.M. walk out of town and then try hitching a ride once you are well beyond the last compounds on the edge of the desert.

At Kargalik the through road goes north of the main part of town. The road heading south toward Tibet is about 3 miles east of the bend in the tarmac at the truck compound. If you continue straight ahead to the east at the intersection, the main route takes you to Khotan. The very wide road diverging at a ninety-degree angle to the east-west route is the road we are going to follow to Tibet. From here to the end of the chapter, distances (when they are known) will be given in both kilometers, seen on the cement mileage markers by the side of the road, and miles. You begin at kilometer zero with the elevation approximately 4,500 feet.

You would be very wise to carry several days' worth of food with you when you travel south of Kargalik. I've been this way twice and carried food but was lucky and did not need much of it because I ate at occasional noodle shops or army canteens with the drivers who were taking me. However, if you encounter a road washout, or get stuck somewhere (not unlikely in this extremely remote country), you will have to fend for yourself and perhaps help feed your fellow travelers as well. Look at any map: you are headed to the back of beyond. Think very carefully before you attempt to travel along this road south of Kargalik. Most trucks do not stop for a hitchhiker because they travel in convoys from Kargalik to Ali. The drivers and their assistants often need to help one another when vehicles break or the road is blocked or barely passable. Once in the Yarkand River Valley the truck I was in broke a drive shaft. The driver put stones behind the wheels, pulled a new drive shaft from the bed of the truck, and replaced the broken one with the aid of his friends.

The wide, straight road leads for a couple of miles past various large government compounds at the edge of Kargalik, then continues due south into wasteland. At kilometer 11 you cross a large irrigation ditch where there will probably be a checkpoint with a gate. (The irrigation canal is crossed by footbridges well to either side of the road, however.) Telephone poles and wires follow the road all the way to Ali, 1,100 kilometers or 682 miles away. Here in the sandy, rocky desert, you have left the large oases of Sinkiang behind. Rolling hills rise to the east, and a spur road leads in that direction toward the oil rigs pumping away at the base of the hills. This is the place where I waited for six hours and was asked by a Uighur sheepherder riding a donkey why I didn't have a vehicle. Low ridges close in on either side of the road, and 70 kilometers (43 miles) from Kargalik is the pleasant town of Kukya (or Kukcha, at 6,500 feet), its main street lined with tall Lombardy poplars, the largest trees you have seen since Kargalik. At Kukya, you'll have your last bowl of thick noodle soup in the Tarim Basin, a gigantic area that includes the Takla Makan Desert. The road bounces across a stream at the edge of town and passes green cornfields beneath a high, eroded gray ridge. Twisting, slithering, the snakelike roadway passes well-irrigated fields, then burrows into dry hills that rise ever higher to either side. A small truck pullout heralds the base of a steep zigzag climb to the first pass, 10,750 feet high at the low point of a narrow ridge.

South of this pass the road drops over 2,500 feet in four long descending swaths to a Uighur-run road maintenance unit called Akaz. Now you are at the bottom of a bone-dry V-shaped gorge with a large turbid stream at the bottom that winds down into the desert near Kargalik. At Akaz, unused kilometer markers sit about: number 309 leans against a building, and 271 forms a low bench piled on two other markers. The road follows the bottom of this narrow trough, heading upstream and passing occasional fields and a few rough-and-tumble homes. Then you reach the small settlement of Khudi (9,400 feet), where an anachronistic modern Chinese army camp replete with cement basketball court has been plunked down in this desolate valley like a space station on the moon. There is a checkpoint here that may or may not be manned. At Khudi you might be able to get a bowl of noodle soup at a local shop, if you can locate the proprietor. Not far beyond the hamlet the stream divides, then splits again. The road begins twisting back and forth up a rocky slope in the narrow canyon, and you gain several thousand feet of altitude. Finally you enter a wide U-shaped valley with north-facing snow-covered ridges to the south, and the road levels out for a few miles. But this is just a brief respite. Your vehicle strains as the road again curls up on a gray hillside. Now the air is decidedly brisk, and you can see that instead of being at the bottom of a gorge, you are approaching the heights of the topography.

The 17,000-foot pass 217 kilometers (135 miles from Kargalik) is called Chiragsaldi in some accounts, but the drivers who cross the ridge call it the Mazar Dawan (*dawan* or *daban* means "pass" in Uighur) after the small settlement where you are headed. Here at the pass you are not more than

40 straight-line miles from K2, the second-highest mountain in the world, on the border with Pakistan, but intervening ridges block any possible view of the peak. The road twists down to 12,400 feet at Mazar (Mazha in Chinese) in the base of the wide, arid Yarkand River valley. Mazar simply means "tomb" in any Islamic region, but for whom these few isolated buildings are named remains a mystery.

At this point the main road turns east, and a side route that leads ultimately to the base of K2 branches off down-valley to the west. This trail is depicted next, then follows the remainder of the journey to the border of Tibet.

The Trail to the North Side of K2 *by Susan Thiele*

[Susan Thiele has lived and taught in Peking and escorts trekking groups in various Asian countries. She has twice gone to the base of K2 from Mazar, and here she describes her first trip into this remote area.]

Where the main road turns left toward Tibet, we swung right at Mazar and stopped for lunch. To celebrate the impending end of our three-day drive from Kashgar, we passed up the usual lunch of hard-boiled egg, stale cookies, sweet bread, and canned mandarin oranges for some delicacies from home. I took out my camera only to see our interpreter's face go ashen: no photographs were allowed near this inconsequential military installation.

Shortly after our city bus recommenced, we were halted by a washout, and an inscrutable heated discussion ensued between the driver, liaison officer, and interpreter. Then the bus and accompanying truck plunged over a low spot in the embankment and proceeded cross-country along the wide gravel bed just above the Yarkand River. It was a jolting ride that put a number of ominous cracks in the windshield. Soon we came to the stream that had washed out the road. As the bus began to cross, I remembered that the gas tank was tied with rope onto the bottom of the bus, since its metal brackets had already broken off. But somehow vehicle and tank survived the 2-foot plunge, and our cross-country trip continued. I had to respect our driver's skill in taking a city bus over terrain that would be difficult even for a four-wheel-drive vehicle.

Eventually we rejoined the road and later that day reached Mazar "Bazaar." Only one old, gutted, whitewashed building exists here. We had hoped to drive beyond, as a party had done before, but a crucial bridge was out, and the presence of nineteen Bactrian camels and their Uighur drivers confirmed that no more cross-country city bus rides were in our future. Camp was made by brushing aside camel droppings on the dusty plain near the lone building. Camel feed and gear were strewn everywhere as negotiations with the Uighur drivers continued into the night.

In the morning as duffles and boxes were laboriously matched into two-sided loads, Uighurs and Westerners sized each other up with amusement and fascination. As one camel team was brought forward to load up, I was surrounded by a dozen reeking camels. The stench was unbearable, yet I dared not move for fear of being bitten or kicked.

Hours later our caravan, which included ten Westerners and nine Chinese and Uighurs, set off along the right bank of the Yarkand River. Over the next week we would be traveling west and south in a stairstep fashion toward our goal. After some time we came to a good bridge, probably built during the 1962 war with India, that led to the left bank. Once there had been a road of sorts here, but in many places it was washed out or covered by landslides. Later in the day we climbed a gorge with high walls, and the trail became extremely narrow. I wondered how the loaded camels would manage, but all was well as we came into the open again near a bridge that took us across the blue-green Surukwat, the stream we would follow south. Here the road hugged canyon walls that resembled the Dakota Badlands.

Camp lay nearby at Illica, a small grove of thornbushes and grass where the camels could graze, firewood could be found, and tents could be erected on the sandy soil. High above camp we found old petroglyphs, probably depicting ibex. In the evening a whirlwind uprooted the eating tent just as a multiplate Chinese meal had been elegantly laid out. The first eager diner to sit down was caught in the twister and ended up coated in stir-fried food and granulated sugar. With the eating tent suspended in air and another whirlwind coming, I dove into my tent as the sides bulged inward 2 feet. One tent, vacant except for 50 pounds of equipment, sailed 40 feet.

On our return we built a mountain sauna here. Making a fire to heat rocks, we selected a sandy place on the river bar and dug a hole nearly 2 feet across and equally deep. Next, shock-corded poles were fashioned into a teepee frame and wrapped with a spare fly. Everyone stripped down to their long johns and positioned themselves inside the teepee. A washbasin was used to ferry the hot rocks from the fire into the pit, the flap was closed, vegetation was laid onto the hot rocks for incense, and water sprinkled slowly onto the rocks. Presto! The tent was full of steam, and giddy with delight, we watched the dirt and sweat of eighteen days pour off our skin.

Next day we left the road for good and climbed a trail well above the right bank of the Surukwat while the camels plodded along the riverbed. It was wonderful to be higher, yet few snow-clad peaks were visible, even though we were headed directly toward them. As we rounded one corner, we saw where the Zug ("false") Shaksgam flowed into the Surukwat below and found a few rocks with well-worn petroglyphs, then followed a steep trail down to the river. We proceeded through intense sun along the stony riverbed to our second camp where a major tributary came in from the west. Pools in the gravel riverbed allowed bathing that probably shocked the modest Chinese and Uighurs, even though we wore swimsuits.

That night several Uighurs generously invited some of us to sit with them and share their dinner. The meat-filled buns they were eating looked delicious until my first bite, when the juice poured over my hand. Rapidly the liquid congealed into mutton fat that was far less tempting.

In the morning we did a test camel ride in preparation for high water to come. You must be a gymnast to mount like the Uighurs, jumping onto the camel's crooked neck, pulling yourself up by the saddle, then spinning around to hop onto the baggage. Our drivers made the complaining camels kneel down to make it easier for us, but it still took some pushing to get those who were less limber aboard. Then came the worst part. The camels stood up on their rear legs first, then their front legs, with an earthquakelike rocking so intense that the ride itself was an anticlimax.

We stayed on the gravel flats of the west bank until cliffs forced us to ford the braided river. Then we crossed a series of long, loose scree slopes that slid directly into the frigid water. Next, we climbed well above the river, which flowed through a gorge with sheer 100-foot walls and again opened out. Here was the dead-end valley mentioned in Shipton's *Blank on the Map,* where steep walls seem to block all further passage until the traveler is directly upon the narrow route leading up toward the Aghil Pass. Suddenly the temperature dropped drastically, and it began to drizzle. Within a few minutes after we had stopped for lunch, Kirghiz nomads rode up one by one on donkeys and greeted us: a man named Oozman and his daughter Zabaguri, a young boy, then a slender man wearing a tall karakul hat. As we offered them tea and learned some basic words in Kirghiz, we wondered where they had come from.

After lunch they left, and we turned toward the hidden defile. Suddenly a weaver at her loom appeared on the dusty plain, her bright red cheeks and red, yellow, and green weaving contrasting sharply with the surrounding dull beige of the riverbed. Soon a family joined us from a nearly invisible yurt that was anchored with rocks and tucked away in a corner. Their weathered faces attested to the rigors of this isolated place, and I was glad when our drivers pulled a watermelon out of one load to give them.

We continued uphill, twice crossing the Surukwat, which was by now a good deal smaller. Our third camp was wide but sloping, and tents and animals shared the same space. Again, about twenty Kirghiz materialized from nowhere. We bought some yoghurt and found that our picture book from a Japanese K2 expedition contained many photographs of these same people, so we tore the pages out as gifts.

This campsite, at approximately 14,015 feet, lay not far below the famous Aghil Pass. Nearly a hundred years before, Francis Younghusband had pioneered the route we had been taking since Mazar during his famous journey from Peiping to Delhi, and Eric Shipton had crossed this pass from the south in 1937 while he was mapping this forbidding region. Unfortunately I was feeling the effects of the altitude and had to endure the ascent from atop a camel. We passed glacier-studded 19,700-foot peaks and a small tarn before reaching the gentle 15,680-foot Aghil Pass. How beautiful it all was and how grand the scale.

It was a long descent, and the rolling, jerking movements of the camel were only exaggerated on the way down. By the time we could see the Shaksgam River, I had revived and dismounted. The steep, winding path straightened out as we approached the final cliff, where the tips of the Gasherbrums near the head of the Baltoro Glacier could be seen. Our party were only tiny specks in this sweeping landscape, and the foreshortened Shaksgam would take a day and a half to hike. The animals had to take a long route, but we found a shortcut through a narrow cleft leading directly to the river. We continued west along the right bank to a ford and waited for the camels to be unloaded and return from the next camping place, a peaceful thornbush thicket. The Shaksgam was far too deep to ford on foot, but its waters weren't swift and the crossing was easy.

Next day we continued downriver, then crossed the braided Shaksgam and followed the right bank to the fifth camp. This spot was windy too, and at the critical moment when my dome tent's poles were taut but the tent was still empty, a gust blew the sphere onto the slopes above. The next day our path led across the river and along its left bank until we reached a clear feeder stream. Here we decided to take what proved to be a strenuous shortcut over a ridge, rather than follow the camels along the bottomland to the Shaksgam's junction with the Sarpo Laggo River. But the view from the top was worth the climb, for though K2 was hidden by clouds, we could look down to the junction of streams flowing from the Sarpo Laggo, Skyang Kangri, and K2 glaciers. In the midst of this gravelly intersection, a huge rock island has been eroded out of the ridge by these turbid rivers. To the north we could see the moving dots of the camel caravan turning into the valley. Suddenly someone yelled "K2" as, ever so momentarily, the clouds parted between us and the grand, elusive peak.

From the valley floor it was still a long haul to Sujet Jangal, the last camp near the terminus of the K2 Glacier. Our eyes were firmly fixed trying to find the thickets, the *jangal* ahead. Then, after the bushes were in view and we thought we had nearly arrived, the most potentially dangerous obstacle of the journey, the river pouring from the K2 Glacier, appeared at our feet. The gray waters weren't wide, but they were deep and awesomely rapid. Now we recalled hearing that a previous expedition had been stuck on the far side for twenty days by high water and that several of their camels had been swept away trying to cross. Still, our drivers were ready to give it a go, and we watched three protesting camels being driven into the torrent. The waters reached their bellies, the critical point where both the drag of the water and buoyancy of the animals can cause them to be torn from their footing, but with several more steps the camels found higher ground.

Suget Jangal on the west bank is not far beyond this crossing, and despite high winds, it was our home for five days. Large canvas tents had been left by the Chinese from a recent expedition, and there was even an earthen oven and the remnant of a vegetable garden. The area is flat and the only practical spot for a large camp, but K2 cannot be seen from here. To see the immense north face of K2 towering over 2 miles above the glacier, you must traverse the hill above camp, *staying low* to a point near the junction of the Skyang Kangri River with the K2 River.

If you plan to trek to the advanced base camp, you must backpack for three days in and one to two back. You can reach the K2 Glacier's snout either by following the K2 riverbed, if the water is low enough, or by climbing the same ridge above camp, then traversing over a steep cliff that descends sharply to the vicinity of the glacier's snout.

Near the snout are several flat places along the west side of the river suitable for camping. The next day, continue up the right side of the glacier on the lateral moraine, watching for cairns leading you high up along the right side. At a place past a small lake on the glacier, you may have two options. In the past, you had to cut directly across to the east side of the glacier, then hike quite a way along this side to a camping spot at the foot of a glacier coming in from the north of Skyang Kangri. But in 1988 the east-side route was too rugged to follow, and climbers set cairns making a long, gradual traverse from the lake up the glacier to this same camping spot on the east side. With caution, the route was not hard to find, and it was safe to cross unroped as the crevasses were all exposed. This last camp should be your advanced trekking camp.

On the third day, follow the cairns to get back on the glacier. In 1983, the cairns began farther up the glacier, but in 1988 they started right from camp. Strike across the glacier until you come to the medial moraine, which serves as a highway as far as you wish to go. A one-day round-trip from this last camp to the official climbers' base camp at the foot of the mountain would be a very ambitious walk; however, the best views of K2 are not from the climbers' base camp, but are found partway along the medial moraine. From the advanced trekking camp, you can return to Sujet Jangal in one to two days.

Cautions: If you decide to ascend the K2 Glacier from Sujet Jangal, you should carry an ice ax and probably crampons. At least one person experienced in glacier travel should be along. If a climbing party has not placed wands along the glacier, you will need more time to find the route and you must be careful not to get lost among the clusters of ice pinnacles along the medial moraine. Beware of sudden weather changes in this region, and understand that this area is practical for trekking only during about a six-week period toward the end of summer—after the K2 River's water level drops in September and before the onset of winter.

From Mazar to Tibet

At Mazar in the Yarkand River valley, the road turns to the east and proceeds upriver along the flat Yarkand River (once also known as the Raskam River). Tan scree slopes to the south are overlain by higher hills of gray. To the north a jumble of buff, charcoal, and white outcroppings rise up to the snows. The river is a swollen torrent in summer, and sometimes the road runs within feet of the opaque waters at places where cliffs make the passage particularly narrow. Then the river angles in a southerly direction toward its source, discovered in 1869 by the rugged British explorer George Hayward, who dressed in local clothing, traveled light, and moved rapidly, like a man possessed. Where the river bends south, the road trends to the northeast up a narrow nala with a clear stream. It was along this stretch that the truck I was riding in broke a drive shaft while straining up the hill. The drivers and their assistants replaced it in two hours, little more time than it had taken them earlier to replace a flat inside-rear tire. Up and up you go to the second 17,000-foot pass, a rounded brown ridge called the Keycha (or Kokart) Daban, 312 kilometers (193 miles) from Kargalik.

The three passes you have traversed all cross the westernmost ridges of the Kun Lun Mountains, a long range that rises up from the southern perimeter of the vast Tarim basin. To the south of the central and eastern stretches of the Kun Lun are the boundless hills, plains, lakes, and wastes called the Chang Tang, which comprise a large part of Tibet. On the eastern side of the Keycha Daban, you descend into a wide valley that loses altitude very slowly. The road crosses several streams that drain upper snowfields and passes small, then larger, then sweeping meadows grazed by sheep and goats. Turning a corner brings you alongside the wide Karakash River and soon to the settlement of Shahidulla (Sai Tu La in Chinese) at 11,900 feet.

Shahidulla's mud-walled compounds house a few Kirghiz herders, as well as a road maintenance post, an army unit, and a gritty trucker's motel and kitchen. Now and always, Shahidulla has been a lonely outpost in a remote valley, but in the 1860s the settlement played a small part in the Great Game, when the Chinese and the British were settling their outermost frontiers. While the Chinese were occupied with a Muslim rebellion, the Maharajah of Kashmir built a small fort here, but the territory was soon reclaimed by the Chinese. George Hayward and the British explorer Robert Shaw passed through Shahidulla on their separate journeys to Yarkand. Francis Younghusband came to Shahidulla in 1889, and Turdi Kol, the chief of the Kirghiz resident there, was only too glad to lead Younghusband along the hidden route to Shimshal Pass, 190 miles away. The previous year eighty-seven Kanjuti men from Shimshal in Hunza had ridden to Shahidulla and raided the Kirghiz, who were anxious to have the British intervene to halt any such additional forays. For traders on the difficult route from Leh in Ladakh to Yarkand, Shahidulla was the place where Chinese customs duties were collected. Presently Shahidulla is merely the last resting spot for two days where it is possible to see green pastures.

The Karakash Valley is several miles wide with snow-covered ridges to the north and south, and you don't have the sense of feeling closed in that you may have experienced while rattling along in the canyons south of the Yarkand River. Widely scattered herds of animals graze among the often-boggy pastures along the broad, flat bottomland. You might see a wild hare with big ears and thick fur. People here catch fish out of the Karakash River. Gradually the meadows give way to stony desert, however, as the valley slowly rises; the wind picks up by afternoon, sending clouds of gray dust sweeping down-valley. The valley divides, and the road drops to cross and leave behind the smaller northern branch of the river. Your driver forces his vehicle along to reach the next motley collection of build-ings: another army base with cement basketball court surrounded by low dormitories and a nearby group of older structures huddled against the wind that are used by the Uighur drivers and a lone goat herder. God only knows where the leather-faced shepherd grazes his small collection of animals, for barely a blade of vegetation is visible.

This bleak place is now called Hong Liu Tan, and it sits at 14,000 feet, 540 kilometers (335 miles) from Kargalik, at the end of the habitable world. One year I arrived in an army truck and went to visit the Uighur side of this small outpost. It was the time of the annual summer festival, when Kashgar was filled with people dressed in their finest and Id Gah Square was a riot of dancers. Here at Hong Liu Tan the fifteen or so Uighur men had decked out a table with sweets, fried wheatcakes, beer, and firewater and were making the best of their isolation. I was immediately invited to join them and we ate, drank, and talked of the festival back home. Later, on my return to the army compound, a Han soldier offered me a slice of the large melon he and the rest of his friends were sharing just outside the front gate. They threw the rinds over their shoulders, knowing the goats would clean them up the next day. Then one man stood up and flung an empty beer bottle against the stone wall.

At Hong Liu Tan you will be rousted out of bed in the middle of the night, for the ride across the high Aksai Chin Plateau is by far the longest day of the trip. Beyond Hong Liu Tan the road climbs to the rolling Chitai Daban, higher than 17,000 feet and 640 kilometers (397 miles) from Kargalik. Both times I've crossed this pass it was on a crisp moonless night, but what a thrill it has been to cross onto what is probably the world's highest plateau. For much of the day, you cross the Aksai Chin, a vast area about 16,000 feet in elevation, claimed by India and shown as part of India on all Indian maps. But the Aksai Chin Plateau was lost to the Chinese during the border war of 1962. China had completed the road you are riding along in the 1950s, before the road was even discovered by an Indian patrol. The northernmost part of the Aksai Chin is called the Soda Plains; this lofty, flat expanse is covered with pebbles, and even in midsummer the occasional small puddles of water by the road are covered with a thin layer of ice. The only companion to the road is the endless line of telephone poles stretching into infinity. As your vehicle skitters across the washboard road surface and dawn becomes daylight, you can see hills in the far distance, but the road cuts in a straight line across the even surface of the arid desert. Errant tire tracks wend their way across the hard, stony desert where bored drivers have wandered, chasing ghosts or their own exhausts.

Far away to either side are lakes, or are they mirages?

The land you are traversing eventually assumes some relief, and the nearby hills become cloaked in subtle pastels. Now you can glimpse a hint of greenery. Hamster-sized rodents dive into their burrows at the vehicle's approach. Small birds float on the still waters of a small lake, and hares crouch, trying to appear invisible. Finally, at the southern limits of the Aksai Chin, near the 718-kilometer marker (446 miles from Kargalik), you cross a 17,500-foot ridgeline. Here a 2-foot-high concrete post demarcates the boundary of Sinkiang and Tibet. You are still 75 miles from Domar, the initial small settlement in Tibet, where you'll first meet nomadic Tibetans, called Drokpas.

The remainder of the account taking this road past Domar, the eastern-most reaches of turquoise blue Pangong Lake, the town of Rudok, and on to Ali, 235 miles from the Tibetan border, is found in "From Sinkiang to Ali" in Chapter 9 of this book's companion volume, *Trekking in Nepal, West Tibet, and Bhutan.* In the same chapter, "Ali and the Way to Mt. Kailas" takes you to sacred Mt. Kailas near the border of Nepal, India, and Tibet.

The Lambardar of Khorkondus in Baltistan's Kondus Valley wears the old style Balti hat called a nhating.

7

Baltistan: Glaciers and Peaked Hats

The mountains of the Central Himalaya and Nepal are beautiful, but the mountains of the Karakoram are powerful and majestic. They inspire awe, not rapture. These peaks pierce through years of formal education and association with high mountains to evoke an echo of primitive fears buried beneath centuries of civilization.
Nick Clinch, on the Baltoro Glacier, 1959

The towering peaks around us were an imposing spectacle, too imposing, in fact, and I wasn't quite sure if it was comfortable to be in the midst of such rugged grandeur.
Suydam Cutting, in the eastern Karakoram, 1940

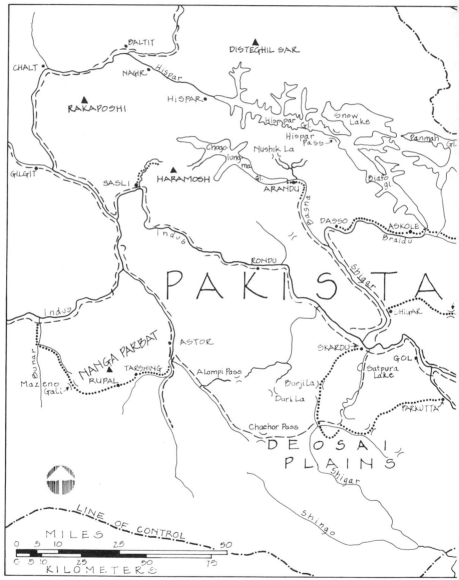

Baltistan

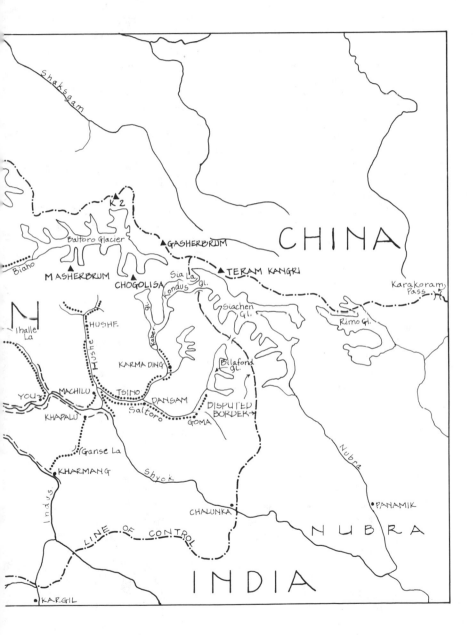

A Mountain Vastness

The Karakoram summits are truly powerful and imposing, but for present-day visitors this grandeur only increases their allure. From the inaccessible reaches of Kampir Dior and Tupopdan in Hunza to the spiked pinnacles of Sherpi Kangri and Teram Kangri above the Siachen Glacier, the towering spires of the Karakoram Range are unique in the Himalayan system of ranges: these mountains and the glaciers descending from them lie in a solid mass extending some 50 by 150 miles and represent the largest system of glaciation outside the polar areas. The majority of these clustered incisor-shaped peaks and curving glaciers lie within the region traditionally called Baltistan, now part of Pakistan's Northern Areas.

Because these mountains were impenetrable by large caravans, Baltistan long remained a cul-de-sac within the greater region crossed by trade routes between the South Asian subcontinent and Turkestan. The deeper valleys of Baltistan produced delicious apricots that were dried and then carried south across the high Deosai Plains to be traded in the bazaars of Kargil and Leh, but this trade was very small in volume and Baltistan had few if any other exports of value. Now a different age is upon us, and the region's mountain vastness holds great interest for hikers and mountaineers. The income gained from portering, guiding, and other work associated with trekking and mountaineering tourism has allowed many Baltis to stay home who would otherwise have to emigrate south to the cities for work.

Little known, little studied, Baltistan is an ancient land of endings and beginnings. Here the Tibetan culture once reached its westernmost point, although Islam has replaced Buddhism in Baltistan for more than five hundred years. The Balti language bears the same resemblance to modern-day Tibetan that Chaucer's language does to contemporary English, and the homespun clothing and page-boy haircuts of men in the upper valleys provide another medieval parallel. Baltis are of mixed stock, and among the various isolated valleys that Baltistan comprises, people of highly dissimilar ethnic strains reside in adjoining houses: a mixture of Islamic, Tibeto-speaking people living in villages that edge on the world's most inaccessible mountain mass.

Uncertain historical evidence indicates that the Baltis once were animists, and that the animism in this land gave way to shamanism, then the Bon Po religion, prior to the people's conversion to Buddhism sometime between the fourth and seventh centuries. Buddhist practice as taught by Padmasambhava was adopted by Baltis and Ladakhis before penetrating eastward into Tibet proper. But the Baltis embraced Shiite Islam in the fifteenth century and have been Shiites ever since.

Baltistan was formerly divided into eight usually squabbling principalities owing greater or lesser fealty to the raja in Skardu. The central marketplace of Baltistan has always been Skardu, with its tenuous southern approaches from the Deosai Plains and along the Indus Valley. The British explorer G. T. Vigne was only the second Westerner to reach Skardu. In 1835 he crossed the high Deosai Plains with Ahmed Shah, then Baltistan's ruler, and later wrote of the view from the edge of the Deosai: "I . . . gazed downwards from a height of six or seven thousand feet upon the sandy plains and green orchards of the valley of the Indus at Skardu, with a sense of mingled pride and pleasure, of which no one but a traveler can form a just conception." Just five years later Ahmed Shah's forces capitulated to the Dogra army of Kashmir, ending Baltistan's centuries of independence. From then until the indigenous revolt of 1947, when Pakistan assumed control, the area was ruled by Kashmir. But because its remoteness and lack of prosperity made internal control of Baltistan less of a priority than it might otherwise have been, the local rulers retained some authority and respect. But local rule has disappeared, and regional differences have lessened as Baltistan has become more closely linked to the rest of the country by daily bus service and plane flights. Regrettably, the upper, glaciated portions of its eastern valleys have been engulfed in warfare with India for control of the Siachen Glacier and the peaks on either side of the Siachen (more about this conflict in the last section of this chapter).

Following Skardu in traditional economic importance were the regions of Khapalu in the Shyok Valley, Shigar (which includes the Basna and Braldu river valleys), and Rondu, the "District of Defiles," along the Indus gorge northwest of Skardu. Of lesser importance were the areas called Kiris, on the Shyok River, and the three fortress principalities of Parkutta, Tolti, and Kharmang (or Khartaksho), upriver on the Indus. To the west, the region called Astor, near the base of the eastern and southern ridges of Nanga Parbat, has at times been loosely connected with Baltistan.

The northern boundary of traditional Baltistan has forever been the trackless Karakoram, and Rondu's defiles set the region's western limits. Its easternmost inhabited gorge lay along the upper Saltoro Valley, and its southernmost settlement was Chalunka, along the Shyok River. At one time, a cairn of rocks near Chalunka marked Baltistan's exact border with the Nubra region in Ladakh. The villages in the Suru River valley south of and including Kargil (now in India) were the former southern limits of Baltistan; people there are called Baltis and speak Balti.

The descriptions in this chapter begin with the road to and town of Skardu. Then follow sketches of the nearby rolling Deosai Plains, some 6,500 feet above Skardu, and Astor, beneath Nanga Parbat to the west of the Deosai. After an account of a typical valley glacier (so you'll know what you're getting in for if you decide to go glacier walking), you will head for Baltistan's glaciated Shigar, Hushe, and Saltoro valleys. Walking routes noted are in open zones unless otherwise indicated. The *Skardu* sheet (NI 43-3) of the U502 Map Series is helpful, with varying degrees of reliability, for most of Baltistan as far east as the Hushe Valley. If you can get into the Kondus or Saltoro valleys, you will need the *Chulung* sheet (NI 43-4). The *Gilgit* sheet (NI 43-2) is necessary if you are going to walk in the area surrounding Nanga Parbat.

Skardu

No matter where you plan to go in Baltistan (with the exception of Astor, a region just to the west), you will go through Skardu to get there. Now that Boeing 737s fly from Rawalpindi-Islamabad to Skardu, most foreigners prefer to take this direct way to reach Baltistan. Flying is a good idea, because the daily buses on the land route from Gilgit to Skardu have to negotiate the twisting road along the Indus gorge.

First, a quick description of the road from Gilgit to Skardu. If you are coming from Gilgit, you can book a jeep instead of the bus. which will shorten the trip time, but the road is the same, no matter which vehicle you take. Figure roughly a six- to eight-hour ride. The road to Skardu leaves the Karakoram Highway, crossing the Gilgit River at the Alam bridge, less than an hour's drive east of Gilgit, just north of the confluence of the Gilgit and Indus rivers. From the bridge it is 88 miles to Skardu, most of them at or near the bottom of the Indus gorge. The route crosses arid, open bottomland, rapidly enters the gorge, and does not emerge until it reaches the large, sandy plain at Skardu. You proceed northeast 10 miles to the town of Sasli (or Sassi), where the river makes a sharp turn to the southeast. The trail up the nala entering from the north at this bend in the river is the route taken by climbers to reach the north face of 24,270-foot Haramosh. Trekkers could walk up this valley for several days and rapidly get into some very high country.

At Sasli, where the river turns to the southeast, the Indus reaches its northernmost point. Until the river bend at Sasli, this great river has been flowing in a rather direct course for over 450 miles from its headwaters, traditionally called the "Lion's Mouth," north of Mt. Kailas in western Tibet (see "To the Headwaters of the Indus" in Chapter 9 of *Trekking in Nepal, West Tibet, and Bhutan*). Upriver from Sasli, the turbid waters flow through a canyon so steep and foreboding that a Swede sent to advise on the building of the road in the 1970s left abruptly, saying, "The only advice I can give you is not to make a road here."

Your arms ache from hanging on to the swaying vehicle, and you may be saying your last prayers as the bus or jeep grinds its gears on the narrow, twisting track that follows near the bottom of the lifeless, vertical walls of this daunting gorge. The Indus River separates the Karakoram Range on the north from the various ranges of the Himalaya to the south. The Indus gorge in this region is considered to be the plane of contact between the former Eurasian landmass to the north and the South Asian subcontinent to the south. Experts in plate tectonics tell us that when the formerly separate landmasses collided in the Oligocene epoch, about forty-five million years ago, what is now the South Asian subcontinent pushed beneath the Eurasian landmass. The line where they meet is this gorge, the "Indus Suture."

You will find precious few villages for over an hour's drive from Sasli, then a few hamlets appear, clinging to life on small alluvial fans. From not far upriver of Sasli until you reach Rondu, the area to the south of the river comprises a large game sanctuary. For a while the walls of the gorge retreat as if to give the traveler some respite, and you pass a few larger villages, including Rondu, the former capital of this "District of Defiles." If you are looking out from the vehicle at the right times, you can see occasional glimpses of snowy peaks high above narrow, enticing defiles to either side of the gorge.

Just before you reach the plain of Skardu, the large Shigarthang Nala empties into the Indus from the south. A mile off the road, behind a moraine, is Katchura Lake, known for its good trout fishing. Also located here is the Shangri La Hotel, Brigadier H. Aslam Khan's centerpiece hotel, an up-scale establishment with many amenities otherwise unavailable north of Islamabad. In addition to the anachronistic red pagoda-roofed cottages that dot the grounds, a DC-3 fuselage also serves as part of the hotel's trappings. Rooms can be booked in Rawalpindi. Up the nala from the hotel, a trail along the Shigarthang Nala leads south, dividing just before Shigarthang pastures, over a day's walk from the hotel. The east fork goes up to the Dari La (about 15,500 feet), beyond which the trail joins another path leading from the Burji La (la means "pass") high above Skardu. This track from the Burji La is noted in "The Unique Deosai Plains," following. The main stream up from Shigarthang eventually reaches the Alam Pir Pass, and to the south of the pass a trail leads down the Bubind Gah (gah, like nala, means "side valley" or "stream") to the Das Khirim Gah, which in turn takes you to the Astor Valley. If you go up the Shigarthang trail, you should consider the Dari La way onto the bewitching Deosai Plains.

The Skardu airport lies in the midst of the 20-mile-long Skardu plain, a desert of sand dunes that shimmers with brilliance during sunny days. Only when shadows lengthen across the waves of sand at either end of the day is this sea of dunes a delicate play of light and shadow. The airport lies 8 sandy miles west of the town's ever-lengthening bazaar. Riding from the airfield into town gives you a little time to adjust to the awesome landscape into which you have flown. Your head swivels, eyeing strata of violet, red, gray, ochre, and brown in the 10,000-foot-high hills surrounding the sandy plain on either side of the Indus River. En route to town you approach and pass south of the 2-mile-long, 1,000-foot-high rock that is a prominent landmark, lying just north of Skardu by a bend in the meandering Indus.

Skardu's bazaar (about 7,700 feet) is a long, rambling affair, stretching from west to east. The western end of the bazaar is called Satellite Town, where you will will find the PIA office, as well as numerous small shops, hotels, and restaurants. Proceeding eastward along this part of the bazaar, you will come to a small traffic island with a memorial to those killed defending the nation. Here also are the Shangrila and Masha Brum hotels, and just off the intersection is the local kerosene (myTTi-kaa Tel) depot, where you can purchase fuel for your stove. North from the traffic island is the walled mazar of Abbas Alamdar, a Shiite saint. Inside are differently colored cloth banners left by pilgrims, as at Baba Ghundi Ziarat in Hunza's Chapursan Valley. A turn to the south from the traffic island leads you in

100 yards to the old bazaar, where you can purchase such neccessities as pots and basic foods. Straight ahead, to the east from the traffic island on the south side of Satellite Town's main street, is the K2 Shop, run by Ghulam Rasul Drasi. Not only is this shop your best local source of trekking and expedition equipment, but Ghulam Rasul is well informed on local contacts in all areas of Baltistan. He formerly oversaw recruitment of expedition porters and, when a sirdar himself, was the best in the region.

Satellite Town extends eastward as far as a fifteenth-century aqueduct, the base of which consists of large granite blocks that must have been brought from elsewhere with great difficulty. East of the aqueduct are the Skardu polo ground and the Askandria Fort, just above the polo field on the eastern foot of Skardu's giant rock. The fort was built by Zowar Singh's Dogra forces following their victory over Ahmed Shah in 1840.

Skardu's tourist officer will be found at the K2 Motel, situated on a low ridge a few hundred yards east of the polo ground. The K2 Motel is operated by PTDC, and expeditions that pass through town often stay there. The tourist officer can be of help with any questions you may have, and he may be able to assist if you are looking for a porter. In addition to asking Ghulam Rasul and the tourist officer about good porters, you might check with the local representative of Waljis Travel or Karakoram Tours, who will have information and perhaps any supplies you may require. Remember that the person you hire to porter and cook for you should be from the area in which you will be trekking.

Books on mountaineering expeditions often picture Balti porters as quarrelsome and apt to strike on a moment's notice. This reputation is by no means universally correct, nor will it be applicable to the person or two you may hire if you are trekking. Most expeditions involve hundreds of porters, so that otherwise mild-mannered people press demands, finding safety in numbers. Also, diplomatic skills in liaison officers and expedition members can be rudely lacking. Doubtless, some locals do become spoiled over time, as they work for well-equipped climbers and try to get whatever they can from the foreigner. The Balti porter-companions I've walked with have been pleasant and hard working (with one exception, a chap pressed on John Mock and myself by the man's smarmy father, who had given us a ride in his vehicle), and most hikers I've met who have walked in Baltistan have had experiences similar to my own. Wages in Baltistan are high, as in Hunza. The difficulty comes in determining how far you will walk in a day. Stages have become set for most routes, particularly those followed by expeditions, and these stages (sometimes called "haltages" in local English, or *pyee* in Balti) may be much closer to a half day's walk than a full day's hike. Good luck in sorting this out if you run up against it. The best thing is probably to discuss stages before you begin, or talk about how far you will walk a day or two ahead of time as you are proceeding. You will probably have to pay per stage, no matter how far you walk in a day. The trick is to know what is and isn't a legitimate stage.

Skardu's residents are Shiites, and the programs you hear on some merchants' radios may be broadcast from Teheran. People in Skardu take part in the annual period of mourning that commemorates the martyrdom in A.D. 680 of Hussain, the grandson of Mohammed the Prophet. Hussain died in the Battle of Karbala near the bank of the Tigris River in what is now Iraq. This observance is called Muharram, and it takes place in the Muslim month of the same name. At the end of this ritual, crowds of men gather in the old bazaar, wailing and flagellating themselves.

The bazaar in Skardu is not as extensive as Gilgit's, but with the KKH completed and the connecting road up the Indus gorge now open, the bazaar has become more reliably stocked. Basic food necessities are available, although occasional shortages of sugar, milk powder, and tinned butter have occurred. Local butter is far superior to that in tins, but you may have to find it in villages or upper pastures, for it may not be available in the bazaar. Since Skardu is not particularly large, it is fairly easy to make arrangements for transport up-country. The second time I went to Skardu, John Mock and I arrived on the plane in the morning, bought cooking pots, kerosene, and food, and were on a jeep to Khapalu by midafternoon with half the rice and dal already cleaned. *Shabash* ("well done")!

Short Walks from Skardu

From Skardu you may take several interesting walking excursions, and they can vary in length as time and energies allow. A stroll around the eastern end of the Skardu rock will take you to the nearby village of Narsok, where you will find a large, pure spring flowing from the base of the monolith. To reach Narsok, walk to the far end of the Skardu polo field and pick up a trail that skirts the rock slopes beneath Zowar Singh's fortress. The mighty Indus snaking along just a few yards beneath your feet among the silvery white sands is an awesome sight. Downriver the braided Indus lazes before reaching the gorges of Rondu that will drop it to the 4,700-foot level and its great swing south at Sasli.

Beckoning you, close to town, is the Askandria Fort. A path follows a convenient wide ledge to its entrance. Once a symbol of Kashmiri rule, the fortress today stands abandoned, its rifle slits guarding only the silent Indus River and occasional grazing sheep.

A climb to the top of the Skardu rock may be undertaken, but this walk is decidedly not for the timid. In 1903 the veteran Karakoram explorer Fanny Bullock Workman reached the top with a porter, but her previously twisted ankle acted up, and thirteen scorching hours elapsed before she could descend. To climb the rock, pass the government college near the western end of Satellite Town and follow a path that diverges from the airport road to the north, paralleling the talus slopes at the base of the rock. Continue past the first slopes to a farther, larger slope that is lighter in hue, with a visible stock trail ascending it. You must keep going up the talus and figure out the difficult route to the left as you approach the top. Several zigzags along exposed ledges require the use of both hands. In the 1830s Ahmed Shah built a well-provisioned fortress on the uppermost knoll, but any easy access route has long since disappeared. Now only the occasional climber or shepherd with his stock will reach the rolling ground above the rock's sheer faces. At the top you will see one last wall of Ahmed Shah's demolished fortress and an intoxicating array of vistas in all directions. To the north the Shigar Valley debouches into the Indus. Here, well above the white dunes and cultivated land at Skardu, you gain a perspective on the degree to which these lower valleys sink beneath the otherwise extremely high ridges and peaks of the Karakoram.

About a mile south of Skardu on the west bank of the Satpura Nala is a tall rock with a vertical, beige-colored northern face. Carved here circa A.D. 900 is a lovely image of a meditating Maitreya Buddha framed by Bodhisattvas.

Walking south up Skardu's alluvial fan takes you to crystalline Satpura Lake some 4 miles from town. To reach the lake by foot, follow the aqueduct and its feeder channel to the jeep road. This road goes directly to the lake, which is well stocked with trout. Reservations for a stay at the lakeside PTDC Motel may be made in Skardu with the tourist officer at the K2 Motel. The road leads beyond the lake to Satpura village, known for its hardworking men, who have served as high-altitude porters on many mountaineering expeditions. Farther along up the road are the Deosai Plains, which you will discover next.

The Unique Deosai Plains

In front of us lay the Deosai, an absolutely treeless wilderness of comparatively level country framed by minor peaks. It gives a unique impression of desolation. I have never seen its equal in this respect elsewhere. Yet the march was very pleasant with many flowers and streams.

Aleister Crowley, 1929

Feeling claustrophobic from walking up the Shimshal gorge, or driving up the Indus Valley to Skardu? Then take a walk (or ride) on the Deosai Plains (sometimes known as the Deosai Plateau), where the rolling grasslands extend far from you in all directions and the snow-covered peaks around the perimeter are only a minor melody in a far greater symphony of open skies and vast distances.

Besides commenting on the Deosai Plains' apparent desolation, Aleister Crowley also said, "It has a devilish reputation for inhospitality," and indeed, some years these high plains have been snow covered for nine months. Heavy frost near streams may occur even during summer nights. This area can be visited most reliably between early to mid-July and late September. The Deosai is also noted for sporadic windstorms that test the stoutest modern tent. Undeniably, though, the Deosai, rarely seen by Westerners, is one of those places with a magic all its own. Nowhere lower than 13,000 feet, the rolling grasslands support no trees or shrubbery, and the Deosai's ruling denizens are scattered colonies of large, vocal marmots. Extending some 40 by 50 miles and surrounded by snow-capped peaks, the Deosai has ultra-pure air that plays tricks on the eyes: clouds above

Balti shepherds in the high pastures make butter inside inflated sheepskins.

appear just beyond reach, and hills that seem nearby retreat as you approach. Shunned by most people, the plains' sole human presence today consists of occasional jeeps and foot travelers crossing from Skardu to Astor during the short summer, when the snows are melted. A few Gujar herders also move across the Deosai with their sheep, goats, and cattle. The Gujars somehow manage to make do with the difficulties raised by lack of wood and occasional windstorms.

From Skardu you have two options for reaching the Deosai (an area that has not been classified by the government's Tourism Division). You can walk or ride on the road that leads up the Satpura Nala beyond Satpura Lake, or you can walk up over the Burji La. Two cautions before you leave, however: first, you would be wise to carry mosquito repellent if you are traveling in midsummer. You will be the only succulent meal for miles in any direction, and humming clouds of mosquitos are apt to become far too cozy for comfort until the sun descends and the air becomes chill. Secondly, be sure not to wander very far south of the road across the Deosai. That would put you toward the Line of Control, the tense, well-guarded, and undemarcated border with India.

Here is a five- to six-day circle trek that will give you an excellent panorama of the central Karakoram (including K2) and allow some walking on the Deosai Plains. The route follows a valley just west of the Satpura Nala, crosses the 15,700-foot Burji La, debouches onto the plains, and circles back, following the little-used jeep road connecting Skardu and Astor. This walking route is best undertaken after you have already done some walking in the region, or at the very least with careful regard for the 8,000-foot rise from Skardu up to the Burji La. In 1912 the English physician and hiker Ernest Neve wrote of the Burji La: "The view from here looking northward is one of the most magnificent in the whole of the Himalayas."

It will take at least two days to reach the Burji La from Skardu. Walking from Skardu, cross the Satpura Nala on the road heading for the airport, then not far beyond the stream, as the road bends to the west, just head cross-country toward the obvious gorge into the hills to the south. The way is narrow at first, and the track continues determinedly up the rocky canyon. Near a shepherds' shelter a couple of thousand feet up, the stream goes underground, so be sure your water container is filled at this point. The stream reappears another hour or two up in a wide, rocky basin. The location of the pass may be a little tricky to determine on this northern side, and the uppermost reaches of the trail are virtually nonexistent from infrequent use. Look for the true low point above a permanent snowbank toward the Satpura (eastern) side of the bowl at the head of the valley. It may be easier to cross the snowfield to a rocky rib just to the west of the pass, then descend the ridge onto the pass itself. Those who don't mind melting snow for water may succumb to the great temptation to camp at the pass to seek an elevated viewing spot on the ridge to the east. Gypsy Davy, who did just that in 1924, said:

> It was such an expanse of immensity as I have hardly imagined. . . . It seems you cannot talk in a matter-of-fact way in a place like that. . . . I thought the Sierras were large, but here, where we could see three or four score miles north, south, east and west, and see only mountains, and most of them above twenty thousand feet, the Sierras seem like sand dunes.

Looking to the south from the pass gives you your first perspective on the rolling Deosai Plains, their color ever changing with the light. The Pangri Range to the distant south ends in the west with Nanga Parbat (unseen from the pass itself), the westernmost mountain of those identified geologically as part of the Great Himalaya Range. Below the pass to left and right are two lapis blue lakes. The trail from the Burji La cuts back and forth down the 400-foot-high south slope, which is pale yellow in the sun but gray in cloudy weather. The path passes the smaller of the two lakes, and the route merges with a wide, larger valley from the west. A previously mentioned pass (called the Dari La on the *Skardu* sheet) in the upper basin of this valley leads down to the Shigarthang Lungma (in Balti, lungma is "stream" or "valley"), a stream that flows into the Indus River not far west of the plain at Skardu. Follow the gently descending valley toward the open grasslands of the Deosai itself. You may be surprised to see trout (stocked by the British in the time of empire) darting into small, dark pools, away from your unexpected presence. This valley you have descended lies just to the west of the Satpura Valley, where the road from Skardu emerges. If you want a more gradual ascent to the Burji La, you could reverse the route and walk up the Satpura Nala.

To the south of and visible from both the Burji and Satpura approaches is a 700-foot hill, on top of which is a 5-foot-high rock cairn. This unnamed hilltop in the northern Deosai commands a clear panorama of the Himalayan Pangri Range and sections of the Karakoram. You could walk to this hill as the southern turning point on your circle. As you climb its gentle, grass-tufted slopes, Nanga Parbat will come into view far to the west of you.

If you want to cross the Deosai and walk to Astor or the southern base of Nanga Parbat, this is entirely possible to do, assuming that the Deosai is free of snow and that you have shelter. You will need food for about a week to reach the Astor River from Skardu, by which time you can resupply essentials. You should also have the *Skardu* (NI 43-3) and *Gilgit* (NI 43-2) sheets of the U502 Map Series or go with a local porter who knows the way. The route into the Astor Valley will be described here, even though it leaves the Deosai, because the way is most easily approached from this side. The route to Astor follows either the road across the Deosai (if there are any bifurcations of the road in the midst of the Deosai, take the northern branch) or the more sporting route over the Burji La. If you are taking this latter trail, as you come out onto the wide plains you will see the old track heading across the undulating grasslands toward the southwest. Follow this route across what could almost be a set for *Lawrence of Arabia*. You will have to ford four crystal-clear streams, the third of which is the Chogo Chu, the "Big Water." When John Mock, our delightfully amiable Balti companion, Ghulam Nabi, and I reached this stream, the day was far enough along and the stream high enough that we decided prudence would dictate camping. Then we crossed the stream in morning's lower water, which proved quite high enough, for the streams were then in spate.

The old track eventually joins the rarely used jeep road near a rock cairn, and you follow the road across the 14,000-foot Chachor Pass, where a wide lake sparkles just before the high saddle that comprises the pass. Here you bid goodbye to the compelling Deosai and enter the Das Khirim Gah, a clear stream that drains into the Astor River; in the distance are forests, which prove to be largely of mixed pines. Ghulam Nabi said that people from Skardu would like to buy the wood, but the men from Astor will not sell. Lower down in the valley you pass the first village, with its small, rectangular houses made of stones and logs. In these uppermost villages, women wear a loose-fitting bonnet with a large curved brim in front, reminiscent of those worn by women in the colonial United States. Continuing down the valley, you enter a realm of tall, scattered pines and finally have your first view of Nanga Parbat towering over the ridge to your left. Below Chilam Chauki (where a better-used road from the south leading to the Line of Control joins the route you are following), jeeps often go empty down-valley, and you may be able to get a quick ride. You can continue down the road to the mouth of the Das Khirim Gah, where it joins the main Astor River at the western base of Nanga Parbat. At the junction of the Das Khirim Gah and the Astor River, you are about 7 miles up-valley from Astor and just a little closer than that down-valley from the Rupal Valley, which leads to the southern base of Nanga Parbat.

But a much more interesting route leads out of the Das Khirim Gah, if you are fit. Just below the town of Gudai, two thirds of the way down the valley, a footbridge crosses to the left bank of the stream. If you cross the bridge and take a footpath up rather steeply several thousand feet, above the small village of Khume, you will reach a pasture with a few small shelters. Chat with the sheepherders here, then take the small path to the west (not the southern trail) up to the ridgetop. At the ridge, WHAM, 26,660-foot Nanga Parbat is spread out before you just a few miles to the west, rising from the low green valley floor in all its majesty. At this ridge you can also see the fields of the Rupal Valley at the southern base of the mountain, a valley you should definitely head for. Scrambling down the hill, go only as far as the first water, then camp wherever you find a flat place (probably on top of a rock). The sunrise on Nanga Parbat from this steep, deserted hill is a sight you will never forget. Continue down the small trail in this valley to the nearby village of Rahimpur (Rampur on old maps) on the far side of the Astor River. The description of the route along the Rupal Valley picks up in the next section.

Astor and the South Face of Nanga Parbat

Astor is a typical western Himalayan valley in that its lower stretches run through a hellishly hot and barren gorge, while its upper reaches are splashed with blissful green meadows and, in Astor's unique case, forests in many places. This valley used to comprise part of the "road" set up by the British that extended from the Kashmir Valley to Gilgit, Hunza, and Kashgar. Astor is usually reached by jeep from Gilgit, but it can also be approached from Skardu across the Deosai Plains, as noted in the last section. If you are in Gilgit and are having trouble getting a ride all the way to Astor (it shouldn't be very hard to find a ride if you ask your hotel manager or the people mentioned in the section on Gilgit in Chapter 5), you could take a vehicle to Jaglot, then switch to a jeep going to Astor. The bridge crossing the Indus River at Jaglot is the beginning of the side road that branches off the Karakoram Highway, goes through the town of Bunji, and southeast up the narrow, arid Astor Valley to the town of Astor. If you come to this region, the *Gilgit* sheet (NI 43-2) of the U502 Map Series will be helpful. People in the Astor region are strict and devout Sunni Muslims. Many men have beards without mustaches, exactly in the style of the Prophet, Mohammed.

Astor village (about 70 miles from Gilgit and 7,500 feet in elevation) is located on a rather steep alluvial fan that is bisected by a deep, glacially fed stream. Astor itself has a large military presence (soldiers from the Northern Light Infantry based in Bunji) and isn't a place to go to as much as through. From Astor you can follow a spur road to the west 1,500 feet up the nala to Rama Meadows, where a splendidly situated rest house has a postcard view of the eastern face of the Nanga Parbat massif. The great eastern ridges of the mountain offer many opportunities for exploring and scrambling about. You could also wander about on the level meadow at Rama or just rest and take in the magnificent view.

The other route you can take up-valley from Astor (aside from the walk across the Deosai, noted in the previous section and easier to take beginning in Skardu) is to the Rupal Valley, just beneath the towering south face of Nanga Parbat. This valley diverges to the west from the main Astor Valley about 12 miles upstream from the town of Astor. The town at the mouth of the Rupal Valley is Rahimpur, a new name for the village formerly called Rampur. When John Mock and I arrived here, several locals questioned whether we should be allowed to proceed up the valley, but John, with his polite, fluent Urdu, was easily able to explain to the men that our intentions were benign. So we stocked up on rations at the small store and continued up-valley. This was in 1982, and many trekkers will have gone this way by now, so you shouldn't have any difficulty with the often-somber locals. To attempt an accurate depiction of this sublime walk would involve superlatives that can often sound meaningless. You walk directly toward Nanga Parbat, from which glacier after glacier cascades down to the valley. The Rupal Nala is quite level, and the trail leads past a couple of tree-shaded villages to the pleasant town of Tarshing, right at the base of the mountain. Just below Tarshing's scattered houses, a gently sloping meadow watered by small springs keeps the grass green, but soggy for pitching a tent.

Right next to Tarshing a lateral moraine bulldozes a ridge across the valley. You climb the moraine along a gentle trail, then cross the rubble-covered Tarshing Glacier (called Chhungphar on the *Gilgit* sheet) on a well-used path. Beyond the glacier is a flower-strewn meadow with cedar trees and the village of Rupal. Some women in this village and in Tarshing still wear old-style hats with floppy crowns made from woven wool dyed red and rear flaps of brown wool resembling beaver tails. John and I stopped for lunch at this meadow surrounding Rupal. Ghulam Nabi had returned home, and it was John's turn to cook the meal. I leaned against a cedar a short distance away to write in my journal, and John began mixing water with the atta (flour) to make roti (wheatcakes). A local came up, hunkered down, and asked John in Urdu where he came from. John, who had been studying Urdu in Lahore, merely said he was from Lahore. Then the man leaned toward John, lowered his voice, and said, "Tell me, how much is the Angrezi paying you to work for him?"

The trail continues gently along until you reach the lateral moraine of the Bazin Glacier. Just before the moraine is a level meadow where expeditions put their base camps if they are climbing the avalanche-prone Rupal face (part of the larger south face) of Nanga Parbat. John and I found an expedition camp here and were kindly treated to some sorely needed protein in the form of sausage and cheese. The path crosses the Bazin Glacier (wider than the Tarshing) and reaches another meadow, called Lutbah by the locals, that stretches for miles. Buy some fresh soft white cheese (locally called *darba*), and butter also, if the herders will sell it. John and I sprawled out on the grass here, chatting with the locals and eating buttery wheatcakes smothered with cheese. We had just finished walking from Goma, the easternmost village in Baltistan, to this awe-inspiring place in about three weeks. Give yourself at least five days from the time you leave Rahimpur to make the round trip to these meadows and back. You can take more time if you want to explore side valleys, walk up-valley to the west, or laze about.

Ever since Tarshing you have been paralleling the base of Nanga Parbat, the tenth-highest peak on earth, an elongated mountain with various ridges and many faces, more a mountain range than a single massif. Nanga Parbat, "Naked Mountain," takes its name from the fact that its sides are so steep they do not hold the snow; another local name for it is Diamir, "Monarch of the Gods." People say when the clouds build up on the slopes, as they do in the summer, that it is just the fairies cooking roti for their daily meal. The mountain was first climbed in 1953 by Hermann Buhl (who died shortly afterward by falling from an overhanging cornice on Chogolisa, a peak overlooking the Baltoro Glacier) and has claimed the lives of more than fivescore mountaineers. Diamir is justly considered one of the most difficult peaks in the world to climb because avalanches rake its many faces and many routes to the top are as steep as the sheer precipices rising some 15,000 feet directly up from the Rupal Valley floor.

If you are comfortable on technical terrain, you could hire a porter-guide and cross the difficult 17,000-foot Mazeno Pass up-valley, a route once taken by men from Chilas in the last century when they raided Rupal, Tarshing, and other villages. The pass is located north of the 9-mile-long Rupal Glacier at the head of the valley. The Mazeno is technically difficult only only for about a 150-foot stretch just below the top on its northern side. On this far side of the pass, a trail leads into the Diamir, then the Bunar Valley, arriving at Bunar village, 14 miles east of Chilas on the KKH (see "The Karakoram Highway up the Indus Valley to Gilgit" in Chapter 5). Allow at least six days to reach the Indus from Tarshing.

Glaciers and Dragons

There are no tigers here, but there are ice-dragons which maul the valleys. This valley was mauled by one, not so long since. . . . He's asleep now, at the head of the Braldoh, shrunk to a mere thirty miles. And his helpers sleep up side nalas.

Gypsy Davy, 1926

Most of Baltistan's upper valleys are glaciated, covered with valley glaciers hundreds of feet thick and up to 45 miles long that descend to between 10,500 and 9,500 feet. Nonmountaineering trekkers are now discovering the phenomenal mountain formations that accompany these glaciers, and many more hikers could walk on glaciers if they chose an accessible one, went with a local, and carried sufficient food. Glaciers are compelling creatures to explore, and walking up them leads to country that is otherworldly, but if you decide to walk on one, you need to be prepared. You should never go onto a glacier alone, and on the upper, snow-covered section of a glacier beyond the moraine, you must always be roped to two or more people.

Novices and veterans alike have run afoul of the deceits that glaciers employ to trap the unwary. Remember the trekker walking by himself on Hunza's Pasu Glacier practically within sight of the KKH: he slipped into a slippery icy funnel with a pool of frigid water at the bottom and emerged soaking and shaken. Arthur Neve, who walked and climbed for over thirty years in the Himalaya earlier this century, had his closest brush with disaster when he fell unroped into a hidden glacial crevasse in the eastern Karakoram: "A few feet lower the crevasse narrowed and was full of water—a black depth. Above was only the broken skylight through which I had fallen." In 1986 Renato Casarotto, one of the top European climbers of the decade, was returning to his base camp, having almost successfully completed a new route to the top of K2. He was walking along the Godwin Austen Glacier at the base of the peak when he fell into a crevasse and shortly thereafter died as a result. Glaciers can humble the experienced mountaineer as well as the neophyte hiker: be extremely careful on them.

Glaciers, like living organisms, have various parts and exhibit predictable curves, slopes, and surfaces along different extremities. People see different views of glaciated terrain and often have incomplete images of glaciers, like the seven blind men who felt different parts of an elephant in the old parable. As we walk along a glacier, we see its life backward, from death to birth. The glacier changes in many ways from its rubble-covered mouth (also called a snout, foot, or toe) to its snowy uppermost cirque. Initially, as you walk toward a glacier and see the massive, menacing mound of creaking ice overlain by pebbles and boulders, your respect may be tempered with disgust at the mess. But find the headwaters of the stream at the glacier's mouth. There, the entire river of glacial waters pours with a roar from beneath an ice cavern. This death of the glacier can be the beginning of a journey to its brilliant white source in a high basin rarely touched by humans.

Before leaving to walk on a glacier, hire at least one local who has been along it and knows the route to carry some weight and cook the food. Wages have become inflated in Hunza and Baltistan because of the many mountaineering expeditions, but with patience and negotiation you can work out an agreeable rate with the person you want to hire. Before leaving Skardu be certain to have enough food and fuel for the period you will be gone: there's no resupplying on a glacier. Check carefully that your companion has adequate protection for snow and ice. He will have a blanket and can use your parka at night, but does he have hat, gloves, socks, and dark glasses or goggles?

Most of the principal glaciers in the Hunza Valley have been mentioned in Chapter 5. Some of Baltistan's numerous glaciers are noted here and elsewhere in this chapter. The Baltoro is Baltistan's best-known glacier, but other major valley glaciers (some of which are more accessible than the Baltoro), are also spectacular, including the Chogo Lungma in the Basna Valley and the Biafo and Panmah in the Braldu Valley. Four shorter glaciers descend south from Masherbrum in the upper Hushe Valley, all of which can be walked upon; in addition, consider the Kondus and Kaberi glaciers in the Kondus Valley, and the Bilafond, Chumik, and Chulung glaciers in the Saltoro Valley.

The 18-mile-long Kondus Glacier in the Kondus Valley of the upper Saltoro Valley is typical of valley glaciers and is an excellent one to walk along. Unfortunately this valley has become a restricted area because of the conflict between India and Pakistan over the Siachen Glacier, which lies just beyond the glaciated pass at the head of the Kondus. However, this is the glacier I am most familiar with, so I will describe the walk along it, both as a guide to the glacier itself should it become derestricted again in the future, and as an example of what glacier walking is like (you can also refer to Jan Zabinski's excellent description of the Baltoro Glacier in the next section).

The Kondus Glacier is located beyond Karma Ding, the last village along the Kondus Valley. Several hours' walk from town along alluvial wastes, pastures, and alfalfa meadows brings you to the mouth of the Kondus Glacier at a rocky and sandy piece of ground called Gronjin, at 10,500 feet. A little farther on, the Kondus River thunders into the daylight from beneath the glacier.

At the mouth of the Kondus, a path leads to the east side of the glacier, here a pile of gray ice and rocks lying about. Typically, such a trail parallels one or both sides of lower glaciers, sometimes following the glacier itself and sometimes along adjacent meadows or slopes. These paths are used by woodcutters and shepherds bringing stock in the summer to graze the intermittent pastures near the glacier, as well as by *Shikaris* (hunters). The trails have stages (pyee in Balti, as already noted), each of which is considered a day's journey. A stage may be somewhat shorter in distance than you may be inclined to walk in a day, but be agreeable with your porter about stopping, unless you are positive of the route ahead, for there may not be another suitable place to camp for quite a distance. Higher up on a glacier, the route always follows the glacier itself, but lower down, the way may be off the creature as much as on. As you begin walking on the rocky, wavelike glacial surface, you quickly realize that you must adapt to a new, tentative way of walking, for there may or may not be melting ice just beneath the rocky skin. Every glacier's lower ablation zone is melting, which means that each step may approximate stepping on a wet banana peel. You are like a ship sailing up and down along a slippery, frozen sea.

Byameparot, the first-stage campground on the Kondus, is the farthest that the villagers take their stock. This rather barren campground lies at the base of a vertical gray granite wall with a view of the junction of the Kondus and Kaberi glaciers. Here you enjoy smashing views of K6, K7, and the Kaberi Glacier leading north straight toward Chogolisa (25,110 feet). The second stage on the Kondus leads to Rahout Chen, the last named camp, of which the initial view is disarmingly foreshortened. This stage is the most strenuous part of the glacier walk because of the hilly, slippery terrain, but you are rewarded by sights of Chilimski Pinnacle, unnamed spires, and numerous subsidiary glaciers—the dragon's wings. Lower down along a glacier, the nalas to the sides may be glaciated, but often these smaller glaciers melt before reaching the main ice flow. Higher up, however, the side glaciers pour directly into the main glacier. Glacial noises range from deep moans and shudders to the ping of a water drop or pebble into a clear pool. Like the ship at sea or the raft in the river, you are on for the ride, and the glacier has you in its grip.

Rahout Chen is a flat, sandy area at 14,000 feet with tarns (small mountain pools) wedged between the Kondus and a glacial icefall from Sherpi Kangri (23,960 feet). At this camp the last grassy areas alongside or above the ice flow begin to disappear, and all higher camps will be on the glacier itself. Above Rahout Chen the Kondus consists of belts of ice alternating with varyingly hued medial moraines, rocky ridges that continue for mile after mile. The medial moraines along the length of the flow become nearly level and are easily walkable, so you can cover more distance in a day here, higher on the glacier. Oddities abound, like shark-toothed seracs, glacial tables (oval rocks supported by squat columns of ice) looking like giant mushrooms, streams that emerge from and vanish into the ice, and strange ice tunnels and caverns. Unlike most long Karakoram glaciers, which are fairly straight in direction, the Kondus makes three grand bends in its down-valley course. A large cirque is the glacier's snow catchment area, its birthplace, and at the head of the Kondus the narrow, heavily crevassed Sia La ("Rose Pass," at about 18,000 feet) leads onto the mighty Siachen, by far the largest Karakoram glacier.

Near the 17,000-foot level on the Kondus, you reach the limit beyond which unroped trekkers should not continue. This limit is not imposed by altitude but is due to the presence of hidden crevasses. Crevasses are long, narrow openings in the otherwise-solid surface of a glacier. They may be over 100 feet deep with sheer, icy walls. If you step off the rocky medial moraine of an upper glacier, every person with you *must* rope up. The lead person *must* have a long pole or ice ax and probe forcefully ahead as you go. *Don't fail to rope up and carry an ice ax.* Hidden, snow-covered crevasses are often invisible. In the cool of the morning, you may cross such crevasses safely, but later in the day, the snow layer will melt, soften, and be thinner: the same step over a hidden crevasse in the afternoon could put you many feet down in a terrible blackness.

Don't make the same mistake I did in 1977, when I almost got myself killed. I was waltzing along unroped, returning back down the Kondus Glacier, 50 yards ahead of my companions. We had failed on our second attempt to cross the gaping crevasses that riddle the Kondus at the Sia La. Suddenly I dropped up to eye level into a hidden crevasse, with one foot providentially perched on a narrow ledge. The crevasse disappeared far below into blackness. John Mock and Mah Jaan (our local friend from Karma Ding, who had been wise enough not to lead ever since we had begun walking on snow) managed, with great difficulty, to pull me out. Three years later when I wrote the first edition of this book, the memory of this foolish, near-fatal mistake was still so horrifying, I could not bear to recount it at all. Please be forewarned: the dragon's skin can be deadly.

The Shigar Valley

The Shigar River is formed by the combined waters of the Basna and Braldu rivers and ends where it joins the Indus River just north of Skardu. The waters of the Shigar come from glaciers in the heart of the Karakoram Range: the Chogo Lungma, Biafo, Panmah, and Baltoro glaciers. Along the latter glacier alone cluster ten of the world's thirty highest mountains, soaring peaks described in superlatives by all who have been there. If you are planning a trek up one of these long valley glaciers, be certain to stock up on essentials in Skardu. This is not the place to get carried away at the last moment and just start walking, as may conceivably be done in the lusher central and eastern Himalaya. Eric Shipton, a titan of Himalayan exploration, once wrote: "Bill [Tilman] and I used to boast that we could organize a Himalayan expedition in half an hour on the back of an envelope. For my first Karakoram venture, with . . . the immense distances involved, the job was rather more exacting."

To reach the uncharacteristically wide and lush Shigar Valley north of Skardu, arrange for transport in Skardu with a jeep driver or a shopkeeper who employs drivers to carry his merchandise. Just a couple of miles east of Skardu, the road to Shigar crosses the Indus to its north side, skimming the white sands of the plain at Skardu both south and north of the river. It takes a little over an hour to reach Shigar (7,700 feet), some 20 miles from Skardu. Shigar boasts the largest polo field in Baltistan. You'll rarely see polo played in the summer, though, because the locals are too busy making money from mountaineering expeditions and the few horses that haven't been traded in on jeeps are grazing in the upper pastures. Once Shigar town was the seat of a strong raja. Polo and archery were played regularly, and the now-crumbling fortress just above town was a true seat of power. Before partition in 1947, the Shigar Valley's dried fruits and delectable apricot nuts had a ready market in bustling Leh Bazaar down the Indus Valley in Ladakh, but now the border is sealed. A hotel-cum-restaurant in the midst of Shigar's small bazaar provides basic meals, and an interesting wooden mosque is nearby.

The Skoro La

Four miles up-valley from Shigar town is the small village of Skoro at the mouth of the Skoro Lungma. At the head of the northern branch of this side valley is the Skoro La (16,715 feet), a difficult pass that has suffered the fate of several others in the region over the past 150 years. Once traversable, these passes are now strictly technical ascents, owing to an overall melting trend. Where snow once permanently blanketed a pass, it has melted to reveal a sheer wall, or where a snow bridge crossed a bergschrund (a crevasse between the edge of a glacier and the adjacent rock), no bridge now exists, and only the mountaineer may cross. This is the case not only with the Skoro La, but with the Nushik La (see below) between Arandu village and the Hispar Glacier, and with the "Old" and "New" Mustagh passes north of the Baltoro Glacier, which may once have been used to reach Turkestan. Paul Fraser, who crossed the Skoro La from north to south, advises that basic mountaineering skills are necessary for crossing the pass. You must rope up, for an avalanche cone on the north side is part of the route. But the tough part is the steep, crevassed glacier, also on the north side of the pass. The Skoro La leads to the upper Braldu River Valley, where you emerge (or leave) just 2 miles above Askole, the last village in the valley. If you want to go this way, allow at least three days to walk between the Shigar and Braldu valleys.

From Shigar to the Shyok Valley Over the Thalle La

The 16,000-foot Thalle La connects the town of Shigar with the green Thalle valley leading to Doghani village in the Shyok River valley near the large town of Khapalu. Aside from various routes onto the Deosai, the Thalle La is one of the few unglaciated high passes in Baltistan connecting separate river valleys. The nala watering Shigar's verdant orchards and fields is called the Bauma Lungma. This sandy side valley leads past a few mills along a stark, narrow gorge to some small huts, where the stream divides. The south-eastern fork contains the trail you follow up to some of Shigar's summer pastures among a large forest of low cedar trees. Above the herdsmen's huts the path disappears in overgrazed pastureland, but the way continues thousands of feet above the trees along the right bank of the stream. If you are using the *Skardu* sheet (NI 43-3) of the U502 Map Series, the map is not very accurate for this route. The way is neither as steep near the pass nor as level along the Bauma Lungma as shown on the map.

Near the rounded Thalle La you can see Haramosh to the west, but views to the highest Karakoram summits are blocked by intervening ridges. To the south and west, just above the highest meadows is the almost-vertical face of a gray peak. Chunks of melting snow slam down from this mountain not far above grazing cattle. East of the pass the way descends along stony highlands, then down long, rolling meadowlands (called *brok* in Balti) where you'll meet shepherds and their flocks of sheep and goats. These pastures are very extensive and were formerly owned by the Raja of Khapalu, whose domain was considered to be Baltistan's most fertile and productive region. The path leads into the wide, U-shaped upper Thalle Valley and turns into a small jeep road that passes many villages with large fields of grain. The valley narrows, and trees increase in number as you descend, going almost due south toward the steep Ladakh Range on the far side of the Shyok River. At the Shyok is the town of Doghani, and a few miles downriver (at the village of Yuu) is a bridge to the south bank of the river. Allow yourself roughly five days to walk between Shigar and Doghani. Khapalu is about 14 miles east of the bridge across the Shyok at Yuu, or you could continue on the dry north bank of the Shyok to the Hushe Valley some 12 miles east, hopefully catching one of the jeeps that ply this road. For continuing routes through this majestic country, see the section below on Khapalu and the Hushe Valley.

The Basna Valley

The Shigar Valley is formed by the confluence of the Basna and Braldu valleys some 20 level miles upriver from Shigar village. Of these two upper valleys, the Braldu is visited far more often by trekkers and climbers, because it is the location of the well-known Baltoro Glacier. The westerly Basna (or Basha) Valley has its own long valley glacier, the Chogo Lungma (that's right, it means "Big Valley"), which is over 25 miles in length. To reach this valley, continue to the bridge across the Shigar River beyond the town of Shigar and cross to the west side of the valley. The vehicular road up the Basna Valley is blocked by avalanches or washed away by the river a half day's walk beyond Tisar, near the valley's mouth. You may be able to hop onto a tractor for the ride as far as the road goes, but even tractors can get bogged down. From Tisar to Arandu, the valley's last town, is about 19 miles, an easy two-day walk, with a superb hot spring en route. Arandu (9,550 feet), originally populated by people from Nagar (the former state in the Hunza Valley to the north), is on the south bank of the Basna just a few hundred feet below the menacing Tipper Gans (or Tippuri) Glacier.

Across the valley north of Arandu is the Kero Lungma, and about 6 miles up the nala is the Kero Lungma Glacier, angling to the northwest. At the westernmost part of the cirque comprising the head of the glacier is the Nushik La, a high pass that leads north to the Hispar Glacier. When the pass was easier to cross, it was used by men from Nagar to reach (and often to ravage) Baltistan, but crevasses on the north side of the pass have made this route difficult to follow. Arthur Neve, who tried to cross this pass in 1895, told of his porters, villagers from Arandu, putting their hands to their throats, saying *"Qatl karo,"* "Slay us," at the prospect of descending the crevassed north side of the pass.

The lengthy Chogo Lungma Glacier ends less than a mile up-valley to the west of Arandu. This glacier angles to the northwest, and one of its upper subsidiary glaciers comes down from Haramosh, south of the Chogo Lungma. To the north of the glacier's head is Golden Peak in the Hispar Valley, the lovely mountain visible near Baltit in Hunza. If you have walked over the Nushik La or up the Chogo Lungma Glacier, do write and tell me about it: I'd like to hear some recent information about these rarely traveled routes.

The Baltoro Glacier and the Trek to Concordia   by Jan Eric Zabinski

[Jan Zabinski is an extremely experienced Hindi-Urdu-speaking trekker who in 1982 walked the entire distance from Kanya Kumari at the southern tip of India to Srinagar in Kashmir. Jan twice has escorted trekking groups along the Baltoro Glacier for Mountain Travel, U.S.A. This is his account of the trek up to and along the Baltoro Glacier (on the *Skardu* sheet) to Concordia at the junction of the Baltoro and Godwin Austin glaciers.]

The approach to the Baltoro Glacier, which covers the upper 30 or so miles of the Braldu Valley, has been considerably shortened in recent decades by politics and road construction. Prior to 1947 the roadhead ended just north of Srinagar in the Vale of Kashmir, and the trek to the Karakoram had to begin there, still three weeks' walk from Dasso (32 miles up-valley from the town of Shigar and the roadhead in the 1970s and early 1980s).

Vittorio Sella's photographs of the Duke of Abruzzi's 1909 expedition to the Karakoram show a line of over three hundred porters crossing the Zoji La out of Kashmir's Sind Valley in April (see "The Zoji La" in Chapter 8). And Filippo Di Filippi's journal from that expedition describes a scene that seems to belong to the Baltoro region itself rather than to the Sind Valley in Kashmir:

> The air was heavy and warmish, just the weather for avalanches. At the foot of the steep ascent we got ahead of nearly all of the coolies, who were toiling through the soft snow, stopping for breath every 200 yards. The scene was a wild and indescribable one, weird and fantastic as a scene in the wildest legend. Our lanterns threw an unearthly light on the features of the coolies resting in long files, with the shapeless loads upon the crutch at their backs, transforming them into strange humpbacked dwarfs. An immense length of black shadow stretched behind them in the snow. The ceaseless murmur of voices and confused shouting came to our ears from the farther groups, who moved restlessly and dimly in the feeble light of the lantern, like men lost and astray in some dreadful gulf shut off on every side by towering cliffs.

The Duke's expedition continued to Dasso via Dras, Skardu, and Shigar, as had Fanny Bullock-Workman's when she did her pioneering exploration of the Chogo Lungma Glacier in 1903. Eric Shipton also used this approach to the Karakoram during his 1937 Shaksgam exploration. However, independence for Pakistan and India in 1947 and the ensuing

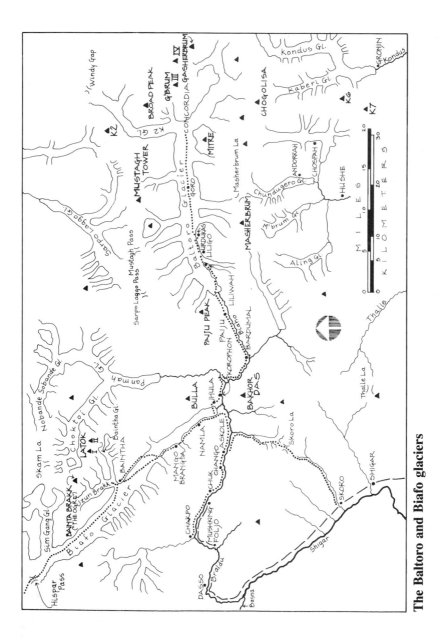

The Baltoro and Biafo glaciers

dispute between the two countries over the fate of Kashmir permanently closed this traditional access to Baltistan from the south. The Zoji La and Dras are now in India, while Skardu, the Braldu, and the Baltoro are in Pakistan.

Modern-day trekkers and expeditions to any region in Baltistan either ride up the KKH or fly from Rawalpindi to Skardu on one of Pakistan International Airline's regularly scheduled Boeing 737 flights. A well-financed expedition, such as the 1978 American K2 expedition, is sometimes able to have its equipment airlifted to Skardu by the Pakistan Air Force.

I have never known a time in Baltistan when jeeps and tractors were not used for local transport. The first time I went to the Baltoro region in 1978, jeeps and tractors would go as far as the bridge to Arandu north of Shigar. Porters would congregate there on news of an expedition, hoping to be hired for the long march to base camp. The first stage was to Dasso, a walk of only about two hours.

For me beginning my first trip up the Baltoro, the journey to Concordia began at the bridge to Arandu. The trailhead is now at the barren campground named Foljo (7,500 feet), a mile beyond the new jeep bridge across the Braldu, slightly beyond Dasso. As of 1988, about half of the new road between Dasso and Askole (the Braldu Valley's last village) had been completed, but soon the new road will reach to Askole. From here on, the description of the route will be by one-day stages.

Foljo to Mushking

Since the construction of the new jeep road from Dasso, the trek from Foljo to Mushking bypasses Chakpo, a small village on the far side of a spur just beyond Dasso that is fast disappearing from the chronicles of travel. The old path crossed the spur 1,000 feet above the river, but the new jeep bridge eliminates this long and laborious climb, recrossing the Braldu and abandoning the old way for the flatter right bank of the river.

Chakpo is an oasis of apricot and poplar trees. Treks and expeditions used to spend their first night above Dasso here, and like the Italian writer and mountaineer Fosco Maraini en route to Gasherbrum IV, people often commented on the poor health of Chakpo's inhabitants. In 1958 Maraini was shocked by the extent of goitre, cretinism, and trachoma in the village. In his book *Karakoram: The Ascent of Gasherbrum IV,* he writes, "The limpid torrents, the crags halfway up the sky, suggested some legendary people, a race of heroes of an age of gold; here was the reality, a wretched sub-race: the humiliated ones."

The trekker who goes along the new jeep road will reach the flat camping place at Mushking (8,500 feet) after about six hours of easy walking from Foljo, but the journey will not be the same as before. The road provides a quick route, but it distances the modern traveler from the great explorers like Shipton and Tilman, whose walk brought them exhaustion and confrontation with the realities of Chakpo.

Mushking to Chuk

The new jeep road to Askole is designed to climb above the right bank of the Braldu River at Mushking and stay there. The left bank is a 1,000-foot-high mass of clay and rubble that continually disintegrates and slides into the river. A jeepable road could never be maintained there, but maintaining the surveyed road is just as questionable. In 1988 the road was blocked by a 50-foot-high wall of compacted snow, the result of a recent avalanche. All passersby were forced to proceed on foot, drop to the river, and cross the Braldu on two flattened logs. The Braldu squeezes through bedrock here in a narrow chasm. With the turbulent water below and apprehension about unstable scree slopes ahead, this defile marks the beginning of the challenge and excitment of walking to Concordia. From this narrow gorge on, it becomes important to walk intelligently, to be aware of footing and balance, and to be ready to react quickly to falling debris and other hazards. This stage is the most dangerous section of the entire route.

The path first cuts across scree, then drops down to hop boulders along the river. If the river is high and the section along its bank impassible, an alternate route high above both the river and the scree becomes necessary. In three round trips through this section I have never had to make this detour and do not wish it on anyone. It's an awful idea to imagine climbing an extra 1,000 feet instead of quickly getting through this short stretch by staying close to the river. In 1988, however, the Braldu was so high that the river route was completely gone. Groups coming back down from Askole were forced to detour higher up but had the option of walking on either the north or south side of the river, since there are new cable crossings farther up the Braldu.

Chuk (9,000 feet), six hours' walk beyond Mushking, is an uninhabited camping spot at the end of the scree section and lies right at the base of a 1,000-foot-high ridge that must be crossed the next day. Chuk is a logical halting place for the night. My only objection to it has always been the water. The small spring is muddy, and when porters are around, it quickly becomes polluted from their washing and toilet activities. But the Braldu is just below camp. Guides from Hunza say that these glacial waters are safe to drink and actually contain healthful properties. They explain that the water is full of dissolved minerals, that it flows past only a few villages after emerging from the higher glaciers, and that those villages are all high on alluvial terraces away from the river. However, this water is terribly cold and perpetually cloudy with a suspension of glacial silt. It is not really very inviting.

Chuk to Askole

In the past the standard stopping spot after Chakpo was Chango. In 1958 Fosco Maraini described the camping spot at Chango as a dank little glade. The stream flowing around it, he said, brought down all manner of filth from a handful of the humblest hovels. Dr. Zeni, the Italian expedition's physician, examined a man's foot. An infection had been treated locally with an application of cow dung. Cleaning the wound, Zeni found a festering sore, the heel half gone because of suppuration. The best he could do for the man was to clean the wound, administer antibiotics and morphine, and inform the man's companions that the patient would die if he was not taken to the hospital in Skardu within two or three days. The man was never taken in for treatment, but he somehow survived, and was in Chango to greet the Italians three months later on their return from Gasherbrum IV.

Over twenty years later I spent a night at Chango. The camping place was in a dusty corral, with drinking water coming from the village irrigation ditches. Late at night Dr. Zeni's scene was played out again in our camp, this time with a man who had a festering sore on his hand, again covered with dung. Our treatments and warnings were the same as Dr. Zeni's, and we were equally uncertain that the patient would ever be taken to Skardu for treatment.

Stopping at Chuk for the night makes a full day to Askole, but it avoids the necessity of spending a night in Chango. The latter then becomes a good place to take lunch, in one of the pleasant shaded areas in the Chango oasis away from the village. Askole is only about 6 miles farther. From Chango the trail remains high on the alluvial terrace, dropping down only when the terrace has been cut into huge blocks by deep ravines coming in from the side. The walking is easy until the edge of one of these blocks is encountered, then it is steeply down and back up the other side. The greatest local attraction is the hot mineral baths 10 minutes' walk up from the trail between Chango and Askole. The pools provide a good opportunity to relax near the end of the day.

Camping in Askole (10,000 feet) is organized by Haji Madhi, the *lambardar,* or headman, of the village. He sells firewood, rents camping space in a corral, and helps with the supply of additional food stocks. If you need chickens, Haji Madhi will sell them to you. If you need a goat to distribute as meat rations to porters at Paiju, Haji Madhi will arrange it. He has a hand in everything and profits from everyone who passes through his village.

Thirty minutes above Askola is an excellent spring. It is well worth the walk to discover its source, for it is away from the village and in a good spot for bathing and laundry. It is also a good vantage point from which to enjoy a late afternoon panorama of the valley. Across the river to the south the route leading to the Skoro La is readily visible. Before partition, expeditions that were finished and in a hurry to return to Srinagar would take the shortcut to Shigar and Skardu via this 16,715-foot pass. They would then continue straight back to Srinagar over the Burji La and the Deosai Plains. The Skoro La is never used for that purpose today, the fastest way out being back to the roadhead and by jeep to Skardu.

Askole to Jhula

Askole is far more important than its modest size would suggest. As long as people continue coming to the Karakoram, Askole will continue to be recorded in the journals of travel, science, and mountaineering. For Askole is both Pakistan's and the subcontinent's final outpost of humanity in this important valley. The new road up the Braldu gorge leads to Askole, not bypassing it, like Chakpo, and consigning it to obscurity.

As you walk out of Askole early in the morning, leaving the last bit of the oasis, it is worth stopping briefly to turn back and imagine the billion people of India and Pakistan now left behind. I have recalled my own journey from Kanya Kumari, the southern tip of the subcontinent, and remembered the intense human interactions that occurred as I walked the length of the subcontinent. And finally, standing just beyond Askole, I've felt the silencing of the last of those billion voices.

Ahead the Braldu River changes its name where it is joined by the torrent issuing from the Biafo Glacier. Above this point in the main valley, the Braldu becomes the Biaho. The route onward to the Baltoro leads first across the Biafo Glacier, whose rubble, ice, and confusion make good practice for the days ahead on the Baltoro. It is wise to pay close attention to the rock cairns. They are a great help in route finding, but they can be misleading. Often paths change as the glacier moves, leaving the old cairns to mark paths leading nowhere. A good strategy is to follow or watch for porters. They negotiate the Biafo on a daily basis and are absolutely familiar with the correct route. It is easy to spot porters, as the trail provides many good vantage points for orientation. Intuition does not work for glacial travel, which is often a walk through a three-dimensional maze.

Somewhere in the middle of this crossing it is good to sit and appreciate the changes in the landscape since Askole. Ahead, Paiju Peak (21,658 feet) stands towering at the very foot of the Baltoro Glacier. Although still hidden by several more twists in the valley, Paiju gives away the secret of the Baltoro. Paiju Peak is the guardian of the door, and this great sentinel marks its position in the sky as clearly from Concordia as it does from the Biafo. Now is a good time to admire the intricate symmetry of the peak, before the senses are overwhelmed with the great towers of the Baltoro just ahead.

Up the Biafo is a 60-mile highway of ice and rock leading directly to Hunza, with the Ogre (23,900 feet), Snow Lake, the Hispar Pass, and the Hispar Glacier along the way.

Just across the mouth of the Biafo is Jhula campsite (10,200 feet). I have always stayed here rather than at Korophon, which is a bit farther on. Jhula offers good water and sheltered camping places. Most large expeditions go on to Korophon because it is a vast open area with room for all the space required of a small city on the move.

Along the Biafo Glacier

If you wish, instead of going up the heavily traveled Baltoro Glacier, you could branch off the main route just before crossing the Biafo Glacier and walk along the valley that contains the Biafo. Should you go beyond the second-stage camp at Mango Brangsa, however, you will cross the Biafo and need to be roped up and ready for glacier travel.

To reach the Ogre's sheer walls, as well as the peaks named Latok I and II (circa 23,440 feet and 22,790 feet, respectively), walk up the west side of the immense Biafo Glacier as far as the first-stage camp, named Namla. Here is an excellent view of both 19,060-foot Bakhor Das, rising straight up from the southern bank of the Braldu River, and also 20,650-foot Bullah, right across the glacier. The next stage, to Mango Brangsa (12,200 feet), is the shortest on this walk. Then proceed across the glacier on the long stage to Baintha camp at 13,870 feet.

As you ascend the glacier beyond Mango Brangsa, ibex may be sighted on the slopes above, particularly in the early morning or evening, for the Biafo is a region where ibex, brown bear, snow leopard, and fox are still known to live. When Galen Rowell came this way, he said, "The Bilafond and Saltoro valleys also had considerably more large granite faces than the fabled Baltoro, but for aesthetics the Biafo won, hands down." He also noted while in this vicinity that "enough major climbs to last several generations were spread around us, untouched and unnamed."

From Baintha camp it is possible to head east off the Biafo, if roped up, onto the Uzun Brakk Glacier leading north to the base of the Ogre, known to Baltis as Bainta Brakk. Or the trekker can walk south from Baintha on the Baintha Lukpar Glacier to the south base of Latoks I and II.

Back on the Biafo, two to three more stages on the glacier itself take the hiker to the southern limits of the gleaming 10-mile-wide basin of snow called Snow Lake, just north of and connected to the Biafo. It was here in 1937 that H. W. Tilman found some startling tracks in the snow. According to Eric Shipton in *Blank on the Map,* "They were eight inches in diameter, eighteen inches apart, almost circular, without sign of toe or heel. The tracks came from a glacier pool where the animal had evidently drunk, and the next day we picked up the spoor on the north side of Snow Lake. The Sherpas judged them to belong to a smaller variety of Yeti, the one which feeds on men, while his larger brother confines himself to a diet of yaks."

Tilman joked with his Sherpas about the yeti (for information on yetis, see "Mammals" in Chapter 13) probably being devilishly hungry, considering that they were Snow Lake's first visitors in thirty years, but the two Sherpas were not amused, standing alone and so exposed on that vast expanse of snow.

Beyond Snow Lake lies the 16,900-foot Hispar Pass, joining the Biafo with the equally long Hispar Glacier in Hunza's Hispar Valley.

Jhula to Paiju

The walk from Jhula has always been one of the most dramatic days of the trek. After being forced onto the cliffside by the Biafo River, the trail drops, as if stunned, onto a gravel bar at the edge of the Dumordo River, a tributary from the north. Here the trail seems impossibly blocked by this vast glacial moat. The icy water is ordinance from the armory of Paiju Peak and the long Panmah Glacier (another side route that can be explored). The Dumordo's channels are impossible to cross when the level is high, and very difficult when the water is lower. Before steel cables and pulley bridges were installed a thirty-minute walk upriver, a decision always had to be made whether to try and cross the Durmordo or to make the two-day detour to the snout of the Panmah Glacier. Trying to evaluate whether to choose potential hazard or certain delay was never an easy decision. The choice between wading and detouring is easier now. All that is at stake is a small toll for a ride in the garroti, the box across the cable, and perhaps some delay if a crowd is trying to cross at the same time.

Currently a cable is stretched across the Dumordo, under the control of Askole's lambardar. It is quite a spectacle when a large expedition arrives at the cable, a fascinating microcosm of South Asia's frenzy and confusion. Somehow each porter is assessed a fee for both himself and his load, and the watchman from Askole tries to keep a running account during the crossing. I once spent several hours with him negotiating the cost for a large group that had just used his cable. Neither of us had an accurate idea of the number of loads and people who had been involved in the crossing. After a while, price became a matter of theatrics, patience, bluff, honor, and imagination, rather than of accounting.

With the cable over the Dumordo in operation, it is now possible to travel from Jhula past the old camp to Paiju (10,200 feet) in one day. If you are trekking on your own with porters here, it is important to note that Bardumal is a traditional halting place and that porters have their wages figured based on the total number of traditional stages that they work. A traditional stage is from Korophon to Bardumal, even though it is quite possible to continue on to Paiju in the same five- to six-hour day. Porters will gladly go on to Paiju, but they are likely to demand two days' wages for their effort. They are not being dishonest, merely expecting payment to follow traditional guidelines. People who are using porters will want to clarify the relation between traditional stages and actual days of walking when the hiring is being done. Traditional stages again become an issue when determining days off and the number of days to be paid for the return journey.

Paiju camp (11,000 feet) could be a wonderful location. It is situated in a nice grove of trees an hour and a half's walk below the mouth of the Baltoro and has the first good views of the glacier and the spires of the Baltoro Cathedrals. Unfortunately, Paiju has become so filthy that professional Western guides now consider it a health hazard. Once known for its beauty, Paiju is now notorious for its gigantic turd fields and garbage dump. The most experienced Western guides are now judging the Baltoro as the filthiest trekking area in Asia, in large part because of Paiju.

In 1982 when an army helicopter flew up the Baltoro, it was cause for celebration. Hearing the chopper blades slicing the thin air, the Balti porters would drop their loads, and as the helicopter darted past, they would dance, wave, and shout, *"Pakistan zindabad!"* ("Long live Pakistan!"). Now helicopters fly by unnoticed, for war has come to the Baltoro and military movements are a daily occurrence. Because of the hostilities between Pakistan and India over control of the Siachen Glacier and the peaks surrounding it, a military fuel dump was established across the river from Paiju in 1984. In 1986 a telephone line was strung the entire length of the Baltoro Glacier, from the fuel dump to the army's advanced position at Gasherbrum Base Camp. (This line corresponds to a similar one on the Indian side stretching up the giant Siachen Glacier.) When the fuel dump was first established, the soldiers assigned to the post were issued weapons and ammunition. Once that first year, they shot and killed over thirty ibex out of boredom.

Paiju to Liligo

Until 1988 the next halting place was Liliwah, a five- to six-hour walk from Paiju after the hiker climbed onto the Baltoro for the first time and crossed it diagonally to camp, just to the south of the glacier. Now Liliwah is gone, totally inundated by an avalanche. There had always been an uneasy sense of impermanence about the camp, what with the rubble lying about that had fallen from the disintegrating walls above. When Liliwah was occupied, these rocks were easily turned into primitive yurts for the porters to sleep in. I suppose the name will survive, because it is associated with a 20,510-foot peak in the vicinity. But I knew Liliwah as the first and last camp of the Baltoro, where the glacier seemed to creak and groan its loudest, with gravity pushing the river of ice in a three-degree slant down toward the distant Arabian Sea. I knew Liliwah because of the incredible lake that formed when the glacier pinched high against the valley walls, creating temporary dams of ice. Liliwah was a beautiful place, and I lament its passing. The first camp next to the Baltoro is now Liligo (12,000 feet), a dusty and inferior campsite two hours' walk along the glacier beyond Liliwah.

Liligo to Urdukas

Beyond Liligo the Baltoro is of far less interest. Its icy rubble and moraines are now merely texture, a foreground of monotony against a background of colossal variety. Until Masherbrum and all the giant peaks appear later on at Concordia, it is the peaks along the northern side of the glacier (collectively known as the northern wall) that dominate. In a single sweep of vision, Uli Biaho Tower and the Trango Towers are captured forever in the mind. The groups of towers are separated from each other by neat glaciers, a scene reminiscent of tidy picket fences, or new driveways between suburban bungalows. A total of six glaciers feed into the Baltoro along this northern wall: Uli Biaho is the first, followed by the Trango, Dunge, Biale, Mustagh, and the Younghusband.

Urdukas (13,000 feet) is located on the south side of the Baltoro across from the Biale Glacier. It is famous as the last bit of green, of flowers, and of life along the Baltoro. For mountaineers descending to this first meadow after months of existence in the stark, hypnotic palette of ice, rock, and high-altitude sky, the green at Urdukas is perhaps the world's most intensely sought-after patch of grass, the place to celebrate the return to a world of living things.

For the trekker, Urdukas is another miserable camp. It too has become incredibly filthy. But it is worth putting up with the mess for the sake of the view. In 1909 Vittorio Sella climbed to a high, snowy ridge above Urdukas at about 17,400 feet and photographed the entire panorama of the northern wall, all the way from Uli Biaho Tower to Marble Peak (20,088 feet). This remarkable panorama was reproduced as a single photograph ("Panorama B") and published as part of the account of the expedition of the Duke of Abruzzi to the Karakoram in 1909. Although it may not be possible to get to the same viewpoint without mountaineering equipment, it is certainly possible to climb way above the camp for an unparalleled view of the northern wall and the Baltoro Glacier.

This viewpoint provides the best look at the Mustagh Glacier and the Mustagh Pass. The latter was the final obstacle for Captain Francis Young-husband, culminating an epic journey in 1887 from Peiping across the Gobi Desert to British India. Never before had the pass been seen by a European, and Younghusband's crossing of it became one of the great moments in Asian exploration and mountaineering. When he reached the top of the pass, Younghusband discovered "nothing but a sheer precipice, and those first few minutes on the summit were full of intense anxiety for me." In smooth, soft leather boots wrapped with handkerchiefs to grip the ice, and with an ordinary pick axe to cut steps, the party began its descent led by Younghusband's guide Wali. The icy slope was pitched as steeply as a roof, and Younghusband knew that one slip from anyone would drag the whole roped party into the abyss. The sun was melting the steps cut by Wali. They quickly became slippery pools of ice, and everyone's boots became slimy on the slick surface.

At the far side of the ice slope, a rock projection marked the beginning of a sheer precipice leading directly to the bottom of the pass. Every scrap of pony rope, turban, and waist cloth was tied together and used to lower a man over the edge. As he descended, he chopped steps in the ice for the other men to use. When he was secure at an intermediate point, the other men descended on the fixed rope. Only the last person was forced to free-climb each of the three final pitches to the bottom. This was one of the slaves Younghusband had released in Yarkand, an incessant grumbler and a rough character, but the best man in the group for this dangerous work.

At the bottom Captain Younghusband discovered that a minor tragedy had occurred at the very moment of success. His baggage had been thrown over the side, and in the process a bottle of brandy had broken, one that he had bought in Peiping and had been hoarding for nine months to cele-brate crossing the Mustagh Pass.

Urdukas to Goro and Goro to Concordia

The final two stages to Goro (13,000 feet) and Concordia (14,000 feet), each about seven hours' walk, purge whatever uncertainty is left about the direction of the route to Concordia. Before Urdukas the Baltoro was con-centrating its final energy in a graceful arc to the south. After Urdukas the

Baltoro is plumb-line straight to Concordia. Before Urdukas the path was furtive, racing across the snout of the glacier, then clinging again tightly to the valley wall. After Urdukas the path steps boldly onto the very center of the Baltoro and marches triumphantly forward to Concordia, the junction of the Godwin Austin Glacier descending from K2 (28,250 feet, locally called Chogo Ri, the "Big Snow Mountain") and the upper Baltoro Glacier, angling in from the southwest. At Concordia the path meets the seven giants of the Baltoro: the Mustagh Tower, K2, Broad Peak, Gasherbrum, the Golden Throne, Chogolisa, and Masherbrum.

Here at this spectacular glacial confluence I remember a Balti porter framed by Masherbrum singing the evening call to prayer, *"Allah-o-Akbar,"* "God is Great." Ahead, travel becomes a journey of the spirit.

The Biafo-Hispar Glacial Traverse   *by Cameron Wake*

[This fine section on the isolated snow world of the Biafo and Hispar glaciers is written by Cameron Wake, a Canadian glaciologist who works with the University of New Hampshire's Glacier Research Group. In 1986, Cameron, a Canadian friend, and two Shimshalis made the first crossing of the Khurdopin Pass between Lupke Lawo (Snow Lake) and the Khurdopin Glacier.]

The walk up the Biafo Glacier to Lukpe Lawo over Hispar Pass (16,900 feet) and down the Hispar Glacier provides an excellent adventure in mountain travel. The trek encompasses a wide variety of terrain, including the dusty, arid gorges of the Braldu and Hispar rivers, the beautiful oases of Askole and Hispar, isolated alpine meadows, chaotic debris-covered ice, steep moraine slopes, smooth white ice, and the wide-open snow expanses of Lukpe Lawo and Hispar Pass. The route provides spectacular views of Baintha Brakk (23,900 feet), the Latok Towers (23,440 and 22,790 feet), and the big peaks that form the north wall of the Hispar Glacier. The journey from Dassu to Askole, up over Hispar Pass and down to Nagar, commonly takes two to three weeks and covers about 110 to 120 miles. Almost two-thirds of this travel is on the Biafo and Hispar glaciers.

On a cautionary note, this trek should only be undertaken by people with experience in glacier travel, crevasse rescue, and routefinding. Don't go if you are at all unsure of your ability to find your own way through the mountains where few trails exist or to deal with the everyday difficulties of travel in remote areas. At these high elevations, altitude sickness can also be a problem. The safest bet is to take it slowly on the trip up the Biafo to provide the time necessary to fully acclimatize. It never hurts to spend a couple of nights at one camp to relax and explore the immediate surroundings in a little more detail, as well as to help with your acclimatization. This is such a beautiful area, there is no sense in rushing through it just to get to civilization on the other side. Enjoy the solitude and the beauty while you can. As a rule of thumb, our small glacier study group rarely slept higher than 1,000 feet above the previous day's camp. If you do begin to feel the symptoms of altitude sickness, descend to a lower elevation for a couple of nights. Going higher will just complicate the problem. Taking it easy on the ascent will allow you to acclimatize and enjoy your existence in the thin air of the high Karakoram.

On one occasion we met a large trekking party from France at the Biafo-Sim Gang junction (15,250 feet). The entourage, which consisted of fifteen Europeans and thirty porters, dwarfed our small party. Nonetheless, we had to organize an evacuation of a woman who was obviously suffering from high-altitude sickness. The whole process took three days and required six porters to carry her to the snout of the Biafo, where a Pakistani army helicopter was flagged down. It still amazes me that a party of forty-five could not organize an evacuation of one of their members! The moral of the story is that the upper sections of the Hispar and Biafo glaciers are very remote, serious places, and a long way from jeep tracks and hospitals. Certainly the most effective method to avoid undertaking an evacuation is not to get sick or hurt; however, you should have a tentative evacuation plan if the need arises. Don't expect any help from the Pakistani army unless you have previously posted a bond with them in Skardu.

It is not uncommon for large storm systems to move into the region during the summer months, resulting in heavy snow accumulation above about 14,000 feet. More than once I have been snowbound in my tent for three to four days waiting for a storm to blow itself out.

The Trek

The hike itself begins with the dusty walk up the Braldu River gorge. In 1987 you could ride a jeep to about 8 miles past Dassu. The locals are optimistic that with a few more years of hard labor they will forge a jeep track through the dirt and rock of the gorge all the way to Askole. Askole is the last place to stock up on supplies, but don't depend on picking up large quantities here because they may not be available. If the harvest has been good you can usually buy some atta (locally ground whole wheat flour); if no major expeditions are in town you should be able to pick up some eggs and chickens; and, if you really want to treat yourself and enjoy eating meat, Askole is a good spot to buy a goat. Discreet inquiries can usually land you any camping or mountaineering equipment—from sleeping bags to ropes—you may have forgotten to bring with you. However, it is a seller's market, and prices can be inflated. Patience and endless cups of tea usually help lower the price. At times I have even been able to purchase canned tuna, sardines, and quality fruit jams in Askole—no doubt remnants of big expeditions. It is also a very good idea to hire a porter or two to carry some extra food and help find the route, at least up to Baintha campground. The going rate in 1988 was about 110 rupees per stage (at 17 rupees to $1 U.S.), for which the porter had to organize his own food. You also have to pay half wages for the porters' return journey. Note that, even if you cover two or three stages in one day, you are still required to pay the porters per stage! (For more on payment versus stages, see "Stages" under "Porters" in Chapter 3.) If you plan to take some porters over Hispar Pass, make sure they have decent footwear, sunglasses, sleeping pad, and a good blanket. If the porters remain with you all the way to Nagar, you should provide for their bus ride to Gilgit and back to Skardu.

The main camping location in Askole is dusty, noisy, and often filled with the garbage from previous expeditions, making it less than desirable. Just to the east of Askole, past the center of town, is an idyllic camping spot in a little green meadow shaded by large trees. Camping here is well worth the few extra rupees you may have to pay the landowner.

The route from Askole to Baintha camp covers three stages. You travel first through the desert to the east of Askole, then turn left up the southwest margin, or edge, of the Biafo Glacier. Just under the large bedrock knoll on the southwest side of the snout are some interesting stone huts. These were built by Ken Hewitt (a British glaciologist inspired by his discussions with Eric Shipton about the region) and his porters for their winter-over scientific expedition in 1961–62. If you walk by these, you have missed the left turn that takes you up the southwest margin of the Biafo. Once on the glacier the majority of the route to Namla and Mango campgrounds is over confused debris-covered ice. Not a very pleasant stroll. The meadow at Mango was my first encounter with a "chapatti western": six local shepherds running around in circles attempting to capture a particularly cunning yak!

Above Mango, the debris cover on the Biafo begins to thin out and walking becomes quite enjoyable on the clean, smooth ice. Baintha campground can be reached by heading diagonally across the glacier to the northeast margin and traversing off the ice into the large ablation valley, then up the ablation valley to camp. (An ablation valley is a small valley that runs parallel to the glacier at its margins. In the Karakoram these valleys, where they exist, usually provide the easiest route up the glaciers.) The porters prefer this route, as their decrepit footwear provides little warmth for their feet while walking on bare ice. However, much of the track in the ablation valley may be flooded following heavy rainstorms or the spring-melt period. Baintha campground can also be reached by heading directly up the glacier and traversing off the ice to the northeast margin before the lateral moraine becomes too nasty. Baintha campground proper, complete with shepherds' huts, is found right at the junction of the Biafo and Baintha glaciers. Access to the Biafo Glacier from this location is difficult at best. We usually set up camp about a mile down glacier from Baintha campground proper, on a beautiful little alluvial fan beside a melt-water pond: just the right size for an afternoon dip. From this camp, access is relatively quick and easy to the smooth, white ice characterizing the middle portion of the Biafo Glacier.

The locals claim it is three stages from Baintha to the junction of the Biafo and Sim Gang glaciers. However, this walk can be completed in one long day if things go well; but be prepared to camp on the ice, as suitable camping locations off-ice are few and far between and access is difficult. Following the large medial moraine provides the most direct route up the middle section of the Biafo Glacier.

A good campsite is located on the rocks at the junction of the Biafo and Sim Gang glaciers, complete with tent platforms and water supply. A crevasse field with some gaping holes guards the entrance to this camp from the glacier. It is easiest to exit to the northeast margin of the Biafo just below the crevasse field. Our research team undertook some radio echo sounding (to determine the thickness of the ice) and surface movement investigations on the Biafo Glacier at this location. We discovered that the ice is almost nine-tenths of a mile thick with an average surface velocity of about 1,000 feet per year.

It is a day's walk from this camp to the top of Hispar Pass, and it is best to leave camp *before* the sun comes up. The crisp, hard snow of the early morning quickly turns to mush in the afternoon, transforming a pleasant stroll into an endless slog. The route toward the pass skirts the southern margin of Lukpe Lawo (British explorer Martin Conway's Snow Lake), revealing excellent views of Lukpe Lawo Brakk (21,630 feet). A look back over the Sim Gang provides a stunning view of Baintha Brakk, rising majestically from the glacier and dominating the scenery. This peak was the scene of Doug Scott's epic seven-day crawl down the Ogre after breaking both of his ankles while abseiling (an abseil is a rapid rappel) from the summit ridge.

Lukpe Lawo is a pristine mountain playground, prime for exploration, ski mountaineering, and some straightforward ascents of peaks in the 18,000- to 21,600-foot range. Lightweight telemark skis and boots are best suited for traveling around Lukpe Lawo; they are light enough for good cruising on the relatively flat, wide-open snow expanses, yet solid enough to allow for carving some turns on the numerous slopes surrounding the basin. Skis are also one of the best preventive measures for keeping yourself on the surface and out of snow-covered hidden crevasses.

Hispar Pass is very broad, extends for over 1 mile, and in good weather is a beautiful spot to set up camp. The pass provides amazing vistas of the peaks surrounding Lukpe Lawo and the Sim Gang, as well as the Latok Towers to the east and Hispar Glacier and Hunza Valley to the west. The safest and most straightforward descent of the pass is via a broad ramp on the north side. This route is also excellent terrain for carving a few turns if you have brought your skis. The first reasonable off-ice campsite is on the western margin of the Khani Basa Glacier where it joins the Hispar. Believe it or not, from Khani Basa to Hispar village is considered eight stages. From this camp it is best to follow the lateral moraine down and back onto the Hispar Glacier. Once down the glacier a little way, the route down to Hispar village consists of walking along the northern margin of the Hispar Glacier through some gorgeous ablation valleys with plentiful alpine flora and clearwater streams. This easy strolling is occasionally interrupted by forced crossings of four tributary glaciers (Jutmau, Taltanus, Pumarikish, and Khiang). These glacier traverses consist of groveling down very steep, loose lateral moraine slopes, traversing chaotic debris-covered ice and climbing back up very steep, lateral moraine slopes on the other side. The walk down the Hispar Glacier combines some of the best and worst hiking the Karakoram has to offer! The ablation valleys provide the location for a number of excellent, very comfortable campsites, with good views of the south wall of the Hispar Glacier and a welcome break from sleeping on snow and rocky platforms. Don't forget to enjoy the fresh rhubarb.

Hispar village is a large oasis situated on a terrace several hundred feet above the Hispar River. The easiest route to the village is via the iron-wire bridge (10 rupees per trip). Otherwise you must undertake yet another traverse across jumbled debris-covered ice on the snout of the Hispar Glacier. Once in Hispar most travelers stay at the rest house. In 1988 this building was in a bad state of repair. You can be sure that your arrival will attract a large gathering of locals in its courtyard. Basic food supplies can usually be obtained from the villagers, and we have always managed to secure some vegetables from the garden in the front yard. A couple of local men usually come by with some nice specimens of sodalite. I have found that great deals are hard to come by in Hispar, as the locals know quite well the value of their stones.

Nagar village is a long one-day or a pleasant two-day walk from Hispar (if you have porters, they will expect pay for three stages). In 1988 the locals were completing the construction of a jeep track most of the way to Hispar village. With a bit of luck you can forgo the dusty walk down the Hispar River gorge and catch a ride on a cargo jeep. If the opportunity arises, definitely stop for a cup of tea or lassi under the big willow tree beside the pond in the little oasis of Huru. Once Nagar is reached, it is relatively straightforward to hop a ride on a cargo jeep or to hike to Hunza and the Karakoram Highway.

Khapalu and the Hushe Valley

To reach the large oasis of Khapalu or the Hushe or Saltoro valleys, it is necessary to travel east from Skardu along the Indus River, then up the Shyok Valley. Jeeps leave Skardu often for Khapalu, a five- to six-hour drive and about 65 miles away; you can get a jeep at midday as easily as in the morning. To remind yourself about the vagaries of jeep travel, read about jeep riding at the beginning of "Chitral's Upper Valleys" in Chapter 4, and be ready for a wild, wooly ride. The sandy road leaves the white Skardu plain at its eastern end and follows the narrow, barren Indus gorge. At the village of Gol, 20 miles from Skardu, a bridge carries the main road to the north bank of the Indus. Just before you reach Gol (sometimes locally spelled Gole) is a large boulder field with several rocks bearing carvings of Buddhist stupas, tridents, and inscriptions in what appears to be Tibetan. A couple of miles beyond the bridge, the Shyok River joins the Indus from the east, effectively doubling the size of the Indus most seasons of the year. The road continues east along the Shyok, while the

Indus bends to the south on its way to Ladakh in India and its headwaters in Tibet.

Upriver along the Indus lie the old Balti fortress principalities of Parkutta, Tolti, and Kharmang. You may (or may not) encounter difficulty in getting south along the Indus Valley, for a checkpost is located along the Indus near its confluence with the Shyok. The disinclination to allow foreigners south of here is because the Line of Control, the disputed border with India, lies to the south (but not close to any of the three towns mentioned). At Parkutta, 8 miles south of the river confluence, an intriguing nala ascends to the west, eventually reaching the 15,050-foot Katicho La. Beyond this pass to the west lie the Deosai Plains; from Parkutta you could take a week-long walk onto the Deosai and down to Skardu via the road or the Burji La (or onward to the Astor Valley and Nanga Parbat, given a few more days).

The first, lowest 15 miles of the Shyok Valley above its junction with the Indus formerly comprised the small state of Kiris, ruled from the town of Kiris, located 3 miles beyond the river junction. Then you enter the former domain of Khapalu's raja, the largest and wealthiest principality within old Baltistan. A bridge across the Shyok takes the main road to the village of Yuu on the south bank. The road continuing east of the bridge along the north bank of the Shyok goes to Doghani, at the mouth of the Thalle Valley, and on past the village of Saling to the west side of the Hushe Valley.

East from Yuu, the main road closely parallels the south bank of the Shyok past several towns with many apricot and apple trees to Khapalu's large, well-shaded alluvial fan (8,400 feet), with its two or three small restaurants-cum-hotels on either side of the nala at the town's modest bazaar. Khapalu's fertile alluvial fan offers many sloping, tree-lined pathways to stroll. This tranquil place is one of Baltistan's loveliest green islands and is a delight to visit away from bustling, dry Skardu, whether or not you will be doing any hiking. In the midst of the oasis next to the polo field is the weathered three-story residence of Khapalu's former raja, still used by his family, an impressive but deteriorating sight here in the remote Shyok Valley.

In addition to walking about Khapalu's environs, in the early morning or late afternoon you could hike up the old jeep road onto the dry spur several hundred feet above town to the east. A climb onto this spur will provide an excellent view of the wide braided plain where the Hushe Valley debouches into the Shyok Valley. The panorama is vast and ever changing with the light at either end of the day, but don't walk up here on a summer afternoon when one of the area's characteristic windstorms sweeps sand across the vastness like a blizzard. Looking north up the Hushe Valley, you can see the massive, symmetrical peak of Masherbrum framed at the head of the valley. Northeast across the wide plain is a flat, low, level ridge hiding the Saltoro Valley, Baltistan's eastern redoubt. Above this ridge, sharp gray spires levitate high over the Saltoro. All in all, given clear weather, this view from above Khapalu is quite grand.

South of town up the Ganse Nala is the 16,500-foot Ganse La, leading to Kharmang in the Indus Valley. This is a tough, steep route and shouldn't be attempted before early July, when most of the snow will have melted. You should take a person from Khapalu to show you the way along this strenuous course and allow four days for the walk to Kharmang. Views north to Masherbrum and other peaks of the Karakoram are spectacular as you climb. This route is not listed by the Tourism Division, for it ends at Kharmang in the Indus Valley (toward but not near the disputed border with India). Just don't go south of Kharmang and you shouldn't step on any authoritarian toes. The Ganse La was crossed from Kharmang to Khapalu by the British explorer Tom Longstaff in June 1908. His Kharmang porters deserted him when snow was encountered 3,000 feet below the pass, so he and his companion Slingsby, along with their two orderlies, shouldered the loads and pushed over the pass through soft, knee-deep snow.

The road east of Khapalu follows the river along the northern base of the spur just noted. For generations, at landings hereabouts determined by the river currents, a *zuk,* the Balti-style frame raft buoyed up by inflated skins, ferried goods, stock, and people back and forth across the Shyok River to the northern riverbank at the base of the Hushe Valley. With every crossing, each sheep- or goatskin had to be reinflated with lung power by blowing into one of the bladder's leather legs. The zuk is used far less now, for bridges up- and downriver carry people and their goods to and from Khapalu. And inner tubes are replacing the inflated skins. The road along the Shyok River continues beyond the base of the spur for several miles, passing a village before reaching the town of Surmo. To the east of Surmo, the Shyok Valley floor narrows as the river turns to the south toward the Line of Control and the Nubra region of Ladakh in India. Just around the river's bend from Surmo is a jeep bridge, which can be used by those who don't want to trust the zuk. If you cross the bridge and turn north, you will be heading up the Hushe Valley as if you had crossed by raft, except that you will be miles to the east on the east bank of the braided Hushe Nala. This is one route to the Saltoro Valley and a longer, alternate route (with little to recommend it) up the Hushe Valley.

The Hushe Valley: To the Base of Masherbrum

The Hushe Valley cuts a straight swath from south to north, from just north of Khapalu to the foot of 25,660-foot Masherbrum. If you can find a jeep going to Hushe Valley or want to book one from Skardu (or possibly Khapalu), it can usually get as far as the last village of Hushe. But it is also fun to walk up the valley because the road is little used and the valley is very gentle, with an elevation rise of only about 1,500 feet in the 20 miles from its mouth to Hushe. The Hushe Valley is usually approached from the road along the north bank of the Shyok, as previously mentioned. Saling and Machilu are the first towns on the west bank of the valley. A bedbuggy rest house at Machilu is not recommended; better to pitch your tent if you stay there. Across the valley from Machilu the Saltoro River sneaks into the valley from the east between two low hills, and not far north of Machilu is a bridge across the Hushe Nala to the village of Balegaon (this bridge is a good approach to the Saltoro Valley).

The villages thin out as you ascend the Hushe Valley, but if you are walking, you can see tantalizing views of snow peaks up narrow nalas ripe for exploration. Tall poplars and the last fruit trees are miniscule next to the sheer walls rising from the east side of the valley in particular. You walk directly toward Masherbrum and have your best views of it before you come too close and it gets foreshortened and hidden behind intervening spurs.

Hushe is the last town, and although it is said to have a population of four hundred, the village isn't anything to write home about. At Hushe, in contrast to Skardu and the large bazaars, some people still wear the traditional round, peaked Balti cap called a *nhating,* made of white wool for men and black wool for women. The first jeep reached Hushe in 1980, horrifying those who had never seen vehicles before. But, according to Pat Emerson, a resident anthropologist, in only three days' time, the Hushepa ("people from Hushe"), including women and children, had gotten used to the noisy moving machine that belched smoke. In 1974 a party of American climbers and their high-altitude porters coming from the Baltoro Glacier to the north surprised the Hushepa by descending from the technical Masherbrum La east of the mountain, a pass the local men thought could not be crossed. (Don't even consider the Masherbrum La unless you have equipment to cross gaping crevasses, for it is a difficult pass.)

North of Hushe, three glaciers extend off the southern slopes of Masherbrum. From west to east, they are the Aling, Masherbrum, and Ghandagoro (or Chundugero). The Hushepa have summer pastures along all of these glaciers, and you can hire a local to show you the way to one or more of the meadows. The meadow at the Ghandagoro Glacier is called Andorrah, and to the east of Andorrah is Ghandagoro Peak, a trekking peak that you can climb in a six-day round trip from Hushe. A fourth glacier, the farthest to the east, the Chogolisa, carries the snows of Masherbrum and Chogolisa (which means "Big Hunting Place" in Balti). A pasture by this glacier is locally known as Chospah. Do some exploring up here: find your own special prominence and name it as you wish. It'll be yours forever.

The Saltoro Valleys: High Spires and Steep Slabs

Across the Hushe Nala from Machilu (on the Hushe's east bank), the Saltoro River slips out from behind a low, beige-colored ridge and empties into the Hushe River. The Saltoro River leads to some fascinating country, and if you walk (or ride) into this valley, you don't need to climb high or walk on a glacier to see sheer walls of granite 2,000 to 4,000 feet high. After the conflict between Pakistan and India over the Siachen Glacier is resolved, you will hopefully again be able to visit the two upper valleys of the Saltoro. The northern fork of the Saltoro is the Kondus Valley, while

Steep spires above the lower Saltoro Valley village of Tsino in Baltistan (photograph by John Mock).

the southern branch keeps the name Saltoro. which means "Giver of Light" in Tibetan, probably referring to the sunlight reflected from the upper valley glaciers. The mouth of the Saltoro Valley is approached most directly via the bridge from Machilu to Balegaon (this latter town is situated not far north of the Saltoro's confluence with the Hushe), as already mentioned. You could also reach the lower Saltoro by crossing the bridge across the Shyok River east of Surmo (noted in the last section) and walking north for a couple of hours. If you want to walk up either upper branch of the Saltoro Valley and perhaps explore higher on one of the local summer pastures, give yourself at least a week to do so. If you walk up, turn directly around at the last village, and return, you will need about five days. Whether you go up the Kondus or Saltoro valley, your return requires retracing your steps to Khapalu.

The main route up the lower Saltoro Valley follows the jeep road on the north side of the river. Halde, the first village on this side of the Saltoro, has a couple of stores and a bridge to the south side of the river, where you can take the flat walk south to the new Shyok bridge. Stay on the Halde side of the river if you are going up the Kondus Valley. If you will be going up the Saltoro Valley, you can either stay on the jeep road or cross the bridge at Halde to the south bank, then follow the trail east above that bank to the junction of the two rivers. The jeep road up the Saltoro Valley continues past Halde on the north side of the Saltoro River, passing through the pleasant, well-shaded towns of Tagas and Tsino (Chino, the westernmost village on the *Chulung* sheet [NI 43-4] of the U502 Map Series) to the few large estates of Brakhor, situated directly across the Saltoro River from the large village of Dansam. If you take the south-bank trail, you will be off the road and have better views of the sharp spires that kiss the sky above Tsino, but the trail is less shaded, with only the village of Paron to pass through. At Dansam (meaning "Three Rivers Meet" in Balti), the Saltoro River divides: the Kondus Valley goes northeast, and the Saltoro angles southeast. The uppermost head of each valley has a crevassed, glaciated pass leading onto the 45-mile-long Siachen ("Red Rose") Glacier.

First, a little about the upper Saltoro Valley. You can reach Dansam at the mouth of the upper Saltoro Valley by the south-bank trail or by crossing the bridge from the jeep road at the junction of the Kondus and Saltoro rivers. Dansam has many thick apricot, apple, mulberry, and poplar trees and several small stores. Just below the old covered footbridge leading to Dansam from the south-bank trail are several boulders with ancient inscriptions of Islamic, Buddhist, and Shaivite motifs, as well as the often-seen ibex. A jeep road heads up-valley as far as the toe of the Bilafond Glacier. For three hours' walk beyond Dansam village you may not encounter any clear water. Then, at the second group of homes comprising Mundik village, the dry, rocky valley is relieved by a spring and a low, flat meadow. The fairly level, U-shaped valley continues through several villages, including Seth. From Seth to the last village of Goma (two towns up), some married women wear hats made of wiry red-dyed sheep wool with a brown beaverlike tail. These chapeaux are undeniably sui generis, and the one I purchased at Seth is easily the most commented-upon hat in my Himalayan hat collection.

If these valleys do open, you may not be permitted to camp beyond Goma, the valley's uppermost village. If you can proceed beyond Goma, interesting nalas lead to the Chulung, Gyong, and Chumik glaciers, but the herds of ibex that once roamed the high country in this area have been decimated by soldiers. The strongest magnet for most hikers would be the sheer walls to the north above the Bilafond ("Butterfly") Glacier that are visible from Goma. These vertical granite walls reaching over 20,000 feet high are part of what is called the Dansam Group, composed of the peaks to the north that you have been passing since the village of Dansam. The Bilafond Glacier leads to the Bilafond Pass (circa 18,000 feet), also called the Saltoro Pass. Beyond this watershed pass, the Lolofond Glacier descends into Indian territory and flows into the middle of the giant Siachen Glacier.

The high ground near the upper reaches of the Saltoro and Kondus valleys has been the improbable arena for the world's highest war, a rarely reported conflict between Pakistan and India for control of the Siachen Glacier and the Karakoram peaks along either side of it. A Pakistani captain talking to Galen Rowell said, "We are fighting Allah and India, and Allah is winning." He could have been speaking for either side with respect to this bizarre, ill-advised war, for both forces have lost more men to avalanches, altitude sickness, the bitter cold, and other causes of death brought on by the altitude and elements than they have to the opposing side. This conflict alternately exploded and hibernated between 1984 and 1988.

More spectacular from the moment you trend north of the enormous slabs of granite at Dansam is the narrow Kondus Valley. Throughout the length of the Kondus, you are without a doubt traveling at the base of a deep, narrow canyon that could only have been chiseled out by the Creator. Towering vertical slabs are visible nearly the entire distance beyond the river junction at Dansam. A long day's walk from Dansam past Thang (called Kondus on the *Chulung* sheet) and Chogron is the last village of Karma Ding. Spires 2,000 feet and higher reach toward infinity at Karma Ding, and pinnacles on K6 to the north mimic the steep, brooding mountains in Walt Disney's *Fantasia*. The 20-mile-long Kondus Glacier, and the tributary Kaberi Glacier leading north from the Kondus toward the southern base of Chogolisa, lie along the upper reaches of this awesome valley. The Kondus Glacier was described in the preceding section "Glaciers and Dragons." For the first two days' walk up the Kondus, the theme of knife-thin peaks plays along either side of the glacier. At the head of the Kondus is Sia Kangri (24,350 feet), with its massive snowfields lying south of the Abruzzi Glacier, an upper extension of the Baltoro Glacier. Beneath Sia Kangri is the Sia La, which provides a crevassed connection across the border to the upper Siachen Glacier.

These Karakoram valleys present a remarkable landscape, but equally wonderful for those fortunate enough to have visited Baltistan's high pastures are the strong, cheerful Baltis in their brown-checked homespun, quietly conversing as they spin thread or make butter in inflated skins. The narrow canyons beneath the vertical walls of the upper Kondus and Saltoro valleys bring to mind Nick Clinch's quotation that begins the chapter. Following those lines, his next sentences read, "Gazing up at sheer walls shrouded by gray clouds, we no longer laughed at the thought of our superstitious ancestors who believed that demons and devils inhabit the highest places of the earth. The line, if any, between us and our chanting Baltis was extremely thin."

8
Kashmir

Though charm, wit and a certain arrogance are there the national trait is, undeniably, dishonesty. . . . All Kashmiris, regardless of religion, distrust one another.

John Keay, 1977

"Is there anything Your Majesty desires?"
"Only Kashmir."

Jahangir, fourth Moghul emperor,
on his deathbed, 1627

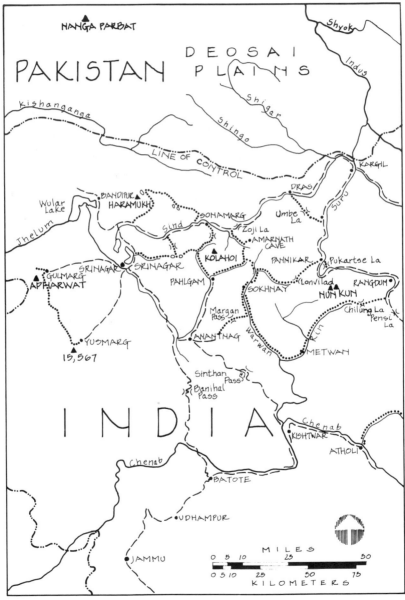

Kashmir

Kashmir's Imperial Past

Like Nepal's Kathmandu Valley, the entire Vale of Kashmir was once a large lake that drained thousands of years ago. Kashmir has been called the "pearl of the Himalaya" since the sixteenth century, when the Moghul emperors began to construct their exquisite formal gardens near the shores of Dal Lake on the west side of the valley. Although the Moghul Empire has long since faded into history, the Shalimar, Nishat, and Chashma Shahi gardens remain for our enjoyment. Each of these symmetrical gardens utilizes water from a large spring as its centerpiece. Particularly well known is the Shalimar Garden east of the lake, created for Shah Jahan in honor of his queen, Nur Mahal, the woman who inspired the Taj Mahal.

Seventy percent of the state of Jammu and Kashmir (J. and K.) is taken up by the high, Tibet-like region of Ladakh (covered in Chapter 9) adjoining the vale to the east, and only part of the remainder of J. and K. lies within the Kashmir Valley. This chapter discusses the famous valley, with an emphasis on trekking possibilities in its verdant, well-known, and often-rained-upon tributaries to the east, and the flower-covered hiking routes over several passes that lead from these monsoon-embraced regions to dry Ladakh.

The oval, 85-mile-long Kashmir Valley (or Vale of Kashmir) is the largest valley within the Great Himalaya Range. Most of the vale's inhabitants are agriculturalists, even if the newly arrived tourist, besieged by touts, believes that the majority of Kashmiris earn their living in the tourist trade. When Europeans began to discover Kashmir, a law was passed that still remains, forbidding foreigners to own land in the valley. Initially, Westerners were not even permitted to winter in the vale. Undeterred, British vacationers originated the idea of constructing extravagant houses atop crudely made barges on the wide canals of the Jhelum River and on 5-mile-long Dal Lake. Thus was born the thriving modern phenomenon of houseboats, where many present-day visitors stay. But Westerners have not been the only people attracted to the vale. For hundreds of years Hindu pilgrims from the populous down-country lowlands have flocked to the Vale of Kashmir for the annual pilgrimage, or yatra, to the tall ice cone at Amarnath Cave believed to be a lingam, a representation of the god Shiva's phallus.

Kashmir's largest town is Srinagar. Webbed by canals and cut by the meandering Jhelum River, Srinagar is said to have been created by order of King Ashoka in the third century B.C. The more recent history of the vale is as colorful as its plane trees in autumn. Islamic dynasties of Kashmiris, Moghuls, and Afghans succeeded each other until 1819, when the Sikh rulers of the Punjab interceded to calm a chaotic situation resulting from Afghan rule. For the next twenty-seven years, Kashmir was administered by Sikh governors. In 1846, the British, desirous of not overextending their direct control in the more remote mountainous regions, signed two treaties with Gulab Singh, the Dogra (a large Hindu ethnic group) Raja, or ruler, of Jammu, involving substantial payment on his part to the British government. The Treaty of Lahore ceded Jammu and Kashmir to the British from the Sikhs. The area ceded included all of greater Kashmir from the Chitral border east to Lahoul and Spiti, including the Gilgit River watershed, Baltistan, and Ladakh. A week later the Treaty of Amritsar recognized Gulab Singh, a Sikh, as Maharaja of Jammu and Kashmir. More recently, the predominantly Muslim Kashmir Valley has been incorporated into the state of Jammu and Kashmir.

The Way to Kashmir

Daily flights on large airbuses fly north-northwest from New Delhi to Srinagar. You may have no other option than flying as long as the situation in the state of Punjab directly south of J. and K. remains unsettled. Sikh separatists have attacked buses crossing the Punjab. Foreigners are sometimes barred from entering Punjab altogether because of the activities of these militants. If you fly to Srinagar, you will land at the airport about 10 miles west of town, where a large sign proclaims: Welcome to the Happy Valley. Soldiers packing automatic weapons, however, lend an ironic note to the signboard.

If Punjab is open and you have the time, go to Kashmir by land. You can always return by air, but if you go north by land you'll get a good look at the route in and have an appreciation for the remoteness of the vale. You can take a direct bus from New Delhi to Srinagar from the Interstate Bus Terminal on Qudsia Marg in the old city of Delhi. Before going there, you should check at either the Government Tourist Office at 88 Janpath in New Delhi or the Kashmir State Government Tourist Office in the Chanderlok Building at 36 Janpath. The state government tourist office in particular will be able to tell you the best bus to take.

It is always possible to book an overnight sleeping berth out of New Delhi from the seating quota that is set aside for tourists. See "New Delhi" in Chapter 3 for the simple procedure involved in getting train reservations from the tourist quota. You will want to get a ticket for Jammu on the Jammu Mail, number "33 Up." This train leaves Delhi every night at 8:55 P.M., arriving the next morning at Jammu Tawi Station. Be very careful with your belongings as soon as you get on this train. Keep an eye on your gear and perhaps put it on your sleeping berth with you, because the bunks allotted to tourists on the train are always the same ones and thievery has occurred here. Directly on the platform of the train station at Jammu Tawi is the booking office of the Jammu and Kashmir Road Transport Corporation. Their buses leave right from the station as soon as they are booked and loaded. You may also go from Jammu to Srinagar by taxi, booking a single seat or the entire vehicle.

Your bus or taxi will quickly leave behind the vast Punjab plains and enter the foothills of the Pir Panjal Range for the twisting, 189-mile trip to Srinagar. These mountains form the southern and western boundaries of the Kashmir Valley, extending in a northwest-to-southeast direction for almost 200 miles. The Pir Panjal parallels the Great Himalaya Range from

the disputed border with Pakistan northeast of Srinagar near the Kishanganga River all the way east to Chamba District on the Ravi River. You
will be crossing the ridges and spurs of this range until your bus descends
into the Kashmir Valley. Before the road to the vale was paved, the overnight stop en route to Kashmir was the village of Batote (5,000 feet) on a
scenic ridge sprinkled with deodar trees between the Tawi and Chenab
rivers. Nowadays, your bus will pause at Batote only for the lunch stop.
A side road leads from Batote to the large town of Kishtwar, the trailhead
for treks north into Ladakh's Zanskar region or south into Chamba. If you
are going to Kishtwar, inquire at Jammu Tawi's rail station for bus information.

From Batote the bus descends 2,500 feet to the deep Chenab River
gorge before climbing a mile up to the Banihal tunnel. When you emerge
from the tunnel, a magnificent sight greets you: the Great Himalaya Range
to the northeast forms a white horizon, while deeper green ridges rise from
chartreuse rice fields below. A sign, Welcome to the Happy Valley, flashes
by, and you begin descending into the Vale of Kashmir. Once on the valley
floor, the bus reaches level ground for the first time since leaving Jammu,
and for the 40 remaining miles to Srinagar, along a road often bordered
with poplars, you feel as if you are flying. If you arrive in late summer,
the air near the town of Pampur will be redolent with the fragrance of
saffron from the nearby fields.

Within twenty-four hours after leaving New Delhi, you will arrive at
the Tourist Reception Center in Srinagar. As you will be tired from the
ride to Srinagar, it is better to find lodging immediately and return to the
reception center the following morning if you need any information.

Srinagar

Do note that the Tourist Reception Center's complex holds all offices
relating to tourism in the valley, including one office at the left rear specifically for trekking and mountaineering. This office sells two inexpensive,
locally produced trekking maps (if they are not out of stock) called *Trekking
Route Map of Jammu and Kashmir*. The maps are at a scale of 1:250,000
(4 miles to the inch) but unfortunately do not have contour lines, thanks
to fusty government regulations. Sheet Number One covers all of the
Kashmir Valley east to Kishtwar and the Suru Valley, and Sheet Number
Two covers most of Zanskar (discussed in Chapter 9). If you don't have
the U502 Series maps, these two maps can be extremely helpful. If you
do have the U502 maps, these locally produced sheets can still provide
good information because they indicate recently built roads and show presently used common names for some places.

The U502 map sheets depicting the regions covered in this chapter are
as follows: *Srinagar* (NI 43-6) covers the northern part of the vale, including Gulmarg, Wular Lake, and Haramukh. *Kargil* (NI 43-7) covers the
Sind Valley, Zoji La, Pahlgam, Amarnath Cave (unmarked), and Lonvilad
Gali Pass. *Punch* (NI 43-10) is useful only for the Pir Panjal Range on the

southwest perimeter of the vale. *Anantnag* (NI 43-11) covers most of Warwan Valley, Kishtwar, Chilung La, Pensi La, and most of the route to the Umasi La.

Visitors to Srinagar usually stay on one of the 1,500 houseboats that are docked on Dal Lake (several hundred tout-filled yards from the Tourist Reception Center); Nagin Lake, a few miles to the north; and various interconnecting canals in different directions. The classes of houseboats are Super Delux, A, B, C, and D (meaning *dhunga,* a smaller type of boat). Prices theoretically are fixed but can be adjusted with bargaining, particularly if you are not looking for accommodation in the busy summer season. The managers of most houseboats will usually quote prices based on full board, and you can negotiate downward if you are not eating every meal on the boat. As I'm a person who prefers dry land and does not appreciate the matter of getting a *shikara* (a small taxi-boat) to the houseboat or being pestered by boat-borne memento-floggers, when I have my druthers I stay at one of the many hotels in town (like the Tibet Guest House) before heading for the hills (as fast as possible).

While you are deciding which area to trek in, you can take several interesting walks in and about Srinagar. The Shankaracharya Hill, also called the Takht-i-Suleman ("Throne of Solomon"), rises 1,000 feet high, just east of the Tourist Reception Center and south of Dal Lake. Trails up the hill lead from near the reception center and from the Boulevard along Dal Lake. At the tree-shaded top, you have an excellent view of Srinagar, Dal Lake, and much of the vale. The small stone Shiva temple on the crest of the hill dates from the sixth century. Shankaracharya Hill is a pleasant place to stroll up and escape the busy city.

To the north of Dal Lake are the walls of Hari Parbat fortress on the low Sharika Hill. It is said that this hill grew after the goddess Parvati dropped a stone on an offending demon. A wall around the hill below Hari Parbat was constructed by Hindustan's ruler Akbar the Great for an Afghan governor in the sixteenth century. As you approach Hari Parbat, you will pass extensive orchards of almond and fruit trees. Sporadically you may hear loud shrieks and shouting from the depths of the orchards, but resist any temptation to intercede in what you may think is assault and battery. The owners of the trees hire men to shout at birds raiding the unpicked fruit.

At Hari Parbat you are close to the old city of Srinagar, much of which was razed in the earthquake of 1885. As with Kathmandu, Srinagar's older sections appear to be imminently ready to collapse, and many roofs support healthy stands of grass. Srinagar probably tops Kathmandu in its collection of mongrel dogs, although they are mostly in the old city, not near the posh houseboats. A stroll through the old city's back streets and passageways can make for a most interesting morning walk. The pagodalike venerable Shah Hamdan Mosque rests on the bank of the Jhelum River. Be certain to remove your shoes before entering to admire the papier-mâché work herein. The mosque itself is handsomely constructed of wood. The Sri Pratap Singh Museum (closed Wednesdays) in Lal Mandi has some fine examples of early Kashmiri artwork. The Srinagar Library is next door. The area called Lal Mandi lies on the left bank of the Jhelum River; to reach it, you will have to take a small ferry across the river or walk well out of your way to a bridge.

Kashmir is known both for the quality and variety of its handicrafts and for the persistence with which they are pressed upon you by guileful salesmen, some of whom paddle about in boats and others of whom follow you down the street. (With more difficulty, the cultured Kashmiri can also be found, like the man who quoted the nineteenth-century English essayist John Ruskin to me as we talked.) You can see finely carved woodwork, leatherwork, embroidery, papier-mâché, carpets, and silver. Be particularly cautious about purchasing anything said to be an antique. Kashmir has been heavily touristed for many years, and it is generally accepted that virtually all antiquities, from coins to Yarkandi shawls, have long since left the valley. Examine the wares offered by several people to get an idea of the qualities and price ranges available; hard bargaining will be in order if you become interested in anything substantial. Because many of the items for sale are made in outlying villages and sold by middlemen, you will find better prices outside Srinagar at the craftspeople's villages. You can reach other towns in the vale by renting a bicycle along the boulevard south of Dal Lake or by taking one of the local buses from the depot in the middle of Srinagar near the Lala Rukh Hotel.

Gulmarg and the Pir Panjal

Gulmarg, the "Meadow of Flowers," was discovered as a tourist destination by the British in the nineteenth century. Prior to that, Moghul emperors vacationed in the Gulmarg area. Today Gulmarg is reached by bus or taxi from Srinagar. If you go by bus, try to get one that goes all the way to Gulmarg, not to Tangmarg, 6 miles by road or 4 miles by bridle path below Gulmarg. Lying some 31 miles west of Srinagar at 8,500 feet, Gulmarg is exquisitely situated in a pine-surrounded basin of the Pir Panjal. It sports a golf course, a nearby tourist office, and a ski hill with several ski lifts and a rope tow.

Gulmarg makes an excellent base for trekking in the northern Pir Panjal Range. Nanga Parbat can be seen to the north from several viewpoints, including Khilanmarg, west and over 1,500 feet up the forested hillside from Gulmarg. From a distance, the Pir Panjal appears somewhat rounded, but when you are actually walking up its slopes, you will find that its smoother peaks rise above evergreen-clad slopes that seem quite equal in steepness to those of the main Himalaya. West and slightly south of Gulmarg is the 13,592-foot peak of Apharwat. This peak is, however, near the disputed India-Pakistan border, called the Line of Control, so check with the tourist office in Gulmarg before you set out for it, or you may meet a perturbed and well-armed member of the Indian Army along the way.

To the south of Gulmarg, a pleasant trek would be to walk up the Ferozepur Nala and beyond to the hamlets of Danwas, Tejjan, and Tosamaidan. For this you will need a porter who knows the way because many stock trails intersect the route. The walk from Gulmarg to Tosamai-dan is considered to be three stages long (see "Stages" in Chapter 3). You may return by way of Riyar and Khag villages or continue south toward Sunset Peak (15,567 feet) and then walk into the foothills along the Romushi Nala to Yusmarg, where a road and bus service connect with Srinagar.

Kashmiris like to trek with ponies as beasts of burden. Using ponies is not always a simple matter, however. For one thing, what begins as a low-key trek can rapidly get out of control unless you are careful to limit the size of your entourage. For another, ponies promised may not in fact materialize. During the busy summer season, many visitors may be riding ponies in such places as Pahlgam or Sonamarg. It is not comforting to find yourself stranded the first night out without your gear and food supplies because the horses have never actually left with them. Said one agent to a peeved trekking-group leader, in attempting an explanation: "Sorry, sahib, not enough horses."

The Sind Valley

Considered by many to be the most beautiful of Kashmir's side valleys, the Sind is also the access route to the Zoji La, the pass crossed by the road to Ladakh. Buses leave from the Tourist Reception Center in Srinagar daily for Sonamarg, 52 miles away in the midst of the Sind Valley. Located northeast of Srinagar, this alpine valley was thoroughly enjoyed by early travelers to Ladakh: "The Sind Valley, which I was now entering, is perhaps the most beautiful valley in Kashmir . . . a perfect paradise" (Sir Francis Younghusband). "One long succession of grass glades and fir trees . . . a wild fairy loveliness" (M. L. A. Gompertz, British traveler and writer). "It would be difficult to imagine more ideal conditions for starting off . . . the glory of the valley is its trees" (Kermit Roosevelt, brother of Teddy). The Sind is not only extremely beautiful, but from it you can leave for or return from some of the best trekking areas to be found in Kashmir.

An excellent base for trekking is Sonamarg (8,990 feet), the "Golden Meadow." In the summer months this meadow area is visited for the day by many down-country tourists from New Delhi and elsewhere. Sonamarg has a small, touristy bazaar and some seasonal restaurants, and the tourist center here is a well of activity with people booking horseback rides or rest houses for the night. Pastel saris trimmed with gold shimmer in the daytime breeze, and many of the gaily dressed city people take the 3-mile horseback ride west, then south, to the Thajiwas Glacier, often led by a tall, somber Gujar. The tourist officer in Sonamarg (who has been G. R. Khan for many years) is at the center during the day and can be of excellent assistance if you have questions or would like to store some saman for several days while you are trekking. Tell him the Angrezi Gujar sent you, but it has been some years now since that lean, lanky nomad has wandered by.

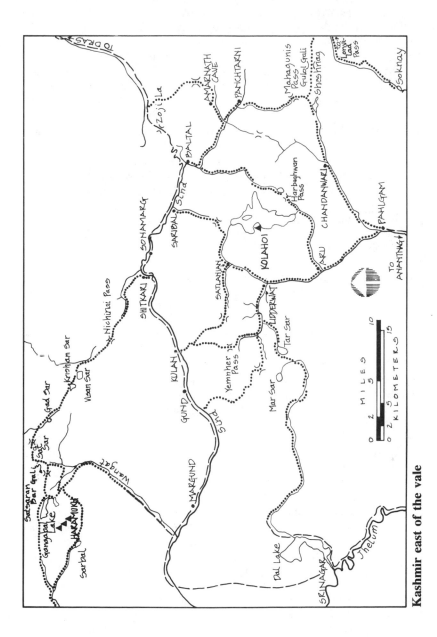

Kashmir east of the vale

Sonamarg to the Vale via Gangabal Lake

A fine walk west of Sonamarg is to cross the Nichinai Pass (13,390 feet) to Gangabal Lake. As always, you would do well to have a local (perhaps recruited at Sonamarg) to accompany you. To reach the trailhead, go 2 miles down-valley from Sonamarg toward Srinagar to the bridge below the tightly clustered houses of Shitkari village, where the road crosses the Sind River. Across the river from this small village, begin walking on the true right bank to the lakes called Krishan Sar and Vishan Sar, and beyond to Gangabal Lake near Haramukh, the highest peak in the vicinity of the Kashmir Valley. From the Shitkari bridge, follow the trail up the ridge into a pine forest where you have your last views of Sonamarg. Keep climbing the ridge 5,000 feet up, mostly through forest, to the barren Nichinai Pass. The trail is well used in the summer and easy to stay with. Two- and three-house summer settlements appear along the way, and you pass encampments of many Gujar, Bakarwal, or Chopan herders in the forests east of the pass.

West of the Nichinai, many animals graze in a large grassy basin sloping gently northward to the Kishanganga River (but don't head toward the river because you would be going toward the disputed Line of Control). The western slopes of the Nichinai Pass will have patches of snow into July, attesting to Kashmir's heavy winter snowfall. Here you are at the head of a tributary of the Kishanganga; to the south lie needle peaks and small glaciers. Walk downward, then angle up to the west across the valley floor to reach two as-yet-unseen lakes. Vishan Sar ("Vishnu's Lake") is found at just over 12,000 feet and is slightly larger than Krishan Sar ("Krishna's Lake") at 12,500 feet. From Krishan Sar, the trail toward Gangabal continues via a zigzag route northwest up the near ridge. Do not take the southwestern trail fork (marked on the U502 map), for it goes up a feeder stream into a narrow cirque that may be snowy. Traveling alone, I took this route and ended up camping on snow, then retracing my steps back to Krishan Sar. Rather, cross the ridge northwest of Krishan Sar, descend to Gad Sar, cross a snow bridge, then rise again to a high ridge that holds the Satsaran Lake, where you have excellent views northward. The trail goes south and crosses the Satsaran Bar Pass and then continues south, then west to Zajibal Pass, where you have a clear view of Gangabal Lake 2,000 feet below, with 16,872-foot Haramukh above.

With technical gear, you could attempt one or more of Haramukh's three principal summits, but walkers will be content to rest by Gangabal Lake. A hundred feet below Gangabal is a smaller lake, Nund Kol, also with excellent shoreline views of Haramukh. The trail from Nund Kol leads 2 miles down to Trunkhal, a camping place at the edge of the forest. Twelve miles down the Wangat Valley from Gangabal via the direct route to the Sind is Narang Nag, a spring. Ruins here date from the time of Ashoka. At Narang Nag you may find a vehicle to take you to the main Sind Valley.

For this alpine trek over the Nichinai to Gangabal Lake and down the Wangat Valley (or the reverse route), you will need about seven days. Alternate routes to Haramukh can also be taken. One good approach route begins by taking a bus from Srinagar to Bandipur. At Bandipur change vehicles or walk to Erin village (4 miles away), and hike up the Erin Valley. At Ishrantar village the valley divides, and you must take either the northern fork, keeping Haramukh to your right, or the southern valley to Sarbal Lake, south of Haramukh. Either way you can get around Haramukh peak to reach Gangabal Lake.

The alpine hills of Kashmir, its "pearls," be they the Pir Panjal or the foothills of the Great Himalaya Range, are extensively populated in the summer months by nomadic herders. Most are Gujars or Bakarwals, but some of the families are Chopan, a smaller ethnic group. Gujars and Bakarwals are found from southern Chitral southeast to the Sutlej River, hundreds of miles away, but most roam south of Nanga Parbat in the hills bordering Kashmir's vale. The Gujars usually herd horses, cattle, and water buffalo; the Bakarwals, sheep and goats. Some herd their own animals, but most care for those of other people, using traditional grazing rights handed down over generations. The differences between Gujars and Bakarwals are indistinguishable to us foreigners. They are tall, lean people, colored like milk coffee, and often often use *khol,* a black coloring, around their eyes. They speak their own languages, which are not understood by Kashmiris. Women wear gold jewelry in their noses and ears, but their most unique feature is painstakingly braided hair. Scores of long braids hang from beneath an embroidered cap, and each braid of oiled hair is composed of three black locks. The men often put henna in their beards, and many have the wise, dignified demeanor of those who have long worked in the hills. Their retinues include pack horses (everything of size is carried by animals), chickens, and chained, ferocious dogs. Like all nomads, the Gujars are usually friendly and have kindly offered me milk or yoghurt for my wheatcakes as I, or they, passed by on the trail.

The Paths to Amarnath Cave

The yatra (pilgrimage) on foot to Amarnath Cave, now considered one of the holiest naturally occurring shrines of the Hindu faith, has continued annually for little more than a hundred years. Extending up 130 feet, Amarnath Cave is high and shallow. Inside the large opening, behind an open-gated iron fence, an underground trickle of water emerges 10 feet up from a small cleft in the sedimentary rock and freezes as it drips to form a tall, smooth cone of ice. This cone was originally called "the formless form," but it has come to have another symbolism. The ice figure is believed to be a lingam, a manifestation of the god Shiva's phallus. On the full moon of the month called Sawan, in July or August, tens of thousands of pilgrims, called yatris, walk from Pahlgam to view the ice phallus and make offerings of food, money, sweets, and garlands of flowers before it.

This unique place is well worth the short trek, but timing is important. The main pilgrimage takes place at the full moon of Sawan, but it is best to visit the cave from mid-June to mid-July, when the trails should be sufficiently clear of snow to be passable and when the seasonal tented inns providing shelter and food are already set up. Also, the ice stalagmite is tallest then, for by pilgrimage time or later the warmer summer air may have melted the ice to a mere foot in height (despite any claims you may read about the lingam waxing and waning with the moon).

Two routes lead to Amarnath Cave in the Amrivati Valley, a small tributary of the Sind Valley. The traditional path is from Pahlgam in the Liddar Valley, 27 miles away over a 14,000-foot pass. In addition, since 1971 a little-publicized but very serviceable 8-mile track that is now paved has connected the cave with the summer settlement of Baltal in the Sind Valley. Baltal (9,500 feet) lies 8 miles up-valley from Sonamarg (described in the preceding section) past the Indian Army's Mountaineering School in a meadow-covered, forest-walled bend of the valley at the foot of the well-traveled switchbacks leading to the Zoji La. In summer you will be able to rent a pony for the short yatra at Baltal or at Domel, 2 miles beyond Baltal. From Baltal, the wide trail climbs somewhat over 3,000 feet to reach the ice pillar of Amarnath in the narrow Amrivati Valley. This makes a very handy approach. Both the path from Baltal and the longer trail to the cave from Pahlgam follow steep gorges with idyllic meadows of wildflowers framed beneath snow peaks. If you trek within three weeks before the yatra, you will be able to buy meals along the way at the numerous temporary tented inns already on the pitch. Finding the way on either of these well-traveled trails to Amarnath is an easy matter, like circling Mt. Kailas in Tibet, or walking on any of Garhwal's yatra routes.

The traditional pilgrimage to Amarnath Cave from Pahlgam in the Liddar Valley is taken in four stages, each a day's journey. (Pahlgam itself is discussed in the next section.) The yatris make the return trip in two days.

Stage 1. Pahlgam to Chandanwari (9,500 feet, the roadhead), 8 miles. This is a jeep road, but most people walk. The way is gentle, leading northeast up the U-shaped East Liddar Valley to this small bazaar and meadow camping place. (An alternate route to the cave leads north up the side valley at Chandanwari and branches into two possible tracks about 5 miles beyond Chandanwari. Nowhere along the way would you find any facilities, or people, for that matter, except an occasional Gujar family. Consult the *Kargil* sheet (NI 43-7) of the U502 Series or Sheet Number One of the trekking route map available in Srinagar for these alternate routes.)

Stage 2. Chandanwari to Shesh Nag (12,200 feet), 7 miles. The road becomes a path leading up the meadow-blanketed valley. Except for one steep zigzag section, the trail is not particularly taxing. Shesh Nag is a glacially fed lake with an opaque blue-green color. A *nag* (serpent) named Janakrani is said to dwell beneath the waters of the lake. South of Shesh Nag are three peaks composed of visibly striated rock similar to the type seen across from Amarnath Cave. Actually, the camping grounds where many people stop are before Shesh Nag at Zojipal or just above Shesh Nag at Wavjan. At Wavjan, a side trail heads easterly to the 15,000-foot Gulol Gali, a good route to the upper Warwan Valley that is described below in the section on the Lonvilad Gali.

Stage 3. Shesh Nag to Panchtarni (11,500 feet), 8 miles. This stage (more strenuous for those who haven't been trekking) takes you past rich green meadows and over 14,435-foot Mahagunis Pass. As you climb the pass, you can smile at signs with encouraging remarks like "Every step is closer to God." At Panchtarni ("Five Springs") campground, Shiva is said to have performed the Tandava Nritya, the "Dance of Destruction." Going east from Panchtarni up the main stream will take you off the pilgrimage route to the head of the valley. A level plain on this pleasant detour reaches gentle alluvial scree fans across from falling glaciers and 16,000-foot peaks.

Stage 4. Panchtarni to Amarnath Cave (13,300 feet), 4 miles. The path leads along the nearly level valley floor to the Amrivati stream diverging northward. Less than a mile along, above the stream's true right bank, is the high opening of Amarnath Cave. The pilgrims reach the cave on the early morning of the fourth day, before the evening of the full moon, called Shravana Poornima. [Note that you can walk up the right (north) bank of this small valley following a route, poorly marked if at all, to a pass that leads you down outside of the Kashmir Valley not far to the east of the Zoji La. Arthur Neve claims to have discovered this route in 1904 and makes the way sound rather sporting. Good luck if you give it a go.]

On the day the yatra procession arrives, both cave and trail are awash with streams of humanity. Outside the cave, the yatris cleanse themselves in the snow-fed Amrivati stream, while within some of the packed multitudes scrape a white calcium substance, a *vibuti* or blessed dust, from the walls. To the left of the ice lingam behind an iron fence is another lower ice formation called Shiva's Tears, where the pilgrims also worship and leave offerings. The crush of yatris is so great that the army must closely guide the proceedings with *lathi* (a long stick) and lung power.

This route from Pahlgam to the holy cave is taken each year by over thirty thousand people on the official days of the yatra. They all follow the Chhari Sahib, the person carrying the gold-plated rod of authority, the emblem of Shiva. A vivid cross-section of India's many-faceted clans and social classes trudge, and in a few cases are carried, along the path from Pahlgam to the cave and back. Foreigners are very welcome to participate, but if you consider going, please understand that you will be only a small part of a vast multitude. You must follow the itinerary of the pilgrimage or go before or after it. No one may precede the Chhari Sahib, and soldiers of the Indian Army are present to assist people and maintain order. Personal privacy is nonexistent during the yatra. Rarely, however, will you have the opportunity to be part of such a vivid procession of people, rich and poor, accompanied by ash-daubed sadhus, both *asali* and *nakali* (real and ersatz). A widely copied advisory for all yatris is published by the government: *"Precautions: In view of the cold weather conditions and the hazardous mountain journey, the intending tourists-cum-pilgrims are advised to be fully equipt with heavy woolens, raincoats, umbrellas, waterproof shoes, walking sticks, torches (flashlights), a thermos containing hot tea or coffee, and tents for shelter. The yatris will have to walk on snow."*

Three weeks before the Sawan full moon, I walked from Sonamarg to

A sadhu from Madras at the ice lingam *in Amarnath Cave, Kashmir.*

Baltal, ate eggs and biscuits purchased from a lone vendor, then continued to within 3 miles of the cave before stopping for the night. The next morning at the cave I met a vacationing Californian and a sadhu from Madras who had been walking up the Pahlgam trail together. The man from Madras had voluntarily left the engineering profession to pursue the life of a wandering religious renunciant. We all wanted to stay in the holy place, but since the high roof of the cave dripped water, we needed to select our sleeping spots carefully. As I cooked parathas for us, the kind, grave sadhu studied my new MSR multifuel stove with a practiced eye, then pointed and said liltingly in his excellent English, "This is all old technology. Only this one part I do not know, for it is new." His words still echo when I look at his photograph: a slim, white-bearded man dressed in white *dhoti* cloth (a dhoti resembles a sarong that passes between the legs) with a grey cotton blanket over his shoulders, standing barefoot on the ice next to the tall ice lingam. He, the Californian, several other sadhus, and myself were the only people sleeping in the holy cave that night.

Pahlgam, the Liddar Valley, and Trails to the Sind Valley

Buses leave several times daily for Pahlgam from the Tourist Reception Center in Srinagar. Pahlgam village, 60 miles from Srinagar and 7,000 feet high in the green, pine-cloaked Liddar Valley, is the starting point for the Amarnath yatra, described above, but other treks can be started here as well. From Pahlgam you can cross to the Sind Valley or the main Vale of Kashmir on foot by means of several routes. Each of these walks begins in the Liddar Valley, then follows one of several variations. These are some of the most popular trekking routes in Kashmir and the entire Himalaya outside of Nepal. Several of these courses will be mentioned here, but other paths are marked on the available maps. If you follow one of the undescribed less-traveled routes, you won't see many trekkers and will be taking a great walk that "isn't in the guide books yet."

The town of Pahlgam (often spelled Pahalgam) is larger than Sonamarg, with a bazaar and numerous hotels scattered about. At the lower end of town is a sign reading Galloping of Horses in the Main Market is Prohibited, while higher up in the main part of town a lean Bakarwal might stride beneath a white banner that proclaims: For the First Time in Pahalgam, Softy Ice Cream. Check with the tourist officer in town if you need any local information or to make reservations for any rest houses in the area. You can take a short day walk from Pahlgam following a pony trail into the hills 3 miles east of town to the meadow of Bhai Saran (7,500 feet), offering a fine valley panorama. If you want to camp, you could continue on 7 miles farther to 12,000-foot Tuliyan Lake.

The Liddar River is the principal conduit for the various trails north to the Sind Valley. A pleasant road through the lower valley follows the east bank of the stream, and there you are very apt to meet Gujars, European couples, Delhi walas on foot or horseback, or a local school or university trekking group or mountaineering team. The first 7 miles, to Aru, are along the nearly level road, and much of the area is wooded. Aru is becoming an offshoot of Pahlgam with a new hotel and more lodges being built. Aru is also the site of the Jawahar Mountaineering and Skiing Institute.

East from Aru, you can walk up a side trail along the Armiun Valley beneath Kolahoi (17,800 feet), the highest peak along the east rim of the Vale of Kashmir. If you keep going up the Armiun Valley (a local guide is recommended, for this route can be tricky), you will reach Arampatri (also called Armiun, at 11,970 feet), where Gujar huts are found beneath steep hills to the north and south. South from Arampati a trail leads to the East Liddar Valley near Pahlgam. But if you continue northeast along the main Armiun nala, you'll cross the 13,200-foot Harbaghwan Pass, then descend to the lake called Har Nag. The valley trail below Har Nag takes you in a little over a day past the paved trail to Amarnath to Baltal in the Sind Valley.

From Aru the main trail up the West Liddar Valley takes you past Gujar huts through forests and meadows to Lidderwat (8,950 feet), once a tranquil meadow where British functionaries on holiday relaxed at the still-standing, but rather run-down, rest house (bookable with the tourist officer in Pahlgam). Teahouses are now being thrown together on Lidderwat's once-untrammeled meadow. First, a quick look at the main Lidder Valley up from here, then a brief mention of several hikes you can take up the large tributary valley to the west of Lidderwat.

At Lidderwat the main valley jogs slightly toward the east, and a pleasant trail follows above the right bank as the river ascends through a mixed forest, where you may possibly sight a family of monkeys. Five miles from Lidderwat is the Gujar encampment of Satlanjan. At Satlanjan a side valley leads northward and branches into two upper nalas, each of which offers routes that go past high lakes, over passes, and far down into the Sind Valley below Sonamarg. Above Satlanjan the Liddar Valley rises gently for several miles until you reach the mouth of the Kolahoi Glacier, which descends from the northern slopes of Kolahoi. Most groups that come up to the glacier from Satlanjan make this a day hike, walking from and returning to Satlanjan in an easy day. You can get a better view of the summit of Kolahoi if you stroll up the slope anywhere just down-valley from the mouth of the glacier to the north of the Liddar's uppermost waters. There you'll more clearly see the sharp, pyramidlike peak, with its horizontal strata alternating with layers of snow.

The first time I came here, I was alone and camped in a grassy place beneath a large overhanging rock that offered some shelter. Several years later, the same spot was covered with sheep dung, indicating how much more use the pastures were then getting from the increasingly large herds of sheep and goats. If you have the freedom to choose your own route, you could climb the ridge on the northern side of the valley. Following the steep meadow up the ridge for 3,000 feet takes you to a 14,000- foot pass that leads to the Sind Valley town of Saribal. Saribal is 4,500 feet below the level of the pass and 5 miles up-valley from Sonamarg. Whether or not you climb the pass from the Liddar Valley (as I enjoyed doing on the first trek), a walk of 1,000 feet or so up from the valley floor gives you a superb, close-in view of Kolahoi and a remarkable perspective on the Kolahoi Glacier as it snakes its way down the mountain's precipitous rock slopes. This glacier resembles a writhing dragon that breathes, not fire, but the freezing headwaters of the Liddar River.

Back down-valley at Liddarwat, the Sekiwas stream valley descends from the west. You can walk up this side valley from Liddarwat and return later in the day, or you can keep going up and cross a pass into the Sind Valley, or another pass leading into the main Vale of Kashmir. Be ready to ford two rapidly flowing streams within the first few hours if you head this way. The first tributary leading south 4 miles upstream at a fork called Dandabari leads to Tar Sar Lake, which is separated from another lake, Mar Sar, by a ridge. As you cross the ridge into the Dagwan Valley, you enter Dachigam National Park, 55 square miles in area. You should not enter the park unless you have a permit from the chief wildlife warden in Srinagar (check with the Tourist Reception Center in Srinagar for the place where you can get the permit).

Beyond Dandabari, up the main Sekiwas nala, you may continue along north of the stream through well-grazed meadows. The sheep and goats you'll see hereabouts in Kashmir's meadows are so used to humans that if you hold out your hand, they will probably come to you thinking that you are offering salt. The place called Sekiwas is a stream junction in the flat meadow. You can follow the near, east, side of the stream to the north to reach the 13,300-foot Yemnher Pass in the low point of the ridge about 3 miles north of Sekiwas. This pass leads down near the Sind Valley town of Kulan, 9 miles below Sonamarg. Once you descend steeply from the pass to the lake and pastures below, you may have difficulty finding the trail down to the main valley because the meadows here are so extensive. If you have trouble and are without a local, ask a herder to show you the way to the trail. He may well delegate the job to his son.

At Sekiwas, you could also ford the main Sekiwas stream and follow the Zajmarg Valley, which leads to the southwest, then angles westerly. Like most upper valleys in Kashmir, these high meadows are apt to be under snow until well into July. The 12,600-foot pass at the upper reaches of Zajmarg barely rises at all from the valley floor. The fun comes on the steep descent to the north, which may have to be made by digging your heels into a steep snowfield. Below the pass, the valley descends in steps down to the floor of the Sind Valley.

The ridge area between the Liddar and Sind valleys has other picture-book lakes and passes as well. The best way to pick a path through the meadow-strewn byways is to have a good map before you reach the trailhead and to hire a local to accompany you.

The Passes from Kashmir to Ladakh

The routes discussed below are described from north to south. They range from the road over the low Zoji La, to the popular Lonvilad Gali at the head of the Warwan Valley, to the high, glaciated Chilung and Umasi passes. Walking from the green meadows of Kashmir across the Great Himalaya Range into the higher, dry reaches of the Suru Valley in the Balti region of western Ladakh or its southerly Buddhist neighbor, the Zanskar District to the south (or hiking these routes in reverse) can make for a wonderful trek. But be sure to carry enough food if you go and, as always, walk with a local who can ease your way and take the mystery out of route finding.

The Zoji La

The principal pass between Kashmir and Ladakh, though no longer a good one for trekkers, has always been the 11,580-foot Zoji La. For centuries, the low Zoji La was the only well-used trade route to cross the Himalayan ranges between the path up the Hunza Valley in the Karakoram Range to the northwest and the trail up the Sutlej Valley 400 miles southeast in the Central Himalaya. The pass is not high, and experienced mail runners once crossed it year round, but it is completely snowed in for five, six, or more months of the year. Now that the road has been built, only the Gujars and Bakarwals with their herds cross the Zoji La on foot, except in spring before the road has been cleared.

The road across Zoji La was built in 1960 and begins its ascent near Baltal in the Sind Valley. The route zigzags up steep, avalanche-prone slopes that have to be plowed out and regraded yearly. As you climb, you have a postcard view south along the beginning of the Amarnath trail, which branches off from the meadow- and forest-carpeted valley leading to Har Nag and the Harbaghwan Pass near Kolahoi. Then the road angles away from the Sind Valley into an almost-level canyon jutting away to the northeast and leading to the Suru Valley just north of Kargil. The meadows in the pass area are treeless but green, the first change away from the rain-drenched Kashmir watershed toward the dry atmosphere of Ladakh. The actual pass is an insignificant rise in the U-shaped basin a couple of miles east of the steep western ascent. Convoys of vehicles can get stalled in the wet bottomland hereabouts, and once I sat on top of a fuel truck here waiting for a mired vehicle to get pulled out of the muck. A hundred yards away across the marshy grasslands, despite the presence of scores of trucks and hundreds of preoccupied humans, a wolf chased a marmot, and just as the marmot was lumbering toward its burrow, the wolf leapt upon it and killed it.

A rarely traveled foot pass leads up from above Amarnath Cave, crossing a high ridge and descending less than 2 miles east of the Zoji La. This route is briefly mentioned in the preceding section "The Paths to Amarnath Cave."

The Lonvilad Gali

The most popular trekking route east out of Kashmir crosses the 14,350-foot Lonvilad Gali (gali means "pass") into the Suru Valley, the westernmost major valley in the Ladakh region (see "The Suru Valley" in Chapter 9). The approach to this pass is from the Warwan Valley, which lies east of Pahlgam and the Liddar Valley. The Warwan Valley itself can be reached from the Vale of Kashmir via several routes, the two most frequented of which are noted here. No matter which way you go, it will take you about a week from where you begin your trek on the Kashmir side until you reach Pannikar village in the Suru Valley. You should trek with a porter-guide. Please be aware that in the past thievery has occurred in the Warwan Valley: tents have been slit in the middle of the night and duffles yanked out. The locals blame the Gujars or Bakarwals, while these nomads finger the locals. Incriminating evidence taints both camps, but this problem seems to have been mitigated in recent years.

The lesser used of the two popular approaches to the Warwan Valley is over the Gulol Gali. This 15,000-foot pass is reached from a path that heads easterly at Wavjan, not far north of Shesh Nag Lake on the main pilgrim track to Amarnath (see Stage 2 of the preceding "The Paths to Amarnath Cave"). This route to the Warwan Valley is shorter, and its roadhead at Pahlgam village is easier to reach than that of the other approach. But the steeper Gulol Gali is usually snow covered and is over 3,000 feet higher than the corresponding Margan Pass, so this route is less often traversed by trekkers. After crossing the Gulol Gali, be sure to keep to the left, the north, and descend along that ridge to the Sain Nala below. The path along the Sain Nala enters the main Warwan Valley 2 miles below the meadow area called Humpet, noted below.

Most individual trekkers and nearly all organized groups that walk into the Warwan Valley approach it via the 11,760-foot Margan Pass, also called Margan "Top." The usual roadhead for this pass is the small hamlet of Lihenwan (8,300 feet), populated by Kashmiris and Gujars and located beyond the spring of Kokernag, east of the large town of Anantnag. If you are traveling on your own, you can get bus or sedan transportation from Srinagar or Anantnag to Kokernag, but going beyond by vehicle may be more difficult, unless you have already booked something (it is at least 10 miles up a gently rising valley along a narrow ribbon of "metalled" road from Kokernag to Lihenwan). Ask for suggestions at Srinagar's Tourist Information Center, or from the tourist officer in Pahlgam. Above Lihenwan, a new road has been constructed across Margan Pass into the Warwan Valley, but this small road sees very little traffic. As you walk up from Lihenwan, be sure to take the correct tributary valley (the same one followed by the road) northward toward Margan and not the main valley, which is a longer route over the Shilsar Pass.

Anywhere you trek in Kashmir, you'll have to be ready for rainy weather, but Margan Top seems to be a focal point for precipitation, so have your bumbershoot or raingear at the ready. The meadow leading up to the pass is long and steep, so go slowly, but the pass itself is wide, even marshy, and nearly level. Your best bet is to stay to the north side as you cross. Several hundred feet below the top is a rest house where you may be able to find shelter. The trail down to the Warwan Valley bottom angles in and out along steep spurs that alternate with forest and meadows. At the bottom of the valley is the village of Inshan (8,100 feet), across the Warwan River. Like the next several towns, it is a clustered village, and a few of its wooden homes are very large and well crafted with steep, shingled roofs. You won't need to cross to Inshan, as the main trail follows the west side of the valley for a day's walk.

The Warwan Valley trends north, gaining elevation quite slowly, and the trail passes several towns populated by Kashmiris who say, "Oh, you're coming from Kashmir," when you say you've come from Lihenwan. The Warwan is a lovely valley with green meadows, a few fields of amaranth, and many of corn and wheat. The last village is Sokhnay (9,000 feet, called Sokhniz on some maps). It was near Soknay that one group lost a duffle to a 2:00 A.M. thief who slashed a tent, and the group I was escorting lost two pairs of handmade trekking boots. Following this dacoity, I felt obliged to loan my good Asolo hiking boots to the group membaar who had not followed careful instructions to protect his boots. For the next two weeks I wore a pair of Indian-made Bata "Hunter" shoes belonging to one of the staff, reminding me of my first few treks when I wore similar shoes and felt every pebble underfoot.

Up-valley from Soknay the main Warwan River is called the Bat Kol, but a day's walk and 2,000 feet higher up, the stream's name changes again to Kainthal. The folded strata as you climb are very pronounced, as in the mountains to the west near Shesh Nag. As you begin the climb, the Warwan Valley jogs to the east and the large Sain Nala enters it from the north; a trail from this nala is the route from the Gulol Gali. Above the V-shaped steep stretch of the climb, the last birch trees are left behind and the valley widens dramatically at the meadow named Humpet, where you are greeted by the shrieking warning of the vocal local marmots. The herders here-abouts may be quite friendly, but their guard dogs definitely are not, so if you approach any camp, do so with a couple of large rocks in your hand and prepare to be aggressive. Better yet, only approach a camp after announcing your presence and making sure the mastiffs are being held or are tied. If a dog charges you with fangs bared, dripping saliva, remember, as it is clamping down on your leg, that it is only doing its job of protecting the camp.

Beyond Humpet, the trail follows the south bank of the stream, passing several springs. A few miles along the wide, meadow-covered valley a small, steeply descending tributary stream enters from the north, near a few Gujar huts above the valley floor that look almost like camouflaged gun emplacements. I imagined this tributary might be the way to the other pass in the area I'd heard about, so I asked our stalwart Kashmiri staff member Ramazan (who does the work of three men) to inquire of a young shepherd about the nala:

"Is there a pass up there?"
"Oh yes, that's the best way to Pannikar."
"Can loaded horses cross that way?"
"No, no, horses can't go over that."

So that pass is out for groups, but if you want to try a higher but surely interesting shortcut that crosses a snowfield, avoiding the crevassed glacier ahead, aim for the Yuranshan Gali, as it is called by the herders here (it is named Bobang Gali on the locally produced map). The last camping area in this upper valley is called Kaintal (11,500 feet), and it lies below the gently descending Bhot Kol Glacier. In the morning, you ascend along the Bhot Kol Glacier to the Lonvilad Gali, a low part of the northerly ridge and the boundary of Kashmir and Ladakh.

The day you cross the Lonvilad Gali will be a long one (unless you make a high camp on the far side of the pass), so get a good start. First of all, be careful of quicksand near the south side of the glacier where you approach it. Be sure you are either on firm ground or rocky moraine; the sandy stretches may want to swallow you, at least up to your knees. The going on the Bhot Kol can be tricky, as always on a glacier, so watch your footing and stay back from the yawning crevasses. If you are making this walk in midsummer or after, the crevasses should be perfectly visible and the snow surface hard. You will be walking onto the glacier from its south side, walking along it for about 3 miles, then angling toward its north side and hiking off the glacier up a rocky south-facing slope toward the low point in the ridge. The top of the ridge is rubble strewn and undulating: the actual Lonvilad Gali could be right where you are standing, or up ahead at the next slight rise. Here on the ridge you are crossing a rare low place (like the Zoji La) along the crest of the Great Himalaya Range just below the prominent Matterhorn-like peak north of the Bhot Kol Glacier.

The descent from the pass follows at first along the top of a dust-and rock-covered moraine, then crosses low, rocky ground and a flat, snowy stretch. Keep your eyes peeled for horse dung or other signs of use, for the best way to traverse this section of the wide, rocky valley. Ahead, the hills turn pink and chalk: tantalizing hints of the tinted hills and dry, sculpted landscape found in Zanskar and Ladakh. As the valley bends to the north, you begin to find a trail among tufts of grass, and the path drops to the camp called Donoru at 11,900 feet in a larger nala. At Donoru you must ford the main stream to the north (left) side, then head several easy hours' stroll down this valley, the Chalong Nala, past a few summer encampments. Keep to the right (south) when you reach the road leading to the Balti village of Pannikar (10,600 feet) at the mouth of the Chalong Nala in the Suru Valley. If by any chance you have walked with Kashmiri horsemen as far as Pannikar, you can be rather sure they will not go any farther. Pannikar and the continuing trek to the east will be discussed in "Pannikar and the Walk Over the Kanji La to Hiniskut" in Chapter 9.

The Chilung La

Are you an experienced hiker who has been complaining that the trails in Kashmir are too frequented by trekkers, that there is no new territory left? Then the path across the 17,050-foot Chilung La may be for you. Just to be sure this book doesn't contribute to cluttering up the trail to this pass with hikers (and since I have no personal knowledge of the way), the route description will be quite brief here. Rarely visited areas are scattered across the Himalaya, and the northern part of the Kishtwar region, which is traversed by this route and the next, is certainly one of these. If you are using the U502 maps, you will need the *Anantnag* sheet (NI 43-11) for this trek and the next walk over the Umasi La. Take a good look at the upper part of this sheet if you want to see some interesting chunks of territory that are virtually never visited by Westerners.

The Chilung La is a tough, glaciated, rarely crossed pass from the Rin Valley, a tributary of the Warwan, to the upper Suru Valley. To reach the Chilung, cross the Margan Pass, mentioned in the last section, and descend to the Warwan Valley, then follow the Warwan 13 miles south to its junction with the Rin. At the mouth of the Rin Valley, head up the Rin to the east and follow the valley up for two days to the major river junction where the Krish (or Krash) Nala joins from the east. You will take this easterly nala. If you are walking with someone who doesn't know the route (as is likely), it would be best to change porters at the last town of Metwan, 5 miles before you reach the junction. The going can be tricky in the upper parts of this valley, so be sure you have an experienced porter-guide, or else hire a local Bakarwal to show you the way. Once you get into the correct glaciated nala leading to the pass, you and your porter can probably figure out a route for yourselves, since the Bakarwals have no occasion to walk to the pass.

On the far, eastern, side of the Chilung Pass, you descend over another glacier into the upper reaches of the Suru Valley, about 8 miles from the Pensi La, which divides the Suru Valley from the Doda Valley in Zanskar. If you are feeling spunky, you can hope for a truck and head south, over the Pensi La to the Doda Valley and Padum in Zanskar. Or you can follow the dusty road north along the nearly level valley to reach Rangdum Gomba, the westernmost bastion of Buddhism in Zanskar or Ladakh. Allow about ten days to reach Rangdum from Lihenwan in the Kashmir Valley. Down-valley from Rangdum are the towns of Pannikar and Kargil, described in "The Suru Valley" in Chapter 9.

The Umasi La

North of the Chenab Valley, southeast of the Warwan, several named cols have been crossed from the Kishtwar region of Jammu District to Zanskar District, the southern portion of Ladakh. None of these passes is easy, and they are rarely crossed by locals. The one exception is the 17,000-foot Umasi La, approached from the large administrative town of Kishtwar. To reach the rolling green Kishtwar plain, take a plane, bus, or train from New Delhi to Jammu, then take a bus from Jammu to Kishtwar.

If you are in Srinagar, you may be able to find a vehicle that is going directly southeast out of the Kashmir Valley on the new road over the 11,700-foot Sinthan Pass. This pass now provides a road link between Kashmir and Kishtwar. Be sure you are fully provisioned at Kishtwar for a trek that can be expected to take about ten days from the roadhead near Gulabgadh (on the new road along the vertiginous Chenab Valley) to Padum in Zanskar's Doda Valley. Kishtwar porters in general do not have a good reputation, so unless you run across a person you are quite certain of, wait until you reach the roadhead to engage someone. In any case, you will probably be changing porters at an upper village near the pass. Do not attempt the Umasi La before the beginning of July, when most of the snow will have melted in the upper areas near the pass.

At Kishtwar take a truck or bus up the Chenab Valley road, which is presently under construction, to the roadhead. Depending on how far the road has been completed by the time you arrive, you will probably reach the village of Atholi with its small shops by vehicle. At Atholi, cross a bridge from the south to the north bank of the raging Chenab River. At the junction of the Bhut and Chenab, and surrounded by them on three sides, is Gulabgadh, once the seat of Gulab Singh, the first Maharaja of Kashmir. At Gulabgadh, you cross the Bhut Nala to its western bank and follow the stream to the northeast. Up this valley you pass waterfalls, villages, and several maidans before reaching the village of Machail, the last large Hindu town, in about two days. Machail has an interesting wooden *mandir,* a Hindu temple. Sapphires were once mined above town, and villagers therefore used to be suspicious whenever an outsider arrived on the scene.

Soon after Machail, the path leads steeply north into the tributary Bhuzas or Zanskar Nala, where the few small villages are inhabited by people originally from Zanskar. Here you are among vertical snow-clad peaks and nearly beyond the last trees. The ascent toward the pass alternates between the ice and snow-covered glacier, rocky moraine, and scree slopes. You will do best along this upper part of the valley if you walk with someone from Machail or, better yet, a Zanskari from one of the small upper villages who knows the route. The way to the pass is not obvious, angling back and forth across these wide snowfields. The Umasi La offers great views into Zanskar and is steeper on the northern side than on the southern approaches. On the snow-covered descent to the north, you can stay on the left side of the Bardar Glacier and walk down the west side of the valley, in which case you could visit the Dzong Khul Gomba. Or you could cross to the right side of the glacier and follow the more traveled route, which would put you slightly closer to Padum, a long day's walk once you reach the wide Doda Valley.

The Guardian of the West keeps his eye on you at Lamayuru's well-furbished monastery in Ladakh.

9

Ladakh and Zanskar

*[The Nubra men] were real "jungli wallahs," mountainmen,
born and bred in the high Himalayas. They were tough as
old leather. They had eyesight that would shame a telescope.
Their clothes were voluminous folds of drab homespun. They
ate a curious grain compound. Their skin, garments, and
food were all of varying shades of brown.*
Theodore Roosevelt, 1926

One pen. One pen. One pen.
Modern Ladakhi mantra spoken
by children to tourists

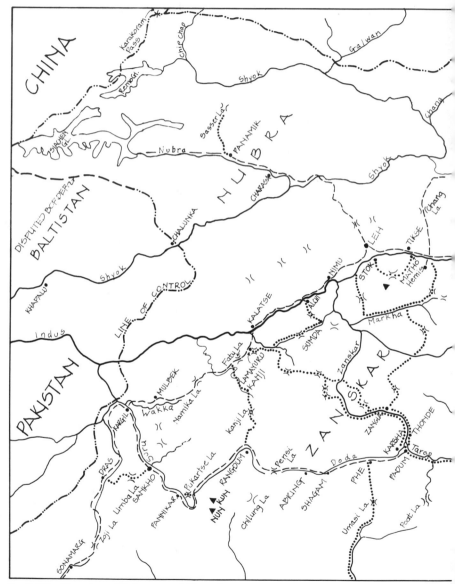

Ladakh, Zanskar, Nubra, and Rupshu

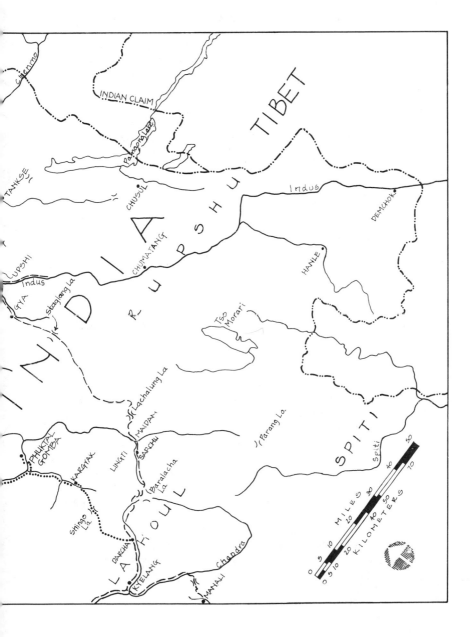

An Untrammeled Tibetan Culture

"Ju'le, ju'le," welcome to Ladakh! When you come to Ladakh, its smiling denizens will greet you, especially in the villages, with the all-purpose Ladakhi salutation of *"Ju'le."* This large region with its high, arid landscape and Buddhist culture is geographically and culturally an extension of western Tibet. The area generally known as Ladakh is presently divided into three administrative districts: Ladakh, Zanskar, and Kargil. Ladakh District comprises the area traditionally called Nubra north of the Indus Valley and the Indus Valley itself. Zanskar constitutes the large chunk of mountainous territory south of Ladakh and north of Lahoul in Himachal Pradesh, while Kargil District consists of the Suru River Valley and its tributaries, regions traditionally called Purig and Baltistan. These three districts together comprise over two-thirds of the state of Jammu and Kashmir, and taken together, they represent the largest single area in India or Pakistan covered in this book.

Nowhere else is the Himalayan mountain system's northwest-to-southeast plunge more rife with rugged but traversable parallel ranges. The Karakoram and Kailas ranges form the northern and eastern borders of Ladakh's three districts, while the main Great Himalaya Range isolates them from the south. The vast majority of Zanskar is covered by the Ladakh and Zanskar ranges, each crowned with scores of 20,000-foot peaks. The passes across the northern Ladakh Range between the Shyok and Indus valleys are 17,000 and 18,000 feet in elevation, while the Zanskar Range's many sharp ridges and torrent-filled defiles limit access to the hardy Changpa nomads forced from their former grazing areas in the west Tibetan plains. The region is so full of precipitous mountains and steep ridges that the word Ladakh means "Land of the Passes." The lowest elevation in all of Ladakh outside the Suru Valley is higher than 9,000 feet, where the Indus flows north into Baltistan.

Ladakh and Zanskar have sandy plains, but only along certain portions of the major valley floors. Foremost among these is the Indus Valley, but communities cluster together in the Nubra, Shyok, Doda, Dras, and Suru valleys as well. Flat land is also found in Rupshu, Ladakh's highest and easternmost area.

Agriculture in these three districts is conducted only where irrigation is possible from glaciers, melting snow, or perennial streams. In Ladakh, a row of poplar or willow trees is a sight to be savored. Horses and donkeys traditionally were sources of income because of their use for transport, and they are still used extensively in Zanskar's inner valleys, but trucks have taken over most hauling along the main valley routes. Zanskaris in particular still make essential and regular trading excursions across mountain passes that most foreigners would hesitate to cross without undertaking an extensive physical training program.

Presently, Muslims form a bare majority of the population of these three districts; most other residents are Buddhist, and all Ladakhis or

Zanskaris are of Mongolian extraction. Most Ladakhi Muslims live in Kargil District and along the Indus Valley. Many are beginning to speak Urdu, learned from religious use and the radio, instead of Ladakhi, which is a dialect of Tibetan. Ladakh's current population of about 130,000 is increasing rapidly, as the polyandry of the Buddhists (which tended to inhibit fertility) is replaced with monogamy and polygamy.

Ladakhis or Zanskaris, no matter what their religious affiliation, are outgoing people who have to work hard during the four months of the growing season, since winters in this elevated region are long and severe. Considering the constraints of the arid landscape and harsh climate, it is remarkable how high the standard of living has been in Ladakh. In traditional Ladakhi culture, a lack of aggression and sense of joy permeate people's lives; young and old work together in a spirit of cooperation underlain by a great joie de vivre.

The old ways and new coexist: here is another Himalayan land where the grandparents dress in traditional fashion while many in their mid-twenties, particularly the men, wear clothes that would not be out of place in New Delhi. The attractive maroon woolen gown called a *coss* remains in style as standard Ladakhi dress for Buddhist or Muslim. And the *jibi* or *sahru* is popular in the countryside. This is a top hat cut out on the front with upturned ear flaps, worn by women or men (who often wear the sahru with flaps akimbo). The larger *perag* headdress has rows of turquoise and a charm box called a *kagu*. Along with the perag is the *tsaroo,* two wings of black sheep's wool, joined on either side of the perag. Once this headpiece was daily fashion for married women, but today it is seen less often in the towns of the main Indus Valley. At festivals, the perag is usually worn only by older women, or by women who have inherited one, for the price of a perag has escalated rapidly.

For more than a thousand years Ladakh was part of the vast region of western Tibet. Buddhism came to Ladakh before it reached central Tibet, for Padmasambhava, the man responsible for the conversion of Tibet from shamanistic Bon Po to Buddhism, traveled from what is now the Swat Valley (in Pakistan) across Tibet from west to east. Ladakh has retained the monastic Buddhism that was forcefully suppressed within Tibet for a generation. In fact, the image of Tibetan culture most Westerners imagine to exist in Tibet is perhaps now more appropriate to Ladakh than to Tibet itself, since the monasteries and temples, the *gomba*s, of Ladakh were never systematically destroyed or closed as they were in Tibet following the Chinese invasion. Large Buddhist monasteries, many sculpted onto rocky prominences, continue to operate in the Indus Valley and within side valleys hidden among saw-toothed ridges throughout Ladakh and Zanskar.

Ladakh was an independent west Tibetan kingdom prior to the fourteenth century. It was ruled by a theocracy, which was beneficent or self-serving, depending on one's point of view. There was and is a royal family both in Ladakh (at Stok) and in Zanskar (at Zangla), and the ancient monasteries continue to survive, prospering in varying degrees. The fourteenth and sixteenth centuries were punctuated by periods of Islamic rule, and conversion to that faith began. Late in the seventeenth century, as Ladakh's power was declining, a deal was struck between the rulers in Srinagar and in Leh whereby, for Kashmiri assurances of protection from invasion, a mosque would be built in Leh. Today this same mosque continues to sound with the call to prayers at the northern end of Leh's main street.

In the early nineteenth century Ladakh was one of several west Tibetan states. The largest of these states, then named Guge, contains the two ancient Sutlej Valley fortress cities Tsaparang and Toling, the former a repository of exquisite frescoes (see "The Lost Cities of Toling and Tsaparang" in Chapter 9 of this book's companion volume, *Trekking in Nepal, West Tibet and Bhutan*). In 1834 Ladakh fell to a Dogra army led by the notorious Zorawar Singh. Since then, this remote, mountainous land has formed some 70 percent of the total area of Jammu and Kashmir.

Great caravans once converged on the caravanserais of Leh from Turkestan, Tibet, and Kashmir. The route from Srinagar to Yarkand crossed the Zoji, Namika, and Fotu passes before it even reached Leh. This part of the journey took two weeks, and beyond Leh five still more perilous passes remained to be crossed. The caravans through Ladakh continued until October 1951, when the passes north were closed by the Chinese authorities, halting the vital north-south trade to Yarkand, trapping a number of Yarkandi merchants in Leh, and effectively paralyzing Leh commercially.

The next jolt to Ladakh's dusty, museumlike atmosphere occurred in 1962 when the border war with China flared and the 272-mile road was rapidly completed from the Kashmir Valley to Leh. The Indian government quickly established large garrisons near Leh and elsewhere, bringing in tens of thousands of troops and changing the economy drastically. There have also been four border wars with Pakistan, the most recent of which smouldered for years in the 1980s (see "The Saltoro Valleys: High Spires and Steep Slabs" in Chapter 7 and "The Nubra Valley," following). In the late summer of 1974 Ladakh was opened to tourism. In 1978 commercial flights began, increasing the flow of tourists and further straining Ladakh's traditional society. The ancient Wheel of Existence on view at the entrance to each Ladakhi gomba must have creaked once again.

Trekking in Ladakh and Zanskar

Ladakh and particularly Zanskar are large, sprawling regions: trails change and crucial bridges are built, washed away, and rebuilt, sometimes in different places, so hiking routes in these areas can often only be outlined. Further, through-paths are often difficult both to describe and to follow on foot in Ladakh and Zanskar for many reasons: trails change according to the time of year (particularly with reference to stream crossings), villages and other recognizable landmarks such as stupas or trees are few, paths are not well marked, and side tracks can mislead anyone who does not have personal knowledge of the proper way. Another complicating factor is the lack of accurate maps. Trekking with one or more locals (who will usually bring one or more donkeys or, more likely, horses, called *sta*) is the most sensible way to hike in these barren, intriguing regions. You will have to pay at least sixty rupees a day for a man and his horse. Before leaving on a trek, be sure you are carrying enough food, because all you are likely to find in the hinterlands aside from milk products is *tsampa* (roasted barley flour), also called *sattu,* or, in Ladakhi, *ngam pe*. If you will be doing a longer trek in Zanskar before mid- to late August when the streams subside, you should probably carry a rope to help with river crossings. You should definitely take along a pair of lightweight running shoes to cushion tender feet in the frigid waters, which are often rapid and in many places flow over sharp rock.

Like the climate in the Hindu Kush or Karakoram in Pakistan, the atmosphere is extremely dry in Ladakh and Zanskar and the sun can be scorching in midsummer (although nights are always chill in the hills). Be sure you drink plenty of fluids, always treat your water with iodine (since boiling usually isn't practical), and don't neglect to take a pinch of salt in your water from time to time to maintain your sodium level. A dawn start and long midday rests should be part of your routine in summer.

As to the U502 maps that depict the large area covered in this chapter, the *Kargil* sheet (NI 43-7) covers the Suru Valley and its tributaries as far west as Mulbek and Rangdum. The *Leh* sheet (NI 43-8) depicts most of Nubra, the Indus Valley, and northernmost Zanskar. The *Martselang* sheet (NI 43-12) shows most of Zanskar, but for southern Zanskar south of Kargyak down to Darcha in Lahoul, you would need the *Palampur* sheet (NI 43-16). Be warned that none of these maps is very reliable for the Zanskar region, but the U502 maps are still as good as any available. Sheets 2, 3, and 5 of the 1:200,000 maps published by Leomann (see Appendix A) have some interesting variations on the information shown on the U502 sheets. No map yet produced has done a good job of accurately portraying the paths across Zanskar's convoluted terrain.

This chapter covers first the air and land routes into Ladakh and Zanskar, followed by the principal land route from the Vale of Kashmir into Leh. Next, Leh and vicinity are sketched in. Then, the monasteries of the Indus Valley and walks beginning and ending in the Indus Valley are noted. Finally, the Suru Valley, Zanskar, Nubra, and Rupshu are each discussed in turn, with the emphasis on trekking routes in the Suru Valley and Zanskar, which are open to trekkers. Note that prior to 1990, the regions of Nubra and Rupshu have been closed to foreigners (with the exception of Indo-foreign mountaineering expeditions in Nubra and jeep safaris to Pangong Lake and Tso Morari). Treks in these areas sometimes go from one region to another, and rather than divide these trails up strictly by region, I have described the walking routes to their natural ending points.

The Road to Leh: Following
the Ancient Caravan Route

Ladakh, once remote, is becoming quite connected with the outside world. Flights on specially modified Boeing 737 jets now fly year round into Leh, Ladakh's only civilian airport. In summer at least five flights weekly are scheduled from Srinagar, as well as frequent flights from both New Delhi (sometimes daily) and Chandigarh (located several hours by bus due north of New Delhi). These planes can often be booked solid with officials, tourist groups, and others with pull. To obtain a seat, you will need to book in advance or engage a large travel agency such as Mercury Travels, Ltd., to assist you in acquiring a confirmed reservation. Flights into Leh are canceled if the weather is bad, which can often happen for several days in a row. Since subsequent flights are sure to be booked, seats can be at a premium and reassignment of confirmed seats follows inscrutable priorities. If the weather is clear, views from the plane are great: flying from the south, you'll cross the snowy, desolate reaches of Zanskar. Flights from Srinagar feature excellent perspectives of Nun Kun's double peak just to the south of the flight path and Nanga Parbat and the Karakoram (including K2) on the northern horizon.

Presently, the principal land route into Ladakh goes from Kashmir. However, summer bus service via an alternate land route has begun into Ladakh from the south. For years an unpaved road has extended from Kyelang and Darcha in Lahoul, Himachal Pradesh, to Upshi in the Indus Valley, not far up-valley from well-visited Hemis Gomba. The route goes north from Darcha via Patseo, the Baralacha Pass, Sarchu, the Lachalung La, the Staglang La, Gya, and Upshi. Most of the way it traverses high, barren desert, skirting the western limits of the high, restricted Rupshu region. This road has been kept open for possible military and civilian use, but prior to 1988 it saw little traffic, primarily because a strong Kashmiri lobby had been successful in seeing to it that all traffic into Ladakh entered from Kashmir. Most years the road could be cleared of snow by the beginning of July (the year I was in the vicinity of the Baralacha Pass, the road was being cleared by the army in the second week of July, but this work is probably done earlier in the year now). The distance from Kyelang (the administrative center of Lahoul—see Chapter 10) to Leh by this route is 223 miles, and because of the long, level stretches in western Rupshu, the journey can be made in an eighteen-hour day. Between Darcha and the Indus Valley, the driver may stop for food at Kilang Serai, about 8 miles north of the Baralacha La, and/or at Pang Serai, some 14 miles beyond the Lachalung La, so go well supplied with your own provisions and liquids. Since this road skirts the Inner Line in the Rupshu region, you may need a permit from the deputy commissioner in Leh (if going south) or Kyelang (if traveling north) before you can buy a ticket for the bus, and you will not be allowed to disembark en route except at the food stop. What an ethereal but exhausting ride this would be.

Most people reach Ladakh by bus or taxi (either a jeep or car) from

Kashmir on a route closely following the ancient fifteen-stage (fifteen-day) caravan track dating back to the days of the Silk Route. Presently, most travelers make the journey in two days, although in a good taxi the trip can be made in one excruciatingly long haul. The usual procedure is to go by bus, leaving from the Tourist Reception Center in Srinagar and going 127 miles to Kargil the first day, then, after a night's rest, proceeding the remaining 145 miles to Leh. All buses take two days to drive between Kashmir and Leh, but you have a choice of three classes of service: super delux, A class, and B class. Super delux buses are fastest and cushy, but one I once traveled in lacked the proper tire iron to fix a flat tire, resulting in a pleasant three-hour hiatus at Mulbek. The A and B class buses are the same size, but A class vehicles are newer, faster models, and have fewer seats.

If you go by bus, you'll leave from Srinagar's Tourist Reception Center. While you wait for the bus to load, try the fresh *puris* with *halwa* sold by vendors who cook them at the depot. A puri is a thin wheatcake cooked in oil, often eaten at breakfast with a sweet farina topping called halwa. Thus fortified, take your seat and watch the Kashmir Valley recede as the bus enters the beautiful wooded Sind Valley (see "The Sind Valley" in Chapter 8). Early lunch will be taken at Sonamarg before the bus proceeds over the 11,580-foot Zoji La into Ladakh.

Military convoys of one hundred to two hundred trucks and civilian transport (goods trucks, oil tankers, buses, taxis, and private cars) share the road into Ladakh, but the two types of vehicles use the road during different hours. While you eat lunch at Sonamarg, a military convoy heading toward Srinagar will undoubtedly rumble past. Your ride to Leh may be interrupted for an hour or so from time to time, due to military vehicles, but the bus drivers know when the road is to be closed and arrange their schedules to minimize delays. Riding to Leh once, we were stopped east of the Zoji La by an approaching convoy. I climbed an embankment near the road and found myself near a mess tent at the edge of a military camp. Turning to leave, I was hailed from a nearby tent: "Sahib, come and take tea."

When your bus reaches the top of the steep Zoji grade and enters a green, U-shaped valley, it will be approaching the pass; you will have crossed the actual Zoji La only when you see a stream flowing eastward, the direction you are traveling. This crossing into Ladakh brings one of the most abrupt climatic changes you are ever likely to see. The Sind Valley pines are gone, and the lush meadows will likewise evaporate before many miles are passed.

The first large village you reach is Dras, a pleasant-enough spot with its green meadows when you pass through in summer, but known for its frigid winters. An ethnologist who once passed the winter in Dras discovered that the town's population suffers from high blood pressure because, with nothing else to do, everyone drinks salted tea to excess. A trail (noted in "The Umbe La" that follows) leaves Dras for the Umbe La and the Suru Valley. The village includes a rest house and a tourist officer, and nearby stands a small checkpoint where all foreigners are required to produce their passports.

East of town just north of the road are four low stone bas-reliefs carved in the seventh century when the area was Buddhist. The road enters a dry narrow gorge, and from here on to the east in Ladakh and Zanskar you will not see greenery unless the land is irrigated. The Dras River, which the road follows, eventually merges with the larger Shingo River, which drains the Deosai Plains. For the 7 miles where the road hugs the Shingo River, the route closely parallels the Line of Control with Pakistan, which runs out of sight along the hill to the immediate north. You can see telephone lines and mule tracks heading up this steep, dry ridge to the disputed border. The Shingo empties into the Suru River very near the Line of Control and less than 20 miles from the Suru's confluence with the Indus.

The important town of Kargil lies on the western bank of the Suru River several miles south of the Shingo River junction. Kargil itself was once considered part of Baltistan, and many people here are Shiites and speak Balti like their brethren in Skardu to the north. Before partition in 1947, Kargil was an important crossroads, with routes leading northward into Baltistan. Now the secondary route is the new road south to Padum in Zanskar District. Kargil is viewed by most travelers as the place where one is awoken at a ghastly hour so the driver can reach the town of Kalatse in the Indus Valley before the military convoy reaches him. The old, stone-paved Kargil bazaar angling down toward the river is well worn, reeking pleasantly of antiquity. A visit there or up the hill to the west past fields of wheat and peas will help to stretch your legs after the long ride. Kargil is the chief town of the Dras, Suru, and Wakka Chu valleys, known collectively as the Purig region. Kargil is also mentioned in "The Suru Valley" that follows.

Your vehicle crosses the bridge over the Suru River just south of town, then climbs up a low dry ridge to enter the valley of the Wakka Chu, a river with a name like a flapper-era background vocal. The road follows lush, irrigated fields bordered with well-trimmed willow trees along the river bottom. Then the valley widens, and at the small village of Mulbek, 25 miles east of Kargil, you see the first evidence of the Buddhist culture to come, aside from the small carvings near Dras. Here at the edge of the fields by the road is a large whitewashed *stupa* (reliquary shrine), and a small monastery rests above on the ridgeline. South of the road behind a new white Buddhist temple stands a tall relief carving of Maitreya, the Buddha-to-come, chiseled from the rock outcropping. This is the largest of several rock carvings in Ladakh. Hereabouts is a sign reading Welcome to the Land of Buddha, placed by Beacon, the branch of the army given the tough job of road construction and maintenance. Beacon does have a sense of humor and along the way, you will see signs like these:

| Go man go but very slow | Overtaker Undertaker |

From Mulbek the road leaves the Wakka Chu and rises to cross the Namika La ("Salt Pass," 12,220 feet), then descends to the town of Bod Kharbu in a tributary valley of the Indus River. At Bod Kharbu, like Dras, there is a large parking area for military convoys, and you will also see a large army camp here. The valley floor is fertile and green from irrigation, but the hills on either side are so barren that even a tiny herd of sheep would have to graze quickly to fend off starvation. Moving up this valley, you pass several small communities, including Hiniskut, just north of and out of sight from the road. As the road begins ascending toward the next pass, look to the south and you can see where the clear stream you have been following disappears into a narrow defile. A trail up this narrow canyon leads to Kanji village and divides, proceeding onward to either Rangdum or Lamayuru monasteries. This trail is described in "The Suru Valley."

Toward the head of the dry valley you are following, you can clearly see the old caravan trail that angles up from the valley floor. Path and road alike cross the third and highest pass between Srinagar and Leh, the 13,430-foot Fotu La. At the pass area and easterly the earth appears bleached. The ancient caravans must have hurried past such inhospitable surroundings. If you wish, you can easily follow the old caravan track south of the road on foot. The path soon disappears out of sight from the road, entering eroded hills and passing old prayer walls and stupas to reach Lamayuru Gomba in about two hours' walk. The trail lies there, forever waiting for you to follow the ancient path of Silk Route caravans.

At the Fotu La you cross the Zanskar Range and begin to drop toward Lamayuru, one of the oldest and most spectacularly situated monasteries in all of Ladakh. Lamayuru is also one of the best managed monasteries: it is clean and well maintained, and its monks are polite and well robed. Perched precariously astride a narrow spur, Lamayuru's buildings are the picture of an exotic Himalayan monastery. Just inside the entrance gate the monks have established a restaurant and inn where you can roll out your sleeping bag and eat the meals provided, gazing at recently painted frescoes of Buddhist divinities. Not far beyond the guest room is the monastery's main kitchen, recognizable by the pile of furze (a low-growing bush) for fuel just outside the door. The large cauldrons inside are sometimes half hidden in billowing smoke. Just outside the *du-khang* (monks' assembly hall) in the central building are excellent-quality wall paintings of the Four Great Kings, also known as the Four Guardians of the Orients, figures often seen at the entrances to assembly halls. These bright, new paintings can be photographed without a flash attachment, a rarely encountered situation, for most monasteries in Ladakh away from the Indus Valley are poorly lit inside.

Several hiking routes begin or end here at Lamayuru and are noted in the section on Zanskar, following. A walk up the parched hill north of the road gives an excellent view of the monastery in its dry valley. If you climb for about a half hour, you will see grey pinnacles to the south in Zanskar, a breathtaking background for Lamayuru, sequestered below. A more level walk would be to stroll up the old caravan trail leading toward the Fotu La. This path is easily visible from the monastery, as it gently curves upward past rows of stupas and long *mani* walls, 5-foot-high stone walls topped with stones inscribed with the sacred Tibetan mantra *Om Mani Padme Hum* ("All Hail the Jewel in the Lotus").

At the small village below the monastery, just as at Mulbek and most villages along the main road, are rudimentary inns run by locals, many of which are cooperative enterprises. If you have time and want to begin to have some insight into life in Ladakh and Zanskar, do pause to stay at some of these lodges. Some of them are directly attached to people's homes, and you can learn some Urdu or Ladakhi and observe family life in these smaller, less frequented inns more easily than in the larger, busier lodges and hotels in Leh. Ladakh and Zanskar and the people who live here are very different from the other hill regions of India, and if you will not be trekking here, the small inns in homes and monasteries near the main road are some of the best places to savor daily life in Ladakh.

In the area between Dras and Lamayuru you may see some people called Dards (strictly speaking, this is not an accurate name for them, but Dard is the term that has come to be used) who are neither Hindu nor Buddhist, although they practice some rituals and observances of each faith as well as their own customs. The women are readily distinguishable, since they wear beads and other small ornaments in their dark red hats. The Dards, who speak their own language, live in towns inhabited by Buddhists and Muslims, but they also have some villages of their own north of the main road.

Near Lamayuru, and especially to the east, the valley becomes a phantasmagoric striated canyon of yellow and bronze wind-eroded rock, leaving no doubt why Ladakh is often called the moonland. The road rapidly descends in scores of hairpin turns to the Indus River, which it crosses to the town of Kalatse (or Khalse), where your driver will probably stop for lunch. Khalse is known for its apricots, which youngsters will try to sell, either fresh or dried, while you eat lunch and watch a convoy of military trucks roll by.

Seven miles east of Kalatse the Indus Valley widens, and you enter the heart of central Ladakh. An additional 25 miles past scattered settlements and larger towns takes you by the village of Nimu, where the Zanskar River flowing from the south bends to join the Indus. This confluence is a remarkable sight: although the Indus headwaters rise more than 400 miles away to the southeast, the river is dwarfed by its so-called tributary. The slate gray Zanskar River is fully three times the size of the languid Indus. At this point you are within 20 miles of Leh, the capital of Ladakh.

Leh

Excitement mounts as your vehicle turns away from the Indus near the small hilltop monastery of Spituk and begins to churn up the wide, dry alluvial fan toward Leh, 5 miles straight ahead. Many visitors approach

Leh (11,400 feet) with the ardor that must have been felt by caravanners of old, and with good reason. Above town, the sixteenth-century Temple of Guardian Divinities perches on Namgyal Peak, and well below, not far above Leh, is the equally old fortresslike royal palace built by Senge Namgyal, the most powerful of Ladakh's kings. The palace is nine stories tall, only five less than the famed Potala in Lhasa. Long streamers of prayer flags that are replaced in a yearly ceremony flutter in the breeze from stupas beside both the imposing castle and the temple above.

Ladakh was opened to tourism when the Indian government wisely removed Zanskar and much of central Ladakh from the Inner Line restrictions that had been enforced prior to mid-1974. Ladakh's opening had been lobbied for by many Ladakhis, and by now over one hundred guesthouses and hotels have sprung up in and near Leh (scores of these are informal establishments without names). Many people utilized spare rooms in their homes, built additions, and later added hotel names to their premises. If you have any question about where to stay, you can stop at the tourist office and ask for recommendations. The tourist office is at the Tourist Bungalow on the side street branching west from the middle of the main bazaar.

Leh's main bazaar runs north to south directly toward the old royal palace on the ridge above. The city's three-hundred-year-old mosque sits just north of the right angle of the bazaar street; in the summer, women in sahru hats sell green vegetables nearby. Before the road to Leh was built, when the bazaar was unpaved and there were no gutters, merchants would close their street-facing doors to permit bazaar-long polo games. Then there was a large sign reading SUB JAIL in the midst of the bazaar. Now the town has changed focus: video shows change daily and instead of the mullah or lama, the superintending engineer is the most respected person about. These days Tibetan refugees, army *jawan*s (soldiers), and foreigners stride along Leh's main street in place of Yarkandis or Baltis. Auto parts, consumer goods, and tourist souvenirs have replaced the pashmina, carpets, and silk of yore, but such necessities as grains, tea, spices, and textiles are still carried in the shops. And chang alley (chang is locally brewed beer made from any of several grains) just east of the main street still offers bottles of the concoction, guaranteed to relieve constipation and introduce unruly new flora into one's system. East of chang alley is a large mani wall with red painted warnings in Tibetan, Urdu, Hindi, and English. The English injunction reads Don't Pass Urine Here.

Beneath Leh's castle, the old city's narrow, twisting lanes and underpasses are reminiscent of any medieval town. More shops line a street along a diverted stream north of the mosque. Follow that street and soon you'll be north of town on a centuries-old path, now paved for some distance, passing stupas and mani walls. While you test how it feels to walk slowly uphill at this rarified level, you can glimpse traditional country scenes along trails that extend miles up the irrigated terracing north of Leh. The first community is Samkar, with its active gomba, and other settlements lie farther along.

Leh's palace on the ridge above town is a scene of disrepair: the building has been abandoned for over two generations, and while the high front wall is relatively unaffected, the roof is riddled with holes and the interior is caked with dust. Reconstruction may begin soon. The smaller temple high on Namgyal Peak is reached from a trail that zigzags upward behind the large, white windowless Avalokitesvara Temple. From the prayer flag-topped ridge are excellent views of Leh, the surrounding settlements, and Spituk Monastery in the distance on the Indus Valley plain. Across the valley to the south is Stok Kangri, a peak you can walk to the base of or higher (see "The Walk From Stok to Matho" that follows). The road east of the temple snaking up the restricted area to the north leads to the 18,380-foot Khardung Pass. Two vertical miles down the far side of the pass lies the junction of the Shyok and Nubra valleys and the Nubra region, described later on. A sign erected by Beacon in Leh at the beginning of this route states that the road is the highest in the world, then says You Can Have Dialogue With God.

As isolated Ladakh began to experience a flood of foreign visitors, villagers living virtually in the Iron Age met Western technology and materialism. The effect was monumental, particularly on young Ladakhis, and many Ladakhis became convinced that Occidental dress and material wealth was to be emulated. In response to this trend, a unique and laudable organization came into being, called the Ladakh Ecological Development Group (LEDeG) and staffed by some well-known and highly respected Ladakhis. The headquarters of LEDeG is located just northeast of the main bazaar in a newly constructed multipurpose building of modified traditional style called the Center for Ecological Development, or, for short, the Ecology Center. This two-story building was inaugurated by Indira Gandhi, then prime minister, and later consecrated by His Holiness the Dalai Lama. The Ecology Center is on the circuit of every visiting politician and all savvy tourists. Here are a restaurant, a bakery, offices, meeting rooms, a museum, a library, and a shop that sells handicrafts made by Ladakhi villagers. A second building houses a workshop where solar ovens, solar water heaters, and components of hydraulic rams (self-operating pumps that force water to a higher level) are constructed. Further, Ladakhis are trained here in the construction of these and other devices utilizing appropriate technology.

LEDeG has other ongoing educational and construction projects designed to assist Ladakhis in entering the modern era through sustainable, harmonious methods. Hydraulic rams and Trombe walls (passive solar heating devices utilizing a painted black wall next to a large south-facing window) have become highly sought after in Ladakh after they proved themselves workable. To see a Trombe wall, look at the front of the Ecology Center. The person who sparked this revolution in appropriate technology in Ladakh is a Swedish linguist named Helena Norberg-Hodge, who helped to found LEDeG and who directs the Ladakh Project, a U.K.-based organization that works closely with LEDeG as well as other groups promoting the traditional culture (such as SECMOL, the Students Educational Cultural Movement of Ladakh). Helena speaks fluent Ladakhi (see her Ladakhi glossary in the back of the book), one of the very few non-Ladakhis to do so, and has justly earned the respect of Ladakhis by emphasing the importance of the traditional society while helping Ladakhis to explore ways to improve their standard of living without social or ecological destruction.

Leh's rapid growth has strained many aspects of life. For instance, the local water supply has been used beyond its limits and fresh water has become a valuable, sometimes nearly nonexistent commodity. One regrettable upshot of increased tourism has been that many outsiders come to Leh for the summer season bringing souvenirs to sell to foreigners, then leave, taking their profits with them. If you get an itchy wallet in Leh, take a close look at what you are tempted to purchase. Was it made in Ladakh, or elsewhere, and who is selling it to you? Those young schlockmeisters wearing jeans who stalk the main bazaar and the carpet sellers in the new emporiums just west of the bazaar are all Kashmiris who merely sell their wares in Leh at a higher price than they would flog the same items in Srinagar.

Trekkers looking for porter contacts in Leh will have to be patient. Outfitters are setting up rudimentary "offices" in Leh, but trekking has been slow to develop here. Most Ladakhis have a lot of work to do at home during the summer, and not everyone is willing to leave and load up his horse for a mere stroll about the hills. Check at the tourist office for references of Ladakhi companies or of individuals who may be able to help you in the area where you want to hike. Artou is a recommended outfitter. If you can locate N.K.L. Chhultim, he is one of the very best local guides. The Ecology Center is another good place to inquire about porter-guide contacts. The Tibetan refugee village of Choklamsar some 6 miles southeast of Leh is also a likely spot to look for porter-guides. Begin asking there at one of the small restaurants or stores. You may find that the best you can manage in Leh is to get a chit written to someone in the roadhead town you want to trek from. In that case, buy supplies and hire a taxi or purchase a ticket for the right bus. Be sure to arrive about an hour ahead of time if you take a bus, so that you can find the right vehicle and locate squeezing room aboard (the bus station is below the taxi stand, not far south of the main bazaar). Buses are always jammed, but this is Ladakh: people are contagiously friendly and, who knows, someone who gets off the bus at your destination may be able to assist you. With the experience you have just shared together, what better introduction can you have to each other?

Monasteries and Short Treks in the Indus Valley of Central Ladakh

Within the wide Himalayan desert of the Indus Valley lie the palaces of Leh, Shey, and Basgo and numerous remarkable monasteries. The monasteries and palaces of Ladakh are its most visited sites, yet few visitors have any meaningful sense of all the paraphernalia they see in these places: the ritual implements, *tangkhas* (scroll paintings), books, murals, mandalas, and images of guardian divinities. It is not within the scope of this book to give more than a brief introduction to Vajrayana (Tibetan) Buddhism, the picturesque monasteries and palaces, and the region's chief festival. To fully understand the meaning of the rich religious panoply, one could study at great length. Most local monks and certainly most Ladakhi Buddhists have only a limited understanding themselves of the Tibetan Buddhist divinities. If the cursory discussion here whets rather than sates your interest, peruse *The Cultural Heritage of Ladakh,* volume one, for monasteries along the Indus Valley (and volume two for information on some monasteries in Zanskar) by David L. Snellgrove and Tadeusz Skorupski.

The monasteries were established for the propagation of the *dharma* (the doctrine or path), as stated by Lord Gautama Buddha. The basis of the doctrine is the Four Noble Truths: suffering, its cause, its suppression, and the Eightfold Path leading to its suppression. All else is but commentary upon the Four Noble Truths, but there has been much to say. Consider that the Tibetan canon, the *Kenjur,* contains 108 books, and that its commentaries, the *Tenjur,* are longer yet. The Vajrayana or "Diamond Vehicle" of Tibetan Buddhism has four schools or orders: the Nyingmapa, Kagyupa, Sakyapa, and Gelugpa. Every monastery you will visit in the Himalaya (unless it is of the Bon Po religion, a precursor of Vajrayana Buddhism) belongs to one of these schools or to a subsect. In central Ladakh, the Kagyupa and the Gelugpa (the branch to which the Dalai Lama belongs) control all but two of the monasteries. The Gelugpa order, a scholarly lineage, was established by Tsong Khapa, while the lineage of the Kagyupas includes Naropa, Marpa the Translator, and Milarepa.

Most large monasteries have both a du-khang, the monks' assembly hall, and a *lha-khang,* the "House of the Gods," or chapel. The du-khang is bigger and usually has multiple rows of cushions for the monks to sit on while praying and performing ceremonies. In smaller monasteries, one room may serve as both the assembly hall and chapel. The du-khang is a monastery's most important meeting place. It is typically reached by a row of steps from a courtyard in front of the main building. Most du-khangs, on the wall of the porch at the entrance, have a painting of the Wheel of Existence.* Inside the du-khang you will see a central image, often Buddha

---

*Grasped by the claws and fangs of Saypo Kolu, Lord of Impermanence and Death (who serves to remind you of the hideousness of clinging to life), the Wheel of Existence is a complex pictorial metaphor of the endless cycle of human life. On the wheel's rim are pictured the phases in the cycle of rebirth, and in the middle circle are a snake, pig, and cock, symbolizing anger, stupidity, and lust or greed, the three vices. The mass of the wheel is divided into six wedges. The upper slice portrays heaven and the lower represents different hells. The remaining wedges represent the worlds of humans, animals, titans, and a purgatory. Buddha, who has escaped from the round of birth and death, is outside the wheel.

Saypo Kolu grasps the Wheel of Life in his fangs and claws. This fresco is at Tikse Monastery in Ladakh's Indus Valley.

in one of his manifestations, between smaller figures of attendants, guardians, or disciples. Rupee and hard-currency offerings are left before the central image in a barley-filled dish. In all large monasteries, seven or more butter lamps burn continuously. Rows of the low tables called *chog-tse* are arranged for the monks to sit at for *puja* (prayers or worship) and other ceremonies. Drums hang from the ceiling, *chenai* (reed instruments like shawms) lie on the tables, five-color Buddhist flags drape low, and the walls are covered with shelves of books, small images, tangkhas, and wall paintings that portray myths of the order governing the monastery. Other rooms in the central building and outbuildings contain images, paintings, the monastery's stores, its kitchen, and the monks' quarters.

Everyone traveling to Ladakh visits some of the monasteries. Most people reach their fill between the second and fifth, but some remain fascinated and continue to see more. The experience you have at a monastery may be different from that of someone traveling with you, and the reception you are accorded today may be quite unlike tomorrow's welcome. If you like a gomba and return more than once, you will learn much more about it. Your demeanor, the person or people you happen to meet, shared language ability, the circumstances under which you meet, the time of day: these variables and more contribute to what will or won't happen. In a smaller gomba, unless prayers are being said in the du-khang, you may not even see anyone immediately. The monks go to their rooms, leave to work on their ancestral property, and perform various religious ceremonies at homes or related monasteries; thus they are not always about when you arrive. Someone will be along soon if you are patient. When people visit a monastery, whether devotees or tourists, the custom has always been to leave a gift of money. The amount given varies entirely with the visitor's means and feeling for the situation. Since there are so many tourists (all of whom are well off enough to travel around the world to visit Ladakh, yet not all of whom are willing to leave donations at monasteries), entrance fees have been established at gombas. Some monasteries are well touristed (in certain rooms), such as Alchi, Spituk, Shey, Tikse, and Hemis, while others are visited less often.

The following list briefly describes most monasteries and palaces outside Leh from west to east along the Indus Valley. The list does not include Lamayuru, which has been mentioned, or Hemis, which is discussed separately below. All gombas are connected with the main Indus Valley road by jeep roads, and most are within an hour's walk of the principal valley bus route.

Additionally, two short hikes are outlined that begin at Tingmo Gang and Stok, respectively. Officially, foreigners are not permitted to walk more than a mile north of the main road along the Indus Valley, except where there are large gombas to be visited. If foreigners were caught trying to enter the Shyok Valley, they would be jailed. However, for the adventurous hiker who wants to have a look north at the Karakoram Range, the trails leading up from nalas above Tingmo Gang, Saspul, Basgo, and Sabu just east of Leh, in the Indus Valley, to the ridgeline of the Ladakh Range do make tempting prospects. On a typically brilliant Ladakh day, a person would have fine views of the eastern Karakoram from most of these passes.

Tingmo Gang. Seven miles east of Kalatse on the main valley road is Nurla village. An hour's walk north of Nurla takes you to one of the old palaces that were held by minor rulers before Ladakh was unified. Tingmo Gang rests in a pleasant setting amongst poplar trees. Although much of the original castle is in ruins, several more interesting shrines can be visited. People from this valley used to hire out as porters for foreign sportsmen and explorers.

A walk of two full or three easy days can be taken along the old trading route beginning at the valley that leads east from Tingmo Gang and proceeds over four low passes to Likir Monastery. Relative to most treks in the region, this one does not involve great climbs and descents, and it can be safely walked as early as May and as late as October, since the elevations reached do not exceed about 12,900 feet. This hike passes some of Ladakh's largest villages, which are quite prosperous since they have enough level, arable places for cultivation and are in relatively low valleys. If you want to break this trek in the middle, walk a couple of hours down-valley from Yangtang and you will arrive at Ri Dzong.

Ri Dzong. An hour's walk north of the main road from Uludrokpo village, Ri Dzong is the newest Gelugpa monastery in Ladakh, built just over a hundred years ago. The du-khang has an image of Tsong Khapa (as do most Gelugpa monasteries) and other statues, primarily of Buddha in his different incarnations. Ri Dzong means "Mountain Fortress."

Alchi. Most monasteries cling defensively to steep ridges or top low outcroppings, yet Alchi, which is the oldest and most iconographically important building complex in Ladakh, sits in a low valley. The side road to Alchi Gomba leads across a bridge over the Indus just west of Saspul. A half-hour walk takes you first to the larger village of Yul Khor, then in another mile to Chos Khor, where buildings rest above the Indus but out of view of the main road. This collection of buildings and shrines collectively known as Alchi "represents an extraordinary survival from the past," according to David Snellgrove. Alchi, like Hemis, is nearly a thousand years old, and was never devastated by invading armies. A hiking route from Lamayuru to Alchi is mentioned in the Zanskar section.

Likir. Likir Gomba is an extremely well kept Gelugpa monastery with many small chapels, a mile and a half north of the main road on the ridge between Saspul and Basgo villages. Within the last century, monks from the Likir Monastery have taken responsibility for the temples several miles away at Alchi.

Basgo. This palace (now largely in ruins) and its still-utilized shrines were once the center of the largest Indus Valley state, before the unification of Ladakh under Leh's authority. Basgo also has a Kagyupa temple, near the road, 5 miles west of Nimu. It is the second oldest gomba in Ladakh after Alchi.

Phiyang. Twelve miles west of Leh, Phiyang is just north of the main Indus Valley road on top of a small hill. A Kagyupa gomba, it is affiliated with Lamayuru. In order to take full advantage of the tourist season, Phiyang's annual festival has been moved to summer.

Spituk. Atop a sheer outcropping near the Indus south of Leh, Spituk Monastery overlooks the airport. This is a Gelugpa monastery with a new du-khang. It is built on several levels of the solid rock crag above Spituk village. A large image of the protector deity Bhairava (as seen also in Kathmandu's Durbar Square) in the gomba has often been misnamed Kali (a Hindu goddess) for the benefit of locally quartered soldiers. As at several other heavily visited monasteries in the valley, pujas have been performed here specifically for tour groups.

Stok. East of Spituk and 6 miles south of Leh is Choklamsar, a village mostly populated by Tibetan refugees, with a new Buddhist Philosophical School. New quarters for His Holiness the Dalai Lama, who now stays here for some time each summer, have been constructed in Choklamsar. Below Choklamsar a bridge crosses the Indus. The road on the south side divides, one branch goes upriver through the long, spread-out village of Shushot to Matho village and gomba. The other branch angles uphill to Stok village, across the wide Indus Valley from Leh. At Stok is the only royal palace that has been maintained and lived in since the 1842 Dogra invasion. The present ranking family member, the Rani of Stok (Gyalmo Diskit Wangmo), was elected to Parliament in New Delhi for one term and presently is involved with many community activities in the area. A small museum at the palace has old tangkhas, traditional ceremonial clothing, and other trappings belonging to the royal family. A pleasant three-day walk from Stok to the village of Matho is described at length, following the list of monasteries.

Shey. Seven miles east of Leh, the ruined palace of Shey sits on a knife-edged ridge with the main Indus Valley road running along its base. The flat valley floor near the palace has scores of stupas. Inside a temple near the road is a two-story image of Buddha. Another temple contains a Buddha that was gilded in bronze by eight Newari craftsmen from Nepal.

Tikse. Since the fifteenth century, monasteries and palaces have been built on hilltops or in unassailable positions so as to be immune from attack. Tikse, about halfway from Leh to Hemis, is one of these, a beautifully situated, multistructured monastery complex best seen from the east. The penultimate story has a roof with a sweeping view overlooking Matho, Shey, and Stakna monasteries, all of which lie above the same wide, irrigated stretch of valley bottom. This is a large monastery with several rooms that are opened for the frequent visitors who come during the day.

I first visited Tikse after the Hemis Festival, arriving late in the day and sleeping outside by a large entrance stupa under brilliant moonlight. In the morning I found a monk doing puja (prayers) in an upper room dominated by a large black image of the dreaded Yidam protector deity named Yamantanka. On either side were Kaladrupa and Mahakala the Great Black God. Like Yamantanka, these gods are so fearsome to human eyes that their faces must be kept covered. When the puja was finished, I was kindly invited to have sattu with the monk. We each ate several bowls of the nutlike toasted barley flour moistened with rich Ladakhi *solja* (tea with salt and butter). For a while, I felt I was truly experiencing Ladakh. About midmorning when I left, the first tour bus arrived, billowing smoke as it climbed the hill. Several years later, I arrived in one of these buses and found myself briefly standing again on the roof, admiring the inspiring views. This time a monk whose job it was to escort tourists had politely learned to say "no problem" when people asked him to pose. Wistfully I recalled my first, far more genuine visit, for this time I was touring both Hemis and Tikse in one wham-bam afternoon.

Stakna. Four miles up the Indus Valley from Tikse, the white buildings of Stakna perch on an isolated, razor-backed outcropping north of the Indus. In the du-khang of this small Kagyupa monastery is a large, silver-gilt stupa built since 1950.

Matho. This gomba above a clump of trees on a low ridge is south of (across) the Indus from Stakna and slightly upriver. Matho, like Stakna, is clearly, if distantly, seen from the roof at Tikse. It is the lone Sakyapa monastery in central Ladakh and well known for its yearly winter festival, during which two monks (who have previously been in solitary meditation) become possessed by a god who temporarily gives them certain extraordinary powers called *siddhi*s.

Chendey. This small Kagyupa monastery is connected with Hemis Gomba and sits across the Indus Valley from Hemis, south of Sakti village.

Trakthok. The name of this monastery means "Top of the Rocks." It is the only Nyingmapa monastery in this part of Ladakh and is situated up the side valley from Karu near Sakti near the road on the way to the restricted Chang La and Rupshu. Trakthok has a small cave in its base said to have been associated with Padmasambhava, founder of the Nyingmapa branch of Vajrayana Buddhism.

The Walk from Stok to Matho

A pleasant three-day walk can be taken from Stok to Matho village passing through narrow lower canyons and over a high pass dividing the nalas that flow past the two towns. This is a good trek if you are in Leh and want to take a short walk, but still test yourself in high elevations. Of course if you have any difficulties with the altitude, you can always retrace your steps back down. You can also try a mountaineering jaunt up Stok Kangri (20,060 feet: yes, above the magic 20,000-foot height) from this route.

The trail from Stok leads gently up beyond town. Looking back you can see Leh and the green fields above town far away across the valley. Slowly the hills converge and the path enters the confines of the gorge. Not far up the canyon, but 500 feet uphill above a bend in the stream, are the ruins of Stang La Khar, "Heavenly God's Palace." This fortress was built during a Mongol invasion, and when the fortifications were under attack, the defenders tossed down tsampa and black bean cakes. When the attackers saw the food raining down, they departed, deceived into believing that the defenders had adequate rations. At that time, a rock-covered underground passage, the ruins of which are still partly visible, led down to the valley stream.

The path up the nala winds farther into the hills, crossing over a rocky spur with a *lap-tse,* a ceremonial pile of stones topped with willow wands and prayer flags. The steep canyon walls are made of thin ribs of hard strata jutting out from softer layers of rock. The trail, nearly invisible on the wider rocky floor, bends again, this time toward the east, then to the south. By now you've gotten up to higher ground: the hills above are more rounded, and there are intermittent flat meadows for camping. Stok Kangri and its eastern outliers lie to the south. You can make a high camp your second day out from Stok village and try for the peak. If you get an early start, have no difficulty with the rapid rise in elevation, and can negotiate the last rather stiff snow slopes (crampons will probably be needed), this walk-up peak may be one you could climb in a long day from your high camp. At the least, you have a sweeping, majestic view of the Indus Valley and the Karakoram to the north if you walk up the lower slopes of the mountain.

Most of us will take the small path up the pink-tinged tributary that angles toward the northeast and the 16,000-foot Matho La. When a group I was escorting stopped at the base of this small feeder stream for the night, two horses belonging to men from Stok died far above camp, having eaten poisonous herbs. The trail down from the pass stays to the south side of the valley and contours horizontally for some distance before angling north and dropping down into the Matho Nala. Down the canyon and east of the trail in a willow grove is a small walled-in courtyard called the Matho Rong Tsan. This is a sacred place where a ceremony having to do with predicting the year's crop is held every year a month after the Hemis Festival (described below). The king's oracle from Stok and the oracle from Hemis arrive, riding white and red horses respectively. During the ceremony each oracle goes into a trance. Year-old juniper branches from Skirbuchan (down the Indus Valley from Khalse) are distributed, and fresh juniper is placed on the two round rock structures called *la tho.* Descending the canyon, views of the wide Indus Valley slowly open out as you emerge from a narrow, twisting defile. You will be west of and below Matho Gomba, noted previously. If you haven't arranged for a vehicle to pick you up at Matho, there is a daily bus or you could walk down to the road a couple of miles toward the river. The road passes through Shushot, a town widely scattered for miles along the river, and perhaps the longest village in this part of the world.

Hemis Gomba and the Hemis Festival

Hemis Monastery belongs to the Kagyupa's Brugpa branch of Vajrayana Buddhism, which is dominant in Bhutan. Hemis is Ladakh's wealthiest monastery, controlling a vast amount of choice farm and grazing land. The gomba sits across the wide valley from Karu village, invisible from the valley floor, and thus fortuitously bypassed, like Alchi, by several invading armies. But Hemis is no longer ignored. Your vehicle will cross the Indus near Karu and slowly meander up the stony, sloping valley floor. Note that at one point the road goes directly through a long prayer wall, but the displaced portion of the high wall has been rebuilt adjacent to the original wall. Hemis lies within protective walls of eroded beige sandstone. If you have time, clamber up the hill above the monastery to fully appreciate the exquisite setting of the gomba, nestled between enfolding strata. Like many monasteries in the Indus Valley, Hemis has a small inn attached to it. Enjoy the view from the monastery roof and be sure to ask to see the large new image of Guru Rimpoche, Padmasambhava, for the monks are very proud of it.

If you are staying at Hemis, consider walking a short hour behind the monastery up a small side valley to Kotsang, a hermitage and shrine that are not directly connected to Hemis. The buildings have been constructed above a sacred cave. The ceiling of this cave slowly oozes a firm, sticky black substance called *shialajit*. Shialajit is said to have curative properties and is taken orally or plastered on the skin. In Leh it costs some thirty rupees a *tola* (10 or 11 grams), but in Germany it can bring 15,000 marks a kilogram. Shialajit is also found in the Indus Valley of Pakistan, particularly near Chilas, and it also comes from one location in the Tirolean Alps, where it is known as "stone oil."

South of Hemis, and mostly in the upper reaches of the Markha Valley (see "The Markha Valley," following) is the 231-square-mile Hemis High Altitude National Park. In this remote region live the ibex, bharal, wolf, and the Pallas cat. This park is also a location where the observant and lucky have one of their best chances anywhere of sighting a snow leopard. For more information about the park, see the district forestry officer in Leh.

The festival at Hemis is held each year on the ninth to eleventh days of the fifth Tibetan month (about late June). Always well attended, the festival now attracts many foreign visitors as well as Ladakhis and Zanskaris, for most other Ladakhi festivals and extended religious ceremonies take place in the winter months when few outsiders are present. For two days the sloping, poplar-covered valley floor near Hemis Monastery sprouts a city of canvas and nylon tents, noodle stalls, and people selling meat *thupa* (soup), *dal-bhaat* (rice, lentils, and vegetables), souvenirs, and tambolo games (similar to bingo). Rajastanis sell medicine, Sikh salesmen offer dentures, puppeteers perform, and of course many teashops operate. You'll see older women wearing perags, bright blouses, and goatskins draped over their shoulders with the fur facing inward. Leh shopkeepers, nomads from Rupshu, Tibetan Drokpas, foreign network broadcasters, journalists, tour group *membaar*s, and others mingle as they eye the wares of the temporary bazaar. The people are part of the show at Hemis, whether you are watching the performance or ordering chow mein in a busy restaurant tent beneath the Lombardy poplars. The blend of new and old is striking: a mod-haired boy in bell bottoms converses with his mother, dressed Ladakhi style, while a polyester-clad Frenchman strides ahead of the members of his group, who exchange amused glances with a Changpa family from Rupshu.

The heart of the festival is a two-day performance by monks in costumes and masks who are surrounded by an audience that sits and stands on roofs, balconies, steps, and the courtyard. Foreigners are now charged to attend the festival. Western-born Lama Anagarika Govinda, who visited Hemis before wheeled vehicles had reached Ladakh, saw these "mystery plays," which were then three days in length. He said of them that "they were far from being merely theatrical performances: they were the coming to life of a higher reality through magic rites, in which . . . performers and spectators are welded into one and have both become active participants. . . . "

The festival's ceremonies are always attended by a selected lama. When the officiating lama is seated, the first play begins. Performers descend from the du-khang between rows of spectators to the music of drums and eight-foot-long horns. The lamas present a series of symbolic scenes including some from Padmasambhava's life; the most dramatic episode depicts the destruction of the ego, which is symbolized by a dough figure that is splattered and kicked into the audience.

During the performance, two Tibetan traditions are carried on: those of the Shirimba and Chabo. The former is an older monk, perfectly typecast, who patrols the perimeter of the performing area. He carries a long whip, which he uses to scatter spectators from areas needed for imminent scenes. He never uses the whip with real force, but older women cackle and smile widely as they make off, much to the evident surprise and delight of the crowd. The Chabo are two young, energetic monks dressed in red-and-yellow robes, red masks, and long false pigtails. Their duty is to dun people for contributions to the monastery. One Chabo throws a *kata* (prayer scarf) over someone's head while the other monk claps his hands to draw playful attention to the victim, who must pay or continue to be pestered. The two Chabo also go beyond the monastery courtyard during the dances, becoming the most familiar masked faces of all.

The Suru Valley

The Suru Valley and its tributaries lie just to the east of Kashmir and comprise the westernmost part of Ladakh. On the bank of the Suru River along the main road from Kashmir to Leh is Kargil, Ladakh's second-largest town after Leh. The only road into the large Zanskar District travels south from Kargil along the length of the Suru Valley, exiting at the Pensi La, the end of the main valley.

The large town of Kargil offers tall poplar trees, a tourist office east above the bazaar, and the last reliable source of any supplies aside from the most basic foodstuffs if you are heading up-valley or toward Zanskar. If you stroll out of town across the footbridge to the east bank of the Suru River and walk up the ridge, you'll see snow-clad peaks to the south, the direction from which the Suru River flows. Kargil does not have the palaces and panache of Leh; it is more an entrepôt to pass through on the way to one of the treks noted below or en route to Zanskar.

In summer there should be at least one bus a day going as far as Pannikar. Check with the tourist officer or at the J. & K. government transport ticket office if you are planning on riding to Rangdum or as far as Padum in Zanskar. If you are going as far as the latter two places, you may have to endure riding on the back of a PWD (Public Works Department) truck or pay to ride in the cab of a private goods truck. You will probably have to arrange the latter by yourself. There is always the far more expensive option of hiring a jeep. If you do this, speak to the tourist officer and try to find out how much you should pay before you start talking to a jeep driver. The road up-valley to the south should be open as far as Pannikar village (42 miles away) by early July unless landslides have blocked it. Beyond Pannikar and Rangdum Monastery, the Pensi La at the head of the valley is generally plowed free of snow by the middle or end of July.

Sankho and the Umba La

Twenty-five miles south of Kargil is Sankho village. Sankho has a little bazaar and a couple of small teashops-cum-restaurants where you can also sleep (like Kargil's hostelries, however, you may find you are sharing your bedclothes with some unwanted intruders; consider pitching your tent on a roof). The town sits at the mouth of the nala descending from the Umba La and directly across the Suru River from a valley leading to the east. First, here is a brief mention of the route to the northwest over the Umba La.

In two to three days you can walk between Sankho and Dras, which is located east of the Zoji La on the main road from Srinagar to Kargil (see "The Road to Leh: Following the Ancient Caravan Route," preceding). As you pass through the several pleasant villages up from Sankho, use some Balti words from the glossary in the back of the book and people will respond with surprise and pleasure, for everyone here is Shiite and Balti is their mother tongue. The last town is Umba; then comes the steep, scree-covered climb to the pass (about 13,500 feet). At the pass you can see Nun Kun, the high double peak to the south, described below. The way down from the pass leads over snow, and afterwards another lower ridge must be crossed before reaching Dras to the northwest. You may also go from Dras to Sankho, but whichever way you walk, take a local to show you the way, particularly the section of the route between the pass and Dras.

Across the Suru River east of Sankho, a valley with numerous villages trends easterly. After a long day's walk up-valley, a route leads up a tributary to the Rasi La, then over a second pass, the Wakka or Sapi La. The path then descends to the Wakka Chu, emerging at Shergol west of Mulbek on the main road into Ladakh east of Kargil. You should allow four to five days for this walk. Be sure to take a local, for none of the maps is much help, and in any case, you would have difficulties here with route finding, particularly between the two passes.

Pannikar and the Walk Over
the Kanji La to Hiniskut

Seventeen miles south of Sankho (and 42 miles from Kargil) is the town of Pannikar (10,600 feet). Pannikar was first mentioned in the last chapter as the village where you emerge after crossing the Lonvilad Gali or the Yuranshan Pass, the passes at the head of Kashmir's Warwan Valley (see "The Lonvilad Gali" in Chapter 8). There is a small inn here and even a tourist office. The homes in Pannikar are dusty brown, the color of the surrounding earth from which they have been made, and few highlights stand out aside from the bright painted woodwork along the eaves of the mosque, the shiny cupolas above, and the green willows along the camping area by the stream that divides the village. The first time I arrived in town, it was the important Muslim holiday of Eid, and the mosque and area around it were crowded with villagers dressed in their best. Some teenage boys wore light sweaters with the words "3 Star," and the ladies had bright yellow, red, or pink shawls over their flower-print loose blouses and baggy pants. But since it was harvest season, a few people were hard at work, each driving a string of horses and cattle in a circle over the recently cut wheat to separate the grain from the stalks. At Pannikar you can hire a horseman to accompany you, or you can walk up-valley. Alternately, there are occasional trucks and the rare bus going up-valley and on to Zanskar.

If you have walked to Pannikar from Kashmir, you can take a vehicle north to Kargil or continue up-valley to the east on a vehicle or by foot. The narrative here assumes you choose to walk. A mile south of town is a footbridge to the east bank of the Suru River. After you ascend the stony hill, you will have to cross the edges of fields to reach a small trail leading up from the base of the ridge you must now cross. This ridge rises up to the Parkacheek or Lago La (12,450 feet), where you have a fine view north to the flat valley and the villages you have just come from, but the spectacular perspective lies beyond the ridge.

To the south rises the steep pyramid of 23,410-foot Nun, while its neighbor, 23,250-foot Kun, lies just beyond. Nun Kun is the highest Himalayan peak in the 450-mile stretch from Nanga Parbat to Nanda Devi. Pouring out from the basin between the peaks is the steep, crevassed Parkacheek or Ganri Glacier, which flows directly into the Suru River below. Arthur Neve called this "one of the grandest views of the world. . . ." This spur you are crossing is fun to walk along; you can go a good distance either way along it, particularly to the east, but you will need to return to the pass to find the small trail leading down to the south, for it is the safest route down. The road follows the river around the base of this long, narrow, fingerlike ridge, but crossing over the top is quicker and far more scenic. Climbers attempting northern routes on Nun or Kun begin at the village of Tangul, across the river from the base of the eastern end of this ridge.

Parkacheek village, the last Balti town in the valley, lies in several clusters at the southern base of the ridge. If you have climbed the ridge for the view but don't want to walk the next stretch, you can wait for a vehicle at the vehicle pullover east of the stream where the trucks stop. Otherwise you will be walking along the level valley floor for the next two days. Not far east of Parkacheek the road is forced practically into the Suru River by a steep ridge, and here you are just across the river from the bottom of the Parkacheek Glacier. The blue glacial ice calves directly off into the river, and chunks of snow and ice float in eddies, then get caught in the current and cruise downstream. The road, which is unpaved beyond Parkacheek, heads into a wider portion of the valley and aims due east. Landslides and mudflows often block the road in summer, and this stretch near Parkacheek is one of several up-valley from Kargil where vehicles can be temporarily halted.

Walking along the road, I noticed an orange steamroller made in Calcutta and approaching it saw that squarely on the front was affixed a color photograph of the frowning visage of Ayatollah Ruhollah Khomeini (whose stern countenance seemed to be telling me to stop enjoying myself). This proved to be the last visible evidence of Shiite influence in the valley. Rolling ground of maidans, bogs, and arid stretches characterize the wide, flat valley floor for the next two days' walk. The large glacier you see to the south is the Shafat Glacier, descending from the Nun Kun massif. Occasional meadows offer pleasant camping spots by the river. Then in the V up the valley far to the east is a glimpse of twisted strata, your first glance at the hills in Zanskar. Soon you pass three stupas with the sacred words "Om Mani Padme Hum" in Tibetan, and you've crossed an invisible boundary demarcating land influenced by the Ayatollah to a region beholden to the Dalai Lama.

In the distance is the small village of Juldo (or Zulidok, 12,600 feet), with its solid whitewashed two-story homes whose flat roofs are piled with what seems to be some of the last scant brushwood to be found in this barren region. Here is an inn with a bright red sign on the roof that must have plopped down from outer space, for it begins Welcome to Disneyland. Beneath the wildly striated ridge you have been approaching is Rangdum Gomba, on a hill that rises barely 100 feet up in the otherwise-flat valley floor. When you walk to Rangdum from Juldo, stay fairly close to the road and resist the temptation to carve a straight line across the flat valley, or you will get into boggy ground. Rangdum is a Gelugpa monastery with about twenty monks. Inside is an image of Tsong Khapa, the founder of the order, and, on the second floor, a good wall painting of the hidden, mythical kingdom of Shambhala.

The main valley floor turns to the south in the vicinity of Rangdum, continuing level past the last village and three large glaciated nalas that debouche from the west. The second of these side valleys leads to the high Chilung La, mentioned in the last chapter. Then the road rises up to the small lakes at the head of the main valley and the level Pensi La (circa 14,450 feet), where you have an excellent view of the Durung Drung Glacier descending from the main Great Himalaya Range. This glacier provides the headwaters of the Doda (or Stod) River and if you cross the pass, you will be in Zanskar and following the Doda toward Padum, Zanskar's district headquarters, noted in the next section.

From Rangdum a four- to five-day walk can be made across the northwestern corner of Zanskar to the vicinity of Hiniskut on the Kargil-to-Leh road. A couple of alternate paths diverge toward the end of this walk, one of which takes you directly to Lamayuru Gomba. This trek from Rangdum can be part of a longer walk from Kashmir through Pannikar, or you can take a vehicle from Kargil and start walking at Juldo or here at Rangdum. The route follows the wide valley that leads east from Rangdum. As you start walking, angle slowly toward the south side of the valley, for the stream percolates down into the stony ground as it flows, and as you continue up, the water can get deeper and more difficult to ford. If the water is low, you can stay on the floor of the valley for a while, but sooner or later you will have to climb up a little and follow a small path above the south bank. The nala narrows, and after you lose sight of the wide main valley, precipices appear below and across the stream. You contour along the small path around many spurs, one of which is a deep maroon color. A tributary enters from the north, but it is the smaller second stream from the north that you will take.

This stream is obvious because it enters the main nala through a deep, narrow slit in the foliated shale. Camp here at this stream junction (about 13,900 feet) and plan on an early start in the morning. The path from here leads north, right through the narrow slot and briefly near the stream, then angles resolutely up a long basin covered with gray and beige rock that opens out as you rise. Look back from time to time and see the snow-covered mountains to the south that rise with you and also the long, lone maroon spur you crossed the day before. At the top is the 16,500-foot Kanji La, but this should not be as high as you go. If you have any energy after resting a bit, walk slowly up to the left (west), and if the clouds haven't settled in for the day, you will have a superb view of the Karakoram to the north, far more sweeping than what you can see from the pass.

North of the pass the route descends steeply over snow, then across stony ground, and gently rises over a sand-colored ridge before dropping to a flat camping spot in the Kang Nala at 14,200 feet. From here, you have only to follow the valley down, but keep your wading shoes at the ready, for there are streams to cross. An hour from camp is the confluence of three wide valleys: a place to dance or sing "Ode to Joy" or the theme from *The Magnificent Seven,* depending on your inclination, even if the local herders think you've been touched by the height. (If you are walking up this valley in the opposite direction, you want to take the valley to the right, the west.) Below this conjunction the valley narrows, zigzagging between soaring walls, and you will have to wade across the gurgling stream several times. Keep your eyes peeled for blue poppies. When the nala widens again, you are not far from Kanji village (12,600 feet), the only town you will see on this side of the pass. People in Kanji are very friendly, and among the village's residents is a respected *amchee,* a doctor

Dawa Norbu from Kanji village hopped on his yak to be photographed.

well versed in Tibetan medical theory and herbal remedies. The gomba in town features a stuffed bear near the entrance.

From Kanji you can continue down-valley a half day's walk to the Kargil-Leh road, passing many rosebushes and beneath a tangle of convoluted strata. Depending on the time of year, you will have to ford the stream from six to twelve times. It may be rough going, particularly in the lower part of the gorge while the water is in spate prior to late August, but now a road has been constructed into Kanji, which will greatly ease the way. At the road down-valley from Kanji you are west of the Fatu La, near the town of Hiniskut, noted in the preceding "The Road to Leh: Following the Ancient Caravan Route." Remember that you can walk the old caravan route, as mentioned in that section, over the pass to Lamayuru Monastery in an easy three hours. (If the stream in the gorge route down-valley from Kanji is too risky to negotiate, an alternate route branches off partway downstream leading to the west over a pass called the Timti La. Take a villager from Kanji with you as guide.)

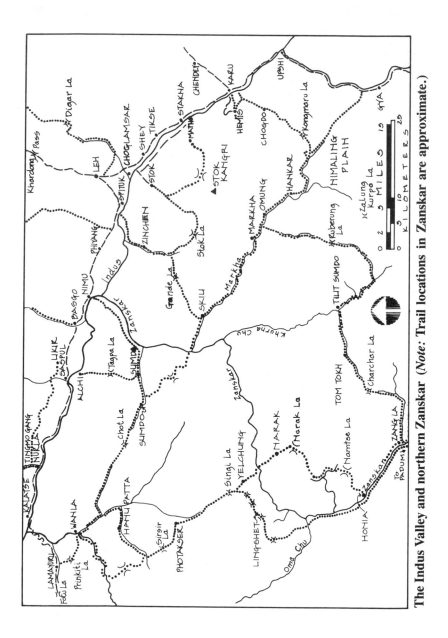

The Indus Valley and northern Zanskar (*Note:* Trail locations in Zanskar are approximate.)

At Kanji you could traverse a different route to the east that goes to Lamayuru Gomba in about two to three days. Take someone from Kanji to show you the way, which begins by crossing the stream below town and traverses past the village barley fields. The route crosses the Shillakong or Yogma La and drops steeply to the narrow Shillakong Tokpo (*tokpo* means "stream" in Ladakhi). Then it follows the Shillakong, crossing and re-crossing it, until the way emerges at the southern base of the Prinkiti La near Wanla village, a path described in "The Zanskar Traverse," following. Here at the base of the Prinkiti La, you are a couple of hours' walk north of Lamayuru.

Remote Zanskar: High Passes and Rushing Torrents

[This region is] an open air geological exhibition running for millions of years with very few spectators.

Kalyan Kumar Bhattacharya, 1989

Aside from the Karakoram glacial vastness, no place in the Himalayan system is so wide and impenetrable as Zanskar District (or Tehsil) in Ladakh. Zanskar lies south of the Indus Valley and north of Himachal Pradesh, comprising some 3,000 square miles: larger than Sikkim and nearly as big as Lebanon. Only since 1978 has a rough, dusty road connected Kargil to the small town of Padum, Zanskar's district headquarters. And the road is usually open only about four months a year. The wide, flat Zanskar and Doda (or Stod) river valleys stretching north and west from Padum respectively represent some of the only large flat surfaces in Zanskar. Unlike the narrow Ladakh Range, the Zanskar Range is wide and complex, and it is a long range, reaching all the way to Nepal. Most of Zanskar's area is rent with high, sharp-edged ridges that catch enough snow to make the steep gorges below very difficult to ford in the short summer months. Alexander Cunningham, the first Western chronicler of Ladakh, tells us that Zangs-kar means "white copper." No large trading routes ever passed through Zanskar, and the region's inhabitants formerly traded only with neighboring Baltis, Ladakhis, Changpas in Rupshu, and Lahoulis to the south. Zanskar's remote areas are some of the best regions in India to see wild mammals, such as ibex, wolf, fox, and possibly the shy snow leopard.

Several routes can be trekked in Zanskar, and some of these will be mentioned, but no currently available map will give you more than a rough estimate of the jagged terrain. Maps that correctly depict Zanskar's convoluted landscape and the trails through the region are yet to be made. So it takes a hardy, adaptable, experienced trekker to strike out along trails far into Zanskar, and all hikers going there will need a local with horses who knows the way, to guide and cook. If you are trekking with just one or two foreigners, you may be able to squeeze by using yak dung or willow branches for fuel, but most people take stoves. When you trek in Zanskar, you should take your own food with you. If not, you will be charged dearly for any food or meals you purchase in villages, as well you should be, for this is a region where people can just feed themselves. In fact, locals may say, *"Kharu,"* which means "give me food" in Zanskari. Your best source-book for information on the monasteries in Zanskar is the second volume of *The Cultural Heritage of Ladakh,* by Snellgrove and Skorupski. And, if you can locate it, the book called *Hiking in Zanskar and Ladakh* by Chabloz and Cremieu (cited in the bibliography) is also helpful.

Zanskaris are engagingly friendly for the most part. The sure way to recognize a man from Zanskar and other outlying regions of Ladakh is by his unique hairdo: traditionally, a man shaves the hair on the front of his head completely off along a line running ear to ear over the top of the head, permitting the remainder of his long tresses to fall loose. The sahru with its upturned flaps is preferred headgear for older Zanskaris. Zanskar's dialect is somewhat different from Ladakhi, but people here should be able to understand any words you use from Helena Norberg-Hodge's Ladakhi glossary in the back of the book, and many men will know some Urdu.

Several routes through Zanskar are mentioned here, beginning with the most popular walk, a north-south traverse of the entire region. Note that this trek can be broken at Padum in the middle, or the walk can be begun or finished in Padum.

First, however, a few words about Padum. Padum's inhabitants are a mixture of Muslims and Buddhists, augmented by a few flatland civil servants who must feel they have been banished to Siberia. An inn of sorts is open in the summer, or you can stay with a family, or camp away from the bazaar. Padum even has a tourist officer. You are supposed to register with him when you arrive, although when I came, it was so early in the year that his office was not yet open. A few stores carry food necessities, and you should be able to purchase kerosene (of possibly uncertain quality), so Padum can be a supply point for basics. Be prepared to encounter vicious midday dust storms in the wide valley up- and downriver from Padum. The day after I arrived in Padum, a chanting, arm-waving demonstration composed of a large maroon-robed crowd of locals and people from up the Tsarap Valley was protesting the misappropriation of funds by a local official. It seems he had bought himself a jeep with money meant for building a bridge and other projects. The angry citizenry had already seen to it that the jeep had been pushed over an embankment and into the river, but this was not enough: people wanted to see the embezzler in jail.

The Zanskar Traverse

The principal trekking route through Zanskar begins (or ends) at Lamayuru, goes through rugged terrain to the Zanskar River, then follows that wide, level valley to Padum, continuing south up the rather gentle Tsarap Valley to the Shingo La and ending at Darcha in the Lahoul region of Himachal Pradesh. The entire trek takes about two and a half weeks, but, as noted above, either half of it can be done up to Padum, or beginning there. Here is a brief account of that walk, with two alternate routes that can be followed south of Yelchung village.

Leaving Lamayuru, drop down into the fields below, walk down-valley and take the first nala to the south, which leads in short order to the dry, white Prinkiti La, a low pass that you descend through a narrow passage to the Shillakong River, where there are several tall poles with prayer flags. Here you have your first choice of routes; your local guide will know which way to go, for he will have asked people which route is being currently used. If the water is high in the Yapola Nala along the main route to the south, you will have to go west up the smaller Shillakong Nala, crossing and re-crossing the stream. From the Shillakong you could also climb northwest to reach Kanji village, but the path toward the Zanskar River and Padum leads south, crossing the Niuche (or Snigutse) La and reaching the main trail at the river and the northern base of the Sirsir La.

The principal path from the bottom of the Prinkiti La leads down past poplar trees, irrigated fields, and a few homes lived in by Dards along the bottom of the Shillakong Nala to the small town of Wanla, with its maroon-and-white monastery perched above town on a knife-edged ridge. Now the path turns south and for some distance follows rosebushes and well-tended fields of mustard and grain along the Yapola Valley. South of Phanjila village, where a tributary enters from the east (see "From Lamayuru to Alchi," following), the trail heads into a narrow gorge where at one point the rushing stream goes beneath old avalanche debris. Recent improvements to the track, which include gouging out large cuts in the steep valley walls, have eliminated some but not all of the fords. Now you turn into a tributary, the Spang Nala, and pass clusters of bushes and Hanupatta village. Overhead the terrain is a rainbow of pastel earth colors, and thin, platelike protrusions of hard strata point to the sky. Then the climb to the first high pass, the Sirsir La, begins.

At the Sirsir La, you can look south across a wide basin to the Singe La, but first comes a steep, then a gentle descent. You walk past Photaksar village, a town with two clusters of homes, green fields, and a gomba above in a dark brown rock outcrop. The way passes through wide yak pastures used by the villagers of Narak (a town on the alternate route described below) and others, but the real homebodies along the undulating hills are the sleek, brown marmots who screech at you, the intruder. The way leads up through snow to the highest pass of the entire route, the 16,950-foot Singe La ("Lion Pass"), with a distinctive, high rocky peak rising directly up east of the pass.

South of the Singe La, the route followed by most individual trekkers and all trekking groups angles over a series of four ridge passes, with relatively (relative for this high, deep country) small drops between them: the Khupte (or Kuba) La, Nietukse (or Murgum) La, Chupkun (or Chapskang) La, and the Haluma (or Hanuma) La. Between the second and third passes is the fair-sized community of Lingshet. Its gomba contains good wall paintings in an old style that shows strong Indian and Kashmiri influence. At the gomba, just as at every gomba in the region, you will be charged for entry. You may be lucky and arrive for the annual festival held sometime in July. After the Haluma La the path descends to the meadows of Snertse, where many animals graze in the summer. Then you drop to the Zingchan (or Oma, "Milk") Chu and climb to the Purfi (or Parfi) La. Now it's down to the west (left) bank of the Zanskar River, and the roller-coaster walk is over. From here you follow the river to Padum. You can walk south as far as Zangla and cross there to the east side of the wide, turbid river. Or you can stay on the same bank of the river for the next two days as far as the large Gelugpa gomba at Karsha, the largest monastery in Zanskar. The monastery's many buildings are clustered above the town and fields of Karsha, along the lowest slopes of a steep ridge not far from the place where the Doda (Stod) River joins the Tsarap to form the Zanskar River and within sight of, but a half day's walk from, Padum.

From south of the Singe La, however, there is an alternate route to the wide Zanskar River valley north of Padum. This way is taken less often because there are fewer settlements, and thus less possible shelter for your local companion, but mainly because it is said to be impossible for pack animals to negotiate. This is the way I have gone, however, so it will be sketched in briefly here. South of the Singe La, the trail goes past the few large homes of Yelchung, then diverges from the better-traveled way. The track stays high to cross one knob, then a second (barely a pass, but marked as such on most maps), then drops abruptly to a sturdy bridge across the Zanskar River, which pours through the narrow opening below. Now you begin a long climb, first to the friendly town of Narak, which has so few fields that the villagers must trade for grain. Here you can just see the Singe La and its distinctive peak, but as you climb higher, the pass and promontory come into clear view, as does the deep gorge you have crossed.

About 4,000 feet above Narak is a notch, but this is a false pass. You must descend slightly, then contour along steep terrain to the true pass, the 15,700-foot Narak La. (If you are coming from the south, be sure not to drop down from the pass, or you'll find yourself in a cul-de-sac and having to slog steeply back up to the trail.) From the pass, curlicue down over slate talus into a substantial stand of willows and an eerie narrow crack in the rock walls where it is said the ice underfoot never melts. This icy stretch is supposed to be the place that horses cannot negotiate. Tall darning needle pinnacles, some with rocks balanced on top, line the dry hills in two places and seem to have been put in place by an imaginative cosmic artist: here, not at Juldo, is the real Disneyland. You descend one nala, then gradually ascend another, fording each stream once or twice. Now a level plain, then the climb to the 14,300-foot Namtse La. Below this pass, the trail descends into a narrow canyon, meeting another small gully 500 feet below the pass. On the slopes above I saw some wild goats that returned my gaze, then returned unconcernedly to their browsing. The small track follows the narrow canyon several thousand feet down to the small hamlet of Honia on the east bank of the Zanskar River.

Now begins the gentle walk south along the rolling bottomland of the wide Zanskar River valley, and you can make great distance-gulping prog-ress. There are few sources of good water hereabouts—*pani mushkeel,* "water difficulty," we said among ourselves. This traverse across Zanskar was part of a far longer walk I did with trekker-climber Arlene Blum and our hardworking Nepali staff, two of whom came with us for five months on no notice at all. The pleasant and attractive town located between high scree slopes and green fields south of Honia is Zangla, where the royal family of Zanskar resides. You can probably meet the king *(gyalpo)* and/or queen *(gyalmo)* if your local companion makes the arrangements, for they are used to seeing visitors. A road extends from Zangla to Padum, but you may have to wait for quite a while to get a lift, unless you are coming from the other direction and can catch a ride in Padum. Just south of Zangla is the Zhumlam Nala, where the difficult route called the Zhumlam begins, the "middle way" to the Markha and Indus valleys (see the next section).

Look hereabouts in the Zanskar Valley for wolf traps: circular, waist-high rings of stones with the topmost layer of rocks cantilevered inward. A lamb is placed inside the 15-foot-wide trap as bait, and any wolf unfortunate enough to jump in cannot leap out. Perhaps you will also see billy goats with wool or burlap aprons tied below their rib cages. These strange garments are used as birth control devices.

South of Zangla is Zozar (or Tsasar) and another small hamlet, then the homes of Thonde. Eight hundred feet above town is Thonde's Gelugpa Gomba, where you'll find superb views of the valley, friendly monks, and a small orchard and gardens watered by a stream that flows from a spring. A trail over the Thonde La that continues into the valley leading to Phuktal Gomba (noted below) ascends above Thonde Gomba. At Thonde the level plod continues straight along the plain past Karsha Gomba (across the valley) and along to Padum on the west bank of the Tsarap Chu. No matter which route you take, the walking time between Lamayuru and Padum is about eight to ten days. It is best to take a local guide on this trek, and although food is available from some houses (at high prices, as noted above), you should bring enough food from Lamayuru (or Padum if traveling north) for the whole trek.

Padum is roughly the midpoint in this trek. The walk south to Darcha in Lahoul can be made in about a week. A road is slowly being built south of Padum; it is supposed to follow the trekking route over the Shingo La, but who knows when and if it will be finished. An hour from Padum is a good camping place with a spring on the main trail; across the river on the eastern bank are the small, intriguing-looking homes of Shila. Then you continue up the narrow valley to Bardun Gomba nestled on its large rock promontory. The road from Padum goes at least this far.

When Arlene and I and our Nepalis arrived at Bardun, we learned that the annual festival was about to occur, so a couple of days later we walked back up from Padum to the monastery for the event, which occurs on Buddha's birthday. We felt extremely fortunate to be the only foreigners at the masked dances. Less than a hundred villagers attended, crowding into the small courtyard and lining the low roofs. Older women wore their turquoise-covered perags, and the girls all had bright pink flowers in their woolen hats. First the lama and a few monks recited some texts, performing ritual purifications for both the monastery and those present. Then the rocks supporting the 30-foot-tall pole in the midst of the courtyard were loosened, the pole tipped onto a roof, and long new white prayer flags were added. The dances began as monks in costume wearing masks whirled and twirled. After a short break for lunch, the forces of good triumphed, and by midafternoon the dance performance part of the festival was over.

The narrow valley opens out near Mune, where there is a Gelugpa gomba. Just north of Mune a trail rarely used by trekkers goes up the Temashut Nala past several pasture areas to a point where you have two options. A small side glacier to the east leads to the Kang La (circa 17,625 feet) and a route down the Miyar Nala in Lahoul (see "Trekking in Lahoul" in Chapter 10). The larger glacier takes you to the difficult Poat La, which provides a route into the upper Dharlang Valley (called the Bhut Nala lower down), the approach route for the Umasi La (see "The Umasi La" in Chapter 8). I once heard a story about a hiker who climbed up to the last shelter on the south side of the Poat La and shared his frigid, windy aerie with a frozen corpse for the night. You'd have to be quite intrepid before attempting either route without a local to see you at least to the pass you were crossing.

South of Mune is Reru, with its own large nala. On the main trail here is a nice camping place with a spring and meadow. Above Reru the dry valley narrows again, and you can make rather good time past the attractive settlement of Itchor up to the several large homes of Pune. If you need supplies at Pune, you will have to pay well for them. At Pune, which lies on the east bank across the river from the main trail, a large river called the Niri (or Tsarap) Chu enters the valley you have been ascending. The Niri Chu is actually the main valley, for it drains a far larger area than the Kargyak River valley to the south that you will follow.

You must be sure to take the hour-and-a-half side walk up the Niri Chu to see Phuktal Gomba, built into the mouth of a large cave, with its many residences perched on steep precipices like a painting in a fairy tale. As you walk around a bend in the narrow gorge and see Phuktal, you will be very glad you made this short pilgrimage. Phuktal is Gelugpa, with sixty or more monks attached to the monastery, although they aren't all present at once because Phuktal has charge of other smaller gombas as well. The important frescoes are in the locked dark red building on the west side of the cave. A tiny spring in the floor of the cave is not supposed to be approached by women. Clamber around on the high buildings for fine perspectives of the complex high above the turquoise stream in the valley floor. When we arrived, we were the first foreigners in six months to visit, for the passes were just then opening. The monks asked about conditions on the Shingo La to the south, where we had come from, because three of their brethren had recently set out over that pass for Lahoul. People here are very friendly and some of them are well traveled, having been as far as Bangalore in south-central India. If you wish, you can take a small, high path from the gomba back down-valley to a cascading stream where the monastery's grain mill is located in a narrow, hidden defile. It is possible to pass the night in the gomba, and you can also arrange for a meal or two.

Up the main path leading south from Phuktal the river is called the Kargyak Chu, and the trail passes several small villages. Excepting a few narrow places, you can make good time to Kargyak, the last village in Zanskar, with about twenty homes, several long rows of mani walls, and excellent yoghurt often available. Here I was invited for tea with a muscular weather-bronzed monk, and we chatted while delicately holding fragile, small cups of chai. At Kargyak the crows are pesky and inquisitive, particularly if food is in evidence, and the doves fly in pairs, whereas down in Padum they swoop in flocks. Not far north of Kargyak a side valley leads to the Phirtse La, an alternate, strenuous route to Lahoul that crosses the Baralacha Pass (see the next chapter) and involves numerous stream crossings, taking several days longer than the main trail. With the exception of the area around Mune, Reru, and Phuktal Gomba, the scenery along this valley isn't as sweeping or awesome as the colorful, convoluted hills and gorges you see between Padum and Lamayuru. But in the vicinity of Kargyak the celestial artist has splashed bright ochres and deep mahogany along the way; the valley opens up and the vistas are grand.

South of Kargyak you angle gently upward through majestic country and soon begin to see the sheer, towering face of an isolated monolith 3,000 to 4,000 feet high that, with only a little imagination, looks like a mammoth sail. You are passing through some of the areas used to pasture Kargyak's rambunctious black yaks, but aside from possibly seeing them and a herder or two, you will likely not see any more Zanskaris, unless, like the monks from Phuktal, they are traveling to Lahoul. The nala leading to the Shingo La is a small, narrow opening on the west side of the wide valley, so you will have to cross the stream to reach it. You may need to climb up the north side of this narrow tributary to reach the grassy slopes above. The way goes west to the camp called Lakong (or Trukur). Then the track turns south up slopes that are sometimes steep and that were several feet deep in snow when we crossed. At the 16,400-foot Shingo La (Shingo refers to an herbal spice that grows hereabouts), a line of stone lap-tse with wind-ripped prayer flags mark the pass and you enter the Lahoul District of Himachal Pradesh.

The way down from the pass first crosses a permanent snowfield and is gentle, then steepens, and the rocky nala becomes narrower as you descend. Coming up from the south, our porters ate ground garlic here to combat the symptoms of altitude sickness, and they all agreed that this was an effective preventative for headaches. As we ascended this uninspiring, snow-covered nala, I had strange night dreams of perpetually walking halfway to a place but never quite reaching it. Chikor (monal pheasants) burbled and swooped, making running landings in the snow as we passed along. Ramjak is the name of the camping place on this side of the pass; you can camp at other places as well, particularly above the lowest part of the nala. The route out of this valley goes on the east side of the canyon well above the stream (unless a new bridge has been built across the difficult-to-ford Barai River) because the stream drops into the larger Barai (or Barhai) Valley below through a slot carved in the rock and there is no room for a path at the bottom.

The trail follows generally along the bottom of the Barai Valley, and you will delight in seeing the initial small clump of silver birches, the first trees for several days' walk, if you are coming from the north. When you reach the few houses called Rarik, you will be an hour's walk from the road at Darcha (locally called Darcha-Sumdo). At Darcha are a couple of small "hotels" where you can get hot food. The daily bus parks at Darcha for the night and leaves for Manali at 6:00 A.M. For more information on this area, see "Trekking in Lahoul" in Chapter 10.

Other Treks in and Adjacent to Zanskar

There are numerous other hikes you can take in Zanskar, some of which are mentioned here. Both because I don't have personal experience with these routes and because of the difficulties in negotiating the rugged terrain and the ecological fragility of the areas, I am loath to publicize them in a book ostensibly meant to guide people into these regions. The hardy and determined will suitably equip themselves, take maps and a local or two, and go, guidebooks be damned, while others are best advised to stick to more well-worn paths. The best guide I've yet seen to the more remote regions of Zanskar are the pullout sheets in *Hiking in Zanskar and Ladakh* by Chabloz and Cremieu, listed in the bibliography. If you want to get well off beaten tracks, try to locate that guide. An exception to my disinclination to publicize remote routes in Zanskar is this first hike below, along the often-trekked Markha Valley (strictly speaking, the Markha Valley is not, in fact, part of Zanskar, but lies out of the Indus Valley on the northern periphery of Zanskar).

The Markha Valley

For those who want a trek that takes about eight to ten days and crosses two to three high passes, getting into some truly high country, the walk from the Indus Valley into and and back out of the Markha Valley has become popular. There are two approaches to the pass leading to the lower reaches of the Markha Valley. The trek to the Markha Valley is usually walked in the direction described here because the initial approach, whichever way you go the first couple of days, is easier going this way and leads to lower ground in the Markha Valley.

The first alternative is a little shorter because it avoids a pass, and it is a good route to take if the streams are not high when you are going in. This walk leaves from Spituk on the main road just south of Leh's airport. At Spitok, cross the Indus on a good bridge and angle southwesterly (down-valley) across the dry landscape until you reach the Zinchen Nala. Walking up this nala, you will have to cross and recross the river, which is difficult if the water is high. First you pass (or possibly camp at) Zinchen village, then after a half day's walk, reach the Rumbak Chu. Here you join the other approach.

If the waters are high, you should walk up the Stok Nala as described above in the first part of "The Walk From Stok to Matho." Two hours up that nala, beyond the place where the old fortress (Stang La Khar) rests high above the stream, angle to the west up a side valley that leads to the Stok La (about 15,900 feet), where there are fine views north to the Indus Valley. The trail south of the Stok La leads steeply into the Rumbak Chu and eventually Rumbak village, not far from the mouth of the valley, where it joins the larger Zinchen Nala.

Now the trail climbs the Zinchen stream to the large home called Yurutse and on to wide meadows at the northern base of the climb up to the next pass. Cross the Ganda La (about 16,200 feet) and descend to the village of Shingo, then proceed past willow trees and rosebushes in a narrow canyon to the Markha River, a tributary of the raging Zanskar River. Here you turn up-valley and in a few hundred yards reach Skiu village. (Note that going down the Markha Valley to the west there is a trail leading to the town of Chiling across the Zanskar River and beyond to either Alchi or farther on to Lamayuru. See "From Lamayuru to Alchi," below.) At Skiu, the path up the Markha Valley begins ascending and there is often lush vegetation along the valley floor, but only dry slopes above. New bridges have been built so that most of the former dicey river crossings can be avoided—assuming, of course, that the bridges haven't been washed out. The day's walk from Skiu to Markha village (circa 12,400 feet) passes hills that often have a deep reddish hue, and the valley opens out shortly after you leave Skiu.

Above Markha village, which has about thirty homes, the nala leading from the Ruberung La, which contains the trail called the Zhumlam (see below), enters the Markha Valley from the south. Just east of this is Markha's gomba on a hill north of the river. Next is the small town of Omung (or Humlung) with its splendid, small gomba 600 feet above the trail below town, then the few homes of Hankar. Here you follow a tributary stream to the north of the main river and rise gently to the grazing meadows of Chachutse. Now, away from the river, you climb to the sweeping pastures of the 16,000-foot-high Nimaling Plain, where thousands of sheep, goats, yaks and cow-yak crossbreeds graze during the summer months. This vast grassland, so high that snow is apt to fall practically anytime during the year, is an idyllic place to wander for a day or two. You will meet herdsmen and women both from down-valley and from villages in the Indus Valley at their movable camps. Rising to the south is 21,000-foot Kang Yurzi ("Nimaling Peak"), a lovely mountain, but not an easy one to climb.

North of Nimaling is the 17,050-foot Kongmaru La, the usual route taken out of the valley. At the pass, views to the Ladakh Range and villages in the Indus Valley to the north are excellent. But the long, steep descent is a stiff one (the reason the valley is better approached from the other direction), and several times the rocky path passes through narrow gorges

The officiating lama at the Hemis Festival in 1977 blesses attendees as he arrives.

where you walk next to or in the stream. The first place to stop north of the pass is Chogdo, but if you keep going another hour you reach Shang Sumdo, where there is an even better camping place. Another stretch of narrow but gradual gorge takes you to the roadhead at Martselang village. Ask about vehicles, but if none is available, continue along the twin ruts gently up to the west for less than an hour and you will be at Hemis Gomba (described above), where you can merely drink tea and grab the first vehicle going to Leh, or order a meal and stay for the night.

From Lamayuru to Alchi

Lamayuru is the trailhead for a trek to Alchi that takes about five days, but this is a strenuous hike that follows a tricky route and has two high passes to cross, so don't be misled by the relatively brief amount of time required for the hike. The route for this walk follows the same course as the traverse of Zanskar (see above) for the first day from Lamayuru to Phanjila. Then you branch east up the Ripchar Valley to the Konke (or Chot) La (circa 16,000 feet) and continue down along a path that can become difficult to follow. The route goes down-valley and reaches the first hamlet called Sumdo. Then, shortly below, a path diverges south and up to the Dundochen La, a track that leads to the Zanskar River and the village of Chiling. Near Chiling a cable across the river supports a garroti (a large wooden box hung from the cable that can be pulled from one side of the river to the other), which can take you to the east bank of the river and the trail up the Markha Valley. From Chiling you could also walk down the Zanskar River valley to its junction with the Indus. Back at Sumdo, a convoluted path leads over a ridge to a tributary from the north where another village named Sumdo is located, not far south of the base of the rise to the 16,200-foot Stakspi (or Tagpa) La, high above the Indus River and Alchi Monastery. Don't fail to walk with a local on this route, for there are several places where you could go entirely off course on rocky ground or along subsidiary paths that lead to pasturing regions. (Note that a slightly shorter but no less difficult alternate route begins at Phanjila and goes up the Ripchar Valley, then diverges north to the hamlet of Urshi and over the 17,200-foot Tar La, descending through Tar and Mang Gyu villages to Gira, west of Alchi.)

The Zhumlam: The "Middle Way"
from the Indus to Zanskar

This rugged route between Zangla, a day's walk north of Padum, and the Indus Valley via the Markha Valley is called the *zhumlam* (or *kunlam*), the "middle way," from Zanskar to the Indus. This is because the route lies between the trail to the west over the Singe La and Lamayuru and the eastern path over the Phirtse La and Rupshu. Before the other trails were improved, this tough pass and gorge route was used occasionally by Zanskaris in spring before the snows began melting and in autumn after the melt was over. As difficult as the passes along the Zhumlam are, the going is also tough underfoot, for there are variously sixty-five to one hundred stream crossings to be made. Mike Searle, an English geologist, made the crossing from north to south in spring with Feeda Hussain from Leh and a bearded fifty-nine-year-old Zanskari from a place called Karnak and his spunky horse. Mike said that without the latter two they could not have made it, and that if they had done the trek a week later that year, the water in one or two of the streams would have been too high. They arrived in Padum on June fifth. Scot ("Bhalu") MacBeth, founding member of the Alpine Stomach Club who can often be found in Khumbu, Nepal, actually escorted a group across this route. He went from south to north, Zangla to Martselang, from September third to the eleventh, and for him the timing was also perfect. Between the Markha Valley and Zangla, you will need to be completely self-sufficient in food. Without doubt a local guide is necessary, as during the middle of the walk you are likely not to see other people for at least five days and the gorges are a veritable maze.

From the north, the shortest route leaves the Indus Valley via Martselang and the Kangmaru La to the Markha Valley. The trail diverges from the floor of the Markha Valley just downriver from Omung village and goes up a nala that is dry up to the 14,400-foot level, the point where the canyon's creek goes underground. Continue upward to the Ruberung La (about 16,100 feet) and follow a twisting route down into the Kurna Chu gorge. (The correct route up this nala from the south is impossible to find without a guide.) If your guide is risking going on the walk with his horse, note that south of the Markha Valley there is precious little forage for three days' walk. Proceed to a place called Tilit Sumdo, then head southwest up a narrow canyon involving scores of icy fords (and a 50-yard stretch where the canyon is so narrow that yaks with wide horns are said to get caught) to the 16,200-foot Char Char La, the last pass you cross before descending the narrow gorge to Zangla village on the Zanskar River. This oversimplified sketch of the seven-to-nine-day walk from Martselang to Zangla may make the hike sound straightforward, but that is not the case. The route cannot be followed by someone who does not know the way, and there is no easy path out if you become lost. This stroll is only for the hardcore hiker with a good local escort who is ready to go at just the right window of time in spring or fall. Milk and cookies will not be served.

Nubra

The Buddhist region of Nubra lies north of Leh across the 18,380-foot Khardung Pass, the first of the five passes on the former trade route from Leh to Turkestan. Nubra consists of two long, deep valleys, the Nubra and upper Shyok, lying beneath the towering eastern Karakoram Range, which contains the highest peaks within Ladakh. The upper Shyok Valley circles south and east of the easternmost peaks in the Karakoram, and the deep furrow of the Nubra Valley lies between two ranges of the Karakoram. At the head of the Nubra Valley is the 45-mile-long Siachen Glacier, the longest glacier in the Karakoram. The full-fledged Nubra River pours from the mouth of the mighty Siachen, carrying the frigid waters of the Siachen, Terong, and other glaciers.

The slate-colored Nubra River merges with the Shyok at 10,000 feet in elevation some 60 miles south of the Siachen. At this river junction you are north of the Ladakh Range and due north of Leh. Near the northern base of the Khardung La, the Nubra Valley is entered via a bridge crossing the Shyok River that leads to Tirit village. The Nubra River snakes back and forth across the 2-mile-wide valley floor, rebounding off the steep walls of the valley. Since the river waters boomeranged off the walls on both sides of the valley, passage to the head of the valley used to be difficult during the high summer waters, but now a road has been blasted all the way up to the mouth of the Siachen. The Nubra Valley was formerly glaciated as far south as Charasa village, practically at the valley's mouth, and thus is U shaped, with steep granite walls along much of its length. Just south of Charasa (where there is a fortress on a large rock) and across the valley on the east bank is the town of Tigur, and up the side valley east of Tigur is an old fortress with Buddhist wall frescoes. Beyond that is Santanling Gomba.

Farther up-valley is the town of Panamik with its nearby springs: red colored, sulphurous, and, at more than 150° F, too hot to immerse oneself in directly. Teddy Roosevelt, who visited the springs in Panamik earlier this century, mentioned seeing a green algae utterly unlike anything seen elsewhere in Ladakh. Panamik village has always been a kind of Ultima Thule: the last place where caravans of yore or today's trekkers (if permitted to freely walk north) would see any trees for at least nine days. If you should ever get here, see if the herd of Bactrian camels that were photographed in the upper valley in 1982 are still alive.

Six miles north of Panamik, at a lone home comprising Sasoma, the old caravan route turns east, up a narrow gorge with mile-high walls, heading for the dicey Sasser La, a high glaciated pass. The Sasser was always considered the most treacherous of the five Leh to Yarkand passes. Early travelers who climbed the hairpin curves traversing its slopes tell of bleached bones alongside the trail: not just a few bones but piles of them, the only remains of animals that could not make the climb or were caught in summer storms.

Once over the Sasser Pass the caravan route descends into the upper Shyok Valley. There, the rare visitor is not far from the Shyok River's origin, at the place where water from the Rimo Glacier meets the Chip Chap River. Not far north from there, along barren, frigid terrain that is level for the most part, is the 18,290-foot Karakoram Pass, the third pass along the route to the north, and the present border with Chinese Sinkiang Province (formerly Turkestan). The pass north of that is the Suget; from there, the former caravaneer descended to Shahidulla, a remote, windswept place described in Chapter 6.

In recent years, three joint Indo-foreign mountaineering expeditions have been permitted to visit Nubra annually. This augurs well for the area being opened, and rumors of the area's impending derestriction have blown about for years. Once the conflict between India and Pakistan for control of the Siachen Glacier basin has been decided (see Chapter 7 regarding this war), it is quite possible that this region may open in midsummer when the Khardung La is traversable, but until then, we will have to content ourselves with reading old accounts of Nubra, or talking with Nubrapa (people from Nubra) in Leh. But if Nubra opens and you are allowed in, go prepared. Even though Nubra itself is a thousand feet lower in elevation than the Indus Valley near Leh, the Ladakh Range between the two valleys is intimidating. The passes over the range are mostly snow covered and between 17,000 and over 18,000 feet in elevation. There can be vicious storms at those elevations any month of the year, and even the main road over the Khardung La must cross a glacier north of the pass en route to the Shyok Valley floor.

Rupshu

Located east of Zanskar, the restricted area of Rupshu is Ladakh's easternmost and most elevated region, blending into western Tibet's high plains. In fact, topographically, but not politically, Rupshu is an integral part of the Chang Tang, Tibet's 600-mile-wide, 15,000-foot-high northern steppes, of which it is the westernmost extremity. Rupshu has majestic, sweeping deserts separated by narrow ranges with lofty passes offering distant views, and a hardy, wide-ranging nomadic people called Changpas. Traders from Lahoul still drive their caravans of sturdy mules across Rupshu into western Tibet, carrying goods such as cloth and costume jewelry and trading for gems, stones, hides, and wool. The lowest point in all of Rupshu is at 13,000 feet along the Indus River near the town of Chumatang. Within Rupshu's 5,500-square-mile area are the peaks of the Ladakh and Zanskar mountains, and several large, crystalline lakes including Tso Morari and Pangong, each framed in wide basins between the two ranges.

The 14,000-foot and 15,000-foot plains of Rupshu support the totally nomadic Changpas. The Changpa economy is geared to the yak, a creature that dislikes descending lower than 12,000 feet in elevation in this region and that provides milk and meat for food, dung for fuel, and wool for clothing and shelter. The Changpas live in black yak-hair tents called *rebu* and traverse a land so high that, as in Nepal's Dolpo region, one of the first requirements for anyone living there is an animal-skin bellows to keep the yak dung fire going in the thin air. Changpas have traditionally subsisted on a hearty but unvarying diet consisting almost entirely of roasted barley flour (here called *phe*), tea, chang, meat, salt, milk, butter, and cheese. The menu most days is phe with solja (tea with butter and salt) and various kinds of soup. The women wear their own version of the Ladakhi perag, and like all women from Ladakh, they buy as much of the imported coral and Tibetan turquoise for their perag as they can afford. Changpas are Buddhist. Like most ethnic Tibetans, they celebrate Losar (the Tibetan New Year) with fervor and gladly travel long distances for celebrations.

Although the once-massive herds of speedy *kyang*, the Tibetan wild ass, are greatly depleted in Rupshu, the marmot colonies have not visibly suffered from poaching. In Rupshu, as in the sweeping Deosai Plains of Baltistan and parts of rugged Zanskar, the sizable, sleek marmots, larger than the groundhogs they resemble, are the real denizens of this high mountain desert.

The traditional path across Rupshu, the first stretch of the Leh-Gartok-Lhasa caravan route, is now a paved road. It diverges north from the Indus at Karu village, climbing the Ladakh Range, across the Indus Valley from Hemis Gomba, to reach the Chang La (18,300 feet), passing several villages and Chendey and Trakthok monasteries. This route now reaches Tankse (Tangtse) 20 miles past the Chang La. Tankse is a village 14 miles south of the Shyok River's southern bend. It used to house Ladakh's easternmost customs post and was the effective limit of Ladakh's inhabited territory. At Tankse, the road continues southeast to the Indus Valley and the border village and military post of Demchok. The large town of Ali in Tibet lies not far beyond (see Chapter 9 in this book's companion volume, *Trekking in Nepal, West Tibet, and Bhutan*). Another nearly level valley leads east from Tankse. Cradled by marble cliffs, this route crosses a low, lake-topped pass and, 25 miles beyond, reaches Pangong Lake (13,917 feet).

Vivid blue Pangong Lake, meaning "great cavity" in Tibetan, is continuous for nearly 100 miles as it crosses into Tibet, reaching as far east as the town of Rudok. Along its shores are still found the occasional black-necked crane, an endangered species with white feathers over its body and a spot of rust on its head. Pangong evokes wonderful images: a solitary, tranquil camp near a glacial stream; drinking tea with a Changpa family; and, come evening, tracking the shy kyang through low lakeside hills. In *The Way of the White Clouds* Lama Anagarika Govinda tells how on first approaching the lake he inadvertently walked into it: "The water was as invisible as the air!" Along the straight shores of the lake, the glacial tributaries can supply drinking water, for here near its western end (unlike its eastern extremity), the lake is salty to the taste and incapable of supporting bacterial life. The water of the Pangong may be invisible near its shore, but in the middle of the lake it assumes a deep, lapis lazuli blue, the blue that is seen over high passes as one crosses Tibet.

Rupshu, like all of Ladakh, abounds in myth and legend, much of it based on fact. Some say that Jesus passed the "lost" years of his life in Hemis Monastery. Lama Govinda received his second spiritual, mystical initiation while resting at Trakthok Monastery on the approach to the Chang La. And Gypsy Davy and Lady Ba camped for three weeks at various places about Pangong Lake in the early 1920s. Once, along the northern side of the lake, Lady Ba's horse, Tomar, disappeared with a herd of kyang. The best shikaris were sent to track him, and they did, across two ranges and a valley. On the third day, Tomar returned "seven years younger than he went out on *shikar*."

Village gods attending a festival in Kulu's Sainj Valley.

10
Himachal Pradesh

The solitude of the mountains had given me back to myself.
Unknown

Honesty is the best policy.

Graffiti on a rock near
Banjar, Tirthan Valley

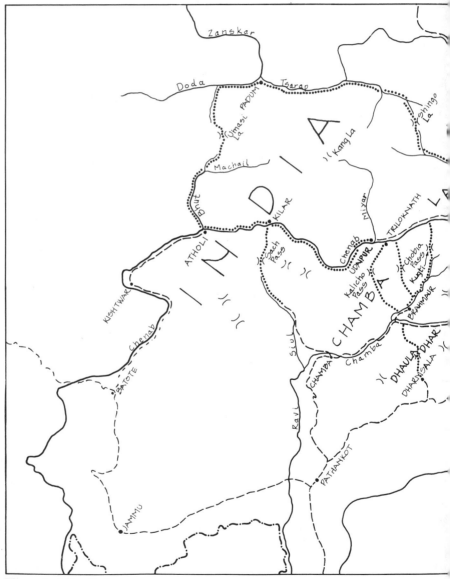

Himachal Pradesh

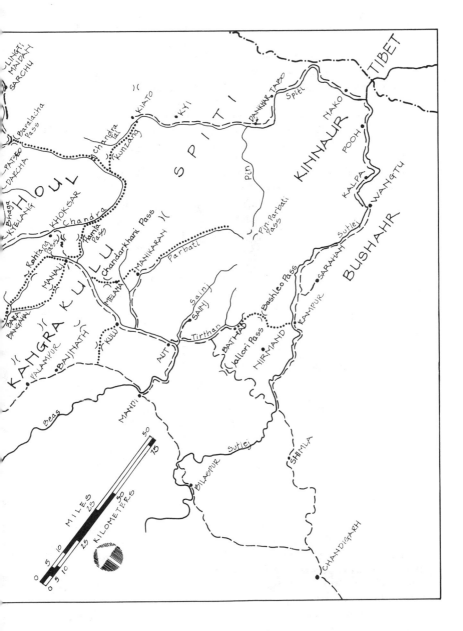

The Northern Districts of "Himalaya State"

With the exception of Kashmir, each region discussed in this book so far has been a fairly arid area, north of ranges that cut it off from the monsoon and rarely touched by rain. But as the descriptions of these Himalayan regions trend easterly, they also move to the south of the main Himalaya Range. The seven regions that provide the grist for this chapter straddle the Great Himalaya Range. Lahoul and Spiti are located north of the main range, just south of Zanskar and Rupshu, while Chamba, Kangra, Kulu, Bushahr, and Kinnaur lie within or south of the highest mountains. These seven regions are the northernmost administrative districts of India's Himachal Pradesh (H.P.), or, in English, "Himalaya State."

Chamba comprises the upper watershed of the Ravi River, Kangra lies in the Beas River valley just to the south of Chamba, the Kulu region is the upper Beas watershed, while Lahoul includes the upper regions of the Chenab River, and Spiti comprises the entire Spiti River watershed. Hilly Bushahr and Kinnaur comprise the section of the deep Sutlej Valley where the Sutlej River descends through the Great Himalaya Range. Chamba, Kangra, Kulu, Bushahr, and Kinnaur in the southerly draining Ravi, Beas, and Sutlej valleys offer lush, monsoon-drenched vistas ribbed with ancient paths that are rewarding for experienced rainy season hikers. People in these more southerly regions are Hindu, whereas in drier Lahoul and Spiti to the north, most people are Buddhist.

Before the British defeated Gulab Singh's army in the mid-1840s, Chamba and Kulu were two independent Himalayan kingdoms. These small states were insulated from the southern plains by the adjacent hill principalities of Kangra, Mandi, Bushahr, and Kinnaur and from the north by their inaccessibility through the Chenab River gorge and the walls of the Great Himalaya Range. As this west Himalayan region was demarcated by the British, neither Chamba nor Kulu was included in southernmost Jammu and Kashmir, Maharajah Singh's domain. Kulu, small in size but strategic because of its direct north-south valley, was an important link in a trans-Himalayan trail used by officials and merchants traveling to or from west Tibet. Bushahr was able to keep its sovereignty as a completely autonomous state until India obtained independence in 1947.

The Buddhist areas of Lahoul and Spiti, north of Chamba and Kulu, were once the farthest reaches of southwestern Tibet. Centuries ago, while the kings of Ladakh were in power, Lahoul and Spiti were united with the kingdom of Ladakh in the Indus Valley by lengthy paths northward through rugged Zanskar and the Rupshu uplands, and it required two weeks to walk from either place to Leh, the capital. Later, the English recognized that Lahoul, Spiti, and Bushahr could provide trade routes to transport the prized pashmina shawl wool and bypass Kashmiri taxation; until 1946, the former two areas were administratively linked with Ladakh. Today, Lahoul and particularly Spiti districts remain tied culturally with Ladakh, although they are administered and approached from the south. Spiti and Kinnaur have been closed to foreign visitors for many years, although there is reliable talk that parts of both regions will open to foreigners before long.

The relatively few Westerners who have walked in Kangra, Chamba, Kulu, or Lahoul know the pleasures of hiking little-known paths through valleys that are equally as scenic as other, more crowded trails, just less publicized. Few areas in the Himalaya (excepting far western Nepal) as large and climatically favorable have so long remained virtually unknown to foreign trekkers. In Himachal Pradesh, you can trek through green valleys in sight of, or among, snowy peaks, meeting locals who have rarely seen foreigners and whose responses are thus refreshingly and delightfully spontaneous. H.P. has panache, and people here still respect their traditions. These are wonderful areas, and if I don't tell about, and thus publicize, too many of the trails, so much the better. In fact, so many paths crisscross these hills that it is impossible to mention all of them. If you have the proper U502 map you can easily figure out a good trekking route, head for a trailhead, and enjoy a fine walk. Still, this chapter gives you suggestions for a few of the better-known routes.

The U502 maps depicting these regions are highly accurate for all the places discussed with the exceptions of Lahoul and Spiti. If you are going to Chamba or Kangra, you should take the *Pathankot* sheet (NI 43-15) and the *Palampur* sheet (NI 43-16). This latter sheet also shows Lahoul and the northern part of the Kulu Valley. The *Simla* sheet (NH 43-4) shows the lower part of the Kulu Valley, including the Sainj, Tirthan, and upper Parbati valleys. This sheet also shows Shimla, the capital of the state, and as much of Kinnaur as you are permitted to trek in. There are also three sheets made in India by the Survey of India called *Trekking Route Map of Himachal Pradesh,* Sheets Number One, Two, and Three. You should be able to find these maps at any sizable tourist office in H.P. Sheet Number One shows Kangra, Chamba, and western Lahoul; Sheet Number Two depicts Lahoul, upper Spiti, and most of the Kulu Valley; and Sheet Number Three shows Shimla and Kinnaur. These maps don't have contour lines, but they do have other important information, such as roads, and indicate some interesting trekking routes. There are also the Leomann maps of the region, mentioned (like all these maps) in Appendix A. The Leomann maps are particularly good for showing the names of peaks in the areas described.

One suggestion that applies to all approaches to H.P. is to go to the Himachal Pradesh Tourism Development Corporation office at the Chanderlok Building, 36 Janpath, in New Delhi. There you can book tickets on direct buses to most major towns in H.P., or at least receive current information on how to best reach a particular place. If you don't fancy hearing one Hindi film after another, try not to get booked onto a bus that shows videos; however, the buses that show these films may also be the most rapid conveyances available (you have been warned).

Another note that applies everywhere in H.P. is to keep in mind that there are many rest houses scattered far and wide throughout the state. These small, pleasant buildings were once used by British forest officers on their rounds. In a few of the rest houses you can see old, old guest registers dating back, in some cases, into the last century. For information on both the locations of these rest houses and where to get a chit for booking them, see the tourist offices in major towns or, alternatively, the local offices of the forestry department or public works department (each department maintains a different group of rest houses). The trekking maps noted above that are produced by the Survey of India show the locations and reservation authority of most of these rest houses. All the rest houses have a chokidar, a guardian whose job it is to let you in and see that you are accommodated, and who may also cook food (either he or his wife will do this). It is best to bring your own basics like cooking oil, dal, rice, spices, and wheat flour, but depending on where you are, when and how you present yourself, and who he is, you may be able to talk the chokidar into cooking you a fine repast.

This chapter will proceed easterly across Himachal Pradesh, beginning in Chamba and continuing with the regions of Kangra, the Kulu Valley, Lahoul, Bushahr, Kinnaur, and Spiti.

Chamba

Hidden behind Kangra District's 15,000-foot-high Dhaula Dhar ridge (see "Kangra," below), Chamba lies between the Kishtwar District of Jammu and Kashmir to the west and Lahoul and Kulu districts to the east. A mountainous, rectangular tract some 60 miles north to south by 70 miles across, Chamba includes the easternmost peaks of the Pir Panjal Range and even a stretch of the deep Chenab gorge downstream from Lahoul (an isolated region called Pangi).

Chamba is reached in two stages from New Delhi. Take a through bus or a sleeper train to Pathankot, located en route to the Jammu Tawi Station on the way to Srinagar. (Note how to book trains in the "New Delhi" section of Chapter 3.) Change at Pathankot for the all-day 75-mile bus or taxi ride to the town of Chamba, passing through the old hill station of Dalhousie, situated on five rounded hilltops. Some visitors like to stop and rest in Dalhousie, at an elevation nearly three times that of Chamba town, but once you've reached Dalhousie, you are only some 25 miles from Chamba.

The town of Chamba (2,380 feet) lies on the north bank of the Ravi River. This big town is the largest in the area, with hotels, a tourist rest house, a large bazaar, and transportation to upper-valley trailheads, where paths lead north to Lahoul, east to Kulu, and south to Kangra. Be sure to stop in the tourist office to get suggestions from the tourist officer as to people up-valley who can assist you with finding a porter. The Bhuri Singh Museum in town is renowned for its art collection, particularly its painted miniatures from Kangra. Chamba has been Hindu for two millennia. This enduring faith is symbolized by the six tall stone temples dedicated to Vishnu and Shiva in Chamba Bazaar, near the long marketplace and promenade. Every August (actually the week leading up to the third Sunday in the month of Sawan), the Minjar Fair celebrates the ripening of the valley's corn, and it is widely attended by hill people who come as much for the grand bazaar and the sociability as for the colorful procession of religious images that climaxes the festival.

The most intriguing and best-traveled denizens of Chamba and Kangra are the Gaddis, a clan of people who are usually seen high on green mountain meadows during the summer with their mixed herds of sheep and goats. The Gaddi men annually travel long distances from their warm, monsoon-blessed southern homeland in Chamba or Kangra, a place they call Gadderan (or Shivbhumi, the "Land of Shiva"), up to the green ridges north of Chamba and the pastures of Lahoul. The women, called Gaddinis, and children often stay at home in the summer to work the fields. Gaddinis wear a full skirt called a *chaura,* so full that it requires twelve yards of cloth if made properly. When I walked in northern Lahoul during the second week of July, the Gaddi shepherds were there, fanning out in the tributaries of the upper Bhaga Valley with their well-trained dogs helping to move the animals. Another clan of seminomadic herders, the Gujars, who roam between Chitral and Kashmir, resemble tall, long-striding, mocha-colored Pathans. But I was in for a surprise when I first saw Gaddis walking near their flocks. These short, deep-brown-complected men dress like mountain sprites in woolen homespun clothing, and when they move they seem to float. While talking with them, I admired their smoke-white woolen robes, called *chola,* which are worn gathered at the waist by many loops of black wool cord. In daytime the garment hangs to the knees like a Muslim's shirt, but at night the robe is let out, providing the warmth of a blanket. During the day as the Gaddis walk, the pocket created above the belt in front of their chola will, like as not, be filled with a tired, snuggled floppy-eared white lamb. If you are invited to tea and warmth by their evening fire, giving some extra matches or tea is a nice way to express appreciation. A book that gives an excellent feel for the Gaddis and their homeland is *Over the High Passes,* by Christina Noble (see the bibliography).

Trekking Possibilities from Chamba

With thousands traveling the favored routes in Nepal and Kashmir each year and others seeking different places to walk, it is reassuring that regions such as Chamba can be the departure point or destination for people who want to hike in the mountains, yet lack the herd instinct. From three areas in Chamba, a profusion of paths leads in all directions to areas as far afield as Kishtwar, Kangra, Lahoul, and the Kulu Valley. Some of the passes in these regions will be referred to by name, others merely alluded to. A good map or two of the area will allow you to pick a route and give it a go, but remember that the trails south into Kangra over Dhaula Dhar, east into Kulu, and north into Lahoul are over ridges usually higher than 15,000 feet, which often involve walking on snow, so don't go too early in the year (usually not before July) or too late (generally not after the end of September, or the first heavy snow of the year). Be sure to stock up on all supplies before leaving the town of Chamba and heading up-valley.

The westernmost area of Chamba centers on the Siul Valley and its

A Gaddi shepherd carries a baby goat en route to the summer pastures in Lahoul (photograph by Jan Eric Zabinski).

tributaries, which lie north of the town of Chamba. Several relatively low-level trails lead west from Chamba's Siul Valley into the Chenab Valley south of the town of Kishtwar. Here, when you descend to the Chenab Valley floor, you reach the road to Kishtwar. Farther north up the Siul Nala, however, are higher passes north to the currently roadless Chenab Valley area called Pangi, between the districts of Kishtwar and Lahoul. The 14,480-foot Sach Pass caps the best-known route to the Pangi region leading directly to its main village, the town of Kilar. From Kilar a trail descends the deep gorge of the Chenab Valley to the roadhead east of Atholi. A high path goes north from Atholi to the Umasi La, a glaciated pass leading to Zanskar. (Note the description of the Umasi La in Chapter 8.)

Bara Bangahal, like Chamba, Kangra, and Kulu, is the name both of a region and of a major town within it. The town of Bara Bangahal is some 60 miles southeast and upriver from Chamba's large bazaar, near the headwaters of the Ravi River, the smallest of the "five fingers" of the Indus. Bara Bangahal, which is probably not yet reached by a road and which has very few shops, is populated by Gaddis, and by following their trails, you can walk over high passes, locally called *jot,* eastward to the Kulu Valley: the Taintu ka Jot (or Tentu, or Solang Jot) leads to the lake known as Beas Kund and down to Solang village; the Sagor Jot and Manali Jot lead to Manali; and there is also the Kali Hind Jot. These passes range from 15,320 feet to 16,385 feet in elevation. South of the Ravi Valley in the region of Bara Bangahal are up to a dozen passes leading south to Kangra District over the high Dhaula Dhar Range that connect Chamba with the towns of Dharmsala, Palampur, and Baijnath (see "Kangra" below).

The last of Chamba's three areas is the northern branch of the Ravi River, the Budhil Nala. The town of Brahmaur, formerly the capital of Chamba State, lies on the Budhil Nala 40 miles east of Chamba Bazaar. Here, as well as in the Ravi Valley to the south, you are in the Gaddis' precipitous homeland, a country with Hindu temples 1,500 years old. From the beautifully situated town of Brahmaur you can walk north over the high Chobia or Kalicho passes to the Chenab Valley in western Lahoul, walks that take four to five days each. The walk over the Kalicho Jot takes you down to Triloknath Temple, noted below under "Lahoul."

The most used pass north to Lahoul's Chenab Valley is the Kugti Jot (16,530 feet). To reach this pass, walk two days east from Brahmaur to the town of Kugti. Then comes a three- or four-day walk over the pass, during which time you will cross a snowfield on the north and probably south side of the pass as well. The walk down from the north side of any of these passes to the floor of the Chenab Valley involves a steep descent of over 6,000 feet, so go slowly, take small steps, and keep your weight over the balls of your feet so you are not continually slipping and falling on your rear end. And, because of the steep rise, think thrice about tackling any of these passes from the north. Check with locals regarding pass conditions if you are going to Lahoul: these cols are high and snowy, even if not actually glaciated. From Bramaur you can also walk to the south over the high ridge called Mani Mahesh Dhar that divides the Budhil Nala from Bara Bangahal along the upper reaches of the Ravi River. Two main trails head south from the Budhil Nala to Bara Bangahal: the Chobu Jot leads from Harser village past sacred Mani Mahesh Lake, and the Nikora Jot goes south from the town of Kugti and drops directly to the village of Bara Bangahal.

Kangra

Kangra formerly was one of the most important west Himalayan hill states, occupying a large area west of the Sutlej. Now Kangra District reaches only from the ridgeline of Dhaula Dhar, "The White Range," south of Chamba, to the Siwalik Hills bordering the Gangetic plains. The Kangra region is replete with many small ancient temples and a dense web of hill trails. The town in Kangra most visited by foreigners is Dharmsala, or more accurately, the smaller town of McLeod Ganj up the ridge, which has been home, since about 1961, to His Holiness the Dalai Lama and his Tibetan government in exile. McLeod Ganj with its inexpensive small restaurants and hotels is a miniature version of the Besantpur or Thamel areas in Kathmandu. The exciting prospect for trekkers is that you can walk right out of town and head for a pass over the daunting but tantalizing Dhaula Dhar ridge just to the north. With a little effort, you will be able to find a local or Tibetan porter-guide who can assist you.

The pass closest to McLeod Ganj is the 14,095-foot Indrahar Pass. To the west, but also approached from McLeod Ganj, is the Minkiani Jot, about 14,430 feet. These crossings both lead into an area of Chamba locally known as Chanota. Be sure to cross either of these passes with a local who knows the way and allow four to five days to reach the Ravi River on the northern side. Numerous other passes also cross Dhaula Dhar, most of which are approached from east of McLeod Ganj. If you take any of these passes from towns like Tikri, Palampur, or Baijnath, you will drop down higher up the Ravi Valley in the Bara Bangahal region. From Bara Bangahal you can either head north over Mani Mahesh Dhar to Brahmaur, or walk up-valley and take another high pass east to the Kulu Valley. In eastern Kangra, a lovely side valley called Chota Bangahal trends northward. From Chota Bangahal, Gaddi trails lead north over high passes to the upper Bara Bangahal region, or you could walk east over the 15,100-foot Bherianga Pass to the Kulu Valley.

The Kulu Valley

Of the seven regions mentioned in this chapter, the Kulu Valley, often called the Valley of the Gods, receives the most tourism by both Indian and Angrezi. The gods referred to are the many village gods that reside in their individual temples scattered in villages throughout the district (and in other districts of H.P. as well). These village gods are generally referred to as *debda* (sometimes written as *devta* or *deota*), but they each have their own specific names. In this part of the Himalaya the gods are not only taken out and consulted via a long-haired shaman, locally called a *gur,* but they are carried from their temple homes on festive occasions and are even willing, dancing participants in these festivals. The debdas are circular objects a couple of feet tall, completely covered ("dressed," you might say) in red felt and costly, shiny silk with about eight to twelve bright silver or gold facial masks, attached so that two or three look out in each of the four directions. Other debdas have their nine or more facial masks all facing in the same direction. Some debdas are protected by an ornate parasol that is attached to the top of their "head."

When a debda is to be brought out from its temple residence, it is propitiated, then carried like a palanquin on two long poles, with one person holding the poles on each end. Once I saw a debda speaking through its gur to a local magistrate who would soon be adjudicating a case concerning land owned by the debda, land that was being claimed by a local resident. The debda requested the magistrate to allow it to keep most of its land. A debda may be consulted by villagers who make an offering, then ask questions through the gur. During this time the image is held aloft on its two long poles, and as it replies, it bounces up and down on these poles and periodically swoops down in the questioner's direction. Then the image is picked up again, not unlike singer James Brown being revived on stage by his backup group the Famous Flames. The devotion and sincerity of people questioning their local god is most evident and extremely touching. Here in Kulu, the gods are wise friends and counselors, not cold, distant concepts.

The largest gathering of the gods occurs during Kulu's annual fall Dussehra Festival, which includes bacchanalian revelry, worship of the gods (including Ragunathji, Kulu's host god), and spirited dance performances by some of Kulu's excellent dance troupes (as well as other troupes imported by tourism officials for the occasion). Dancers in Kulu's troupes, bless their souls, are not always just male, as you see in most parts of South Asia, but the well-costumed dancers may be of both sexes, and the better troupes know many intricate dances. It is truly a joy (to Western eyes) to see men and women dancing together unself-consciously, as can be observed at the Dussehra Festival and other festivals during the year.

As well as for its approachable gods and its autumn festival, Kulu is known for its lovely women, its extensive pine forests, its bountiful harvest of apples and other fruits and vegetables, and its network of hill trails. And Kulu has earned a reputation for something else as well. Due partly to the beauty, ambiance, and relative accessibility of Kulu and its tributary valleys, small colonies of foreign travelers (particularly British, French, and Italian) have congregated here over the years for the high-quality *charas,* or *bung* as it is locally called. In English we call charas (a Hindustani word) by its Arabic name: hashish. Serious aficionados, whether local or Angrezi, call themselves *charasi* and go to considerable effort rubbing the mature resinous flowering tips of wild cannabis plants between their palms to collect their own charas. Or they purchase it only from trusted friends, because adulteration has increased in recent years. In addition to its use as a euphoric (or, with overuse, a soporific), charas has often been used by long-distance walkers and mountain climbers in the Himalaya to relieve fatigue, increase flagging appetite, or aid the onset of sleep at high elevation. Charas has long been a cash crop for the hill people, who collected it for centuries before Westerners began buying it in quantity during the late 1960s, although its value has increased greatly since then. Note, however, that the Kulu Valley has no monopoly on charas. In the Tribal Areas of the North-West Frontier Province, and in Chitral, Swat, Kashmir, Garhwal, Kumaon, Nepal, and Sikkim, the wild or cultivated cannabis plant is rubbed for hashish and/or cut for *ganja* (marijuana) despite its illegality.

The Kulu Valley is approached directly by bus from New Delhi, and you can make bus reservations at the H.P. Tourism Development Corporation office at 36 Janpath in New Delhi. Buses into the valley may be delayed for long hours during the summer monsoon, as I found out one warm night at the Mandi bus depot en route: the overnight express leaving Manali was forced to halt, doubling its journey time to New Delhi, while ochre-colored avalanche debris 6 miles away was bulldozed from the road. The twelve-to-twenty-hour bus ride from Delhi to Manali brings on what one exhausted traveler called "inevitable sleeping-position weirdness." There is a small airstrip at Bhuntar, 6 miles south of Kulu town, which is serviced by Vayudoot Airlines. Flights are scheduled daily in the summer from New Delhi via Chandigarh, but they are booked well in advance and are apt to be canceled by bad weather.

Manali

The larger town of Kulu (formerly known as Sultanpur) is the administrative center of Kulu District, but the upper valley town of Manali (6,300 feet) is the most popular place to begin or end a trek in the Kulu Valley. Trails out of Manali lead to passes connecting with Chamba and with Lahoul's Chandra Valley. Manali's tourist officer can provide you with maps, advise you about the region's most frequented paths, and if you need a porter or crew, he can direct you to one of the several trekking outfitters in town (see Appendix B). The Mountaineering and Allied Sports Institute is located across the Beas River from town on the east bank and about a mile south of town. People there can also assist you with information on treks, but hikes outfitted by them tend to be rather pricey.

Manali is not a hill station for the gentry like Dalhousie or Shimla. The long bus ride from New Delhi and lack of sweeping views and abundant luxury hotels limit, to some extent, the number of people who visit the Kulu Valley. Still, Manali has grown from a few shops in the 1950s to an eclectic hodgepodge of new and newer stores, hotels, and lodges. During the summer season the bazaar teems with Pahari-speaking Kulu walas, Lahoulis, Nepali laborers, Tibetan refugees, and foreign and downcountry tourists. The people of Kulu, slightly built and congenial, raise excellent fruits of many varieties in addition to the valley's renowned, succulent apples. Men from this valley and from Lahoul wear distinctive pillbox hats, which have changed in recent years: the front-facing material of the hats was formerly subdued velvet but is now cloth with a bright, multicolored pattern. In winter when the valley is snow blanketed, Manali hibernates as people stay at home spinning and weaving wool for the costly, elegant Kulu shawls of pashmina and Angora.

Manali is the trailhead for many walks and excursions. The pagoda-roofed Hadimba Temple housing an image of goddess Hirma Devi is sheltered in a grove of gargantuan deodar on a low spur just northwest of the bazaar. A road out of the upper bazaar leads to a trail up through this cedar forest, but the 400-year-old temple can also be approached from the south. To do so, take the trail out of Manali bazaar that goes up to Sial village, situated on a knoll just west of town. At Sial you'll see typical Kulu (and H.P.) homes with one or two lower stories of mud plaster topped by an upper story cloaked in wood from the roof to the porch that surrounds the building's perimeter. The roofs of homes here are made of wooden shake. In Sial ask for the way to Sonoghee, the next village up the path. Sonoghee lies on the north bank of a small ravine, a fifteen-minute walk from Manali. Rest and take tea at Sonoghee, or continue on the wide trail, contouring up-valley within the evergreen-clad folds of the vail. Ten minutes away is the tall, forbidding Hadimba Temple.

Many people, arriving in Manali after a trek or the long ride from New Delhi, will at once hire a taxi or walk 2 miles to the baths at the hot springs of Vashist. To reach Vashist on foot from Manali, cross from the bazaar to the left bank of the Beas River, where large signs announce the beginning of the 295-mile Manali-to-Leh road (see "The Road to Leh: Following the Ancient Caravan Route," in Chapter 9). Continue northward along the road, then up an easterly spur road to the place where the tourism department has erected bathing cubicles and a cafe. If you wish to use the old baths in the village, carry on along the paved road to Vashist Bazaar. These original baths, where locals go regularly to wash, are less well maintained than the newer spa and not for those who dislike an occasional green waterplant floating through their tub.

Solang, one of the last settlements up the Kulu Valley, can be reached directly by hired jeep or by taking a bus from Manali to Palchan village and then continuing up-valley to the northwest by foot. Solang has a rest house that can be booked with the tourist officer in Manali. From here, you can take a day hike to the lake called Beas Kund or begin your trek westward over the high Taintu ka Jot to Bara Bangahal in Chamba.

Beyond Palchan on the road to the Rohtang Jot is the turnoff for Kothi village. Kothi's rest house is the last accommodation below treeline in the pass area. Near the rest house the Beas River flows through an extremely narrow, 100-foot-deep gorge. During the monsoon-filled summer, snowfields above Kothi pour cascades of water over slate faces framed in tall pine forests. The stretch of road from Kothi on up to the high collection of summer teashops and small restaurants called Mahri offers scenery reminiscent of the Swiss Alps. Tourists from the industrial Punjab who have never been into the mountains take taxis or the special daily round-trip bus to the top of the 12,970-foot Rohtang Jot a full 30 miles by road from Manali but barely out of sight high above town. A separate pathway up the Rohtang remains in use for the tens of thousands of animals and their Gaddi herdsmen who yearly cross and recross the wide, rolling pass. When former U.S. Supreme Court Justice William O. Douglas traversed the Rohtang near the end of July 1951, he encountered a torrential rainstorm on the approach to Kothi and the next day on the pass saw cattle and horses killed by a freak snow. Beyond the Rohtang Pass, which is Kulu's border with Lahoul, are road connections along the Chandra Valley to Spiti District and the towns of Kyelang and Udiapur (see "Lahoul," below). Note that a tunnel beneath the Rohtang Pass is presently under construction.

A good stiff hike east right from the town of Manali leads to the Hamta Jot (14,000 feet). While the Rohtang has a vehicle road, the Hamta Pass will continue to be negotiated exclusively by the occasional donkey train going to Spiti, local shepherds with their flocks, and a few random trekkers. From the top of the pass, 19,690-foot Deo Tibba and its 20,405-foot twin Indra Sen north of it on the Kulu-Lahoul boundary are visible.

From Manali the walk toward Hamta Jot crosses the Beas River to the east bank right at town, passes the Mountaineering Institute, then heads into the Alaini Nala, which is called the Hamta Nala higher up. Alternatively, you could take a bus or hire a taxi to leave you off at a place closer to the beginning of the footpath. Walk up the Alaini Nala and climb to Hamta village, then continue more gradually as you rise. You may stop at the level, grassy camping place called Chikka, or continue farther to a place known as Bhalu Ka Ghera, "The Bear's Den." This southern approach to the pass is steady, but not nearly as steep as the talus drop-off you find on the northern side of the pass.

You would be wise to hire someone for this walk, if only to have him show you the best route for the difficult northern descent from the pass. Once you reach the U-shaped tributary valley leading north into Lahoul, you descend gradually to the place called Chhatru, where there is a small PWD rest house. From here you can either walk a half day down-valley on the little-used road to Gramphu or Koksar on the main Manali-to-Kyelang road north of the Rohtang Pass, or, if you are well-supplied, walk up the Chandra Valley toward Chandra Tal or even as far as the Baralacha Pass (see "Trekking in Lahoul," below). This walk from Manali to Chhatru and the main road will take about three to four days.

Kulu's Side Valleys

Most visitors to Kulu follow particular roads and take them only to the well-touristed places. It is as though seeing Kulu's pine-covered ridges beneath meadows fed by snowmelt is so grand that one shouldn't dare intrude farther. But once you have made the journey to the Kulu Valley, you are amid the scenery, not regarding the view from afar as you would at a hill station. Grazing trails in profusion thread the slopes, and the plucky walker who wants to tramp through the hills may want to explore onc or more crossings between Kulu's numerous idyllic side valleys, many of which are well forested.

Kulu's tributary valleys generally enter the Beas Valley at right angles, like the branches of an evergreen tree, with the southern streams longer than those to the north. The larger feeder valleys are generally on the eastern side of the main valley. Two of the larger valleys are the Sainj and Tirthan, which debouch near Aut village in southern Kulu, some 50 miles below the headwaters of the Beas. Each of these valleys, like many of the others, have little-used roads up them, and also (particularly the larger Tirthan and its main town of Banjar) have scheduled bus service. During the British Raj, there were many large "reserved forests" in the upper-valley regions of Kulu's eastward-trending tributary valleys. In 1984 several of these former reserved forests in the upper regions of the Sainj and Tirthan valleys were incorporated into Himachal's largest protected area, the Great Himalayan National Park (669 square miles). For more information about this new park, contact the district forestry officer in the town of Kulu.

Between the Rohtang Pass and the Sainj and Tirthan valleys in lower Kulu are about fifteen tributary valleys (and more that are tributaries of these), all of which lead either to passes or to snow-covered summits of the Pir Panjal and Himalayan ranges. If you have time for a trek of several days or more, check with the tourist officer in Manali and perhaps collect a few chits for rest houses in the area where you will be walking, then take a bus or walk into a southern valley and begin heading from one valley to another, crossing ridges as you go. If, on the other hand, you want only one or two nights out, you may decide to leave from a northern town and return to it through a nearby nala. The possibilities are limitless, and serendipity plays a great part in producing memorable events during such excursions.

The Parbati Valley

Kulu's largest tributary valley is the Parbati, a long vale north of the Sainj Valley, which stretches to the east as far as the restricted Pin-Parbati Pass, which divides Kulu from Spiti's Pin Valley. This is a lovely valley with high relief and pines ascending to the skies, where the terrain becomes steeper and steeper as you proceed up-valley The mouth of the Parbati Valley is 5 miles south of the town of Kulu and just north of the valley's airstrip at Bhuntar.

The best-known town in the Parbati Valley is Manikaran (6,000 feet), connected to Kulu town by bus. Tall snowy spires point to the heavens above town, while flowing from the earth are a number of very large and very hot springs. One evening beneath threatening skies, I made a quick trip on foot to Manikaran, walking across the footbridge into town toward high clouds of steam that had been visible for some distance. Here, over some of the largest springs, is the immense Guru Nanak Gurdwara (a gurdwara is a Sikh temple) with signs saying No Uncovered Heads, No Smoking Please. My glasses fogged immediately on entering the steamy gurdwara, right at a gents' bathing pool. It was elbow to knee with tall, hirsute Sardarjis (a Sikh may be politely referred to as *Sardarji*), none of whom were as nonplussed at seeing me as I was at seeing them, all in a mass, saying "Come, join us."

Near the gurdwara is a geothermal project, and then come the old buildings in Manikaran, consisting of a collection of large smoke-blackened log homes strung along east of the several sources of hot-water springs. Manikaran has for some years been one of several towns in Kulu frequented by shabbily dressed European world travelers, often referred to amongst themselves as freaks, who smoke the excellent local charas with cheap, harsh tobacco in pipes called *chelums*. I got a quick eyeful of the withdrawn, unwelcoming freak community that evening in a small, smoke-filled restaurant. Walking away from that bizarre ambiance into the rainy night to the haunting voice of the Doors' Jim Morrison, I cogitated on the two highly disparate sets of long-haired pilgrims who were attracted to Manikaran: the freaks and the Sikhs.

Six miles east of Manikaran is the Tos Nal, leading north from the Parbati Valley. At the head of the valley is the difficult Sara Umga Pass, about 16,500 feet high, which leads to the Chandra Valley. It is not an easy trek to cross this high ridge above a valley glacier, so the hike should only be undertaken by the experienced who are going with a knowledgeable guide. When you cross the pass and descend, you will be a couple of hours' walk up-valley from Chhatru, where the route from the Hamta Pass reaches the Chandra Valley. You could add on more walking in the upper Chandra Valley (see "Trekking in Lahoul" below) to this hike, or head down-valley for the road descending from the Rohtang Pass. Take at least five days of rations for this walk.

Somewhere up-valley from Manikaran along the Parbati Valley, probably near the entrance to the Tos Nal, you will pass a checkpost beyond which you are not supposed to proceed. The upper valley has no permanent villages, only glaciated streams that water pastures for the herds of animals that feed there during summer.

A walk that has become quite popular is the crossing of the Chandra-khani Pass between the towns of Melana in a tributary of the Parbati Valley and Nagar in the Beas Valley. Of course you can cross the pass from either side, but the route will be described here from Melana to Nagar. Ten miles down-valley from Manikaran is the forest rest house of Jari, where this walk has traditionally begun. A road partway up the side valley toward Melana has been built, and if you want, you could hire a vehicle to take you as far as the road extends. Otherwise, cross the Parbati River at Jari and take the trail up the narrow Melana Nala, where a frothy white stream thrashes below slabs of gray rock spotted with pines. The path follows the bottom of the gorge, then rises directly up some 1,500 feet to the curious town of Melana.

People in Melana consider themselves to be Thakur Rajputs, high-caste ultra-pukka Hindus who speak a Tibetan dialect (a fact I confirmed by trying some Tibetan words and counting from one to ten in Tibetan with a couple of the more approachable residents) and are quite removed from other villages in Kulu. You should be prepared for a chilly welcome in Melana and had better not wear any visible pieces of leather when in town (I wore rubber flip-flops, which was fine). Stay on the main trail and be sure not to pause and rest on or even touch the inviting, large rock slab platforms that you'll see, for these are considered quite sacred. There is one rock that only the village gur can sit upon, and he was doing that the day I visited, communing with the gods to stop some unseasonable rain.

The homes in Melana are large two- and three-story houses of wood and stone arranged in three clusters. The well of activity is in the middle section where two community-owned buildings sit across from the sacred stone platform. The right-hand building is the place where the elected council of eleven elders meet, many of whom wear the Melana-style hat, shaped like a hat from Kulu, but utilizing only gray homespun material with a black border along the edge. The local god is called Jamlu. In Kulu he is considered to be a very powerful, even feared, god, and in keeping with the standoffish nature of his worshippers, when he goes to the fall Dussehra Festival, he sits alone across the river from the rest of the debtas present. At meetings of the elected council in town, Jamlu has the final say. Most people in town don't fancy their children being educated. As a result, the schoolmaster assigned to the village leads a lonely life and his classroom is practically empty. Melana has at least one hospitable family: the home of Sankta Ram, belonging to the theoretically "low-caste" Harijan clan, one of a very few Harijan families who live at the far end of the third group of homes. Sankta is a very fine man who has worked for the Mountaineering Institute in Manali and who knows a great deal about hiking routes in Kulu.

The trail to the pass from Melana goes quite directly up over 2,000 feet from town through forest and past some overhanging rocks that can provide shelter from rain. At the top of the ridge is the 11,617-foot Chandrakhani Pass. You can head rather steeply down the northern side of the pass, or you can follow the top of the roller-coaster grassy and rocky ridge to the west for about a mile, enjoying the wonderful wooded views, then descending to the north. Either way, the path you follow will take you into a forest of towering pines and down past several villages toward the town of Nagar, where the Russian artist Nicholas Roerich lived and painted for some years in the 1930s. A small art gallery occupies the house where he once lived. Rooms in the nearby castle, with legends galore of its own, can be booked by making a reservation with the tourist officer in Kulu. If you are heading up for the Chandrakhani Pass from this side, be sure to take a local with you at least far enough to get you onto the right path for the pass, otherwise you may wander about for some time among various interconnecting trails.

Lahoul

The large region of Lahoul lies just north of the Kulu Valley across the wide Rohtang Pass. Officially Lahoul and Spiti are different subdivisions of the same district, but the two regions are different enough in terms of location, accessibility to foreigners (Lahoul is permitted, Spiti is not), and the makeup of their inhabitants that they will be discussed separately here. To reach Lahoul, you must take the daily bus leaving in the morning from the town of Kulu or Manali. Until the tunnel beneath the Rohtang is completed, you will take a rest above the treeline at Mahri, then head up the twisting road past the headwaters of the Beas River for the Rohtang Jot (12,970 feet). This pass is open generally from about the end of May until the first heavy snow (probably in October). It is crossed on foot by locals virtually every month of the year, but not without periodic loss of life. From the top of the pass you can look directly across the deep Chandra Valley to the Sonepani Glacier and, to the west, the double peak of Gyephang (19,195 feet). This mountain is Lahoul's most sacred peak and has several important myths attached to it.

Like Kashmir's Zoji La, the Rohtang Jot is both an important climatic and a cultural watershed. South in the Kulu Valley are large stands of forest, while to the north in Lahoul, few trees brighten the significantly drier landscape. Kulu's *paharis* (hill people) are Hindu, while most of Lahoul's population is Buddhist. The uninformed traveler might imagine Lahoul, remote and isolated by high ranges, to be economically bereft or scenically desolate. The latter impression is quashed first, as soon as the visitor reaches the northern slopes of the wide Rohtang Pass and sees the wide mass of mountains that comprises the central part of Lahoul. Soon after the new arrival descends from the pass and comes across large homes and well-dressed Lahoulis, the first misconception is also lain to rest, for people in Lahoul are often more prosperous than any of their neighbors.

To reach Kyelang from Kulu, you descend from the Rohtang Pass into the Chandra Valley, go downriver to the junction of the two rivers, then proceed a little way up the Bhaga. Many hairpin turns, knee-cramped hours, and mind-boggling glimpses beyond Manali, you arrive in Kyelang (about 10,000 feet and 71 miles from Manali). The green oasis of Kyelang in the Bhaga Valley has been the administrative capital of Lahoul for enough years now to warrant construction of a second generation of utilitarian government buildings. During the summer months buses run daily to Kyelang from Manali and the town of Kulu over the weather-lashed Rohtang Pass, when it is clear of snow for road travel. But it is interesting that even in late fall and early spring, bus service within Lahoul continues in the lower valleys, when the roads are free of snow, even though Lahoul is cut off from the regions to the south (when the tunnel beneath the pass is completed, Lahoul should be accessible year round). Kyelang's modest bazaar offers only basic necessities at regulated prices. A new fifty-bed tourist hostel has been built, and several plain restaurants serve meals. Kyelang's square, stolid houses are built Tibetan style, three or more stories tall, with flat roofs, like homes throughout Lahoul. There is a gomba above Kyelang and a larger one, named Kardong, at the site of Lahoul's former capital, higher up and visible across the deep Bhaga Valley.

From Kyelang daily buses travel west to towns in the Chenab Valley at least as far as Udaipur. A daily bus also runs from Kyelang north up the Bhaga Valley to Darcha-Sumdo, the roadhead for the trek north into Zanskar. In mid- to late summer, a bus runs two or three times weekly from Kyelang to Leh in Ladakh. The 223-mile ride takes over eighteen hours if there are no complications, such as avalanches, swollen streams or washed-out bridges. Check at the tourist office in Manali if you plan to go this way, since you may need to get permission from the deputy commissioner in Kyelang before you can take the bus (have two photographs handy). For more information on this recently opened route, look at the beginning of the section called "The Road to Leh: Following the Ancient Caravan Route," in Chapter 9.

Lahoul has three principal valleys. The area called Pattan is in western Lahoul's deep Chenab River gorge east of and upriver from Chamba's Pangi region. At a place called Tande Sumdo at the upper, eastern end of Pattan, the Chenab divides into two valleys, the Bhaga and the Chandra. These gorges, emanating from their respective sources west and east of the Baralacha Pass, resemble the thumb and forefinger of the upturned left hand touching, where the thumb is the Bhaga, the forefinger is the Chandra, and the arm is the Chenab. From Tande Sumdo, the junction of the two valleys, a bus road extends along Lahoul's main Chenab Valley beyond the town of Udiapur, but the road down the Chenab Valley continuing west from Udiapur to Kishtwar and the city of Jammu may not be completed before the turn of the century.

Traditionally Lahoul has been divided into six regions, with five or six local dialects. The keeper of the one-room Him-Sagar restaurant-cum-hotel at Darcha-Sumdo in the Bhaga Valley remarked that he has difficulty understanding the Lahouli dialect of people from Gondla in the Chandra Valley, fewer than three hours away by bus. Irrespective of locality, the women of Lahoul, some of whom are extremely attractive, wear an embroidered, pleated maroon or brown dress that reaches to within a foot of the ground. To this may be added large, old-style earrings of turquoise and brass, nose rings, and heavy leggings, though some prefer modern silver earrings and stockings. The younger women wear various styles of necklaces, while their mothers prefer neckpieces of alternating coral and turquoise. Every woman uses a scarf to provide sun protection and color. All ladies have a part in the center and a single long braid of hair. The old-style hairdo of married women involves removing hair above the forehead in an area the shape of a V, with the apex of the V at the part.

Seed potatoes grow well in Lahoul's bracing climate, and from that crop alone some Lahoulis have become wealthy enough to buy choice tracts of land in Kulu for winter residences. Another unlikely but profitable source of income for Lahoulis is the harvesting of wild herbs. The plant called *kuth (Sausserea lappa)* is a fine example: oil extracted from its roots is valuable as a fixing agent for perfumes, and it has medicinal uses as well. The most recently introduced crop that has benefited Lahoul is hops. India once had to import hops to make beer, but now hops are grown extensively in Lahoul.

The districts of Lahoul and Spiti have been allied by both proximity and their common Buddhist culture. Ancient upland trails crossed both regions to Leh and Lhasa. Today only ruined buildings remain of what were once vast wholesale bazaars at Patseo in Lahoul and Losar in Spiti. The barren plains of Patseo and Losar were resting places for great caravans while their goods were bartered by traveling merchants from Kulu, Ladakh, Yarkand, and Tibet. Some Lahoulis continue to transport goods by mule over the Baralacha Pass to the high plains of Rupshu and even into Tibet, but most people in Lahoul are farmers or work for the government.

Trekking in Lahoul

People who like walking in sparsely inhabited high mountain valleys with well-grazed pastures will appreciate Lahoul, but they must choose their season. The upper valleys and high passes are not clear of snow before the Gaddis bring their herds in during July, but by that time the monsoon has begun, and although the rains here are lighter than in Kulu, hikers do need to be prepared for precipitation. The summer months are good ones for walking, nonetheless, as the rain that does reach Lahoul often tends to fall at night.

The Pattan area of the Chenab Valley in western Lahoul is reachable by a daily bus from Kyelang, as noted above. As you proceed west down the Chenab, in about 11 miles you reach Shansha, the hamlet at the base of the hike to the high Kugti Jot, the most frequented pass south to Chamba. The next junction with a trail south is the village of Bima, where the route to the Chobia Jot diverges. Shortly afterwards is Triloknath at the base of a nala leading to the glaciated Kalicho Pass. Both the trail from Triloknath and the path over the high Chobia Pass beginning at Bima lead to the town of Brahmaur in Chamba. Check with locals to be certain the pass you want to cross has already been in use that year before you attempt it. These paths to Chamba are usually not passable until mid-July (see also the preceding "Trekking Possibilities From Chamba"). The town of Triloknath has an ancient temple containing a multi-armed white marble image of Triloknath ("Lord of Three Worlds"), another name for the Bodhisattva Avalokitesvara, also known as "Glancing Eye." This image is considered to be closely related to the white marble image of Chuku at the gomba of the same name on the west side of Mt. Kailas in western Tibet (see "The Walk Around Mt. Kailas" in Chapter 9 of this book's companion volume, *Trekking in Nepal, West Tibet, and Bhutan*).

Just a few miles beyond Triloknath is the larger town of Udaipur. Udaipur has its own well-known temple, named Mrikula Devi, with excellent wood carvings. Udaipur sits at the base of the long Miyar Nala. This northward-trending valley has high passes leading east to the Bhaga Valley and west to the Saichu Nala, another tributary of the Chenab. The upper 12 miles of the Miyar Nala are glaciated, and at the head of the valley is the Kang La (circa 17,625 feet), which leads to the Temashut Nala above Mune Gomba in Zanskar's Tsarap Valley (see "The Zanskar Traverse" in Chapter 9). If you are considering trying this pass, take someone with you;

the last permanent habitation in the valley is the small hamlet of Khanjar. The Kang La has been crossed by Westerners in both summer and winter. If you attempt or cross the pass, I'd certainly like to hear about your experience.

A good trek in Lahoul for the hardy walker is to walk all or part of the upper Bhaga and/or Chandra valleys, which connect at the high Baralacha Pass. First, the Chandra Valley approach: The Chandra Valley can be entered from the Hamta Pass (already briefly described at the end of the "Manali" section preceding). An easier approach to the Chandra Valley is from the northern side of the Rohtang Pass, either at the place called Gramphu, where the small road up the Chandra Valley diverges from the main road, or a couple of miles farther down at Koksar where there are several small restaurants and where you may be able to get the occasional vehicle up-valley in mid- to late summer. Buses go from Manali to Spiti in midsummer, and foreigners may be able to take the bus as far as the Kunzang Pass, the border of Spiti. These buses leave the main Manali-to-Kyelang road at Gramphu.

If you begin the trek from the Chandra Valley, you can start walking at Gramphu or Koksar, or you may leave right from Manali and cross the Hamta Pass into the Chandra Valley. The Chandra Valley goes eastward, past Chhatru, then another 10 or so miles along is a camping ground called Puti Runi, "Broken Stone," which refers to a single split boulder that is 30 feet high. Just to the east of Puti Runi is the long Bara Shigri Glacier (the "Large Glacier"), which enters from the south. Here the valley turns to the north. Half a day's walk north from this turning, the jeep road crosses to the east bank of the river and begins climbing toward the Kunzang La. This pass, about 14,500 feet high, is actually the head of and westernmost point in the restricted Spiti Valley. Vehicles cross the pass in summer between Lahoul and Spiti. You can legally walk up to the pass, which lies in reddish brown country, then angle northwest and cross another low point in a ridge called the Balamo La, which leads to Chandra Tal ("Moon Lake," about 14,100 feet) in the Chandra Valley. Alternatively, near the floor of the Chandra Valley where the road begins angling up toward the Kunzang Pass, you can take the footpath up-valley and either continue along near the river or take an upper trail to reach Chandra Tal ("not to be missed," say those who have been there). The three-quarter-of-a-mile-long lake lies in a meadow area across the Chandra Valley from the Sumandar Tapu (or Dingkarmo) Glacier.

From Chandra Tal the way proceeds north for two more stages, first to Tokpo Yogma (or Likhim Gongma), then to Tokpo Gogma (or Baralacha Ban). Going up this wild valley, with its rushing streams and meadows inhabited by Gaddi shepherds and their flocks, you may have to wait until early morning, when the water is lower, to cross the streams at these camps. Finally comes the Baralacha Pass (see below). This route up the Chandra Valley is best done after late July or August, when most of the snow will have melted. High water, particularly in the afternoons, can be a hazard in this valley, so you should take a rope to help with stream crossings. At the Baralacha La, you meet the route that ascends the Bhaga Valley (described below). The entire walk from Manali over the Hamta and Baralacha passes to the roadhead at Darcha takes about twelve days; figure a couple of days less if you walk from Koksar or Gramphu (and somewhat less again if you get a lift partway up the Chandra Valley).

Once at Patseo (see below), I met an English couple who had nearly finished this walk. They were tired, having hiked without a porter and carried all their food, but they were also most satisfied. The long climb from Manali to the Hamta Pass was the most difficult part of the trek, but their muscles firmed up along the Chandra Valley, where they waded many glacial streams and communicated by sign language with Gaddi herders by the shepherds' evening fires. Chandra Tal was, for them, the most beautiful spot on the trek. With their heavy packs, they went slowly at first, then sped up, taking eleven days from Manali over the Hamta and Baralacha passes and to the roadhead at Darcha.

The other way you can approach this walk is from Darcha-Sumdo (just called Darcha by Westerners) in the Bhaga Valley. Starting at Darcha, you pass through higher, drier country: sere ochre- and magenta-splashed mountain desert. You could make the whole circle, or just go up from Darcha to the Baralacha La and back. To reach Darcha, take the daily 4:00 P.M. bus from Kyelang. But before leaving Kyelang, stop at the SDO's office behind the PWD rest house and request a chit that will allow you to stay at the Patseo rest house.

Leaving Darcha for Patseo and the Baralacha, you first walk along the foot trail angling up to the north, then meet the road that goes up-valley. You are entering a land populated in summer by shepherds and their scattered herds of sheep and goats and traversed by infrequent mule trains from Manali or Kyelang going to Rupshu and sometimes on to Tibet. The mule trains stop at the green meadow by Patseo, "Stone Bridge," on the east bank of the valley, 8 miles beyond Darcha. Here is a small two-room rest house with a tiny chokidar's hut in back. Beyond Patseo the mule caravans continue, as you do, taking the shortcuts past the old campground called Zing Zing Bar and across the main stream to the north side, up some more gravelly hills to a higher meadow at Suraj Tal, "Sun Lake," the source of the Bhaga River, just a mile before the pass. The Baralacha Pass (about 16,100 feet) is less a pass than a wide, flat stretch of high land, higher along its southern reaches at the head of the Chandra Valley. This is the place where three valleys meet: the Bhaga, Chandra, and the Yunan. The Yunan River is a tributary that flows north into the Tsarap River, which eventually flows past Phuktal Gomba and down to Padum in Zanskar (see "The Zanskar Traverse" in Chapter 9). The meaning of *baralacha* is either "the pass with crossroads on top" or "the twelve-horned pass." Here at the pass you could be in Tibet: there are no trees or bushes, and locals must carry wood or use dung chips for fuel. This walk from Darcha to the pass and back takes about four days, but you might plan on an additional day for exploring the high country near the Baralacha.

Oddly enough, however, you are still in H.P. if you continue north from the pass. In another 20 miles via the road (some of which you could undoubtedly cut off, just as you were doing en route to the pass) you reach the border of H.P. at Sarchu on the vast Lingti Maidan (circa 13,900 feet). Here, in this wide tract inhabited only by Gaddis and a few lonely jawans at an army outpost, is the actual border between Lahoul and Zanskar. In theory, walking north on the road is restricted. If you are taking the Phirtse La route to Zanskar, don't cross the bridge to the eastern side of the Yunan, but stay on the true left bank of the Yunan and when you meet the Lingti Chu, head west. But only go this way with a local as guide.

Finally, in Lahoul, is the trail from Darcha in the Bhaga Valley to the Shingo La (about 16,400 feet) that most trekkers follow to reach Zanskar from Lahoul (or the reverse). This route has been described at the end of "The Zanskar Traverse" in Chapter 9. You would be best off if you go with a local and his horse, but don't wait until you reach Darcha to make arrangements, or you will definitely pay a premium (unless you get lucky at Darcha and meet someone from Zanskar who has accompanied a trekker southward over the pass and is returning). Don't expect to find anything aside from basic hot meals in Darcha, and possibly a dry place to sleep (which may be crowded and smoky). If you are headed for either the Shingo La or the Baralacha, but particularly the Shingo (as the ascent is so steep), take it slow and don't neglect to acclimatize, and possibly temporarily retrace your steps if you go up too fast. See the section on altitude sickness in Chapter 14 if you are having any difficulties with adjusting to the elevation. If you are in Darcha with a day to spare, take lunch and wander across the Bhaga Valley and along the intriguing valley to the east.

Bushahr

Directly to the east of Kulu on the Indo-Tibetan border are Bushahr and Kinnaur, Himachal Pradesh's easternmost regions. Here is the narrow, steep-walled valley of the Sutlej River, a waterway that has its origins on the southern slopes of Mt. Kailas in Tibet. The Sutlej flows from Tibet into India through a deep gap in the Great Himalaya Range in an area formerly known as Pooh. South of Pooh was the region once called Kunawar, now known as Kinnaur, and south of this region was the former princely state of Bushahr. This state was never under the suzerainty of Kashmir like most small kingdoms to the west, and the ruling family traced its unbroken lineage back 123 generations. Thus, Bushahr was in existence since the time when the Hindu epic the *Mahabharata* was written, and in fact the founder of the state was said to have been the grandson of Lord Krishna. Here, you will travel up-valley from Bushahr to Kinnaur.

To reach first Bushahr, then Kinnaur, you must fly from New Delhi to Shimla or Chandigarh (below in the plains) or take a direct bus from New Delhi to Shimla, H.P.'s capital. At Shimla, on its 6,300-foot-high ridge, you will need to transfer to a second bus or another vehicle to reach Rampur (about 3,000 feet), the former capital of Bushahr, 90 miles away, along what is known as the Hindustan-Tibet Road.

Rampur, actually located south of Kinnaur District in Shimla District, is a compact town (with a dire shortage of hotel accommodations) in the bottom of the steep Sutlej River gorge. The annual festival here is the three-day Lavi Fair, which occurs in November. Rampur's most unique building is the large, multigabled Padam Palace, whose foundation stone (made in Lahore) announces that it was laid in 1919 by H. H. Maharaja Padam Singh Sahib Bahadur. A few people really lived in luxury in those days, including H.H.M.P.S.S.B., as you can see if you tour about the palace. High above the the raja's ornate circular *durbar* room (where he received his subjects) are carved wooden panels with slits that allowed the raja's wives, who were in purdah, to observe the proceedings below. Outside is a gazebo on the spacious palace grounds, the only open place in town.

Near the bus stop at the north end of Rampur on the west side of the main street is an old gomba, an incongruous sight in this lowland town with its several mandirs (Hindu temples). Inside the damp lha-khang, lit by a guttering oil lamp, is an outsized prayer wheel, Tibetan-style books in cupboards, and three images covered in red satin. The temple's one improbable object is a rock with the sacred mantra *"Om Mani Padme Hum"* said to be inscribed in minute lettering one *crore* (ten million) times.

You can take a nice walk directly from Rampur to the Tirthan Valley in Kulu. First, get chits from the PWD office in Rampur for the rest houses at Arsu and Sarahan. Then cross the Sutlej on the footbridge below town and take the path heading up the west (true right) side of the tributary valley directly across from Rampur to Pali village, then continue on to the ridge. Here at the ridge you enter the area called Outer Saraj in Kulu District. A short descent leads to the rest house at Arsu. Here you are up-valley from Nirmand, a town that can also be reached by a spur from the main road along the Sutlej Valley (not far south of Rampur). Nirmand is a cultural center known for its temples and its well-educated populace. From Arsu, follow the small dirt road for a ways, then angle up, taking the western tributary to the town of Sarahan, with its rest house at the edge of the forest just beyond town. Near Sarahan's rest house is an old wooden chalet-style temple dedicated to the god Shring Rishi that sits alone in an idyllic meadow dotted by willow trees and cut by a clear, meandering brook.

The trail above Sarahan leads gently through the parklike meadow, then directly up through a forest of conifers. Partway up the ridge on this path I met an older man resting and smoking a *beedie* (a small conical cigarette of cheap tobacco rolled in the leaf of the ebony tree). "Namaskar," I said. Then, "Is this a one- or a two-beedie hill?" He laughed, and as we chatted, I learned he was a retired forester from Kulu who had little respect for the present authorities in his former department. He allowed that some of the employees of the department were on the take and that the hills were rapidly losing their forest cover as a result. Certainly the hills *are* being rapaciously cut in Garhwal just to the east, and also in parts of Kulu. But later I met a man two valleys north who pointed to the hillside about us that was covered with new forest growth. He said that the same hillside had not been wooded when he was a child.

The pass at the top of the ridge is called the Bashleo Pass (10,660 feet), and it takes you from the region called Outer Saraj to Inner Saraj, from outer to inner Kulu, one might say. Some 10 miles to the west along this twisting, wooded ridge is the Jallori Pass (10,280 feet), which is crossed by a road. If you are in Shimla and want to take the shortest route to Kulu in distance (but longer timewise), the Jallori route is the way you will go. From the Bashleo Pass, the path drops some 4,500 feet through forest to the small community of Bathad in an upper tributary of the Tirthan River valley. An easy day's walk along the road from Bathad takes you down to Banjar, where there is bus service to the town of Kulu. It will take you two short days, staying at the rest houses, then one long day over the pass to walk from Rampur to Bathad.

Up the Sutlej Valley from Rampur and above the narrow valley floor is the town of Sarahan (a different Sarahan than the one mentioned above), connected by its own link road. Sarahan is the village where Bushahr was founded, and it served for some generations as Bushahr's capital. This is a lovely spot with a rest house that has excellent views to the north; the rest house can be reserved at the PWD office just south of Rampur. While you are there, you might check with the PWD office for other rest houses under its jurisdiction. Many relatively small but steep, green side valleys lie up the Sutlej Valley from Rampur which just waiting to be explored by the inquisitive trekker who is seeking lovely hiking terrain unvisited by foreigners.

Approximately 40 miles beyond Rampur on the main Hindustan-Tibet Road is Wangtu Bridge, near the boundary of Kinnaur, the farthest that foreigners have been permitted to proceed for many years. Here the sacrosanct Inner Line may be pushed back to allow foreign visitors to savor the glories of Kinnaur. Beyond Wangtu is the Baspa River, a large river valley that enters the Sutlej from the southeast. The Baspa is fed by many glaciers in its upper reaches, and maps show many tantalizing passes leading out of the valley, both north to the Tidang Gad and south into Uttar Pradesh's Tons River valley. The Baspa and its neighboring valleys are in Kinnaur proper, whose district headquarters is the town of Kalpa. Beyond Kalpa, and quite close to the Tibetan border, is the confluence of the large Spiti River with the Sutlej in the border region formerly called Pooh. Pooh was once a tiny independent princely state known for its delicious apricots and grapes, its excellent wood carvings, and its large stands of deodar trees.

Kinnaur   *by Tashi D. Lek*

[The following information on Kinnaur is kindly provided by Tashi D. Lek. Mr. Lek has traveled repeatedly through Kinnaur, and his contacts among the worldwide Tibetan community are many and diverse.]

The district of Kinnaur straddles the Sutlej River as this great waterway flows south from its headwaters at Mt. Kailas across the Tibetan border toward Bushahr. Kinnaur is one of the many transitional areas of the

Himalaya: it begins in its lower reaches with an essentially Hindu population and ends many score miles to the north in an area whose cool, dry, clustered towns are at 10,000 feet and whose people are rooted in the Tibetan Buddhist tradition.

The pleasures of Kinnaur come in many forms: its natural beauty, its unusually pleasant people, its architecture, and its historically important temples would make for a multifaceted Himalayan journey if its valleys and paths were available to foreign pilgrims. A succession of side valleys with lush waterfalls leading to snow-capped mountains and orchards of apples, apricots, and almonds makes one realize that parts of Kinnaur have received more than their fair share of nature's gifts. The people of upper Kinnaur, whose pleasing personalities are legendary, would be the first to agree.

In the *Mahabharata*, India's epic poem, the Pandavas (five brothers who battle their cousins) were forced into twelve years of exile in the forests. The terms of the exile were that if they should be discovered during this time, they must then pass another twelve years in the forest. Local legend records that a portion of their exile was lived in the village of Moorang just above the eastern bank of the Sutlej in upper Kinnaur.

During the eleventh century, Kinnaur was the southernmost region of the Kingdom of Guge. Remnants of this era can be found in the villages of Riba, Ropa, and Pooh, each of which contain gombas attributed to Rinchen Zangpo of Guge (see "The Temples of Spiti," following). Several hundred years ago, Kinnaur was part of Bushahr. In fact, the village of Sangla along the Baspa River in lower Kinnaur was once the capital of Bushahr, and you can still see the former rulers' palace above town.

The drive up the main Sutlej Valley from Kalpa to Pooh takes about five hours. For those inclined to nervousness, these five hours are hours of taut muscles as the driver negotiates scores of blind turns, sometimes thousands of vertical feet above the Sutlej, while the brown waters of the mighty river whoosh and swirl far below. The road itself is another testimonial to Indian engineering and road-building capabilities: in several places it is quite literally carved across the exposed face of a precipice.

One of Kinnaur's most pleasant villages is Kannum. Here in the early nineteenth century the well-traveled Hungarian scholar Csoma de Koros (who once lived in Vung Tau, Vietnam) compiled the first English-Tibetan dictionary. Kannum is tenuously connected with the main road by a theoretically jeepable road that zigzags its way about 2,200 feet above the Sutlej. If you make it, the richness of Kinnaur's temple architecture, apricot groves, and welcoming inhabitants are all well represented.

Kinnaur's border with Spiti lies beyond the town of Nako on the Spiti River near the small village of Sumdo, so Kinnaur and its people extend fully 20 miles up the Spiti River valley. At Nako, high above the east side of the river, is a temple commissioned by Rinchen Zangpo, whose original murals and statues remain intact. Nako can reward you for the time you pass there and is a proper introduction to Spiti itself.

Full-on upper Kinnaur formal dress in Nako village resembles that of Tibet just to the north, except for the Bushahr-derived pillbox hat (photograph by Tashi D. Lek).

Spiti

Visiting the Spiti Valley in 1956, David Snellgrove wrote that "Spiti has completely preserved its Tibetan character." However, that was before the road was built into Spiti from the Sutlej Valley. By 1977 a newspaper squib related that regular bus service was due to begin from the Hindustan-Tibet Road in the Sutlej Valley to Tabo in Spiti, "known in archaeological circles as the Ajanta of the Himalayas." There is great curiosity among foreigners about this Tibet-like district because of the artwork in Spiti's gombas, the few photographs published of its dry canyons, and the lure of its unvisited valleys, but for many years now, all of Spiti (locally called Piti) has been restricted from nonnationals, and even Indians have to get a permit (usually easily obtained if they have good reason to enter) to travel beyond the Inner Line into Spiti. Spiti means "The Middle Province," because it lies between Tibet, Kulu (once in British India), Lahoul, Kinnaur, and the former state of Bushahr.

The barren Spiti Valley is connected by road over the Kunzang Pass with Lahoul's upper Chandra Valley to the west. The lower and more accessible bus approach to Spiti is from Shimla through Kinnaur, in the deep gorge of the Sutlej Valley. If Spiti and Kinnaur were derestricted, you would be able to take a bus from Shimla to Kinnaur's district headquarters of Kalpa in the Sutlej Valley and there change vehicles to reach the Spiti Valley.

Until 1630 the Spiti Valley was the southwesternmost province of the west Tibetan kingdom called Guge, which stretched to the entrepôt village of Taklakot near the present Indo-Nepalese border. In those times, people in Spiti practiced polyandry and all married women wore the perag, a local version of the Ladakhi or Tibetan headpiece of coral and turquoise. Befitting the valley's high elevation, the principal crops were and still are barley, buckwheat, and peas. When Guge disintegrated, for a time Lahoul and Spiti came under the suzerainty of Leh's royal family. The Spiti Valley has not been prosperous since the days of the great trans-Himalayan trade caravans, when one branch of the ancient Hindustan-to-Tibet route utilized Spiti's high valley as a connecting link from Tibet to Kulu and the southern path to Kashmir. Now, under pressure from locals, much of Spiti may soon emerge from behind the Inner Line.

All passes into Spiti from the south were once snowed in for about half the year. Presently, however, the road that has been built into Spiti from the Sutlej Valley would remain open most of the year. But if Spiti is ever derestricted, you will have a choice of other routes into the region besides the roads that enter at either end of the valley. A few footpaths cross into Spiti over high ridges from the south, although they are rarely used now except by herders. The principal trail into Spiti south of the Kunzang La crosses the Pin-Parbati Pass (about 15,000 feet). Named for the valleys it connects, the Pin-Parbati Pass is approached from the west by taking a bus from the Kulu Valley town of Kulu to Manikaran in the Parbati Valley. From there, it is about a 25-mile walk to the pass and an equal distance past the traditional towns in the Pin Valley before reaching a jeepable road leading down to the main road near Spiti's old capital of Dankhar. Spiti's borders with Lahoul, Kulu, and Kinnaur are mostly marked by a concatenated strand of white, 20,000-foot peaks. The few additional recognized routes into Spiti originate in Kinnaur, between those summits, but they too are restricted.

Several gombas in Spiti merit attention, both for their spectacular settings and for the images and particularly the paintings within them. Proceeding upriver from the lower valley, the four best-known gombas begin with the temple of Nako, actually in Kinnaur. This shrine is built over a rock with an imprint alleged to be of Padmasambhava's foot.

Farther along are the most important temples in the valley, the buildings at Tabo. From the outside these buildings, which are situated on a dry plain, are unremarkable cubical mud structures: nothing special. But the plain exteriors have served their purpose because the temples have not been plundered by invaders. Inside are room after room of frescoes painted in different centuries, beginning with the eleventh. These are Gelugpa sect temples, and their frescoes may well have been executed by the same group of Kashmiri craftsmen who worked on the temples to the north in the Indus Valley at Alchi in Ladakh and at Toling and Tsaparang easterly up the Sutlej Valley in western Tibet.

The third temple in Spiti is at Dankhar—two small buildings on the north side of the valley containing sixteenth-century frescoes. The original Dankhar Gomba is across the valley near the mouth of the Pin Valley. Above the Dankhar monastery sits the old fortress capital of Spiti. In 1849 a British major named Hay wintered at Dankhar and wrote an account of his experience. The meaning of the word *dankhar* derives from the seventeenth, eighteenth, and nineteenth centuries when Spiti was often invaded by its neighbors, all of whom were more powerful than the lightly populated Spitipa. During an invasion, people would be warned by fires built on particular mountaintops, then some men would go high up to hidden redoubts called dankhars, where they would meet and decide what to do. Often the families would take food and valuables and hide in the unpopulated upper pastures until danger was past. Some 25 miles beyond Dankhar is the Kyi Gomba, situated just as you could hope to find the highest monastery in a remote valley: the small white buildings of Kyi rest on a knoll above the trail and seem to float before the high, stratified escarpment like a miniature city.

Spiti's upper valley is splashed with deep reds and browns. In caravan days, travelers through Spiti knew they were nearing Lahoul and the green vale of Kulu when they passed the perpendicular walls of the maroon canyon where the valley turns due west at Kiato. Spiti has many serpentine side valleys trending either to the southwest or northeast. The southwest valleys are usually culs-de-sac, but several tributaries heading northeast from upper Spiti lead to the Tsarap River, here called the Malung, which flows through the Lingti Maidan on the Manali-to-Leh road north of the Baralacha Pass. Maps show a trail going north just east of Kiato and another better-known path over a pass called the Parang La to the valley of the Para Chu. The Parang La trail is the direct Spiti-to-Rupshu route, the kind of trek that inveterate hikers like to dream about in front of the home fire. The Para Chu Valley leads onto Rupshu's high plains: to the great salt lake of Tso Morari and the trail to Hanle and Tashigang in the upper Indus Valley. All of these treks, however, will have to wait until the areas are derestricted, which could only happen if an international border with Chinese-occupied Tibet were ever demarcated.

The Temples of Spiti   *by Tom Pritzker*

[Tom Pritzker has visited numerous interesting regions of the Himalaya, from northwestern Nepal to far-eastern Bhutan. He is particularly interested in the artistic heritage of tenth- to thirteenth-century Tibet and in the course of his study has visited Spiti three times. Here is his depiction of Spiti's most artistically important temples.]

The Spiti Valley, largely unchanged through the centuries, houses what is perhaps the most important collection of ancient Tibetan monasteries in the world today. In the eleventh century, after a dark age of Tibetan Buddhism, the religion was reinvigorated and reimported from India by the kings of the western Tibetan kingdom of Guge. At the time, Spiti lay along the southwestern frontiers of Guge. Today, almost a thousand years later, the people of Spiti still follow the culture and traditions to which they have clung for centuries. Five major temples display that cultural heritage of the Western Himalaya from the eleventh through the twentieth centuries. Spiti is truly a treasure trove of art, history, and culture.

Unfortunately all of Spiti is off-limits to foreigners. Current plans, however, include an airstrip and an easing of restrictions for Indian groups. For the optimist, these plans foreshadow hope for changes in government policy regarding general foreign visitors.

Road access to Spiti is, in itself, a challenge to the mind and body. A jeepable unpaved road covers the breadth of this east-west river valley. But to experience this pleasure one must choose between the cliff-hanging engineering feat along the Sutlej River through Kinnaur (a three-day drive from Shimla) or the perils of the road over the Rohtang and Kunzang passes (a two-day drive from Manali). The latter route is open during the summer season: sometimes.

Traveling from Shimla, you enter Spiti officially at the village of Sumdo, west of the confluence of the Spiti and Sutlej rivers. At this point you are at an altitude of 10,500 feet and well into the moonscape typifying most of Spiti. Geologically this area is known as the Trans-Himalaya and is earthquake prone, having suffered a bad quake in 1975. The rocks, dust, and sand seem endless and in fact are nearly so since the great Tibetan Plateau lies just to the north and east of this remote valley.

The people are of Tibetan stock, and those who wear traditional clothing dress much like the people of Kinnaur, wearing gray and maroon homespun and Bushahr-style pillbox hats. While the road has brought bus service and mail, the roughly 7,500 people of Spiti live a basic agricultural existence much the same as their ancestors have lived for the last millennium. The Indian government's efforts, both in bridge building and horticulture, have made visible strides that have resulted in the availability of food and clothing as well as the potential for an improving standard of living in an area that is inhabited in spite of its incredibly desolate topography.

About 19 miles west of Sumdo is Tabo, the most important of Spiti's temple complexes. Almost appearing as an afterthought along the road, the houses of Tabo are made of stone, wood, and mud and sit atop a flat plateau just above the Spiti River. This stark setting camouflages the paradise of color, history, and imagery that is housed in the eight temples within the walls of the monastery.

Among the eight, the du-khang (assembly hall) alone contains an inscription that dates it to the end of the tenth or beginning of the eleventh century. It was during this period—prior to the development of sects within Tibetan Buddhism—that Yeshe Od, the King of Guge, sent the young monk known as Rinchen Zangpo (958–1055) to India with the mission of bringing the dharma back to western Tibet. By the end of his life, Rinchen Zangpo, known also as the Great Translator, had translated 158 of the holy scriptures from Sanskrit into Tibetan. His works laid a foundation for a second diffusion of Buddhism throughout Tibet. In addition to his translations, Rinchen Zangpo's biography alludes to his having constructed 108 gombas and stupas. Tabo is specifically mentioned as one of these works. As a final contribution, the Great Translator is credited with having imported thirty-two Kashmiri artisans and with them a painting style that is lost in present-day Kashmir.

Upon entering the du-khang at Tabo, the visitor is met with a staggering room of frescoes done in the style of eleventh-century Kashmir. The room is roughly 35 by 65 feet, with ceilings higher than 20 feet. In the rear of the hall is a free-standing three-sided chapel with a fully frescoed walkway that allows the worshipper to circumambulate the chapel. The frescoes are laid out in three horizontal bands around the du-khang. The lowermost band, done in a less refined fashion, depicts Buddhist legends and stories from the life of Buddha. The middle register is punctuated by thirty-two stucco figures of seated goddesses, while the upper register is the realm of a series of Buddhas and Bodhisattvas who can only evoke feelings of paradise. At the head of a series of columns sits a four-bodied stucco figure of Vairocana that, in the seated position, reaches over 13 feet in height. In fact, the entire room is laid out in a fashion that places the visitor in the midst of a three-dimensional mandala. This room is truly one of the great treasures of the Himalaya.

Within yards of the du-khang are a series of free-standing buildings that house the remaining temples of Tabo. While the history of the du-khang makes it of unique interest, the remaining temples house some of the finest artistic accomplishments of fifteenth- through eighteenth-century Tibet. The frescoes throughout the buildings make Tabo a living museum of art styles of Tibet through the ages. Due to the efforts of a *geshe* (a teacher with a doctorate in philosophy) from the eastern Tibetan region of Kongbo, Tabo now lays claim to a school of painting, a school of Buddhist philosophy, and thirty-two monks.

Another 25 miles to the west, the next temple of note is that of Dankhar. Dating to sometime in the sixteenth or seventeenth century, Dankhar sits as a mountain fortress along the precipice of a jagged collection of mountains over 1,000 feet above the Spiti River. The temples' activities are minimal, but it overlooks a village whose population must number in the hundreds.

As you continue along the valley, about forty minutes off the main road, the village of Lalung harbors an important temple attributed to Rinchen Zangpo. While the frescoes have been repainted, the walls are covered from head to foot with lyrical stucco figures modeled in the unmistakable style of the eleventh century. About 150 feet from the main temple is a small room housing a slightly inferior version of Tabo's stucco figure of a four-bodied Vairocana.

Farther down the river, but before Kaza, which is the administrative headquarters of Spiti, is a bridge straddling the Spiti River. Over this bridge the road continues for about 12 miles to a second valley angling to the southwest, known as the Pin Valley. This picturesque valley contains numerous villages of whitewashed stone and mud houses set above fields of green peas and barley. In the winter, snow prevents all movement in the valley. To provide entertainment, the entire village gathers in a different house each day. The host is responsible for the food and drink for his assigned day. While most of the population of Spiti adheres to the Gelugpa sect of the Dalai Lama, the population of Pin follows the earlier traditions of the Nyingmapa sect.

Just beyond the village of Gungri is a temple complex consisting of three buildings. While we have no hard evidence to prove it, tradition holds that the oldest of these buildings predates Tabo.

Among its other attributes, the Pin Valley is famous for its horse breeding as well as the ibex that lurk on the cliffs high above the valley floor. Along the valley floor, life gets interesting when you go to visit other villages. To cross the Pin River, many of the population carry with them a yak-hair girdle attached to a hollowed-out yak bone. The apparatus is attached to your legs on one end and then to a cable that stretches across the river. Combined with a pulley system, this mode of transport is quite invigorating for the first-time visitor.

The fifth important temple in the main Spiti Valley is known as Kyi Gomba. Located less than an hour west of Kaza, Kyi is the home of the nineteenth (and current) incarnation of Rinchen Zangpo, Lo Chen Tulku, from Nako in Kinnaur. The temple complex is built atop the pinnacle of a cone-shaped hill that itself sits at the foot of a 1,600-foot-high sheer cliff. The temple's paintings would indicate a foundation dating to sometime around the sixteenth century. Today, Kyi is the most active monastery in Spiti with about one hundred and fifty monks and an active school of Buddhist philosophy.

From Kyi it is about a three-hour drive to Losar, the westernmost village of the Spiti Valley. From there the road climbs to the 14,700-foot Kunzang Pass, at the end of the Spiti Valley.

While Spiti has numerous villages and temples not mentioned in this account, its uniqueness lies in the preservation of its traditions and the history of an area that many centuries ago was part of a thriving caravan route through Tibet, India, and Central Asia. Today as you journey through Spiti you are constantly reminded of the long journey of Buddhism and the role of this small enclave in that great journey.

At Rupkund Lake during the 1987 Nanda Devi Raj Jat Yatra (Photograph by Swami Sundarananda).

11

Garhwal's Sacred Mountains

A hundred divine epochs would not suffice
to describe all the marvels of Himachal.
As the dew is dried up by the morning sun,
so are the sins of mankind by the sight of Himachal.
                                    Skanda Purana, fifth century A.D.

Body is the temple of God.
                          Graffiti near Bageshwar, Almora District

Garhwal and Kumaon

TO TAKLAKOT

Lipu Lekh La

SHANG TANG KALOPANI
Kuthi Yankti

GARBYANG

PEAKS, GLACIERS & MEADOWS

Milam gl.

MILAM

Darma

Mahakali

PANCH CHULI

DUNAGRI

MAPONG

Dhauliganga

NANDA DEVI

TAWAGHAT

LATA
Rishi Ganga

NANDA KOT

Gori

Ganga

MANTOLI Pindari gl.

MUNSIARI

DARCHULA

TRISUL

Rupkund

JAULJIBI

Nandakini

HILLS & VILLAGES

WAN

KAPKOTE

Ramganga

JHULAGHAT

GHAT

MUNDOLI

Pindar

DEBAL

PITHORGARH

GWALDAM

BAGHESHWAR

Sarju

ALMORA

M I L E S
0   5   10   20

0 5 10   20   30
K I L O M E T E R S

Garhwal and Kumaon

The deep gorge of the Sutlej River in the eastern part of Himachal Pradesh provides the generally accepted line of division through the Great Himalaya Range demarcating the Western and Central Himalaya. This chapter covers the Central Himalaya across the hill portions of the state of Uttar Pradesh (U.P.), "Northern State": from the Tons River (a major tributary of the large Yamuna River), not far east of the deep Sutlej River gorge, to the Mahakali River (usually called the Kali), which forms the border between India and Nepal. Uttar Pradesh is India's most populous state, with a population exceeding any country in Europe. The hill regions mentioned in this chapter comprise only a small part of the state and an even smaller fraction of the populated areas in U.P. In going from the Sutlej to the Tons River, you cross from the watershed of the mighty Indus to the drainage of the holy Ganges River, a wide basin stretching 700 miles east to Nepal's eastern border with the Indian state of Sikkim.

The upper stream valleys of the Ganges and its principal tributary, the Yamuna, contain hundreds of ancient shrines, usually constructed of large blocks of stone, sacred to Hindu devotees of Krishna, Vishnu, and especially Shiva. The upper Ganges also has a pilgrim path to Hemkund Lake, sacred to members of the Sikh faith. Trails forbidden to foreigners lie east of Nanda Devi's summit in the Kumaon region, and some lead toward Tibet, where Indian pilgrims, called *yatris* in Hindi, now travel again to Lake Manasarowar and sacred Mt. Kailas, the "Crown Chakra of the Earth," the world's most sacred mountain for Tibetan Buddhist and Hindu alike. The pilgrim, or yatra, routes to the principal shrines in Garhwal (*garh* means "fortress") will be described, but first some background.

The previous seven chapters, as a whole, have covered a vast oval area layered in ranges, including the Hindu Kush, Karakoram, Pir Panjal, Zanskar, Ladakh, and Kailas ranges in addition to the main Great Himalaya Range. From the Karakoram Pass in Ladakh's Nubra region to the area of Uttar Pradesh where the Bhagirathi River (the western tributary of the Ganges) enters India from Tibet, the disputed Indo-Chinese border caroms in a basically north-to-south direction. East of the Bhagirathi, the border between India and Tibet bends to a southeasterly slant for a couple of hundred miles to the boundary of Nepal. The point where the Bhagirathi enters India from Tibet means more to the map reader and trekker than a border shift to the southeast, however. To the north and west of the Bhagirathi, the area of the Western Himalaya, Karakoram, Hindu Kush, and their subranges forms a wide jigsaw mosaic of ridges and valleys stretching into infinity. East of the Bhagirathi, however, the mountainous areas south of Tibet include only the Great Himalaya Range and its southern protectors, the Mahabharat and Siwalik ranges, and the high peaks, as often as not, provide the border between India and Tibet.

The valleys east of the Sutlej and south of the Himalaya receive more rain and have more vegetation than the lands to the northwest. These valleys of the Central Himalaya are folded into steep, narrow gorges that can be traversed by people, but until quite recently, they could not be negotiated by large pack animals or vehicles. The valleys generally run from the mountains in the north to lower hills in the south, and up-valley they lead toward the frontier rather than to neighboring valleys. The Tibetan border either demarcates the Himalayan crest or parallels it just north of the main peaks.

Those who have seen the upper areas of the Yamuna and Ganges river valleys, described in this chapter, are invariably astonished at the beauty of these lush, craggy regions. Few of us now interested in Himalayan trekking can remember the era in the 1930s when Shipton and Tilman were having what Shipton called a "Himalayan Heyday," exploring and climbing in the Garhwal area. Since then, excepting Arnold Heim and August Gansser's epic 1936 sojourn through Garhwal and Kumaon, the four-person 1950 Scottish expedition to peaks around Nanda Devi, and very few other expeditions, India's Central Himalaya was closed to foreigners for many years north of the large hill stations, such as Shimla and Almora. In 1974, when the Inner Line was relocated northward and many new areas were opened to visitors, most foreigners focused their interest on Ladakh. Only slowly have people become aware that the 200-mile stretch from the Sutlej to the Mahakali is an area equal in scenic grandeur to any in the Himalaya. In Uttarakhand, "Northern Region," as the Ganges headwater area has traditionally been called, paths lead to vistas unsurpassed for mountain scenery. And in the many holy places of this region, India's legions of yatris practice traditions that are millennia old.

In the eighteenth century, this area was divided into two principal hill states. Kumaon lay between the peak of Nanda Devi and the Mahakali River; its capital was the ridge-straddling town of Almora. The other, much larger, hill state within Uttarakhand was Garhwal, and its last capital, Srinagar (different from Srinagar in Kashmir), is still on a flat plain by the Alaknanda River, the eastern branch of the Ganges. West of Garhwal were two groups of small princely states, the Bara ("Twelve") and Attara ("Eighteen") Thakurai. These thirty states were vest-pocket size compared to Garhwal and Kumaon, for they did not extend beyond the Sutlej and together comprised a strip of territory roughly 30 miles wide extending from the Tibetan frontier south to the Punjab plains. In the beginning of the nineteenth century, the Gurkha army from Nepal defeated first the forces of Kumaon, then the army in Garhwal, moving the western border of Nepal to the Sutlej. By the time the tough Gurkha forces reached the last ridge before the Sutlej, however, their supply lines were so long and their cumulative injuries so debilitating that their campaign began to run aground against the motley forces of the thirty princely states. The border of Nepal remained at the Sutlej until the conclusion of the British-Gurkha War in 1816, when the Treaty of Sagauli established the boundary at its present location along the Mahakali River.

The people of Garhwal and Kumaon are descended from both Aryan and Mongol stock, and many villages still have families with distinct racial heritages. Most villagers you meet speak local dialects, but they also know as much Hindi as you will have learned from John Mock's "Introduction to Hindustani (Hindi-Urdu)" in the back of the book. Dotials (like those who portered with the Scots in 1950) and other Nepalis migrate to the Garhwal and Kumaon hill country for summer work, and if you speak some Nepali, you can use it with them. A Nepali will not likely have a local's knowledge of hill trails, but Nepalis are usually excellent porters. Some of this area's most interesting denizens are the Tibetan-descended Bhotia villagers from the upper valleys, who resemble their brethren in Nepal but who, unlike other Bhotias, are Hindu and usually worship Shiva, the Lord of Himachal, whose throne is atop Mt. Kailas.

The majesty of the Central Himalaya lies in its ruggedness, and the juxtaposition of monsoon-drenched valley floors with soaring rock buttresses dusted in snow is repeated like a fugue in Garhwal. But when the summer monsoon strikes in June, these fantastic gorges can become as difficult to reach as the mythical Shangri La. So walking in late spring (April and May, until the beginning of the monsoon, about the middle of June) and in fall (from early September until the first snow sometime in November) is best in Garhwal and Kumaon unless you are prepared for rain.

The hills of Uttar Pradesh, like Himachal Pradesh, have a vast number of interconnecting trails, and only the best known can be described or even hinted at here. Some of the region's most enchanted places lie along unheralded paths, none of which will be revealed here. Your best assist to discovering these hidden vales is a good map, which will not itself portray every trail, but will indicate the existence of a valley that, with a local villager, you can explore for yourself.

The U502 Series maps are quite accurate for most of the regions in Uttar Pradesh because in the early part of this century these areas were controlled by the British, whose early surveys form the basis for U502 maps. From west to east, the following four maps in the U502 Series contain most of the information about hill regions in Uttar Pradesh: The *Chini* sheet (NH 44-1) shows the upper Tons Valley (poor reliability) and a few of the northernmost sections of the Bhagirathi River; Yamnotri Temple is just on the bottom of the map. The *Dehra Dun* sheet (NH 44-5) depicts the Yamuna and Bhagirathi rivers, Gangotri and Kedarnath temples, and the Alaknanda Valley as far north as 20 miles beyond the town of Chamoli; Badrinath Temple is just on the eastern edge of the sheet. If you are going up the Alaknanda Valley, you should also have the *Nanda Devi* sheet (NH 44-6), which shows the town of Joshimath and the Dhauliganga, Rishiganga, Pindar, upper Nandakini, upper Gori, and Darma river valleys. The *Almora* sheet (NH 44-10) depicts Almora town and most of the unrestricted hill regions of Kumaon (including a good-sized chunk of far western Nepal as far east as the town of Silgarhi). Although these maps are generally accurate, they do not have up to date road information, for which you will need a map supplied by the U.P. tourist authorities. By now, there are most likely trekking maps along the lines of those made for J. and K. and H.P. Check for these at an office of U.P. Tourism (locations of which are noted just below).

Before leaving New Delhi for Uttar Pradesh, be sure to stop in at the Uttar Pradesh Government Tourist Department at the Chanderlok Building, 36 Janpath, New Delhi. If you are going to U.P. from elsewhere, there are also tourist offices at Uttarkashi, Dehra Dun, Mussoorie, Hardwar, Rishikesh, Kotdwar, Pauri, Srinagar, Joshimath, Ranikhet, Naini Tal, Almora, and Pithoragarh (you may find others as well). Offices in the larger towns will be far better staffed to assist you than the others. Should you want to fly from New Delhi, the best airport to reach is at Dehra Dun. But remember that U.P. is closer to New Delhi than any other region in the Indian Himalaya. If you are going from New Delhi by road to the Tons or Yamuna valleys, you will want to take a bus to Dehra Dun, then switch for another bus north. Those going by land from New Delhi to the Bhagirathi, Alaknanda, or Pindar valleys should take a bus to Rishikesh and change there. If you are going to a large enough town, there may be a direct bus. For instance, direct buses go from New Delhi to Pithoragarh in Kumaon. Check with the U.P. Tourist Department at the above address to learn the exact options available to you when you want to travel.

Uttar Pradesh, like H.P., has many rest houses, both those operated by the Public Works Department (PWD) and the Forestry Department. The PWD rest houses tend to be larger and located in more trafficked places, and they tend to be more fully booked with visiting officials. The forest rest houses are often less expensive, only a couple of rooms in size, and can be in rather out-of-the-way locations. You should get a chit for every night you plan to stay at any rest house, but the individual chokidar of each one (particularly the smaller Forestry Department rest houses) may possibly decide to let you stay without one, depending on whether any rooms are available, on how his last few experiences with foreigners went, and on the degree of politeness with which you present yourself. It is definitely best to get a *pukka* (proper) chit. Then you can be certain of staying. The reservation authority for rest houses is usually a day or more south of the accommodation itself, so a little planning can help here. Stop at district tourist offices, district PWD offices, or district forestry offices as you travel north to get chits to stay at these rest houses. Some of the various reservation authorities will be noted below in the separate sections.

The Hill Stations

Before proceeding up-country to the more northerly and sacred mountainous regions of Garhwal and Kumaon, the hill stations must definitely be mentioned. Frankly, I am not an experienced guide to these islands of old Angleterre, for almost without exception, I have bused past these pleasant towns with their views of the distant mountains to get into the mountains, not gaze upon them from afar. But these towns offer trekkers an excellent chance to revive from the heat of the plains before a hike, or to recover from the rigors of the trail afterward. The hill stations are an essential part of the Indian Himalaya, and more of them are to be found in the hills of Uttar Pradesh than anywhere else.

During the British Raj, these hill towns were built in English resort style, with hotels, villas, cottages, restaurants, shops, and cinemas. Each hill station also has its mall. Until the early 1960s, successive generations of civil servants—British, then Indian—moved the state seats of government to the various hill stations seasonally to avoid administrative paralysis in the early summer premonsoon oven. The most accessible and representative of these in India (aside from Shimla in H.P. and Darjeeling in West Bengal north of Calcutta) are in the hills of U.P., north to northeast of New Delhi. These inland islands bear as much relation to the surrounding villages as Disneyland does to Orange County, but they remain popular, enjoyed today by city families on holiday to escape the summer heat. And for some whirlwind tourists, a quick taxi ride to Shimla or Mussoorie may be the entirety of their fling with the Himalaya.

These quasi-Elizabethan, neo-Indian hill towns are buzzing throughout the busy spring and summer seasons, but off-season, especially during a clear midwinter full moon, a hill station offers mountain lovers a quiet, comfortable place to stroll and reflect while regarding the snow mountains. In Shimla, Mussoorie, Ranikhet, Naini Tal, and Almora, all manner of cuisine, particularly delicious regional Indian food, is available in restaurants adjacent to the hotels and lodges. Each of these hill towns is situated on a ridgetop, and most offer their own lookout point with a wide Himalayan panorama. For a look-see at one of the hill stations less visited by Westerners, try Lansdowne, Pauri (and consider the trail to Almora from there), Naini Tal, Ranikhet, or Chakrata, northwest of Mussoorie, hidden over near the H.P. border.

From these towns, paths for day, overnight, and weekend-long walks extend into the nearby hills. Some people overcome their initial reservations about trail walking with a hike to the nearby hilltop, or *tibba*, as they are often called. Shimla, "the queen of the hill stations" in H.P., with its Jakoo Hill overlook and large mall, was once the summer home of the central government during the British Raj. Not far from Mussoorie is Benog Hill, and you can take overnight walks to 8,570-foot Top Tibba and 9,915-foot Nag Tibba. The hilltops near Almora are known for the temples atop them, harking to pre-British days when Kumaon was ruled by the Chand dynasty from Almora.

Mussoorie's 7,026-foot Gun Hill viewing point is approachable from the mall below by walkway or suspended gondola. I once stood on the deserted Gun Hill observation deck late one January afternoon, trying to discern a few summits not entirely cloud hidden and reflecting on a just-completed fifteen-month Himalayan sojourn. The peaks from Bandarpunch to Nanda Devi were cloaked in gray stratus, but, to the west, glowing clouds graced the beginning of a glorious sunset.

The Holy Yatra Trails

Much of Hinduism's myth and tradition stems from the Vedas: sacred writings compiled between 3,500 and 4,000 years ago. Many of the Vedas' legends about Vishnu, Krishna, and especially Shiva speak of places in the Himalaya. The most important collection of story-hymns, called *Rig-Veda*, describes the veneration of rivers in terms of their physical and spiritual properties. Shiva, one of the three principal gods worshipped as a manifestation of Atman (the Ultimate Essence), is considered to dwell in the Himalaya. His throne is atop sacred Mt. Kailas, and from the strands of his long, matted hair flows the holiest of rivers, the Ganga, or Ganges. Since prehistory the natural wonders of the Uttarakhand area in particular have been identified by Hindus as manifestations of the gods themselves, or of places where mythic events took place. When you trek in Uttarakhand (or visit Amarnath Cave in Kashmir, Muktinath in Nepal, or any Buddhist gomba), you too will be a yatri, a pilgrim, going on yatra, or doing *naykor*, "going around places," as the Tibetans say, a new generation of pilgrim from the West.

With the passing of time, six Himalayan sites have come to be of undisputed importance for Hindu yatris. Of these, four will be discussed in this section, for they lie in Uttarakhand. The fifth, Amarnath Cave, is covered in Chapter 8. The last, Mt. Kailas, is described at length in Chapter 9 of this book's companion volume, *Trekking in Nepal, West Tibet, and Bhutan*. The traditional path to Mt. Kailas through Kumaon is once again being used by Hindu yatris, so it is briefly mentioned in this chapter, even though it lies wholly within an area restricted for non-Indians. The four most important *dham*s, "an abode of God, a sacred dwelling place," or *tirth*s "a place of pilgrimage," are Yamnotri, Gangotri, Kedarnath, and Badrinath. Yamnotri and Badrinath are associated with Vishnu, the redeemer and preserver, a force who shakes his fist at time; Gangotri and Kedarnath are shrines for Shiva, the destroyer and transformer. There are far more shrines than these four, and if you wanted to, you could bus and walk for month after month, going to temple upon temple in Uttarakhand.

In the summer the four principal dhams are visited by thousands of yatris from all parts of India. Devotees approach the holy shrines to perform *puja*, worship ceremonies that involve recitation of scriptures and ritual presentations of grains, oils, spices, or precious objects to the deity. These ceremonies, which have evolved over many generations, are important both to assure the soul's future life and to honor those now dead. The ritual cleansings that preceed the puja are designed to wash away any sins from the past and are performed in traditionally sacred locations adjacent to the temples. Yamnotri and Badrinath even have hot springs in which to cleanse oneself of sins. Both the bathing rituals (which you may also see in Varanasi—also called Benares or Kashi—and numerous other locations in India and Nepal) and the puja ceremonies (some of which may continue for hours) might seem different from Western practice until you consider Christian multitudes in church kneeling for the weekly blessing, or a congregation receiving communion. And the baptism ceremony of Christians is not at all unlike bathing purification rites that Hindus practice in traditional, unself-conscious fashion throughout their lives.

In Varanasi on the hot Ganges plains, I had been reluctant to bathe due to the turbidity (read pollution) of the water. When I visited Badrinath, however, I saw steam rising from the hot spring called Tapta Kund and realized that here was the perfect spot to first immerse myself in India. Leaving the *bhavan*, the pilgrim rest house where I was staying, I walked to the hot spring early in the morning when the bathers were few, left my clothes in a pile by the side and, wearing briefs like the other male bathers (women bathe in a nearby enclosure), enjoyed a warm, neck-deep soak in the large covered pool. There is nothing like participation to remove the "me-they" feeling, and afterward as I walked away from the ancient bathing tank, returning the smiles and nods of the nearby sadhus, I too was a Badrinath yatri.

Until roads were built into Garhwal in the 1950s, yatris needed to walk for weeks to reach a single tirth. Nowadays paved roads lead to within a few miles of each of the four spiritual places, and Gangotri and Badrinath can be reached directly by road. The order in which the four tirths are discussed here is from west to east: Yamnotri, Gangotri, Kedarnath, and Badrinath. These tirths are described, as well as other paths in their vicinity, whether or not these other trails are directly associated with any pilgrimage site. The pilgrim trail to the Tibetan border that leads to Mt. Kailas is briefly mentioned later, for it lies in Kumaon very near the border with Nepal.

Yamnotri

You can reach Yamnotri by either of two routes. You can take a bus from Hardwar (or Rishikesh just to the north) past Deoprayag (or Devaprayag), where the Bhagirathi and Alaknanda join to form the Ganges, to Tehri, then continue on past Dharasu to Barkot in the Yamuna Valley and north to the roadhead at Hanuman Chatti (a *chatti* is a pilgrim's rest house; originally chattis were usually plain, open-sided structures). Or you can begin at Dehra Dun and go to Mussoorie (where accommodations can be booked at Yamnotri's small rest house) up the Yamuna Valley past Barkot to Hanuman Chatti. Hanuman Chatti can also be reached on foot from Dodi Tal by a route mentioned in "The Walk to Dodi Tal and Beyond," following. Allow yourself two to three days from Hanuman Chatti for visiting the temple (allow more time for side trips) and expect to find basic food supplies available in the summer season. Note the route up the Hanuman Ganga east of Hanuman Chatti leading in two days to Dodi Tal (see "The Walk to Dodi Tal and Beyond").

Yamnotri Temple lies 8 miles beyond Hanuman Chatti on a trail that passes Phul Chatti and Janki Chatti en route. Less than a mile off the short section between Phul and Janki chattis is the village of Kharsali with its own small temple. Do walk to Kharsali as you proceed. Here you will have a better view of the peaks in the vicinity, like Bandarpunch, than at the main temple itself, since Yamnotri sits cut off from most perspectives at the base of a ridge. Kharsali is the home of Yamnotri's *pujaris* and *pandas*. All four of these holy shrines have pujaris, Brahmin-caste priests responsible for worship in the temples, and pandas, Brahmins who guide pilgrims and assist them in performing the appropriate rituals. With the lengthening of the roads and widening of trails, the pandas have fallen on hard times, as they are needed by yatris for less time than before. After Janki Chatti the path ascends gently, then steeply, to Yamnotri (10,000 feet), 3 miles up the valley.

For people going to each of the four dhams, Yamnotri should theoretically be visited first, since the traditional order in which the shrines are supposed to be visited is from west to east. The temple lies at the base of a spur below Saptrishi Kund (meaning "Lake of the Seven Rishis," or sages), a glacier-fed lake considered to be the headwaters of the Yamuna River. Yamnotri is the smallest and least visited of the four holy places, and it has two special features sometimes associated with these shrines: a *shila*, a large rock with mythic associations, here connected to Vishnu, the temple deity, and a spring hot enough to boil rice (which then becomes *prasad*, consecrated food). A second hot spring is diverted into two tanks for bathing. Yamnotri sits near the base of sacred 20,720-foot Bandarpunch, the "Monkey's Tail." This peak is named for Hanuman, the powerful, mythical monkey god who was the faithful servant of the king Rama (an avatar of Vishnu) in the epic *Ramayana*. From Yamnotri there are two places above and beyond the temple to go. A small path to Saptrishi Kund leads up the west side of the narrow ravine leading north from the temple. After passing a waterfall, you must cross the stream to the east side to reach the sparkling lake, the headwaters of the Yamuna. Contrast this lovely scene with the wide, muddy Yamuna flowing past New Delhi.

The other route beyond Yamnotri is a small path leading up the high ridge to the north, a path that finally disappears in scree and snow. With a local guide you can find the way over the high ridge (circa 17,000 feet) into the upper Tons River valley and down to the valley floor. Descending this valley, the uppermost part of the Tons River, you come to Osla, the valley's uppermost village. From Osla (where there is a forest rest house) you can head up another tributary, the Ruinsara Gad, to the meadow camping area called Har-ki-Dun (11,695 feet). This place has been compared to the lovely "Valley of Flowers" in the Alaknanda Valley to the east (see below), which should be enough said to the discerning hiker.

The Tons River and Har-ki-Dun

Most people won't approach the upper Tons Valley from Yamnotri, however. The usual route to the Tons is to take a bus from Dehra Dun to Mussoorie, then to Nowgaon in the Yamuna Valley and over the ridge to the roadhead town of Naintwar (or Netwar, 4,595 feet) in the Tons Valley. From Naintwar to the last town of Osla (8,395 feet) is a two-day hike, and from Osla it is another day to Har-ki-Dun. There are three forest rest houses

along the way; check at Mussoorie about booking them. The Govind
Sanctuary comprises 368 square miles of the upper Tons Valley, including
Har-ki-Dun, Bandarpunch, and several other peaks north of Bandarpunch.

The Tons is considered to be a branch of the Yamuna, but like the
Zanskar River above its confluence with the Indus in Ladakh, the Tons is
larger than the river of which it is supposedly a tributary. Here, the Tons
Valley has many chir (long-needle) pines. When I stayed at a forest rest
house near Sheona down-valley from Naintwar, a plaque read: Forests—
1898. Would that there were an active protector of the forests here now,
for when I ascended the nearby tributary, I saw clearcutting on an unforgiv-
ably massive scale. Towering piles of trimmed timber, usually sawn by
Nepali women, were piled on the denuded hills. Long wooden sluices
carried the timber down the side valley to the Tons, where it would be
floated farther down to be collected for eventual sale by the contractors
who had purchased it.

The men in the Tons Valley wore hats that I thought of as being Kulu
style. But when I asked, I was told that these pillbox hats are considered
by locals to be Bushahr style. Many homes in the Tons are several stories
tall and have flagstone courtyards. A few glances at a map of the area will
give you some good ideas for long off-the-beaten-path treks. Let's hope
these routes don't get in the damn guidebooks.

The Bhagirathi Valley

*The Bhagirathi is different from the Yamuna, the Alaknanda and the
Saraswati, just because she is Ganga.*

From a local guide to Uttarakhand

The western branch of the Ganges River is the Bhagirathi, and it drains
remarkably beautiful and hilly country in the midst of Garhwal, some of
which is cloaked with thick forest. Numerous routes can be followed
by hikers, both south of Gangotri and up-valley from the small but well-
known temple. Some of the better-known trails leading away from the
Bhagirathi Valley will be mentioned as you proceed northward toward
Gangotri.

The shortest route to reach Gangotri by road is from Rishikesh (meaning "The Sage's Hair") at the edge of the southernmost hills, via Tehri and
the town of Uttarkashi (about 3,300 feet). Uttarkashi is a short day's drive
from Hardwar (or Haridwar, "Shiva's Gate," the gateway to the abode of
the gods) or Rishikesh. At Uttarkashi you will have to change buses.
Uttarkashi, the "Northern City of Light," on the Bhagirathi River, is an
architectural and human amalgam: *dharmsalas* (pilgrims' rest houses) old
and new sit next to old stone homes and shacks of corrugated tin. The
ancient Hanuman and Vishwanath mandirs are not far from rows of newly
built shops and the Vishwanath Talkies. Across the river is the giant new
Maneri-Bhali power project, while a mosque sits just above town. Youngsters or young men energetically play cricket on an open field in the midst

of town while soldiers, shopkeepers, students, and sadhus, sadhus, and more sadhus live here. During the winter, some sadhus who stay at or near Gangotri join those who more or less live in Uttarkashi, and all are given food and shelter, accounting for the many faded orange robes of the *sannyasi,* the renouncing individuals, that you see. Some of Uttarkashi's sadhus are of the nakali, ersatz, variety, but others are serious renunciates or true jungly ascetics with a wild look of knowing carved into their mien. One man whom I traded nods with several times could have been a professor or bank president, so distinguished was his countenance.

There is a large Tourist Bungalow in town where you may stay. Uttarkashi is also the location of the Nehru Mountaineering Institute, which has been overseen for some years by the very capable Col. Balwant S. Sandhu. You can get good information and should be able to find porter and/or guide contacts through the institute. In Uttarkashi at the Tourist Bungalow, you can book a room at the Tourist Bungalow in Gangotri. Also, at the Forestry Department in Uttarkashi, you can book a room at the forest rest houses at Gangotri or Dodi Tal and you can get a fishing permit for Dodi Tal as well.

The Walk to Dodi Tal and Beyond

Dodi Tal is a lake at about 9,700 feet known for its fishing and the surrounding forest of pine and deodar. The lake is approached up the Binsi (or Asi Ganga) Valley, which debouches into the Bhagirathi just 2 miles up-valley from Uttarkashi at the hamlet of Gangori. In all seasons of the year you can drive some distance up the Binsi Valley by road. If the road is dry, you can go as far as the village of Kalyani by jeep or truck. Then you walk past the last village of Agoda (or Agora) and up the main valley another 10 miles to the lake. Allow a minimum of four days for this walk to and from Dodi Tal. There has been no little controversy as to whether a road should be built up to the lake. If you go to Dodi Tal, you will see whether the forces for preservation have won out over those who would build yet another road merely for the benefit of a few vacationers who don't care to walk.

If you wish to take a lesser-used path, head up-valley from Dodi Tal. An easy day hike rising less than 2,500 feet up from the lake takes you to the top of the ridge, the 12,100-foot Alneha Pass over Pandrasu Dhar (*dhar* means "ridge"). From here you have a magnificent view of Bandarpunch at the head of the Hanuman Ganga Valley. If you have supplies and go with a local to point out the way, you can add on one more day's walk from the pass and descend westerly along the Hanuman Ganga Valley to Hanuman Chatti, the roadhead for the walk to Yamnotri.

Trails East from Malla

Seventeen miles up the Bhagirathi Valley from Uttarkashi is the village of Malla. Before roads were built into the hills of Garhwal, Malla was the village where pilgrims walking between Gangotri and Kedarnath arrived at or departed from the Bhagirathi, depending which way they were proceeding. At Malla you can walk easterly into the hills crossing three ridges to reach the Bhilangana River. Both higher and lower routes lead through this hilly, wooded area, and before you strike out into it, you would do well to hire a porter-guide who knows the region, either at Uttarkashi or at Malla (if at Malla, perhaps go with someone who was recommended to you at Uttarkashi).

Given nine or ten days, you could take a fine upper-level hike from Malla skirting the highest ridges to reach the temples at Trijugi Narayan, a town not far from Kedarnath in the Mandakini Valley, east of the Bhilangana. En route you would be able to visit some of the many small upper lakes found among the higher ridges, like the well-known Shastru Tal (14,760 feet) high above the ridge west of the Bhilangana River. Adding on at least four days to this walk, you could hike up to the glaciated headwaters area of the Bhilangana. To walk along this high route, you should carry food, for there are few villages. At the headwaters of the Bhilangana you are due south of Gangotri and surrounded by numerous peaks, many higher than 20,000 feet. Two of the best known summits are the sheer peak of Thalay Sagar to the north and Kedarnath Dome to the east. Shepherd's camps are found scattered up this narrow valley, even along the side of the upper Khatling Glacier that descends from the northwest. It is said that near the Khatling Glacier is a cave with an ice lingam similar to that found at Amarnath in Kashmir. Your local porter-guide will have to point this place out to you, if it exists.

A lower foot trail east of Malla is the traditional yatra path to the dham of Kedarnath. This walk passes through villages with ancient chattis, some now virtually unusable from age and neglect. From west to east, the names of the villages and chattis en route go something like this (every map has different versions of the names): Malla, Sari, Chhuna Chatti, Belak, Pangrana, Jhala Chatti, Budhakedar (a roadhead on the Bal Ganga River), Bhairo Chatti (or Bhairgaon), Ghuttu,* Panwali Kanta, Tali, Mhangu (or Maggu) Chatti, Trijugi Narayan, and Sonprayag. At Trijugi Narayan a fire called Akhand Dhuni has been burning, so it is believed, since Shiva and Parvati were married at this spot thousands of years ago. From Gaurikund just north of Sonprayag, you can walk north to Kedarnath, described in the following section "Kedarnath: Shiva's Abode." Allow about a week for this walk along the pilgrim route from Malla to Sonprayag and expect to be able to purchase basic foods from villagers along the way, especially at the roadheads. Autumn is a fine time for this trek, but if you were prepared for the monsoon's rain, you could certainly do this hike in summer.

---

*Ghuttu is the roadhead in the Bhilangana Valley and is reached by bus from the large town of Tehri in the Bhagirathi Valley, 38 miles north of Rishikesh. You could walk up the Bhilangana Valley to the Khatling Glacier and back from Ghuttu in about six to eight days. But err on the long side provisionwise if you want to explore about the upper reaches of the valley, which must be a grand locale.

Expect to meet and enjoy traveling with sadhus on this lower, traditional yatra route. Everyone is a yatri who walks along this trail, except the locals, and the few who still do this yatra on foot are part of the centuries-old tradition of pilgrimage from temple to temple. As you go, you will see substantial stone temples with stone or metal images inside, called *murti*, and also small wayside shrines, perhaps consisting of just a few piled stones with a single flower or a few grains of rice left as an offering. Walking in this vicinity, I saw a dog weighted down by a metal collar with triple rows of sharklike teeth designed to protect him from bears. Some women wear silver bracelets, and one I met carried a lovely round bamboo basket with porcupine quills as ribs.

The Temple of Gangotri

In the Bhagirathi Valley north of Malla, the road continues north into the narrowing gorge past the town of Gangnani, known for its hot springs (which may be a bit sulfurous for some). In this region during the monsoon of 1978, a large avalanche temporarily formed a dam across the river, inundating 9 miles of road. Now you zip past tantalizing side valleys and up a series of hairpin turns to a sweeping vista of peaks at the town of Suki. Not far beyond Suki the Bhagirathi bends to the east, levels out, and you reach Harsil, virtually as far north as you will get. Harsil (about 8,400 feet) was once the adopted home of an Englishman named George Wilson who introduced apple and apricot trees. Two intriguing valleys with pasturelands and glaciers in their upper reaches debouch into the Bhagirathi from the north at Harsil, but these tempting valleys may or may not be considered out of bounds. Better check, if you decide to get off the main road, for hereabouts you are quite close to a disputed chunk of land in the border region with Tibet.

To the east of Harsil, the Bhagirathi River receives the waters from the equally large Jadh Ganga, entering the valley from the frontier area. Then the Bhagirathi begins angling to the east-southeast, now that it is north of many high peaks in the region. The narrow canyon roars with the waters of the river, and shortly you reach the roadhead just below the small temple of Gangotri (about 10,300 feet), 60 miles from Uttarkashi. Here, in a forest of deodar that is rapidly and lamentably becoming severely denuded, hotels built by enterprising entrepreneurs and "dharmsalas" constructed by both the pecuniary and good-hearted have sprouted to house the many yatris who now come each year.

The small stone temple of Gangotri (Gangotri means "Ganges Flowing North," and it does just that near its mouth) was built in the eighteenth century by the Gurkha general Amar Singh Thapa near the sacred shila called Bhagirath. On that same large boulder many, many years ago, King Bhagirath had meditated intently for years, and by doing so, the king caused the holy waters of the Ganga to descend from heaven into Shiva's piled hair. After further meditation by King Bhagirath, Shiva was pleased and allowed the most sacred river Ganga to appear on earth at three sources in the heart of his Himalayan abode. The principal source of the Ganges

River is at Gamukh, where the waters from the Gangotri Glacier emerge up-valley from Gangotri Temple.

In such an auspicious location you can see yatris from the vast breadth of Mother India, and you may meet highly disciplined and accomplished sannyasis as well. One of these, a man who has passed several winters here at his small cottagelike quarters called Kuteer, is Swami Sundarananda. The swami is a disciple of Swami Tapovanam, a highly venerated author, naturalist, and Sanskrit scholar. Photographs of Swami Sundarananda in his youth reveal an intense young man who both taught yoga and practiced difficult yogic postures. Now, he has metamorphosed into a white-haired elder with an unmistakable smile of beauty and bliss. Truly a renaissance man among renunciates, the swami has trekked to uncountable pilgrimage sites and, unlike most yogis and lamas, he has been willing to climb numerous technical peaks in addition to receiving nourishment by contemplating them. He is also known as the "Clicking Swami" for the thousands of photographs he has taken over the years. You may have a meeting with the swami or walk and talk with other sadhus (like the man from Madras mentioned in the section on Amarnath in Chapter 8), and wherever or whenever these visits occur, they may well be some of your most memorable experiences in these sacred hills.

Treks from Gangotri

Both near Gangotri and up-valley from the temple are numerous places for the trekker-yatri to visit. The principal sights and walks are noted here, going up the valley from west to east. First, however, just a few hundred yards downriver from the temple is the falls called Gaurikund, the "Shining Source." Here is the legendary location where the Ganges initially descended into Shiva's topknot and then dropped more gently from his matted locks to earth. If Shiva had not first caught the mighty river and slowed its force, it would have split the earth. At Gaurikund, the waters of the Bhagirathi arc to a lower level from numerous troughs naturally carved from solid rock.

Just over a mile west of Gangotri, the tributary Rudugaira Gad enters the river from the south. You can walk up this steep side valley and about 3,000 feet up will find the summer pasture of Rudugaira in an upper basin between 21,000-foot peaks. A glacier with the same name as the pasture and river fills the higher portions of the valley. A technical pass called Auden Col, over 18,000 feet in elevation, forms the low point at the valley's head and leads across the main range to the upper catchment area of the Khatling Glacier at the head of the Bhilangana Valley. For some inscrutable reason, this pass may still be considered closed, even though it lies south of the Inner Line.

A valley that is visited more often is the Kedar Ganga, which parallels the Rudugaira Gad and joins the Bhagirathi just across the river from Gangotri Temple. Here, a stiff uphill pull of 4,000 feet through a pine, then a birch, forest and beyond takes you to another shepherds' camping ground. A herd of bharal has made this and the neighboring valley its home, if the animals haven't received too much unwanted attention from the increasing numbers of visitors in recent years. Not far beyond the mouth of the upper valley glacier is Kedar Tal, well above the last sources of wood, where you can camp if you wish. Leading up to the west of the lake is a high path that crosses to the Rudugaira Valley. The peak to the southeast is 22,218-foot Bhrigupanth, and to the south is the sharp spire of Thalay Sagar, which mirrors its neighbor Shivling (which you must walk up the main valley to see). If you want, you can walk south of the lake and go still farther up the valley glacier to the base of the peaks surrounding you. Allow at least three days for this trek if you want to reach Kedar Tal and return.

Formerly the walk up the main valley from Gangotri was a difficult scramble over broken terrain once the pilgrim got beyond the dense deodar forest, but now the way has been eased by a well-graded trail with tea stalls en route. You can join the yatris and eat with them in the few dharmsalas that are found as far along as Gamukh, but if you intend to proceed beyond Gamukh, you should bring your own foodstuffs and a stove. If you are coming directly from Uttarkashi to Gangotri, food prices will be lower and items like ghee and good milk powder more likely to be available in Uttarkashi; otherwise you can get basics in small quantities as far up as Gangotri. The first halting place beyond Gangotri is Chirbasa, "The Pine Grove," a long half day's walk from Gangotri. Half as far away is the next way station, Bhojbasa, "The Birch Grove," where Swami Lal Behari Baba feeds and shelters yatris at his *ashram* (an ashram usually connotes that an accomplished yogi or sannyasi is in charge). It can be most enjoyable to join the yatris at these chattis, ashrams, or dharmsalas, but be sure to leave a generous offering after you avail yourself of the amenities provided.

Above Bhojbasa the valley continues bending to the south, the trail levels out, and you have new views of meadows and the many high peaks you are approaching, including the narrow point of 21,460-foot Shivling, "Shiva's Phallus." A short hour's walk takes you from Bhojbasa to Gamukh (12,650 feet), the mouth of the 25-mile-long Gangotri Glacier, a place revered as the "Cow's Mouth," the font of the Bhagirathi and principal source of the holy Ganga, the Ganges River. Gamukh is an awesome place: here, hunks of ice splash into the river emerging full bore from the glacier, yatris endure more chilling cleansings, and sadhus perform longer rituals. How different this spot is from similar glacial mouths in Muslim Pakistan. Each yatri finds for himself or herself the meaning of the tribute to Gamukh by author and Tibetologist Marco Pallis: "It is useless to try to describe the grandeur of the scene: there are perfections about which the only eloquence is silence."

Near Gamukh is a sandy beach where you can camp. Figure two easy days up from Gangotri to Gamukh and one day back. However, Gamukh need not be your ending point. If you have food and shelter, you can proceed farther into the midst of the mass of mountains about you. One walk to take is along the Raktvarn Glacier. Paralleling the north side of

A sadhu at Gamukh, the source of the Ganges River, performs a water puja (photograph by Swami Sundarananda).

the Gangotri Glacier, you can turn left, easterly, after a mile, and walk up a tributary valley to the Raktvarn (or Raktwan) Bamak (*bamak* means "glacier" in Garhwali), which leads to 22,300-foot Mana Parbat. Farther on up the glacier is 22,737-foot Sri Kailas peak (there are several peaks named Kailas, so don't confuse this one with Mt. Kailas in Tibet).

A popular trek above Gamukh is the day hike to the meadows at Tapovan, at the base of Shivling. To reach Tapovan, you must cross the main Gangotri Glacier from north to south, then continue 3 miles up the south side of the glacier to the camping area and shepherds' pasture at Tapovan. Notice how Shivling changes perspective, becoming even more pointed as you proceed. If you wish, you can continue beyond Tapovan to Kirti Bamak, the first large side glacier joining the Gangotri from its left (west) side. Here you have circled to the east of Shivling and can see 22,770-foot Kedarnath Dome to the south. From Tapovan to the Kirti Bamak and back adds on another day. And you can just keep going across the Kirti Bamak and along the Gangotri Glacier if you really want to traverse more boulder fields and get farther away from the now nonexistent crowds.

The last direction to head beyond Gamukh is the pasture area called Nandanvan. Nandanvan (14,800 feet) can be reached from Tapovan by walking about a mile up-valley parallel to the Gangotri Glacier (toward the Kirti Bamak), then crossing the rugged, rocky, and probably crevassed surface of the glacier to the campground of Nandanvan at the northern foot of the Bhagirathi massif. Alternatively, you could reach this camp from Gamukh by following the right (east) side of the Gangotri Glacier past the Raktvarn tributary and across the Chaturangi Bamak, the "Glacier of Four Colors." Walking parallel to the southern side of this side glacier takes you to another lake, Vasuki Tal, north of Vasuki Parbat. Look for bharal on the slopes above as you walk and boulder hop in this area.

Continuing up along the Chaturangi Bamak is a restricted route over 19,510-foot Kalindi Khal, "Kalindi Pass." This prohibited and technical route leads to the Saraswati River, the main branch of the Alaknanda, the Ganges' eastern fork, which flows past Badrinath (see the section following). To cross this pass you need special permission, not at all easily obtained from the Ministry of Home Affairs (Lok Nayak Bhavan, Khan Market, New Delhi). The first time Swami Sundarananda crossed this difficult pass, he fell into a deep crevasse, but since then he has traversed this route nine times. Jai Swamiji!

Kedarnath: Shiva's Abode

The third dham is Kedarnath, the Abode of Shiva. Pilgrim buses with their fuming exhausts began plying newly built roads through these sacred mountains in the 1950s and 1960s, but before that time all yatris who visited the temples followed specific trails and stayed at the dharmsalas and chattis along the way. Now the shortest southern approach to Kedarnath is from Rishikesh via Rudraprayag in the Alaknanda River valley, the eastern branch of the Ganga.

The roadhead for Kedarnath Temple is at Gaurikund, the place where Shiva found his consort, Parvati. This is the auspicious place where Parvati meditated for millennia before marrying Shiva. Isn't it wonderful that in the days when the gods lived on earth they had "world enough and time" to undergo the proper preliminaries before joining in union? No short betrothal for Shiva and Parvati. They knew the meaning of eternity.

The stolid Kedarnath Temple (11,700 feet) is 9 miles beyond Gaurikund; the mandir itself is composed of large, molded blocks of rock and was built eight hundred years ago over a stone considered to be the remains of a "self-born" manifestation of Shiva as Nandi the bull. This rock (believed to be the top of Nandi's humped back) is worshipped daily by pilgrims infused with *bhakti* (adoration for the godhead). In the morning the image is honored in its natural or unadorned form with offerings of ghee and milk. In the evening the image is adored in its ornamental form; under a gold canopy it is covered with flowers and brightly colored offerings.

Not far above the temple is the small lake called Gandhi Sarovar, where some of Mahatma Gandhi's ashes were scattered, just as they were at holy Lake Manasarovar near Mt. Kailas in Tibet. Kedarnath is also the place where the important philosopher-guru Shankaracharya died. A temple to Shankaracharya sits on the low hill just east of Srinagar in Kashmir. An entire order of sannyasi devoted to the study and practice of Shankaracharya's teachings has been in existence for hundreds of years. One of the prominent members of this order is Khaptad Baba (mentioned in this book's companion volume), who lives north of Silgarhi in western Nepal.

If you wish, you can follow a small path up-valley from Kedarnath along the Chorabari Bamak toward the southern base of Kedarnath Dome. Another high-level route passes several lakes to the west of Kedarnath. This path is followed by yatris who wish to do cleansing pujas at the various lakes, called Vasuki Tal (the first lake, 3,000 feet above Kedarnath), Pain Tal, and, farther west, Masuri Tal (about 15,000 feet in elevation), lying above the Bhilangana Valley. If you could find a panda or porter (often called *coolie* in Hindi, despite its connotation of a person staggering under an insufferably heavy load) who both knew the route and was up for the rigors of the trip, you could have your own high-altitude yatra. From Masuri Tal, a prominent ridge heads southwest, then south. This ridge can be followed (although there might be difficulty with finding water) to the place called Bhasam, 12,304 feet on the U502 *Dehra Dun* sheet (NH 44-5). Here you are on the old yatra path between Malla and Trijugi Narayan (referred to in the last section), a mile above and a long half day's walk from Trijugi Narayan. This must be an inspiring walk. Do let me hear about it if you go that way.

Four additional pilgrimage sites are associated with Kedarnath, all of which are in high, scenic locations, and all of which have their own myths attached. With a copy of the U502 sheet noted above, you can be a real Shiva devotee and visit some or all of these. None of these temples is connected by road, so to visit any of them, you must walk. Lacking the U502 sheet, just get one of the inexpensive locally produced booklets, follow directions, and ask the way, as Indian yatris do. In addition to Kedarnath, these sites, called the Panch Kedar, are Madhyameshwar, Tungnath, Rudranath, and Kalpeshwar.

Every one of the four principal tirths is too far north to be open in winter, and each of the four main pilgrimage locations has a winter seat, where a representative image is propitiated during the snowy season. These murties are carried down in the fall and returned in the spring with great ritual. The opening and closing of each principal tirth is usually noted in the New Delhi papers. Kedarnath's winter seat is at Ukhimath (sometimes written Okhimath), as is the winter seat of Madhyameshwar and Rudranath. During the winter, an image belonging to each of these temples resides in Ukhimath, a temple similar in style to Kedarnath, but smaller in size. The image belonging to Kedarnath is a mustachioed man with a cobra around his neck. Five pujaris stay at Ukimath in winter, and along with the images temporarily in residence, they disperse to the various temples where they are resident in summertime.

The guard at Ukhimath is a formidable brown mastiff named Lalu. During the day, Lalu lazes about the temple's stone courtyard, sleeping and slowly raising his large head in the direction of familiar faces to be patted. But when dusk falls, Lalu comes alive and is on duty at his station in the temple's entranceway. His throaty growls and deep, loud bark wakes sleeping pilgrims in the nearby dharmsalas and frightens away all interlopers. Lalu knows his job and does it well.

Badrinath: The Home of Lord Vishnu

Badrinath, the tirth dedicated to Lord Badri Vishal, or Vishal Badri, (Vishnu) is reached from Rishikesh via the Alaknanda River Valley. Continuing upriver from the plains along the twisting Alaknanda Valley, your bus plows past towns with names ending in *prayag,* which indicate that they are sacred river *sangams,* "confluences." In fact, en route from Rishikesh to Badrinath, you pass all the Panch Prayags: Devaprayag (the most important sangam, for this is the junction of the Bhagirathi and Alaknanda to form the holy Ganga); Rudraprayag (where the road to Kedarnath diverges); Karnaprayag (at the junction of the Pindar Valley, discussed below); Nandprayag (at the base of the Nandakini River, which leads to the west face of Trisul, about which more later); and Vishnuprayag (far below Joshimath at the sangam of the Alaknanda and the Dhauliganga). All buses stop at the large town of Joshimath, 150 miles from Rishikesh, magnificently situated up and down along a ridge over 1,000 feet above the river.

More will be said about Joshimath (6,500 feet) under "Josimath and Its Bugyals," following, but for now, imagine yourself changing buses with the other yatris and continuing headlong the next morning for Badrinath to finish your yatra to the four major dhams. In doing this, you will also pass the roadhead town of Gobind (or Govind) Ghat, between Joshimath and Badrinath, where you can leave for the Valley of Flowers and Hemkund Lake, a hiking route covered in the next section. Now your ardor for the pilgrimage to Badrinath cannot be delayed. From a gate at Joshimath, the pilgrim-packed buses set out daily in the morning at an officially appointed hour (about 6:30 A.M.). The road is too narrow to accommodate two-way traffic, so convoys of vehicles alternately ply the relatively short but horrifyingly circuitous 30-mile stretch. The buses roar down to the bottom of the gorge on the one-way road, then race each other over 1,000 feet up the other side and onward to Badrinath in a spectacle that must be undergone to be wholly appreciated.

Badrinath Temple (10,300 feet) is probably the most visited tirth. Badri refers to a wild fruit said to have been eaten by Vishnu during his long period of ascetic meditation. Badrinath's temple and town, both of which are closed in winter, lie west of the Alaknanda. You follow the cement path past meditating and alms-seeking sadhus, cross a bridge, and continue north to the centuries-old shrine through narrow, winding galis, past restaurants, souvenir and puja-accessories shops, and more sadhus. All pilgrims will have taken a holy dip in the hot Tapta Kund before entering the temple and taking part in one of the numerous pujas offered morning and afternoon. Reserve Your Pujas Here, reads one sign in English, and with good reason, for the brilliantly painted temple is small and people have to wait before having *darshan* (an audience) with Sri Badrinath. Unlike the custom with the stone at Kedarnath, the image of Lord Badrinath (Vishnu) is worshipped adorned for the entire summer season and worshipped unadorned during the winter when only the gods have their darshan.

Like the Panch Kedars, there are also Panch Badris, but these are at generally less exhalted elevations. The Panch Badris are Vishal Badri, the main shrine; Yogdhyan Badri at Pandukeshwar (just north of Gobind Ghat, noted in the next section); Bhavishya Badri, the "Future Badri," above the road in the Dhauliganga Valley; Bridha (or Vridha) Badri, not far south of Joshimath; and Adi Badri, near Karnaprayag. Even with the Panch Kedars, Panch Prayags, and Panch Badris, you are still only beginning to get an appreciation for the many temples in Uttarakhand. This is an ancient, ancient land with traditions going back thousands of years and a complex, interwoven system of beliefs. As with many regions in the Himalaya, you could pass years in Garhwal and only learn a fraction of the ceremonies and myths connected with this remarkable area.

Directly west of Badrinath is a side valley that rises to the base of the white spire called Nilkanth, or "Blue Throat" (21,640 feet). Nilkanth is one of the 1,008 names of Shiva, and it refers to the time Shiva drank Halahal, the world's poison, and held it in his neck, saving mankind from the forces of decay and death. The British climber Frank Smythe called Nilkanth "The Queen of Garhwal," reversing the mountain's ascribed sex, but no matter, it is a very lovely peak as seen from the east bank of the river at Badrinath. Take a day hike up the tributary valley from Badrinath village toward Nilkanth's base. Walking up this nala directly from bustling Badrinath, you approach glacial features quickly, for within hours of leaving the village you are on morainal debris that leads toward the Himalayan snows. You will have excellent views of a series of steep talus slopes beneath towering buttresses that are layered like massive snowcakes, the peak more than a neck-craning mile above. If you don't want to walk that far, then head uphill from Badri Vishal for Charanpaduka, a rock with the imprint of Vishnu's foot and lying within view of both the temple and Nilkanth.

To the north of Badrinath the trekking possibilities are excellent, although unlike the other three dhams, these trails up-valley from Badrinath are beyond the hallowed Inner Line and thus can't be pursued. This fact I had clearly pointed out to me early one morning when I tried to visit Vasudhara Falls north of Badrinath. The route to sacred Vasudhara lies through a military camp, and I was politely but firmly advised to retrace my steps by an official-looking man whose face was well lathered with shaving cream. In the area beyond the Inner Line are other extremely sacred locations along the Alaknanda. Here a tributary takes the name of the main river, while the larger stream continues directly north and is called the Saraswati. Vasudhara Falls is near the base of the tributary called the Alaknanda on the way to Satopanth Glacier, the glacial source of the Alaknanda, which corresponds to Gamukh at the mouth of the Bhagirathi (but doesn't seem to be as important as Gamukh). Up the glacier is Satopanth Lake, where the divine trinity of Brahma, Vishnu, and Shiva are said to meditate beneath 23,420-foot Badrinath Peak (Chaukhamba) and Swargarohini, the peak dividing the two glacial sources of the Ganga, a mountain called the Path to Heaven.

Rising up on the east side of the valley just south of the Tibetan border is Kamet: at 25,447 feet, the third-highest mountain in India. Demarcating the Tibetan frontier due north of Badrinath at the end of the valley is the 17,900-foot Mana Pass, crossed by Krishna in the "Age of the Gods." Below rolling high desert plains not far north of Mana Pass is the ancient temple city of Tsaparang in the Sutlej Valley, where early Christian missionaries discovered a thriving city (see "The Lost Cities of Toling and Tsaparang" in Chapter 9 of this book's companion volume).

Hemkund and the Valley of Flowers

Twelve miles north from Joshimath in the Alaknanda Valley on the Badrinath road are the unpretentious teahouses of Gobind Ghat. From this stopping place you can walk into the midst of the Central Himalaya at its most precipitous, following a path that leads to the Sikh pilgrimage spot of Hemkund (or Sri Hemkund Sahib), a cobalt-colored lake at 14,200 feet. The path to both Hemkund and the beautiful vale that Frank Smythe named the Valley of Flowers crosses the Alaknanda River at Gobind Ghat and rises into the Laxman Ganga Valley. Before you lengthen your stride in

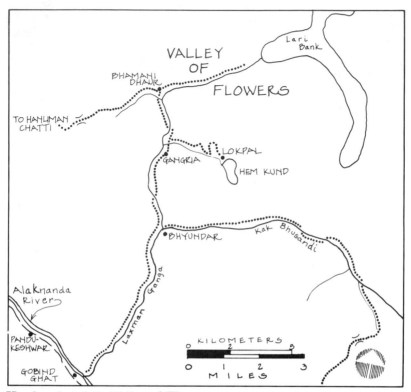

Hemkund and the Valley of Flowers

anticipation, after crossing the footbridge at Gobind Ghat, you may need to register with the police at the *chaulki* (police post). A few yards beyond the police chaulki is a Sikh-run gurdwara, a temple and rest house freely provided for all pilgrims. If you have arrived during the hours when meals are offered, you will be served delicious Punjabi food (gratis, but offerings are appreciated), a heartening prelude to, or reward after, the walk.

From Gobind Ghat, at 6,000 feet in elevation, the trail rises for 10 spectacular green miles. The constantly ascending path passes seasonal teahouses, for many pilgrims on this trail are Delhi-walas or people unused to hiking who live in the flat plains of the Punjab and who often need to rest and refresh themselves. Consequently, the tea sellers along the warm lower trail do a good business during "the rush" in August and September. Along the way, 6 miles from the roadhead at Gobind Ghat, is the small, neat village of Bhyundar at the junction of the Laxman Ganga Valley you have been following and a tantalizingly beautiful, tree-cloaked tributary called the Kak Bhusandi Valley. Later, when you return by way of Bhyundar village, you might hire a porter-guide to show you the little-known way back to either the Dhauliganga Valley or to Joshimath via the Kak Bhusandi and the snowy trails beyond, some of which are glaciated.

Ten miles from Gobind Ghat, at 10,500 feet, is another Sikh-operated gurdwara called Gangria (also called Gobind Dham, "Gobind's Holy Place," after Guru Gobind Singh, who is connected with Hemkund). At the gurdwara, accommodating volunteers provide meals at fixed times and lodging as well (donations are accepted and should definitely be forthcoming from foreigners, as at Gobind Ghat). Nearby, private teashops dispense chai any time of day, in the cool of the pine-shaded valley floor. Just beyond Gangria, the trail divides. Those going to Hemkund take the steep path to the right (east), a well-maintained zigzagging trail 3 miles and nearly 4,000 feet up to the lake, the headwaters of the Laxman Ganga. This dham is sacred to the memory of Guru Gobind Singh, the tenth and final Sikh prophet, who created the Khalsa order, the "Pure Ones." A new gurdwara has been constructed lakeside, dedicated to Guru Gobind Singh, who once meditated here in a past life at the lake surrounded by seven snow peaks.

The large circular metal building was partially completed when I walked up in early June (about as early in the year as you will find the trail cleared of snow). Inside the gurdwara I observed two Sikh brethren complete a ceremony that involved chanting and the draping of the Adi Granth Sahib, the holy scripture of the religion, with layers of cloth. Outside, the trail had been cleared of snow by an army platoon, which was just then departing. Soon the soldiers were followed down by the two Sikh worshippers, who had kindly given me fistfuls of sweet prasad. Thirty yards from the large, unfinished gurdwara I saw a tiny, low-roofed chatti dedicated to the Hindu deity Laksman, for, to Hindus, this high place is known as Lokpal, the place where Lord Ram's younger brother Laksman once meditated. As I was the only person left at Hemkund that evening, I happily brewed tea to drink with the sugary prasad and settled in for the night, a very satisfied yatri, feeling protected by both Laksman and Guru Gobind Singh.

The alternate route from Gangria is a wide trail that leads up by the main stream, here called the Pushpawati, and through a narrow rocky defile into the upper valley. This is the Valley of Flowers that Frank Smythe crossed into from the north after he made the first ascent of Kamet. Smythe also called the valley "a place of escape from modern civilization," and he wrote about it in his book *The Valley of Flowers*. The spring I saw it, forty-six years later, it was in much the same pristine splendor: a narrow, U-shaped vale terraced with green spring growth and washed with narrow waterfalls, one after another, draining unseen snowfields far above. I was fortunate to visit early in the season, for during a full day's time in this exquisite place I saw only a single herdsman with his sheep, far across the way. My only other companions were several hawks floating far aloft.

The valley is now the 33.5-square-mile Valley of Flowers National Park. If you want to camp there overnight, you will have to get permission from the DCF for Joshimath District, in Chamoli, the district headquarters.

This uninhabited upper valley has by now been well studied by botanists, who have found literally hundreds of wildflower varieties. Local legend tells of Bhaman Dhaur, "Bhaman's Cave," where a saint once meditated, sanctifying the vale. The cave is there: a massive slanting rock with walled entrance and a dry, straw-covered floor. Looking toward the rock cave from the trail, you will see a pasture angling steeply upward beyond the rock. If you follow the animal paths 1,500 feet up, you will reach a shepherds' camp. An additional 1,700-foot rise will take you to a col 7,000 knee-smashing feet above Hanuman Chatti, situated a few miles south of Badrinath.

Joshimath and Its Bugyals

Joshimath is the northernmost large bazaar in the valley, and the town is very busy in the summer season. Yatri and mountaineer alike rest here en route to their destinations farther north. The pious Hindu pilgrim will visit some of the many shrines in Joshimath, particularly the Durga Temple and Jyotirmath Temple, connected with Shankaracharya, who attained enlightenment here in a cave. Joshimath is also the town where the representative image of Badri Vishal rests in winter. The mountaineer or hiker will send or collect mail, purchase provisions, and get ready to be off for the hills. Several outfitters are available in Joshimath, and arrangements for guides and/or porters can be made here. The town is scattered about on many levels, both above and below the main bazaar. In the midst of the bazaar, the road divides, just as the river does far below. One fork of the road follows the Alaknanda River to Badrinath and the areas covered in the two previous sections. The other branch of the road goes easterly up the Dhauliganga Valley toward the Rishiganga Valley and the Nanda Devi area and beyond to the north. Along the Dhauliganga Valley are remarkably beautiful scenes of the lush forest and high granite typical of Garhwal's vertiginous hills.

If you have limited time or want to warm up for a longer trek, hike for a day or make an overnight camp somewhere on the ridge up from Joshimath, which offers excellent viewpoints. As you walk up from Joshimath's bazaar, you will see farther up both the sacred Alaknanda Valley and along the Dhauliganga to the tributary Rishiganga gorge, which drains the hidden Nanda Devi Sanctuary. Good trails take you from Joshimath up to the *bugyal* (grazing meadow) called Auli and on to Gorsin Bugyal. If you are walking up for the day only, take water, lunch, and an umbrella to divert sun or rain. For a superb overnight hike, carry shelter and camp where you wish: there are many sites. With a good start from Joshimath one morning, you can walk up and camp, then leave the next day to walk toward the triangulation point at 12,458 feet on the *Nanda Devi* U502 sheet (NH 44-6). From that remarkable spot, you have a 360-degree view. You can see Kamet, Nilkanth, the Badrinath peaks, the 20,000-foot peaks near Hemkund, Lata Peak, and some of the renowned summits that encircle the Nanda Devi Sanctuary, such as Hanuman, Dunagiri,

Bethartoli (unclimbed until 1977), Trisul, and Nanda Devi herself, standing majestically apart.

These lovely meadows above Joshimath may entice you for a leisurely walk of several days. Beyond Auli and Gorsin is a web of trails leading from pasture to pasture, with dramatic, changing vistas throughout. Three miles south of the 12,458-foot point is the well-traveled Kuari Pass (12,140 feet), once crossed by Lord Curzon, the governor general of India, and in 1950 by the Scots with their Dotial porters. You could make a nice circle trek of several days either beginning or ending at Joshimath and crossing the Kuari Khal, the "Doorway Pass," into, or out of, the Birehi Valley to the south. This valley branches east from the main Alaknanda about 4 miles north of the large district headquarters town of Chamoli.

An additional 3 miles east from Kuari Khal is the high summer village of Delisera, another gently rolling grazing area, frequented by herds from the south that are driven over the Kuari Pass. More than 6,000 feet down from Delisera and the pass is the small town of Tapoban with its sacred hot springs. A circle route can be followed from Joshimath to the grazing areas and a high point or two, then down to Tapoban, a walk that takes three to five days. Continue by bus from Tapoban to Joshimath, a short ride through the precipitous lower Dhauliganga gorge.

Into the Nanda Devi Sanctuary

The wide, inner meadows of the "secret shrine," the Nanda Devi Sanctuary, lie 18 miles as the lammergeier soars from Lata village up the once-impenetrable Rishiganga gorge (the Rishiganga is named for the seven Rishis who are said to have retreated to the sanctuary of the headwaters area of the river and who are also connected with Saptrishi Kund above Yamnotri). The sanctuary, a series of rolling meadows surrounded by a 45-mile ring of high peaks, including Nanda Devi, had never known human footsteps until 1934, when Shipton and Tilman, with their small band of Sherpas and Dotials, forced a precarious route up the primeval valley to the vast meadowlands inhabited by secretive musk deer, herds of goral (a wild goat-antelope), bharal (the blue sheep), and that shy monarch the snow leopard. The trail to the sanctuary is barely discernible in places, but it can be traversed. After 1974 when the Rishiganga Valley, which leads to the sanctuary from the west, emerged from behind the Inner Line, numerous trekking groups and mountaineering expeditions began to make their way into the sanctuary. The once-pristine inner meadows quickly became the focus of too much attention from locals and foreigners, with the poaching of musk deer, the rapid acceleration of human visitation, and the fact that in 1979 a man named Unmed Singh of Paing village in the lower Rishiganga Valley discovered an alternate route into the sanctuary and began taking goats there to graze. He was soon followed by others with increasingly large herds.

In 1980 Nanda Devi National Park (243 square miles) was established, and practically at the same time the park was closed to all entry. The prohibition on entry has been extended at least until 1992. For up-to-date information, contact either the DCF for Nanda Devi National Park in Chamoli, the local district headquarters, or the Indian Mountaineering Foundation (IMF), Anand Niketan Road, New Delhi 110 022. (The IMF is located a ten-minute taxi ride from Indira Gandhi International Airport in New Delhi.)

In mid-May 1977, with only the scantiest of information about the Nanda Devi Sanctuary and the route to it, I found myself with a new friend and a porter from Joshimath (who would quickly prove to be of little help) on the local bus from Joshimath to Lata, little expecting what the next eighteen days would bring. We hoped we had enough food; we thought, correctly, we might be ahead of most groups going into the valley; and we expected a real trail, not the frail paths connecting narrow ledges that we were about to find.

The traditional route into the sanctuary is divided into eight stages between Lata village, a half hour's walk above the road, and the sanctuary. Half the stages are less than 2 miles in straight-line distance, but compensating for their brevity, these stages have steep inclines or thin ledges that make walking difficult and hazardous in places. What follows (leaving aside most of the interesting aspects of my own trip) is a brief description of the stages into the sanctuary, should the area once again be opened for entry by responsible parties.

Lata is a typical mountain village in Garhwal. The word Lata refers to *lat,* meaning "leg": the leg of the Goddess Nanda Devi's resting place (more about this powerful goddess later). In this town you'll find homes constructed of wood, mud, and stone, and friendly, accommodating people who celebrate a yearly festival. Many men from Lata know the trail into the sanctuary, for they have accompanied numerous trekking and mountaineering parties. The first stage from Lata to Lata Kharak (*kharak* means "pasture area") involves a 4,400-foot climb in and out of shade to the pasture at timberline atop a spur high above the village. Lata Kharak is nearly as high as Lata Peak, a rounded 12,624-foot promontory at the end of this spur guarding the mouth of the Rishiganga gorge.

The second stage climbs from Lata Kharak high over the Dharanshi Pass (Dharanshi means "The Open Ridge") and down to Dharanshi camp, no easy walk in spring when most of the route is covered in snow. An hour's push above Lata Kharak takes you to a sweeping view of the entire trail back to Lata Kharak and to Tapovan and the Kuari Pass down-valley and the Badrinath peaks farther to the northwest. Heading to Dharanshi Pass, the trail angles upward across rocky, snowy slopes, but once across the ridgeline that forms the pass, the route practically requires technical aids in the precipitous terrain, crossing couloirs and contouring around several knife-edged spurs. This stage and the last two stages before the sanctuary represent trekking at its most dangerous: hiking that varies somewhere between foolhardiness and exhilaration.

Dharanshi camp is located either high on the ridge or 2,000 feet lower

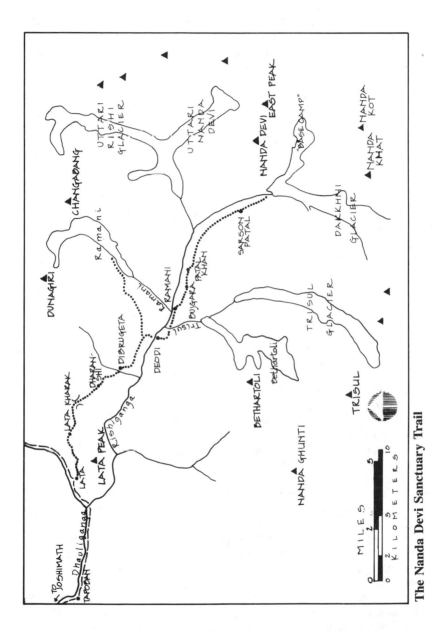

The Nanda Devi Sanctuary Trail

in a large basin, depending on snow conditions. The third stage is relatively short, leading either down from upper Dharanshi, or up, then down, from the sheep pens in the lower bowl. From the rock cairns on the eastern rim of the bowl above lower Dharanshi is a view that stretches from the high peaks in the Gangotri area to Nanda Devi herself, floating above her secluded haven. The cairns also mark the path leading nearly 3,000 feet downward to tree-shaded Dibrugeta campground.

Dibrugeta means "The Small Meadow of the Stone God." From here the path climbs steeply, turning onto an exposed southern face with good perspectives of the primeval gorge. The track continues up-valley, seesawing to avoid vertical rock ribs. Just before the path drops down to the Rishiganga River for the first time, a small side track angles upward to pastures at the headwaters of the Ramani Nala and the base of Dunagiri (23,184 feet) and shark's-toothlike Changabang ("The Shining Mountain," the peak that gives Nanda Devi light, 22,520 feet). A worn log bridge at the end of this short stage takes the path across the Rishiganga to Deodi camp on the south bank of the Rishi, where the route remains.

Deodi, "The Vestibule," the fourth camp, is a clearing by the river near several cabin-sized boulders. Again the trail strikes up the wall of the canyon in unrelenting fashion, and in an hour it levels out beneath streamers of Spanish moss that frame Nanda Devi. At a pleasantly situated rocky overlook, the Trisul side valley comes into view ahead. This tributary leads to 20,840-foot Bethartoli and 23,360-foot Trisul, "Nanda's Trident," climbed by British explorer Tom Longstaff in 1907, the highest summit yet scaled at that time and one of the world's better-known high walk-up peaks. The towering ridgeline on the eastern side of this nala is the "inner curtain," the wall that was finally surmounted by Unmed Singh and his goats. At this overlook you can also see the stupendous walls of the upper Rishiganga gorge with its 2-mile-high stone slabs. Longstaff climbed Trisul, but he could not penetrate this upper gorge. Shipton, Tilman, and their small crew took nine days of probing to force a way through these last 4 miles into the sanctuary.

Dropping to cross the roaring Trisul stream, the path then rounds a low evergreen-dotted ridge and angles down to Ramani campground (*ramani* means "joyous" or "beautiful," and is the place where the Rishis first found refuge). Ramani is a sandbar beneath an overhanging cliff and is as far as sheep or goats can travel on the traditional route. The next two stages feature a path that is slight at best, difficult to locate in places, and continually rising or falling with tricky footing and highly exposed sections. Few trees and little brush are found beyond Ramani because of this inner curtain of solid rock. Only trail-marking cairns grow in this vertical stretch, and each cairn is well above the last.

Bujgara camp ("Birch Tree"—there are, or were, a few birches here) is a series of rocky terraces five hours' clamber above Ramani. This stage is the most difficult walk yet, exceeded only, perhaps, by the first couple of hours of the next. The thread-thin route from Bujgara crosses providentially placed ledges, rounds fatally exposed corners, and climbs, climbs,

climbs, to the remaining camping spot in the gorge. It was along this stretch as I was edging along a precipice, hanging on for dear life, while carrying a heavy backpack, that my understated British companion Jean informed me of the definition of "fatal exposure": if you fall, you die.

The horizontal distance from Bujgara to Patal Khan, the seventh camping place, is less than a mile. The aerie called Patal Khan, "Flat Stone Quarry," lies not far above another possible camp called Tilchaunani. From Patal Khan you have an excellent view of Nanda Devi's pyramid-shaped top, as well as several 20,000-foot peaks on the northeastern perimeter of the mountain ring that encircles the sanctuary. A rock overhang provides shelter, and even inside it you have a fine perspective of the glaciated northern branch of the Rishiganga, the less well known fork of the sanctuary.

Carrying on from Patal Khan, corridor after corridor and slab after slab of scree and rock must be traversed, and several low ridges have to be gained. Then, quite unexpectedly, rounding yet another spur, there is grass underfoot, and the trail does not drop off again but bends south and glides onto a series of alpine meadows: the Nanda Devi Sanctuary. These rolling fields, roughly 13,000 feet in elevation, continue for miles, falling away steeply only toward the southern fork of the Rishiganga. Some distance along the meadows is the place called Sarson Patal, the last camp except for the "base camp" at the southern foot of Nanda Devi.

Here in the sanctuary, I witnessed Sherpas with a trekking group that followed us who were harassing and frightening away a herd of virtually tame bharal. This was only a dash of the depredations that were to follow, but it is what I observed, and for me, some shred of youthful innocence died that day. Knowing now of the invasion by humans and herds that followed, I don't hesitate to agree with the closure of the sanctuary.

Just east of the sanctuary and the Rishiganga, a succession of buttresses rises in one concatenated, near-vertical sweep to the summit of 25,645-foot Nanda Devi, the second-highest mountain in India and the highest summit in the Central Himalaya. Nanda Devi is the "Bliss Giving Goddess," the most important deity in Garhwal. This, her dwelling place, is even clearly visible to the northeast from sacred Mt. Kailas. Nanda Devi is usually associated with the kindly, lovely qualities of Shiva's consort Parvati (of whom she is an incarnation), but when aroused, as with her need to protect the seven Rishis who came to her feet for protection from the demons, she can take on the frightening, wrathful aspects of Durga. She is surrounded by peaks associated with her, such as Nanda Khat, her bed; Nanda Kot, her castle; Nanda Ghunti, her veil or headdress; Nanda Pal, her glance; Rishi Kot, "The Rishi's Fortress"; and Gauri Parbat, "The Mountain of the Fair (or Golden) Goddess."

In recent history a new chapter has been added to the ancient myth of Nanda Devi. American mountaineer Willi Unsoeld initiated an expedition to Nanda Devi, and part of the preparation for the expedition was done by his daughter Nanda Devi Unsoeld, a lovely woman who had been named for this, the most beautiful peak Willi had ever seen. When Devi died abruptly high on the peak (of what we Westerners would call acute altitude sickness), local legend quickly accepted the idea that the goddess, loving the woman, or wanting her as a devotee or friend, took Devi into her own ethereal realm. An alternate belief holds that the goddess had previously caused herself to be reborn as golden-haired Nanda Devi Unsoeld and that Devi very naturally and inevitably returned once again to her heavenly abode.

The Pindar Valley, Rupkund, and the Raj Jat Yatra

On the well-traveled pilgrim road to Joshimath and Badrinath lies the town of Karnaprayag at the sacred confluence of the Alaknanda and the Pindar rivers. The Pindar is a long valley, extending 50 miles east of Karnaprayag and catching runoff from such summits as Trisul, Nanda Khat, Nanda Ghunti, and Nanda Kot, which form the southerly bastion of the mountain ring about Nanda Devi. In its middle region the Pindar Valley leaves Garhwal and enters western Kumaon. Two destinations known to trekkers (other fine hiking routes can be surmised from map perusal) may be reached from the Pindar Valley: Rupkund, a small, high mountain lake on the slopes of the Trisul massif; and the Pindari Glacier, at the head of the Pindar River.

Rupkund, a small 15,670-foot-high lake, actually drains into the Nandakini Valley to the west of Trisul and can be approached by taking a bus up the Nandakini Valley to the roadhead at Ghat from Nandaprayag, located up the Alaknanda Valley at the Nandakini-Alaknanda sangam. But Rupkund is usually approached from the Pindar Valley to the south, along an old pathway from the towns of Debal and Wan. To reach this trail, take the daily (perhaps twice-daily) bus from Karnaprayag up the Pindar Valley to the small bazaar of Debal. Plan to walk for a total of eight to twelve days in this area, depending on whether you intend to reach Rupkund or go beyond to Homkund. The approach from Ghat in the Nandakini Valley is about equally as far from Rupkund as the walk-in from Debal or the roadhead 12 miles beyond Debal at Mundoli. You will be able to purchase basic staple foods at Debal, so it isn't necessary to lug everything from elsewhere. Just east of Debal is the traditional border of Garhwal and Kumaon, but this walk to Rupkund lies wholly within Garhwal.

Going north from Debal, a path takes you in a day to the rest house at the ridgeline village of Lhajum (or Lohajung or Loharjang), where you have good views of several peaks, including Trisul, surrounding Nanda Devi. The next day's walk carries you from the land of small shops and out of sight of the road into a narrower valley, reaching Wan (about 9,000 feet), with its homespun-clad denizens. Going to Wan is like walking back in time. The day I stayed there, a Devi Puja occurred involving the cutting of two sheep and the making of many puris for the villagers to eat, along with chunks of mutton and gobs of halwa. No one seemed bothered by

A woman from Harsil village in Garhwal (photograph by Swami Sundarananda).

my presence as I accompanied a number of men and children up to the mandir, which to my unknowing eyes looked merely like an empty shed, without even a murti. This was sacred ground, however, and we all removed our shoes as we approached the mandir. Here the docile, small black ewe was sprinkled with rice and ghee thirty seconds before her life ended.

Approximately every twelve years a rare four-horned ram is born in the vicinity, usually to the west of Wan. After it is two or three years old, it is invested with the Goddess Nanda Devi and ceremonially leads a large procession of people, most of whom live in the hills of Garhwal and Kumaon. This yatra, called the Nanda Devi Raj Jat Yatra, begins at the village of Nauti north of Karnaprayag and proceeds by slow stages to Rupkund. The many symbolic aspects of the yatra include both Hindu and other associations, and they are quite complex. The last Raj Jat Yatra was in late August and early September 1987. Those who usually accompany the four-horned ram were present, such as pujaris, thousands of villagers (some carrying gaily embroidered ceremonial umbrellas), sadhus (including Swami Sundarananda), and several silver images of Nanda Devi carried in palanquins. But, adding a touch of the modern world, a crew of cinematographers also went on the pilgrimage.

The yatra wended its way past Wan, through thick coniferous forest, then over high bugyals with small but important lakes and temples. Rupkund, tucked away high on the northern side of a ridge, was barely thawed that year, like most years, and snow still descended to its shores around part of its perimeter. Pujas were performed at this small lake where numerous human bones and skulls are scattered about, usually beneath the often-present snow and ice. Whether these bones are from a former yatra (during which something must have transpired to enrage the goddess, causing her to unleash a heavy storm) or from another event is not certain, and several theories exist. Carbon dating has placed these remains as being about six hundred years old. The occasional Western trekker who makes it to Rupkund (the headwaters of the Rup Ganga, a tributary of the Nandakini) may turn around here. But the yatris continue along a narrow path that takes them over the steep Jiura Gali and down a scree slope to lush meadows in the upper reaches of the Nandakini Valley near the precipitous western face of Trisul. Then they contour to Homkund, another lake, not as high as Rupkund. Above Homkund, the ram, who is decorated with ornaments, is released to continue on its way up into the arms of Shiva.

Of the many glaciers in Garhwal, the Pindari at the head of the Pindar Valley is one of those best known to Westerners. A series of six PWD bungalows are available at stages along the Pindar and Sarju valleys, beginning with a bungalow at the roadhead of Kapkote in the Sarju Valley, south of the Pindar and reached from Almora. But you can also reach the Pindari Glacier by bus from the roadhead at Mundoli 12 miles from Debal in the Pindar Valley. Expect to take about six days from Mundoli to reach the glacier, high up in its narrow gorge. The Pindari Glacier, like most in the Central Himalaya, is strictly a falling glacier (one that is steep, with broken chunks of ice) that requires ropes and ice equipment for climbing. It has

no interminably long valley moraines like glaciers in the Karakoram, or
the Gangotri Glacier, but is instead a massive tangle of ice chunks seem-
ingly frozen in free-fall that extends only a few miles from the catchment
area to the glacier's mouth. At the top of the Pindari Glacier is a highly
technical 17,700-foot col named Traill's Pass for the British administrator
and explorer who first crossed over it into the Gori Valley.

Kumaon's Gori and Darma Valleys

Kumaon is far less well known to foreign trekkers than Garhwal,
primarily because its more interesting regions in the upper Gori and Darma
valleys are located north of the Inner Line. East of Nanda Devi in Kumaon
this line is located, for the most part, 30 to 40 miles south of the border,
and it's a real pity, because these valleys would be fascinating to visit. But
don't try sneaking into these regions, for if you do, it will not be long
before you are face to face with a member of the crack Indo-Tibetan Border
Police, usually known as the ITBP, and you will also be under arrest.

Still, there are some lovely regions you can visit in Kumaon, and if
you want to do some hiking in the winter or spring, the hills in Kumaon
are delightful places to wander. You'll never be too far from a town where
you can purchase basic foods, and you needn't worry that you will be
tripping over other foreigners. In the spring you can enjoy the rhododendrons that bloom in the hills, usually displaying the most brilliant of reds
with the snows of the himals to the north as a backdrop.

The Gori and Darma valleys in northern Kumaon are tributaries of the
Mahakali River (often called the Kali), which demarcates the western boundary of Nepal. Along with the more northerly Kuthi Yankti Valley, which
also flows into the Kali, these deep, parallel gorges are walled by high
peaks and crested with caravan passes leading toward the former entrepôt
of Gyanima Mandi, to Taklakot, and to holy Mt. Kailas in western Tibet.
The north bank of the Gori and the entire Darma and Kuthi Yankti valleys
lie north of the Inner Line and have rarely been visited by foreigners.

Two fine book-length accounts of travels in these valleys (and others)
have been published. Arnold Heim and August Gansser, the two members
of the 1936 Swiss expedition to this area, and W. H. Murray of the four-
person 1950 Scottish Himalayan expedition wrote about their respective
expeditions. Check the bibliography for information about these fine books.
Both of these groups were notable for their small size, for their members'
wide-ranging interests, for their good rapport with locals, and for their
discovering the advantages of eating the local diet and traveling as lightly
as possible. Murray tells us that close to the village of Mapong (on the Gori
River very near today's Inner Line) at the base of the deep canyon between
Nanda Kot and Panchchuli's row of five summits, there was once a stone
marker inscribed, All land north of this stone is Tibet. Harish Kapadia
trekked more recently in these upper valleys and over a high pass between
them, writing about his experience in volume 39 of *The Himalayan Journal,* the always-informative annual that he edits (see the bibliography).

Harish hails from Bombay and is one of India's top experts on trekking. From Kashmir to Nubra, Zanskar, Lahoul, Kulu, Kinnaur, Garhwal, and northern Kumaon, he has trekked and climbed in regions that we foreigners cannot get permits to enter. More power to him, and let's hope his informative, flavorful articles keep coming to continue whetting our appetites.

Kumaon's forested midlevel valleys south of the restricted area are particularly colorful during the harvest season, when Bhotias from the upper villages move southward on their annual migration from the snows. Perhaps the best-known Bhotia of an earlier generation to come from this area was Nain Singh, from Milam village in the upper Gori Valley. Known as "Number 1," he was the most accomplished of the early surveyors, called the pundits, having reached Lhasa after traveling and keeping clandestine observations through 1,200 miles of unmapped Tibetan territory. Today Milam-walas and others attend local autumn harvest fairs, such as the Jouljibi Fair at Munsiari in November (Munsiari is just south of the restricted region), but for now the days of wide-open travel to Tibet by the Garhwal Bhotias are over.

For cognoscenti of the remote (and politically unreachable), here are several notes on the far northeast corner of this area of the Himalaya, around the northern reaches of the Mahakali. The snowfields that feed the Mahakali's source lie below the high Lepu Lekh La, once the busiest summer pass to Taklakot and holy Mt. Kailas (see below). This pass is still shown on the cheap maps you can buy of the yatra routes through Uttarakhand. An upland tributary of the Mahakali that exceeds it in size above their confluence is the Kuthi Yankti. The Kuthi Valley includes two other passes to Tibet and Shang Tang (21,262 feet), first climbed by a Swiss team. Clustered Kuthi village, with its finely carved wooden homes, is at 12,300 feet said to be the highest permanently inhabited town in the Central Himalaya.

The Yatra Path Toward Mt. Kailas

The most sublime "Throne of the Gods," "The Crown Chakra of the Earth," and "Shiva's Throne," Mt. Kailas in southwestern Tibet is revered by Tibetan Buddhist, Bon Po, Jain, and Hindu alike as the physical and metaphoric center of the world. Kailas is situated north of Kumaon and the two Tibetan lakes called Manasarowar ("Mapham" in Tibetan) and Rakas Tal. Since 1981, groups of Indian yatris have once again been permitted to make the pilgrimage to holy Mt. Kailas, this most sacred mountain on earth for Hindus. People are chosen annually by lottery from thousands of applicants, and about eight groups of twenty-five, called "batches," make the trip every summer. Each group meets in New Delhi, then proceeds by a special bus directly to Kumaon, crossing the Inner Line at Jauljibi, a small town on the northern bank of the Gori River where it meets the Mahakali River. They continue north along the Indian side of the Kali by bus past the large town of Darchula to the roadhead at Tawaghat (about 3,500 feet), 25 miles beyond Jauljibi, located in a deep, green gorge just north of the point where the Darma River joins the Kali.

Here the yatris begin their *paydal yatra,* their hike on foot. Now the path rises over and swoops down from the high, forested ridges that plunge into the narrow gorge of the Kali. The yatris are accompanied by physicians who keep a close eye on their progress, and if a person is having too much difficulty on the strenuous trek, he or she is not permitted to continue. After about five days' walk, the path levels out for a stage as the pilgrims hike through Garbyang village and past the mouth of the Kuthi Yankti River. Then the yatris reach Kalopani, "Black Water," the last camp in India. Here they bid goodbye to their ITBP hosts, bundle up, and begin a long pull up the wide, stony nala that now curves to the east. At the top of this basin is the frontier with Tibet, the 17,000-foot Lipu Lekh Pass, which is practically within shouting distance of the Indo-Nepal boundary, the northeasternmost point of Uttar Pradesh. You can meet the yatris again in the section called "The Walk Around Mt. Kailas" in Chapter 9 of this book's companion volume as they perform their *parikrama,* their circumambulation of holy Mt. Kailas.

Woman from Lachen in northern Sikkim.

12

Sikkim

Metok-chharp, blossom-rain, how lucky for you! In Tibet, when there's rain and sunshine at the same time, we call it "blossom-rain" and think it extremely auspicious. How lucky for you to have blossom-rain just as you are entering Gangtok. It means you are going to be very happy in Sikkim.

Tessla Dorji (wife of Bhutan's then prime minister) to Nari Rustomji as he was nearing Gangtok to take up his appointment as dewan (a high official position), 1954

[Much of this chapter was written by Carmi Weingrod, a Seattle resident and travel writer who has made several treks in different regions of the Himalaya.]

An Infinite Variety of Green

Sikkim sits between Nepal and Bhutan, yet most of its eastern border is not with Bhutan, but with Tibet's wedge-shaped Chumbi Valley. Smaller than Yellowstone National Park, India's tiniest and least populous state measures only 40 to 80 miles and is isolated from Nepal, Tibet, and the rest of India by high ridges. Joined to the British Empire by treaty and its northern boundary demarcated in 1890, Sikkim became an Indian protectorate in 1949 and an Indian state in 1975.

Sikkim is composed of the immensely luxuriant Ranjit and Tista river basins, whose thick forests range from sal in the deep southern gorges to conifer and birch in the upper tributaries. The varied vegetation includes literally thousands of plants, among them magnolia, tree fern, wild strawberry and raspberry, woody creeper, primrose, bougainvillea, crimson and yellow rhododendron, poinsettia, and hundreds of orchid varieties. Sikkim's "endless diversity of green" is best seen during the monsoon. Butterflies and leeches also abound in the wet summers. Cardamom plants provide Sikkim with one of its largest export crops. Tiny and black, the seeds of this plant have become a very popular spice in Asia, Europe, and North America.

Sikkim's population of about a quarter million is largely composed of ethnic Nepalis, whom the British urged to emigrate to fill the need for administrators and cultivators. Until Sikkim became an Indian state, it was ruled for five centuries by the Buddhist Namgyal dynasty. The Namgyals are Lepcha, formerly the region's most powerful ethnic group. More than fifty Buddhist monasteries are scattered across Sikkim, primarily in the more densely populated south.

Trekking in Sikkim

The U502 Series maps covering Sikkim are the *Kanchenjunga* sheet, NG 45-3, including western Sikkim, and *Phari Dzong,* NG 45-4, depicting Gangtok, Rumtek, and the eastern part of the state. In addition, a good map of Sikkim is published by the Association of American Geographers, noted in Appendix A.

Sikkim is a restricted area within India, and permission to go there must be secured by a special permit months before your intended arrival. Individual travelers should begin the application process at least four months prior to arrival by requesting a restricted area permit application from any Indian embassy or consulate. This application is separate from the standard Indian visa form and requires three photographs; there is no additional charge. You can apply to visit Sikkim in New Delhi at the Sikkim Tourist Office on the first floor of the Hansalaya Building at 15

Barakhamba Road, not far from Connaught Place, but the process will still take two to three months.

You will not receive a Sikkim endorsement in your passport. Instead, you will be notified by mail when the process is completed, and the actual permit must be picked up in Darjeeling, on the border with Sikkim in the state of West Bengal. When you apply for the standard Indian visa, you must state your intention to visit Darjeeling by printing DARJEELING along the top of your application. A separate endorsement for Darjeeling will be stamped beside the visa in your passport.

Tourists are granted a seven-day tourist permit to visit Sikkim. A tourist permit does not entitle you to trek, however. A separate trekking permit must be obtained before entering Sikkim, and the regulations for trekking are quite rigid: only one trekking route is open, and you must be with a group of six or more persons accompanied by a licensed Indian guide. No exceptions are made. Because of these regulations, it is advisable to make your arrangements through a tour operator in the United States or England. Group trekking permits are valid for fifteen days.

To reach Darjeeling, you must first travel to Siliguri in the Indian state of West Bengal. Siliguri (New Jalpaiguri) can be reached by train from Calcutta in about thirteen hours. You can also fly to Siliguri's Baghdogra Airport from Calcutta or New Delhi. From Baghdogra, the bus trip to Darjeeling, including a snack stop in Kuresong, takes about four and a half hours. Groups of three or four can hire a taxi, which although slightly more expensive is quicker and safer (the road can be treacherous). The famous Toy Train—a narrow-gauge railway that runs from New Jalpaiguri to Darjeeling—makes the 76-mile scenic journey in eight to twelve hours. If you aren't in a hurry and the train is running (the tracks are often damaged by recurring landslides), the trip can be an enjoyable experience, but be ready for a cinder dust coating. Darjeeling, a hill station at 7,500 feet, commands a fine view of Sikkim's most sacred peak, Kangchenjunga (at 28,146 feet the third-highest mountain in the world), 40 miles to the north, on the border of Nepal and Sikkim.

Travel from Darjeeling to Sikkim is possible via public bus, taxi, or hired jeep. The journey is spectacular, as the winding road first descends through fertile terraces and rhododendron forests to the Tista River before climbing back up to the hills of Gangtok, Sikkim's largest town and administrative headquarters. Permits are inspected at a checkpoint in Rongphu, on the Sikkim border.

At Gangtok you can obtain a three-day extension of your seven-day tourist permit at the Foreigners' Registration Office by completing a single form. If you have a trekking permit, you must spend at least two days in Gangtok, and you are encouraged to visit nearby Pemayangtse and Tashiding, two of Sikkim's most famous monasteries, now only open to trekking parties. You do not need a trekking permit to visit Rumtek, one of the area's best-known monasteries, situated high on a ridge just across the valley from Gangtok. This monastic community was home to the late Gyalwa Karmapa, leader of the Kagyupa branch of Tibetan Buddhism.

Each May, ritual masked dances are performed at Rumtek similar to the dances that take place at Hemis in Ladakh and at Thame and Tengboche monasteries in Nepal.

The single trek permitted foreigners in Sikkim begins at the quiet village of Yoksum (5,800 feet), a couple of hours' drive west of Gangtok. At Yoksum your group will be assigned its Indian guide, who will accompany you for the duration of the trek, a ten-day round-trip from Yoksum to the Goecha La, a 16,500-foot pass with superb views of Kangchenjunga. The route is currently being enlarged into a loop trail that will cross the Goecha La and terminate near Gangtok, making it a twelve-day trek.

From Yoksum the path climbs through an enchanted forest of towering rhododendron, pine, azalea, orchid, and giant oak. Moss-covered branches —like a swinging haven for Tarzan and Jane—hang low over the trail. Monkeys, birds, and butterflies abound. The track follows the high valleys up toward the pass, crossing raging green rivers on well-maintained bridges.

Western Sikkim is largely uninhabited. One day's walk from Yoksum is Tshoka (9,400 feet), the only village on the trek and home to several Tibetan refugee families. You can stop at this friendly village and have a cup of salted butter tea with one of the families. At Dzongri ("Mountain Fortress," 13,200 feet) are a few cabins that house seasonal yak herders and an occasional pilgrim, but no permanent residents. Considered sacred to the Sikkimese, Dzongri is one of the very special places along the trek. Open and windswept, the land is dotted with chortens where relics of ancient kings are sequestered. You can join the wandering yaks here and meander up to a number of scenic high points adorned with prayer flags.

Unlike trekking in Nepal and other places in the Indian Himalaya, few local travelers are encountered on the trail, and the land is pristine and unspoiled. Spectacular views of Kangchenjunga, Pandim, and other peaks of the Singalila Ridge separating Sikkim from Nepal are visible for the entire trek. Above treeline (14,000 feet) enormous black boulders rise above scree, and the landscape is stark and otherworldly. White peaks, jagged and glacial, form a permanent backdrop as you climb toward the Goecha La. For clear skies and the best views, trek in autumn. If you are attracted by Sikkim's abundant vegetation and wildlife, go during spring.

Travel from and to Nepal

If you are in Nepal and want to go to Darjeeling or Sikkim, the only place you can cross the eastern border of Nepal into India is near Siliguri, at Kakarbhitta on Nepal's main east-west road. The Indian border point here is named Raniganj. You may well have to have a special stamp in your passport, which you can get at the Indian High Commission in Kathmandu. Be sure to check before you leave Kathmandu for the border. If you are crossing from India into Nepal, two photographs and $10 should get you an immediate one-week visa (if regulations do not change).

13
Himalayan
Natural History

by Rodney Jackson

Introduction

Since the Himalaya's origin less than 25 million years ago, it has molded the region's fauna and flora by limiting Indian species from moving northward and Tibetan species from moving southward. Because of its youthfulness in geological terms the Himalaya has not yet evolved plant and animal life uniquely adapted to its terrain; flora and fauna are instead an amalgam of forms native to India, Southeast Asia, the Mediterranean, and Europe. Himalayan rivers were in place before the mountains were; consequently, the courses of the rivers have remained unchanged while they have cut ever-deeper gorges. These valleys have provided the main avenues of contact between Indian and Eurasian wildlife. Animals adapted to cold climes, such as wolves, brown bears, and rose finches, moved south from Eurasia, while tropical species moved north into the foothills, eventually meeting in the high mountains.

The main Himalaya, stretching for 1,900 miles and varying in width from 50 to nearly 200 miles, really consists of three parallel ranges. The low hills of the Outer Himalaya, or Siwaliks, adjoin the Indian plain and in few places exceed 3,000 feet in height and 30 miles in width. For much of their length the Siwaliks are separated from the main Himalaya by elongated *duns*, or flat valleys, such as the Vale of Kashmir. The Middle Himalaya forms the southern edge of the Inner or Great Himalaya Range, which extends from Kashmir to Bhutan and China. The Middle Himalaya's peaks vary in height from roughly 6,000 to 14,000 feet. This zone supported extensive and magnificent forests of conifers, oaks, maples, laurels, and magnolias until intensive woodcutting in recent years decimated them. The Inner Himalaya is distinguished, of course, by its high peaks, which abut the so-called Trans-Himalaya Range, in reality not a range but a series of ridges, ranges, and plateaus forming the southern edge of Tibet. Examples of individual ranges considered part of the Himalaya include the Zanskar Range, the various Ladakh ranges, the Hindu Kush, and the Karakoram.

The Himalaya is a biological wonderland. To the north lies Tibet, the Roof of the World, a vast area of plains, mountains, and gorges that is only now being explored by naturalists. Neither altitudinal nor latitudinal factors hold much sway, given the region's high base elevation and rigorous climatic regime. Harsh winters, a short growing season, and paucity of moisture have far-reaching effects on the vegetation and wildlife. Ladakh and the more northerly parts of Pakistan, such as the Khunjerab or Shimshal areas, which border the Tibetan Plateau, tend to have a similar flora and fauna. They differ, however, in having decidedly more broken and rugged terrain. A sparse mantle of vegetation—mostly spiny and contorted shrubs or ephemeral annuals—provides a meager supply of food for the wild and domestic grazers of the area. There are no or very few trees, more because of insufficient soil moisture than other factors. Most of the trees, poplars and willows, grow along the margins of man-made irrigation ditches. Like Tibet, this is a region of harsh and bleak winters, daily winds, and a notable paucity of monsoon rainfall or even winter snow—except in those few places bordering the main Himalayan ranges or where deep gorges penetrate the massifs, allowing moist air to penetrate.

Tropical heat and arctic cold are telescoped into a span only 40 miles wide in the Himalaya of Sikkim and Bhutan, and the region as a whole boasts a richness and variety of plants and wildlife that is perhaps unequaled in the world. On a circuit of the Annapurna massif you will pass from tropical forest to the barren mountain desert of the Tibetan Plateau: two major biogeographical zones. Botanists have estimated that at least 6,500 species of flowering plants grow in Nepal alone. India and Pakistan are not without their own biotic diversity and uniqueness. Although the British botanist Joseph Hooker cataloged many Himalayan plants in the mid-nineteenth century, the region's fauna is not well known. A new order of amphibians was discovered in Nepal in the early 1970s, and only recently have the first field studies been conducted on large ungulates (hoofed animals), such as the bharal, or blue sheep.

This trekking guide obviously cannot provide more than a brief glimpse of the area's natural history. The number of plants and animals that can be described here is quite limited, and the descriptions that are included suffer from incompleteness. But if this account stimulates the reader to explore further, it will have served its purpose. In the bibliography you will find references to the most useful natural history books, field guides, and magazine articles. For flowering plants, I recommend Polunin and Stainton's *Flowers of the Himalaya*, with its excellent plates and descriptions. For birds, the latest edition of the *Birds of Nepal* will enable you to identify most species present in India and many of those in Pakistan. Prater's *The Book of Indian Mammals* remains the only mammal guide for the Indian Himalaya; since it was written in 1965—before any field studies were made of the mountain species—it has some misleading information. However, the plates will help you identify any large mammal you are likely to see. Roberts's *The Mammals of Pakistan* is more recent and very informative, but it is too large to take on a trek. Other sources of information are the numerous articles on Himalayan wildlife and natural history appearing in popular magazines published by the world's many conservation groups and zoological societies. One day the Himalayan trekker will be able to take along a completely portable library, making identification of plants and animals routine. Until then, interest, ingenuity, and perseverance will be the primary tools for exploring life in the Himalaya.

Life Zones

Biologists recognize a number of vertical (or altitudinal) and horizontal (or regional) zones that support distinctive fauna and flora (see accompanying diagram). The eastern Himalaya is considerably wetter than the western (Kashmir and Kumaon) or northwestern (Hindu Kush and Karakoram) Himalaya because as the yearly monsoon moves northwestward from the Bay of Bengal, the moisture it carries is rapidly dissipated. And the north-

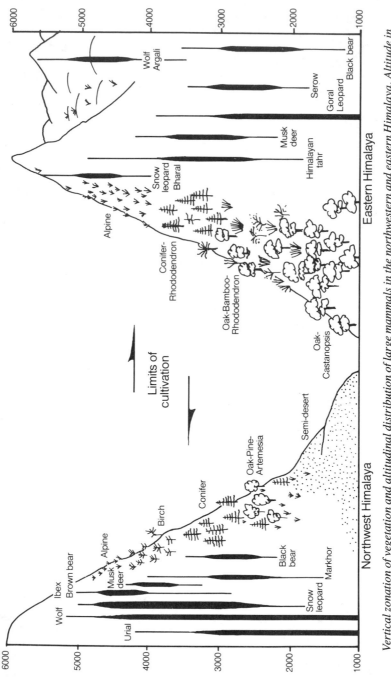

Vertical zonation of vegetation and altitudinal distribution of large mammals in the northwestern and eastern Himalaya. Altitude in meters. (Reproduced courtesy of University of Chicago Press, 1977.)

ern slopes of the Himalaya and the Tibetan Plateau, sequestered in a rain shadow beyond the monsoon's reach, are dry and practically rainless. As one would expect, then, forests, flowering plants, and wildlife are most diverse and prolific in the east. The eastern Himalaya supports lush tropical montane forests, while at the same elevations in the west is found subtropical thorn or sage scrub. In the north, coniferous or deciduous forests grow on some of the more moist slopes, yet other slopes are entirely unforested. In arid Ladakh, for example, the only trees are those planted near villages and along irrigation ditches. The change from east to west is not abrupt, however. Most biologists recognize the Kali Gandaki River as the eastern boundary and the Sutlej River as the western boundary of a gradient along which plant life changes significantly, with Southeast Asian species to the east and Mediterranean-Eurasian ones to the west.

Vertical zonation results from changes in temperature and moisture with increasing elevation. Temperature decreases while moisture increases to a point and then, at higher levels, decreases. In general, the temperature drops about 3.5 degrees Fahrenheit for every 1,000-foot rise, and the timberline seems to coincide with elevation levels having mean temperature of about 50° F for the warmest day of the year. Timberline varies from about 12,000 to 13,500 feet; it is higher on southern than on northern slopes, and higher in the west than the east.

Equally dramatic is the effect of aspect. Steep north-facing slopes receive substantially less sunshine than those that face southward. It is not unusual to cross from hot, oak-covered or bare slopes over a ridge into the snowbound cool of a north-facing fir or birch forest. Even in the dead of winter, you may see grasshoppers and agamid lizards feeding or basking in the sun on one slope, while a few yards away the ground is covered by deep snow and all animals are hibernating.

The permanent snow line is another limit that determines plant and animal populations. Its height varies according to summer temperatures, amount of snowfall, and exposure, fluctuating greatly even within the same range. In the central and western Himalaya the permanent snow line may be 2,000 feet lower on a north slope than on a south slope and in the eastern Himalaya, perhaps as much as 3,000 feet lower on a north slope. Precipitation actually may be less on the higher peaks, and conditions are generally more severe than in temperate America or northern Europe because the steep slopes and strong winds of the Himalaya usually prevent deep accumulation of snow, with its moderating effect.

Five major vertical zones have been recognized. From highest to lowest, they may be briefly described as follows:

aeolian (snow line and higher)

alpine (timberline to snow line)

subalpine (a narrow transition zone)

temperate (a broad belt)

subtropical and tropical (warmer, low-lying belts)

The accompanying table shows how the location of each zone varies in elevation from region to region and notes the dominant plant life of each zone. (In the table, the temperate and subtropical/tropical zones are further subdivided.) The elevations given in the table should serve only as a general

Simplified Vertical Zonations of Himalayan Vegetation

Zone	Northwest [a]	West [b]	East–Central [c]
Aeolian	lower limit unknown bacteria, fungi, lichens	15,000 ft. plus bacteria, fungi, lichens	15,000 ft. plus bacteria, fungi, lichens
Alpine	alpine meadows 9,600–? ft. pioneer plants	alpine meadows 11,700–15,000 ft. pioneer plants	alpine meadows 11,400–15,000 ft. pioneer plants
Subalpine	subalpine scrub 9,000–11,400 ft. birch, juniper, sagebrush	subalpine scrub 10,200–12,000 ft. birch, juniper, fir, rhododendron, willow	subalpine scrub 10,200–12,000 ft. birch, juniper, rhododendron
Temperate	temperate coniferous forest 6,000–10,200 ft. pine, Himalayan edible pine, west Himalayan fir	temperate coniferous forest 7,500–10,500 ft. deodar (Himalayan) cedar, west Himalayan fir, Himalayan hemlock, blue pine, cypress	conifer-rhododendron forest 7,500–10,500 ft. blue hemlock, east Himalayan fir, spruce
	forest and sage steppe 6,000–8,400 ft. chir (long-needled) pine, sagebrush	temperate mixed forest 6,000–9,000 ft. oak, deodar (Himalayan) cedar, spruce	temperate evergreen forest 4,500–7,500 ft. oak, rhododendron, magnolia, maple
Subtropical and Tropical	subtropical, semi- desert scrub 1,800–6,000 ft. *Capparis, Pistacia,* wild olive	pine forest 2,700–6,000 ft. chir (long-needled) pine	subtropical montane forest 2,400–4,500 ft. chilaune, chestnut, oak, alder
	subtropical thorn 1,800 ft. acacia, *Zizyphus*	subtropical thorn 2,400 ft. acacia, bauhinia, *Albizzia*	tropical evergreen rain forest 150–2,400 ft. sal, bauhinia, *Terminalia*

[a] Northwest = Pakistan, Jammu, and Kashmir

[b] West = Himachal Pradesh, Uttar Pradesh, and western Nepal

[c] East-Central = Nepal east of Kali Gandaki Valley to Bhutan

guide to the zones and their characteristic plant communities, for they vary considerably as a result of exposure, soil depth and moisture, the underlying rock type, and such human influences as logging, burning, and grazing. Although the transition from one zone to the next is gradual rather than abrupt, the change may be dramatic if steep slopes and strong shifts in aspect prevail or if man has removed the original plant cover.

Aeolian Zone

The permanent snow line is considered the lower limit to this zone. Flowering plants are absent here, and life is limited to bacteria, fungi, insects, and crustaceans that subsist upon airborne food particles blown up from below. Much ground is exposed because snow seldom accumulates evenly. Lichens encrust rocks, and spiders, springtails, and glacier fleas are able to survive in protected microclimates among the rocks and in the soil. Jumping spiders have been found at the 22,000-foot level on Mt. Everest, presumably preying upon other insects that live beneath the snow or that are blown there by the wind. Microorganisms have even been found in soil sampled from the very top of Mt. Everest. At the 19,000-foot level, temporary glacial pools in the eastern Himalaya are known to support large populations of fairy shrimp. And birds and mammals are occasional though transient visitors; the snow leopard, for example, may use high passes to move from one valley to another, and such flocking birds as snow pigeons and cloughs frolic in the thermals. Some birds may rest on high cols as they migrate across the Himalaya, although their flights are usually nonstop.

Alpine Zone

The alpine zone extends from timberline to snow line. It is a zone characterized by harsh winters, short summers, shallow stony soils, strong winds, and a lack of moisture. At the upper limits of vegetation, a few pioneering rock plants grow in sheltered places—beneath rocky ledges and beside protective boulders—where they form small cushions. Typical plants include the stonecrops and rock jasmines, which have basal rosettes of succulent leaves, and the drabas or stoneworts with their densely matted, cushionlike stems. *Stellaria decumbens* has been found at 20,129 feet and is listed in the *Guinness Book of World Records* as the highest plant in the world; however, the rock-encrusting *Arenaria bryophylla* has been recorded at 20,277 feet. Delicate purple or red primroses are often seen flowering immediately adjacent to melting snow. The plants are typically widely scattered and, unless they are in bloom, easily overlooked. The alpine zone also supports such plants as the edelweiss or sow's ear, having fuzzy, hairy leaves and a tufted, or clustered, growth pattern (adaptations to the scarcity of water in a form available to plants).

In sedge and grass meadows, wildflowers often form spectacular displays. These profusions of color are greatest where snowmelt collects and where deeper soils have developed over the ages. Some species bloom into late summer, especially at higher elevations and on more exposed sites.

Anyone familiar with the mountain flora of North America or Europe will recognize many genera: there are buttercups, anemones, larkspurs, everlasting flowers, asters, dandelions, thistles, saxifrages, cinquefoils, louseworts, geraniums, lilies, and gentians. The diversity is staggering; in Nepal alone more than sixty-seven species of primrose occur, many of them in the alpine zone. Worth looking for are the sky blue *Meconopsis* poppy—the so-called queen of Himalayan flowers—and the delicate purple gentians and poisonous monkshood. Carpets of wildflowers are all the more remarkable in the northwestern Himalaya, where soils are absent or thin and water very precious. Small and vulnerable hanging alpine meadows relieve the otherwise-barren landscape of this region.

Alpine scrub is found along streams and in U-shaped valleys. Typical species include the *Cotoneaster*, a rigid and much-branched shrub that produces an abundance of red berries in the fall; *Caragana*, a member of the pea family that bears thorns and is widespread in central Asia; *Ephedra* or Mormon tea; rose; and several species of procumbent (a flattened growth form) rhododendrons, junipers, and cinquefoil. This community is characteristic of the dry valleys behind the main range, such as Dolpo, Ladakh, and large parts of Tibet. In Bhutan, relatively lush stands of rhododendron, grasses, and sedges prevail.

The high Deosai Plains of Baltistan are vegetated by sagebrush and willow, with moist grassy meadows along the watercourses. In contrast, the alpine zone in Ladakh has very little plant life and virtually no trees, except those people have planted and the odd, stunted juniper that grows in protected places. All plants in this region are adapted to conditions of extreme dryness. Much of the Karakoram consists either of barren scree or arid steppe in which sagebrush is the chief ingredient.

The animals found in the alpine zone tend to be of Eurasian origin, with preexisting adaptations to the severe conditions of northern latitudes. Typical mammals include bharal, pikas, marmots, red foxes, weasels, voles, and mice. Snow leopard, lynx, wolves, and brown bears are found near the Tibetan border, and in this zone in the western Himalaya the ibex is a characteristic ungulate. A few large birds, such the snow cock and snow partridge, are permanent residents. In summer there is a dramatic influx of songbirds, which breed in the grassy meadows. Snakes and lizards are typically scarce.

Subalpine Zone

The subalpine zone is most accurately considered a transition between the temperate coniferous forest and the alpine belt, in effect delineating the timberline. Stunted, windblown birch, juniper, and rhododendron characterize this zone, except in the northwest, which has, instead of rhododendron, sagebrush, poplar, and willow. Fir, pine, or spruce trees are interspersed with these shrubs, and some north-facing slopes support pure birch forests. Birch is easily identified by its pale, peeling bark, which in times past provided the main source of paper.

The birch forest and scrub of the subalpine zone are vital habitat for the arboreal birch mouse and the dwindling population of musk deer.

Temperate Zone

Below an elevation of 12,000 feet is a more or less continuous forest belt. Conifers such as fir, hemlock, pine, cypress, and cedar occupy the higher levels. Undergrowth is sparse in most places, consisting of rhododendron, a variety of shrubs, and in the east, bamboo. In Bhutan, Sikkim, and as far west as central Nepal, a lush, temperate evergreen forest grows between elevations of 3,000 to 5,000 feet. Almost pure stands of evergreen oaks are interspersed with laurels, chestnuts, maples, magnolias, and other trees that rarely exceed 60 feet in height. In spring the forest is ablaze with white magnolia and white, pink, or red rhododendron blossoms. Mosses and lichens clothe every oak, and numerous orchids and other epiphytes add to the "cloud forest" setting. These forests are frequently shrouded in mist, and they may be remarkably cool even in summer. Some of the steeper slopes support almost pure stands of alder, a tree with deciduous branches that break off easily and lack the moss festoons so characteristic of the oaks in the area. Alders seem to invade areas prone to landsliding and probably play a vital role in stabilizing areas that have slid. Numerous wildflowers, ferns, and orchids occur, especially in moist ravines and near streams. Look for yellow balsams, purple violets, touch-me-nots, begonias, and Solomon's seals. The flora and fauna of this temperate-zone belt are truly Himalayan in composition, but they have been little explored, cataloged, or described.

In West Nepal, Kumaon, and parts of Kashmir, the temperate forests consist mainly of oak, blue pine, and west Himalayan fir with some deodar cedar. Magnolias are absent, rhododendrons sparse, and maples occur primarily near streams or along cool northerly slopes. Farther west yet, the coniferous forests at the same elevation are patchy and steppelike with such species as oak and sage in the understory.

The northwestern Himalaya is semiarid to arid at this altitudinal zone. Forests, if present, are small and scattered. There are few conifers, and the barren landscape is dominated by shrubs.

The Himalaya is famous for its variety of "rose-trees"—rhododendrons. The greatest number of species is found in Bhutan and Sikkim. About twenty-nine species are found in Nepal, and most of these are east of Kathmandu. One, *Rhododendron arboreum*, is the national flower of Nepal. Rhododendrons range from trees 45 feet tall to low, creeping shrubs and even epiphytic climbers. Flower color is not a reliable means of identification, for a single species can exhibit shades from white and pale pinks to scarlet. The displays are best seen between late March and early May.

Conifers become increasingly abundant as one climbs higher. In the west, the forests are dominated by the five-needled Himalayan blue pine (*Pinus wallichiana*) and the west Himalayan silver fir (*Abies pindrow*), a species with a smooth, silvery bark. Other trees include the famous deodar, a magnificent Himalayan cedar that grows as high as 150 feet, with a girth of 35 feet. Also look for the hemlock (*Tsuga dumosa*), a delicate conifer, and the west Himalayan spruce (*Picea smithiana*), with its flattened leaves (in contrast to the needlelike leaves of firs) and pendulant cones. Spruce branches droop conspicuously. The Himalayan silver fir (*Abies spectabilis*) is found from Kashmir to Bhutan but is most abundant in central Nepal and westward. It is differentiated from its western cousin by its rough, fissured bark and lower leaf surfaces that have two dark bands rather than one. Another pine, the Himalayan edible pine (*Pinus gerardiana*), provides food for people in the Hindu Kush and parts of the Karakoram; the seeds, which are protected by thick scales, contain much oil. The leaves occur in clusters of three. Yet another pine that is found in almost-pure stands in the central and western Himalaya—the long-needled or chir pine (*Pinus roxburghii*)—is best distinguished by its long, light green needles (in bundles of three) and deeply fissured bark. This relatively fire-tolerant fir is common in west Nepal at elevations of 2,700 to 6,000 feet. On limestone outcrops you may well find dense stands of Himalayan cypress (*Cupressus torulosa*).

Spruce and hemlock are more likely to be found on cool, moist, north-facing slopes, especially in the drier parts of the Himalaya (for example, north of the Annapurna and Dhaulagiri massifs). Larches (*Larix* spp.) are found only from central Nepal eastward, while the Himalayan cypress occurs only west of the Kanjiroba Himal of Nepal. Junipers (*Juniperus* spp.) are characteristic of the more arid higher elevations throughout the Himalaya, although they are more common in the alpine or subalpine belts.

The fauna of the temperate zone is diverse and in many respects rather unique. Large mammals include the serow; goral; the takin of Bhutan, Burma, and China; and the Himalayan tahr. At lower elevations macaque monkeys forage on the ground; the langur monkey, which spends much of its time in trees, is found up to around the 12,000-foot level. Less frequently seen wildlife includes Himalayan black bears, forest leopards, yellow-throated martens, red pandas, and a number of small cats. There are numerous small rodents, from wood mice to flying squirrels. Frogs, toads, and snakes, few of which are cataloged, also occur. But the greatest variety is in the avifauna. Most trekkers will attest to mysterious and wonderful calls from birds heard but not seen. The presence of trees, shrubs, and ground vegetation provides many foraging niches for birds that would otherwise compete with one another. Laughing thrushes, babblers, and minias flit about the ground and tangled brush, while nuthatches and tree creepers comb conifer branches for food. Tits and warblers forage among the foliage, and woodpeckers work on dead or dying trees. If you sit quietly on a trailside log, you'll be well rewarded for your patience. Many species will come close enough for you to see without field glasses.

Subtropical and Tropical Zones

Subtropical montane forests occupy the foothills of the Himalaya. Common trees include the chestnut (*Castanopsis* spp.) with yellow flowers and spiny acornlike fruits; *Schima* spp.—locally called *chilaune*—with fragrant white flowers and a nutlike fruit; and in west Nepal, the horse chestnut and walnut. Oaks are also abundant, and alders grow along drainages and on recent landslide scars.

West of Nepal's Karnali River are almost monotypic stands of long-needled pine, which at higher elevations merges with oak forests. The pines are sometimes 100 feet tall, and without an understory of shrubs or vines, the forest has a parklike appearance. Most trees bear witness to past wildfires, to which this pine is specially adapted.

The subtropical fauna is decidedly Indian in composition. For example, this zone, like much of India, has chital deer, tigers, water buffaloes, and hog deer, and in times past there were elephants. However, unless you make a special trip to a tropical reserve such as the Chitwan, you are unlikely to see these animals. And because most of these animals are not truly Himalayan, they will not be discussed further.

Below the subtropical is the tropical zone, which extends up to 4,500 feet in the east. Until the terai region of Nepal was developed, the tropical forests extended in a continuous belt along the country's southern border. They are now very fragmented. The canopy is composed of many deciduous and evergreen hardwoods, including bauhinia and teak, although sal (*Shorea robusta*) is the major species. Its large, rounded leaves, 6 to 10 inches long and a shiny yellowish green, make it an easy species to identify. Although never quite leafless, sal sheds much of its foliage during the dry season. Its flowers are yellow, and it is an important timber and fodder species. Until recently, sal trees formed an almost-continuous forest belt along the base of the Himalaya, but in many areas branches have been repeatedly lopped off and the leaves collected for firewood and livestock feed, with the result that the sal's form is typically straight and gaunt. The shrubs, bamboos, palms, and ferns that cover the forest floor decrease in density as you move west so that the sal forest becomes increasingly parklike, until it is replaced by thorn scrub in India and Pakistan. Among the arid scrubs, acacia, *Zizyphus*, and other thorny species dominate.

Himalayan Fauna

Mammals

Langur monkeys, Himalayan orange-bellied squirrels, pikas, and marmots are the mammals most commonly seen on a trek in the Himalaya. Many hikers remark on the paucity of large animals, and certainly the water buffaloes or yaks you see will be domestic rather than wild ones. To see such wildlife as the Himalayan tahr, musk deer, or urial, you must go either to a national park or one of the few remaining sparsely populated valleys of the Himalaya. Even in such places wildlife may be under considerable pressure. There are a few strongholds outside the confines of a national park: examples include Ladakh and Zanskar in India and the Shimshal Valley in Pakistan. Here wild game is relatively widespread thanks to the rugged terrain, sparse human population, or in the case of Ladakh, the strong Buddhist influence. Because almost all species are on the decline, do not participate in their demise by purchasing wild-animal skins or horns—it may in fact be illegal to do so (and impossible to import without a special permit). Also, you'll simply encourage the local people to hunt all the more.

A few of the larger or more conspicuous mammals you may find on a trek are listed below with brief descriptions. Except where stated otherwise, the species occur throughout the Himalayan chain.

Primates. Langurs (*Presbytis entellis*) are long-limbed, long-tailed gray monkeys with distinctive black faces. They live in troops of as many as fifty and are the most commonly seen species in the Himalaya. Like the rhesus macaque, this species is sacred to many Himalayan peoples, and even the monkeys that raid agricultural fields are not killed. The rhesus macaque (*Macaca mulatta*) occurs at lower elevations and is brownish red, has a squat form with short limbs, and spends much of its time on the ground. Often seen in towns and villages.

Yeti (Abominable Snowman to some). Protected by the government of Nepal, the yeti has yet to be classified by scientists. Since its possible presence was first reported by British Resident Brian Hodgson in 1832, accounts of this ape have been numerous in eastern Nepal and occasionally as far west as the Karakoram (though its existence there is even more open to question). In 1951 mountaineer Eric Shipton took pictures of "yeti tracks" on the Menlung Glacier, near Everest; these pictures are now considered the "type photos" of the yeti's apelike footprints. Eyewitness accounts generally describe the yeti as a stocky ape 5 feet or taller, with coarse reddish or grayish brown fur, a large head with a pointed crown, hairless face, and robust jaw. Its arms reach to the knees, and it moves bipedally with a shuffling gait. If the yeti exists—some evidence is tantalizing—some experts speculate it probably does so in the dense montane forests of the middle elevations. Since "yeti tracks" have usually been found on or near strategic passes, it is assumed that yetis use passes to move from one valley to another. During their mating season, snow leopards communicate with piercing, eerie "yowls": villagers sequestered in a high mountain hut during a winter snow storm would naturally think of the yeti! But more tangible evidence, in the form of scats, hair, or a conclusive photograph, is needed to decide whether this creature is real or a fancy of the human imagination. Many expeditions have endeavored to do so, and all have failed.

Hares. Look for the woolly hare (*Lepus oiostolus*) while driving across the Tibetan plains; in many places in the south, it is the only form of wildlife you will see because everything else has been hunted out. The black-napped hare (*L. nigricollis*) takes its place in the Himalayan region.

Pika (*Ochotona* spp.). This delightful relative of the hare is easily found amongst rocks and along mani walls above the tree line. Also known as the mouse-hare, the pika has a short muzzle, rounded ears, and no visible tail. It lives in loose colonies, spending summer days collecting grass and forbs, which it stores under rocks for the winter. Will allow you to approach closely.

Marmot. Marmots live in large colonies, excavating deep burrows in which they hibernate during winter. They feed outside burrows during summer and give loud whistles when sighting an intruder. Most commonly encountered above timberline. The Himalayan marmot (*Marmota bobak*) is about 2 feet long with a 5-inch tail and occurs along the Tibetan Plateau throughout the Himalaya. The long-tailed marmot (*M. caudata*), whose tail exceeds one-third of its total body length, has a rich golden orange pelage. Found in the wetter areas of Pakistan and Kashmir; common on the Deosai Plains, and in various areas of Zanskar.

Red fox (*Vulpes vulpes*). Its sign is often seen, because the red fox tends to use the same trails people do. Fairly shy, but not infrequently observed by trekkers. Preys on small rodents, such as pikas and voles. In appearance the same as the European or North American red fox.

Dhole, jackal, and wolf (*Canis alpinus, Canis aureus,* and *Canis lupus*). Jackals and dholes are larger than foxes, with black-tipped tails. The dhole, or Indian wild dog, is the larger of the two and is best identified by its bushy tail and black cheek patch. Both are widely distributed in the Himalaya but are nonetheless rare. The familiar wolf may be seen in small packs in Zanskar, Hunza, Dolpo, and other border areas in the Himalaya and is widespread in the rolling mountains of Tibet. Because wolves often kill many domestic animals, they are usually shot or trapped by villagers.

Bears. The brown bear (*Ursus arctos*) inhabits wetter alpine or subalpine meadows and scrub in Tibet and the far western Himalaya but is very rare along the central or eastern parts of the range. Its pelage (fur) is sandy or reddish brown, and it has a conspicuous hump of longish hair over the shoulder. Uses forefeet for digging out bulbs, grass, and the occasional marmot. The Himalayan black bear (*Selenarctos thibetanus*) is a widespread denizen of temperate forests at elevations of 4,000 to 12,000 feet. Black in color with a conspicuous cream-colored V on the chest. If you visit the lowlands, you may see the sloth bear (*Melursus ursinus*). Give all bears plenty of room—every year locals are severely mauled by bears disturbed intentionally or accidentally.

Spotted cats. If you are exceptionally lucky, you may see a forest leopard (*Panthera pardus*) while hiking through a forest, or even the legendary snow leopard (*P. uncia*) while traversing a high meadow. Either is rarely seen, of course, but to find their sign along the trail is possible—look for the tracks in the snow or mud, and areas scraped bare with droppings nearby. The large cat tracks winding through a village at about 7,000 feet probably belong to a forest leopard (looking for dogs to eat!). Those seen at the 12,000-foot level and away from forests probably belong to the snow leopard or the lynx. The forest leopard may weigh as much as 150 pounds and usually inhabits forests lower than 10,000 feet.

Until Gary Ahlborn, myself, and our Nepali associates radio collared and tracked five snow leopards in the Langu Valley, almost nothing was known about the habits of this magnificent cat. The elusive snow leopard can melt away unseen and invariably spots the human intruder first. Over four years of study, we saw it only eighteen times. Its pelt is smoky gray with a tinge of yellow, its spots forming open rosettes. Best identified by its 3-foot-long tail and its size—about that of a large dog. Snow leopards rarely descend into the coniferous forest belt and are most frequently glimpsed north of the main Himalaya along the Tibetan border. Ibex and bharal are primary food items in large parts of their range, but with the depletion of native ungulates, snow leopards have turned to livestock for sustenance. This almost guarantees them a short life. Strongly solitary, they nevertheless communicate to each other through such signs as scrapes, scats, and scent-sprayed rocks. Look for their distinctive scrapes—shallow depressions scuffed in the ground, usually with a pile of dirt at one end—along the edge of sharp ridgelines, atop rocky promontories, and along river bluffs near stream confluences. Snow leopards rarely number more than a half dozen in a particular valley complex. Places like the Langu Valley of Nepal's Shey-Phoksumdo National Park in Nepal support as many as twelve or more cats per 80 square miles. Zanskar in Ladakh is another stronghold for the species.

The lynx (*Lynx lynx*) inhabits the barren uplands of Ladakh, the Karakoram, and Tibet, avoiding forests and deep valleys. Several other species of small cat also dwell in the Himalaya, but you are not likely to encounter them. In the bleakest places in Ladakh and Baltistan, look for Pallas's cat (*Felis manul*), which is about the size of a large domestic cat with a cheshirelike face and thick, grizzled silvery buff fur and a long tail, ringed near the tip.

Large Indian civet (*Viverra zibetha*). May be seen in forests and scrub at low elevations. About 30 inches in length, with black-and-white-striped tail and two white throat patches. Short legs, silvery gray fur.

Martens and weasels. Species are too numerous for all to be described. The stone marten (*Martes foina*) inhabits the higher mountain steppe, avoiding forests; forests are the primary domain of the Himalayan yellow-throated marten (*M. flavigula*), which, as its name denotes, is yellow throated. Its pelt is greatly prized for making hats. The weasel (*Mustela* spp.) is a small, slender animal with a sinuous body. Frequently bold and inquisitive, a weasel may approach a quietly sitting person. Feeds on voles and other small rodents and occurs throughout the Himalaya, usually in or near meadows and brush fields.

Red panda (*Ailurus fulgens*). The red or lesser panda of the eastern Himalaya is easily recognized by its white face, dark eye patches, rich chestnut back, dark limbs, and faintly ringed tail. It's rarely seen but worth keeping an eye out for reclining on a branch, for these pandas are not as uncommon as previously thought.

Tibetan wild ass, or kiang (*Equus kiang*). The wild ass of the Tibetan plains and surprisingly common in some parts of Ladakh. A small herd was recently found near Khunjerab National Park in Pakistan. Unmistakable. Regarded as the world's most handsome and horselike wild ass, the kiang is almost 4 feet at the shoulder, with a pale chestnut or almost reddish summer coat. Typically occurring in herds of five to ten (occasionally more than a hundred), kiang feed upon the sparse desert grasses and shrubs. Said to rut in later summer, but like other Tibetan ungulates, their social life is only now being studied in the wild by George Schaller. Although able to exist under extremely harsh conditions, they have disappeared from many places at the hands of man.

Muntjac, or barking deer (*Muntiacus muntjak*). Found at lower elevations in montane forest. Recognized by its reddish brown body with short, dainty legs. The distinctive doglike bark may be repeated at regular intervals. Partial to rocky, wooded ravines.

Musk deer, or kasturi (*Moschus chrysogaster*). The musk deer is a primitive deer about as large as a medium-size dog. It has large, rounded ears, no visible tail, and an arched back, with long hind limbs. The male sports long upper canines or tusks and has a highly prized musk gland, the contents of which are literally worth their weight in gold. Musk deer are solitary and shy most of the time, and you are more likely to see piles of their droppings than catch a glimpse of an animal. They prefer birch forests and scrub in the upper temperate and alpine zones. Local people hunt them with dogs, snares, and poisoned spears, and for some villagers they provide a major source of income. Where protected, they can become extremely tolerant of human presence—a breeding pair essentially lives within the village of Phortse in Sagarmatha National Park, and sightings are guaranteed for those willing to spend a few hours looking.

Tibetan gazelle (*Procapra piticaudata*). An inhabitant of plateau grasslands and barren steppes, the Tibetan gazelle is probably the most widespread of Tibet's wild ungulates and is also found in a small part of Ladakh. Stands about 2 feet at the shoulder and is best distinguished by S-shaped horns 11 to 15 inches in length and a pale, slaty gray coat with distinctive white rump and buttocks. Both sexes have horns. Usually seen singly, in pairs, or small groups.

Tibetan antelope, or chiru (*Pantholops hodgsoni*). A handsome antelope found in the extreme eastern parts of Ladakh, an area presently closed to trekking. Adult males stand about 36 inches at the shoulder and sport dark, saberlike horns (20–28 inches), a black face, pale tawny pelage with reddish tinges to the flanks, a white rump patch, and short tail. Females are hornless. Curious nasal sacs when inflated give muzzle a swollen appearance. Used to occur in large herds, but now very rare.

Goral (*Nemorhaedus goral*). A widespread inhabitant of the south-facing slopes of the Himalaya to as high as the 14,000-foot level in India, but lower in Pakistan. Stands 2 feet at the shoulder. Horns short, pointed, and present in both sexes. Color variable, but usually grayish. Solitary, but may be seen in groups of up to five. Usually the goral waits until you are nearly upon it before bounding uphill in a zigzag route and disappearing quickly.

Serow (*Capricornis serow*). Goatlike, standing about 3½ feet at the shoulder, with a stocky body, thick neck, large head and ears, and short limbs. Horns stout and conical, pointed backwards, and present in both sexes. Color generally black or reddish chestnut, with white on limbs. Inhabits forests and wooded gorges, using cliffs for escape. Usually solitary. Found at 6,000 to 10,000 feet.

Bharal (*Pseudois nayaur*). Sheeplike in appearance, the bharal exhibits the behavior of a goat. Males stand about 3 feet at the shoulder and are best identified by their slaty blue body color, black flank stripes, and dark chests. Cylindrical horns curve outward; in older animals, tips are directed backward. Females lack stripes and have thin horns. Bharal are an essentially Tibetan species found north of the main range from Zanskar to Bhutan. Easily seen in India's Nanda Devi Sanctuary, in the Hemis High Altitude Park of Ladakh, and the Shimshal area of Pakistan. They occur in herds of more than eighty individuals, though groups of a dozen or so are more typical. Found from elevations of 9,000 to around 20,000 feet on the north slopes of Mt. Everest. Bharal are an important item in the diet of snow leopards.

Himalayan tahr (*Hemitragus jemlahicus*). A large, handsome goat that is very partial to the steepest cliffs. Males stand around 3 feet at the shoulder and sport large, shaggy shoulder ruffs that are straw colored, contrasting with the black or coppery brown body color. Horns are about 12 inches long, close set, and curving backward. Females lack the ruff and are much smaller. Tahr are found within a narrow, but highly discontinuous band of land along the southern slopes of the Himalaya from west Kashmir to Sikkim.

Ibex (*Capra ibex sibirica*). Easily identified by the large scimitar horns and beard so characteristic of the goat genus. Females lack the beard and have smaller horns; males stand about 40 inches at the shoulder. Like all ibex, the Asiatic ibex have a strong predilection for the steepest cliffs. They are excellent climbers, though easily killed by hunters in the winter when deep snows hinder their movements. They spend summers at 16,000 feet or higher if grassy hanging meadows are available, and their escape is always to cliffs. The most widespread ungulate of the mountains of Pakistan, occurring as far east as the Sutlej River of India.

Markhor (*Capra falconeri*). Another wild goat, with a straight or flaring set of corkscrew horns, a flowing, whitish gray ruff, and a dark flank stripe. Very localized occurrence in Chitral, Gilgit, Astor, and Indus areas. They live in herds like urial and ibex. Essentially an inhabitant of the low-lying cliffs that receive little moisture and support a dry, shrubby vegetation.

Urial, or shapu (*Ovis orientalis*). A sheep found in the large river valleys of the Karakoram and the Indus drainage, preferring gently rolling to steeply rolling terrain, up to the 14,000-foot level (though usually found much lower). A large animal, grayish in color with a long black chest ruff and white bib. Horns massive and strongly corrugated, forming an open half circle that turns inward at the end. Often seen at the lower end of such valleys as the Braldu, Shigar, and Shyok. Now much depleted.

Argali (*Ovis ammon*). The wild sheep of the rolling hills and mountains of Tibet, ecological equivalent of the Rocky Mountain bighorn. Stands about 3½ feet high, is sandy colored, with massive horns and a white rump patch. Occurs in small herds; very vulnerable to human disturbance. A few can be seen in the Hemis High Altitude Park, Ladakh. Far more impressive is the Marco Polo sheep (*Ovis ammon poli*), a subspecies found along the border regions of Pakistan and China. It is easily recognized by its very long (up to 75 inches) outward-spiraling horns.

Wild yak (*Bos grunniens*). The legendary yak or "grunting ox" is far rarer in the wild than in captivity. Apparently now only found in the most remote, uninhabited valleys of Tibet or the Chinghai area of China. Used to occur in the Changchenmo Valley of Ladakh's Rupshu region. Wild bulls may weigh twice as much as yaks seen in the Tibetan villages of the Himalaya. Probably migratory, wild yaks occur in herds of several dozen or more. Males may be solitary or form small "bachelor" herds. Female groups appear deceptively similar to unattended yaks belonging to Tibetan nomads and may be superficially identified by their obvious wariness of man. Domesticated yaks play a vital role as transport animals to people of Tibetan ancestry.

Birds

The Himalaya is an ornithological paradise, with at least 800 species. Depending upon whose tally one takes, this compares favorably with the 1,200 to 1,800 species found in the entire Indian subcontinent. The abundance of birdlife reflects the diversity of life zones and habitats, as well as the central position of the Himalaya between two major biogeographical zones: the Kali Gandaki River of Nepal is usually considered the dividing line between the eastern and western avifauna. Himalayan birdlife was virtually terra incognita until recently. When Nepal opened to outsiders in the early 1950s, several species new to science were discovered, and the habitat of the spiny babbler, a common bird, was finally determined.

Visitors from Europe and America may recognize a few species from home: the golden eagle and house wren, for example. However, the vast majority of species will be new, sporting such names as crested serpent eagle, large-necklaced laughing thrush, three-toed golden-backed woodpecker, satyr tragopan, hoary barwing, Tibetan twite, white-capped river chat, Hodgson's frogmouth, Mrs. Gould's sunbird, and Guldenstadt's redstart. Birds can be seen even at the highest elevations, and many migrate over the Himalaya. Mountaineers have encountered choughs at 27,000 feet, heard snipes flying over the highest peaks at night, marvelled at geese returning from their Tibetan breeding grounds, and found dead birds on windy cols.

With one of the recently published field guides and a pair of lightweight binoculars, novice and expert alike can look forward to many hours of exquisite birdwatching. If you are interested in numbers, you can expect to enumerate lists at least as long as those back home, even restricting yourself to narrow altitudinal ranges. For the serious ornithologist, spring and summer are the best times to visit the Himalaya because birds are in their breeding plumages and generally much more approachable. You can spend hours watching rose finches, accentors, pipits, and many others amid carpets of alpine wildflowers. However, a word of caution: because of late storms or the monsoon's arrival, it may be wet and, at high elevations, cold.

For those trekkers without benefit of binoculars or field guide, opportunities for observing and appreciating are still ample. Most will surely sight a lammergeier—the bearded vulture—as it glides low over Bhotia villages and across knife-edged ridges, or will flush an impeyan pheasant on its downhill race. A few of the birds you may see are very briefly described below according to their preferred habitat. This introduction obviously cannot mention more than a few, nor can the descriptions provided allow identification of any species with certainty. The emphasis here is on alerting you to birds that are widespread and of prominent size, color, or behavioral features.

Alpine Meadows and Slopes

Rose finches (*Carpodacus* spp.). Gregarious small birds with thick bills and notched tails that are among the most common breeders in alpine meadows. Many species; most brownish with crimson or reddish breasts in males.

Impeyan pheasant, or danphe (*Lophophorus impejanus*). A bird of nine iridescent colors. Invariably glides noisily downhill when disturbed. A heavy bird, the male is easily recognized by its white rump and tan tail. The female is a nondescript brown bird with a white rump. Found on steep grassy or rocky slopes or in winter fir forests.

Grandala (*Grandala coelicolor*). Unmistakable glistening blue robin of steep rocky slopes well above tree line.

Redstarts (*Phoenicurus* spp.). Robinlike birds with dark heads and chests and chestnut brown abdomens and tails.

Pipits (*Anthus* spp.) **and wagtails** (*Motacilla* spp.). Long-legged birds partial to grassy meadows. Pipits are heavily streaked, while wagtails have whitish or yellow breasts and constantly pump their tails.

Snow cocks. Giant partridges that escape by running uphill. Feed in groups and found as high as 18,000 feet. The Tibetan snow cock (*Tetraogallus tibetmanus*) is brownish with white underparts, while the Himalayan snow cock (*T. himalayensis*) is gray with rufous neck streaks and a chestnut chest band. Cannot be mistaken for the snow partridge (*Lerwa lerwa*), which is much smaller and barred gray and white.

Accentors (*Prunella* spp.). Sparrowlike ground-feeding birds with long square tails. They hop about. Many species; most gray or brownish, with dark face mask.

Streamside Habitats (above 8,000 feet)

White-capped river chat (*Chaimarrornis leucocephalus*). Black-and-maroon bird with white cap, seen skimming from rock to rock. Also pumps tail.

Plumbeous redstart (*Rhyacornis fuliginosus*). Tame, slaty blue bird that constantly moves its tail up and down. Female with conspicuous rump, male with rufous (reddish) tail.

Dippers (*Cinculus* spp.). Plump birds that feed by walking underwater. The white-breasted dipper (*C. cinculus*) has a white throat and breast. The brown dipper (*C. pallasii*) is all chocolate brown. Both bob up and down while standing on rocks.

Forktails (*Enicurus* spp.). Black-and-white birds with forked tails. The spotted forktail (*E. maculatus*) has a spotted back and a long tail that it lifts up and down slowly. The little forktail (*E. scouleri*) is a small bird seen moving amongst rocks in rushing streams.

Ibisbill (*Ibidorhyncha struthersii*). Large gray bird with prominent, decurved bill. Breeds in glaciated valleys. Bobs head and tail.

Oak and Conifer Forests

Blood pheasant (*Ithaginis cruentus*). Pheasant with coral red legs found east of Dhaulagiri. Quite tame near Tengboche Monastery, where flocks of several hundred are known to congregate in winter.

Tragopan pheasants (*Tragopan* spp.). Brilliant and very rare crimson pheasants with blue-and-black faces. Found in dense forests.

Great Himalayan barbet (*Megalaima virens*). Green, brown, and dark blue with large yellow bill and red beneath tail. Several may gather at a fruiting tree.

Himalayan jay (*Garrulus glandarius*). Medium-size gregarious bird that has a white rump obvious in flight. Lacks the dark crest of the blue-throated jay, which occurs in oak forests.

Yellow-billed blue magpie (*Cissa flavirostris*). Yellow bill and long blue tail distinguish this bird from its lowland cousin with a red bill.

Himalayan tree pie (*Dendrocitta formosae*). Noisy bird that feeds in scattered parties. Recognized by its dark gray body and white wing patch. The closely related nutcracker (*Nucifraga caryocatactes*) of pine and fir forests is a large dark bird that continuously flicks its tail, showing white patches.

Minivets (*Pericrocotus* spp.). Brightly colored (red, orange, or yellow) long-tailed birds seen feeding amid dense foliage.

Bulbuls. Robin-size birds that perch conspicuously on trees and shrubs. The red-vented bulbul (*Pycnonotus cafer*) is found at lower elevations, often in gardens. Note the red patch under its tail. The black bulbul (*Hypsipetes madagasciensis*) has a bright coral red bill and feeds in excited parties that keep up a constant chatter.

Laughing thrushes (*Garrulax* spp.). Noisy, myna-size birds; prefer areas of dense vegetation; form large feeding parties. Many species. The white-throated laughing thrush (*G. albogularis*) is olive brown with a large throat patch. The white-crested (*G. leucolophus*) has a "turban" and a brown eye streak. The white-spotted (*G. ocellatus*) is profusely spotted with white. The striated (*G. striatus*) is rich cinnamon with narrow white streaks and is usually found in shady ravines.

Black-capped sibia (*Heterophasia capistrata*). Common, light rufous bird with dark head and crest that is raised upon alarm. Jerks tail up and down and has a beautiful clear whistle.

Blue-headed rock thrush (*Monticola cinclorhynchus*). Usually found in pine forests and open shady places. The male is an outstanding cobalt blue and orange with a white wing patch evident in flight.

Mountain thrushes (*Loothera* spp.). Common inhabitant of fir forests and small forest glades. Brown or olive brown with heavily spotted breast and abdomen. Spends much time on the ground.

Whistling thrush (Myiophoneus caeruleus). Blue-black bird with bright yellow bill, often seen near rushing streams and deep cover. Song (consisting of sustained silvery notes at dawn) penetrates above sound of waterfall.

Coal tits (*Parus* spp.). Minute black birds with white cheek patches and dark crests.

Scarlet finch (*Haematospizma sipahi*). Male a brilliant scarlet with brown wings and tail; seen in heavy forest at low elevations.

Not mentioned are the cuckoos, flycatchers, warblers, leaf warblers, bush robins, nuthatches, woodpeckers, and creepers. Some are extremely numerous and so often sighted; many are difficult to identify without field guide and glasses; and others are simply inconspicuous.

Steppe of Ladakh and Pakistan

Lack of food and cover, in the way of ground plants, limits the diversity of birds able to exploit the windswept plains. Ground-nesting songbirds, many migratory and nondescript with brown or tawny plumages, dominate the avifauna.

Look for the Tibetan partridge (*Perdix hodgsoniae*) among *Caragana* shrubs (when disturbed it calls loudly, preferring to run uphill). In rocky ravines you are bound to see the chukor partridge (*Alectoris graeca*), a heavily barred gray-and-buff partridge with orange legs and bill. Its shrill call almost resembles its name. The Tibetan sandgrouse (*Syrrhaptes tibetanus*) congregates in small flocks and inhabits very stony country. If you are exceptionally lucky, you will see the black-necked crane (*Grus nigricollis*) during its migration to lake breeding grounds; it is now very scarce in western Tibet and Ladakh. The Tibetan owlet (*Athene noctua*) is also rare; it is recognized by its relatively long legs and boldly barred (streaked) and spotted body.

The dominant birds, however, are such songbirds as the short-toed lark (*Calandrella cinerea*), Hume's lark (*C. acuttirostris*), and the horned lark (*Eromophila alpestris*), a species familiar to North Americans. Larks have melodious songs, usually sung during impressive courtship flights, and they walk or run on the ground rather than hop. The skylarks (*Alauda* spp.) are masters of song in flight. There are many accentors (see above) and several species of snow finch (*Montifringilla*), a flocking songbird related to sparrows and difficult even for the experts to separate. The Tibetan twite (*Acanthis flavirostris*) is a finchlike pale brown bird that is both tame and able to survive in the bleakest of areas.

The hoopoe (*Upupa epops*), a widespread species of Africa, Asia, and Europe, is important to Tibetans, for its arrival signifies the onset of summer. It is unmistakable with its distinctive cinnamon coloration and fan-shaped black-tipped crest.

In addition you may see ducks, plovers, sandpipers, and snipe along the permanent rivers where vegetation or mudbars occur. Around villages look for the noisy pied magpie, a large black-and-white bird with a long green-gloss tail.

Other Common Species

These birds are likely to be found in a variety of habitats. Soaring birds you may see are the lammergeier, or bearded vulture (*Gypaetus barbatus*), with its 9-foot wingspan and long, wedge-shaped tail; the Himalayan griffin vulture (*Gyps himalayensis*); the golden eagle (*Aquila chrysaetos*), recognizable by its white wing patches and white at the base of the tail, which distinguishes it from the steppe eagle; and a variety of buteos or buzzards that have rounded wings and fan-shaped tails. In winter, gray or brown harriers (*Circus* spp.) can be seen hovering over open areas.

Fast-flying kestrels and other falcons literally streak by, while snow pigeons (*Columba leuconota*) wheel about in large flocks and feed in open fields like the common rock dove, from which they are unmistakably distinguished by their pale necks and abdomens. Near villages you will see ravens or crows, the common myna (*Acridotheres tristis*), house sparrows (*Passer domesticus*), and swifts. The raven (*Corvus corax*) is a large black crow with a distinctive, wedge-shaped tail and an unmistakable call: *gorak . . . gorak*. Crows (*Corvus* spp.) are small and lack the shaggy throat feathers of the raven. Choughs fly about in very large flocks; there are two species, the yellow-billed (*Pyrrhocorax graculus*) and the red-billed (*P. pyrrhocorax*).

Look as well for ducks, geese, and cranes flying over in spring and fall. High mountain lakes provide resting sites for waterfowl, though few species breed there.

Reptiles and Amphibians

Although some seventy species of reptiles and amphibians inhabit Nepal, only thirty of these are typically found in the mountains. Of these, less than a dozen are found above 8,000 or 9,000 feet. Amphibians, like frogs and toads, occur primarily in the tropical zone and the warmer, lower, temperate forest belts, although some live in hot springs at amazingly high altitudes. The number of species also declines as you move westward to the Karakoram. Salamanders are rare but were recently discovered in the forests of east Nepal. If you are observant, you may find the Himalayan rock lizard, the *Agama* (males have orange heads with bright blue throats), the long-legged *Japalura* lizard of brushy slopes, or the skink species *Leiolopisma ladacense*, which holds the record for being the highest lizard in the world, found at 18,000 feet.

Unless you visit the hot and humid lowlands or know where to look, you are unlikely to find any snakes in the Himalayan regions. Typical snakes include the rat snakes and racers, which are fast moving with large eyes, slender necks, and broad heads; water snakes, which are, indeed, partial to the aquatic environment; and the mountain pit vipers, which are uniformly dark with triangular heads. Most of the snakes are nonpoisonous. The cobra is occasionally encountered at low elevations. The only other venomous species are pit vipers; fortunately, they too are relatively rare and not often seen.

Although reptiles and amphibians have not been studied in Sikkim and Bhutan, it is likely that numerous species thrive in the favorable conditions found there.

A World in Transition:
The Future of Himalayan Wildlife

Alas, as remote as the Himalaya or the Karakoram may seem, you will be lucky to see much wildlife—unless you are trekking in one of the national parks or reserves that have been recently established. Throughout the Himalayan region the numbers of all large mammals have been greatly decimated and their populations fragmented as former habitat is converted to agriculture, forests felled, pastures grazed beyond their ability to sustain grass, and predators ruthlessly hunted because they had no choice but to take someone's sheep to survive. Other forces are at work altering the habitat or directly affecting the wildlife: for example, many species have suffered as a result of border wars and the presence of so many armed persons in formerly sparsely inhabited regions. As I write, India, Pakistan, and China are at relative peace with each other, but a protracted guerrilla war has massed weapons and refugees along the Afghanistan border with Pakistan.

Another problem is the way in which local people perceive the politics of conservation. While the numbers of tourists to the stupendous mountains of Nepal, Bhutan, India, Pakistan, and Tibet soar upward, few of the local inhabitants benefit from the influx of dollars, marks, or pounds—yet their freedom to graze their animals at will is increasingly restricted as authorities tackle the problem of too many livestock or pastures that receive too little rest from domestic sheep, goats, and cattle. With these conflicts and few tangible benefits, it is no wonder that so many local residents view a national park with apprehension or openly flout its regulations.

As tourism increases it is a tragedy that few will see a musk deer, a Himalayan tahr, or a kiang. This need not be the case. Thanks to recent efforts by conservationists, including a new cadre from Asia itself, we have the basic information to reverse the downward spiral. Now, politicians and the government need the commitment to follow through with innovative approaches to ensuring that man and wildlife can coexist to mutual benefit. It is imperative that the villagers participate in planning and management, that they benefit directly and significantly from the tourists who have come halfway around the world to see their sacred snow-clad peaks.

Despite their limited resources, countries like India and Pakistan have or are embarking on ambitious conservation programs. India, for example, has established a large number of high-altitude reserves for species like the snow leopard, while Pakistan is seeking to develop its Khunjerab National Park in concert with Taxkorgan Reserve on the Chinese side of the border. Those fortunate enough to see a Marco Polo sheep racing across the rolling hills, a diminutive musk deer daintily feeding on forest floor lichens, or massive Himalayan tahr standing calmly on a small cliff ledge, its coppery brown ruff catching the sinking sun, cannot fail to go home with memories to match the world's highest peaks. How high their feelings might soar if they could but glimpse a snow leopard! I am convinced these images need not be idle phantasy. Thanks to the efforts of many, wildlife is returning in the face of protective measures. And where there is prey, the mythical snow leopard may not be far behind. Your support of international and regional conservation organizations can make this possible. I urge you to let them know how or where you would like your donation spent. Let the people of the Himalaya know your interest in wildlife does not exclude providing for their basic needs. And visit national parks or reserves like Hemis and Dachigam in India, or the Khunjerab and Chitral Gol in Pakistan.

A man in Baltit, Hunza, spins wool using a drop spindle.

14

A Himalayan Medical Primer

by Peter H. Hackett, M.D.

Preparation

Discussions of Asian travel invariably turn to matters of health. The returning traveler is asked by the inexperienced, "Did you get sick?" and by more experienced friends, "How sick did *you* get?" Infectious diseases are the most feared, and are much more common in developing countries that do not yet have adequate sewer systems, immunizations, and a high standard of living. As a result, travelers frequently have minor illnesses, many of which are no longer found in developed countries. Other problems are related to the unique environment trekkers seek: high altitude, precipitous trails, glaciers, jungle, and desert. The chances of a traveler becoming seriously ill, however, are not great. Recent statistics gathered from 1984 to 1987 by David Shlim, medical director of the Himalayan Rescue Association, may be of some interest to those planning a trip. He calculated that the risk of dying while trekking was 14 per 100,000. Most deaths were from trauma (falling off trails). For comparison, the risk of dying in a car accident in North America each year is 24 per 100,000, and of being murdered in Miami, Los Angeles, or New York, 20 per 100,000.

Adventure travel in this fascinating area of the world should result in increased vitality and enrichment of life. Even persons with diabetes, high blood pressure, heart disease, and other problems have done quite well on treks in the Himalaya. Others who were perfectly well have suffered dire consequences because of pushing themselves when they shouldn't have and, in general, not anticipating what they were getting into. Proper preparation, simple precautions, knowledge of basic medical treatment, and a proper medical kit can effectively treat minor illnesses before they become serious.

More detailed sources on the subject of travel medicine and trip preparation include your physician; the U.S. Public Health Service Centers for Disease Control, Atlanta, Georgia; your local public health clinic; special travelers' medicine clinics, which are now appearing in most large cities in North America; and university medical centers. In such clinics you can obtain expert advice, any necessary immunizations, and updated information for each country. While it is impossible in this chapter to discuss all potential medical problems that may occur on a Himalayan trip, there are a number of useful medical books that are small enough to be taken along. Especially recommended are Wilkerson's *Medicine for Mountaineering*, Darvill's *Mountain Medicine*, Auerbach's *Medicine for the Outdoors*, and Hackett's *Mountain Sickness: Prevention, Recognition and Treatment*.

A routine physical exam before trekking is of minimal value for the healthy person. However, even minor, nagging kinds of problems—such as tendinitis, headache, recurrent sinusitis, cough, or unexplained aches and pains—should be evaluated because they could easily flare up in a remote environment where adequate diagnosis and treatment may not be available. If you are under a physician's care for a special medical problem, you should of course discuss your travel plans with your doctor. Most physicians are, understandably, not familiar with special Third World or altitude problems and may refer you to an immunization clinic or a colleague with special expertise. Or you may wish to offer your doctor excerpts from this chapter or other materials to assist in your preparation. Medications should be discussed with your physician and adequate supplies prescribed for the trip. It is also a good idea to carry a small card with your passport listing medications and dosages, allergies, and past medical problems and even containing a miniature version of an electrocardiogram (EKG) for those who have had previous cardiac problems. Such cards can be invaluable.

Some trekking companies recommend stress electrocardiograms for men over age forty and women over age fifty. Unfortunately, the stress EKG is notorious for false positive results in healthy people, which can lead to unnecessary, expensive, and sometimes risky further testing. The best indicator that your heart is able to take on the stress of a trek is that it can handle similar stress before you go. In other words, the best stress test is a hiking or backpacking trip over rugged terrain and into high-altitude areas. If you experience no difficulty with that back home, you are unlikely to have any difficulty with trekking in the Himalaya, even though the mountains are considerably higher. Exercise stresses the heart much more than altitude per se. A special caution to the sedentary individual who decides to take up trekking in mid- or late life: get in shape first.

A dental checkup is advisable. Dental problems may develop because of high altitude (air trapped in cavities expands), tooth trauma, or cracked fillings, and dental care is difficult to obtain and unreliable throughout most of these regions. I have had to send more than one trekker back to civilization because of tooth problems (they didn't want me to just yank out a tooth!).

Physical conditioning may or may not be important, depending on the type of trip envisioned. Plenty of sedentary folks are able to tolerate short, easy treks without any particular problem. It's important to choose a trek suited for your level of comfort and your level of conditioning. Most Himalayan treks, however, follow a course across steep ridges and valleys, and demand a high level of fitness. Proper physical conditioning makes trekking easier and much more enjoyable. Fit persons will be bothered less by minor illnesses, for example, whereas a trekker struggling into camp each day will have little reserve left to deal with illness. A conditioning program should be started months ahead of time and should consist primarily of walking. Walking up and down steep hills, not necessarily with loads, is best. Building-bound workers in the city can get in shape by running or walking up and down flights of stairs during lunch hour. Running is excellent for cardiovascular conditioning, as are cross country skiing, swimming, and other aerobic activities. Being able to run a mile in under ten minutes is probably evidence of adequate cardiovascular conditioning for a trek. However, the principle of specificity applies to trekking as it does to any other sport: there are specific muscles and joints used for trekking, and the more these can be conditioned prior to the trip, the more effective the training. There is no specific training for altitude. Persons living at high altitude have the advantage of partial acclimatization. Aerobic fitness is important but will not lessen the time necessary for acclimatization and does not protect against altitude illness.

Every trekker should carry a small medical kit. You should discuss your particular needs with your physician. A list of recommended items for the kit is included at the end of this chapter. Contents will vary depending upon your medical sophistication, whether there's a trip physician, the number in the party, length of the trip, and availability of local services.

If possible, identify health facilities in your region of travel beforehand, as well as telegraph offices, radios for sending emergency messages, and airstrips. If you are not trekking with a local tour outfitter or agent, it is wise to register with your country's local consulate. Most Westerners working in remote regions of Nepal and India, for example, will leave emergency contacts with the American consulate, and many will leave a deposit in case a helicopter or some sort of evacuation is needed.

All trekkers, particularly those who go with groups, should consider insurance coverage. Some of the newer policies include trip cancellation insurance, default protection, supplemental collision damage waivers, and emergency medical expenses. Default protection reimburses you should a tour operator default. Trip cancellation insurance reimburses you for cancellation penalties or extra cost incurred if you must change your plans before or during a trip because of circumstances beyond your control, including illness. Any sickness qualifies that prevents you from traveling and that your doctor is willing to certify. Some emergency medical policies are reimbursement plans, which means that you still have to pay up front, while some companies provide direct payments to foreign hospitals and doctors. Excellent coverage can be obtained for $3 to $5 a day per person, or sometimes even less. Baggage insurance, helicopter evacuation, trip cancellation insurance, and medical insurance are sometimes all provided by one policy for a slightly greater cost. Always inquire whether a policy will cover emergency transportation, such as a helicopter. Determine whether your current health insurance covers foreign travel and emergency evacuations. (For more on the vagaries of helicopter evacuation, see "Rescue," below.)

Immunizations

Immunizations offer an easy and effective way to avoid some of the major illnesses associated with international travel. You need to discuss with your doctor or a travelers' clinic the particular immunizations you will need. The following is a guide to the most important ones:

Cholera. The risk of cholera is very low. The vaccines are not very effective, and vaccination is not recommended for tourists. Some countries, however, do require a booster within six months of entry for travelers arriving from infected areas. These countries are listed by the U.S. Public Health Service.

Diptheria-tetanus. Your immunization should be current (a booster shot within the last ten years).

Gamma globulin. Immune serum globulin (ISG, gamma globulin) is unquestionably effective and necessary for travel in this part of the world. The dose is 2 milliliters (ml) intramuscularly for a trip of three months or less and 5 ml every four months for longer trips. ISG prevents hepatitis A, which is endemic throughout all of central Asia, and also has some effects against tetanus, rabies, and measles. Persons with a previous history of hepatitis A are immune for life and do not require this immunization. Gamma globulin is not a vaccine. It provides passive immunity because it provides antibodies from another person's blood. A recent conference of the World Health Organization established that there has not been a case of AIDS in over 20 million doses of gamma globulin and that no chance of contracting the AIDS virus exists with this immunization. Hepatitis B vaccine is not ordinarily recommended for travelers, except for medical personnel whose work requires handling body fluids or those who expect to have sexual contacts in areas where hepatitis B is highly endemic, such as Southeast Asia.

Influenza and pneumococcal pneumonia. Two vaccines commonly overlooked by public health authorities and travelers' clinics are influenza vaccine and pneumococcal vaccine. Both are very effective with minimal side effects and should be considered by every traveler. Influenza and pneumococcal pneumonia are found throughout the world. All persons with chronic lung disease, diabetes, splenectomy, or over sixty-five years of age should receive a once-a-lifetime Pneumovax for prevention of pneumococcal pneumonia and a yearly influenza shot at the start of the flu season, usually in October. Travelers should probably have these vaccinations as well.

Measles. Anyone born after 1956 who did not receive measles vaccine after age one and does not have a documented history of infection should receive a single dose of vaccine before traveling.

Meningococcus. Because of a meningococcal epidemic in Nepal in 1984, the U.S. Public Health Service has been recommending the vaccine. The epidemic seems to be over in 1989. However, you should seek the current advice of the Public Health Service.

Polio. All travelers who have previously completed a primary series should receive a booster dose of oral polio vaccine or inactivated polio vaccine.

Rabies. The rabies vaccine is recommended only for those anticipating contact with animals that may have rabies or prolonged residence where rabies is a constant threat, such as in Nepal or India. The current vaccine is presently much easier, more comfortable, and more efficient than previous vaccines but not necessary for the general trekker.

Typhoid. Typhoid vaccine is recommended for all travelers to this part of the world, although it is not fully protective. The vaccine often causes one or two days of pain at the injection site, sometimes accompanied by fever, headache, and general malaise.

Yellow fever. Vaccination is not necessary for this part of the world.

Many of these immunizations can be given together. A measles shot has to be given two weeks before a gamma globulin shot, which is given one to two weeks before departure. Pregnant women should not receive any type of live virus (measles, trivalent polio). Cholera and typhoid vaccines are also best avoided during pregnancy, especially in the first trimester. Vaccines that pose no problems during pregnancy or breast feeding include gamma globulin, hepatitis B, rabies, diptheria, tetanus, and oral chloroquine (see "Prevention of Malaria," below).

Most experts recommend a stool examination upon return from, or just before leaving, Asia (it's much cheaper in Asia). Even if you have no symptoms, you may have acquired worms or parasites. Also recommended is a tuberculosis skin test prior to departure and a repeat after return if the initial test result was negative.

Although international health certificates are no longer required throughout most of the world, they do provide documentation for those few places where they may be mandatory and also provide a useful place for recording your immunizations.

Prevention of Malaria

Malaria is a particular problem in the lower-altitude areas of South and Southeast Asia. Since recommendations change with changing resistance in strains of malaria, you should obtain updated information just prior to travel. There is little danger of contracting malaria in Himalayan treks, since the anopheles mosquito penetrates Himalayan river valleys only to an altitude of about 3,000 feet. However, the traveler may be entering the Himalaya through malarial areas, such as the terai of Nepal, or India, Thailand, or Burma. Travel through any malaria-infested area generally requires preventive medication—for adults, usually 500 milligrams (mg) of chloroquine phosphate (one tablet) beginning one week before entering and continuing six weeks after leaving the risk area. If you are traveling in rural Thailand or Burma, you may be advised by your physician to take chloroquine plus fansidar or, alternatively, 100 mg of doxycycline once a day during exposure, since strains totally resistant to chloroquine and 80 percent resistant to fansidar have now emerged in these countries. Probably more important than medication for prevention of malaria is applying mosquito repellent when in malarious areas, using mosquito netting during sleep, and wearing long pants and sleeves when out at dusk, the time of day when the anopheles mosquito feeds.

On Trek

Diarrhea

Although usually not more than nuisance, diarrhea does affect a large number of travelers and can be especially serious in children; the smaller the child, the more quickly dehydration develops. Dehydration due to diarrhea is still the major cause of death in Asian children.

The reason infectious diarrhea is so common in Asian countries is the lack of sewer systems. The same diarrheas were prevalent in the United States and Europe a hundred years ago. Developed countries now efficiently dispose of feces, separate wastes (sewage) from the drinking supply, and disinfect tap water. These precautions have not yet become the rule throughout much of Asia and, as a result, intestinal illness transmitted by the fecal-oral route is quite common. Fecal contamination is found in the soil, raw food, on flies, on the hands of some food servers, and in the water, to mention a few places.

Diarrhea is generally not a serious illness, and "diarrhea neurosis" can ruin a trip because of excessive worry. A few sensible precautions in disinfecting water, avoiding contaminated food and beverages, and maintaining personal hygiene, will help prevent diarrhea, or at least "cut the losses."

Water Disinfection

All water in the "turd" world is suspect and requires disinfection. Even tap water in places like Rawalpindi or New Delhi should not be trusted, although tap water is apparently good in Thailand. Simple disinfection techniques include the following:

Heat. The often-repeated recommendation of boiling water for five to ten minutes at sea level is only for complete sterilization and is unnecessary for disinfection. Giardia and amoeba cysts (parasites) both are killed in two to three minutes at 140°F; intestinal viruses are killed within seconds at 176° to 212°F; and intestinal bacteria are killed within seconds at 212°F (the boiling point of water at sea level). The higher the temperature, the less time required for disinfection. Bringing water to a boil is adequate for disinfection of all intestinal-disease-causing organisms. Although boiling point decreases with increasing altitude—the boiling point of water at 14,000 feet is 187°F; at 19,000 feet it's 178°F—these temperatures are still adequate for disinfection. The problem with using heat is fuel consumption and time: a pressure cooker saves both at any elevation.

Filtration and clarification. Water-filtering devices are limited in their efficacy by the size of their pores, which must be small enough to catch all infectious particles. Parasitic eggs and larvae and giardia and amoeba cysts are large enough to be caught in a filter, but it is very difficult for bacteria and nearly impossible for viruses, which are only 0.1 microns in size, to be caught. Filtering does remove particulate debris, however, thereby allowing a lower dose of disinfecting agents, and does improve the appearance and taste of "dirty" water, but filters clog quickly if water is dirty or has a lot of suspended particles. The appearance of water can also be improved by sedimentation—that is, by allowing large particles to settle out over a period of several hours.

Charcoal resins are commonly incorporated into multiple-layered filters to improve the color, taste, and smell of water after chemical disinfection. However, charcoal does not remove microorganisms and is therefore not itself a disinfectant.

Recommended water disinfection devices (effective for all except viruses) are Katadyne Pocket Filter, First-Need Purifier, and Water Tech Water Purifier.

Chemical disinfecting agents. Chlorine and iodine are the most commonly used disinfecting agents. Both effectively kill bacteria and viruses and giardia and amoeba cysts. The rate and percent of organism death depends on the concentration of the disinfecting agent and the exposure time.

$$organism\ death = contact\ time \times concentration\ of\ agent$$

Since "death" is a constant, doubling the contact time will allow half the amount of disinfecting agent to be used. For example, if sixteen drops of iodine solution are needed to disinfect a quart of water in thirty minutes, eight drops will disinfect in one hour, and only four drops are needed to disinfect the water in two hours. (Four drops are probably about the lowest amount of iodine that can be used to disinfect a quart of water.) In very cold water or if there is organic matter in the water, the dose needs to increase (chlorine and iodine are absorbed and therefore become less active in cloudy or polluted water). Taste can be improved by adding drink flavoring *after* adequate contact time or by pouring the water through a charcoal resin after disinfection. *Note:* The potency of some tablet and crystal forms of iodine and chlorine is affected by heat and moisture. Tablets deteriorate within a few months after the bottle is opened.

Chlorine is used in all municipal water systems and is very effective, even for giardia. For water disinfection, chlorine can be used in the form of Halazone tablets or liquid bleach.

Iodine has some advantages over chlorine since iodine is less affected by debris in the water. It is effective in low concentrations if there is adequate contact time, and the taste is better at these low levels than is the taste of chlorine. Iodine is quite safe but should not be used by people with unstable thyroid disease or iodine allergy, or during pregnancy.

Iodine in tablet form is easiest to use while trekking, but tablets come in only one strength (8 mg). Iodine in solution form—for example, the povidone-iodine preparation Betadine—is very handy since it can double as a disinfectant for wounds. Iodine crystals are also commonly used to produce a saturated solution. My own experience is that iodine solutions invariably leak in luggage—pack them with great care! I personally prefer Betadine since it's an essential ingredient of the first aid kit as well.

The accompanying table gives dosages and contact times for the various forms of chlorine and iodine. Become familiar with one system and use it regularly.

Food and Beverage Contamination

Contamination of food products is common. The motto for Third World travelers is "Cook it, peel it, boil it, or forget it." Foods freshly cooked that are still warm and have not had time to be contaminated by flies, etc., are perfectly safe. Fruits that can be peeled are safe, as is anything that can be boiled. Yogurt, one of the tastiest foods in Asia, is a

Water Disinfection by Chemical Agents

Agent	Form		Concentration/time per quart water
Chlorine	tablet	p-dichlorosulfamoyl benzoic acid (Halazone)	5 tabs/10 min. (1 tab/glass of water) or 2.5 tabs/30 min.
	solution	sodium hypochloride (bleach) 1% 4%–6%	10 drops/30 min. 2 drops/30 min.
Iodine	tablet	tetraglycine hydroperiodide (EDWGT, Potable Aqua, Globaline)	1 tab/10 min.
	solution	10% povidone-iodine (Betadine)	8 drops/15 min. or 4 drops/30 min.

Information courtesy of Howard Backer, M.D.

Note: If water is cold (less than 60° F) or cloudy, double the dose or the contact time. If both cold and cloudy, double both the dose and the contact time.

pure culture of lactobacillus and is therefore generally safe unless it has been exposed to flies; in that case the top layer can be scraped off. Bottled soda drinks and beer are considered safe because of the carbonation. (Carbonation makes the pH too acid for infectious organisms, plus carbon dioxide itself kills some organisms.) Milk is safest if pasteurized or scalded. It is not necessary to actually boil it. A particular problem is home-brewed liquor. Rakshi, as it is called in Nepali (arak in Sherpa or Tibetan), is a distilled product and generally safe. Chang (Tibetan beer) is a problem since it is prepared by pouring untreated water through fermented rice, barley, or corn mash. Although chang may be unsafe, it is often unavoidable because of its role in local custom, and you might be considered rude to refuse it. Many times I have gulped down chang with a little mantra chanted to ward off illness.

Another source of contamination can be recreational drugs. I met one trekker who had bought some local hashish on a trek and decided to eat it rather than smoke it, to save the wear and tear on his lungs. It didn't take long after his eating the hashish to make a presumptive diagnosis of severe bacterial diarrhea. When I looked at the hash, it was obvious that it must have been 50 percent cow dung!

Hygiene on organized treks with reputable trekking companies is quite good. The staff usually provide boiled water so that chemical disinfection is unnecessary, and precautions in preparing food are adequate. Washing your own hands after bowel movements is important in limiting disease as well. All toilet paper should be burned or buried, both for hygiene and to avoid the visual pollution. It is a good sign to see all the kitchen help in camp washing their hands frequently. All in all, one has to use a moderate ration of common sense. Persons concerned to the point of wanting to wear disposable rubber gloves, disinfect all eating utensils before eating, and being afraid to shake hands with friendly residents, touch children, etc., are probably better off staying at home in their more secure environment. Be sensible, relax, and enjoy your trek.

Treatment of Diarrhea

Despite adequate preventive measures, diarrhea may still occur. Diarrhea is defined as a change in frequency and liquidity of stools. Dynsentary is diarrhea that is associated with abdominal pain, straining at stool, and blood and mucous in the stool. Fever may be present with either. In cities, stool tests may be easily available and cheap, and establishing the exact diagnosis and subsequent exact treatment is worthwhile. In the field setting, however, determining the cause of diarrhea is difficult. In any case, it is generally safe to wait one to two days after the onset of any diarrheal illness to see if it resolves quickly and spontaneously.

While waiting twenty-four to forty-eight hours to see if the diarrhea stops, you can take a number of measures to help limit the unpleasant effects. First of all, since diarrhea generally means increased fluid loss, it is important to increase fluid intake: with voluminous stools, liters of fluid may be necessary to avoid dehydration. Water is mostly what is needed, but if the diarrhea is severe, electrolyte solutions (containing sodium, potassium, chloride, and bicarbonate) and sugar also become important. Throughout Asia, rehydration packets provided by the World Health Organization are available. In Nepal the product is called Jeevan Jal, which is an electrolyte solution made by mixing one packet in a liter of treated water. Rehydration is particularly important for children, who can very quickly get dehydrated.

Agents that slow the intestines—such as tincture of opium, deodorized tincture of opium (paregoric), diphenyxolate (Lomotil), or loperamide (Immodium)—help reduce fluid loss as well as reduce the frequency of stools and cramps. The correct dosage of Lomotil is two tablets after each loose bowel movement, and no more than ten tablets in twenty-four hours. Also effective is Pepto-Bismol, a nonprescription product in liquid or tablet form that works by an unknown mechanism. Two tablets can be taken four times a day. Pepto-Bismol contains an aspirinlike product and therefore should be used with caution by people already on aspirin or who have problems with aspirin. Kaopectate and other kaolin or pectin products are useless in treating diarrhea.

If the diarrhea is not resolving or if it is particularly severe, especially with a high fever, it's worthwhile to attempt a more definitive treatment based on some guess as to the cause of the illness. In Nepal, diarrhea-causing agents include, in order of frequency, bacteria (shigella, salmonella, and campylobactor), parasites (including giardia and amoeba), viruses (enterovirus, reovirus, and others), and worms (unusual). Unfortunately, there is little correlation between symptoms—such as blood and mucous in the stool, foul-smelling burps and gas, the color of the stool, or other easily identifiable factors—and the pathogen. Therefore, field treatment is usually blind. A good initial treatment that will cover all bacterial diarrheas (the majority of diarrheas) is the new drug ciprofloxacin, known by the trade name Cipro in the United States. One 500 mg tablet taken twice a day for five days is very effective and acts quickly. Another useful antibiotic is trimethoprim/sulfamethoxazole (Septra DS or Bactrim DS), also taken twice a day for five days. This is a sulfa drug and must be avoided by people allergic to sulfa. So many of the bacterial diarrheas are now resistant to ampicillin, amoxicillin, or tetracycline that these drugs are now unreliable.

The use of antibiotics for prevention of diarrhea is controversial and is generally not recommended by experts. Liberal use of antibiotics in this manner produces more organisms resistant to the drugs, which is an increasing problem all over the world with these bacterial diarrheas. Since the treatment is relatively simple and effective, antibiotics probably should be reserved for actual diarrheal illness treatment, not used for prevention. Pepto-Bismol is a wiser choice for prevention, since it is not an antibiotic and does not induce resistance.

If diarrhea does not respond to the antibiotic within two to three days, the cause is more likely a parasite or a virus. There is no specific treatment for viral diarrhea; the body sheds itself of viral illnesses within a week or so, and the treatment is directed to decreasing cramps and fluid loss. The two most common parasites in central Asia are giardia and amoeba, both of which are treated with a drug called tinidazole. This drug is not available in North America yet, but it is readily available in Asia; in Nepal and India it is sold as Tiniba. The dosage for giardiasis is a single, one-time dose of 2 grams (gm); for amoebiasis the dosage is 2 gm per day for three days.

Sulfurous burps and foul-smelling gas are often ascribed to giardiasis, but these are actually relatively nonspecific symptoms. Giardiasis takes two weeks to incubate and develop, whereas bacterial infections develop much more quickly. Therefore, if you've been in Asia for only a short time—i.e., less than two weeks—your diarrhea is more likely to be bacterial or viral rather than giardia. If after treatment with an antibiotic and an antiparasitic agent there is still diarrhea, especially associated with upper abdominal pain, worms should be considered, although they are not as common a cause of diarrhea as the others. However, worms can be treated rather easily with mebendazole, in the dosage of one tablet (100 mg) twice a day for three days.

Diarrhea may also be due to food poisoning. If a toxin that has been produced in a food substance is ingested (common where there is no refrigeration), it may cause immediate vomiting and diarrhea. More than once, unfortunately, I have been at dinner with a friend who quite suddenly became pale (with a greenish tint) and immediately vomited, sometimes on the table. This kind of acute explosive illness, often occurring in the first day or two in Asia, is food poisoning caused by a toxin. Fortunately, it usually lasts only a few hours, but sometimes it can continue up to twelve hours. Usually by the time a person is strong enough to seek help, he or she is already starting to get better. The fluid losses, however, can leave people weak for a few days.

Trekkers with severe abdominal pain and tenderness when the abdomen is pressed upon, especially without diarrhea, should be evacuated to the nearest hospital for evaluation for appendicitis or other potential surgical conditions.

There are other approaches to diarrhea in this part of the world: shamans treat by appeasing evil spirits, and many village health care workers treat with herbal remedies, some of which appear to be very effective. Once on a BBC yeti hunt, of which I was a deputy leader, we ran into a crisis when the cameraman was unable to go on because of severe diarrhea. I had treated him with antibiotics and antiparasitic agents, yet he continued to become weaker and weaker and finally was not able to move. As a result, we had to halt the entire expedition (at great cost) and wait for his recovery. A village health worker came over to our camp and asked to see the doctor. He asked me if I had any of the new American ulcer medicines, since he had a stomach ulcer and was always interested in new ulcer treatments. I was glad to share some of my medication, and then I asked him for a consult on the cameraman. He examined our prostrate comrade and asked for a stool sample, which was not hard to obtain. A quick look at the stool in a tin can, and he made an immediate diagnosis. He then administered a series of herbal medications and also prescribed alternating hot and cold compresses to the abdomen (which, of course, I thought were useless). He told us that within twenty-four hours all diarrhea would stop and that within forty-eight hours the victim would be strong enough to go on. Sure enough, the diarrhea stopped within twenty-four hours, and in forty-eight hours the cameraman had a remarkable recoup of his strength. Ever since then, I have had more respect for herbal remedies and have used them more often myself.

Another time, in the upper Arun Valley, for the purposes of a movie, a shaman went into a trance directed toward my diarrheal illness. After his trancelike state, he diagnosed my diarrhea as being from fear I had experienced earlier that day when crossing a particularly bad bridge made of willow strands. He said that it would be gone the next day. Well, my diarrhea was gone the next day, and I still have no idea if that was the real cause or not.

Respiratory Infections

The common cold is called common for a reason. It's likely that trekkers will pick up local viruses. The combination of jet lag, new environment, thermal extremes, dust and other particulate matter, and suppressed immunity because of high altitude and ultraviolet light can result in frequent upper respiratory infections. These are best treated, if necessary, with decongestants, such as pseudoephedrine (Sudafed), and aspirin or acetaminophen for pain and fever. With fever and facial pain indicating sinusitis, an antibiotic should be administered. Bronchitis that produces green or yellow sputum associated with fever should also be treated with an antibiotic, especially at high altitudes, since it may predispose to high-altitude illness. Sore throats are best treated with hard candies and throat lozenges to keep the throat moist and aspirin, acetaminophen, or ibuprofen for pain. At high altitude, always be aware of the possibility of pulmonary edema in yourself or others with any kind of cough or chest complaint (see "High Altitude Pulmonary Edema," below).

Headaches are common at high altitude but if associated with fever or a stiff neck, they must be taken very seriously because of possible meningitis. Rather uncomfortable muscle aches and pains associated with a bad headache and a high fever that goes on for days and days may very well be typhoid fever, which has been on the increase in Nepal. It tends to have a course of more than one week and can cause progressive, prostrating illness; it may or may not be associated with diarrhea. Anyone with muscle aches and pains, fever, headache, and shaking, bone-rattling chills away from medical care should be treated for typhoid fever. The drugs currently used are chloramphenicol or ampicillin in a dose of 500 mg four times a day.

Snow Blindness

Snow blindness is a burn of the cornea caused by excessive exposure to ultraviolet (UV) light. It is entirely preventable by wearing adequate glasses or goggles that filter 90 percent of UV-B radiation and reduce exposure from the sides also. UV light penetration increases by 5 percent for every 1000-foot gain of altitude, so there is 75 percent more ultraviolet penetration at 15,000 feet then there is at sea level. Reflection of this much UV light off snow or water can produce a burn in only two hours. Even on cloudy days, exposure is adequate for damage. Snow blindness is extremely painful and can last forty-eight hours or longer. Porters, who usually don't have adequate goggles, are the most likely victims. Makeshift goggles can be improvised by taping a piece of cardboard over the eyes, with small horizontal slits through which the porter can see but which will also block most of the UV reflection. If preventive measures are inadequate and snow blindness occurs, the eyes need to be patched to prevent the extreme irritation caused by the eyelids moving across the injured cornea. Cold compresses should also be applied and pain pills given. Earlier generations of climbers used drops of mineral oil under the eyelids to provide some increased lubrication across the cornea. Antibiotic eyedrops or antibiotic ophthalmic ointment can be applied for the same purpose and also prevents infection.

Women's Health Concerns

Gynecologic problems need to be anticipated. Some women are particularly prone to yeast infections, especially during antibiotic use, and should carry appropriate medications, since antibiotics may have to be taken for diarrhea or some other cause.

Irregular menstrual periods are common when changing multiple time zones, exercising strenuously, and going to high altitude. This should not be a concern unless there is any chance of pregnancy. The first period after missing a few may be abnormally heavy. Note that tampons and pads are not available in the hill areas.

Some authors have irresponsibly written that birth control pills should be discontinued at high altitude. Studies that I conducted in Nepal found no increased incidence of altitude problems or any other problems in women trekkers on birth control pills. It may be wise for women expeditioners who will be at 18,000 feet or above for months at a time to discontinue the pill because of the slight increased risk of vascular problems. For everyone else it is best to stay on the pill.

Little information is available about the effects of short-term high-altitude exposure during pregnancy. Conservative advice is to limit exposures to less than 15,000 feet, for periods of only a few weeks, and to take extra time to acclimatize. Pregnant trekkers need to realize the consequences of having a complication far from medical care and transportation.

Trauma

It is impossible in the space of this chapter to cover diagnosis and management of trauma in the back country. Suffice it to say that falling off the trail is the most common cause of death, injury, and helicopter evacuation in Nepal. Concentrate on walking when walking, and scenic viewing when resting or stopping. Every trekker should have sterile bandages, adhesive tape, wraparound gauze, safety pins, and elastic bandages for treatment of common injuries (see "Medical Kit for Himalayan Trekking," below).

Wounds

Most wounds can be treated adequately on trek. Extensive facial injuries that might cause a cosmetic problem, open fractures, or penetrating wounds of the abdomen, chest, or head call for evacuation to a hospital. The most important principle in the treatment of wounds is adequate cleansing and disinfection anytime the skin is broken. Small wounds can be cleaned by scrubbing with iodine solutions. After the wound has been thoroughly cleansed, it should be covered with an antibiotic ointment and bandaged; the bandage should be left in place for a long time to maintain the initial cleanliness. Larger wounds that cause gaping of the skin need to be thoroughly cleansed by irrigation with disinfected water; at least a liter should be irrigated into the wound to wash out any debris and to kill bacteria. Gaping wounds can then be taped shut and carefully bandaged. Wounds that are very extensive, going down to the bone or across tendons, or wounds that are difficult to clean properly need antibiotics as well. Penicillin, erythromycin, or cephalosporins can be administered in dosages of 250 mg four times a day for five days. Likewise, wounds not initially needing antibiotics but which later become infected should also be treated with antibiotics four times a day for five days.

Animal bites are a particular problem in central Asia because of the danger of rabies. Rabies is not carried by rodents, such as rabbits, squirrels, mice, rats, and picas. Dogs, bats, wolves, monkeys, and foxes are the common rabies carriers. All animal bite wounds first need to be treated like any wound with thorough cleansing and bandaging. The following measures must then be taken if rabies is a consideration. First, if at all possible, the animal must be captured and watched for ten days (good luck!). If there is no sign of illness in the animal in ten days, there is no danger of rabies. If it is not possible to catch the animal and observe it, the conservative measure is to proceed to the nearest urban center where rabies vaccine is available. The postexposure treatment involves five injections of HDCV (human diploid cell vaccine) over a period of one month, plus a one-time injection of rabies antibodies (rabies immunoglobulin, RIG). This injection is given as soon as possible to provide some protection while the body is making antibodies in response to the vaccine. This postexposure treatment in Kathmandu, for instance, costs more than $500. If you have had a preexposure immunization series of three injections for prophylaxis, you still must have the postexposure treatment, but only an additional two shots. These treatments can be very difficult to obtain in Asia.

The rabies problem is a particularly troublesome one. Prevention is obviously the best solution. When faced with a growling dog, pick up a rock or just pretend to pick up a rock, and the dog will usually run away with its tail between its legs. Walking sticks and umbrellas are also handy.

The Nitty-Gritty: Lice, Fleas, Bedbugs, and Scabies

In addition to gut trouble, picking up unwanted passengers on your body or in your clothes is one of the undesirable but possible events connected with trekking. Maybe you'll get them; probably you won't. You may be exposed to these little critters from contact with people, animals, or places where the parasites have already found a home. You're more likely (but it's far from inevitable) to become infested if you sleep in people's homes or remain near animals (as many people with dogs or cats for pets already know). Other than the "ugh" factor and temporary itchiness, the worst aspect of these insects is that they can spread disease. Protecting yourself from parasites is one very good reason for sleeping in your own tent.

Lice are small, oblong, shiny white insects that move very sluggishly and are usually found in the seams of your clothing (unless they are head lice found in your body hair). They are fairly subtle when they bite, and at first you may be tempted to think you merely need a bath, but you can see a small temporary welt after they have bitten you, and you can see the lice. Fleas are small, dark brown insects that move by leaping great distances at a single bound. Their bite can be painful and may itch for up to a week. Bedbugs are relatively larger, up to ¼ inch in length; you can definitely feel them when they move (in bed at night), and they can move rather rapidly. They live in cracks in furniture or the walls, and like fleas, they may want to take up residence in your sleeping bag or sleeping sheet. If you've been bitten by a bedbug or flea, you'll know it. Scabies, caused by tiny mites that burrow under the skin, produces intense itching; the mites are too small to be seen.

Temporarily dropping our good Buddhist strictures against the taking of life, how do we get rid of these unwanted guests? You can kill lice between your thumbnails. The tricky part is doing the same thing to their shiny eggs (nits), which are very tiny and may be numerous, but which are visible only in good light. Both lice and nits expire with a satisfying *pop*. A good way to get rid of lice, fleas, or bedbugs is to do as the locals do: shake and air out in the sun your bedclothes (in your case, your sleeping sheet and bag). All three of these pests hate sunlight. Washing your clothing also helps but does not usually get rid of lice. And be sure to keep yourself clean, too.

You can also get lethal bug powder in Asia and *carefully* dust your garments. Bug powders in Asia contain ingredients that are long gone from such preparations at home, so wash your hands after using. Malathion is generally considered safe (compared to DDT, for example). Body lice and the mites that cause scabies can be killed by using Kwell, Gamene, or Gammexane, which are 1% solutions of gamma benzene hexachloride (also known as lindane 1%) and come as cream, lotion, or shampoo. Gamma benzene hexachloride (lindane) is toxic and should not be applied to the face or open wounds. Follow directions carefully when using. One dose should kill head lice or scabies mites, but if not, wait a week for the second application. Itching may continue for days, even after all the parasites are killed. Nits should be combed out of hair after treatment. Kwell can be purchased only by prescription in the West. In Asia, however, as with all drugs, you can readily purchase the generic formula at pharmacies. Other drugs effective for lice (but not scabies) are 1% permethrin (Nix) and pyrethrins with piperonyl butoxide (Rid, XXX, and others).

Altitude Problems

There are a few medical conditions that preclude traveling to high altitude: these are pulmonary hypertension, moderate to severe chronic lung disease, unstable angina, unstable cardiac arrhythmias, cerebrovascular malformations, sickle cell anemia, congestive heart failure, and high-risk pregnancies. Persons with well-controlled blood pressure and heart problems and normal pregnancies seem to do just fine at high altitude but must exercise some caution. For all trekkers, not just those with medical problems, I seriously recommend a trial of high-altitude exposure before traveling to high areas on expensive and time-consuming trips. For example, you can sleep at 10,000 to 12,000 feet in the Rocky Mountains and the Sierra Nevada in North America or the volcanoes in Mexico and South America, or camp out near the tops of some European peaks. A person's response to high altitude (given the same rate of ascent) is generally predictable from one time to the next. So if you do well sleeping at 12,000 feet in North America, you will probably do well at that altitude in Asia. Doing well at 12,000 feet will make it easier to acclimatize to higher altitudes, and you should have little trouble.

As the Himalayan Rescue Association likes to point out, "The Himalaya starts where other mountains leave off." Too few trekkers seem to realize that it is the sleeping altitude that makes the critical difference in terms of the hypoxic (lack of oxygen) stress. In Tibet the *lowest* sleeping altitudes are generally 13,000 to 14,000 feet—the same as many summits in North America and Europe. For this reason the Himalaya deserves much more respect and much more knowledge of prevention and treatment of altitude illness. Recent studies have shown that approximately 30 to 40 percent of all trekkers in the Mt. Everest area develop some degree of altitude illness, with about one-third of this group becoming sick enough to change plans and not reach their destination. About 10 percent of this sick group develop life-threatening illnesses that require evacuation and/or medical attention. Only prior experience at these altitudes may help predict how your body is going to react. The three factors that determine whether you acclimatize well or become ill are (1) the altitude, (2) the rate of ascent to that altitude, and (3) your individual susceptibility to altitude illness. Men and women are equally susceptible to acute mountain sickness, and children may be somewhat more susceptible. Older folks seem to do just fine. What is hard for young, fit persons to understand is that superior physical conditioning grants absolutely no protection from altitude illness.

Prevention of Altitude Illness

The surest way of preventing altitude illness is by allowing the body adequate time to acclimatize. Avoid flying directly to altitudes over 9000 feet unless you can allow three or four days to adjust to the altitude before proceeding higher. For any mode of ascent, it is best to spend three or four days between 10,000 and 12,000 feet, acclimatizing until you feel stronger and less breathless; you should do the same between 14,000 and 15,000 feet, and again between 17,000 and 18,000 feet. Above these altitudes, it is best to get up and down as quickly as possible since the body's ability to acclimatize within the short period of time that most trekkers are exposed is limited.

Responsible trek leaders and guides will gear the rate of ascent to the people who acclimatize slowly. Everyone's physiology is different, and there is nothing to be ashamed of if you acclimatize more slowly than others. Some of the greatest mountain climbers in the world are poor acclimatizers but are able to make it up the peaks because they spend the necessary time acclimatizing before going for the summit. Other leaders and guides have no idea of the acclimatization process and consider performance at altitude a matter of strength or weakness rather than acclimatization. Unfortunately, this attitude is still too common. Acclimatization makes all the difference in the world. This is one reason I like to call altitude the great equalizer. Persons who are out of shape and not very athletic at sea level may acclimatize well and surpass marathon runners who are too incapacitated to move on the trail. Once the initial period of acclimatization is over, of course, the marathon runner will be superior in performance. But during the time of rapid adjustments in the body, when altitude sickness is likely to be debilitating, fitness is no protection, and the ones who go fast are the ones most likely to suffer.

Sometimes rapid ascent cannot be avoided. For example, the only way to enter Tibet is either by flying directly to Lhasa at 12,000 feet or by driving over the Sepo La pass from Kathmandu, which is an even worse stress. The road goes from 4000 feet in Nepal to over 17,000 feet and then down to 14,000 feet at Xegar in a matter of a day and a half or so. No wonder so many people get altitude sickness in Tibet! When faced with this kind of forced rapid ascent, especially if you know you are susceptible to altitude illness, preventive medication is prudent.

The drug of choice for preventing altitude sickness is acetazolamide (Diamox), which is a sulfa drug. Acetazolamide causes the blood to be slightly more acid, which stimulates breathing. It is also a mild diuretic. It hastens the natural processes of acclimatization, which are to increase breathing, reduce alkalinity, and diurese fluids. Therefore, acetazolamide does not mask the illness or cause any false sense of wellness. It produces changes in a few hours that normally take a few days. Acetazolamide should not be taken by people who are allergic to sulfa or during pregnancy. It can be used by both children and adults. The usual regimen is 125 to 250 mg twice a day starting twenty-four hours before ascent and continuing through the first twenty-four hours at altitude. Although this may be only four or five doses, it is very effective in speeding acclimatization and is all that is necessary. The drug can be restarted at any time if symptoms of altitude sickness develop (see below).

Adequate hydration is also helpful in preventing altitude illness. The body loses tremendous amounts of fluid from the lungs and the skin in the high, dry environment. You should drink enough to maintain a clear and copious urine output. Other measures include eating a diet high (greater than 70 percent) in carbohydrates, and going higher during the day and coming back down to sleep. Avoid sleeping near the top of passes. It's also best for acclimatization to have some mild or moderate activity rather than just to lie around. Exercise stimulates the circulation and respiration and helps the body adapt.

Your body usually offers plenty of warning signs that it doesn't like being at altitude and that you need to slow down and give it a little more time to acclimatize. However, no matter how slowly they go, some rare individuals do not acclimatize well and if not aided by acetazolamide will just have to go down. The secret is to listen to your body and heed the warning signals discussed below.

Acute Mountain Sickness

Acute mountain sickness (AMS) is the most common form of high altitude illness. Its typical symptoms are headache, lack of appetite, nausea, sometimes vomiting, and a feeling of tiredness. The initial symptoms are almost exactly like an alcohol hangover. One reason alcohol should be avoided in the first days at high altitude is that it can blur the distinction between acute mountain sickness and hangover. Another reason is that alcohol aggravates the effects of altitude and can actually impair acclimatization and make people more ill. (Contrary to popular opinion, alcohol does not exert any more effect on the brain at altitude than it does at sea level.) This stage of mild mountain sickness can be treated with aspirin or acetaminophen for headache, and perhaps other medication, such as promethazine hydrochloride (Phenergan) or prochlorperazine (Compazine), for the nausea and vomiting. However, even a headache alone must be taken as a warning sign that the body needs more time to acclimatize.

In treating acute mountain sickness, keep in mind three cardinal rules: (1) stop ascending if symptoms develop; (2) go down if they become worse instead of better with treatment; and (3) go down immediately if there is trouble with coordination, change in consciousness, or evidence of fluid in the lungs.

Rule 1: Stop ascending in the presence of symptoms. If ascent is stopped, mountain sickness will usually resolve within twenty-four to forty-eight hours but sometimes takes up to three or four days, depending on the rate of ascent, the altitude, and other factors. Acetazolamide should be administered in the same doses as for prevention to speed acclimatization. If, despite these measures, there is no improvement or symptoms become worse, you must descend.

Rule 2: Descend in the presence of worsening symptoms despite treatment. If started early enough, descent does not have to be very far; a 1,000- to 3,000-foot drop in altitude may be enough to reverse the process and induce rapid resolution. The bottom line is to descend as far as necessary for results. In Tibet in particular it may be very difficult to drop in altitude since there is no quick way off the plateau and a descent may involve going up even higher over a pass. In such circumstances it is best to treat medically and try to find oxygen. Oxygen is available in Xegar, Shigatse, and Lhasa and may be available in other places as well. If you are responsible for a group, it behooves you to inquire about the availability of oxygen in areas of travel or to carry oxygen with you. One cylinder, good for four to eight hours depending on flow rate, may save a life and a lot of problems.

Rule 3: Descend immediately if severe mountain sickness or pulmonary edema develops. The single most reliable sign of onset of severe acute mountain sickness is loss of coordination. Coordination can be tested by having the sick person walk a straight line heel to toe. A well person should be able to accomplish this feat without the maneuvers of a tightrope walker or falling off the line (and an unquestionably well person can always be used for comparison). Anyone who stumbles off the line and is obviously having difficulty with coordination needs immediate medical attention with administration of oxygen, dexamethasone (Decadron), and descent. Other symptoms associated with severe mountain sickness are recurrent vomiting, severe headache, loss of interest in all activities and surroundings, hallucinations, bizarre behavior and thinking processes, paralysis, seizures, and unconsciousness. This type of severe mountain sickness is also called high altitude cerebral edema (HACE). Dexamethasone, which reduces brain swelling, should be given to people this ill in a dosage of 4 to 8 mg initially and then 4 mg every six hours, either by mouth or injection, depending on whether there is vomiting. Descent is mandatory.

High Altitude Pulmonary Edema

High altitude pulmonary edema (HAPE) is the form of altitude illness that most often results in death. HAPE is caused by fluid accumulating in the lungs so that the air sacs become filled with fluid instead of air, resulting in suffocation from lack of oxygen. The key to avoiding death and serious illness is anticipation and early recognition. The early symptoms of pulmonary edema are dry cough, decrease in exercise ability, longer recovery time from exercise, and excessive breathlessness and rapid heartbeat during exercise. As the illness progresses, shortness of breath develops even with small amounts of effort, the cough becomes worse, and fingernail beds become a dusky gray or blue color. In the late stages of the illness, the victim is breathless even at rest, usually with a resting respiratory rate greater than 24 breaths per minute and a resting heart rate greater than 100 beats per minute. The fingernails are always bluish or gray, a gurgling sound can often be heard in the chest, and the cough becomes wet and finally productive of pink, frothy sputum. At this stage, death may only be a few hours away.

If high altitude pulmonary edema is recognized early, prompt treatment can result in very rapid recovery. Treatment includes oxygen and/or descent. If oxygen is available, it should be given immediately, especially in serious cases. If the illness is discovered early, descent without oxygen is adequate and sometimes even rest alone without further ascent will make the pulmonary edema resolve, but this usually takes days. With descent, recovery is remarkably fast. For example, I have had patients who were unconscious at 14,000 feet wake up during the one-hour helicopter evacuation to 4,000 feet. By the time we landed they felt so well that they refused to pay the helicopter bill, claiming the illness was not severe enough to have warranted the helicopter! In reality, they would have been dead in another twelve hours or so at high altitude. This fast response to descent is one of the more puzzling, but satisfying, elements of the disease.

Other measures for treating pulmonary edema include keeping the victim warm, since cold will increase the pulmonary artery pressure and cause more fluid in the lungs; keeping the victim in a sitting position rather than lying so that breathing is easier; and avoiding overexertion. It is always easiest to have the person walk down on his or her own power—but without carrying a load and perhaps being carried on the uphill sections to avoid overexertion. Medications are not very useful for treating high altitude pulmonary edema. Oxygen and descent are the mainstays of treatment, and early recognition is the key to saving lives.

Most people who die or need to be evacuated from altitude illness have early warning signs but choose to ignore them and continue on. Often this foolhardiness is the result of group pressure: trekkers in large groups are therefore more likely to get in trouble than are individual trekkers, who are more free to change the itinerary as necessary. It is very important not to deny symptoms of altitude sickness. Although mountain sickness may be difficult to differentiate from conditions that may have the same sort of symptoms—such as alcohol hangover, flulike illnesses, bronchitis, pneumonia, exhaustion, dehydration, and hypothermia—the trekker needs to make the best judgment possible and if unsure of the cause of illness, to assume that it is due to high altitude. You must keep in mind that altitude illness, if ignored, can lead to death. Unfortunately, there is no way to tell at the first onset of symptoms whether the illness will be short and trivial or likely to progress. The best way to guarantee a progression of illness, however, is to continue on despite feeling ill.

Rescue

Evacuation from remote areas of the Himalaya is very difficult at best. The trekker must assume primary responsibility for himself or herself: the trouble you get into is the trouble you have to get out of. However, if there is an injury or a significant illness, help is usually available in the form of other trekkers or mountaineers not too far away, local villagers, porters, or guides.

The first priority is to establish the extent of injury and incapacity. You have to evaluate the situation much more carefully than if you were in the backcountry in the States because of the greater difficulty and expense of evacuation. Probably the most important determination is if the injured or sick person is well enough to move on his or her own power. If someone has fallen down a cliff, for example, and complains of pain in the lower back, you don't immobilize the victim on some sort of board and call for a helicopter and wait for help; you try to get the person to stand up and walk. Many people have been able to walk out of the mountains to the nearest airstrip with compression fractures of the vertebrae and other injuries that they might not normally have walked out with in North America. Head, neck, and spine injuries are particularly troublesome since at home we have a paranoia about possibly doing further damage by moving somebody with this type of injury. The truth is that having a person move under his or her own power is not going to cause anywhere near the stress of the initial fall or injury. Sore necks can be splinted with cut-up sleeping pads; scalp lacerations can be closed by cleaning the wound and tying the hair together across it; and people can walk out with injured backs as long as there is no paralysis or nerve damage. It is too often a fatal mistake to keep a victim of pulmonary edema at high altitude while waiting for a helicopter instead of starting right away, which is the definitive treatment and immediately effective.

Evacuation can be a very difficult problem in the mountainous regions of Pakistan and India, especially since trekkers are usually in remote areas with slow transport, poor communication, and a real lack of health facilities.

Both countries utilize helicopters in the mountains for military purposes, and the military does fly evacuation missions in suport of trekking and mountaineering groups, but the arrangements can be difficult to make and are expensive (in 1980 in India, for instance, the cost of a helicopter for one hour was 4,000 rupees, about $600 U.S.). In Pakistan, a deputy commissioner, who may be far from the scene of a trekking accident, is required to arrange for an evacuation by the army, and the injured party is required to pay for the helicopter.

For individual travelers, the best opportunity for quick medical evacuation in Pakistan is along the Baltoro Glacier. As long as the conflict with India over the border in the Siachen Glacier area continues, Pakistan army helicopters fly daily between Skardu and Gasherbrum Base Camp (to the southwest of Concordia), and these choppers have been known to transport foreigners back to Skardu or even to Gilgit. It would be indiscreet, however, and assuming too much to expect that this service will automatically be available. Flying foreign civilians is unauthorized and is completely at the discretion of the individual pilot.

Evacuation in Pakistan is complicated by the fact that pack animals are not used to transport loads. Porters do all the carrying, so in case of injury, an evacuation using people must be devised. In the Kalash Valleys of Chitral, for example, a hiker severely injured by a rockfall was carried out on a *charpoy,* the local wood frame bed strung with rope.

In India, horses or yaks are often available to transport an injured person to a railhead. In Zanskar, for example, a woman member of an organized group suffered internal injuries and had to ride a horse for four days to Padum, where the district commissioner and superintendent of police were contacted for evacuation. However, the prospects for air transport were too uncertain, so the woman had to go out to Kargil in the cab of a truck. If a helicopter had been arranged, it would have required using the wireless in Padum to contact the army base in Leh, which would have made a decision based on the strength of the need.

The greater the risks, the more important is the need for an organized system of evacuation, but, as has been shown above, these systems are rarely in place. Individual travelers, without organized logistical support to arrange for a quick evacuation, need to minimize their risks as much as possible.

Should a fatality occur, local authorities (police) must be notified. An investigation of sorts is usually required before disposal of the body. Cremation, if wood is available, crevasse burial, or other burial is best done on location. All details of the death should be recorded, and belongings and passport should be brought back to the consular section of the person's embassy.

The Trekker's Medical Kit

Following is a list of suggested medical supplies for Himalayan trekking. Specific items and amounts needed will vary according to medical sophistication, the number in your group, and length of trip. This list includes prescription items: in all cases their advisability, proper use, and side effects need to be discussed with your physician. How to use these drugs and proper precautions are also covered in the medical books recommended at the beginning of this chapter.

Water disinfectant: iodine or chlorine tablets, iodine tincture, povidone-iodine (Betadine), bleach, or filter

Sunscreen: sun protection factor (SPF) 10 to 15

Mosquito repellent: very important in malarial areas

Wound disinfectant: povidone-iodine (Betadine), 1-oz. plastic spout or dropper bottle (more if doubling for water disinfection)

Blister treatment: moleskin, Second Skin, or cloth adhesive tape

Adhesive strips:
  Band-Aids, #10
  ¼" or butterfly tapes, 1 package

Gauze pads: 3", #4

Gauze roll: 3" roll

Cloth adhesive tape: 2" roll

Elastic bandage: 3" roll

Thermometer

Scissors: Swiss-army type adequate

Safety pins

Matches: windproof, waterproof

Space blanket

Analgesics:
  aspirin or acetaminophen (Tylenol), #20
  acetaminophen with codeine (Tylenol with codeine), 30 mg, #10

Anti-inflammatories: ibuprofen (Advil, Rufen, or Motrin), 200 mg or 400 mg, #20

Antibiotics:
  trimethoprim/sulfamethoxazole (Bactrim DS or Septra DS) double strength (160 mg/s 800 mg), #14
  enteric-coated erythromycin, 250 mg, #28
  ciproflaxacin (Cipro), 500 mg, #10
  gentamicin (eyedrops or ophthalmic ointment)
  skin antibiotic/antifungal ointment

Antidiarrheals:
  diphenoxylate HCl with atropine sulfate (Lomotil), #30
  Pepto-Bismol tablets, #50 (more if using for prevention of diarrhea)

\# = quantity

Antinausea drugs:
  promethazine HCl (Phenergan), 50 mg tablets, #4, *or*
  prochlorperazine (Compazine), 10 mg tablets, #5

Antihelminthic (for worms): mebendezole, 100 mg, #6

Malaria prophylaxis: individualized for traveler and trip

Antihistamine:
  diphenhydramine HCl (Benadryl), 50 or 25 mg, #4 or #8, *or*
  chlorpheniramine

Decongestant: pseudoephedrine HCl (Sudafed), 60 mg

High-altitude trips:
  acetazolamide (Diamox), 250 mg or 500 mg long-acting, #20
  dexamethasone (Decadron), 4 mg, #10

Appendices

Appendix A

Maps

I am told that there are people who do not care for maps,
and I find it hard to believe.

Robert Louis Stevenson

The maps in this book are all drawn to scale, but they are meant primarily for general orientation and as aids to interpreting the descriptions of treks. For a very few people, these maps will be sufficient. But for most hikers, these maps lack sufficient detail to be relied on for route-finding when a person is actually trekking. The best thing to do when you are trekking away from main trails is to walk with a local who knows the way, for no map can provide as much information as a person who lives in the area. This appendix is designed to point out, from west to east, the principal maps depicting in greater detail every region described in this book. Outlets for purchasing these maps are given under "Map Ordering" at the end of this appendix.

The best single overall map of the Himalaya is the 1:4,000,000 sheet entitled *Indian Subcontinent,* published by John Bartholomew & Son, Ltd., of Edinburgh, Scotland. This map, in Bartholomew's World Travel Series, is widely distributed and available at most large map stores. All the areas discussed in this book are depicted on this excellent topographic map.

The best overall series of maps covering the Himalaya outside Tibet is the U.S. Army Map Service (AMS) U502 Series. These maps have a scale of almost 4 miles to the inch (1:250,000) and a contour interval of 250 or 500 feet, depending on the sheet. The U502 Series was completed prior to 1960, so it does not have current road information. But virtually all villages in the hill areas are shown, and these maps can be very helpful, especially if you are trekking off the main routes. The sheets covering Pakistan and India are quite accurate in most areas, excepting the Zanskar region of northern India. The sheets depicting Hunza and Baltistan are spotty in reliability, but these maps remain the best generally available. Good quality *color* copies (far better than black and white) of U502 Series maps may be ordered from Michael Chessler Books. Copies of most U502 sheets can also be ordered from foreign map houses, including Zumsteins, Geo Center, and Libreria Alpina. Black-and-white copies of these maps should be highlighted for easier readability: try to emphasize the ridgelines and principal rivers with different-color marking pencils.

The available U502 sheets covering the accessible mountain areas of Pakistan and India are, from west to east (and north to south):

- NJ 43-13 *Mastuj*   Tirich, Turikho, Yarkhun, Ghizar, and Yasin
                             valleys
- NI 43-1 *Churrai*   Golen and Shishi valleys, upper Swat, Kandia
- NJ 43-14 *Baltit*   Ishkuman Valley and most of Hunza Valley
- NI 43-2 *Gilgit*   Indus gorge, Gilgit, Astor
- NI 43-6 *Srinagar*   Kaghan Valley, northern Vale of Kashmir
- NJ 43-15 *Shimshal*   Khunjerab, Shimshal Valley, Hispar Glacier
- NI 43-3 *Mundik*   Biafo & Baltoro glaciers, Deosai, Skardu,
                             Thalle, Hushe
- NI 43-7 *Kargil*   Sind, Liddar, Suru valleys, Amarnath, Kargil
- NI 43-11 *Anantnag*   lower Warwan; Chilung, Pensi, Sach passes,
                             Kishtwar
- NI 43-15 *Pathankot*   Chamba, Dhaula Dhar, Dharmsala
- NI 43-4 *Chulung*   Kondus and Saltoro valleys, Siachen, upper
                             Nubra
- NI 43-8 *Leh*   Nubra, Leh, Ladakh's Indus Valley
- NI 43-12 *Martselang*   Umasi La, most of Zanskar, Hemis Gomba
- NI 43-16 *Palampur*   eastern Chamba, Kulu and Spiti valleys, Lahoul
- NH 43-4 *Simla*   Lower Kulu Valley, Shimla, Rampur, Kinnaur
- NI 44-13 *Tso Morari*   Spiti Valley, southern Rupshu
- NH 44-1 *Chini*   Sutlej, Baspa, Tons, and upper Bhagirathi rivers
- NH 44-5 *Dehra Dun*   Mussoorie, Gangotri, Kedarnath, Badrinath
- NH 44-6 *Nanda Devi*   Joshimath, Rishi Ganga, Pindar, Dhauliganga
                             rivers
  NH 44-10 *Almora*   Almora, Pithoragarh, Kumaon's hills
  NG 45-3   *Kanchenjunga*   Western Sikkim
  NG 45-4   *Phari Dzong*   Eastern Sikkim

The Operational Navigational Charts (ONC Series) at a scale of 1:1,000,000 are a series of maps made for pilots. These maps cover the entire world, and the information shown on them is obtained from satellites. Surficial information (mountains, lakes, rivers) is excellent, but it's best to be highly skeptical regarding what these sheets say about either roads or towns. The ONC G-7 sheet covers all the areas of southwestern Sinkiang described in Chapter 6. ONC Series maps are inexpensive and are carried by many agents in the United States. They can also be ordered direct from NOAA.

Two atlas-size books published in Japan by Gakushukenkusha, Ltd. (Gakken), contain many large-scale maps of areas covered in this book. The two books are part of a series, Mountaineering Maps of the World, edited by Ichiro Yoshizawa. The individual volumes are titled *Himalaya* (1977) and *Karakorum, Hindu-Kush, Pamir and Tien Shan* (1978). Each of these books has a text in Japanese and color photographs. These volumes have, respectively, twenty-three and twenty-five two-page shaded relief maps that cover many Himalayan regions. The books can be difficult to locate, but when found their maps may be copied for use in the field and are particularly useful for areas with the highest concentrations of peaks.

Two maps depicting Kashmir, Zanskar, and most of Ladakh at a scale of 1:250,000 but without contour lines have been produced in India. These sheets are called *Trekking Route Map of Jammu and Kashmir*. Sheet Number One is to the west of Sheet Number Two. These maps are available at the Trekking and Mountaineering Office in the Tourist Reception Center in Srinagar, Kashmir.

Three maps similar to those above in scale and type but depicting Himachal Pradesh (*Trekking Route Map of Himachal Pradesh*) are available at larger tourist offices, such as Shimla and Manali, in Himachal Pradesh. Both these maps and those noted in the previous paragraph seem to be basically copies of U502 sheets without contour lines and minus many place names, but with up-to-date road information included and place names updated to current usage.

A series of eighteen three-color maps at 1:200,000 scale by various cartographers that depict the Hindu Kush, Karakoram, and parts of the Himalaya (as far east as Garhwal) were published in Japan between 1972 and 1977. These sheets are available from either Geo Center or Libreria Alpina.

A series of 1:200,000 Indian Himalaya Maps has been produced by Leomann Maps. These maps basically appear to be taken from the U502 Series and the Japanese maps referred to in the previous paragraph. The best information they add is their careful depiction of peaks. On the reverse of the sheets are some trek descriptions (of varying accuracy) and other information. The sheets are:

Sheet 1	*Jammu & Kashmir*	Kashmir Valley and Kishtwar
Sheet 2	*Jammu & Kashmir*	Kargil, Nun Kun, and western Zanskar
Sheet 3	*Jammu & Kashmir*	Leh and eastern Zanskar
Sheet 4	*Himachal Pradesh*	Dhaula Dhar, Chamba, Pangi, and western Lahoul
Sheet 5	*Himachal Pradesh*	Kulu and Parbati valleys, Lahoul
Sheet 7	*Garhwal*	Gangotri, Har-ki-Dun, Mussoorie
Sheet 8	*Kumaon*	Badrinath, Nanda Devi area

Two excellent but expensive maps of the Garhwal region in India are available with a contour interval of 100 meters and a scale of 1:150,000. These sheets, published in 1978 by Ernst Huber, are named *Garhwal-Himalaya-Ost* and *Garhwal-Himalaya-West*. The *Ost* (east) sheet covers the Nanda Devi area, and the West sheet covers from Mussoorie east to Joshimath, including the four sacred pilgrimage places of Yamnotri, Gangotri, Kedarnath, and Badrinath. These two maps can be purchased from German map houses. Keep in mind, though, that the U502 maps for these places are very accurate, giving good coverage of these regions.

A map of Sikkim by Pradyumna Karan at the scale of 1:150,000 was published in 1969 by the Association of American Geographers. This map can be ordered for $3.00 by writing to the Program Director of Geography, George Mason University, Fairfax, VA 22030.

An extremely accurate series of maps covering India (and Nepal) with a contour interval of 100 feet at a scale of one inch to the mile (1:63,360) has been printed by the Survey of India. These excellent maps are highly restricted, however, and though they are coveted by many, they are unlikely ever to become generally available.

Map Ordering

In addition to the maps already listed, a few other good maps of specific areas have been published. The following sources will send lists or catalogues of the maps they sell. Ordering maps takes time, so begin the process well in advance to allow time for correspondence, particularly with the Library of Congress or overseas map sellers.

Michael Chessler Books
P.O. Box 2436
Evergreen, CO 80439
Telephone (800) 654-8502; (303) 670-0093
At last: a breakthrough in color U502 sheet availability. This company sells a wide variety of maps for Himalayan regions (such as the Leomann maps), including excellent color reproduction copies of most maps in the U502 Series from Pakistan and India. Chessler also carries a good 1:100,000 Italian map of the Baltoro Glacier.

Geo Buch Verlag
Rosental 6
D-8000 München 2
West Germany
A large map house and bookseller.

Geo Center GmbH
Honigwiesenstrasse 25
Postfach 80 08 30
D-7000 Stuttgart 80
West Germany
One of the biggest map houses; it also sells books.

Library of Congress
101 Independence Avenue
Washington, D.C. 20540
U502 Series maps cost a minimum of $8.50 per sheet, plus postage. If you know which map sheets you want, you can write directly to the Photo-duplication Division. But if you have any questions about which map to order, you'll have to first contact the senior reference librarian at the same address. This latter process takes two steps and requires at least eight weeks, so plan ahead. The color copies available from Michael Chessler are far superior to the black-and-white copies you can get from the Library of Congress.

Libreria Alpina
Via C. Coroned-Berti, 4
40137 Bologna, Zona 3705
Italy
Excellently stocked map and book seller with a fine catalog.

NOAA Distribution Branch (N/CG33)
National Ocean Service
Riverdale, MD 20737
>   Sells the ONC Series of maps, if you can't find copies in your area.

Stanford International Map Centre
12-14 Long Acre
London WC2E 9LP
England
>   Sells black-and-white copies of some U502 sheets.

Zumsteins Landkartenhaus
Liebkerrstrasse 5
8 München 22
West Germany
>   A well-stocked map seller.

Appendix B

Trekking Outfitters in Pakistan and India

There are far fewer well-established trekking outfitters in Pakistan and India than are to be found in Nepal, and prices for arranged treks tend to be higher in Pakistan and India. The following outfitters can make full arrangements for you if you have informed them *at least* three months ahead of time (six months ahead is much preferable). Alternatively, if you don't want to write directly to an overseas outfitter, an organized trek can be planned for you (for a higher fee of course) through an established tour operator at home. The tour operator will, in turn, probably contact one of these outfitters (sometimes called an agent, especially when referred to by a tour operator). On the other hand, if you are already in Gilgit, Skardu, Srinagar, Manali, or Joshimath and merely want a porter-guide, you can try to make arrangements on the spot with a local outfitter or the office of one of these companies. If you have any particularly positive or negative experiences with any of these outfitters, do let me know. These are only some of the trekking outfitters in Pakistan and India, but these firms are either long established or come highly recommended.

Pakistan

Adventure Pakistan
10, Khayaban-e-Suharwardy
P.O. Box 1088
Islamabad
Pakistan
Telephone (051) 823963 or 812151; telex 5769 or 5836 WALJI PAK
    This is the trekking and mountaineering branch of Travel Waljis, Ltd., the best-established travel agency in Pakistan.

Karakoram Tours
1, Baltoro House
Street 19
Sector F-7/2
Islamabad
Pakistan
Telephone 29120
    Run by a Balti, this company specializes in Baltistan.

Pakistan Tours Ltd.
Flashman's Hotel
The Mall
Rawalpindi
Pakistan
Telephone 64811

The government-owned tourism company and mountaineering and trekking outfitter. Sayeed Anwar, Pakistan's trekking expert, is in charge of the trekking wing.

Sitara Travel, Ltd.
P.O. Box 63
25–26, Shalimar Plaza, off the Mall
Rawalpindi
Pakistan

Nazir Sabir Expeditions
P.O. Box 1442
Islamabad
Pakistan
Telephone 92-51-853672; telex 5811 NAIBA PK

Nazir Sabir, one of Pakistan's most accomplished and respected mountaineers, has set up his own company, which handles both trekking and mountaineering groups.

India

Arventures Adventure Holidays (P) Ltd.
Post Bag No. 7
Dehra Dun 248 001
India
Telephone 29172; telex 585-268 HMB IN

Run by experienced Himalayan climbers and trekkers Rahul and Rekha Sharma, Arventures is a new company that will arrange treks anywhere in the Indian Himalaya. Their specialty is Garhwal.

Choomti Trekkers, Pvt. Ltd.
Houseboat King's Marina
67 the Bund
Srinagar, Kashmir
India

This company outfits treks in Kashmir and is recommended by those who have used its services.

Kashmir Travels
Trueman Building, Suites 4 and 5
Polo View
P.O. Box 108
Srinagar 190001, Jammu and Kashmir
India

Sohrab Rigzin is the Ladakhi owner of this small company that comes well recommended; they outfit treks in Kashmir and Ladakh.

Tiger Mountain Pvt. Ltd.
1/1 Rani Jhansi Road
New Delhi 110 055
India
Telephone 522004, 520030, 523057; telex 315061 TREK-IN

P.O. Box 428
Srinagar, Kashmir
Telephone 73550

A well-established company (also known as Tiger Tops, Mountain Travel India), their office in Kashmir is at Star of Zanzibar Houseboat, the Bund, near Zero Bridge, Srinagar.

West Himalayan Holidays
10 Barley Mow Passage
London W4 4PH
England
Telephone 01-995-3642; telex 9419369

Summer address:
Indventure Travel
P.O. Box 1
Manali, Kulu District, Himachal Pradesh
India

A long-established and very reliable firm that organizes and outfits treks in the region bounded by Chamba, Lahoul, the Kulu Valley, and Shimla.

Appendix C
Afghanistan!

"Staray mashasy." *"May you never be tired."*
"Kwar mashay." *"May you never be poor."*
Traditional Afghan greeting

*In recent years whenever I have been asked which of the
countries I have seen I would most prefer to visit again, I
have invariably said Afghanistan. I remember it as an exciting, violent, provocative place. . . . It was . . . "One of the
world's great cauldrons."*
James A. Michener, 1963

Not for the first time in its glorious and gory history has Afghanistan been
invaded, but since the Russian invasion of 1979, Afghanistan has endured genocide
and the calculated bombing and ruination of many villages. It will be years before
Afghans in the hills can accord foreign travelers the gracious hospitality they were
once accustomed to providing the visitor: *"mosafar aziz-e-khodast"* ("the traveler
is beloved of God"). But Afghanistan lives, particularly for those of us who have
known its compelling desert landscape, its intensely green oases, and its tough and
genuine people. We long for Afghanistan. We pray for the Afghans and their
ravaged land. In our hearts we feel an unquenchable yearning for Afghanistan.

Irresistible. Compelling. These words express for many both the land and its
people. Visiting Afghan mountain people, many foreigners feel as if they have met
long-forgotten kith and kin who grew up on a different continent, speak another
language, yet are separated only by an accident of birth. From the pretentious,
conceited youngbloods to the grave, magnanimous nobility of the white-bearded
elder, to the reserved graciousness of the wife in purdah (who may only be seen
by the female visitor), the people of Afghanistan weave a spell over those fortunate
enough to visit their homeland.

This severe, enthralling land lies north and south of the cold, sere Hindu Kush,
the westernmost extension of the Himalayan mountain system. Like a shepherd's
melodic song, or a dimly heard flutist by a mountain brook, the names of Afghanistan's desert and mountain strongholds vibrate in one's memory: Registan,
Shibarghan, Badakhshan, Nuristan, Wakhan, Bamiyan. Likewise, Afghanistan's
clans comprise a varied, fascinating mosaic: Pushtun, Baluch, Brahui, Hazara,
Uzbek, Aimaq, Turkoman, Tajik, Nuristani, Farsiwan.

But Afghanistan has been scourged and burned, its hard-won irrigation systems bombed into wastelands and its tools, draft animals, and seed stock largely
decimated. It will take untold years to resurrect the land and people from a decade

of war. The land must be purged of millions of antipersonnel mines still lying on and buried in the earth. But it will take generations to extinguish the intense hatreds born of political and interpersonal feuds. Afghanistan will phoenixlike rise from ashes, but not without help and not without time. How many of us have dared to dream, "Shall I give of myself to go and assist with reconstruction?"

A Short Bibliography on Afghanistan

As Afghanistan opens again to visitors, we can learn about it by reading some of the many excellent articles and books that have been written about this harsh, hauntingly beautiful land and its enigmatic, hospitable people. A few of the better books in English are listed below. The volumes by Louis Dupree and Edelberg and Jones have especially thorough bibliographies. Many fine books and periodicals about Afghanistan have been written in German, particularly those published by Akademische Druck-u. Verlagsanstalt in Graz, Austria.

Abercrombie, Thomas J. "Afghanistan, Crossroad of Conquerors." *National Geographic,* September 1968, 297–345.
Excellent photography; a fine overview of the land and its people.

Chaffetz, David. *A Journey Through Afghanistan: A Memorial.* Chicago: University of Chicago Press, 1981.
"This book is a recounting of a journey through Western Afghanistan by two young Americans who wanted to explore and experience the lonely, hermetic world of the Afghan nomads . . ." (from the preface).

Denker, Debra. "Along Afghanistan's War-torn Frontier." *National Geographic,* June 1985, 772–97.
The war's bitter toll told in personal terms. Debra Denker visited Afghan friends in Pakistan's North-West Frontier and traveled across the border into Afghanistan as well.

Dupree, Louis. *Afghanistan.* Princeton: Princeton University Press, 1980.
The most complete, authoritative information source on the country's geography, history, folklore, and lives of the people. With many photographs, charts, and eight appendices.

Dupree, Nancy Hatch. *An Historical Guide to Afghanistan.* Kabul: Afghan Tourist Organization, 1977.
An excellent, lively guide to Afghanistan already exists. Here's hoping this fine book will be reissued as soon as possible. My favorite photograph is captioned "A Shah Buz or King Goat Leading a Herd Across the Dasht-i-Laili."

Edelberg, Lennart, and Schuyler Jones. *Nuristan.* Graz, Austria: Akademische Druck-u. Verlagsanstalt, 1979.
The best evocation in writing, drawings, and photographs of a unique region, since ravaged by bombardment.

Hodson, Peregrine. *Under A Sickle Moon.* New York: Atlantic Monthly Press, 1987.
Well-written, at times poetic, account of a journey through war-torn Afghanistan.

Kessel, Joseph. *The Horsemen.* New York: Farrar, Straus, and Giroux, 1968.
Excellent novel about *buzkashi,* the national sport of "goat grabbing"; the action ranges across northern Afghanistan.

Michaud, Roland, and Sabrina Michaud. *Afghanistan*. London: Thames and Hudson, 1980.
    Exquisite photographs, primarily of people.
———— . *Caravans to Tartary*. London: Thames and Hudson, 1985. A photographic account of northern Afghanistan, particularly of the Michauds' trip into the Wakhan.
Michaud, Sabrina, and Roland Michaud. "Bold Horsemen of the Steppes." *National Geographic*, November 1973, 634–69.
    The Turkomans of northern Afghanistan in all their rugged and delicate glory.
———— . "Winter Caravan to the Roof of the World." *National Geographic*, April 1972, 435–65.
    Winter travel with the Kirghiz along the Wakhan Corridor; a page from history.
Michener, James. *Caravans*. New York: Fawcett Crest, 1963.
    Novel based on memory and other accounts. A page turner.
Newby, Eric. *A Short Walk in the Hindu Kush*. New York: Penguin, 1981.
    A classic travel book. Newby and friend feign interest in bagging a peak, but they really want to visit Nuristan.
Toynbee, Arnold J. *Between Oxus and Jumna*. London: Oxford University Press, 1961.
    Toynbee skillfully blends travel and history. As he circles Afghanistan and visits Pakistan as well, he notes, "In every journey, there are as many objectives missed as there are objectives obtained."

Bibliography

Included in this bibliography are only a few of the books you can find about the mountainous regions of Pakistan and India, but these few can be especially helpful. Most of the books listed should not be difficult to locate, given access to a well-stocked library, although those published overseas may be obtainable only in the country of publication. You can find further information about nearly every region mentioned in this book from one or more of the titles below, and by perusing their bibliographies, you can vastly expand your list of sources.

General Books on the Karakoram and the Western and Central Himalaya

Barrett, Robert LeMoyne, and Katherine Barrett. *The Himalayan Letters of Gypsy Davy and Lady Ba*. Cambridge: W. Heffer and Sons, 1927.
A poetic tale of a year's travels in Ladakh and Baltistan. Hard to find, but very informative about the way things were.

Bernbaum, Edwin. *Sacred Mountains of the World*. San Francisco: Sierra Club Books, 1990.
A fascinating compilation in words and photographs of sacred mountains in the Himalaya and elsewhere.

Braham, Trevor. *Himalayan Odyssey*. London: George Allen & Unwin, Ltd., 1974.
From Chitral to Sikkim, the author has his eyes on the peaks, but he makes a few comments on the approaches as well.

Cleare, John. *The World Guide to Mountains and Mountaineering*. London: Mayflower Books, 1979.
Facts about peaks, passes, access, maps, and references, intelligibly presented. Cleare picks up at the snowline, where this book leaves off. Fifty pages of the book describe the Himalaya.

Longstaff, Tom. *This My Voyage*. New York: Scribners, 1950.
Good suggestions on routes in Garhwal, Baltistan, and the Gilgit River valleys by an early master of the small expedition.

Mason, Kenneth. *Abode of Snow*. Seattle: The Mountaineers, 1987.
The basic history of Himalayan exploration and mountaineering.

Newby, Eric. *A Short Walk in the Hindu Kush*. New York: Penguin Books, 1981.
A classic account of trekking in the Panjshir Valley and Nuristan, Afghanistan, written with insight and humor. Find this one: it's a must.

Shipton, Eric. *The Six Mountain-Travel Books*. London: Diadem; Seattle: The Mountaineers, 1985.
Contains *Nanda Devi* and *Blank on the Map* with its account of roaming southwestern Sinkiang and Baltistan's northern glaciers.

———. *That Untravelled World*. London: Hodder and Stoughton, 1969.
Superb autobiographical writing by a master of the small expedition, about Baltistan, Kashmir, Garhwal, and elsewhere.

Singh, Madanjeet. *Himalayan Art*. New York: Macmillan, 1968.
An overview of wall painting and sculpture from Ladakh to Bhutan. Contains many photographs; the text is often quite technical.

Thesiger, Wilfred. *The Last Nomad*. New York: Dutton, 1980.
Although this book is only in part about the Himalaya, Thesiger has an interesting if self-righteous approach to travel in Asia. He roamed at length and visited many remote peoples and places. Excellent photographs.

Tichy, Herbert. *Himalaya*. Translated by Richard Rickett and David Streatfeild. Vienna: Anton Schroll, 1970.
Brief but captivating accounts of voyages by Tichy and others from Chitral to Assam. Tichy has a wonderful, "insider's" feel for the land and people.

Tilman, H. W. *The Seven Mountain-Travel Books*. London: Diadem; Seattle: The Mountaineers, 1983.
Contains *The Ascent of Nanda Devi* and *China to Chitral*.

Younghusband, Francis. *The Heart of a Continent*. Hong Kong: Oxford University Press, 1984.
A classic book telling of several journeys through the Karakoram, Ladakh, and Kashmir.

Pakistan

Adamson, Hilary, and Isobel Shaw. *A Traveller's Guide to Pakistan*. Islamabad: The Asian Study Group, 1981.
The best overall guide to Pakistan. Hard to locate out of Pakistan, however. A completely revised version of this book entitled *Pakistan Handbook* is to be published in 1990 by the Guidebook Company, Hong Kong.

Ali Haqiqat. *Trekker's Guide to Hunza*. 3d ed. Karachi: Self-published, 1988.
A unique book in that it is the first trekking guide for any part of the Himalaya written by a person from the hills: Haqiqat Ali is a Wakhi from Gujal, Hunza. Lists many intriguing trekking possibilities; the third edition includes some interesting color photographs.

De Fillippi, Fillipo. *Karakoram and the Western Himalaya: An Account of the Expedition of H. R. H. The Duke of Abruzzi*. New York: Dutton, 1912.
This is a rare book about one of the first Western expeditions to the Baltoro Glacier with a fascinating separate collection of wide, wide panoramic photographs depicting the region.

Fairley, Jean. *The Lion River: The Indus*. New York: John Day, 1975.
Factual account of the mighty Indus and the peoples on its shores.

Fleming, Peter. *News from Tartary*. Los Angeles: J. P. Tarcher, 1982.
The epic 1935 journey from Peking to Kashmir includes Kashgar and Hunza in its last section.

Hurley, James. "The People of Baltistan." *Natural History,* October 1961, 19–27; November 1961, 56–69.
Excellent information on Baltistan and its people in this two-part article.

Jettmar, Karl. *Rock Carvings and Inscriptions in the Northern Areas of Pakistan*. Islamabad: Institute of Folk Heritage, 1984.
Describes every location in the Gilgit River valleys and Baltistan where you can see petroglyphs.

Keay, John. *The Gilgit Game*. Hamden, Connecticut: Archon, 1979.
Interesting narrative of exploration in the Gilgit River valleys during the latter half of the last century. Check out the photograph of George Hayward.

———. *When Men and Mountains Meet*. Hamden, Connecticut: Archon, 1981.
Well-wrought history of European exploration in the Karakoram Range and Kashmir from 1820 to 1875.

Maraini, Fosco. *Karakoram: The Ascent of Gasherbrum IV*. New York: Viking, 1961.
Tale of an expedition to the head of the Baltoro Glacier that includes far more than what happened above base camp.

———. *Where Four Worlds Meet*. Translated by Peter Green. London: Hamish Hamilton, 1964.
Well-written account of an expedition in Chitral. Includes an early excursion to the Kalash valleys.

Miller, Keith. *Continents in Collision*. London: George Philip, 1982.
Informative accounting of activities in "Hunza proper" and elsewhere by the 1980 International Karakoram Project.

Neve, Arthur. *The Tourist's Guide to Kashmir, Skardo, Etc*. Lahore: The Civil and Military Gazette Ltd., undated (circa 1935).
Covering Gilgit, Baltistan, Ladakh, and Kashmir, this little red book shows that the understated British of a bygone era were there before us: what we call "technical," they called "sporting." May still be found in Gilgit shops.

Rowell, Galen. "Baltistan: The 20th Century Comes to Shangri-La." *National Geographic*, October 1987.
Traditional Baltistan joins the modern age by fits and starts. Includes a short section on the Siachen war. The author has been to Baltistan five times.

———. *In the Throne Room of the Mountain Gods*. San Francisco: Sierra Club Books, 1987.
Photographs of the Baltoro Glacier that make you want to forget everything and go. The text about the Baltoro is very informative.

Schomberg, R. C. F. *Between the Oxus and the Indus*. Lahore: Al-Biruni, 1976.
Useful background information on early travel in the Gilgit River valleys.

Shor, Jean Bowie. *After You, Marco Polo*. New York: McGraw Hill, 1955.
An attempt to retrace Marco Polo's route; some facts on Hunza as it used to be.

Staley, John. *Words for My Brother*. Karachi: Oxford University Press, 1982.
The best book on this list for insightful, anecdotal information on Chitral, Hunza, Gilgit, Kohistan, and the valleys in between. The author and his wife Elizabeth traveled with and among local people, drawing them out, and the resulting book is excellent.

India

Chabloz, Ph., and N. Cremieu. *Hiking in Zanskar and Ladakh*. Geneva: Olizane, 1986.
Contains thirteen handy pullout sheets with descriptions of different routes in Ladakh and Zanskar; has good black-and-white photographs. The best guide to remote regions in Zanskar. For those who want to order, the ISBN is 2-88086-031-8.

Deacock, Antonia. *No Purdah in Padam*. London: George G. Harrap, 1960. A fine narrative of the first women's overland journey in 1958 from England to Zanskar.

Douglas, William O. *Beyond the High Himalayas*. Garden City: Doubleday, 1952.
An account of a 1951 trip from Kulu to Leh. Brief mention of Hunza.

Govinda, Lama Anagarika. *The Way of the White Clouds*. Boston: Prajna, 1985. A man who was born in the West and eventually became an initiated lama describes his travels in Ladakh and Tibet with many insights into Tibetan Buddhism.

Heim, Arnold, and August Gansser. *The Throne of the Gods*. Translated by Eden and Cedar Paul. New York: Macmillan, 1939.
A fine book on Garhwal and Kumaon with many excellent photographs. Heim and Gansser traveled light, appreciating the people and their land.

Keay, John. *Into India*. London: John Murray, 1973.
Good, anecdotal cross-cultural insights that give a flavor of the vast cauldron that is India.

Mehta, Ved. *Portrait of India*. New York: Farrar, Straus & Giroux, 1970. Excellent anecdotes; has a substantial section on the Himalaya.

Murray, W. H. *The Scottish Himalayan Expedition*. London: J. M. Dent & Sons, 1951.
A perceptive book; the Scots enjoyed the locals and describe well the areas traversed. Lots of information about Garhwal and Kumaon.

Noble, Christina. *Over the High Passes: A Year in the Himalayas*. Glasgow: Collins, 1987.
The author, who has lived in the Himalaya for many years, tells us about the migratory Gaddis as they roam between Kangra, Chamba, Kulu, and their summer pastures in Lahoul's rolling uplands.

Pallis, Marco. *Peaks and Lamas*. 3d ed. London: The Wc'urn Press, 1974.
Much anecdotal and well-written information on Tibetan Buddhism with an account of visits to Bushahr, Sikkim, and Ladakh in 1936.

Schettler, Margret, and Rolf Schettler. *Kashmir, Ladakh and Zanskar*. South Yarra, Australia: Lonely Planet, 1985.
This guide to Kashmir, Ladakh, and Zanskar includes trekking information.

Snellgrove, David L., and Tadeusz Skorupski. *The Cultural Heritage of Ladakh*, vol. 1. Boulder: Prajna Press, 1977.
Excellent, authoritative data about the Indus Valley in Ladakh. Many photographs.

Snellgrove, David L., and Tadeusz Skorupski. *The Cultural Heritage of Ladakh*, vol. 2. London: Aris and Phillips, 1981.
Primarily covers the large monasteries in Zanskar.

Thukral, Gurmeet, and Elizabeth Thukral. *Garhwal Himalaya*. New Delhi: Frank Bros., 1987.
A fine guide to Garhwal with excellent photographs. Some chapters have been written by veteran trekker Bill Aitken.

Weare, Garry. *Trekking in the Indian Himalaya*. South Yarra, Australia: Lonely Planet, 1986.
Good information about treks in Kashmir, Ladakh, Himachal Pradesh, and Garhwal.

In addition, two journals often offer articles by hikers about India's Himalayan regions: The *Indian Mountaineer,* the semiannual journal of the Indian Mountaineering Foundation, Benito Juarez Road, New Delhi, 110 021, India; and *The Himalayan Journal,* the annual publication of the Himalayan Club, P.O. Box 1905, Bombay 400 001, India.

Medical Information

Auerbach, Paul. *Medicine for the Outdoors.* Boston: Little, Brown, 1986.

Bezruchka, Stephen. *The Pocket Doctor.* Seattle: The Mountaineers, 1988.
Written for the layman with disease prevention in mind, this compact book includes information on medication and dosages.

Darvill, Fred T. *Mountaineering Medicine: A Wilderness Medical Guide.* 11th ed. Berkeley: Wilderness, 1985.
Small in size, this condensed guide to first aid has diagrams and describes everything from bandaging scratches to reducing a dislocated shoulder and setting broken bones in the hills.

Hackett, Peter H. *Mountain Sickness: Prevention, Recognition and Treatment.* New York: The American Alpine Club, 1980.
The most authoritative word on altitude sickness.

Wilkerson, James A., M.D., ed. *Medicine for Mountaineering.* 3d ed. Seattle: The Mountaineers, 1985.
The most complete how-to medical book; covers nearly everything. Too heavy to carry, however.

Natural History

Ali, Salim. *Field Guide to the Birds of the Eastern Himalayas.* New Delhi: Oxford University Press, 1978.
Covers Sikkim and Bhutan, describing 535 species and illustrating 366. Detailed natural history information.

Fleming, Robert L., Sr., Robert L. Fleming, Jr., and Lain S. Bangdel. *Birds of Nepal.* Bombay: Vakil and Sons, 1979.
Compact field guide describing about 800 species, including some from Kashmir and Sikkim. Definitely the best available, but has some misleading illustrations.

Hooker, J. D. *Himalayan Journals.* London, 1854 (available in reprint editions).
Account by the first botanist to visit the Himalaya and study it in depth.

Inskipp, Carol, and Tim Inskipp. *A Guide to Birds of Nepal.* Dover: Tanager Books, 1985.
Based on reported sightings and museum collections, this book provides basic information on the distribution, habitat, behavior, and breeding of 835 species. Although illustrated with 676 distribution maps, it is not a field guide.

Israel, Samuel, and Toby Sinclair. *Indian Wildlife.* Singapore: APA, 1987.
An overview of wildlife in India, Nepal, and Sri Lanka, this book (written and photographed by various contributors) contains sections on birds, mammals, and selected national parks.

Jackson, Rodney. "Snow Cats of Langu Gorge." *Animal Kingdom,* July/August 1987, 45–53.
An account of Rodney Jackson's study of the snow leopard.

Jackson, Rodney, and Darla Hillard. "Tracking the Elusive Snow Leopard." *National Geographic,* June 1986, 793–809.
A fuller account of Rodney Jackson's lengthy research on the behavior of snow leopards in a remote Himalayan region.

Majupuria, Trilok C., ed. *Wild Is Beautiful.* Kathmandu: S. Devi, 1981.
Introduction to the fauna of Nepal, written by Nepalese experts. Some chapters suffer from inaccurate information. Available in Kathmandu bookstores.

Mierow, Dorothy, and Tirtha Bahadur Strestha. *Himalayan Flowers and Trees.* Kathmandu: Sahayogi Press, 1978.
Portable guide with many color photographs of trees, shrubs, and wildflowers of Nepal, for those wanting something lightweight to carry. Illustrates some of the commonly encountered species.

Polunin, Oleg, and Adam Stainton. *Flowers of the Himalaya.* Delhi: Oxford University Press, 1984. 580 pp.
The guide to the flowering plants of the Himalaya, from Kashmir to Nepal. Illustrated by 690 color plates, it describes 1,500 plants found above elevations of 4,000 feet. Though somewhat heavy and expensive, you'll be able to identify most plants encountered. An abridged edition is also available.

Prater, S. H. *The Book of Indian Mammals.* Bombay: Bombay Natural History Society, 1965. 324 pp.
Describes all large mammals of the Indian subcontinent. Recent research has changed much of our knowledge on the natural history of many primates, cats, wild sheep, and goats. Plate illustrations. Not a field guide.

Roberts, T. J. *The Mammals of Pakistan.* London: Ernest Benn, 1977.
Detailed descriptions of Pakistan's mammals, illustrated by line drawings. Very informative and reasonably up to date, but too large to serve as a field guide. Difficult to find outside of a library.

Schaller, George B. *Mountain Monarchs: Wild Sheep and Goats of the Himalaya.* Chicago: University of Chicago Press, 1977.
Detailed facts about Himalayan sheep and goats. Technical but readable.

———. *Stones of Silence: Journeys in the Himalaya.* New York: Viking Press, 1980.
Well-written, factual information on the author's fieldwork in southern and northern Chitral, Hunza, Baltistan, and elsewhere.

Stainton, J. D. A. *Forests of Nepal.* London: John Murray, 1972. 181 pp.
Out-of-print account of the forest types of Nepal, applicable to much of the Himalaya.

Vaurie, Charles. *Tibet and Its Birds.* London: H. F. & G. Witherby, 1972. 407 pp.
Lists birds known to occur in Tibet, based on museum records. Includes informative accounts of the region's geography, climate, and zoogeography, with an account of early scientific explorations.

Glossaries

Glossary of Foreign Words Used in the Text

Speak to people in their own language.
Mushkeel Baba, 1990

This glossary is a list of foreign words found in the text. The most frequently used languages and dialects are abbreviated, as follows:
Ba = Balti. **Br** = Burushaski. **D** = Dari. **H** = Hindustani (Hindi or Urdu. Note: Hindi/Urdu words are often used in some of the included dialects. Some of these Hindustani words are taken directly from Sanskrit.) **K** = Khowar. **Kz** = Kirghiz. **L** = Ladakhi. **T** = Tibetan. **U** = Uighur. **W** = Wakhi.

aghost (?)	a pass
ah cha (H)	"good," "okay," "yes" (often said with a side-to-side wiggle of the head)
Allah-o-Akbar (Arabic)	"God is Great"
alu (H)	potato
amchee (T)	doctor who practices Tibetan medicine
an (K)	pass or high ridge
angotee (K)	visitor's guest room in a traditional Chitrali home
Angrezi (H)	foreigner (strictly speaking, an Englishman)
aq oey (Kz)	"white dwelling," a yurt
arak (Br)	distilled spirit made from mulberries
asali (H)	genuine; the real thing (compare with **nakali**)
'ash (U)	soup with thick noodles, vegetables, and maybe a few pieces of meat
ashram (H)	rest house for pilgrims; usually an ashram has a spiritually respected person in charge (may also be a retreat for sages and their students)
ata (Kz,W)	father
ataliq (K)	man who formerly tutored the ruling **mehtar** in Chitral
atha (U)	tomorrow
atta (H)	wheat flour
ayran (Kz)	curdled milk drink
baba (H)	"old man"; can be used as term of respect for older people

-bad (H)	suffix meaning "town"
baipash (K)	main room in a traditional Chitrali home
bamak (Garhwali)	glacier
bar (K, Shina)	stream
barasahib (H)	boss, an important person
battering (Br)	dried apricots (Hunza's are the sweetest anywhere)
bazha (U)	bazaar
beedie (H)	cheap conical cigarette with inexpensive tobacco rolled in ebony tree leaf
bhakti (H)	devotion and love for God
bhavan (H)	rest house for pilgrims
bingguan (Chinese)	upscale guesthouse
brok (Ba)	upper-elevation grazing area
bugyal (Garhwali)	pasture or meadow used by grazing animals
burka (H)	veil worn by Muslim women
burus (Br)	delicious fresh white cheese
buzkashi (D)	"goat grabbing," the national sport of Afghanistan, in which two teams mounted on horses vie to carry a headless goat into a small circular goal
chai (H)	tea
chaikhana (H,D)	teahouse (sometimes connotes a place where food is served and people may sleep)
chai-wala (H)	tea seller
chandra (H)	moon
chang (T)	homemade beer (may be made with impure water)
chapati (H)	flat wheatcake
charas (H)	hashish
charasi (H)	smoker of hashish
charpoy (H)	"four legs"; wooden frame bed, usually strung with rope
chatta (H)	umbrella
chaulki (H)	small police post
chaura (Gaddi)	full skirt worn by Gaddinis
chenai (H)	single-reed instrument played at polo games, marriages, and other occasions when music is enjoyed
cheo (Kalash)	black homespun dress worn by Kalash women
chogha (K,Br)	long men's cloak worn in Chitral and Pakistan's Northern Areas
chogo (Ba)	big
chog-tse (T)	low table used in Ladakhi and Tibetan homes and monasteries
chokidar (H)	watchman and/or caretaker of a property
chola (Gaddi)	white woolen robe worn by Gaddi men
chorten (T)	Tibetan Buddhist reliquary shrine (same as **stupa**)
coolie (H)	porter
coss (L)	maroon woolen gown worn in Ladakh

crore (H)	10 million
dahi (H)	yoghurt
dal (H)	cooked or uncooked lentils
dal-bhaat (H)	literally, "lentils and rice," but usually means a meal including vegetables and garnishes
dalda (H)	vegetable oil (a brand that has become a generic name)
dankhar (probably T)	sequestered place for hiding
darba (Ba)	fresh white cheese
darshan (H)	the "auspicious sight" of a deity's image or a revered person
dawan or **daban** (U)	pass
debda, also **devta** or **deota** (Pahari)	female deity
dekun-malda (W)	crumbled wheat bread, cheese, and yoghurt
dham (H)	abode or dwelling place of God
dhar (H)	high ridge
dharma (H)	the doctrine or path; religious law or duty
dharmsala (H)	pilgrim's rest house
dhoti (H)	garment of white cloth wrapped around a man's midsection
dhunga (Kashmiri)	small partially enclosed boat in Kashmir used as an inexpensive sleeping quarters
diltar (Br)	buttermilk
doko (Nepali)	woven basket carried on the back with a tumpline
dol (K)	drum
du-khang (T)	monks' assembly hall in a Tibetan Buddhist temple
durbar (H)	to give audience, or the place where a ruler gives an audience
dut (W)	rope or wire bridge
esphad (Kalash)	"greetings," "hello"
fakir (H)	Muslim mendicant; religious ascetic
gah (?)	side valley or stream; same as **nala**
gali (H)	narrow lane in a city that is usually too small for vehicles
gang shar lam khyer (T)	"to bring to the path (of enlightenment) whatever may happen"
ganga (H)	tributary of the sacred Ganges (Ganga) River
ganja (H)	marijuana
garem chashma (H)	hot spring
garh (Garhwali)	fortress
garroti (H)	box (hanging beneath a cable) that carries people or things across a river
geshe (T)	teacher with a doctorate in philosophy
ghee (H)	clarified butter
gol (K)	stream or side valley
gomba (T)	Tibetan Buddhist temple or monastery

gotsil (Br)   irrigation channel in "Hunza proper"
gul (H)   flower
gur (Pahari)   shaman in the Kulu region
gurdwara (H)   Sikh temple
gyalmo (T)   queen
gyalpo (T)   king
haj (Arabic)   the pilgrimage to Mecca (also, anyone who has
                             made the pilgrimage)
halwa (H)   sweet made from farina and sugar
hanee (Br)   almondlike edible apricot seed
havildar (H)   low-ranking noncommissioned officer in the Indian
                             army
hel (W)   meadow
imam (Arabic)   leader of prayers at a mosque; if capitalized, an
                             Imam is a divinely appointed, infallible successor
                             of Mohammed in the Shiite tradition
inshallah (Arabic)   "if God wills," loosely means "maybe"
jai (H)   hail
jangal (H,U)   trees: sometimes in a forest, but maybe just two or
                             three trees or bushes
jawan (H)   soldier
jelabie (H)   sweet shaped somewhat like a pretzel
jerab (W)   valley with a permanent stream
jhola (H)   small shoulder bag
-ji (H)   honorific suffix indicating respect
jibi (L)   man's or woman's top hat with upturned brim (same
                             as **sahru**)
jot (?)   pass
ju (Br)   apricot
kagu (L)   charm box
kai-tik (U)   yoghurt
karai (H,D)   eggs fried with tomatoes, onions, and spices
kata (T)   prayer scarf given to a friend embarking on a
                             journey, when meeting an important monk or lama,
                             or placed on an image
keema (H)   ground meat with spicy sauce
khaanaa (H)   food
khana (H,D)   house
kharak (Garhwali)   upland pasture or meadow
kharu (Zanskari)   "give me food"
khol (H)   black coloring used like mascara
khot (K)   cloud
kund (H)   a lake or source of water
kurut (D,W)   flavoring made by boiling buttermilk with wheat
                             flour and drying the residue
kuth (?)   plant whose roots are used for medicinal and other
                             purposes

kyaa haal chaal hay? (H) — "how are you?"; the basic greeting in Urdu-speaking areas and in Pakistan—usually abbreviated to **"kyaa haal hay?"**

kyang or **kiang** (T) — Tibetan wild ass

la (T) — high pass

lambardar (B) — headman in a Balti village

lap-tse (T) — ceremonial pile of rocks, usually found on tops of passes in regions of Tibetan culture; lap-tses often include carved stones, animal horns, and/or prayer flags

lasht (K) — plain

lassi (H) — in the summer pastures, this is buttermilk; in a restaurant, it is a drink made with yoghurt and water that can be "sweet," with sugar, or "sour," left plain

lat (H) — leg

la-tho (L) — ceremonial rock structures in the Matho Nala

lha-khang (T) — "house of the gods"; a chapel in a monastery

lingam (H) — representation, often in stone, of Shiva's phallus

lisa or **lissah** (B) — hunting place

lungma (B) — stream or valley; same as **nala**

maidan (H) — flat open place, usually a meadow

mala (H) — string of prayer beads, like a rosary

malang (H) — Muslim religious ascetic

maltash (Br) — butter

mamu (Br) — milk

mandlr (H) — Hindu temple

mani wall (T) — wall of stones, the top row of which is carved in Tibetan with the sacred mantra "Om Mani Padme Hum"

marg (H) — street (in Kashmir, means "meadow")

masur dal (H) — orange dal that is easy to cook at upper elevations

mazar (Arabic) — tomb of a Muslim saint or revered person

mee sha (U) — hashish

mehtar (K) — governor of Chitral in former days

mel (Br) — apricot wine

melph (K) — black

membaar (H) — member of a trekking group

Mir (Persian) — ruler of Hunza State in former days

mogh (K) — the best-quality handwoven woolen fabric in Chitral

mujahedeen (Arabic) — "holy warrior," freedom fighter in Afghanistan

murti (H) — metal or stone image of a god or goddess

mushkeel (H) — difficulty, problem

mustagh (Turkic) — ice mountain

muzzafer or **mosafer** (Arabic) — traveler

muzzafer khana (D,H) — travelers' inn

myTTi-ka tel (H)   kerosene

nag (H)   serpent

nakali (H)   ersatz, false (compare with **asali**)

nala (H)   stream or side valley

namaste or **namaskar** (H)   hello or goodbye; literally, "I honor the godhead within you" (namaste is less formal)

nan (H,D,Kz,U)   large, slightly raised wheat bread cooked in a clay oven

nasphe (Ba)   roasted barley flour, a basic food in the highland areas (same as **ngam phe, phe, sattu,** or **tsampa**)

naykor (T)   "going around places," pilgrimage

ngam phe (L)   roasted barley flour, a basic food in the highland areas (same as **nasphe, phe, sattu,** or **tsampa**)

nhating (Ba)   traditional peaked Balti hat

pahari (H)   hill person from the Central Himalayan region; may also refer to various hill languages

paisa (H)   generally means "money"; 100 paisa equal a rupee

pakol (K)   Chitrali-style hat

pamir (W)   grassy, high-altitude pasture area

panch (H)   five (considered an auspicious number)

panda (H)   Brahmins who assist pilgrims in different ways, including performing sacred rituals

pani (H)   water

parai (Kalash)   used with a destination, it means "I'm going to _____"

paratha (H)   large, flat wheatcake cooked in oil (of which the author is extremely fond)

parbat (H)   high mountain

parikrama (H)   circumambulation, whether of a temple or sacred place

pashmina (H)   cashmere: the best-quality shawl wool (from the underbelly of an upland sheep or goat)

patta nahi (H)   "I have no information," "I don't know"

paydal (H)   on foot

perag (L)   large traditional headpiece with rows of turquoise and pieces of coral; worn by Ladakhi and Zanskari women (see also **tsaroo**)

peri (K,Br)   fairy (a large anthropomorphic type that may be capricious)

phe (L)   roasted barley flour (same as **nasphe, sattu,** or **tsampa**)

phiti (Br)   inch-and-a-half-thick bread made in Hunza (same as **putok**)

pir (Arabic)   hereditary religious leader in the Ismaili sect

pradesh (H)   state

-prayag (H)   suffix attached to the name of certain sacred river confluences

prusht (Kalash)	"good," "okay"
puja (H)	worship that usually includes offerings to a deity
pujari (H)	Brahmin priest who conducts worship services in temples
pukka (H)	proper, good
puri (H)	thin wheatcake fried in oil
putok (W)	bread made in Gujal (same as **phiti**)
puttee (H,B,K)	handwoven woolen fabric about a foot wide
pyee (Ba)	"stage," traditional day's walk in Baltistan
qatl karo (Ba)	"slay us"
qwawali (H)	Islamic devotional music, often up-tempo
raj (H)	reign; as in the British Raj
raja (H)	king or local potentate
rakh-med (U)	"thank you"
ramani (Garhwali)	joyous, beautiful
rassi (H)	rope
rebu (T)	black yak-hair tent
ri (Ba)	snow-covered mountain
roti (H)	wheat bread; like a small **nan**
saddar (H)	cantonment; the British-built part of a city with a grid system of streets
sadhu (H)	literally, "excellent"; a Hindu ascetic: some are genuine, others less savory
sahib (H)	loosely means "sir" (don't be mesmerized by its use)
sahru (L)	man's or woman's hat with upturned brim (same as **jibi**)
Salaam alekwm (Arabic)	"peace be with you"; the international Muslim greeting
saman (H)	belongings, luggage, gear
sangam (H)	confluence of two rivers, often considered a sacred place
sannyasi (H)	renouncing individual, a Hindu ascetic who has left the world behind
sar (Persian, W)	"head"; a mountain peak
sattu (H,L)	roasted barley flour, a basic food in the highland areas (same as **nasphe**, **ngam phe**, or **tsampa**)
serai (H,D)	inn, usually composed of rooms surrounding an open courtyard
shabash (H)	"well done"
shalwar (H)	baggy pants with a drawstring
shalwar-kameez (H)	baggy trousers with long-tailed shirt (national dress in Pakistan)
sherab (H)	wine, or, loosely, alcohol
sherrin (Persian, H)	sweet
shialajit (Persian)	stone oil (for a more complete definition, see "Hemis Gomba and the Hemis Festival" in Chapter 9)

shikara (Kashmiri)   small boat used as a taxi in Kashmir

shikari (H)   hunter of game

shila (H)   large rock with mythic associations

siddhi (H)   (spiritually related) mental or physical powers

sirdar (H)   the man in charge of the people that accompany a trekking group (he may also be called a guide)

solja (L)   salted Tibetan tea with butter

sta (T,L)   horse (pronounced sTTah)

stupa (H)   Buddhist reliquary shrine (same as **chorten**)

tangkha (T)   Tibetan Buddhist painted scroll

tharing (Br)   goatskin used to make butter

thik (or **teek**) (H)   "okay," "all right"

thik hay? (H)   "is it okay?"

Thum (Br)   Hunza's ruler (same as **Mir**) in former days

thupa (T)   general name for soup

tibba (Garhwali)   hilltop

tirth or **tirtha** (H)   place of pilgrimage

tirthayatra (H)   pilgrimage; a journey to a sacred place (often called **yatra**)

tokpo (L)   stream

tola (H)   measurement of weight; originally the weight of a silver rupee, about 11.4 grams, a tola is often considered now to be 10 grams

toori til (H)   mustard oil for cooking (low quality; it tastes fishy)

tsampa (T)   roasted barley flour, a basic food in the highland areas (same as **nasphe, ngam phe,** or **sattu**)

tsaroo (L)   two winglike appendages of black sheep's-wool attached to the **perag**

vanaspati (H)   cooking oil

vibuti (H)   "blessed dust"; often sprinkled on or given to supplicants by a guru

wala (H)   maker, possessor, keeper, inhabitant, or doer of anything (paratha wala, Delhi wala, trekking wala)

yak sher (U)   "very good"

yatra (H)   pilgrimage; journey to a sacred place (also called **tirthayatra**)

yatri (H)   pilgrim

yeti (H,T)   as yet undocumented apelike animal inhabiting dense forests and alpine regions (see Chapter 13, "Himalayan Natural History")

zhumlam (L)   middle path

ziarat (H)   shrine dedicated to a Muslim saint or revered person

zindabad (Arabic)   "long live"

zuk (Ba)   old-style Balti raft kept afloat by inflated goat or sheepskins (innertubes are often used now)

Introduction to Hindustani (Hindi-Urdu)

by John Mock

Hindustani is the lingua franca of the South Asian subcontinent, understood from the Khyber Pass to Calcutta. It is a nonstatus, colloquial language used in informal everyday situations. Above all, it is highly functional. In Pakistan, it is written in modified Arabic script and always called Urdu. In India, where it is called Hindi or Urdu, it is usually written in Devanagari, the Sanskritic script.

Pronunciation

Unless you're a native speaker of a Sanskrit-derived language, it can be difficult to master the sound system of spoken Hindustani. Listening closely to native speakers and watching how they make the different sounds will help you wrap your tongue around this new language. The following romanized transcriptions will get you started.

Vowels

Vowels are pronounced as follows:

a	as in "*a*bove," "*u*p"
y	as in "b*i*t"
w	as in "p*u*t," "l*oo*k"
e	as in "s*a*fe"
o	as in "g*o*"
aa	as in "f*a*ther"
i	as in "s*ea*t"
u	as in "p*oo*l"
ay	as in "b*ai*t"
aw	as in "l*aw*"

A **(hãy)** denotes nasalization of a vowel sound. Nasalization of "Hyndwstaani" vowels is the same as in Nepali, or as in French words like *bon-bon, bien, comment*.

Consonants

Hindustani distinguishes between a dental and a retroflex *t, d,* and *r*. The dental versions start with the tip of the tongue on the backside of the front teeth. The retroflex versions—transcribed with capital letters—start with the tip of the tongue lightly curled back (retroflexed) to touch the roof of the mouth.

Hindustani consonants may also be aspirated or unaspirated. Aspirated consonants get a puff of air. Unaspirated consonants get hardly any breath. An *h* after a consonant is used to transcribe aspirates.

Dental and Retroflex Consonants

t	dental
th	dental, aspirated (not like *th* in "the"—Hindi has no *th* like English)
T	retroflex
Th	retroflex, aspirated
d	dental
dh	dental, aspirated
D	retroflex
Dh	retroflex, aspirated
R	retroflex
Rh	retroflex, aspirated

Unaspirated/Aspirated Consonants

k	unaspirated, as in **kaanaa** ("one-eyed person")
kh	aspirated, as in **khaanaa** ("food")
g	unaspirated, as in **garam** ("hot")
gh	aspirated, as in **ghar** ("home")
c	unaspirated (like English *ch* in "*ch*urch"), as in **char** ("four")
ch	aspirated, as in **chhe** ("six")
j	unaspirated, as in **juThaa** ("defiled by eating")
jh	aspirated, as in **jhuThaa** ("untrue")
p	unaspirated, as in **pyr** ("Monday" in Urdu)
ph	aspirated, as in **phyr** ("again")
b	unaspirated, as in **baag** ("garden")
bh	aspirated, as in **bhaag** ("run away")

Other Consonants

l, m	pronounced close to English, as in **log** ("people"), **maa** ("mother")
n, r	similar to English, as in **naam** ("name"), **raastaa** ("road"); the *r* can be trilled
s, sh	as in **sab** ("all"), **shab** ("night" in Urdu)
y	as in **yaar** ("buddy")
v	pronounced like a cross between English *v* and *w,* as in **vo** ("she," "he," or "that")
f, z	occur in loan words from English and Farsi, as in **fon** ("phone"), **baazaar** ("market")

Sentence Structure

Where is the verb in an English sentence? It's in the middle. In Hindustani the verb always ends the sentence. The subject begins the sentence, and everything else comes in between. The basic sentence order in Hindustani is:

Subject	Object	Verb
ham	**chay**	**pite hãy**
We	tea	drink

Adjectives precede nouns, and adverbs precede verbs.

acchaa	**sastaa**	**khaanaa**
good	cheap	food

jaldi	**kijiye**
quickly	do it

The simplest sentence in Hindustani is an unconjugated verb—i.e., an infinitive. It conveys an imperative sense. It is not polite, but it is also not abusive: it is neutral. For example, **aanaa** means "come!" The word **mat** preceding such an infinitive makes it negative. For example, **mat dekhna** means "don't look!" **Mat** as a negative is used only with imperatives.

The Verb "To Be"

The verb **honaa**—"to be"—is the most common verb in Hindustani, as it is in English, essential for talking about anyone or anything. In the present tense, the singular **hay** and the plural **hãy** correspond to English "is" and "are." The difference between the two Hindustani words is that the plural form is nasalized, whereas the singular isn't. In addition, there is the special form **hũ** for the first person, corresponding to English "am."

Singular		*Plural*	
am	**hũ**	are	**hãy**
is	**hay**		

I am John
jaan	**hũ**
John	am

It is Kashmir.
kashmir	**hay**
Kashmir	is

Minu and Wally are there.
mynu	**awr**	**wali**	**wahãã**	**hãy.**
Minu	and	Wally	there	are

Negative

The word **nahĩ** before the verb makes a sentence negative.

This is not ghee.
ye	**ghi**	**nahĩ**	**hay**
this	ghee	not	is

Pronouns

Any noun or nouns can be used as subject for an appropriate form of **honaa** to make a simple "is/are" sentence. Pronouns can also be subjects. The pronouns are:

Singular		Plural	
I	**mãy**	we	**ham**
		you (polite)	**aap**
she, he, it (present)	**ye**	they (present)	**ye**
she, he, it (absent)	**wo**	they (absent)	**we**
who	**kawn**		

In Hindustani the third-person pronouns are the same as the words for "this," "that," "these," and "those":

Singular		Plural	
this	**ye**	these	**ye**
that	**wo**	those	**we**

I am John.

may	**jaan**	**hũ**
I	John	am

This is Kashmir.

ye	**kashmir**	**hay**
this	Kashmir	is

You are here.

aap	**yahãã**	**hãy**
you	here	are

What is that?

wo	**kyaa**	**hay?**
that	what	is

Possessives

Adding the suffix /**kaa** to nouns or pronouns makes them possessive, like English " 's" or "of."

Where is Minu's house?

minu/kaa	**ghar**	**khãã**	**hai?**
Minu's	house	where	is

What is the price of sugar?

chinii/kaa	**daam**	**kyaa**	**hai?**
sugar's	price	what	is

Note the exceptions for possessive pronouns:

	Singular			*Plural*
my, mine	**meraa**		our	**hamaaraa**
his, hers, its (present)	**ys/kaa**		their (present)	**yn/kaa**
of this	" "		of these	" "
his, hers, its (absent)	**ws/kaa**		their (absent)	**wn/kaa**
of that	" "		of those	" "
whose	**kys/kaa**		whose	**kyn/kaa**

What is the price of this?

ys/kaa	**daam**	**kyaa**	**hay?**
this/of	price	what	is

What is your name?

aap/kaa	**naam**	**kyaa**	**hay?**
your	name	what	is

Verb Conjugation

Hindustani verbs have three parts:

- the stem, which carries the meaning
- the ending, which carries the number and gender
- the tense marker at the very end, often a conjugated form of **honaa**

The endings **rahaa** (masculine singular), **rahe** (masculine plural), and **rahi** (feminine singular and plural) can often be used for both present and future tenses and must be followed by the form of **honaa** appropriate for the subject.

I am going to Ladakh tomorrow.

mãy	**kal**	**ladaakh**	**jaa/rahaa**	**hũ**
I	tomorrow	Ladakh	going (m.s.)	am

You are drinking tea.

aap	**chay**	**pii/rahii**	**hãy**
you	tea	drinking (f.)	are

Where are they coming from?

we	**kahãa/se**	**aa/rahe**	**hãy?**
they	where/from	coming (m.pl.)	are

He isn't looking at you.

wo	**aap/ko**	**nahĩ**	**dekh/rahaa**	**hay**
he	you/at (to)	not	looking (m.s.)	is

Simple Present Tense

The endings **/taa** (masculine singular), **/te** (masculine plural), and **/ti** (feminine singular and plural) when added to a verb stem and followed by the tense marker form the simple present tense.

We want to go to Leh.

ham	**le**	**jaanaa**	**chahaate**	**hãy**
we	Leh	to go	want (m.pl.)	

I live in America.

mãy	amerykaa/mẽ	rahtaa	hũ
I	America/in	live (m.s.)	

Simple Past Tense

Transitive verbs: add /ne to the subject and the ending /aa to the verb stem.

I saw him.

mãy/ne	ws/ko	dekhaa
I	him	saw

We ate food.

ham/ne	khaanaa	khaayaa
we	food	ate

Intransitive verbs: just add the endings /aa (m.s.), /e (m.pl.), /i (f.s.), or /ī (f.pl.) to the verb stem, depending on the number and gender of the subject.

We lived in Pakistan for two years.

ham	paakystaan/mẽ	do	saal	rahe
we	Pakistan/in	two	years	lived

Note special forms for **jaanaa** ("to go"):

gayaa	he went
gaye	they (m.pl.) went
gayi	she went
gayī	they (f.pl.) went

Past of tense marker **honaa:**

thaa	was (m.s.)
the	were (m.pl.)
thi	was (f.s.)
thī	were (f.pl.)

Who was it?

kawn	thaa?
who	was (it)

She was there.

wo	wahãa	thi
she	there	was

We were ill.

ham	bimaar	the
we	ill	were

Future Tense

Future tense endings go right on the stem. There is no additional tense marker.

/egaa (m.s.)
/egi (f.s.)

/**ēge** (m.pl.)
/**ēgi** (f.pl.)

In Skardu, everything will be available.

skaardu/mē	**sab kwch**	**mylegaa**
Skardu/in	everything	will be available

Will you go with us?

aap	**hamaare/saath**	**jaaēge?**
you	us/with	will go

Postpositions

In Hindustani prepositions follow the noun. They are:

in	/**mē**
on	/**par**
from	/**se**
of	/**kaa**
up to, until	/**tak**

She/he is in the house.

wo	**ghar/mē**	**hay**
she/he	house/in	is

How far is it from here up to Shimshal?

yahāā/se	**shymshaal/tak**	**kytni**	**dur**	**hay?**
here/from	Shimshal/up to	how much	far	is

Some useful postpositions have two words: the first is always /**ke**, a form of the possessive postposition /**kaa**. Remember that some pronouns have special forms with this postposition.

/**ke lyye**	for (sake of)
/**ke pass**	have (a thing)
/**ke saamne**	in front of
/**ke saath**	with (a person)
/**ke baad**	after
/**ke upar**	above

What do you have?

aap/ke	**paas**	**kyaa**	**hay?**
you	have	what	

Make tea for us!

hamaare/lyye	**chay**	**banaanaa!**
us/for	tea	make

Ko Constructions

Many extremely useful Hindustani expressions are impersonal constructions, formed by adding the postposition **ko** to the subject or pronoun. Remember that the following pronouns change form when followed by a postposition:

I	**mwjh/ko** (often contracted to **mwjhe**)
this/that	**ys/ko**
he/she/it	**ws/ko**
these/those	**yn/ko**
they	**wn/ko**

/ko chaahyye expresses need or want for an object:

What do you need?

aap/ko	**kyaa**	**chaahyye?**
you	what	need

We need a room.

ham/ko	**kamaraa**	**chaahyye**
we	room	need

/ko infinitive **hay** expresses having to do something:

I have to go now.

mwjhe	**abhi**	**jaanaa**	**hay**
I	now	to go	(have)

/ko malum hay expresses knowing:

Do you know my name?

aap/ko	**meraa**	**naam**	**malum**	**hay?**
you	my	name	know	

/ko pasand hay expresses liking:

He/she likes tea.

ws/ko	**chay**	**pasand**	**hay**
he/she	tea	likes	

/ko pyaas hay	thirst
/ko nind hay	sleepiness
/ko jaldi hay	haste/hurry
/ko bwkhaar hay	fever
/ko bhukh hay	hunger
/ko Dar hay	fear
/ko kushi hay	happiness
/ko zwkaam hay	a cold

Helpful Phrases

Greetings	**namaste** (Hindu)
	salaam alekwm (Muslim)
How are you (doing)?	**kyaa haal chaal hay?**
How are you?	**aap kayse hãy?**
I'm fine.	**mãy Thik hū**
Everything else OK?	**awr sab Thik hay?**

Where are you going?	aap kahãa jaa/rahe hãy?
Where do you want to go?	aap kahãa jaanaa chaahate hãy?
Where is _____ ?	_____ kahãa hay?
What is your name?	aap/kaa naam kyaa hay?
My name is _____ .	meraa naam _____ hay
What is her/his name?	ws/kaa naam kyaa hay?
Her/his name is _____ .	ws/kaa naam _____ hay
What is that?	vo kyaa hay?
That is a _____ .	vo _____ hay
Who is that?	vo kawn hay
That is my friend.	vo meraa dost hay
Where is _____ available?	_____ kahãa myltaa hay?
I need/want (a thing).	mwjhe _____ chaahyye
Give me _____ .	mwjhe _____ denaa
	mwjhe _____ dijyye (polite)
How much is _____ ?	_____ kytne payse hãy?
That's too much.	wo zyaadaa hay
Please make it less.	kwch kam kijyye
What time is it?	kytne baje hãy?
It's eight o'clock.	aaTh baje hãy
Please go straight.	sidhe jaayye
Please turn right.	dahyne jaayye
Please turn left.	baayē jaayye
Please stop here.	yahãa rwkyye
Enough! OK.	bas! Thik hay!

Vocabulary

Time

half-past	saRhe
o'clock	baje
today	aaj
tomorrow	kal
yesterday	kal
day after tomorrow	parsõ
day before yesterday	parsõ

Numbers

one	ek
two	do
three	tin
four	char
five	paanch

(Numbers, continued)

six	chhe
seven	saat
eight	aaTh
nine	naw
ten	das
eleven	gyaaraa
twelve	baraah

Food

apple	seb
banana	kelaa
bread	roTi
butter	makkhan, ghi
carrot	gaajar
cauliflower	gobhi

chickpea	chanaa
egg	anDaa
food	khaanaa
fruit	phal
lentils	daal
mango	aam
milk	dudh
orange	santaraa
pea	maTar
peanut	mwmphali
pepper	myrch
potato	aalu
rice	chaval
salt	namak
spice	masaalaa
vegetable	sabzi
whole-wheat flour	aaTaa
yoghurt	dahi

Colors

black	kaalaa
blue	nilaa
green	haaraa
red	laal
white	safed
yellow	pilaa

Relations

father	pytaa
mother	maataa
brother	bhaai
sister	bahyn
friend	dost
woman	awrat
man	maard
person	aadmi
people	log

The Body

ear	kaan
eye	ãankh
hand	haath
head	syr
nose	naak
stomach	peT
tooth	dãanT

Other Nouns

blanket	kambal
candle	mombaTTi
chair	kwrsi
cloth, clothes	kapRaa
cup	pyaalaa
hat	Topi
kerosene	myTTi/kaa Tel
key	chaabi
lock	taalaa
luggage, stuff	samaan
metal plate	thaali
moon	chand
mountain	parbaat
needle	sui
path, trail	raastaa
room	kamaraa
shoe	jutaa
soap	saabwn
spoon	chamach
store	dwkaan
street	saRak
sun	swraj
tailor	darji
thing	chiz
thread	taagaa
water	paani
wind	hawaa

Adjectives

a little	thoRaa
all	har
bad, no good	kharaab
beautiful	swndar
below	nichaa
big	baRaa
cheap	sastaa
closed	band
cold	Thandaa
difficult	mwshkyl
dirty	ganDaa
dry	sukhaa
easy	aasaan
empty	khaali
enough	kaafi
finished	khatam

forbidden	manaa
fresh	taazaa
genuine	asali
not genuine	nakali
good	acchaa
heavy	bhaari
high	wnchaa
hot	garam
ill	bimaar
important	khaas
inside	andaar
light	halkaa
little, small	chhoTaa
long	lambaa
necessary	zaruri
new	naayaa
old	pwraanaa
open	khulaa
ready	tayyaar
separate	alag
straight	sidhaa
strong	mazbut
sweet	mIThaa
too much	zyaadaa
true	sach
useless	bekaar
very, many	bahwt
weak	kamzor
well made, ripe	pakkaa
not well made, unripe	kaccha
wet	gilaa
wrong	galat

Verbs

ask (a question)	puchhnaa
ask (for something)	mãangnaa
bathe	nahaana
bring	laanaa
burn	jalaanaa
buy	kharidnaa
climb	chaaRhnaa
come	aanaa
do	karnaa
drink	pinaa
eat	khaanaa

(Verbs, continued)

fall	girnaa
give	denaa
go	jaanaa
hear, listen	swnnaa
learn	sikhnaa
look	dekhnaa
meet, be available	mylnaa
move	chalnaa
read, study	paRhnaa
remain, reside	rahnaa
sit	bayThnaa
sleep	sonaa
speak	bolnaa
take	lenaa
understand	samajhnaa
want	chaahanaa
wash (clothes)	dhonaa
write	lykhnaa

Adverbs

again	phyr
ahead	aage
always	hameshaa
behind	pichhe
in front	saamne
here	yahãa
in the middle	bich/mē
near (close)	nazdik
right now	abhi
on foot	paydal
outside	baahar
slowly	dhire
sometimes	kabhi
then	tab
there	wahãa
totally	bylkwl

Question Words

how much/many?	kytnaa
how?	kaysaa
what?	kyaa
when?	kab
where?	kahãa
which one?	kawnsaa
who?	kawn

| whose? | kys/kaa |
| why? | kyō |

Conjunctions

and	awr
but	lekyn
or	yaa
maybe	shayad
because	kyōki
yes	hãã
no	nahī

Introduction to Afghan Dari

by Stephen Shucart

Afghan Dari is a Persian dialect akin to classical Persian, or Farsi. It is spoken by millions of Afghan refugees living in Pakistan, as well as by many Chitralis.

Many believe Afghans to be the most hospitable of all Muslim people. The Afghans have never been conquered, and as Afghanistan was not subject to the British Raj, travelers are rarely likely to meet Afghans who speak English. The principal exceptions are merchants in the cantonment area of Peshawar, where many of Kabul's infamous Chicken Street tourist shops have relocated since the Russian invasion of December 1979.

While exploring the Chitral area, especially around Garam Chashma, you will encounter many Afghans, especially battle-hardened Mujahedeen: proud, fierce warriors who are more than happy to share their tea and food in mud *chaikhana*s (teahouses) and *caravanserai*s (square inns with an inner courtyard). A more friendly and open people are not to be found. Soon the time will come when trekkers can once again explore the glorious scenery and unique tribal life of the Hindu Kush in a free Afghanistan.

Pronunciation

Vowels

a	as in "f*a*ther"
e	"*e*very"
i	as in "*i*ll"
o	as in "*o*rbit"
u	as the double *oo* in "b*oo*t"
aa	as in "m*a*rket" or "g*a*rden"
ai	as the long *i* in "*i*ce"
au	as the *ou* in "*ou*r"
dj	as in "plea*s*ure"

Consonants

Most consonants are pronounced as in the West, but please note the following:

g	is always hard, as in "good"
q	is not followed by *u;* it is an explosive, breathy sound, as in "*kh*aki"
kh	a throaty, coughing sound, like the *ch* in the Scottish "lo*ch*"
gh	a back of the throat, glottal stop

Sentence Structure

The basic sentence order in Dari is:
    Subject   Object   Verb
Modifiers follow the noun.

Nouns

Plurals are formed by adding the ending *-ha*.

tefal	child
tefelha	children

A word is attached to its modifier by adding the suffix *-e*.

tefel-e khub	good child

Prepositions

Prepositions perform most other functions:

ba	to, at, into, on
bas	with, by means of
dar	in
az	from

Pronouns

Personal

man	I	**maa**	we
tu	you (intimate: for child, servant, insult)	**shomaa**	you (general)
o	he, she		
iin	it, this		
aan	it, that	**aanha**	they

Possessive

Add *-e* to the thing possessed:

ketaab-e man	my book
ketaab-e shomaa	your book
ketaab-e o	his, her book

Objective

Objective (accusative) forms are indicated by **raa**:

ma raa	me	**maa raa**	us
tu raa	you (intimate)	**shomaa raa**	you (general)
o raa	him, her		
iin raa	it, this		
aan raa	them, that	**aanhaa raa**	them

Dative

Use the preposition **ba** ("to") or **baraay** ("for")

ba man	to me	**baraay maa**	for us
ba tu	to you	**baraay shomaa**	for you
ba o	to him, to her		
ba iin	to this, to it		
ba aan	to that, to them	**baraay aanhaa**	for them

Verbs

The verb forms given in this glossary are based on the infinitive and the first person singular of the present tense:

didan, mebinam	to see, I see
raftan, merawam	to go, I go

Only three forms of the verb are essential: past, present, and imperative.

Past Tense

Past tense is formed by dropping the *-an* ending from the infinitive and adding the personal ending:

man raftam	I went	**maa raftem**	we went
tu rafti	you went	**shomaa rafted**	you went
o raft	he, she went	**aanhaa raftand**	they went
iin raft	it went		
aan raft	that went		

Present Tense

Present tense is usually indicated by the prefix *me-*, but the forms are often so different from the infinitive that the present tense is given along with the infinitive in the verb list under "Vocabulary."

raftan	to go	**man merawm**	I go
		tu merawi	you go
		etc.	

Imperative

Imperative is indicated by the prefix *be-*. Three forms are used: (1) is extremely short, used to inferiors or animals, and often in anger; (2) is polite; and (3), used with **loftan** ("please"), is the ultimate in politeness.

raftan	to go	(1) **boro!**	go away!
		(2) **berawed**	go
		(3) **loftan berawed**	please go

Future Tense

Future tense can be indicated by using the present tense with such future words as **fardaa** ("tomorrow"), **hafta-e bad** ("next week"), or **dar aayenda** ("in future").

fardaa ba Chitral merawam   Tomorrow I will go to Chitral.

Adjectives

Comparison is similar to English:

khub	good
khubtar	better
khubtarin	best
kalaan	big
kalaantar	bigger
kalaantarin	biggest

Vocabulary

Colors

black	**siyaah**
blue	**aabi**
brown	**naswaari**
gray	**khaaki**
green	**sabz**
pink	**golaabi**
purple	**benafsh**
red	**sorkh**
yellow	**zard**

Relations

father	**padar**
mother	**maadar**
brother	**braadar**
sister	**khuaahar**
husband	**shauhar**
wife	**khaanom**
son	**pesar**
daughter	**dokhtar**
boy	**bacha**
girl	**dushiza**
widow	**bewa**
orphan	**yatim**

The Body

arm	**bazu**
beard	**rish**
blood	**khun**
brain	**maghz**
ear	**gosh**
elbow	**aronj**
eye	**chasm**

(The Body, continued)

face	**ruy**
hand	**dast**
head	**sar**
knee	**zaanu**
leg	**leng**
mouth	**daan**
nose	**bini**
stomach	**meda**

Time

o'clock	**baja**
hour	**saa'at**
minute	**daqiqa**
second	**saniya**
day	**roz**
night	**shab**
yesterday	**diroz**
last night	**dishab**
today	**emroz**
tonight	**emshab**
tomorrow	**fardaa**
tomorrow night	**fardaa shab**
day after tomorrow	**pas fardaa**
every day	**har roz**
every night	**har shab**
morning	**sobh**
noon	**chasht**
week	**hafta**
month	**maah**
year	**saal**
Friday	**juma**
Saturday	**shanbe**
Sunday	**yak shanbe**
Monday	**du shanbe**
Tuesday	**se shanbe**
Wednesday	**chaar shanbe**
Thursday	**panj shanbe**
spring	**bahaar**
summer	**taabestan**
fall	**khazaan**
winter	**zemeztaan**

Numbers

zero	**safer**
half	**nim**
one, first	**yak, awal**
two, second	**du, dowom**
three, third	**se, sowom**
four, fourth	**chaar, chaarom**
five, fifth	**panj, panjom**
six, sixth	**shash, shashom**
seven, seventh	**haft, haftom**
eight, eighth	**hast, hashom**
nine, ninth	**noh, nohom**
ten, tenth	**dah, dahom**
eleven	**yaazdah**
twelve	**duaazdah**
thirteen	**sezdah**
fourteen	**chaardah**
fifteen	**paanzdah**
sixteen	**shaanzdah**
seventeen	**hafdah**
eighteen	**hajdah**
nineteen	**nozdah**
twenty	**bist**
twenty-one	**bist-o yak**
twenty-two	**bist-o du**
thirty	**si**
forty	**chel**
fifty	**pinja**
sixty	**shasht**
seventy	**haftaad**
eighty	**hashtaad**
ninety	**nawad**
one hundred	**sad**
one thousand	**hazaar**

Food

almond	**badaam**
apple	**seb**
apricot	**zardaalu**
beans	**lubiya**
beet	**lublabu**
bread	**naan**
butter	**mas'ka**
carrot	**zard ak**
corn	**jawaari**
cream	**sar-e shir**

(Food, continued)

date	**khormaa**
egg	**tokhom**
flour	**aard**
fruit	**mewa**
grape	**angur**
lentils	**daal**
meat	**gosht**
melon	**kharbuza**
milk	**shir**
onion	**piyaaz**
orange	**naraanj**
pear	**naak**
peas	**moshang**
pepper	**mirch**
potatoes	**kachaalu**
raisin	**keshmesh**
rice	**brenj**
salt	**namak**
spinach	**paalak**
tea	**chaay**
tomato	**baanjaani rumi**
vegetable	**tarkaari**
watermelon	**tarbuz**
yoghurt	**mast**

Nouns

bathroom	**tashnaab**
blanket	**kambal**
book	**ketaab**
camel	**shotar**
candle	**sham**
carpet	**qaalin**
city	**shahr**
clothes	**lebaas**
emerald	**zamarod**
goat	**boz**
gun	**tofang**
hashish	**charas**
hemp	**ganjah**
holy war	**jahad**
holy warrior(s)	**mujahad/ mujahadeen**
horse	**asp**
house	**khaana**
knife	**kaard**

lapis lazuli	**laajward**	*(Adjectives, continued)*	
matches	**gogered**	happy	**khosh masrur**
moon	**maah**	heavy	**sangin**
mountain	**koh**	helpless	**becharra**
pass	**kotal**	high	**beland**
river	**daryaa**	hot	**garm**
room	**otaaq**	hungry	**goshna**
ruby	**yaaqut**	important	**mohem**
sheep	**gosfand**	intoxicated	**nashe**
star	**staara**	(stoned)	
street	**sarak**	large	**kalaan**
sun	**aaftaab**	left side	**dast-i chap**
thing	**chiz**	less	**kam**
war	**jang**	light	**roshan**
water	**aab**	little	**khord**
		a little	**yak kame**
		long	**daraaz**

Adjectives

		many	**bisyaar**
ahead	**pesh**	mistaken	**ghalat**
alive	**zenda**	more	**digar**
all	**hama**	necessary	**laazemi**
bad	**kharaab**	new	**nau**
beautiful	**qashang**	old	**qadim**
beginning	**shoro**	old person	**pir**
below	**zer**	open	**waaz**
big	**kalaan, bozorg**	ordinary	**aadi**
cheap	**arzaan**	poor	**gharib**
closed	**basta**	ready	**tayaar**
cold	**sard**	rich	**daulatmand**
crazy	**dewana**	right side	**dast-i rast**
dead	**morda**	several	**chanin**
dirty	**chatal**	short	**kotaah**
dry	**khashk**	sick	**naajor, mariz**
easy	**aasaan**	small	**kochak**
empty	**khali**	snowy	**barfi**
enough	**bas**	straight ahead	**ru-ba-ru**
equal	**baraabar**	(go)	
excellent	**besyaar khub**	sweet	**shirin**
expensive	**qimat**	tight	**tang**
false	**drogh**	tough	**sakht**
far	**dur**	true	**rast**
fast	**zud**	ugly	**badrang**
fat	**chaaq**	very	**besyaar, khele**
fresh	**taaza**		**ziyaad**
full	**por**	weak	**za´if**
genuine	**asel**	wet	**tar**
good	**khub**	wide	**bardaar**

Verbs

Infinitive given first, followed by first person singular:

be	**budan, hastam, mebaasham**
buy	**kharidan, mekaram**
bring	**awordan, mearam**
burn	**sokhtan, mesuzam**
come	**aamadan, me'aayam**
cut	**boridan, meboram**
do	**kardan, mekonam**
drink	**nushidan, menosham**
eat	**khordan, mekhoram**
fall	**oftidan, meoftam**
fight	**jangidan, mejangam**
give	**daadan, medeham**
go	**raftan, merawam**
hear	**shonidan, meshnawam**
know	**danestan, medanam**
learn	**yaad greftan, yaad megiram**
make	**saakhtan, mesaazam**
put	**maandan, memaanam**
read	**khaandan, mekhaanam**
run	**dawidan, medawam**
say	**goftan, megoyam**
see	**didan, mebinam**
sell	**frokhtan, mefrosham**
sleep	**khaabidan, mekhaabam**
take	**greftan, megiram**
think	**feker kardan, feker mekardam**
understand	**fahmidan, mefahamam**

Adverbs

after	**baad**	last	**sakher**
again	**digar-baar**	maybe	**momken**
ago	**pesh**	middle	**wasat**
ahead	**ru-ba-ru**	near	**nazdik**
always	**harwaqt**	no	**ne**
as far as	**taa**	now	**hala**
behind	**dar posht**	no matter	**parwaanest**
besides	**bar-alaawa**	often	**barhaa**
enough	**bas**	out	**birun**
front	**pesh**	side	**taraf**
here	**iinja**	slowly	**ba-aahestagi**
		sometime	**wagte**

suddenly	**yakbaar**	*(Interrogatives, continued)*	
then	**pas**	who?	**ki?**
there	**aanja**	whom?	**ki-raa?**
therefore	**azaan sabab**	whose?	**azki?**
until	**taa**	why?	**cheraa?**
yes	**balé**		

Interrogatives

Conjunctions and Prepositions

		about	**darbaara**
how?	**chetaur?**	and	**wa, o**
how many?	**chand?**	because	**zera chunke**
how much?	**cheqadar?**	but	**magar**
what?	**che?**	if	**agar**
which?	**kodam?**	or	**ya**
when?	**kai?**	with	**baa**
where?	**kojaa?**		

Phrases

Greeting: place your right hand over your heart and bow slightly:

Peace be upon you.	**salaam alaikom**
The reply:	**alaikom-e salaam**
How are you?	**chetaur hasted?**
Are you well?	**khub hasted?**
Is your body well?	**jani juraas?**
How is it?	**che hal dared?**
Thank you very much.	**bisyaar tashakor**
Goodbye:	
Go in the safety of God.	**ba aman-e Khodaa**
God be your protector.	**Khodaa haafez**
What is your name?	**nam-e shomaa chist?**
My name is Steve.	**nam-e man Steve ast**
Where are you from?	**shomaa az kojast?**
I'm from America.	**man as Amrika ast**
What is this?	**iin che ast?**
What is that?	**aan che ast?**
What do you want?	**che mekoned?**
How many people are with you?	**baa shomaa chand nafar ast?**
Where is the bathroom?	**tashnaab kojast?**
Excuse me.	**bubakshed**
How much is the price?	**chand qimat?**
It is too much money.	**iin pul ziyaad ast**
It is expensive.	**qimat ast**
I don't understand.	**man nafahmam**
What did you say?	**shomaa che gofted?**
Is this the road to Chitral?	**iin sarak-e Chitral ast?**
Why not?	**chera nist?**
What time is it?	**chand baja ast?**

It is one o'clock.	**yak baja ast**
How many wives do you have?	**chand khaanom daared?**
I have two wives.	**man du khaanom daaram**
I'm very sorry.	**bisyaar afsos**
Where is it from?	**az kojast?**
It's from Mazar-i-Sharif.	**iin az Mazar-i-Sharif ast**
Go there!	**aanja boro!**
Stop!	**baash!**
Come here!	**iinja biyaa!**
Sit!	**beshi!**
Don't shoot!	**fair nakon!**

Khowar Glossary

by John Mock

Khowar, the language of the Kho, is the chief language throughout the district of Chitral, though most side valleys have their own dialects and educated Chitralis also speak Urdu and Persian. Khowar is generally understood in the Kalash valleys and the Lutkoh Tehsil. Pushtu has penetrated the southern valleys. The Chitralis of Turikho are considered to speak the purest Khowar, and it is the first tongue for many in the Ghizar and Yasin valleys, which are upriver from Gilgit district. Khowar is an Indo-European variant that shows significant Iranian influence, and it is included in the language group known as Dardic.

Vowel Pronunciation

The diacritical marks here and in the vocabulary lists indicate long vowels.

a	as in "*a*bove"
ā	as in "*fa*ther"
i	as in "b*i*t"
ī	as in "s*ea*t"
u	as in "p*u*t"
ū	as in "p*oo*l"
o	as in "g*o*"

Grammar

To briefly sketch the grammar, Khowar has no gender. A plural is formed by adding -*an* to the singular. Adjectives precede nouns and show no change in gender or number. Khowar has postpositions (prepositions placed after their objects). Its verbs are mostly regular. Infinitive forms end in -*ik* or -*ek*.

The present-tense endings to regular verbs are as follows:

	Singular	Plural
First person	-*iman*	-*isian*
Second person	-*isan*	-*imian*
Third person	-*iran*	-*inian*

Vocabulary

Pronouns

I	**awā**	we	**ispa**
you	**tū**	you (plural)	**pissa**
it, she, he (near)	**hess**	they (near)	**hāmit**
it, she, he (far)	**hassa**	they (far)	**hāttet**

me, my	mā
your	tā
his	here
our	ispā
their	hattetan

Colors

black	shā
blue	otch
green	sauz
red	krūī
white	ishperū
yellow	zech

Relations

father	tāt
mother	nān
brother	brar
sister	īspusār
husband	mosh
wife	bok
boy	daq
girl	kumorū
woman	kimerī
man	mosh

The Body

blood	leh
ear	kar
eye	ghech
hand	host
head	sor
nose	niskār

Time

morning	chūchī
noon	pishin
afternoon	chaghnass
day	anūss
midnight	chūī barābar
today	hanūn
yesterday	dush
tomorrow	chūī
day after tomorrow	pingā

(Time, continued)

day before yesterday	otirī

Numbers

one	ī
two	jū
three	troī
four	chor
five	ponj
six	choī
seven	sāt
eight	āsht
nine	nyuf
ten	jush
eleven	jush ī
twelve	jush jū
twenty-one	bishīr ī
thirty	bishīr jush
forty	jū bishīr
fifty	jū bishīr jush
sixty	troī bishīr
one hundred	ī shor

Food

apple	palogh
apricot	zhūlī
dried apricot	chambor
apricot nut	zhor
bread	shāpik
butter	māskah
buttermilk	shatū
cheese (white)	shapināk
cream	kambakkh
egg	aiyukūn
grape	dratch
meat	pashūr
milk	shir
mulberry	mratch
dried mulberry	kiturī
pear	tang
rice	grinj
salt	trupp
walnut	birmogh
whole-wheat flour	peshīrū
yoghurt	machir

Other Nouns

ball	plinj
bed	zhen
blanket	zhīl
clothes	chellai
cow	leshū
fire	angār
hat	khoī
Chitrali-style hat	pakol
hawk	yurj
hemp	bong
herd	rom
horse	istor
house	dūr
ibex	
male	ushūng
female	mūrū
ice	yoz
mallet	ghal o tsun
moon	mas
mountain	zom
pass	ān
plain	lāsht
polo	ghol
polo field	jinalī
river	galogh
side	waltī
sun	yor
valley	gol
water	ūgh

Adjectives

all	chīk
bad	dish
beautiful	chust
big	lut
cold	ushak
good	jam
high	zhang
hot	petch

(Adjectives, continued)

left-side	kholī
long	drung
many, very	bo
right-side	hosk
sweet	shirin

Verbs

be	assik
be able	bīk
bring	angīk
come	gīk
do	korīk
drink	pīk
eat	zhibīk
give	dīk
go	bīk
know, understand	hushkorīk
look	lolīk
read	rek
sit	nishīk
sleep	oreil
speak	lūdīk
take	ganīk

Adverbs

after	āchār
ahead	prushtī
certainly	khā mā khā
how	kicha
now	hanisen
probably	albātt
slowly	lash
when	kia wat
where	kura
who	kā
why	ko

Conjunctions

and	oche
because	kokī

Phrases

How are you?	tu kīcha asus?
How are you?	jam tāzā kosī hau ā?
Fine, thanks.	bo jam, mehrbānī
Fine, brother, and how are you?	jam brār ā, tū tāzā asūs a?
Where are you coming from?	kurār gītī asūs?
I don't know.	mā te malūm nikī

Burushaski Glossary

by John Mock

Burushaski, unrelated to any other spoken language in the world, is the language of Hunza and Nagar. Pronunciation varies from the Hunza side of the valley to the Nagar side. In parts of the Yasin Valley, where the Burusho people also live, the closely analogous Werchikwar is spoken. But in the lower-elevation Gilgit River Valley that separates Hunza from Yasin, Shina, an Indic language, is spoken.

Burushaski has four classifications of nouns: male and female (human) and animate and inanimate (nonhuman). Correct word order places the subject first and the verb last. Sibilant consonant clusters give the language a unique sound.

Vowel Pronunciation

a	as in "*a*bove"
ā	as in "f*a*ther"
i	as in "b*i*t"
ī	as in "s*ea*t"
u	as in "p*u*t"
ū	as in "p*oo*l"
o	as in "g*o*"
e	as in "t*a*ke

Vocabulary

Pronouns

I	**je**
you	**un**
he	**ine**
she	**inagus**
we	**mi**
they	**ne**
this	**ine**
that	**kine**

Relations

father	**uy**
mother	**mī**
woman	**gus**
man	**hir**
boy	**hiles**
girl	**dasin**

(Relations, continued)

infant	**giyas**
uncle	**nun**
shaman	**bitān**

The Body

blood	**multān**
hand	**ring**
head	**yatis**
ear	**ltumal**
eye	**lchin**

Colors

black	**matum**
green and blue	**shiqam**
red	**bardum**
white	**burūm**

Food

apple	bālt
apricot	jū
dried	batering
apricot nut	hāni
large bitter nut	balānimah
apricot varieties	
very sweet	Alisakākas
whitish, best quality	Brumdrū
white	Kabuli
yellow and sweet	Habidrū
barley	hari
bread	shapīk
bread cooked in coals	kemishdon
bread soaked in ghee	chamūrikī
thick wheat bread	phitī
wide wheat cake	giyal
buckwheat	barū
butter	maltāsh
buttermilk	diltār
cheese	
hard cheese, reddish	rakpin
hard cheese, whitish	kurūt
white	burūs
cream	irān
egg	tingān
meat	chāp
milk	māmū
mulberry	biranch
pea	gark
pear	phesho
rice	bras
salt	bayū
soup	daudho
walnut	balring
water	tsil
whole-wheat flour	diram

Other Nouns

animal	haiwān
bird	balas
bridge	brosh
cloud	kuronch
day	gunts
fire	pfū

(Other Nouns, continued)

glacier	haguts
goat	
he-goat	haldyn
she-goat	tsier
hat	pfartsin
hawk	bāz
herd	dun
horse	haqur
house	hā
ice	gamū
mountain	chhish
night	thup
pass	haguts-e-kuns
path, way	gun
river	daryā
rope	gashk
sky	aiyesh
snow	geh
stone	dūn
sun	sāh
tree	tom
tent	gut
valley	bar
wind	tish

Adjectives

all	yon
bad	gunikish
beautiful	daltās
big	uyum
cold	chhāgurum
far	mathān
good	shuā
high	thānum
left-side	ghawum
long	gusānam
many, very	būt
near	asir
new	thosh
old (thing)	diganum
right-side	dowum
small	jut
true	tsān

Verbs

bathe	tum delus
climb	dusas, kairkinus
come	juwus
do	etas
drink	minas
eat	shius
give	uyas
go	niyas
sit	hurūtas
sleep	guchaiyas
speak	yanas
understand	henas
walk	gutsāras

Adverbs

after	īljī
again	dā
ahead	yar
here	khole
how	be
now	mū
on foot	gatal
side	pachīmo
slowly	thalā
there	ele
therefore	ītetsum
when	ke
where	am
who	āmīn
why	bes

Conjunctions and Prepositions

and	ke
because	beseke

(Conjunctions, continued)

but	thī
with	ka

Time

today	khūlto
tomorrow	jīmale
yesterday	sā ati
day after tomorrow	hī pulto
day before yesterday	yā bulto

Numbers

one	hin
two	ālto
three	usko
four	wālto
five	tshundo
six	shindo
seven	talo
eight	altar
nine	huncho
ten	torum
eleven	turmahan
twelve	turnalto
twenty	yalta
twenty-one	yaltahan
thirty	altar han
forty	altu walta
fifty	altu walta torum
sixty	ski altar
seventy	ski altar torum
eighty	walti altar
ninety	walti altar torum

Phrases

How are you?	besan hāl bilā?
	be mei bā?
I'm good.	shuā bā
What's your name?	gwik besan bilā?
Where are you going?	ām nichen?
I'm going to _____ .	je _____ nichā bā
Is this the road to _____ ?	_____ niyas gan bī?
Let's go!	gusar chen!

Wakhi Glossary

by Haqiqat Ali

Wakhi is a dialect of archaic Iranian. In Pakistan, Wakhi is spoken in the Gujal region of the upper Hunza Valley, in the northern regions of the Ishkuman and Yasin valleys, and in the upper Yarkhun Valley of Chitral. In Afghanistan, Wakhi is spoken in parts of northeastern Badakhshan. These are also the areas where you are likely to meet Wakhi families. Wakhi, along with all other Indo-Iranian languages, uses subject-object-verb word order.

Vocabulary

Pronouns

I	**woz**
you	**tu**
he	**yā ayā**
she	**yā hooinān**
we	**sak**
they	**ayasht**

Relations

name	**nong**
father	**tāt**
mother	**nān**
woman	**hoolnān**
man	**day**
boy	**kash**
girl	**perchod**
infant	**za zamān**
shaman	**betān**

The Body

blood	**wikhan**
ear	**gish**
eye	**kak**
hand	**dast**
head	**sar**
heart	**pezove**

Time

today	**wodeg**
tomorrow	**piga**
yesterday	**yez**

(Time, continued)

day before yesterday	**bo ror ter miss**

Numbers

one	**yew**
two	**bui**
three	**trui**
four	**tsaboor**
five	**panz**
six	**shaadh**
seven	**hube**
eight	**hath**
nine	**nau**
ten	**dhas**
eleven	**dasyiw**
twelve	**dasbui**
twenty	**wisth**
thirty	**wisthdas**
forty	**sbo wist**
fifty	**bo wiste das**
sixty	**thru wiste**
seventy	**thru wiste das**
eighty	**tsabor wiste**
ninety	**tsabor wiste das**
hundred	**saad**

Food

apple	**mur**
apricot	**chuan**
apricot nut	**kutuk**

barley	**yurk**
bread	
bread cooked in mold	**qemichdun**
inch-thick bread	**shapīk putok**
thick wheat bread	**dildungi**
wheat cake cooked in ghee	**chamuriki**
wide wheat cake	**giral garal**
buckwheat	**burvi**
buttermilk	**deegh**
cheese	
dry	**qurut**
hard	**raqpin**
cream	**mirik**
egg	**tukhmurge**
food	**shapīk**
herb tea	**chamuru**
kernel	**serk**
meat	**gosht**
midmorning meal	**pizvan**
milk	**bursh mau jarj**
mulberry	**biranje**
pea	**shakh**
pear	**peshow**
rice	**gerange**
salt	**namak**
soup	**moch**
tea	**choi**
walnut	**tor**
water	**yupek**
whole-wheat flour	**doram semem**
yoghurt	**piee**

Other Nouns

bird	**parinda**
cloud	**vitish**
day	**ro**
desert	**dasht**
fire	**rakhnigh**
goat	
he-goat	**buch**
she-goat	**tugh**
hat	**sikied**
hawk	**baz**
herd	**kala**
house	**khun khon**

(Other Nouns, continued)

ice	**yikh**
juniper	**yarz**
lake	**zhuy**
moon	**zhumak**
mountain	**kho**
night	**naghed**
pass	**wiyin**
pathway	**fidek**
river	**darya**
rope	**shivan**
snow	**zem**
spring (of water)	**kuk**
star	**stor**
stone	**ghar**
sun	**yier**
tent	**chodir**
tree	**darakht**
valley	**dooe dara hagh**
village	**garya**
wind	**dama shemol**

Adjectives

all	**khukht**
bad	**shak**
beautiful	**khushroy**
big	**lup**
cold	**sur**
good	**buft**
small	**zaqik timiker**
true	**rost**
very many	**ghafeh**

Verbs

bathe	**wizan din ghusl**
climb	**senak**
come	**wease**
do	**tsar gokh**
sit	**nazes**
sleep	**rukhupen**
speak	**khan qisatsar**
understand	**dish**
walk	**chaw**

Adverbs

after	**tsabasen**
again	**dubora woz**
ahead	**tur purut**

here	drem
how	tsumar
now	nive
on foot	sik pood pioda
side	gena taraf
slowly	asta muloim
their	drah tra
therefore	aska skam
	yemedastan
when	tsoghdy tsoghdar
where	komar

(Adverbs, continued)

| why | chizer |
| who | koy kuy |

Conjunctions and Prepositions

and	woz
because	chizarki
but	laiken, magar
with	dan da qiti

Phrases

How are you?	chiz holi?
How do you do?	kumeresh rech tueshkumar rech?
What are you?	tua t chize ti kaspe chize?
What is your name?	ti nunge chize?
Where have you come from?	tuet khumaran et wezg?
Fetch me milk.	jarj mazhar wuzum
Give me a glass of water.	yi gloss yupk ma er rand
Do you eat apricots?	chuan esh yawa?

Balti Glossary

by John Mock

Balti is the language spoken throughout Baltistan, whose administrative center is Skardu. Balti is similar to Ladakhi, another Tibetan language, but is more archaic in that its pronunciation corresponds closely to its spelling. Such is not the case in the modern Lhasa dialect of Tibetan.

Balti ascribes gender only to animate beings. The suffix *-po* indicates male; *-mo*, female. Like other Tibetan languages, Balti uses subject-object-verb word order.

Pronunciation

Ng is nasal, pronounced as a single sound like the *ng* in "si*ng*ing." The consonant clusters, *kh*, *khs*, *ts*, and *dz* are also pronounced as single units.

Vowels

Long vowels are indicated by a horizontal superscript (**dyū**).

a	as in "*a*bove"
ā	as in "f*a*ther"
i	as in "b*i*t"
ī	as in "s*ea*t"
u	as in "p*u*t"
ū	as in "p*oo*l"
o	as in "g*o*"
e	as in "t*a*ke"

Vocabulary

Demonstratives

this	**dyū**
these	**dyung**
that	**do**
those	**dong**
what	**chī**
which	**go**
who	**sū**

Numbers

one	**chīk**
two	**ngīs**
three	**khsūm**
four	**bjī**

(Numbers, continued)

five	**gā**
six	**truk**
seven	**bdun**
eight	**bgyad**
nine	**rgu**
ten	**phchū**
eleven	**chūschīk**
twelve	**chongas**
thirteen	**chuksum**
fourteen	**chubjī**
fifteen	**chogā**
sixteen	**churuk**
seventeen	**chubdun**

eighteen	chubgyad	(Relations, continued)	
nineteen	churgu	woman	bostring
twenty	ngī-shū	man	mī
thirty	khsum-chū	boy	bū
forty	ngī shū ngīs	girl	bong o
fifty	ngī shū ngīs na phchū	headman	trang pā
sixty	ngīshū khsum		
seventy	ngīshū khsum na phchū		
eighty	ngīshū bjī	**Food**	
ninety	ngīshu bjī na phchū	apple	kūshū
one hundred	byā	apricot	chūlī
		dried	pading

Time

Sunday	adid
Monday	tsandār
Tuesday	angāru
Wednesday	batu
Thursday	brespot
Friday	shukuru
Saturday	shingsher
dawn	sharka
morning	zantus
midday	tro fed
early afternoon	pishin
late afternoon	phiro
sunset	ngima nub
evening	gonghin
moonrise	lzod sher
night	tshan
today	diring
tomorrow	bela
yesterday	gonde
day after tomorrow	snang la
day before yesterday	kharchak la

Colors

black	nākpo
green	sngonpo
red	mārpo
white	kārpo

Relations

father	ātā
mother	āmā

Food (continued)

barley flour	nas fe
bread	khurbā
butter	mar
cheese (whey)	darbā
egg	bjabjum
food	zachas
meat	shā
milk	omā
pea	pokshān
rice	bras
salt	payū
salt tea	payū chā
tea	chā
walnut	stargāh
whole-wheat flour	bay fe

Other Nouns

clothes	gonchās
hat	nāting
ice	gang
moon	zod
mountain	brak
path, way	lām
rain	charphā
river	gyamtso
skin	markhor
snow	khā
spring	chhūmik
sun	ngīmā
valley	lungbā
water	chhū
yak	dzo

Adjectives

beautiful	**rgāshe**
big	**chhogo**
cold	**grākhmo**
good	**lyakhmo**
hot	**tronmo**
left	**khen**
little	**tsūntse**
long	**ringmo**
new	**sarfā**
old	**sningmā**
right	**trang**
very good	**zhyumbo**

Verbs

drink	**thūngmā**
eat	**zā**
go	**shākspā**
sit	**dukpā**
speak	**zerba**

Adverbs

here	**dyūwā**
how	**chī-byāse**
near	**ngīmore**
when	**nām**
where	**gār**

Phrases

How are you?	**chī khabar?**
It's good.	**lyākhmo dū**
Where are you from?	**kyang gar pai īn?**
I'm from _____ .	**_____ pai īn**
Who are you?	**khyang sū īn?**
What is this?	**dyū chī īn?**
How is the road?	**lām-po chīna yod?**

Ladakhi Glossary

by Helena Norberg-Hodge

Ladakhi is classified as a dialect of Tibetan, but though the two are very closely related, they are sufficiently different that Ladakhis and Tibetans often speak Hindi-Urdu with one another. The written language found in traditional (mainly religious) texts is classical Tibetan.

Ladakhi will seem quite difficult to start with (and it is), but it doesn't require much effort to learn a few words, and any effort will be rewarded ten times over. If nothing else, be sure to greet everyone with a **"ju´le"** and you'll see faces light up with a broad smile as they answer **"ju´le"** back.

Pronunciation

It would be much too complicated to give a precise phonetic rendering of the words in the glossary, so the following is nothing more than a rough sketch. (Aspirated sounds, for example, are not distinguished from nonaspirated ones.) It should nonetheless be sufficient for making oneself understood.

Zh is the equivalent of French *j* as in *"jour."*

Long vowels are marked with a horizontal superscript (**lō**).

Accented syllables are marked with an acute accent (**kule´a**).

Word Order

Word order is as in Tibetan: subject-object-verb. Adjectives (other than demonstratives) follow the nouns they modify; adverbs precede verbs.

I am now reading a good book.

nga	**specha**	**galla**	**chik**	**daksa**	**sillat**
I	book	good	one	now	am reading

Verbs

Verbs can be very tricky indeed. However, by dropping the infinitive ending *-ches* and adding the following endings to the root, you should be able to get by:

Present and Future Tense

First person: *-at*

> **yong-ches**   **yong-at**   **nga yongat:**   I am coming

Second and third person: *duk*

> **yong-ches**   **yong-duk**   **khong yongduk:**   he is coming

Past Tense

Usually first person: *(s)pin*

> **yong-ches**   **yong-(s)pin**   **nga yongspin:**   I came

Second and third person: *-s*

yong-ches   **yong-s**   **khong yongs:**   he came

Vocabulary

Pronouns

I	nga
you	nyerang
he,she	khong
it	ibo
we (including you)	ngatang
you (plural)	nyeranggun
they	khonggun
my	nge
your	nyerang´i
his, hers	knong´i
our	ngazhe
their	khong´guni

Colors

black	nakpo
blue	ngonpo
green	ljangku
red	marpo
white	kharpo
yellow	serrpo

Relations

mother	amma
father	abba
older brother	acho
older sister	ache
younger brother	no
younger sister	nōmō
brother	mingbo
sister	shingmo
grandfather	mēmē
grandmother	abbī

Time

day	zhak
week	dun´zhak
month	da´wa
year	lō
time (o'clock)	chutsot´
morning	ngamo, ngatok´
evening	pittok´
day before yesterday	kartsan´zhak

(Time, continued)

yesterday	dhang
today	dring
tomorrow	tōre
day after tomorrow	nangs´la
sun, daylight	nyima
night	tsanīsan

Numbers

one	chik
two	nyiss
three	sum
four	zhī
five	shnga
six	tuk
seven	rdun
eight	rgyatt
nine	rgu
ten	stchu
eleven	chukshik´
twelve	chuknyiss´
thirteen	chuksum´
fourteen	chubzhī´
fifteen	chonga´
sixteen	churuk´
seventeen	chubdun´
eighteen	chubgyatt´
nineteen	churgu´
twenty	nishu´
thirty	sumchu´
forty	zhipchu´
fifty	ngapchu´
sixty	tukchu´
seventy	rdunchu´
eighty	gyattchu´
ninety	rgupchu´
one hundred	gya
one thousand	stongchik
two thousand	stongnyiss

Food

barley flour (roasted)	tsampa, ngampe´
bread	tagī´
butter	mar

buttermilk	ta´ra
cheese (dry)	churpe´
food	zachess, kardjī´
kerosene	samar´
meat	sha
milk	ōma
rice	dass
soup	tuk´pa
sugar, sweets	ka´ra
vegetables	tsod´ma
water (drinking)	tungchu´
wheat flour	pakpe´
yoghurt	zho

Other Nouns

assembly hall (in temple)	dukhang´
buddha	sang´gyas
Buddhist	nang´pa
cup	ko´re
goat	ra´ma
horse	sta
house	khang´pa
hotel	donkhang´
illness	nat, zur´mo
kettle	tibril
masked dances	cham
medicine	sman
monk	ta´ba
paper	shugu´
table	chog´tse
prayer	monlam´
prayer recitation	yangs´
prayer wall	mendong´
room	nang
school	lop´ta
sheep	luk
shoes	pa´bu
spoon	turrmangs´
student	loptuk´
teacher	lopon´
temple	lhakhang´
trail, road	lam
water	chu
wind	lungspo´
wood	shing

Adjectives

bad	tsokpo
beautiful	rdemo
big	chenmo
breakable	tholmo
cold	tangmo
dark	mundik´
difficult	kakspo
easy	lamo
far	takring´
fast	gyogs´pa
good	gyalla
happy	thatpo, skittpo
heavy	ichinte
high	tonnpo
hot	tsan´te
light	salpo
little	nyungun´
low	mamo
many	mangpo
near	nyemo
sad	tser´ka, dukpo
slow	kule´a
small	chungun´
strong	shante, shetchan´
thick, fat	rompo
thin	tamo
warm	tonmo

Verbs

arrive	lep´ches
buy	nyo´ches
come	yong´ches
cook	skol´ches
do	choches´
drink	tung´ches
eat	za´ches
eat, drink	donches´ (polite)
leave, go	chaches
pay	skyakches´
say	zer´ches
see	thong´ches
sew	tsem´ches
get sick	zur´moyongches
stay, sit (polite)	dukches, zhukches

steal	shkun´ma, shku´ches	
take	nam´ches (polite)	
talk	spe´ratangches,	
	moll´ches (polite)	
teach, learn	lap´ches	
understand	hago´ches	

Adverbs

early, before	snganla
later	stingne
now	daksa

Phrases

Yes: affirmative of whatever verb is being used	e.g., ī´nok
No: negative of whatever verb is being used	e.g., mā´nok
Hello, goodbye, thank you, please.	ju´le!
O.K.	digches īnok
Where are you going?	nyerang´ ka´ru skyo´dat?
I'm going to (Leh).	nga (Le)´a chat
How many (kilometers) to Leh?	ine´le´a (kilometer) tsam ī´nok?
Hi, come in.	skyo´dang
What's your name?	nyerang´i tsan´la chī zhuchen?
My name is _____ .	nge minga´ _____ zerchen
How old are you?	nyerang´ lo tsam īn?
I'm (forty).	nga lo (zhipchu)´ īn
Where do you live?	nyerang´ kā´ru zhuk´sat?
I live in (Leh).	nga (Leh)a dū´gat
Where do you come from?	nyerang´ kā´ne īn?
I'm from (America).	nga (America)ne īn
How much does a kilo of (apricots) cost?	(patting´) ki´loa tsam ī´nok?
Where can I buy _____ ?	_____ nyo´sa kāne yot?
Do you have any _____ ?	_____ zhibmo yo´da?
How much does that cost?	pene tsam song?
That's expensive.	ma rinchan´ rak
Where is the water?	chu ka´ne yot?
Is this drinking water?	ī´bo tungchu´ īna?
The food is very good.	karjī´ ma zhim´po rak
Where is the path to the gomba?	gon´pa cha´se lam ka´bo īn?
Does this path go to (Zanskar)?	ī´bo (Zanskari) lam ī´ na?
How long does it take?	nyi´ma tsam go´rin?
It takes (nine) days.	nyi´ ma (rgu) go´rin
(Two) passes must be crossed.	la (nyiss) gyab goshen´
Do you have horses?	sta yo´da?
Yes, I have horses.	sta yott
Each horse costs (sixty) rupees a day.	sta rea, nyi´me khir´mo (tukchu´) cho chen´
I want a guide.	nga lamgyus´pa chik gō´sat
He is a very good man.	mi ma gyall´a yot

Index

Numbers in italics refer to photographs.

A Note to the Reader

Readers are invited to send updated information and corrections for any title in the Sierra Club Adventure Travel Guide series to the author, c/o Travel Editor, Sierra Club Books, 730 Polk Street, San Francisco, CA 94109.